CW00919952

# Honda VFR400R & RVF400R
# Service and Repair Manual

## by Matthew Coombs

**Models covered**

VFR400R (NC30). 399cc. 1989 to 1998
RVF400R (NC35). 399cc. 1994 to 1998

*(3496-272-3Z1)*

ABCDE
FGHIJ
KLMNO

Printed in USA

**Haynes Publishing**
Sparkford, Nr Yeovil, Somerset BA22 7JJ, England

**Haynes North America, Inc**
861 Lawrence Drive, Newbury Park, California 91320, USA

**Editions Haynes**
Tour Aurore – IBC, 18 Place des Reflets
92975 Paris La Defense 2 Cedex, France

**Haynes Publishing Nordiska AB**
Box 1504, 751 45 UPPSALA, Sweden

# Contents

## LIVING WITH YOUR HONDA VFR/RVF

### Introduction

### Daily (pre-ride checks)

## MAINTENANCE

### Routine maintenance and servicing

# Contents

# The Birth of a Dream

by Julian Ryder

There is no better example of the Japanese post-War industrial miracle than Honda. Like other companies which have become household names, it started with one man's vision. In this case the man was the 40-year old Soichiro Honda who had sold his piston-ring manufacturing business to Toyota in 1945 and was happily spending the proceeds on prolonged parties for his friends. However, the difficulties of getting around in the chaos of post-War Japan irked Honda, so when he came across a job lot of generator engines he realised that here was a way of getting people mobile again at low cost.

A 12 by 18-foot shack in Hamamatsu became his first bike factory, fitting the generator motors into pushbikes. Before long he'd used up all 500 generator motors and started manufacturing his own engine, known as the 'chimney', either because of the elongated cylinder head or the smoky exhaust or perhaps both. The chimney made all of half a horsepower from its 50 cc engine but it was a major success and became the Honda A-type. Less than two years after he'd set up in Hamamatsu, Soichiro Honda founded the Honda Motor Company in September 1948. By then, the A-type had been developed into the 90 cc B-type engine, which Mr Honda decided deserved its own chassis not a bicycle frame. Honda was about to become Japan's first post-War manufacturer of complete motorcycles. In August 1949 the first prototype was ready. With an output of three horsepower, the 98 cc D-type was still a simple two-stroke but it had a two-speed transmission and most importantly a pressed steel frame with telescopic forks and hard tail rear end. The frame was almost triangular in profile with the top rail going in a straight line from the massively braced steering head to the rear axle. Legend has it that after the D-type's first tests the entire workforce went for a drink to celebrate and try and think of a name for the bike. One man broke one of those silences you get when people are thinking, exclaiming 'This is like a dream!' 'That's it!' shouted Honda, and so the Honda Dream was christened.

## 'This is like a dream!' 'That's it' shouted Honda

Mr Honda was a brilliant, intuitive engineer and designer but he did not bother himself with the marketing side of his business. With hindsight, it is possible to see that employing Takeo Fujisawa who would both sort out the home market and plan the eventual expansion into overseas markets was a masterstroke. He arrived in October 1949 and in 1950 was made Sales Director. Another vital new name was Kiyoshi Kawashima, who along with Honda himself, designed the company's first four-stroke after Kawashima had told them that the four-stroke opposition to Honda's two-strokes sounded nicer and therefore sold better. The result of that statement was the overhead-valve 148 cc E-type which first ran in July 1951 just two months after the first drawings were made. Kawashima was made a director of the Honda Company at 34 years old.

The E-type was a massive success, over 32,000 were made in 1953 alone, but Honda's lifelong pursuit of technical innovation sometimes distracted him from commercial reality. Fujisawa pointed out that they were in danger of ignoring their core business, the motorised bicycles that still formed Japan's main means of transport. In May 1952 the F-type Cub appeared, another two-stroke despite the top men's reservations. You could buy a complete machine or just the motor to attach to your own bicycle. The result was certainly distinctive, a white fuel tank with a circular profile went just below and behind the saddle on the left of the bike, and the motor with its horizontal cylinder and bright red cover just below the rear axle on the same side of the bike. This was the machine that turned Honda into the biggest bike maker in Japan

**Honda C70 and C90 OHV-engined models**

The CB250N Super Dream became a favorite with UK learner riders of the late seventies and early eighties

ready for the TT. In 1959 the factory entered five riders in the 125. They did not have a massive impact on the event being benevolently regarded as a curiosity, but sixth, seventh and eighth were good enough for the team prize. The bikes were off the pace but they were well engineered and very reliable.

The TT was the only time the West saw the Hondas in '59, but they came back for more the following year with the first of a generation of bikes which shaped the future of motorcycling - the double-overhead-cam four-cylinder 250. It was fast and reliable - it revved to 14,000 rpm - but didn't handle anywhere near as well as the opposition. However, Honda had now signed up non-Japanese riders to lead their challenge. The first win didn't come until 1962 (Aussie Tom Phillis in the Spanish 125 GP) and was followed up with

with 70% of the market for bolt-on bicycle motors, the F-type was also the first Honda to be exported. Next came the machine that would turn Honda into the biggest motorcycle manufacturer in the world.

The C100 Super Cub was a typically audacious piece of Honda engineering and marketing. For the first time, but not the last, Honda invented a completely new type of motorcycle, although the term 'scooterette' was coined to describe the new bike which had many of the characteristics of a scooter but the large wheels, and therefore stability, of a motorcycle. The first one was sold in August 1958, fifteen years later over nine-million of them were on the roads of the world. If ever a machine can be said to have brought mobility to the masses it is the Super Cub. If you add in the electric starter that was added for the C102 model of 1961, the design of the Super Cub has remained substantially unchanged ever since, testament to how right Honda got it first time. The Super Cub made Honda the world's biggest manufacturer after just two years of production.

Honda's export drive started in earnest in 1957 when Britain and Holland got their first bikes, America got just two bikes the next year. By 1962 Honda had half the American market with 65,000 sales. But Soichiro Honda had already travelled abroad to Europe and the USA, making a special point of going to the Isle of Man TT, then the most important race in the GP calendar. He realised that no matter how advanced his products were, only racing success would convince overseas markets for whom 'Made in Japan' still meant cheap and nasty. It took five years from Soichiro Honda's first visit to the Island before his bikes were

The GL1000 introduced in 1975, was the first in Honda's line of Goldwings

a world-shaking performance at the TT. Twenty-one year old Mike Hailwood won both 125 and 250 cc TTs and Hondas filled the top five positions in both races. Soichiro Honda's master plan was starting to come to fruition, Hailwood and Honda won the 1961 250 cc World Championship. Next year Honda won three titles. The other Japanese factories fought back and inspired Honda to produce some of the most fascinating racers ever seen: the awesome six-cylinder 250, the five-cylinder 125, and the 500 four with which the immortal Hailwood battled Agostini and the MV Agusta.

When Honda pulled out of racing in '67 they had won sixteen rider's titles, eighteen manufacturer's titles, and 137 GPs, including 18 TTs, and introduced the concept of the modern works team to motorcycle racing. Sales success followed racing victory as Soichiro Honda had predicted, but only because the products advanced as rapidly as the racing machinery. The Hondas that came to Britain in the early '60s were incredibly sophisticated. They had overhead

**Carl Fogarty in action at the Suzuka 8 Hour on the RC45**

cams where the British bikes had pushrods, they had electric starters when the Brits relied on the kickstart, they had 12V electrics when even the biggest British bike used a 6V system. There seemed no end to the technical wizardry and when in 1968 the first four-cylinder

CB750 road bike arrived the world changed for ever. They even had to invent a new word for it: superbike. Honda raced again with the CB750 at Daytona and won the World Endurance title with a prototype DOHC version that became the CB900 roadster. There was the six-cylinder CBX, the first turbocharged production bike, they invented the full-dress tourer with the Goldwing and came back to GPs with the revolutionary oval-pistoned NR500 four-stroke, a much-misunderstood bike that was more rolling experiment than racer. It was true, though, that Mr Honda was not keen on two-strokes - early motocross engines had to be explained away to him as lawnmower motors! However, in 1982 Honda raced the NS500, an agile three-cylinder lightweight against the big four-cylinder opposition in 500 GPs. The bike won in the first year and in '83 took the world title for Freddie Spencer. In four-stroke racing the V4 layout took over from the straight four, dominating TT, F1 and Endurance championships and when Superbike arrived Honda were ready with the RC30. On the roads the VFR V4 became an instant classic while the CBR600 invented another new class of bike on its way to becoming a best-seller.

And then there was the NR750. This limited-edition technological tour-de-force embodied many of Soichiro Honda's ideals. It used the latest techniques and materials in every component, from the oval-piston, 32-valve V4 motor to the titanium coating on the windscreen, it was - as Mr Honda would have wanted - the best it could possibly be. A fitting memorial to the man who has shaped the motorcycle industry and motorcycles as we know them today.

**An early CB750 Four**

## The NC30 and NC35

They're methodical at Honda – not predictable but certainly methodical. Having built a world-beating 750 V4 they then miniaturised it and produce a 400 cc version. Come to think of it, even when their V4s weren't accepted as modern miracles of production engineering in the pre-VFR750 days, they still produced smaller versions.

The reason is simple: the Japanese licensing system. Until very recently, it was all but impossible to buy and run a big bike in Japan. Potential motorcyclists have to jump through an astonishing number of hoops to be licensed for lower capacity levels, but for a big bike there were tests with very low pass rates and such sneaky little extras as testing your ability to pick your bike up from lying on its side. The effective top capacity level that it was possible to qualify for without vast amounts of time, money and anabolic steroids was 400 cc. And so all four big manufacturers built scaled-down versions of the superbikes they made for their export markets.

Some of these bikes escaped from the home market, such as the VF400 of 1983, a scaled down middle-of-the-road motorcycle that got rave reviews but only lasted for a short time in the UK market mainly due to the fact it cost 25% more than a bike like Kawasaki's GPz305 workhorse. Even a bike like the VF500 that was made for export had a scaled down 400 cc version back home – and in typical Honda fashion it wasn't just a sleeved-down 500, both the bore and the stroke were different.

The British market got its first proper 400 when Honda UK took the brave step of importing the scaled-down version of the RC30 (or VFR750R) built for Superbike racing homologation, the 400 cc NC30 (or VFR400R). This wasn't the first VFR400, the VFR400R and VFR400Z (NC21 and NC24) models had been available in Japan since

**The RVF400 NC35**

1986. The NC30, though, was a real RC30 replica (are you following this?) a whole 18 kg lighter than the previous model and a dead ringer for the bigger bike. As you'd expect, it handled with ultimate precision and the motor was happiest at five-figure rotational speeds – max torque happened at 10,000 rpm and peak power at 12,500! Again everyone agreed that this was a gem of a motorcycle but the British market balked at the price tag of £5899 that was up to over £6500 by April 1991, 18 months after the bike's introduction. The recently revamped Honda CBR600FM cost under £5000 at the start of 1991, so despite the aluminium chassis, twin headlamp fairing, single-sided swingarm, gear-driven camshafts and drop-dead gorgeous looks, the bike was a sales failure.

The sales success came with the '90s phenomenon of the grey import, boatloads of second-hand Japanese home-market bikes that were difficult to keep legal (that Japanese system again) and shipped to the UK where they were sold at attractive prices. Most grey importers will have derestricted the 59 bhp Japanese-spec bikes, a procedure that involves some electronic trickery.

The NC30 was introduced in 1989 on the Japanese market and was joined in 1994 by the RVF400 (NC35). The NC35 still had the gear-drive-camshaft 55 x 42 mm lump but now had upside-down front forks and 17-inch wheels front and back. And of course it looks just like its 750 cc big brother. Basically, Honda's 400 cc V4 is ten years old. Most motorcycles would be pensionable by now. The NC30 and its relatives manage the near-impossible trick of still being totally up to date and as trick as the day it was first launched. And why shouldn't it? An RC30 still looks the business, doesn't it?

# Acknowledgements

Our thanks are due to Elliott Motorcycles of Swindon for supplying the VFR400R featured in the photographs and for providing technical support and encouragement for this manual. The RVF400R was supplied by Bike Direct of Bristol.

We would also like to thank NGK Spark Plugs (UK) Ltd for supplying the colour spark plug condition photos and the Avon Rubber Company for supplying information on tyre fitting.

The introduction, "The Birth of a Dream" was written by Julian Ryder. The cover photographs were taken by Paul Tanswell.

# About this Manual

The aim of this manual is to help you get the best value from your motorcycle. It can do so in several ways. It can help you decide what work must be done, even if you choose to have it done by a dealer; it provides information and procedures for routine maintenance and servicing; and it offers diagnostic and repair procedures to follow when trouble occurs.

We hope you use the manual to tackle the work yourself. For many simpler jobs, doing it yourself may be quicker than arranging an appointment to get the motorcycle into a dealer and making the trips to leave it and pick it up. More importantly, a lot of money can be saved by avoiding the expense the shop must pass on to you to cover its labour and overhead costs. An added benefit is the sense of satisfaction and accomplishment that you feel after doing the job yourself.

References to the left or right side of the motorcycle assume you are sitting on the seat, facing forward.

**We take great pride in the accuracy of information given in this manual, but motorcycle manufacturers make alterations and design changes during the production run of a particular motorcycle of which they do not inform us. No liability can be accepted by the authors or publishers for loss, damage or injury caused by any errors in, or omissions from, the information given.**

## Frame and engine numbers

The frame serial number is stamped into the right-hand side of the steering head. The engine number is stamped into the top of the crankcase on the right-hand side of the engine. Both of these numbers should be recorded and kept in a safe place so they can be furnished to law enforcement officials in the event of a theft. There is also a carburettor identification number on the intake side of each carburettor body, and a colour code label on the top of the rear mudguard under the passenger seat.

The frame serial number, engine serial number, carburettor identification number and colour code should also be kept in a handy place (such as with your driver's licence) so they are always available when purchasing or ordering parts for your machine.

The procedures in this manual identify the bikes by type (ie VFR or RVF), then if necessary by model code (eg K, meaning a 1989 production year model). The model code or production year is printed on the colour code label, which is located on the top of the rear mudguard under the passenger seat.

| Model | Year | Code | Initial engine no. | Initial frame no. | Carb ID no. |
|---|---|---|---|---|---|
| NC30 – grey import | 1989 | K | NC13E-1200001 | NC30-1000001 | VDE3A A |
| NC30 – grey import | 1990/91 | L | NC13E-1300001 | NC30-1050001 | VDE3D A |
| NC30 – grey import | 1992-on | N | NC13E-1400001 | NC30-1100001 | VDE3D B |
| NC35 – grey import | 1994/95 | R | NC13E-1500001 | NC35-1000001 | VP90A A |
| NC35 – grey import | 1996-on | T | NC13E-1600001 | NC35-1100001 | VP90A A |
| NC30 – UK spec | 1990/91 | L | NC13E-2100007 | NC30-2000006 | VDE3B A |
| NC30 – UK spec | 1991-93 | M | NC13E-2200001 | NC30-2100001 | VDE3F A |

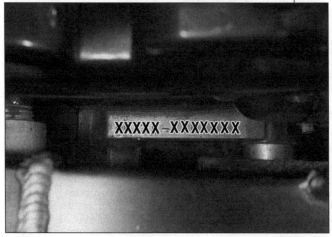

The engine number is stamped into the top of the crankcase on the right-hand side of the engine

The frame number is stamped on the right-hand side of the steering head

## Buying spare parts

Once you have found all the identification numbers, record them for reference when buying parts. Since the manufacturers change specifications, parts and vendors (companies that manufacture various components on the machine), providing the ID numbers is the only way to be reasonably sure that you are buying the correct parts.

Whenever possible, take the worn part to the dealer so direct comparison with the new component can be made. Along the trail from the manufacturer to the parts shelf, there are numerous places that the part can end up with the wrong number or be listed incorrectly.

Parts for unofficial (grey) import machines can be obtained from dealers specialising in imports or from certain Honda dealers. Note that many of the NC30 import parts will be the same as those fitted to the UK NC30 model. Certain items, such as spark plugs, lubricants, chains, tyres, batteries and brake pads can be obtained from non-specialist dealers.

Used parts can be obtained for roughly half the price of new ones, but you can't always be sure of what you're getting. Once again, take your worn part to the breaker for direct comparison.

Whether buying new, used or rebuilt parts, the best course is to deal directly with someone who specialises in parts for your particular make.

## Unofficial (grey) imports

The majority of VFR400R (NC30) and all RVF400R (NC35) machines in the UK are unofficial (grey) imports. These second-hand machines are imported directly from the Japanese market and are allocated age-related licence plates for UK use; the licence plate letter reflects the production year in Japan.

Common changes made prior to sale in the UK are the disabling of the rev-limiter device (or more correctly 'speed-limiter' device), which is fitted to comply with Japanese market regulations. The device is located in the speedometer head and is linked to the ignition control unit to cut the ignition when 180 kmh (112 mph) is reached. The importers have several methods of disabling the device, either fitting a plug-in unit at the speedometer head or ignition control unit, or by modifying the limiter mechanism.

Speedometers calibrated in kilometres (kmh) must have a miles per hour (mph) scale applied. This can be done simply by applying a suitable overlay to the speedometer lens or a more professional approach is to fit one of the replacement dial faces to the speedometer itself. In each case it is important that the correct size overlay or dial face is used.

The ratings of certain bulbs (headlight, sidelight, brake/tail light and turn signal lights) differ from those normally used on UK market machines. Of these, the brake/tail light bulbs will most likely have been replaced with the regulation 21/5W UK fitment.

Note that restrictor kits can be fitted to the VFR and RVF engines to reduce their power output to 33 bhp (25 kW) to comply with the UK full standard category A licence. Kits can be obtained from and fitted by grey importers.

Professional mechanics are trained in safe working procedures. However enthusiastic you may be about getting on with the job at hand, take the time to ensure that your safety is not put at risk. A moment's lack of attention can result in an accident, as can failure to observe simple precautions.

There will always be new ways of having accidents, and the following is not a comprehensive list of all dangers; it is intended rather to make you aware of the risks and to encourage a safe approach to all work you carry out on your bike.

## Asbestos

● Certain friction, insulating, sealing and other products - such as brake pads, clutch linings, gaskets, etc. - contain asbestos. Extreme care must be taken to avoid inhalation of dust from such products since it is hazardous to health. If in doubt, assume that they do contain asbestos.

## Fire

● Remember at all times that petrol is highly flammable. Never smoke or have any kind of naked flame around, when working on the vehicle. But the risk does not end there - a spark caused by an electrical short-circuit, by two metal surfaces contacting each other, by careless use of tools, or even by static electricity built up in your body under certain conditions, can ignite petrol vapour, which in a confined space is highly explosive. Never use petrol as a cleaning solvent. Use an approved safety solvent.

● Always disconnect the battery earth terminal before working on any part of the fuel or electrical system, and never risk spilling fuel on to a hot engine or exhaust.

● It is recommended that a fire extinguisher of a type suitable for fuel and electrical fires is kept handy in the garage or workplace at all times. Never try to extinguish a fuel or electrical fire with water.

## Fumes

● Certain fumes are highly toxic and can quickly cause unconsciousness and even death if inhaled to any extent. Petrol vapour comes into this category, as do the vapours from certain solvents such as trichloro-ethylene. Any draining or pouring of such volatile fluids should be done in a well ventilated area.

● When using cleaning fluids and solvents, read the instructions carefully. Never use materials from unmarked containers - they may give off poisonous vapours.

● Never run the engine of a motor vehicle in an enclosed space such as a garage. Exhaust fumes contain carbon monoxide which is extremely poisonous; if you need to run the engine, always do so in the open air or at least have the rear of the vehicle outside the workplace.

## The battery

● Never cause a spark, or allow a naked light near the vehicle's battery. It will normally be giving off a certain amount of hydrogen gas, which is highly explosive.

● Always disconnect the battery ground (earth) terminal before working on the fuel or electrical systems (except where noted).

● If possible, loosen the filler plugs or cover when charging the battery from an external source. Do not charge at an excessive rate or the battery may burst.

● Take care when topping up, cleaning or carrying the battery. The acid electrolyte, evenwhen diluted, is very corrosive and should not be allowed to contact the eyes or skin. Always wear rubber gloves and goggles or a face shield. If you ever need to prepare electrolyte yourself, always add the acid slowly to the water; never add the water to the acid.

## Electricity

● When using an electric power tool, inspection light etc., always ensure that the appliance is correctly connected to its plug and that, where necessary, it is properly grounded (earthed). Do not use such appliances in damp conditions and, again, beware of creating a spark or applying excessive heat in the vicinity of fuel or fuel vapour. Also ensure that the appliances meet national safety standards.

● A severe electric shock can result from touching certain parts of the electrical system, such as the spark plug wires (HT leads), when the engine is running or being cranked, particularly if components are damp or the insulation is defective. Where an electronic ignition system is used, the secondary (HT) voltage is much higher and could prove fatal.

---

# Remember...

✗ **Don't** start the engine without first ascertaining that the transmission is in neutral.

✗ **Don't** suddenly remove the pressure cap from a hot cooling system - cover it with a cloth and release the pressure gradually first, or you may get scalded by escaping coolant.

✗ **Don't** attempt to drain oil until you are sure it has cooled sufficiently to avoid scalding you.

✗ **Don't** grasp any part of the engine or exhaust system without first ascertaining that it is cool enough not to burn you.

✗ **Don't** allow brake fluid or antifreeze to contact the machine's paintwork or plastic components.

✗ **Don't** siphon toxic liquids such as fuel, hydraulic fluid or antifreeze by mouth, or allow them to remain on your skin.

✗ **Don't** inhale dust - it may be injurious to health (see Asbestos heading).

✗ **Don't** allow any spilled oil or grease to remain on the floor - wipe it up right away, before someone slips on it.

✗ **Don't** use ill-fitting spanners or other tools which may slip and cause injury.

✗ **Don't** lift a heavy component which may be beyond your capability - get assistance.

✗ **Don't** rush to finish a job or take unverified short cuts.

✗ **Don't** allow children or animals in or around an unattended vehicle.

✗ **Don't** inflate a tyre above the recommended pressure. Apart from overstressing the carcass, in extreme cases the tyre may blow off forcibly.

✔ **Do** ensure that the machine is supported securely at all times. This is especially important when the machine is blocked up to aid wheel or fork removal.

✔ **Do** take care when attempting to loosen a stubborn nut or bolt. It is generally better to pull on a spanner, rather than push, so that if you slip, you fall away from the machine rather than onto it.

✔ **Do** wear eye protection when using power tools such as drill, sander, bench grinder etc.

✔ **Do** use a barrier cream on your hands prior to undertaking dirty jobs - it will protect your skin from infection as well as making the dirt easier to remove afterwards; but make sure your hands aren't left slippery. Note that long-term contact with used engine oil can be a health hazard.

✔ **Do** keep loose clothing (cuffs, ties etc. and long hair) well out of the way of moving mechanical parts.

✔ **Do** remove rings, wristwatch etc., before working on the vehicle - especially the electrical system.

✔ **Do** keep your work area tidy - it is only too easy to fall over articles left lying around.

✔ **Do** exercise caution when compressing springs for removal or installation. Ensure that the tension is applied and released in a controlled manner, using suitable tools which preclude the possibility of the spring escaping violently.

✔ **Do** ensure that any lifting tackle used has a safe working load rating adequate for the job.

✔ **Do** get someone to check periodically that all is well, when working alone on the vehicle.

✔ **Do** carry out work in a logical sequence and check that everything is correctly assembled and tightened afterwards.

✔ **Do** remember that your vehicle's safety affects that of yourself and others. If in doubt on any point, get professional advice.

● If in spite of following these precautions, you are unfortunate enough to injure yourself, seek medical attention as soon as possible.

# 1 Engine/transmission oil level

**Note:** *The daily (pre-ride) checks outlined in the owner's manual covers those items which should be inspected on a daily basis.*

## Before you start:
✔ Take the motorcycle on a short run to allow it to reach normal operating temperature.

***Caution: Do not run the engine in an enclosed space such as a garage or workshop.***

✔ Stop the engine and support the motorcycle in an upright position, using an auxiliary stand if required. Allow it to stand undisturbed for a few minutes to allow the oil level to stabilise. Make sure the motorcycle is on level ground.

## Bike care:
● If you have to add oil frequently, you should check whether you have any oil leaks. If there is no sign of oil leakage from the joints and gaskets the engine could be burning oil (see *Fault Finding*).

## The correct oil
● Modern, high-revving engines place great demands on their oil. It is very important that the correct oil for your bike is used.
● Always top up with a good quality oil of the specified type and viscosity and do not overfill the engine.

| Oil type | API grade SE, SF or SG |
|---|---|
| Oil viscosity | SAE 10W40 |

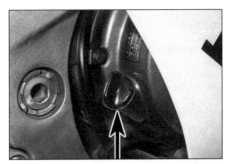

**1** Unscrew the oil filler cap (arrowed) from the right-hand crankcase cover. The dipstick is integral with the oil filler cap, and is used to check the engine oil level.

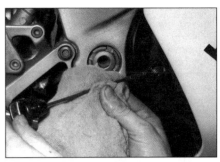

**2** Using a clean rag or paper towel, wipe off all the oil from the dipstick. Insert the clean dipstick back into the engine, but **do not** screw it in.

**3** Remove the dipstick and observe the level of the oil, which should be somewhere in between the upper and lower level lines (arrowed).

**4** If the level is below the lower line, top the engine up with the recommended grade and type of oil, to bring the level up to the upper line on the dipstick. Do not overfill.

# 2 Legal and safety checks

## Lighting and signalling:
● Take a minute to check that the headlight, tail light, brake light, instrument lights and turn signals all work correctly.
● Check that the horn sounds when the switch is operated.
● A working speedometer is a statutory requirement in the UK. If the speedometer is calibrated in kilometres, make sure that a suitable mph indicator is stuck to its face for the UK market.

## Safety:
● Check that the throttle grip rotates smoothly and snaps shut when released, in all steering positions. Also check for the correct amount of freeplay (see Chapter 1).
● Check that the engine shuts off when the kill switch is operated.
● Check that sidestand return spring holds the stand securely up when retracted.

## Fuel:
● This may seem obvious, but check that you have enough fuel to complete your journey. If you notice signs of fuel leakage – rectify the cause immediately.
● Ensure you use the correct grade unleaded or low-lead fuel – see Chapter 4 Specifications.

# 3 Brake fluid level

> ⚠ **Warning: Brake hydraulic fluid can harm your eyes and damage painted surfaces, so use extreme caution when handling and pouring it and cover surrounding surfaces with rag. Do not use fluid that has been standing open for some time, as it absorbs moisture from the air which can cause a dangerous loss of braking effectiveness.**

## Before you start:

✔ Support the motorcycle in an upright position, using an auxiliary stand if required, and turn the handlebars until the top of the front brake master cylinder is as level as possible. If necessary, tilt the motorcycle to make it level. The rear master cylinder reservoir is located below the seat cowl on the right-hand side of the machine.

✔ Make sure you have the correct hydraulic fluid. DOT 4 is recommended.

✔ Wrap a rag around the reservoir being worked on to ensure that any spillage does not come into contact with painted surfaces.

✔ Access to the front reservoir cap screws is restricted by the windshield. A short or angled screwdriver is required to access the screws.

## Bike care:

● The fluid in the front and rear brake master cylinder reservoirs will drop slightly as the brake pads wear down.

● If any fluid reservoir requires repeated topping-up this is an indication of an hydraulic leak somewhere in the system, which should be investigated immediately.

● Check for signs of fluid leakage from the hydraulic hoses and components – if found, rectify immediately.

● Check the operation of both brakes before taking the machine on the road; if there is evidence of air in the system (spongy feel to lever or pedal), it must be bled as described in Chapter 7.

**1** The front brake fluid level is visible through the reservoir body – it must be between the UPPER and LOWER level lines (arrowed).

**2** If the level is below the LOWER level line, remove the two reservoir cap screws and remove the cover, the diaphragm plate and the diaphragm. On RVF models, first remove the screw securing the cap clamp.

**3** Top up with new DOT 4 hydraulic fluid until the level is above the lower mark. Take care to avoid spills (see **Warning** above).

**4** Ensure that the diaphragm is correctly seated before installing the plate and cover.

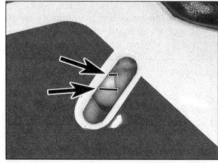

**5** The rear brake fluid level is visible through the reservoir body via the aperture in the right-hand side of the seat cowling – it must be between the UPPER and LOWER level lines (arrowed).

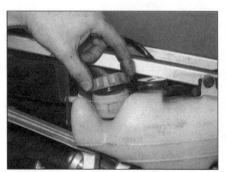

**6** If the level is below the LOWER level line, remove the seat cowling (see Chapter 8). Unscrew the reservoir cap and remove the diaphragm plate and diaphragm.

**7** Top up with new clean hydraulic fluid of the recommended type, until the level is above the lower mark. Take care to avoid spills (see **Warning** above).

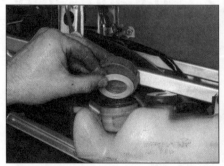

**8** Ensure that the diaphragm is correctly seated before installing the plate and cap. Tighten the cap securely, then install the seat cowl (see Chapter 8).

# 4 Coolant level

> **Warning: DO NOT remove the radiator pressure cap to add coolant. Topping up is done via the coolant reservoir tank filler. DO NOT leave open containers of coolant about, as it is poisonous.**

## Before you start:
✔ Make sure you have a supply of coolant available (a mixture of 50% distilled water and 50% corrosion inhibited ethylene glycol anti-freeze is needed).
✔ Always check the coolant level when the engine is at normal working temperature.

Take the motorcycle on a short run to allow it to reach normal temperature.
*Caution: Do not run the engine in an enclosed space such as a garage or workshop.*
✔ Support the motorcycle in an upright position, using an auxiliary stand if required, whilst checking the level. Make sure the motorcycle is on level ground.

## Bike care:
● Use only the specified coolant mixture. It is important that anti-freeze is used in the system all year round, and not just in the winter. Do not top the system up using only water, as the system will become too diluted.
● Do not overfill the reservoir tank. If the coolant is significantly above the UPPER level line at any time, the surplus should be siphoned or drained off to prevent the possibility of it being expelled out of the overflow hose.
● If the coolant level falls steadily, check the system for leaks (see Chapter 1). If no leaks are found and the level continues to fall, it is recommended that the machine is taken to a Honda dealer for a pressure test.

**1** The coolant reservoir is located under the seat cowling on the right-hand side. The coolant UPPER and LOWER level lines are visible by looking up from below the cowl.

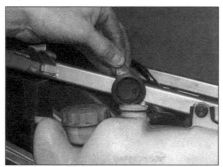

**2** If the coolant level is not in between the UPPER and LOWER markings, remove the seat cowl (see Chapter 8), then remove the reservoir filler cap.

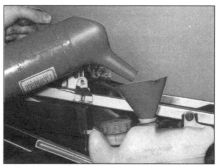

**3** Top the coolant level up with the recommended coolant mixture. Fit the cap securely, then install the seat cowl (see Chapter 8).

---

# 5 Suspension, steering and drive chain

## Suspension and steering:
● Check that the front and rear suspension operates smoothly without binding.
● Check that the suspension is adjusted as required.

● Check that the steering moves smoothly from lock-to-lock.

## Drive chain:
● Check that the drive chain slack isn't excessive, and adjust if necessary (see Chapter 1).
● If the chain looks dry, lubricate it (see Chapter 1).

# 6 Tyre checks

### Tyre care:
● Check the tyres carefully for cuts, tears, embedded nails or other sharp objects and excessive wear. Operation of the motorcycle with excessively worn tyres is extremely hazardous, as traction and handling are directly affected.

● Check the condition of the tyre valve and ensure the dust cap is in place.

● Pick out any stones or nails which may have become embedded in the tyre tread. If left, they will eventually penetrate through the casing and cause a puncture.

● If tyre damage is apparent, or unexplained loss of pressure is experienced, seek the advice of a tyre fitting specialist without delay.

### Tyre tread depth:
● At the time of writing UK law requires that tread depth must be at least 1 mm over 3/4 of the tread breadth all the way around the tyre, with no bald patches. Many riders, however, consider 2 mm tread depth minimum to be a safer limit. Honda recommend a minimum of 1.5 mm on the front and 2 mm on the rear.
● Many tyres now incorporate wear indicators in the tread. Identify the location marking on the tyre sidewall to locate the indicator bar and replace the tyre if the tread has worn down to the bar.

### The correct pressures:
● The tyres must be checked when **cold**, not immediately after riding. Note that low tyre pressures may cause the tyre to slip on the rim or come off. High tyre pressures will cause abnormal tread wear and unsafe handling.

● Use an accurate pressure gauge.

● Proper air pressure will increase tyre life and provide maximum stability and ride comfort.

| Loading | Front | Rear |
|---|---|---|
| Rider only | 33 psi (2.25 Bar) | 33 psi (2.25 Bar) |
| Rider and passenger | 33 psi (2.25 Bar) | 36 psi (2.50 Bar) |

**1** Check the tyre pressures when the tyres are **cold** and keep them properly inflated.

**2** Measure tread depth at the centre of the tyre using a tread depth gauge.

**3** Tyre tread wear indicator bar and its location marking (usually either an arrow, a triangle or the letters TWI) on the sidewall (arrowed).

# Chapter 1
## Routine maintenance and servicing

## Contents

**1**

## Degrees of difficulty

| | | | | |
|---|---|---|---|---|
| **Easy,** suitable for novice with little experience  | **Fairly easy,** suitable for beginner with some experience  | **Fairly difficult,** suitable for competent DIY mechanic | **Difficult,** suitable for experienced DIY mechanic | **Very difficult,** suitable for expert DIY or professional  |

## Engine

Cylinder numbering (as viewed from riding position)

FRONT ↑

|   |   |
|---|---|
| 2 | 4 |

|   |   |
|---|---|
| 1 | 3 |

| | |
|---|---|
| Front right .................................................... | no. 4 |
| Front left ..................................................... | no. 2 |
| Rear right .................................................... | no. 3 |
| Rear left ..................................................... | no. 1 |

Spark plugs

| | |
|---|---|
| Type | |
| Standard .................................................. | NGK ER9EH or Nippon denso Y27FER |
| For extended high speed riding ......................... | NGK ER10EH or Nippon denso Y31FER |
| Electrode gap .............................................. | 0.6 to 0.7 mm |
| Engine idle speed ............................................. | 1300 ± 100 rpm |
| Carburettor synchronisation – max. difference between carburettors .. | 40 mm Hg |

Valve clearances (COLD engine)

| | |
|---|---|
| Inlet valves ................................................. | 0.12 to 0.18 mm |
| Exhaust valves ............................................. | 0.21 to 0.27 mm |
| Cylinder compression ....................................... | 157 to 213 psi (10.8 to 14.7 Bar) |
| Oil pressure (with engine warm) ............................. | 71 to 85 psi (5.0 to 6.0 Bar) @ 5000 rpm, oil @ 80°C |

## Miscellaneous

| | |
|---|---|
| Drive chain slack ............................................ | 15 to 25 mm |
| Clutch cable freeplay ....................................... | 10 to 20 mm |
| Throttle cable freeplay ...................................... | 2 to 6 mm |

| Tyre pressures (cold) | Front | Rear |
|---|---|---|
| Rider only ................................................. | 33 psi (2.25 Bar) | 33 psi (2.25 Bar) |
| Rider and passenger ...................................... | 33 psi (2.25 Bar) | 36 psi (2.50 Bar) |

## Torque settings – specific components

| | |
|---|---|
| Spark plug .................................................. | 9 Nm |
| Engine/transmission oil drain plug .......................... | 35 Nm |
| Engine/transmission oil filter ............................... | 10 Nm |
| Timing inspection cover ..................................... | 18 Nm |
| Steering stem nut ........................................... | 140 Nm |
| Top yoke fork clamp bolts .................................. | 11 Nm |
| Rear wheel bearing holder pinch bolt ........................ | 55 Nm |

## Torque settings – non-specified components

**Note:** *Where a specific setting is not given for a particular bolt/nut, these general settings apply. The dimension given applies to the diameter of the thread, not the head.*

| | |
|---|---|
| 5 mm bolt/nut .............................................. | 5 Nm |
| 6 mm bolt/nut .............................................. | 10 Nm |
| 8 mm bolt/nut .............................................. | 22 Nm |
| 10 mm bolt/nut ............................................. | 35 Nm |
| 12 mm bolt/nut ............................................. | 55 Nm |
| 6 mm flange bolt with 8 mm head ........................... | 9 Nm |
| 6 mm flange bolt/nut with 10 mm head ...................... | 12 Nm |
| 8 mm flange bolt/nut ....................................... | 27 Nm |
| 10 mm flange bolt/nut ...................................... | 40 Nm |

## Recommended lubricants and fluids

| | |
|---|---|
| Engine/transmission oil type ................................. | API grade SE, SF or SG motor oil |
| Engine/transmission oil viscosity ........................... | SAE 10W40 |
| Engine/transmission oil capacity | |
| Oil change ................................................ | 2.4 litres |
| Oil and filter change ..................................... | 2.5 litres |
| Following engine overhaul – dry engine, new filter .............. | 3.0 litres |
| Coolant type .............................................. | 50% distilled water, 50% corrosion inhibited ethylene glycol anti-freeze |
| Coolant capacity | |
| Radiator and engine ...................................... | 2.1 litres |
| Reservoir ................................................ | 0.2 litre |
| Brake fluid ................................................. | DOT 4 |
| Drive chain ................................................ | SAE 80 or 90 gear oil |
| Steering head bearings ...................................... | Lithium-based multi-purpose grease |
| Swingarm pivot bearings .................................... | Molybdenum disulphide grease |
| Suspension linkage bearings ................................ | Molybdenum disulphide grease |
| Bearing seal lips ........................................... | Lithium-based multi-purpose grease |
| Gearchange lever/clutch lever/rear brake pedal pivots ............. | Molybdenum disulphide grease |
| Front brake lever pivot and piston tip ........................ | Molybdenum disulphide grease |
| Cables .................................................... | 10W40 motor oil |
| Sidestand pivot ............................................ | Molybdenum disulphide grease |
| Throttle grip ............................................... | Multi-purpose grease or dry film lubricant |

**Note:** *The daily (pre-ride) checks outlined in the owner's manual covers those items which should be inspected on a daily basis. Always perform the pre-ride inspection at every maintenance interval (in addition to the procedures listed). The intervals listed below are the intervals recommended by the manufacturer for each particular operation during the model years covered in this manual. Your owner's manual may have different intervals for your model.*

## Daily (pre-ride)
See *'Daily (pre-ride) checks'* at the beginning of this manual.

## After the initial 600 miles (1000 km)
**Note:** *This check is usually performed by a Honda dealer after the first 600 miles (1000 km) from new. Thereafter, maintenance is carried out according to the following intervals of the schedule.*

## Every 600 miles (1000 km)
☐ Check, adjust and lubricate the drive chain (Section 1)

## Every 4000 miles (6000 km) or 6 months (whichever comes first)
☐ Check and adjust the idle speed (Section 2)
☐ Check the brake pads (Section 3)
☐ Check and adjust the clutch (Section 4)
☐ Check the spark plug gaps (Section 5)
☐ Lubricate the clutch/gearshift/brake lever/brake pedal/sidestand pivots and the throttle/choke/clutch cables (Section 6)

## Every 8000 miles (12,000 km) or 12 months (whichever comes first)
*Carry out all the items under the 4000 mile (6000 km) check, plus the following*
☐ Replace the engine oil and filter (Section 7)
☐ Check the fuel system and hoses (Section 8)
☐ Check the battery terminals (Section 9)
☐ Check and adjust the throttle and choke cables (Section 10)
☐ Replace the spark plugs (Section 11)
☐ Check/adjust the carburettor synchronisation (Section 12)
☐ Check the cooling system (Section 13)
☐ Check the brake system and brake light switch operation (Section 14)
☐ Check and adjust the headlight aim (Section 15)
☐ Check the sidestand (Section 16)
☐ Check the suspension (Section 17)

## Every 8000 miles (12,000 km) or 12 months (whichever comes first) (continued)
☐ Check and adjust the steering head bearings (Section 18)
☐ Check the tightness of all nuts, bolts and fasteners (Section 19)
☐ Check the condition of the wheels and tyres (Section 20)

## Every 12,000 miles (18,000 km) or 18 months (whichever comes first)
*Carry out all the items under the 4000 mile (6000 km) check, plus the following*
☐ Replace the air filter element (Section 21)
☐ Change the brake fluid (Section 22)

## Every 16,000 miles (24,000 km) or two years (whichever comes first)
*Carry out all the items under the 8000 mile (12,000 km) check, plus the following*
☐ Check and adjust the valve clearances (Section 23)

## Every 24,000 miles (36,000 km) or two years (whichever comes first)
*Carry out all the items under the 12,000 mile (18,000 km) and 8000 mile (12,000 km) checks, plus the following*
☐ Replace the coolant (Section 24)

## Non-scheduled maintenance
☐ Check the cylinder compression (Section 25)
☐ Check the engine oil pressure (Section 26)
☐ Check the wheel bearings (Section 27)
☐ Re-grease the steering head bearings (Section 28)
☐ Re-grease the swingarm and suspension linkage bearings (Section 29)
☐ Replace the brake master cylinder and caliper seals (Section 30)
☐ Replace the brake hoses (Section 31)
☐ Replace the fuel hoses (Section 32)
☐ Change the front fork oil (Section 33)

1

**Component locations on right-hand side**

1  Rear brake fluid reservoir
2  Coolant reservoir
3  Spark plug access for rear cylinder
4  Throttle cable upper adjuster

5  Front brake fluid reservoir
6  Brake lever span adjuster
7  Radiator pressure cap
8  Front brake pads

9  Front cylinder coolant drain plugs
10  Timing inspection cover
11  Engine/transmission oil filler plug/dipstick

12  Rear brake light switch
13  Rear brake pads

**Component locations on left-hand side**

1  Clutch cable upper adjuster
2  Steering head bearings
3  Air filter
4  Idle speed adjuster
5  Spark plug access for rear cylinder
6  Battery
7  Drive chain
8  Coolant drain plug
9  Engine/transmission oil drain plug
10  Clutch cable lower adjuster
11  Engine/transmission oil filter
12  Front brake pads

**1**

1 This Chapter is designed to help the home mechanic maintain his/her motorcycle for safety, economy, long life and peak performance.

2 Deciding where to start or plug into the routine maintenance schedule depends on several factors. If your motorcycle has been maintained according to the warranty standards, you may want to pick up routine maintenance as it coincides with the next mileage or calendar interval. If you have owned the machine for some time but have never performed any maintenance on it, then you may want to start at the nearest interval and include some additional procedures to ensure that nothing important is overlooked. If you have just had a major engine overhaul, then you may want to start the maintenance routine from the beginning. If you have a used machine and have no knowledge of its history or maintenance record, you may desire to combine all the checks into one large service initially and then settle into the maintenance schedule prescribed.

3 Before beginning any maintenance or repair, the machine should be cleaned thoroughly, especially around the oil filter, spark plugs, valve covers, body panels, carburettors, etc. Cleaning will help ensure that dirt does not contaminate the engine and will allow you to detect wear and damage that could otherwise easily go unnoticed.

4 Certain maintenance information is sometimes printed on decals attached to the motorcycle. If the information on the decals differs from that included here, use the information on the decal.

# Every 600 miles (1000 km)

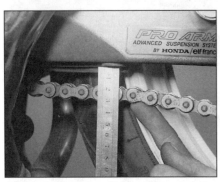

**1.3 Push up on the chain and measure the slack**

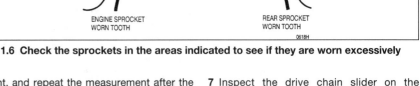

**1.6 Check the sprockets in the areas indicated to see if they are worn excessively**

## 1 Drive chain and sprockets – check, adjustment and lubrication

### Check

1 A neglected drive chain won't last long and can quickly damage the sprockets. Routine chain adjustment and lubrication isn't difficult and will ensure maximum chain and sprocket life.

2 To check the chain, place the bike on its sidestand and shift the transmission into neutral. Make sure the ignition switch is OFF.

3 Push up on the bottom run of the chain and measure the slack midway between the two sprockets, then compare your measurement to that listed in this Chapter's Specifications **(see illustration)**. As the chain stretches with wear, adjustment will periodically be necessary (see below). Since the chain will rarely wear evenly, roll the bike forwards so that another section of chain can be checked; do this several times to check the entire length of chain.

4 In some cases where lubrication has been neglected, corrosion and galling may cause the links to bind and kink, which effectively shortens the chain's length. Such links should be thoroughly cleaned and worked free. If the chain is tight between the sprockets, rusty or kinked, it's time to replace it with a new one. If you find a tight area, mark it with felt pen or paint, and repeat the measurement after the bike has been ridden. If the chain's still tight in the same area, it may be damaged or worn. Because a tight or kinked chain can damage the transmission bearings, it's a good idea to replace it.

*Caution: If the machine is ridden with more than 40 mm of slack in the drive chain, the chain will contact the frame and swingarm, causing severe damage.*

5 Check the entire length of the chain for damaged rollers, loose links and pins, and missing O-rings and replace it if damage is found. **Note:** *Never install a new chain on old sprockets, and never use the old chain if you install new sprockets – replace the chain and sprockets as a set.*

6 Remove the engine sprocket cover (see Chapter 6). Check the teeth on the engine sprocket and the rear wheel sprocket for wear **(see illustration)**.

7 Inspect the drive chain slider on the swingarm for excessive wear and replace it if worn (see Chapter 6).

### Adjustment

8 Rotate the rear wheel until the chain is positioned with the tightest point at the centre of its bottom run. If available, raise the rear wheel off the ground using an auxiliary stand or support.

9 Slacken the bearing holder pinch bolt **(see illustration)**.

10 Using the pin spanner tool provided in the toolkit or a suitable drift located in one of the notches in the adjuster, turn the bearing holder until the proper chain tension is obtained **(see illustration)**. Having completed the adjustment, on VFR models check the alignment of the tip of the sprocket tooth with the wear decal on the swingarm, and on RVF models check the alignment of the front of the

**1.9 Slacken the bearing holder pinch bolt (arrowed)**

**1.10a Turn the bearing holder using the tool provided or a suitable drift as shown**

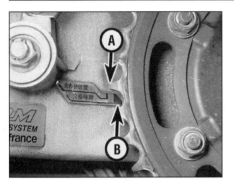

1.10b On VFR models, if the sprocket tooth (A) aligns with the red zone (B), replace the chain

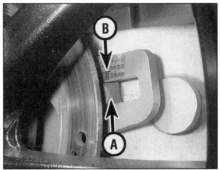

1.10c On RVF models, if the front of the block (A) aligns with the red zone (B), replace the chain

1.11 Tighten the pinch bolt to the specified torque

block on the inside of the swingarm with the wear decal on the slider section of the brake caliper bracket **(see illustrations)**. If either aligns with the red REPLACE CHAIN zone, the drive chain has stretched excessively and must be replaced.

**11** Tighten the bearing holder pinch bolt to the torque setting specified at the beginning of the Chapter **(see illustration)**.

### Lubrication

**12** If required, wash the chain in paraffin (kerosene), then wipe it off and allow it to dry, using compressed air if available. If the chain is excessively dirty it should be removed from

the machine and allowed to soak in the paraffin (see Chapter 6).
*Caution: Don't use petrol (gasoline), solvent or other cleaning fluids which might damage the internal sealing properties of the chain. Don't use high-pressure water to clean the chain. The entire process shouldn't take longer than ten minutes, otherwise the O-rings could be damaged.*
**13** For routine lubrication, the best time to lubricate the chain is after the motorcycle has been ridden. When the chain is warm, the lubricant will penetrate the joints between the sideplates better than when cold. **Note:** *Honda specifies SAE 80 to SAE 90 gear oil*

*only. If you use an aerosol chain lube make sure that it is suitable for O-ring or X-ring (sealed) chains; if it isn't, the solvents could damage the chain's sealing rings.* Apply the oil to the area where the sideplates overlap – not the middle of the rollers.

> **HAYNES HiNT** *Apply the oil to the top of the lower chain run, so centrifugal force will work the oil into the chain when the bike is moving. After applying the lubricant, let it soak in a few minutes before wiping off any excess.*

# Every 4000 miles (6000 km) or 6 months

### 2 Idle speed –
check and adjustment

**1** The idle speed should be checked and adjusted before and after the carburettors are synchronised (balanced) and when it is obviously too high or too low. Before adjusting the idle speed, make sure the valve clearances and spark plug gaps are correct. Also, turn the handlebars back-and-forth and see if the idle speed changes as this is done. If it does, the throttle cables may not be adjusted or routed correctly, or may be worn out. This is a dangerous condition that can cause loss of control of the bike. Be sure to correct this problem before proceeding.

**2** The engine should be at normal operating temperature, which is usually reached after 10 to 15 minutes of stop-and-go riding. Place the motorcycle on its sidestand, and make sure the transmission is in neutral.

**3** The idle speed adjuster is located in between the fairing side panel and the frame on the left-hand side **(see illustration)**. With the engine idling, adjust the idle speed by

turning the adjuster screw until the idle speed listed in this Chapter's Specifications is obtained. Turn the screw clockwise to increase idle speed, and anti-clockwise to decrease it.

**4** Snap the throttle open and shut a few times, then recheck the idle speed. If necessary, repeat the adjustment procedure.

**5** If a smooth, steady idle can't be achieved, the fuel/air mixture may be incorrect (see Chapter 4) or the carburettors may need synchronising (see Section 12).

2.3 Idle speed adjuster screw (arrowed)

### 3 Brake pads – wear check

**1** Each brake pad has wear indicators that can be viewed without removing the pads from the caliper. On the front brake caliper, the pad wear indicator grooves are visible by looking up at the lower edge of the pads **(see illustration)**. On the rear brake caliper, the pad wear indicator cutouts are visible by

3.1a Front brake pad wear indicator groove

1

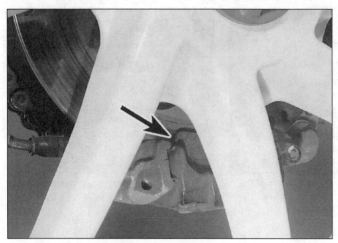

3.1b Rear brake pad wear cutout is located in the side of the pad

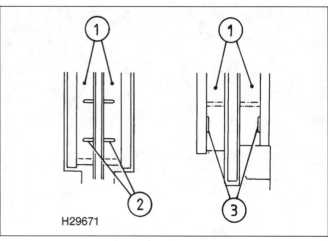

3.2 Pad wear indicators

*1 Pad friction material   2 Front pad grooves   3 Rear pad cutouts*

looking at the top edge of the pads **(see illustration)**.

**2** If the pads are worn to or beyond the bottom of the grooves (front pads) or to or beyond the beginning of the cutouts (rear pads), they must be replaced **(see illustration)**. If the pads are dirty or if you are in doubt as to the amount of friction material remaining, remove them for inspection (see Chapter 6). **Note:** *Some after-market pads may use different indicators to those on the original equipment as shown.*

**3** Refer to Chapter 7 for details of pad replacement.

## 4  Clutch – check and adjustment

**1** Check that the clutch cable operates smoothly and easily.

**2** If the clutch lever operation is heavy or stiff, remove the cable (see Chapter 2) and lubricate it (see Section 6). If the cable is still stiff, replace it. Install the lubricated or new cable (see Chapter 2).

**3** With the cable operating smoothly, check that the clutch lever is correctly adjusted. Periodic adjustment is necessary to compensate for wear in the clutch plates and stretch of the cable. Check that the amount of freeplay at the clutch lever end is within the specifications listed at the beginning of the Chapter **(see illustration)**.

**4** If adjustment is required, loosen the adjuster lockring at the top of the cable and turn the adjuster in or out until the required amount of freeplay is obtained **(see illustration)**. To increase freeplay, turn the adjuster clockwise. To reduce freeplay, turn the adjuster anti-clockwise. Tighten the locking ring securely.

**5** If all the adjustment has been taken up at the lever, reset the adjuster to give the maximum amount of freeplay, then set the correct amount of freeplay using the adjuster on the lower end of cable. The lower adjuster is set in a bracket on the alternator cover on the left-hand side of the engine. Use the nuts on each end of the threaded section in the cable to adjust freeplay **(see illustration)**. Remove the lower fairing to access the adjuster nuts (see Chapter 8). To increase freeplay, slacken the front nut and tighten the rear nut until the freeplay is as specified, then tighten the front nut. To reduce freeplay, slacken the rear nut and tighten the front nut until the freeplay is as specified, then tighten the rear nut. Subsequent adjustments can now be made using the lever adjuster only.

## 5  Spark plug gaps – check and adjustment

**1** Make sure your spark plug socket is the correct size before attempting to remove the plugs – a suitable one is supplied in the motorcycle's tool kit which is stored under the seat.

**2** To access the front cylinder spark plugs, remove the fairing side panels (see Chapter 8), then remove the upper radiator lower mounting bolts and swing the radiator forward.

**3** The rear cylinder spark plugs are accessed via the cutouts in the front of the seat cowl.

**4** Clean the area around the plug caps to prevent any dirt falling into the spark plug channels.

**5** Check that the cylinder location is marked on each plug lead, then pull the spark plug

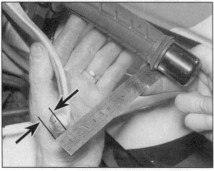

4.3 Measuring clutch cable freeplay

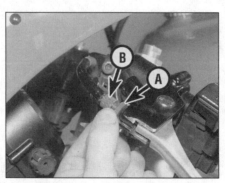

4.4 Slacken the lockring (A) and turn the adjuster (B) in or out as required

4.5 Clutch cable lower adjuster nuts

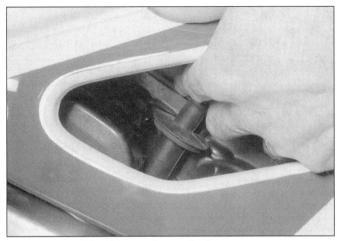

5.5a  Remove the spark plug cap . . .

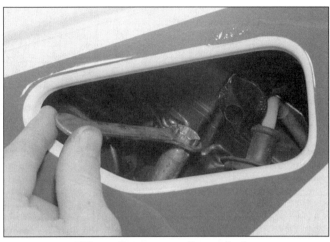

5.5b  . . . then unscrew the spark plug

cap off each spark plug **(see illustration)**. Clean the area around the base of the plugs to prevent any dirt falling into the engine. Using either the plug removing tool supplied in the bike's toolkit or a deep socket type wrench, unscrew the plugs from the cylinder head **(see illustration)**. Lay each plug out in relation to its cylinder; if any plug shows up a problem it will then be easy to identify the troublesome cylinder.

**6** Inspect the electrodes for wear. Both the centre and side electrodes should have square edges and the side electrodes should be of uniform thickness. Look for excessive deposits

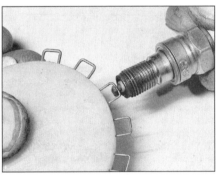

5.9a  Using a wire type gauge to measure the spark plug electrode gap

and evidence of a cracked or chipped insulator around the centre electrode. Compare your spark plugs to the colour spark plug reading chart at the end of this manual. Check the threads, the washer and the ceramic insulator body for cracks and other damage.

**7** If the electrodes are not excessively worn, and if the deposits can be easily removed with a wire brush, the plugs can be re-gapped and re-used (if no cracks or chips are visible in the insulator). If in doubt concerning the condition of the plugs, replace them with new ones, as the expense is minimal.

**8** Cleaning spark plugs by sandblasting is permitted, provided you clean the plugs with a high flash-point solvent afterwards.

**9** Before installing the plugs, make sure they are the correct type and heat range and check the gap between the electrodes **(see illustrations)**. Compare the gap to that specified and adjust as necessary. If the gap must be adjusted, bend the side electrodes only and be very careful not to chip or crack the insulator nose **(see illustration)**. Make sure the washer is in place before installing each plug.

**10** Since the cylinder head is made of aluminium, which is soft and easily damaged, thread the plugs into the heads turning the tool by hand **(see illustration)**. Once the plugs are finger-tight, the job can be finished

with a spanner on the tool supplied or a socket drive **(see illustration 1.5b)**. Tighten the spark plugs to the specified torque setting where possible – do not over-tighten them. If using the tool provided in the bike's toolkit to tighten the spark plugs, tighten them first by hand and then a further 120° for a new plug, or 30° for a used plug, using the tool handle.

> **HAYNES HINT** *As the plugs are quite recessed, slip a short length of hose over the end of the plug to use as a tool to thread it into place. The hose will grip the plug well enough to turn it, but will start to slip if the plug begins to cross-thread in the hole – this will prevent damaged threads.*

**11** Reconnect the spark plug caps, making sure they are securely connected to the correct cylinder. Install all other components previously removed.

> **HAYNES HINT** *Stripped plug threads in the cylinder head can be repaired with a Heli-Coil insert – see 'Tools and Workshop Tips' in the Reference section.*

**1**

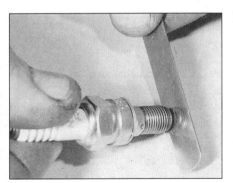

5.9b  Using a feeler gauge to measure the spark plug electrode gap

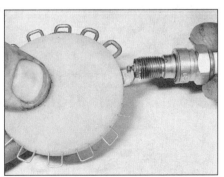

5.9c  Adjust the electrode gap by bending the side electrode only

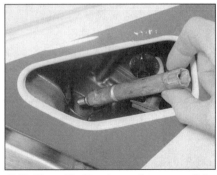

5.10  Thread in the plug as far as possible turning the tool by hand

## 6 Stand, lever pivots and cables – lubrication

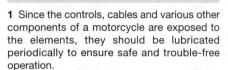

1 Since the controls, cables and various other components of a motorcycle are exposed to the elements, they should be lubricated periodically to ensure safe and trouble-free operation.

2 The footrests, clutch and brake levers, brake pedal, gearshift lever linkage and sidestand pivots should be lubricated frequently. In order for the lubricant to be applied where it will do the most good, the component should be disassembled. However, if chain and cable lubricant is being used, it can be applied to the pivot joint gaps and will usually work its way into the areas where friction occurs. If motor oil or light grease is being used, apply it sparingly as it may attract dirt (which could cause the controls to bind or wear at an accelerated rate).
**Note:** *One of the best lubricants for the control lever pivots is a dry-film lubricant (available from many sources by different names).*

3 To lubricate the cables, disconnect the relevant cable at its upper end, then lubricate

**6.3a Lubricating a cable with a pressure lubricator. Make sure the tool seals around the inner cable**

the cable with a pressure adapter and aerosol lubricant, or if one is not available, using motor oil via the set-up shown **(see illustrations)**. See Chapter 4 for the choke and throttle cable removal procedures.

4 The speedometer cable should be removed (see Chapter 9) and the inner cable withdrawn from the outer cable and lubricated with motor oil or cable lubricant. Do not lubricate the upper few inches of the cable as the lubricant may travel up into the instrument head.

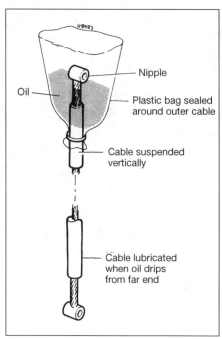

**6.3b Lubricating a cable with a makeshift funnel and motor oil**

# Every 8000 miles (12,000 km) or 12 months

*Carry out all the items under the 4000 mile (6000 km) check, plus the following:*

## 7 Engine oil and oil filter change

*Warning: Be careful when draining the oil, as the exhaust pipes, the engine, and the oil itself can cause severe burns.*

1 Consistent routine oil and filter changes are the single most important maintenance procedure you can perform on a motorcycle. The oil not only lubricates the internal parts of the engine, transmission and clutch, but it

also acts as a coolant, a cleaner, a sealant, and a protectant. Because of these demands, the oil takes a terrific amount of abuse and should be replaced often with new oil of the recommended grade and type. Saving a little money on the difference in cost between a good oil and a cheap oil won't pay off if the engine is damaged. The oil filter should be changed with every oil change.

2 Before changing the oil, warm up the engine so the oil will drain easily. Remove the lower fairing (see Chapter 8).

3 Put the motorcycle on its sidestand, and position a clean drain tray below the engine.

Unscrew the oil filler cap from the right-hand crankcase cover to vent the crankcase and to act as a reminder that there is no oil in the engine **(see illustration)**.

4 Next, unscrew the oil drain plug from the bottom of the engine and allow the oil to flow into the drain tray **(see illustrations)**. Check the condition of the sealing washer on the drain plug and replace it with a new one if damaged or worn.

5 When the oil has completely drained, fit the plug to the sump, using a new sealing washer if necessary, and tighten it to the torque setting specified at the beginning of the

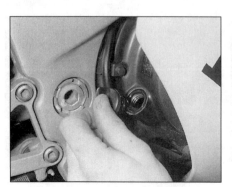

**7.3 Unscrew the oil filler cap . . .**

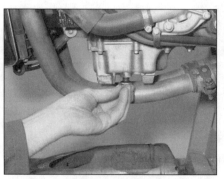

**7.4a . . . and the oil drain plug . . .**

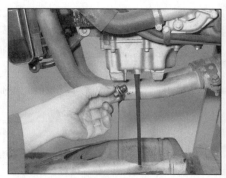

**7.4b . . . and allow the oil to completely drain**

7.5 Tighten the drain plug to the specified torque setting

7.6a Unscrew the filter using a filter removing tool (chain type shown) . . .

7.6b . . . then allow the oil to drain . . .

Chapter **(see illustration)**. Avoid overtightening, as damage to the sump will result.

**6** Now place the drain tray below the oil filter. Remove the bolt securing the bottom of the lower radiator to its bracket and swing the radiator forward. Unscrew the oil filter using a filter removing strap- or chain-wrench and tip any residual oil into the drain tray **(see illustrations)**. Remove the filter by manoeuvring it between the two front downpipes and the lower radiator.

**7** Smear clean engine oil onto the rubber seal on the new filter, then manoeuvre it between the two front downpipes and the lower radiator and screw it onto the engine **(see illustrations)**. Tighten it to the specified torque setting using a filter wrench, or if one is not available, tighten the filter as tight as possible by hand **(see illustration)**. Install the radiator mounting bolt and tighten it securely.

**8** Refill the engine to the proper level using the recommended type and amount of oil (see *Daily (pre-ride) checks*). With the motorcycle vertical, the oil level should lie between the upper and lower level lines on the dipstick (see *Daily (pre-ride) checks*). Install the filler cap **(see illustration 7.3)**. Start the engine and let it run for two or three minutes (make sure that the oil pressure light extinguishes after a few seconds). Shut it off, wait a few minutes, then check the oil level. If necessary, add more oil to bring the level up to the upper

level line on the dipstick. Check around the drain plug and the oil filter for leaks.

> **HAYNES HINT** *Saving a little money on the difference between good and cheap oils won't pay off if the engine is damaged as a result.*

**9** The old oil drained from the engine cannot be re-used and should be disposed of properly. Check with your local refuse disposal company, disposal facility or environmental agency to see whether they will accept the used oil for recycling. Don't pour used oil into drains or onto the ground.

> **HAYNES HINT** *Check the old oil carefully – if it is very metallic coloured, then the engine is experiencing wear from break-in (new engine) or from insufficient lubrication. If there are flakes or chips of metal in the oil, then something is drastically wrong internally and the engine will have to be disassembled for inspection and repair. If there are pieces of fibre-like material in the oil, the clutch is experiencing excessive wear and should be checked.*

7.6c . . . and remove the filter

## 8 Fuel system – check

> ⚠️ **Warning: Petrol (gasoline) is extremely flammable, so take extra precautions when you work on any part of the fuel system.** *Don't smoke or allow open flames or bare light bulbs near the work area, and don't work in a garage where a natural gas-type appliance is present. If you spill any fuel on your skin, rinse it off immediately with soap and water. When you perform any kind of work on the fuel system, wear safety glasses and have a fire extinguisher suitable for a Class B type fire (flammable liquids) on hand.*

**1**

7.7a Smear clean oil onto the filter seal . . .

7.7b . . . then install the filter . . .

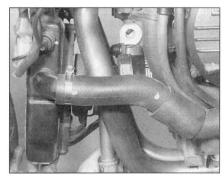

7.7c . . . and tighten it as described

### Check

**1** Remove the fuel tank (see Chapter 4) and check the tank, the fuel tap and the fuel and vacuum hoses for signs of leakage, deterioration or damage; in particular check that there is no leakage from the fuel hoses. Replace any hoses which are cracked or deteriorated.

**2** If the fuel tap is leaking, tighten the assembly screws (see Chapter 4). If leakage persists unscrew the screws and disassemble the tap, noting how the components fit. Inspect all components and replace any that are worn or damaged. Some components are available individually, though it may be necessary to replace the whole tap.

**3** If the carburettor gaskets are leaking, the carburettors should be disassembled and rebuilt using new gaskets and seals (see Chapter 4).

### Filter cleaning

**4** Cleaning or replacement of the fuel filter is advised after a particularly high mileage has been covered. It is also necessary if fuel starvation is suspected.

**5** The fuel filter is mounted in the tank and is integral with the fuel tap. Remove the fuel tank and the fuel tap (see Chapter 4). Clean the gauze filter to remove all traces of dirt and fuel sediment. Check the gauze for holes. If any are found, a new filter should be fitted (check for availability – it may be necessary to replace the whole tap). Check the condition of the O-ring and replace it if it is in any way damaged or deteriorated.

### 9 Battery – check

**1** All models covered in this manual are fitted with a sealed battery, and therefore require no maintenance. **Note:** *Do not attempt to remove the battery caps to check the electrolyte level or battery specific gravity. Removal will damage the caps, resulting in electrolyte leakage and battery damage.* All that should be done is to check that its terminals are clean and tight and that the casing is not damaged or leaking. See Chapter 9 for further details.

**2** If the machine is not in regular use, disconnect the battery and give it a refresher charge every month to six weeks, as described in Chapter 9.

### 10 Throttle and choke cables – check

### Throttle cables

**1** Make sure the throttle grip rotates easily from fully closed to fully open with the front wheel turned at various angles. The grip should return automatically from fully open to fully closed when released.

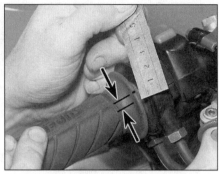

**10.3 Throttle cable freeplay is measured in terms of twistgrip rotation**

**2** If the throttle sticks, this is probably due to a cable fault. Remove the cables (see Chapter 4) and lubricate them (see Section 6). Install the cables, making sure they are correctly routed. If this fails to improve the operation of the throttle, the cables must be replaced. Note that in very rare cases the fault could lie in the carburettors rather than the cables, necessitating the removal of the carburettors and inspection of the throttle linkage (see Chapter 4).

**3** With the throttle operating smoothly, check for a small amount of freeplay in the cables, measured in terms of the amount of twistgrip rotation before the throttle opens, and compare the amount to that listed in this Chapter's Specifications **(see illustration)**. If it's incorrect, adjust the cables to correct it.

**4** Freeplay adjustments can be made at the throttle end of the cable. Loosen the locknut on the accelerator cable where it leaves the handlebar **(see illustration)**. Turn the adjuster until the specified amount of freeplay is obtained (see this Chapter's Specifications), then retighten the locknut.

**5** If the adjuster has reached its limit of adjustment, reset it so that the freeplay is at a maximum, then remove the fuel tank and air filter housing (see Chapter 4) and adjust the cable at the carburettor end. On VFR models, the adjuster is on the upper cable in the bracket, and on RVF models, the adjuster is on the lower cable. Slacken the adjuster locknut, then screw the adjuster out, making sure the lower nut remains captive in the bracket, thereby threading itself down the

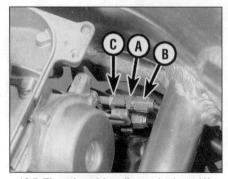

**10.5 Throttle cable adjuster locknut (A), adjuster (B) and lower nut (C) – carburettor end (VFR model shown)**

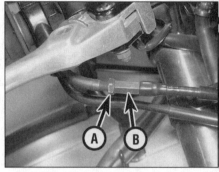

**10.4 Throttle cable adjuster locknut (A) and adjuster (B) – throttle end**

adjuster as you turn it, until the specified amount of freeplay is obtained, then tighten the locknut **(see illustration)**. Further adjustments can now be made at the throttle end. If the cable cannot be adjusted as specified, replace the cable (see Chapter 4).

 **Warning: Turn the handlebars all the way through their travel with the engine idling. Idle speed should not change. If it does, the cables may be routed incorrectly. Correct this condition before riding the bike.**

**6** Check that the throttle twistgrip operates smoothly and snaps shut quickly when released.

### Choke cable

**7** If the choke does not operate smoothly this is probably due to a cable fault. Remove the cable (see Chapter 4) and lubricate it (see Section 6). Install the cable, routing it so it takes the smoothest route possible.

**8** If this fails to improve the operation of the choke, the cable must be replaced. Note that in very rare cases the fault could lie in the carburettors rather than the cable, necessitating the removal of the carburettors and inspection of the choke plungers (see Chapter 4). Make sure there is a small amount of freeplay in the cable before the plungers move. If there isn't, check that the cable is seating correctly at both the lever and the carburettor ends. If it is, then slacken the choke outer cable bracket screw on the carburettor and slide the cable further into the bracket, creating some freeplay **(see illustration)**. Otherwise, replace the cable.

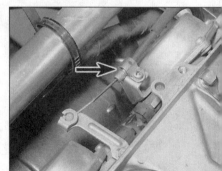

**10.8 Slide the outer cable end (arrowed) further into the bracket to create some freeplay**

## 11 Spark plugs – replacement

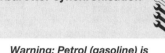

1 Remove the old spark plugs as described in Section 5 and install new ones.

## 12 Carburettor synchronisation

**Warning: Petrol (gasoline) is extremely flammable, so take extra precautions when you work on any part of the fuel system. Don't smoke or allow open flames or bare light bulbs near the work area, and don't work in a garage where a natural gas-type appliance is present. If you spill any fuel on your skin, rinse it off immediately with soap and water. When you perform any kind of work on the fuel system, wear safety glasses and have a fire extinguisher suitable for a Class B type fire (flammable liquids) on hand.**
**Warning: Take great care not to burn your hand on the hot engine unit when accessing the gauge take-off points on the intake manifolds. Do not allow exhaust gases to build up in the work area; either perform the check outside or use an exhaust gas extraction system.**

1 Carburettor synchronisation is simply the process of adjusting the carburettors so they pass the same amount of fuel/air mixture to each cylinder. This is done by measuring the vacuum produced in each cylinder. Carburettors that are out of synchronisation will result in decreased fuel mileage, increased engine temperature, less than ideal throttle response and higher vibration levels. Before synchronising the carburettors, make sure the valve clearances are properly set.
2 To properly synchronise the carburettors,

you will need a set of vacuum gauges or calibrated tubes to indicate engine vacuum. The equipment used should be suitable for a four cylinder engine and come complete with the necessary adapters and hoses to fit the take-off points. **Note:** *Because of the nature of the synchronisation procedure and the need for special instruments, most owners leave the task to a Honda dealer. Also access to the synchronisation screws is very difficult as they are on the underside of the carburettors - a flexi-drive screwdriver helps.*

**Warning: The engine and carburettors will be hot. With the restricted access to the screws, great care must be taken not to burn yourself while synchronising the carburettors.**

3 Remove the lower fairing (see Chapter 8).
4 Start the engine and let it run until it reaches normal operating temperature, then shut it off.
5 Disconnect the vacuum hose from the vacuum take-off stub on the no. 3 cylinder intake manifold. Apply a vacuum to the hose and seal it off using a clamp. This ensures the fuel tap is open and can supply fuel to the carburettors. Remove the blanking screws from the intake manifolds of the remaining carburettors **(see illustration)**.
6 Connect the vacuum gauge adapters to the intake manifolds. Make sure they are a good fit because any air leaks will result in false readings.
7 Start the engine and adjust the idle speed (see Section 2). If using vacuum gauges fitted with damping adjustment, set this so that the needle flutter is just eliminated but so that they can still respond to small changes in pressure.
9 The vacuum readings for all of the cylinders should be the same. If the vacuum readings vary, proceed as follows.
10 The carburettors are adjusted by turning the synchronising screws situated in-between the carburettors, in the throttle linkage. **Note:** *Do not press up on the screws whilst adjusting them, otherwise a false reading will be obtained.*

**12.5 Intake manifold blanking plug (arrowed)**

11 On VFR models, first synchronise no. 4 carburettor to no. 2 using the synchronising screw between the two front cylinder carburettors, until the readings are the same **(see illustration)**. Then synchronise no. 1 carburettor to no. 3 using the left-hand synchronising screw (that next to no. 1 carburettor) between the two rear cylinder carburettors, and finally synchronise nos. 1 and 3 carburettors to nos. 2 and 4 carburettors using the right-hand synchronising screw (that next to no. 3 carburettor) between the two rear cylinder carburettors.
12 On RVF models, first synchronise no. 3 carburettor to no. 1 using the synchronising screw between the two rear cylinder carburettors, until the readings are the same **(see illustration)**. Then synchronise no. 2 carburettor to no. 4 using the right-hand synchronising screw (that next to no. 4 carburettor) between the two front cylinder carburettors, and finally synchronise nos. 1 and 3 carburettors to nos. 2 and 4 using the left-hand synchronising screw (that next to no. 2 carburettor) between the two front cylinder carburettors.
13 When all the carburettors are synchronised, open and close the throttle quickly to settle the linkage, and recheck the gauge readings, readjusting if necessary.

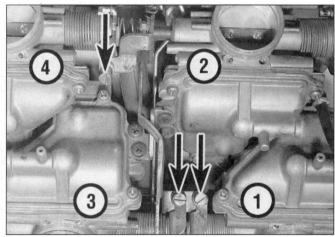

**12.11 Synchronisation screws and carburettor identification – VFR model (arrowed)**

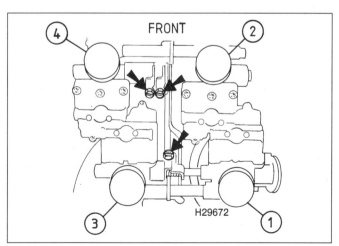

**12.12 Synchronisation screws and carburettor identification – RVF model (arrowed)**

**14** When the adjustment is complete, recheck the vacuum readings, then adjust the idle speed by turning the throttle stop screw (see Section 2) until the idle speed listed in this Chapter's Specifications is obtained. Stop the engine.

**15** Remove the vacuum gauges. Release the clamp on the fuel tap vacuum hose and connect it to the take-off stub on the no. 3 cylinder intake manifold. Fit the blanking screws into the remaining intake manifolds, making sure that their sealing washers are in place.

**16** Install the lower fairing (see Chapter 8).

## 13 Cooling system check

**Warning: The engine must be cool before beginning this procedure.**

**1** Check the coolant level (see *Daily (pre-ride) checks*).

**2** Remove the lower fairing (see Chapter 8). The entire cooling system should be checked for evidence of leakage. Examine each rubber coolant hose along its entire length. Look for cracks, abrasions and other damage. Squeeze each hose at various points. They should feel firm, yet pliable, and return to their original shape when released. If they are dried out or hard, replace them with new ones.

**3** Check for evidence of leaks at each cooling system joint. Tighten the hose clips carefully to prevent future leaks.

**4** Check the radiators for leaks and other damage. Leaks in the radiators leave tell-tale scale deposits or coolant stains on the outside of the core below the leak. If leaks are noted, remove the radiator (see Chapter 3) and have it repaired or replace it with a new one.

*Caution: Do not use a liquid leak stopping compound to try to repair leaks.*

**5** Check the radiator fins for mud, dirt and insects, which may impede the flow of air through the radiator. If the fins are dirty, remove the radiators (see Chapter 3) and clean them using water or low pressure compressed air directed through the fins from the rear side of the radiator. If the fins are bent or distorted, straighten them carefully with a screwdriver. If the air flow is restricted by bent or damaged fins over more than 30% of the radiator's surface area, replace the radiator.

**6** Remove the pressure cap from the upper radiator filler neck by turning it anti-clockwise until it reaches a stop **(see illustration)**. If you hear a hissing sound (indicating there is still pressure in the system), wait until it stops. Now press down on the cap and continue turning the cap until it can be removed. Check the condition of the coolant in the system. If it is rust-coloured or if accumulations of scale are visible, drain, flush and refill the system (See Section 24). Check the cap seal for cracks and other damage. If in doubt about the pressure cap's condition, have it tested by a Honda dealer or replace it with a new one. Install the cap by turning it clockwise until it reaches the first stop then push down on the cap and continue turning until it can turn no further.

**7** Check the antifreeze content of the coolant with an antifreeze hydrometer. Sometimes coolant looks like it's in good condition, but might be too weak to offer adequate protection. If the hydrometer indicates a weak mixture, drain, flush and refill the system (see Section 24).

**8** Start the engine and let it reach normal operating temperature, then check for leaks again. As the coolant temperature increases, the fan should come on automatically and the temperature should begin to drop. If it does not, refer to Chapter 3 and check the fan and fan circuit carefully.

**9** If the coolant level is consistently low, and no evidence of leaks can be found, have the entire system pressure checked by a Honda dealer.

## 14 Brake system – check

**1** A routine general check of the brake system will ensure that any problems are discovered and remedied before the rider's safety is jeopardised.

**2** Check the brake lever and pedal for loose connections, improper or rough action, excessive play, bends, and other damage. Replace any damaged parts with new ones (see Chapter 7).

**3** Make sure all brake fasteners are tight. Check the brake pads for wear (see Section 3) and make sure the fluid level in the reservoirs is correct (see *Daily (pre-ride) checks*). Look for leaks at the hose connections and check for cracks in the hoses. If the lever or pedal is spongy, bleed the brakes (see Chapter 7).

**4** Make sure the brake light operates when the front brake lever is pulled in. The front brake light switch, mounted on the underside of the master cylinder, is not adjustable. If it fails to operate properly, check it (see Chapter 9).

**5** Make sure the brake light is activated just before the rear brake takes effect. If adjustment is necessary, hold the switch and turn the adjuster ring on the switch body until the brake light is activated when required **(see illustration)**. The switch is mounted on the inside of the rider's right-hand footrest bracket, just ahead of the master cylinder. If the brake light comes on too late, turn the ring clockwise. If the brake light comes on too soon or is permanently on, turn the ring anti-clockwise. If the switch doesn't operate the brake light, check it (see Chapter 9).

**6** The front brake lever has a span adjuster which alters the distance of the lever from the handlebar **(see illustration)**. Each setting is identified by a notch in the adjuster which aligns with the arrow on the lever. Pull the lever away from the handlebar and turn the adjuster ring until the setting which best suits the rider is obtained. There are two settings.

## 15 Headlight aim – check and adjustment

**Note:** *An improperly adjusted headlight may cause problems for oncoming traffic or provide poor, unsafe illumination of the road ahead. Before adjusting the headlight aim, be sure to consult with local traffic laws and regulations – for UK models refer to MOT Test Checks in the Reference section.*

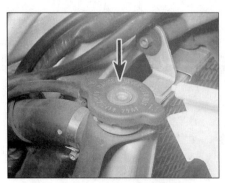

**13.6 Cooling system pressure cap (arrowed)**

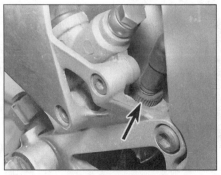

**14.5 Rear brake light switch adjuster ring (arrowed)**

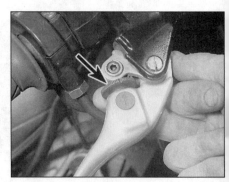

**14.6 Front brake lever span adjuster ring (arrowed)**

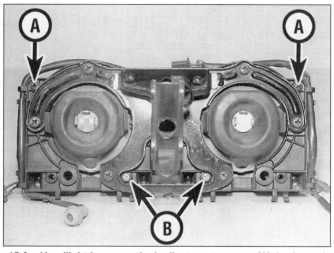

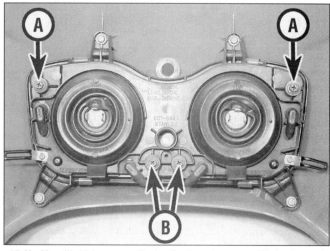

**15.2a Headlight beam vertical adjustment screws (A), horizontal adjustment screws (B) - VFR models**

**15.2b Headlight beam vertical adjustment screws (A), horizontal adjustment screws (B) - RVF models**

**1** The headlight beam can adjusted both horizontally and vertically. Before making any adjustment, check that the tyre pressures are correct and the suspension is adjusted as required. Make any adjustments to the headlight aim with the machine on level ground, with the fuel tank half full and with an assistant sitting on the seat. If the bike is usually ridden with a passenger on the back, have a second assistant to do this.

**2** Vertical adjustment is made by turning the adjuster screw on the top outer corner of each headlight unit **(see illustrations)**. Turn it clockwise to move the beam up, and anti-clockwise to move it down.

**3** Horizontal adjustment is made by turning the adjuster screw on the bottom inner corner of each headlight unit **(see illustrations 15.2a and b)**. Turn it clockwise to move the beam in, and anti-clockwise to move it out.

## 16 Sidestand – check

**1** The sidestand return spring must be capable of retracting the stand fully and

holding the stand retracted when the motorcycle is in use. If the spring is sagged or broken it must be replaced.

**2** Lubricate the sidestand pivot regularly (see Section 6).

**3** On VFR models, check the condition of the sidestand rubber. If it is worn down to or beyond the wear limit line, replace it with a new one **(see illustration)**.

**4** On RVF models, the sidestand switch prevents the motorcycle being started if the stand is extended. Check its operation by shifting the transmission into neutral, retracting the stand and starting the engine. Pull in the clutch lever and select a gear. Extend the sidestand. The engine should stop as the sidestand is extended. If the sidestand switch does not operate as described, check its circuit (see Chapter 9).

## 17 Suspension – check

**1** The suspension components must be maintained in top operating condition to ensure rider safety. Loose, worn or damaged

suspension parts decrease the motorcycle's stability and control.

### Front suspension

**2** While standing alongside the motorcycle, apply the front brake and push on the handlebars to compress the forks several times. See if they move up-and-down smoothly without binding. If binding is felt, the forks should be disassembled and inspected (see Chapter 6).

**3** Inspect the area around the dust seal for signs of oil leakage, then carefully lever up the dust seal using a flat-bladed screwdriver and inspect the area around the fork seal **(see illustration)**. If leakage is evident, the seals must be replaced (see Chapter 6).

**4** Check the tightness of all suspension nuts and bolts to be sure none have worked loose.

### Rear suspension

**5** Inspect the rear shock for fluid leakage and tightness of its mountings. If leakage is found, the shock should be replaced (see Chapter 6).

**6** With the aid of an assistant to support the bike, compress the rear suspension several times. It should move up and down freely without binding. If any binding is felt, the worn or faulty component must be identified and replaced. The problem could be due to either the shock absorber, the suspension linkage components or the swingarm components.

**7** Support the motorcycle using an auxiliary stand so that the rear wheel is off the ground. Grab the swingarm and rock it from side to side – there should be no discernible movement at the rear **(see illustration overleaf)**. If there's a little movement or a slight clicking can be heard, inspect the tightness of all the rear suspension mounting bolts and nuts, referring to the torque settings specified at the beginning of the Chapter, and re-check for movement. Next, grasp the top of the rear wheel and pull it upwards – there

**16.3 Replace the sidestand rubber if it is worn to or beyond the line (arrowed)**

**17.3 Check above and below the dust seal for signs of oil leakage**

**1**

17.7a Checking for play in the swingarm bearings

17.7b Checking for play in the rear shock mountings and suspension linkage bearings

18.4 Checking for play in the steering head bearings

should be no discernible freeplay before the shock absorber begins to compress (see illustration). Any freeplay felt in either check indicates worn bearings in the suspension linkage or swingarm, or worn shock absorber mountings. The worn components must be replaced (see Chapter 6).

8 To make an accurate assessment of the swingarm bearings, remove the rear wheel (see Chapter 7) and the bolt securing the suspension linkage assembly to the swingarm (see Chapter 6). Grasp the rear of the swingarm with one hand and place your other hand at the junction of the swingarm and the frame. Try to move the rear of the swingarm from side-to-side. Any wear (play) in the

18.5 Slacken the right-hand bolt (A) and the left-hand bolt (B)

bearings should be felt as movement between the swingarm and the frame at the front. If there is any play the swingarm will be felt to move forward and backward at the front (not from side-to-side). Next, move the swingarm up and down through its full travel. It should move freely, without any binding or rough spots. If any play in the swingarm is noted or if the swingarm does not move freely, the bearings must be removed for inspection or replacement (see Chapter 5).

## 18 Steering head bearings – freeplay check and adjustment

1 This motorcycle is equipped with caged ball steering head bearings which can become dented, rough or loose during normal use of the machine. In extreme cases, worn or loose steering head bearings can cause steering wobble – a condition that is potentially dangerous.

### Check

2 Support the motorcycle in an upright position using an auxiliary stand. Raise the front wheel off the ground either by having an assistant push down on the rear or by placing a support under the engine.
3 Point the front wheel straight-ahead and

slowly move the handlebars from side-to-side. Any dents or roughness in the bearing races will be felt and the bars will not move smoothly and freely.
4 Next, grasp the forks and try to move them forward and backward (see illustration). Any looseness in the steering head bearings will be felt as front-to-rear movement of the forks. If play is felt in the bearings, adjust the steering head as follows.

> **HAYNES HiNT** *Freeplay in the fork due to worn fork bushes can be misinterpreted for steering head bearing play – do not confuse the two.*

### Adjustment

5 Slacken the right-hand fork clamp bolt in the top yoke and remove the left-hand clamp bolt, noting the clutch cable guide secured by the bolt (see illustration). The handlebar clamp bolts can remain in place.
6 Prise the cap off the steering stem nut and remove the nut using a 41 mm socket or spanner (see illustrations).
7 Gently ease the top yoke upwards off the fork tubes and position it clear of the head bearings, using a rag to protect the tank or other components (see illustration).
8 Prise the lockwasher tabs out of the

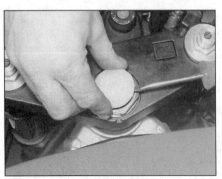

18.6a Prise off the nut cap . . .

18.6b . . . then unscrew the nut . . .

18.7 . . . and ease the yoke up off the forks

**18.8a Bend down the tabs securing the locknut . . .**

**18.8b . . . and remove the locknut**

**18.9a Adjust the bearings using either a C-spanner . . .**

notches in the locknut **(see illustration)**. Unscrew the locknut using either a C-spanner or a suitable drift located in one of the notches **(see illustration)**. Remove the lockwasher, bending up the remaining tabs to release it from the adjuster nut if necessary. Inspect the tabs for cracks or signs of fatigue. If there are any, discard the lockwasher and use a new one; otherwise the old one can be re-used.

**9** Using either the C-spanner or drift, slacken the adjuster nut slightly until pressure is just released, then tighten it until all freeplay is removed, yet the steering is able to move freely **(see illustrations)**. The object is to set

the adjuster nut so that the bearings are under a very light loading, just enough to remove any freeplay.

**Caution: Take great care not to apply excessive pressure because this will cause premature failure of the bearings.**

**10** With the bearings correctly adjusted, install the lockwasher, using a new one if the tabs are weakened or cracked, onto the adjuster nut and fit two tabs into the slots in the adjuster nut **(see illustration)**.

**11** Hold the adjuster nut to prevent it from moving, then install the locknut and tighten it finger-tight **(see illustration 18.8b)**. Tighten

the locknut further until its notches align with the remaining lockwasher tabs. Secure the locknut in position by bending up the lock washer tabs into its notches **(see illustration)**.

**12** Fit the top yoke to the steering stem **(see illustration 18.7)**, then install the nut and tighten it and both the fork clamp bolts to the torque settings specified at the beginning of the Chapter **(see illustration)**. Do not forget to secure the clutch cable guide with the left-hand fork clamp bolt **(see illustration)**. Fit the cap over the stem nut.

**13** Check the bearing adjustment as described above and re-adjust if necessary.

**18.9b . . . or a drift**

**18.10 Use a new lockwasher if the tabs on the old one are fatigued or cracked**

**18.11 Bend the tabs up into the notches in the locknut**

**1**

**18.12a Tighten the steering stem nut to the specified torque**

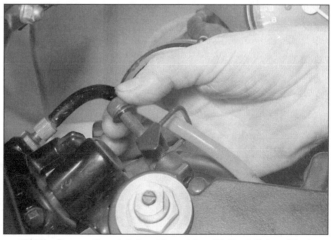

**18.12b Secure the clutch cable guide with the left-hand fork clamp bolt**

## 19 Nuts and bolts – tightness check

1 Since vibration of the machine tends to loosen fasteners, all nuts, bolts, screws, etc. should be periodically checked for proper tightness.
2 Pay particular attention to the following:
  Spark plugs
  Engine oil drain plug
  Gearshift pedal bolt
  Footrest and stand bolts
  Engine mounting bolts
  Shock absorber and suspension linkage bolts and swingarm pivot bolts
  Handlebar clamp bolts
  Front axle bolt and axle clamp bolts
  Front fork clamp bolts (top and bottom yoke)
  Rear wheel nut and bearing holder pinch bolt

**19.3 Torque wrenches are available in various ranges**

  Brake caliper mounting bolts
  Brake hose banjo bolts and caliper bleed valves
  Brake disc bolts
  Exhaust system bolts/nuts
3 If a torque wrench is available, use it along with the torque specifications at the beginning of this and other Chapters **(see illustration).**

## 20 Wheels and tyres – general check

### Tyres

1 Check the tyre condition and tread depth thoroughly – see Daily (pre-ride) checks.

### Wheels

2 Cast wheels are virtually maintenance free, but they should be kept clean and checked periodically for cracks and other damage. Also check the wheel runout and alignment (see Chapter 7). Never attempt to repair damaged cast wheels; they must be replaced with new ones. Check the valve rubber for signs of damage or deterioration and have it replaced if necessary. Also, make sure the valve stem cap is in place and tight.

# Every 12,000 miles (18,000 km) or 18 months

Carry out all the items under the 4000 mile (6000 km) check, plus the following:

## 21 Air filter – replacement

**Caution: If the machine is continually ridden in wet or dusty conditions, the filter should be replaced more frequently.**

1 Remove the fuel tank (see Chapter 4).
2 Release the clamp securing each sub air cleaner hose to the union on the back of the housing and detach the hoses **(see illustration).**
3 On VFR models, release the clamp securing the drain hose to the left-hand side of the housing and detach the hose **(see illustration).**

4 Remove the seven screws securing the air filter cover to the filter housing and remove the cover **(see illustrations).** Remove the filter element from the housing and discard it **(see illustration).** Check the condition of the sub air cleaner element, and clean or replace it as required **(see illustration).**

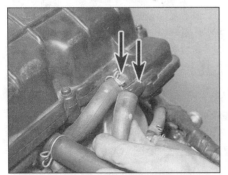

**21.2 Detach the sub-air cleaner hoses (arrowed) . . .**

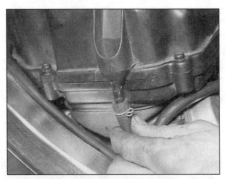

**21.3 . . . and on VFR models, the drain hose**

**21.4a Remove the cover screws . . .**

**21.4b . . . then lift off the cover . . .**

**21.4c . . . and remove the air filter**

**21.4d Check the condition of the sub air cleaner element**

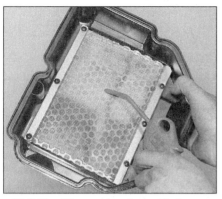

21.6 The filter can be cleaned between intervals using compressed air

5 Install the new filter by reversing the removal procedure. Make sure the filter is properly seated, then install the cover and attach the sub air cleaner hoses and drain hose (VFR models only), securing them with the clamps. Install the fuel tank (see Chapter 4).

6 To clean the filter in between replacement service intervals, tap the filter on a hard surface to dislodge any dirt and use compressed air to clear the element, directing the air from the inside **(see illustration)**.

## 22 Brakes – fluid change

1 The brake fluid should be replaced at the prescribed interval or whenever a master cylinder or caliper overhaul is carried out. Refer to the brake bleeding section in Chapter 7, noting that all old fluid must be pumped from the fluid reservoir and hydraulic line before filling with new fluid.

> **HAYNES HINT** *Old brake fluid is invariably much darker in colour than new fluid, making it easy to see when all old fluid has been expelled from the system.*

# Every 16,000 miles (24,000 km) or two years

*Carry out all the items under the 8000 mile (12,000 km) check, plus the following:*

## 23 Valve clearances – check and adjustment

1 The engine must be completely cool for this maintenance procedure, so let the machine sit overnight before beginning.
2 Remove the spark plugs (see Section 5).
3 Remove the lower fairing (see Chapter 8) and the valve covers (see Chapter 2). Each cylinder is referred to by a number (see Specifications).
4 Make a chart or sketch of all valve positions so that a note of each clearance can be made against the relevant valve.
5 Unscrew the timing inspection cover from the right-hand crankcase cover **(see illustration)**. Discard the cover O-ring as a new one must be used. The engine can be turned using a 14 mm spanner or socket on the starter clutch bolt and turning it in a clockwise direction only **(see illustration)**. Alternatively, place the motorcycle on an auxiliary stand so that the rear wheel is off the ground, select a high gear and rotate the rear wheel by hand in its normal direction of rotation.

6 Turn the engine until the "T1" mark on the timing plate aligns with the static timing mark on the crankcase cover, and the index lines on the right-hand end of the camshafts on the rear cylinder head are facing away from the head **(see illustrations)**. If they are facing towards the head, rotate the engine clockwise one full turn until the "T1" mark again aligns with the static timing mark. The camshaft index lines will now be facing away and the no. 1 cylinder is at TDC on the compression stroke.

23.5a Remove the timing inspection cover

7 With no. 1 cylinder at TDC on the compression stroke, check the clearances on the no.1 cylinder inlet and exhaust valves. Insert a feeler gauge of the same thickness as the correct valve clearance (see Specifications) between the rocker arm and shim of each valve and check that it is a firm sliding fit – you should feel a slight drag when the you pull the gauge out **(see illustration)**. If not, use the feeler gauges to obtain the exact clearance. Record the measured clearance on the chart.

23.5b Turn the engine clockwise using a 14 mm socket on the starter clutch bolt

**1**

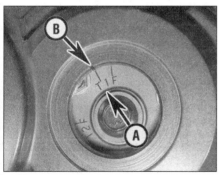

23.6a Turn the engine until the T1 mark (A) aligns with the static mark (B) . . .

23.6b . . . and the camshaft index lines (arrowed) face away from the head

23.7 Measure the valve clearance using a feeler gauge as shown

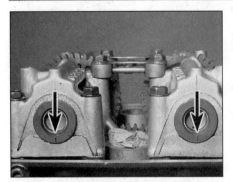

**23.8 Camshafts shown with the index lines (arrowed) facing towards the head**

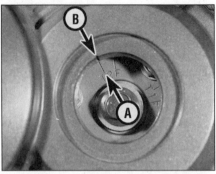

**23.9 Align the T2 mark (A) with the static mark (B)**

**23.12a Slide the rocker arm across . . .**

**8** Now rotate the engine clockwise until the "T1" mark on the timing plate again aligns with the static timing mark on the crankcase cover, and the index lines on the right-hand end of the camshafts on the rear cylinder head are facing towards the head **(see illustration)**. The no. 3 cylinder is now at TDC on the compression stroke. Measure the valve clearance of the no. 3 cylinder valves using the method described in Step 7.

**9** Rotate the engine clockwise until the "T2" mark on the timing plate aligns with the static timing mark on the crankcase cover **(see illustration)**, and the index lines on the right-hand end of the camshafts on the front cylinder head are facing away from the head **(see illustration 23.6b)**. The no. 4 cylinder is now at TDC on the compression stroke.

**23.12b . . . to access the shim**

Measure the valve clearance of the no. 4 cylinder valves using the method described in Step 7.

**10** Rotate the engine clockwise until the "T2" mark on the timing plate again aligns with the static timing mark on the crankcase cover, and the index lines on the right-hand end of the camshafts on the front cylinder head are facing towards the head **(see illustration 23.8)**. The no. 2 cylinder is now at TDC on the compression stroke. Measure the valve clearance of the no. 2 cylinder valves using the method described in Step 7.

**11** When all clearances have been measured and charted, identify whether the clearance on any valve falls outside the specified range. If any do, the shim between the rocker arm and the valve must be replaced with one of a thickness which will restore the correct clearance.

**12** Make sure the cylinder being worked on is at TDC on the compression stroke before removing the shim. Place rags over the spark plug holes and the cam gear train holes to prevent a shim from dropping into the engine on removal. To access the shim being replaced, slide the rocker arm above that shim along its shaft and against the pressure of the spring, until the shim is accessible **(see illustrations)**.

*Caution: If the valve clearance is tight, it is possible that the shim may pop out when the rocker arm is slid across.*

**13** If available, use a magnet to remove the

shim **(see illustration)**. Otherwise, put a dab of grease onto a small screwdriver and remove the shim – it will stick to the grease **(see illustration)**. Do not allow the shim to fall into the engine.

**14** Measure the shim using a micrometer to determine its size **(see illustration)**.

**15** Calculate the required replacement shim by using the formula $a = b - c + d$, where $a$ is the required shim size, $b$ is the measured valve clearance, $c$ is the specified valve clearance, and $d$ is the existing shim thickness. For example:

*The measured clearance of a no. 1 cylinder inlet valve is 0.20 mm, so b = 0.20.*

*The specified clearance range for an inlet valve is 0.12 to 0.18 mm, the mid-point being 0.15 mm, so c = 0.15.*

*The thickness of the existing shim is 2.200 mm, so d = 2.2.*

*Therefore, the required replacement shim a = 0.20 – 0.15 + 2.2 (a = 2.25 mm)*

**Note:** *If the required replacement shim is greater than 2.800 mm (the largest available), the valve is probably not seating correctly due to a build-up of carbon deposits and should be checked and cleaned or resurfaced as required (see Chapter 2).*

**23.13a Remove the shim using a magnet . . .**

**23.13b . . . or a screwdriver with a dab of grease**

**23.14 Measure the shim using a micrometer**

**16** Shims are available in 0.025 mm increments from 1.200 mm to 2.800 mm. Obtain and install the replacement shim in the recess in the top of the valve spring retainer **(see illustration 23.12b)**, noting that the shim should be lubricated with molybdenum disulphide oil (a 50/50 mixture of molybdenum disulphide grease and engine oil).

**17** Make sure the shim is correctly seated, then slide the rocker arm onto the shim, making sure it doesn't catch the edge of the shim, and that it is centrally positioned. Repeat the process for any other valves until the clearances are correct.

**18** Rotate the crankshaft several turns to seat the new shim(s), then check the clearances again.

**19** Install all disturbed components in a reverse of the removal sequence. Use a new O-ring on the timing inspection cover and

23.19a  Fit the cover using a new O-ring . . .

23.19b  . . . and tighten it to the specified torque

smear it and the cover threads with molybdenum disulphide oil (a 50/50 mixture of molybdenum disulphide grease and engine

oil) **(see illustration)**. Tighten the cover to the torque setting specified at the beginning of the Chapter **(see illustration)**.

# Every 24,000 miles (36,000 km) or two years

*Carry out all the items under the 8000 mile (12,000 km) check, plus the following:*

## 24 Cooling system – draining, flushing and refilling

⚠️ *Warning: Allow the engine to cool completely before performing this maintenance operation. Also, don't allow antifreeze to come into contact with your skin or the painted surfaces of the motorcycle. Rinse off spills immediately with plenty of water. Antifreeze is highly toxic if ingested. Never leave antifreeze lying around in an open container or in puddles on the floor; children and pets are attracted by its sweet smell and may drink it. Check with local authorities (councils) about disposing of antifreeze. Many communities have collection centres which will see that antifreeze is disposed of safely. Antifreeze is also combustible, so don't store it near open flames.*

### Draining

**1** Remove the lower fairing and the right-hand fairing side panel (see Chapter 8). Remove the pressure cap by turning it anti-clockwise until it reaches a stop **(see illustration 13.6)**. If you hear a hissing sound (indicating there is still pressure in the system), wait until it stops. Now press down on the cap and continue turning the cap until it can be removed.

**2** Position a suitable container beneath the water pump. Remove the coolant drain plug and its sealing washer and allow the coolant to completely drain from the system **(see illustrations)**. Retain the old sealing washer for use during flushing.

**3** Position the container beneath the front cylinders, then remove the drain plugs and

sealing washers and allow the coolant to completely drain from the engine **(see illustrations)**. Retain the old sealing washers for use during flushing.

### Flushing

**4** Flush the system with clean tap water by inserting a garden hose in the radiator filler

neck. Allow the water to run through the system until it is clear and flows cleanly out of the drain holes. If the radiator is extremely corroded, remove it (see Chapter 3) and have it cleaned by a specialist.

**5** Clean the drain holes then install the drain plugs using the old sealing washers.

**6** Fill the cooling system with clean water

24.2a  Remove the drain plug from the water pump (arrowed) . . .

24.2b  . . . and allow the coolant to drain

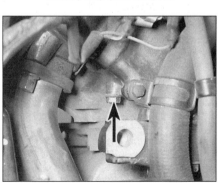

24.3a  Remove the drain plug from each front cylinder (arrowed) . . .

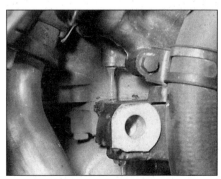

24.3b  . . . and allow the coolant to drain

**1**

mixed with a flushing compound. Make sure the flushing compound is compatible with aluminium components, and follow the manufacturer's instructions carefully.

**7** Start the engine and allow it to reach normal operating temperature. Let it run for about ten minutes.

**8** Stop the engine. Let it cool for a while, then cover the pressure cap with a heavy rag and turn it anti-clockwise to the first stop, releasing any pressure that may be present in the system. Once the hissing stops, push down on the cap and remove it completely.

**9** Drain the system once again.

**10** Fill the system with clean water and repeat the procedure in Steps 7 to 9.

### Refilling

**11** Fit a new sealing washer to each drain plug and tighten them securely.

**12** Fill the system with the proper coolant mixture (see this Chapter's Specifications).
**Note:** *Pour the coolant in slowly to minimise the amount of air entering the system.*

**13** When the system is full (all the way up to the base of the upper radiator filler neck), start the engine and allow it to idle for 2 to 3 minutes. Flick the throttle twistgrip part open 3 or 4 times, so that the engine speed rises to approximately 4000 – 5000 rpm, then stop the engine. This process will bleed any trapped air bubbles from the system.

**14** If necessary, top up the coolant level to the base of the upper radiator filler neck and install the pressure cap **(see illustration)**. Also top up the coolant reservoir to the UPPER level mark (see *Daily (pre-ride) checks*).

**15** Start the engine and allow it to reach normal operating temperature, then shut it off. Let the engine cool then remove the pressure cap as described in Step 1. Check that the coolant level is still up to the base of the upper radiator filler neck. If it's low, add specified mixture until it reaches the base of the filler neck. Refit the cap.

**16** Check the coolant level in the reservoir and top up if necessary.

**24.14 Make sure the pressure cap locates properly under the rim of the filler neck**

**17** Check the system for leaks.

**18** Do not dispose of the old coolant by pouring it down the drain. Instead pour it into a heavy plastic container, cap it tightly and take it into an authorised disposal site or service station – see **Warning** at the beginning of this Section.

# Non-scheduled maintenance

## 25 Cylinder compression – check

**1** Among other things, poor engine performance may be caused by leaking valves, incorrect valve clearances, a leaking head gasket, or worn pistons, rings and/or cylinder walls. A cylinder compression check will help pinpoint these conditions and can also indicate the presence of excessive carbon deposits in the cylinder heads.

**2** The only tools required are a compression gauge and a spark plug wrench. A compression gauge with an 8 mm threaded adapter for the spark plug hole will be required. Depending on the outcome of the initial test, a squirt-type oil can may also be needed.

**3** Make sure the valve clearances are correctly set (see Section 23) and that the cylinder head bolts are tightened to the correct torque setting (see Chapter 2).

**4** Refer to *Fault Finding Equipment* in the Reference section for details of the compression test.

## 26 Engine – oil pressure check

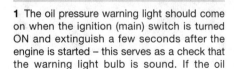

**1** The oil pressure warning light should come on when the ignition (main) switch is turned ON and extinguish a few seconds after the engine is started – this serves as a check that the warning light bulb is sound. If the oil

pressure light comes on whilst the engine is running, low oil pressure is indicated – stop the engine immediately and carry out an oil level check *(see Daily (pre-ride) checks).*

**2** An oil pressure check must be carried out if the warning light comes on when the engine is running yet the oil level is good (Step 1). It can also provide useful information about the condition of the engine's lubrication system.

**3** To check the oil pressure, a suitable gauge (which screws into the crankcase) will be needed. Honda provide a tool (part no. 07501-4220100) for this purpose.

**4** Warm the engine up to normal operating temperature then stop it.

**5** Remove the oil pressure switch (see Chapter 9) and swiftly screw the adapter into the crankcase threads. Connect the oil pressure gauge to the adapter.

**6** Start the engine and briefly increase the engine speed to 5000 rpm whilst watching the gauge reading. The oil pressure should be similar to that given in the Specifications at the start of this Chapter.

**7** If the pressure is significantly lower than the standard, either the pressure regulator is stuck open, the oil pump is faulty, the oil strainer or filter is blocked, or there is other engine damage. Begin diagnosis by checking the oil filter, strainer and regulator, then the oil pump (see Chapter 2). If those items check out okay, chances are the bearing oil clearances are excessive and the engine needs to be overhauled.

**8** If the pressure is too high, either an oil passage is clogged, the regulator is stuck closed or the wrong grade of oil is being used.

**9** Stop the engine and unscrew the gauge and adapter from the crankcase.

**10** Install the oil pressure switch (see Chapter 9). Check the oil level (see *Daily (pre-ride) checks*).

## 27 Wheel bearings – check

**1** Wheel bearings will wear over a period of time and result in handling problems.

**2** Support the motorcycle upright using an auxiliary stand so that the wheel being checked is off the ground Check for any play in the bearings by pushing and pulling the wheel against the axle **(see illustration)**. Also rotate the wheel and check that it rotates smoothly.

**3** If any play is detected in the hub, or if the wheel does not rotate smoothly (and this is not due to brake or transmission drag), the wheel bearings must be removed and inspected for wear or damage (see Chapter 7).

**27.2 Checking for play in the wheel bearings**

## 28 Steering head bearings – re-greasing

**1** Over a period of time the grease will harden or may be washed out of the bearings by incorrect use of jet washes.
**2** Disassemble the steering head for re-greasing of the bearings. Refer to Chapter 6 for details.

## 29 Swingarm and suspension linkage bearings – re-greasing

**1** Over a period of time the grease will harden or dirt will penetrate the bearings due to failed dust seals.
**2** The swingarm is not equipped with grease nipples. Remove the swingarm and suspension linkage as described in Chapter 6 for greasing of the bearings.

## 30 Brake caliper and master cylinder seals – replacement

**1** Brake seals will deteriorate over a period of time and lose their effectiveness, leading to sticking operation or fluid loss, or allowing the ingress of air and dirt. Refer to Chapter 7 and dismantle the components for seal replacement.

## 31 Brake hoses – replacement

**1** The hoses will in time deteriorate with age and should be replaced regardless of their apparent condition.
**2** Refer to Chapter 7 and disconnect the brake hoses from the master cylinders and calipers. Always replace the banjo union sealing washers with new ones.

## 32 Fuel hoses – replacement

⚠ **Warning: Petrol (gasoline) is extremely flammable, so take extra precautions when you work on any part of the fuel system. Don't smoke or allow open flames or bare light bulbs near the work area, and don't work in a garage where a natural gas-type appliance is present. If you spill any fuel on your skin, rinse it off immediately with soap and water. When you perform any kind of work on the fuel system, wear safety glasses and have a fire extinguisher suitable for a Class B type fire (flammable liquids) on hand.**

**1** The fuel delivery and vacuum hoses should be replaced regardless of their condition.
**2** Remove the fuel tank (see Chapter 4). Disconnect the fuel hoses from the fuel tap and from the carburettors, noting the routing of each hose and where it connects (see Chapter 4 if required). It is advisable to make a sketch of the various hoses before removing them to ensure they are correctly installed.
**3** Secure each new hose to its unions using new clamps. Run the engine and check for leaks before taking the machine out on the road.

## 33 Front forks – oil change

**1** Fork oil degrades over a period of time and loses its damping qualities. Refer to Chapter 6 for front fork removal, oil draining and refilling, following the relevant steps. The forks do not need to be completely disassembled.

**1**

**Notes**

# Chapter 2
# Engine, clutch and transmission

## Contents

## Degrees of difficulty

| Easy, suitable for novice with little experience |  | Fairly easy, suitable for beginner with some experience | | Fairly difficult, suitable for competent DIY mechanic |  | Difficult, suitable for experienced DIY mechanic | | Very difficult, suitable for expert DIY or professional | |

## Specifications

### General

Type . . . . . . . . . . . . . . . . . . . . . . . . . . . . . . . . . . . . . . Four-stroke 90° V-four
Capacity . . . . . . . . . . . . . . . . . . . . . . . . . . . . . . . . . . . 399 cc
Bore . . . . . . . . . . . . . . . . . . . . . . . . . . . . . . . . . . . . . . 55.0 mm
Stroke . . . . . . . . . . . . . . . . . . . . . . . . . . . . . . . . . . . . 42.0 mm
Compression ratio . . . . . . . . . . . . . . . . . . . . . . . . . . . 11.3 to 1
Firing order . . . . . . . . . . . . . . . . . . . . . . . . . . . . . . . . . 1-4-3-2
Cylinder numbering
  Rear left . . . . . . . . . . . . . . . . . . . . . . . . . . . . . . . . . . 1
  Front left . . . . . . . . . . . . . . . . . . . . . . . . . . . . . . . . . . 2
  Rear right . . . . . . . . . . . . . . . . . . . . . . . . . . . . . . . . . 3
  Front right . . . . . . . . . . . . . . . . . . . . . . . . . . . . . . . . . 4
Cooling system . . . . . . . . . . . . . . . . . . . . . . . . . . . . . . Liquid cooled
Clutch . . . . . . . . . . . . . . . . . . . . . . . . . . . . . . . . . . . . . Wet multi-plate
Transmission . . . . . . . . . . . . . . . . . . . . . . . . . . . . . . . . Six-speed constant mesh
Final drive . . . . . . . . . . . . . . . . . . . . . . . . . . . . . . . . . . Chain

FRONT

2

## Camshafts

Inlet lobe height
Standard . . . . . . . . . . . . . . . . . . . . . . . . . . . . . . . . . . . . . . . . . 32.717 to 32.957 mm
Service limit (min) . . . . . . . . . . . . . . . . . . . . . . . . . . . . . . . . . . . 32.670 mm
Exhaust lobe height
Standard . . . . . . . . . . . . . . . . . . . . . . . . . . . . . . . . . . . . . . . . . 32.428 to 32.668 mm
Service limit (min) . . . . . . . . . . . . . . . . . . . . . . . . . . . . . . . . . . . 32.38 mm
Journal diameter
VFR400
Standard . . . . . . . . . . . . . . . . . . . . . . . . . . . . . . . . . . . . . . . . . 27.939 to 27.960 mm
Service limit (min) . . . . . . . . . . . . . . . . . . . . . . . . . . . . . . . . . . . 27.93 mm
RVF400
Standard . . . . . . . . . . . . . . . . . . . . . . . . . . . . . . . . . . . . . . . . . 27.959 to 27.980 mm
Service limit (min) . . . . . . . . . . . . . . . . . . . . . . . . . . . . . . . . . . . 27.93 mm
Journal holder diameter
Standard . . . . . . . . . . . . . . . . . . . . . . . . . . . . . . . . . . . . . . . . . 28.000 to 28.021 mm
Service limit (min) . . . . . . . . . . . . . . . . . . . . . . . . . . . . . . . . . . . 28.03 mm
Journal oil clearance
VFR400
Standard . . . . . . . . . . . . . . . . . . . . . . . . . . . . . . . . . . . . . . . . . 0.040 to 0.082 mm
Service limit (max) . . . . . . . . . . . . . . . . . . . . . . . . . . . . . . . . . . . 0.092 mm
RVF400
Standard . . . . . . . . . . . . . . . . . . . . . . . . . . . . . . . . . . . . . . . . . 0.020 to 0.062 mm
Service limit (max) . . . . . . . . . . . . . . . . . . . . . . . . . . . . . . . . . . . 0.072 mm
Runout (max) . . . . . . . . . . . . . . . . . . . . . . . . . . . . . . . . . . . . . . . . . 0.03 mm

## Rockers

Rocker arm bore diameter
Standard . . . . . . . . . . . . . . . . . . . . . . . . . . . . . . . . . . . . . . . . . 8.500 to 8.515 mm
Service limit (max) . . . . . . . . . . . . . . . . . . . . . . . . . . . . . . . . . . . 8.53 mm
Rocker arm shaft diameter
Standard . . . . . . . . . . . . . . . . . . . . . . . . . . . . . . . . . . . . . . . . . 8.466 to 8.484 mm
Service limit (min) . . . . . . . . . . . . . . . . . . . . . . . . . . . . . . . . . . . 8.46 mm

## Valves, guides and springs

Valve clearances . . . . . . . . . . . . . . . . . . . . . . . . . . . . . . . . . . . . . . See Chapter 1
Inlet valve
Stem diameter
Standard . . . . . . . . . . . . . . . . . . . . . . . . . . . . . . . . . . . . . . . . . 4.475 to 4.490 mm
Service limit (min) . . . . . . . . . . . . . . . . . . . . . . . . . . . . . . . . . . . 4.47 mm
Guide bore diameter
Standard . . . . . . . . . . . . . . . . . . . . . . . . . . . . . . . . . . . . . . . . . 4.500 to 4.512 mm
Service limit (max) . . . . . . . . . . . . . . . . . . . . . . . . . . . . . . . . . . . 4.56 mm
Stem-to-guide clearance
Standard . . . . . . . . . . . . . . . . . . . . . . . . . . . . . . . . . . . . . . . . . 0.010 to 0.037 mm
Service limit (max) . . . . . . . . . . . . . . . . . . . . . . . . . . . . . . . . . . . 0.09 mm
Seat width . . . . . . . . . . . . . . . . . . . . . . . . . . . . . . . . . . . . . . . . . . 1.70 to 2.30 mm
Valve guide height above cylinder head . . . . . . . . . . . . . . . . . . . . . 10.0 mm
Exhaust valve
Stem diameter
VFR400
Standard . . . . . . . . . . . . . . . . . . . . . . . . . . . . . . . . . . . . . . . . . 4.465 to 4.480 mm
Service limit (min) . . . . . . . . . . . . . . . . . . . . . . . . . . . . . . . . . . . 4.46 mm
RVF400
Standard . . . . . . . . . . . . . . . . . . . . . . . . . . . . . . . . . . . . . . . . . 4.475 to 4.485 mm
Service limit (min) . . . . . . . . . . . . . . . . . . . . . . . . . . . . . . . . . . . 4.46 mm
Guide bore diameter
Standard . . . . . . . . . . . . . . . . . . . . . . . . . . . . . . . . . . . . . . . . . 4.500 to 4.512 mm
Service limit (max) . . . . . . . . . . . . . . . . . . . . . . . . . . . . . . . . . . . 4.56 mm
Stem-to-guide clearance
Standard . . . . . . . . . . . . . . . . . . . . . . . . . . . . . . . . . . . . . . . . . 0.020 to 0.047 mm
Service limit (max) . . . . . . . . . . . . . . . . . . . . . . . . . . . . . . . . . . . 0.12 mm
Seat width . . . . . . . . . . . . . . . . . . . . . . . . . . . . . . . . . . . . . . . . . . 1.70 to 2.30 mm
Valve guide height above cylinder head . . . . . . . . . . . . . . . . . . . . . 10.0 mm
Valve springs free length (inlet and exhaust)
Inner spring
Standard . . . . . . . . . . . . . . . . . . . . . . . . . . . . . . . . . . . . . . . . . 31.4 mm
Service limit (min) . . . . . . . . . . . . . . . . . . . . . . . . . . . . . . . . . . . 30.2 mm
Outer spring
Standard . . . . . . . . . . . . . . . . . . . . . . . . . . . . . . . . . . . . . . . . . 34.4 mm
Service limit (min) . . . . . . . . . . . . . . . . . . . . . . . . . . . . . . . . . . . 33.2 mm

## Cylinder head
Warpage (max) ......................................... 0.10 mm

## Clutch
Friction plates .......................................... 10
Plain plates ............................................ 9
Friction plate thickness
    Standard ........................................... 2.92 to 3.08 mm
    Service limit (min) .................................. 2.8 mm
Plain plate warpage (max) .............................. 0.3 mm
Spring free height (set of three together)
    Standard ........................................... 5.3 mm
    Service limit (min) .................................. 4.8 mm
Clutch housing ID at guide bore
    Standard ........................................... 29.000 to 29.021 mm
    Service limit (max) ................................. 29.06 mm
Clutch housing guide OD
    Standard ........................................... 28.967 to 28.980 mm
    Service limit (min) .................................. 28.93 mm
Clutch housing guide ID
    Standard ........................................... 21.995 to 22.015 mm
    Service limit (max) ................................. 22.05 mm

## Lubrication system
Oil pressure ........................................... see Chapter 1
Oil pump
  VFR400
    Inner rotor tip-to-outer rotor clearance .................... 0.15 mm
    Outer rotor-to-body clearance ......................... 0.15 to 0.22 mm
    Rotor endfloat ...................................... 0.04 to 0.09 mm
  RVF400
    Inner rotor tip-to-outer rotor clearance
      Standard ........................................ 0.15 mm
      Service limit (max) ............................... 0.20 mm
    Outer rotor-to-body clearance
      Standard ........................................ 0.15 to 0.21 mm
      Service limit (max) ............................... 0.35 mm
    Rotor endfloat
      Standard ........................................ 0.02 to 0.09 mm
      Service limit (max) ............................... 0.10 mm
Oil pump drive sprocket ID
    Standard ........................................... 29.025 to 29.075 mm
    Service limit (max) ................................. 29.11 mm

## Cylinder bores
Bore
    Standard ........................................... 55.000 to 55.015 mm
    Service limit (max) ................................. 55.07 mm
Warpage (max) ......................................... 0.10 mm
Ovality (out-of-round) (max) ............................ 0.10 mm
Taper (max) ............................................ 0.10 mm
Cylinder compression ................................... see Chapter 1

## Connecting rods
Small-end internal diameter
    Standard ........................................... 14.016 to 14.034 mm
    Service limit (max) ................................. 14.05 mm
Small-end-to-piston pin clearance
    Standard ........................................... 0.016 to 0.040 mm
    Service limit (max) ................................. 0.06 mm
Big-end side clearance
    Standard ........................................... 0.1 to 0.3 mm
    Service limit (max) ................................. 0.4 mm
Big-end oil clearance
    Standard ........................................... 0.028 to 0.052 mm
    Service limit (max) ................................. 0.07 mm

**2**

## Pistons

Piston diameter (measured 10 mm up from skirt, at 90° to piston pin axis)

| | |
|---|---|
| Standard . . . . . . . . . . . . . . . . . . . . . . . . . . . . . . . . . . . . . . . . . . . . . . . . . . . | 54.970 to 54.990 mm |
| Service limit (min) . . . . . . . . . . . . . . . . . . . . . . . . . . . . . . . . . . . . . . . . . . | 54.92 mm |

Piston-to-bore clearance

| | |
|---|---|
| Standard . . . . . . . . . . . . . . . . . . . . . . . . . . . . . . . . . . . . . . . . . . . . . . . . . . . | 0.010 to 0.045 mm |
| Service limit (max) . . . . . . . . . . . . . . . . . . . . . . . . . . . . . . . . . . . . . . . . . . | 0.10 mm |

Piston pin diameter

| | |
|---|---|
| Standard . . . . . . . . . . . . . . . . . . . . . . . . . . . . . . . . . . . . . . . . . . . . . . . . . . . | 13.994 to 14.000 mm |
| Service limit (min) . . . . . . . . . . . . . . . . . . . . . . . . . . . . . . . . . . . . . . . . . . | 13.98 mm |

Piston pin bore diameter in piston

| | |
|---|---|
| Standard . . . . . . . . . . . . . . . . . . . . . . . . . . . . . . . . . . . . . . . . . . . . . . . . . . . | 14.002 to 14.008 mm |
| Service limit (max) . . . . . . . . . . . . . . . . . . . . . . . . . . . . . . . . . . . . . . . . . . | 14.02 mm |

Piston pin-to-piston pin bore clearance

| | |
|---|---|
| Standard . . . . . . . . . . . . . . . . . . . . . . . . . . . . . . . . . . . . . . . . . . . . . . . . . . . | 0.002 to 0.014 mm |
| Service limit (max) . . . . . . . . . . . . . . . . . . . . . . . . . . . . . . . . . . . . . . . . . . | 0.04 mm |

## Piston rings

Ring end gap (installed)

Top and second rings

| | |
|---|---|
| Standard . . . . . . . . . . . . . . . . . . . . . . . . . . . . . . . . . . . . . . . . . . . . . . . . . . . | 0.18 to 0.33 mm |
| Service limit (max) . . . . . . . . . . . . . . . . . . . . . . . . . . . . . . . . . . . . . . . . . . | 0.65 mm |

Oil ring side-rail

| | |
|---|---|
| Standard . . . . . . . . . . . . . . . . . . . . . . . . . . . . . . . . . . . . . . . . . . . . . . . . . . . | 0.20 to 0.80 mm |
| Service limit (max) . . . . . . . . . . . . . . . . . . . . . . . . . . . . . . . . . . . . . . . . . . | 0.95 mm |

Ring-to-groove clearance

Top ring

| | |
|---|---|
| Standard . . . . . . . . . . . . . . . . . . . . . . . . . . . . . . . . . . . . . . . . . . . . . . . . . . . | 0.015 to 0.050 mm |
| Service limit (max) . . . . . . . . . . . . . . . . . . . . . . . . . . . . . . . . . . . . . . . . . . | 0.10 mm |

2nd ring

| | |
|---|---|
| Standard . . . . . . . . . . . . . . . . . . . . . . . . . . . . . . . . . . . . . . . . . . . . . . . . . . . | 0.015 to 0.045 mm |
| Service limit (max) . . . . . . . . . . . . . . . . . . . . . . . . . . . . . . . . . . . . . . . . . . | 0.10 mm |

Ring identification

| | |
|---|---|
| Top ring . . . . . . . . . . . . . . . . . . . . . . . . . . . . . . . . . . . . . . . . . . . . . . . . . . . . . | 'R' (facing up) |
| 2nd ring . . . . . . . . . . . . . . . . . . . . . . . . . . . . . . . . . . . . . . . . . . . . . . . . . . . . . | '•' mark or 'RN' (facing up) |

## Crankshaft and bearings

Main bearing oil clearance

| | |
|---|---|
| Standard . . . . . . . . . . . . . . . . . . . . . . . . . . . . . . . . . . . . . . . . . . . . . . . . . . . | 0.025 to 0.049 mm |
| Service limit (max) . . . . . . . . . . . . . . . . . . . . . . . . . . . . . . . . . . . . . . . . . . | 0.07 mm |
| Runout (max) . . . . . . . . . . . . . . . . . . . . . . . . . . . . . . . . . . . . . . . . . . . . . . . . | 0.03 mm |

## Transmission

Gear ratios (no. of teeth)

VFR400

| | |
|---|---|
| Primary reduction . . . . . . . . . . . . . . . . . . . . . . . . . . . . . . . . . . . . . . . . . . . . | 2.117 to 1 (72/34T) |
| Final reduction . . . . . . . . . . . . . . . . . . . . . . . . . . . . . . . . . . . . . . . . . . . . . . . | 2.666 to 1 (40/15T) |
| 1st gear . . . . . . . . . . . . . . . . . . . . . . . . . . . . . . . . . . . . . . . . . . . . . . . . . . . . . | 2.928 to 1 (41/14T) |
| 2nd gear . . . . . . . . . . . . . . . . . . . . . . . . . . . . . . . . . . . . . . . . . . . . . . . . . . . . | 2.166 to 1 (39/18T) |
| 3rd gear . . . . . . . . . . . . . . . . . . . . . . . . . . . . . . . . . . . . . . . . . . . . . . . . . . . . . | 1.800 to 1 (36/20T) |
| 4th gear . . . . . . . . . . . . . . . . . . . . . . . . . . . . . . . . . . . . . . . . . . . . . . . . . . . . . | 1.591 to 1 (35/22T) |
| 5th gear . . . . . . . . . . . . . . . . . . . . . . . . . . . . . . . . . . . . . . . . . . . . . . . . . . . . . | 1.435 to 1 (33/23T) |
| 6th gear . . . . . . . . . . . . . . . . . . . . . . . . . . . . . . . . . . . . . . . . . . . . . . . . . . . . . | 1.318 to 1 (29/22T) |

RVF400

| | |
|---|---|
| Primary reduction . . . . . . . . . . . . . . . . . . . . . . . . . . . . . . . . . . . . . . . . . . . . | 2.117 to 1 (72/34T) |
| Final reduction . . . . . . . . . . . . . . . . . . . . . . . . . . . . . . . . . . . . . . . . . . . . . . . | 2.533 to 1 (38/15T) |
| 1st gear . . . . . . . . . . . . . . . . . . . . . . . . . . . . . . . . . . . . . . . . . . . . . . . . . . . . . | 3.307 to 1 (43/13T) |
| 2nd gear . . . . . . . . . . . . . . . . . . . . . . . . . . . . . . . . . . . . . . . . . . . . . . . . . . . . | 2.352 to 1 (40/17T) |
| 3rd gear . . . . . . . . . . . . . . . . . . . . . . . . . . . . . . . . . . . . . . . . . . . . . . . . . . . . . | 1.875 to 1 (30/16T) |
| 4th gear . . . . . . . . . . . . . . . . . . . . . . . . . . . . . . . . . . . . . . . . . . . . . . . . . . . . . | 1.591 to 1 (35/22T) |
| 5th gear . . . . . . . . . . . . . . . . . . . . . . . . . . . . . . . . . . . . . . . . . . . . . . . . . . . . . | 1.435 to 1 (33/23T) |
| 6th gear . . . . . . . . . . . . . . . . . . . . . . . . . . . . . . . . . . . . . . . . . . . . . . . . . . . . . | 1.318 to 1 (29/22T) |

Input shaft 5th and 6th gears ID

| | |
|---|---|
| Standard . . . . . . . . . . . . . . . . . . . . . . . . . . . . . . . . . . . . . . . . . . . . . . . . . . . | 28.000 to 28.020 mm |
| Service limit (max) . . . . . . . . . . . . . . . . . . . . . . . . . . . . . . . . . . . . . . . . . . | 28.04 mm |

Input shaft 5th and 6th gears bush OD

| | |
|---|---|
| Standard . . . . . . . . . . . . . . . . . . . . . . . . . . . . . . . . . . . . . . . . . . . . . . . . . . . | 27.959 to 27.980 mm |
| Service limit (min) . . . . . . . . . . . . . . . . . . . . . . . . . . . . . . . . . . . . . . . . . . | 27.94 mm |

Input shaft 5th and 6th gears gear-to-bush clearance
    Standard . . . . . . . . . . . . . . . . . . . . . . . . . . . . . . . . . . . . . . . . .   0.020 to 0.062 mm
    Service limit (max) . . . . . . . . . . . . . . . . . . . . . . . . . . . . . . . . . .   0.10 mm
Input shaft 5th gear bush ID
    Standard . . . . . . . . . . . . . . . . . . . . . . . . . . . . . . . . . . . . . . . . .   24.985 to 25.006 mm
    Service limit (max) . . . . . . . . . . . . . . . . . . . . . . . . . . . . . . . . . .   25.03 mm
Input shaft OD at 5th gear bush point
    Standard . . . . . . . . . . . . . . . . . . . . . . . . . . . . . . . . . . . . . . . . .   24.967 to 24.978 mm
    Service limit (min) . . . . . . . . . . . . . . . . . . . . . . . . . . . . . . . . . .   24.96 mm
Input shaft-to-bush clearance at 5th gear bush point
    Standard . . . . . . . . . . . . . . . . . . . . . . . . . . . . . . . . . . . . . . . . .   0.007 to 0.039 mm
    Service limit (max) . . . . . . . . . . . . . . . . . . . . . . . . . . . . . . . . . .   0.06 mm
Output shaft 2nd, 3rd and 4th gears ID
    Standard . . . . . . . . . . . . . . . . . . . . . . . . . . . . . . . . . . . . . . . . .   28.000 to 28.020 mm
    Service limit (max) . . . . . . . . . . . . . . . . . . . . . . . . . . . . . . . . . .   28.04 mm
Output shaft 2nd, 3rd and 4th gears bush OD
    Standard . . . . . . . . . . . . . . . . . . . . . . . . . . . . . . . . . . . . . . . . .   27.959 to 27.980 mm
    Service limit (min) . . . . . . . . . . . . . . . . . . . . . . . . . . . . . . . . . .   27.94 mm
Output shaft 2nd, 3rd and 4th gears gear-to-bush clearance
    Standard . . . . . . . . . . . . . . . . . . . . . . . . . . . . . . . . . . . . . . . . .   0.020 to 0.062 mm
    Service limit (max) . . . . . . . . . . . . . . . . . . . . . . . . . . . . . . . . . .   0.10 mm
Output shaft 2nd gear bush ID
    Standard . . . . . . . . . . . . . . . . . . . . . . . . . . . . . . . . . . . . . . . . .   24.985 to 25.006 mm
    Service limit (max) . . . . . . . . . . . . . . . . . . . . . . . . . . . . . . . . . .   25.03 mm
Output shaft OD at 2nd gear bush point
    Standard . . . . . . . . . . . . . . . . . . . . . . . . . . . . . . . . . . . . . . . . .   24.967 to 24.978 mm
    Service limit (min) . . . . . . . . . . . . . . . . . . . . . . . . . . . . . . . . . .   24.96 mm
Output shaft-to-bushing clearance at 2nd gear bush point
    Standard . . . . . . . . . . . . . . . . . . . . . . . . . . . . . . . . . . . . . . . . .   0.007 to 0.039 mm
    Service limit (max) . . . . . . . . . . . . . . . . . . . . . . . . . . . . . . . . . .   0.06 mm

## Selector drum and forks

Selector fork end thickness
    Standard . . . . . . . . . . . . . . . . . . . . . . . . . . . . . . . . . . . . . . . . .   5.93 to 6.00 mm
    Service limit (min) . . . . . . . . . . . . . . . . . . . . . . . . . . . . . . . . . .   5.80 mm
Selector fork bore ID
    Standard . . . . . . . . . . . . . . . . . . . . . . . . . . . . . . . . . . . . . . . . .   12.000 to 12.021 mm
    Service limit (max) . . . . . . . . . . . . . . . . . . . . . . . . . . . . . . . . . .   12.04 mm
Selector fork shaft OD
    Standard . . . . . . . . . . . . . . . . . . . . . . . . . . . . . . . . . . . . . . . . .   11.969 to 11.980 mm
    Service limit (min) . . . . . . . . . . . . . . . . . . . . . . . . . . . . . . . . . .   11.95 mm

## Torque settings – specific components

Engine mountings
    Adjuster bolts . . . . . . . . . . . . . . . . . . . . . . . . . . . . . . . . . . . . . .   11 Nm
    Adjuster bolt locknuts . . . . . . . . . . . . . . . . . . . . . . . . . . . . . . . .   55 Nm
    Lower rear mounting bolt nut
        VFR models . . . . . . . . . . . . . . . . . . . . . . . . . . . . . . . . . . . . . .   40 Nm
        RVF models . . . . . . . . . . . . . . . . . . . . . . . . . . . . . . . . . . . . . .   65 Nm
    Left-hand mounting bolts . . . . . . . . . . . . . . . . . . . . . . . . . . . . .   40 Nm
    Right-hand mounting bolts . . . . . . . . . . . . . . . . . . . . . . . . . . . .   40 Nm
Valve cover bolts . . . . . . . . . . . . . . . . . . . . . . . . . . . . . . . . . . . . . .   10 Nm
Camshaft holder bolts . . . . . . . . . . . . . . . . . . . . . . . . . . . . . . . . . .   12 Nm
Timing inspection cover . . . . . . . . . . . . . . . . . . . . . . . . . . . . . . . . .   18 Nm
Rocker arm shaft plugs . . . . . . . . . . . . . . . . . . . . . . . . . . . . . . . . .   8 Nm
Camshaft drive gear assemblies
    Mounting bolts . . . . . . . . . . . . . . . . . . . . . . . . . . . . . . . . . . . . .   36 Nm
    Crankcase bolt . . . . . . . . . . . . . . . . . . . . . . . . . . . . . . . . . . . . .   12 Nm
Cylinder head 6 mm bolts . . . . . . . . . . . . . . . . . . . . . . . . . . . . . . .   12 Nm
Cylinder head 8 mm bolts . . . . . . . . . . . . . . . . . . . . . . . . . . . . . . .   36 Nm
Starter clutch cover bolts . . . . . . . . . . . . . . . . . . . . . . . . . . . . . . .   28 Nm
Starter clutch bolt . . . . . . . . . . . . . . . . . . . . . . . . . . . . . . . . . . . . .   85 Nm
Right-hand crankcase cover bolts . . . . . . . . . . . . . . . . . . . . . . . . .   10 Nm
Oil pump driven sprocket bolt . . . . . . . . . . . . . . . . . . . . . . . . . . . .   15 Nm
Clutch nut . . . . . . . . . . . . . . . . . . . . . . . . . . . . . . . . . . . . . . . . . . .   85 Nm
Oil pump cover bolts . . . . . . . . . . . . . . . . . . . . . . . . . . . . . . . . . . .   12 Nm
Oil pump mounting bolts . . . . . . . . . . . . . . . . . . . . . . . . . . . . . . . .   12 Nm
Selector drum cam pin bolt . . . . . . . . . . . . . . . . . . . . . . . . . . . . . .   23 Nm

**2**

**Torque settings** – specific components (continued)

| | |
|---|---|
| Gearchange shaft centralising spring locating pin | 23 Nm |
| Selector drum guide plate bolts | 12 Nm |
| Crankcase 6 mm bolts | 12 Nm |
| Crankcase 8 mm bolts | 23 Nm |
| Crankcase 10 mm bolt | 40 Nm |
| Connecting rod cap nuts | 24 Nm |
| Selector fork shaft bolt | 12 Nm |

**Torque settings** – non-specified components

**Note:** *Where a specific setting is not given for a particular bolt/nut, these general settings apply. The dimension given applies to the diameter of the thread, not the head.*

| | |
|---|---|
| 5 mm bolt/nut | 5 Nm |
| 6 mm bolt/nut | 10 Nm |
| 8 mm bolt/nut | 22 Nm |
| 10 mm bolt/nut | 35 Nm |
| 12 mm bolt/nut | 55 Nm |
| 6 mm flange bolt with 8 mm head | 9 Nm |
| 6 mm flange bolt/nut with 10 mm head | 12 Nm |
| 8 mm flange bolt/nut | 27 Nm |
| 10 mm flange bolt/nut | 40 Nm |

## 1 General information

The engine/transmission unit is a liquid-cooled 90°V-four. The sixteen valves are operated by double overhead camshafts which are gear driven off the crankshaft. The engine/transmission assembly is constructed from aluminium alloy. The crankcase is divided horizontally.

The crankcase incorporates a wet sump, pressure-fed lubrication system which uses a chain-driven oil pump, an oil filter and by-pass valve assembly, a relief valve and an oil pressure switch. On UK VFR L and M models, the lubrication system includes a cooling circuit fed by a second rotor in the oil pump.

The alternator is on the left-hand end of the crankshaft and the starter clutch is on the right-hand end. The oil pump is chain driven off the crankshaft, and the water pump is driven by the oil pump.

Power from the crankshaft is routed to the transmission via the clutch. The clutch is of the wet, multi-plate type and is gear-driven off the crankshaft. The transmission is a six-speed constant-mesh unit. Final drive to the rear wheel is by chain and sprockets.

## 2 Operations possible with the engine in the frame

The components and assemblies listed below can be removed without having to remove the engine/transmission assembly from the frame. If however, a number of areas require attention at the same time, removal of the engine is recommended.

Valve cover
Camshafts and rockers
Camshaft drive gears
Cylinder heads
Ignition rotor and pulse generator coil
   assembly
Clutch
Gearchange mechanism (external
   components)
Alternator
Oil filter and oil cooler (where fitted)
Oil sump, oil pump, oil strainer and oil
   pressure relief valve
Starter motor
Starter clutch
Water pump

## 3 Operations requiring engine removal

It is necessary to remove the engine/transmission assembly from the frame to gain access to the following components.

Pistons, piston rings and cylinder bores
Transmission shafts
Selector drum and forks
Crankshaft and bearings
Connecting rods and bearings

## 4 Major engine repair – general note

1 It is not always easy to determine when or if an engine should be completely overhauled, as a number of factors must be considered.
2 High mileage is not necessarily an indication that an overhaul is needed, while low mileage, on the other hand, does not preclude the need for an overhaul. Frequency of servicing is probably the single most important consideration. An engine that has regular and frequent oil and filter changes, as well as other required maintenance, will most likely give many miles of reliable service. Conversely, a neglected engine, or one which has not been run in properly, may require an overhaul very early in its life.
3 Exhaust smoke and excessive oil consumption are both indications that piston rings and/or valve guides are in need of attention, although make sure that the fault is not due to oil leakage.
4 If the engine is making obvious knocking or rumbling noises, the connecting rod and/or main bearings are probably at fault.
5 Loss of power, rough running, excessive valve train noise and high fuel consumption rates may also point to the need for an overhaul, especially if they are all present at the same time. If a complete tune-up does not remedy the situation, major mechanical work is the only solution.
6 An engine overhaul generally involves restoring the internal parts to the specifications of a new engine. The piston rings and main and connecting rod bearings are usually replaced and the cylinder walls honed during a major overhaul. Generally the valve seats are re-ground, since they are usually in less than perfect condition at this point. The end result should be a like new engine that will give as many trouble-free miles as the original.
7 Before beginning the engine overhaul, read through the related procedures to familiarise yourself with the scope and requirements of the job. Overhauling an engine is not all that difficult, but it is time consuming. Plan on the motorcycle being tied up for a minimum of two weeks. Check on the availability of parts

**5.3 Each fairing bracket is secured by a bolt (arrowed)**

**5.6a Remove the lower radiator with its lower bracket . . .**

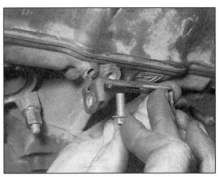

**5.6b . . . then remove the upper bracket from the front cylinder head**

and make sure that any necessary special tools, equipment and supplies are obtained in advance.

**8** Most work can be done with typical workshop hand tools, although a number of precision measuring tools are required for inspecting parts to determine if they must be replaced. Often a dealer will handle the inspection of parts and offer advice concerning reconditioning and replacement. As a general rule, time is the primary cost of an overhaul so it does not pay to install worn or substandard parts.

**9** As a final note, to ensure maximum life and minimum trouble from a rebuilt engine, everything must be assembled with care in a spotlessly clean environment.

## 5  Engine –
removal and installation

*Caution: The engine is very heavy. Engine removal and installation should be carried out with the aid of at least one assistant; personal injury or damage could occur if the engine falls or is dropped. An hydraulic or mechanical floor jack is advised to support and lower or raise the engine.*
**Note:** *A peg spanner is required to slacken and tighten the adjuster bolt locknuts on two of the engine mounting bolts. If the Honda*

*service tool (Part no. 07HMA-MR70200) is not available, a suitable one will have to fabricated out of a piece of 30 mm (OD) steel tubing, or an old 22 mm socket.*

### Removal

**1** Support the bike securely in an upright position using an auxiliary stand. Work can be made easier by raising the machine to a suitable working height on an hydraulic ramp or a suitable platform. Make sure the motorcycle is secure and will not topple over (see *Tools and Workshop Tips* in the Reference section).

**2** If the engine is dirty, particularly around its mountings, wash it thoroughly before starting any major dismantling work. This will make work much easier and rule out the possibility of caked on lumps of dirt falling into some vital component.

**3** Remove the lower fairing (see Chapter 8). Also remove the rear lower fairing bracket on each side to improve clearance when removing the engine **(see illustration)**.

**4** Drain the engine oil (see Chapter 1). Also drain the cooling system (see Chapter 1).

**5** Remove the fuel tank (see Chapter 4).

**6** Remove the radiators (see Chapter 3). When removing the lower radiator, leave the lower mounting bracket attached to the radiator and remove the bolt securing its bracket to the engine **(see illustration)**. Also

remove the lower radiator upper mounting bracket to improve clearance **(see illustration)**.

**7** Remove the exhaust system, including the rear cylinder header pipes to improve clearance when removing the engine (see Chapter 4).

**8** Remove the carburettors (see Chapter 4). Plug the engine inlet manifolds with clean rag.

**9** Remove the thermostat housing (see Chapter 3).

**10** Disconnect the negative (–ve) lead from the battery **(see illustration)**.

**11** Trace the alternator wiring from the left-hand side of the engine and disconnect it at the white connector in the bracket on the right-hand side of the engine **(see illustrations)**. Release the wiring from any clips or ties, noting its routing, and coil it so that it does not impede engine removal.

**12** Trace the ignition pulse generator, neutral switch and oil pressure switch wiring from the right-hand side of the engine and disconnect it at the black connector(s) in the bracket on the right-hand side of the engine **(see illustrations 5.11a and b)**. Release the wiring from any clips or ties, noting its routing, and coil it on top of the crankcase so that it does not impede engine removal.

**13** On VFR models, to improve access to the engine mounting bolt, remove the bolt

**2**

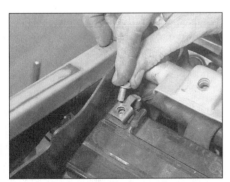

**5.10 Disconnect the negative lead from the battery**

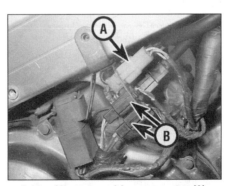

**5.11a Alternator wiring connector (A), pulse generator, neutral and oil pressure switch connectors (B) – VFR models**

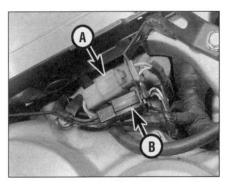

**5.11b Alternator wiring connector (A), pulse generator, neutral and oil pressure switch connector (B) – RVF models**

5.13  Remove the bolt (arrowed) securing the bracket and position it clear

5.14  Pull all four HT leads off the spark plugs

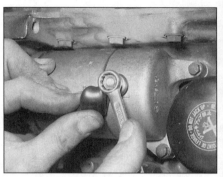

5.15  Pull back the cover and remove the nut securing the starter motor lead

securing the connector bracket to the underside of the frame and position the bracket clear of the engine **(see illustration)**. The remaining connectors and headlight relay (where fitted) can be left in the bracket or disconnected as required.

**14**  Disconnect all the HT leads from the spark plugs and secure them clear of the engine **(see illustration)**. If the HT leads don't have their cylinder number marked on them, label each lead to ensure correct reconnection.

**15**  Pull back the rubber cover on the starter motor terminal, then unscrew the nut and disconnect the lead **(see illustration)**.

**16**  Note the alignment punch marks between the gearchange linkage arm and the shaft so that they can be correctly aligned on installation. Unscrew the linkage arm pinch bolt and slide the arm off the shaft **(see illustration)**.

**17**  Unscrew the bolt securing the clutch cable bracket to the alternator cover, then detach the bracket and slip the cable end out of the release lever on the engine sprocket cover **(see illustration)**.

**18**  Remove the front sprocket (see Chapter 6).

**19**  On VFR models, remove the rubber heat guard from between the top of the engine and

the front of the frame, noting carefully how it fits.

**20**  On UK VFR L and M models, unscrew the two bolts securing each oil cooler pipe union to the crankcase. Also unscrew the pipe bracket bolts, then detach the pipes from the engine. If preferred, remove the entire oil cooler with its pipes (see Section 7).

**21**  At this point, position an hydraulic or mechanical jack under the engine with a block of wood between the jack head and sump. Make sure the jack is centrally positioned so the engine will not topple in any direction when the last mounting bolt is removed. Take the weight of the engine on the jack.

**22**  Unscrew the nut on the left-hand end of the lower rear engine mounting bolt **(see illustration)**. Unscrew the adjusting bolt locknut on the right-hand end of the bolt using a suitable peg spanner (see **Note** above), then unscrew the adjusting bolt and the mounting bolt together using an Allen key in the mounting bolt head, which engages with the adjuster bolt **(see illustrations)**. Withdraw the mounting bolt with the adjuster bolt from the right-hand side. Note the spacer between the engine and the frame, and retrieve it after the engine has been moved forward **(see illustration 5.26a)**.

**23**  Unscrew the upper rear mounting bolt, then unscrew the adjusting bolt locknut using the peg spanner. Unscrew the

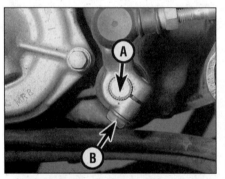

5.16  Note the alignment of the punch marks (A), then remove the bolt (B) and slide the arm off the shaft

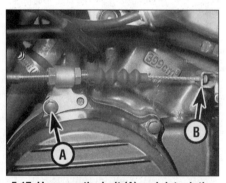

5.17  Unscrew the bolt (A) and detach the cable end (B) from the lever

5.22a  Remove the nut from the left-hand end of the bolt . . .

5.22b  . . . then remove the locknut . . .

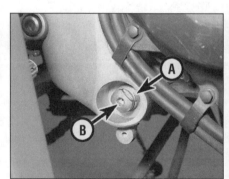

5.22c  . . . and unscrew the adjuster bolt (A) and the mounting bolt (B) together

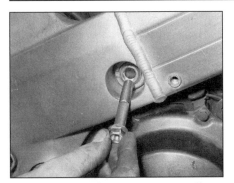

5.23a Remove the upper rear mounting
bolt . . .

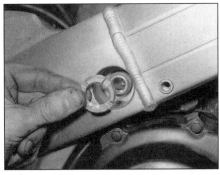

5.23b . . . the locknut . . .

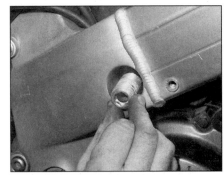

5.23c . . . and the adjuster bolt

adjuster bolt using an Allen key (see
illustrations).
24 Make sure the engine is properly
supported on the jack, and have an assistant
support it as well. On VFR models, remove the
front, middle and upper rear mounting bolts
on the left-hand side, noting the spacer fitted
with the middle bolt, and that the front bolt
also secures the radiator/front cylinder coil
bracket (see illustrations). Now remove the
front and middle bolts on the right-hand side,
noting that each has a spacer (see
illustrations). On RVF models, remove the
upper and lower front mounting bolts on the
left-hand side, noting the spacers, and the
upper rear mounting bolt (see illustrations).
Also remove the upper and lower front
mounting bolts on the right-hand side, noting
the spacer fitted with the lower bolt.
25 The engine can now be removed from the
frame. Check that all wiring, cables and hoses
are well clear, then carefully lower the engine
and manoeuvre it out of the side of the frame
(see Caution above). In our experience, the
easiest way to manoeuvre the engine out is to
have two people physically manhandle it
rather than to lower and move it on the jack.
Support the engine between you and remove
the jack, then move the engine forward, lower
it a bit, lift the front of the engine up, then
lower the engine out of the frame (see
illustration). In some cases, depending on
what type of stand is being used to support

5.24a On VFR models note the spacer
(arrowed) fitted with the middle bolt . . .

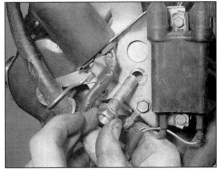

5.24b . . . and how the front bolt secures
the bracket

5.24c Remove the front bolt and its
spacer . . .

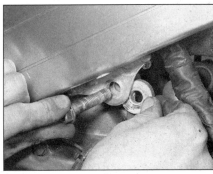

5.24d . . . and the middle bolt and its
spacer

2

5.24e On RVF models, remove the front
mounting bolts on each side (arrowed) . . .

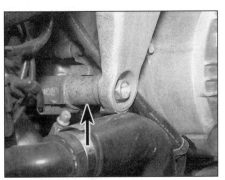

5.24f . . . noting the spacers where fitted

5.25 Manoeuvre the engine as
described

5.26a Do not forget to install the spacer

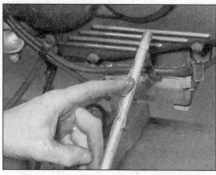

5.26b Grease the mounting bolt . . .

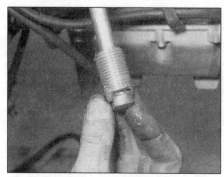

5.26c . . . then engage the adjuster bolt with the mounting bolt head . . .

5.26d . . . and thread the adjuster bolt finger-tight into the frame

5.26e Tighten the upper . . .

5.26f . . . and lower adjuster bolts to the specified torque

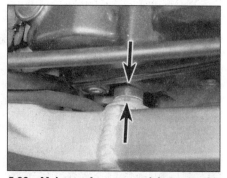

5.26g Make a reference mark between the upper adjuster bolt and the frame (arrows) . . .

5.26h . . . and tighten the locknut to the specified torque

5.26i Now make a reference mark between the lower adjuster bolt and the frame (arrows) . . .

5.26j . . . and tighten the locknut to the specified torque

the bike, it may be easier, or necessary, to lift the bike frame up off the supported engine.

## Installation

26 Installation is the reverse of removal, noting the following points:

a) Make sure no wires, cables or hoses become trapped between the engine and the frame when installing the engine.

b) Many of the engine mounting bolts are of different size and length. Make sure the correct bolt is installed in its correct location. Do not forget to install the spacer between the engine and frame on the lower rear mounting on the right-hand side (see illustration 5.26a).

c) Apply a thin coat of grease to the lower rear mounting bolt, then slide the adjuster bolt onto the mounting bolt and engage them (see illustrations 5.26b and c). Slide the mounting bolt with the adjuster bolt fully into the frame from the right-hand side, making sure the spacer remains in place and the bolt passes through it - tighten it finger-tight (see illustration 5.26d).

d) Next install the adjuster bolt into the upper rear right-hand mounting and tighten it finger-tight (see illustration 5.23c).

e) Install the three left-hand side mounting bolts. On VFR models, make sure the 15 mm spacer is fitted with the middle bolt and that the front bolt secures the radiator/front cylinder coil bracket, and tighten them finger-tight *(see illustrations 5.24a and b)*. On RVF models, make sure the spacers are fitted with the front bolts *(see illustrations 5.24e and f)*.

f) Install the two right-hand side mounting bolts. On VFR models, make sure the 9 mm spacer is fitted with the middle bolt and that the 3.5 mm spacer is fitted with the front bolt, and tighten them finger-tight *(see illustrations 5.24c and d)*. On RVF models, make sure the spacer is fitted with the lower bolt.

g) Tighten the upper adjuster bolt using an Allen key, and the lower adjuster bolt using the head of its mounting bolt, to the torque setting specified at the beginning of the Chapter *(see illustrations 5.26e and f)*. Make a reference mark between each adjuster bolt and the frame as a check against the adjuster bolt turning while the locknut is being tightened, then fit the locknuts and tighten them to the specified torque setting using the peg spanner *(see illustrations 5.26g, h, i and j)*. Check that the reference marks still align – if they don't, repeat the installation and tightening procedure. Now fit the bolt into the upper adjuster bolt, and the nut onto the left-hand end of the lower mounting bolt *(see illustrations 5.23a and 5.22b)* and tighten them to the specified torque setting.

h) Tighten the remaining mounting bolts, three on the left-hand side and two on the right-hand side to the specified torque setting.

i) Use new gaskets on the exhaust pipe connections.

j) Align the punch marks on the gearchange lever linkage arm and shaft when installing the arm onto the shaft, and tighten the pinch bolt securely *(see illustration 5.16)*.

k) Make sure all wires, cables and hoses are correctly routed and connected, and secured by any clips or ties.

l) Refill the engine with oil and coolant (see Chapter 1).

m) Adjust the throttle and clutch cable freeplay and idle speed (see Chapter 1).

n) Adjust the drive chain (see Chapter 1).

o) Start the engine and check that there are no oil or coolant leaks before installing the fairing panels.

## 6 Engine disassembly and reassembly – general information

### Disassembly

**1** Before disassembling the engine, the external surfaces of the unit should be thoroughly cleaned and degreased. This will prevent contamination of the engine internals, and will also make working a lot easier and cleaner. A high flash-point solvent, such as paraffin (kerosene) can be used, or better still, a proprietary engine degreaser. Use old paintbrushes and toothbrushes to work the solvent into the various recesses of the engine casings. Take care to exclude solvent or water from the electrical components and inlet and exhaust ports.

 **Warning: The use of petrol (gasoline) as a cleaning agent should be avoided because of the risk of fire.**

**2** When clean and dry, arrange the unit on the workbench, leaving suitable clear area for working. Gather a selection of small containers and plastic bags so that parts can be grouped together in an easily identifiable manner. Some paper and a pen should be on hand to permit notes to be made and labels attached where necessary. A supply of clean rag is also required.

**3** Before commencing work, read through the appropriate section so that some idea of the necessary procedure can be gained. When removing components it should be noted that great force is seldom required, unless specified. In many cases, a component's reluctance to be removed is indicative of an incorrect approach or removal method – if in any doubt, re-check with the text.

**4** An engine support stand made from short lengths of 2 x 4 inch wood bolted together into a rectangle will help support the engine **(see illustration)**. The perimeter of the mount should be just big enough to accommodate the sump within it so that the engine rests on its crankcase.

**5** When disassembling the engine, keep 'mated' parts together (including gears, cylinder bores, pistons, connecting rods, valves, etc. that have been in contact with each other during engine operation). These 'mated' parts must be reused or replaced as an assembly.

**6** A complete engine/transmission disassembly should be done in the following general order with reference to the appropriate Sections.

Remove the valve covers
Remove the camshafts and rockers
Remove the cylinder heads
Remove the starter clutch
Remove the clutch
Remove the alternator (see Chapter 9)
Remove the starter motor (see Chapter 9)
Remove the water pump (see Chapter 3)
Remove the pulse generator coil assembly (see Chapter 4)
Remove the gearchange mechanism external components
Remove the oil sump
Remove the oil pump
Separate the crankcase halves
Remove the connecting rods and pistons
Remove the crankshaft
Remove the transmission shafts
Remove the selector drum and forks

**6.4 An engine support made from pieces of 2 x 4 inch wood**

### Reassembly

**7** Reassembly is accomplished by reversing the general disassembly sequence.

## 7 Oil cooler and pipes (UK VFR L and M models) – removal and installation

**Note:** *The oil cooler can be removed with the engine in the frame. If the engine has been removed, ignore the steps which do not apply.*

### Removal

**1** Remove the lower fairing panel (see Chapter 8).

**2** Drain the engine oil (see Chapter 1).

**3** To remove the cooler without its feed and return pipes, unscrew the bolts securing the cooler to the pipe unions and detach the pipes. Now unscrew the cooler mounting bolt and remove the cooler. Discard the union O-rings as new ones must be removed.

**4** To remove the cooler with its feed and return pipes, unscrew the two bolts securing each pipe union to the crankcase. Also unscrew the pipe bracket bolts, then detach the pipes from the engine. Now unscrew the cooler mounting bolt and remove the cooler and pipes. Discard the union O-rings as new ones must be used.

**5** To remove the pipes but leave the cooler in place, unscrew the bolts securing the pipe unions to the cooler, then unscrew the two bolts securing each pipe union to the crankcase. Also unscrew the pipe bracket bolts, then detach the pipes from the engine and cooler and remove them. Discard the union O-rings as new ones must be used.

### Installation

**6** Installation is the reverse of removal, noting the following:

a) Always use new O-rings on the pipe unions.

b) Check the condition of the cooler mounting grommet and replace it if it is damaged or deteriorated.

c) Fill the engine with oil (see Chapter 1).

**2**

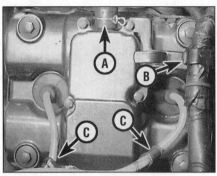

**8.3 Detach the breather hose (A) from its union, and the wiring loom (B) and HT leads (C) from their clips**

**8.4 Pull the caps off the spark plugs**

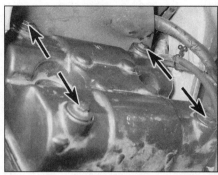

**8.5 The valve covers are secured by four bolts (arrowed)**

## 8 Valve covers – removal and installation

**Note:** *The valve covers can be removed with the engine in the frame. If the engine has been removed, ignore the steps which do not apply.*

### Removal

**1** Remove the lower fairing (see Chapter 8).

**2** To access the front cylinders valve cover, remove the radiators (see Chapter 3).

**3** To access the rear cylinders valve cover, remove the fuel tank (see Chapter 4). Release the clamp securing the breather hose to the breather and detach the hose. Also release any cables, leads and hoses from their clips **(see illustration).**

**4** Disconnect the spark plug caps from the plugs and secure them clear of the engine, noting which fits where **(see illustration).**

**5** Unscrew the four bolts securing the valve cover then lift the cover off the cylinder head **(see illustration).** If it is stuck, do not try to lever it off with a screwdriver. Tap it gently around the sides with a rubber hammer or block of wood to dislodge it. Also remove the gasket. Note the rubber washers fitted in the cover and remove them if they are loose.

### Installation

**6** Examine the valve cover gasket and the rubber washers for signs of damage or deterioration and replace them if necessary.

**7** Clean the mating surfaces of the cylinder head and the valve cover with lacquer thinner, acetone or brake system cleaner.

**8** Apply a smear of a suitable sealant into the grooves in the valve cover. Install the gasket onto the valve cover, making sure it fits correctly into the groove, and that the arrow next to the "IN" mark points to the same side as the "IN" mark on the top of the front cylinder valve cover or the breather hose union on the top of the rear cylinder cover **(see illustrations).**

**9** The front cylinders valve cover must be installed with the "IN" mark to the rear, facing the inlet side. The rear cylinder valve cover must be installed with the breather hose union pointing to the front. Position the valve cover on the cylinder head, making sure the gasket stays in place **(see illustration).** If removed, fit the rubber washers into the cover, using new ones if required, and making sure they are installed with the "UP" mark facing up **(see illustration).** Install the cover bolts and tighten them to the torque setting specified at the beginning of the Chapter **(see illustration).**

**10** Install the remaining components in the reverse order of removal.

**8.8a Make sure the gasket locates in the groove . . .**

**8.8b . . . and the arrow next to the IN mark faces the inlet side of the cover as described**

**8.9a Install the valve cover, noting the IN mark (arrowed) on the front cover**

**8.9b Make sure the UP mark faces up . . .**

**8.9c . . . then install the bolts and tighten them to the specified torque**

**9.2a Remove the timing inspection cover**

**9.2b Turn the engine clockwise using a 14 mm socket on the starter clutch bolt**

## 9 Camshafts – removal, inspection and installation

**Note:** *The camshafts can be removed with the engine in the frame. Place clean rags over the spark plug holes and the cam gear train holes to prevent any component from dropping into the engine on removal. To make installation and setting the timing easier, it is advised that the front and rear cylinders are worked on separately, ie the camshafts are not all removed at the same time.*

### Removal

**1** Remove the valve covers (see Section 8).
**2** Unscrew the timing inspection cover from the right-hand crankcase cover **(see illustration)**. Discard the cover O-ring as a new one must be used. The engine can be turned using a 14 mm spanner or socket on the starter clutch bolt and turning it in a clockwise direction only **(see illustration)**. Alternatively, place the motorcycle on an auxiliary stand so that the rear wheel is off the ground, select a high gear and rotate the rear wheel by hand in its normal direction of rotation.
**3** To remove the front cylinder head camshafts, turn the engine until the "T2" mark on the timing plate aligns with the static timing mark on the crankcase cover, and the index lines on the right-hand end of the camshafts are facing away from the head and aligning with the index mark on the camshaft holders **(see illustrations)**. The no. 4 (front right) cylinder is at TDC on the compression stroke (all valves closed).
**4** To remove the rear cylinder head camshafts, turn the engine until the "T1" mark on the timing plate aligns with the static timing mark on the crankcase cover, and the index lines on the right-hand end of the camshafts are facing away from the head and aligning

with the index mark on the camshaft holders **(see illustration and 9.3b)**. The no. 1 (rear left) cylinder is at TDC on the compression stroke (all valves closed).
**5** Before disturbing the camshaft journal holders, check for identification markings. For the front cylinder head, the inlet camshaft holders are marked A (right-hand cylinder) and B (left-hand cylinder) and the exhaust camshaft holders marked C (left-hand cylinder) and D (right-hand cylinder). For the rear cylinder head, the inlet camshaft holders

are marked A (left-hand cylinder) and B (right-hand cylinder) and the exhaust camshaft holders are marked C (right-hand cylinder) and D (left-hand cylinder). The letter corresponding to each holder is also stamped into the cylinder head. These markings ensure that the holders can be matched up to their original locations on installation. If no markings are visible, mark your own using a felt pen. If necessary, make a sketch of the layout as a further aid for installation **(see illustration)**.

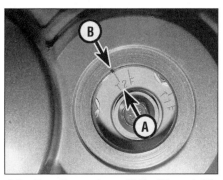

**9.3a Turn the engine until the T2 mark (A) aligns with the static mark (B) . . .**

**9.3b . . . and the index lines (arrowed) face away from the head**

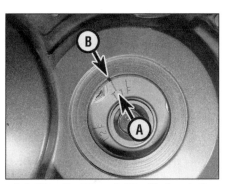

**9.4 Align the T1 mark (A) with the static mark (B)**

**9.5 Note the letter marked in the middle of each holder and its corresponding letter on the cylinder head (arrows)**

2

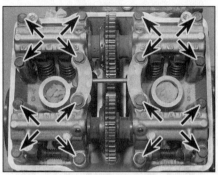

9.6a Camshaft holder and oil pipe assembly bolts (arrowed)

9.6b Remove the oil pipe assembly . . .

9.6c . . . then lift off the camshaft and holders together

**6** Unscrew the camshaft holder bolts for the camshaft being worked on and all the bolts securing the central oil pipe and plate assembly, evenly and a little at a time in a criss-cross pattern, until they are all loose **(see illustration)**. Remove the bolts, noting their different sizes, and the oil pipe plates and the oil pipes, then lift off the camshaft holders and camshaft together, noting how they fit **(see illustrations)**. To separate the camshaft from the holders, align the cam lobe with the lobe-shaped hole in the holder, then remove the camshaft, noting how it fits **(see illustration)**. Retrieve the dowels from either the holder or the cylinder head if they are

loose. The camshafts are marked for identification. For the front cylinder head, the inlet camshaft is marked FR IN and the exhaust camshaft is marked FR EX. For the rear cylinder head the inlet camshaft is marked RR IN and the exhaust camshaft is marked RR EX **(see illustration)**. **Note:** *To avoid the possibility of confusing related camshafts and holders, do not separate them unless required for inspection. If they are separated, make sure that all front cylinder components are stored separately from the rear cylinder components.*

**Caution: If the bearing cap bolts aren't loosened evenly, the camshaft may bind.**

### Inspection

**7** Inspect the bearing surfaces of the camshaft holders and the corresponding journals on the camshaft. Look for score marks, deep scratches and evidence of spalling (a pitted appearance) **(see illustration)**.

**8** Check the camshaft lobes for heat discoloration (blue appearance), score marks, chipped areas, flat spots and spalling **(see illustration)**. Measure the height of each lobe with a micrometer **(see illustration)** and compare the results to the minimum lobe height listed in this Chapter's Specifications. If damage is noted or wear is excessive, the camshaft must be replaced. Also, be sure to check the condition of the rockers (see Section 10).

**9** Check the amount of camshaft runout by supporting each end of the camshaft on V-blocks, and measuring any runout using a dial gauge. If the runout exceeds the specified limit the camshaft must be replaced.

9.6d Separate the camshaft from the holders if required

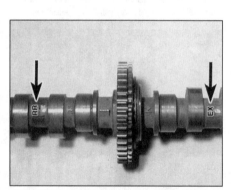

9.6e Each camshaft is marked according to its location (arrows)

> **HAYNES HiNT** *Refer to Tools and Workshop Tips in the Reference section for details of how to read a micrometer and dial gauge.*

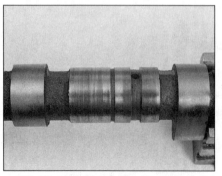

9.7 Check the journal surfaces of the camshaft for scratches or wear

9.8a Check the lobes of the camshaft for wear – here's an example of damage requiring camshaft repair or renewal

9.8b Measure the height of the camshaft lobes with a micrometer

9.10 Measure the cam bearing journals with a micrometer

9.12 Apply molybdenum oil to the camshaft journals and holders

9.13 The index line on the right-hand end of each camshaft must face the top of the holder

**10** Next, check the camshaft bearing oil clearances. Measure the diameter of the camshaft journal with a micrometer **(see illustration)**. Measure the journal holder diameter with an internal micrometer or telescoping gauge. To determine the journal oil clearance, subtract the holder diameter from the journal diameter and compare the result to the clearance specified. If the clearance is greater than specified, compare the measurements of the camshaft journal and the holder to those specified and replace whichever component is beyond its limit.

**HAYNES HiNT** *Before replacing camshafts or the journal holders because of damage, check with local machine shops specialising in motorcycle engine work. In the case of the camshafts, it may be possible for cam lobes to be welded, reground and hardened, at a cost far lower than that of a new camshaft. If the bearing surfaces in the holders are damaged, it may be possible for them to be bored out to accept bearing inserts. Due to the cost of new components it is recommended that all options be explored before condemning them as trash!*

**11** Check the camshaft drive gear on the drive gear assembly and the driven gear on each camshaft for wear, cracks and other damage, replacing them if necessary. The driven gears are integral with the camshafts, whilst the drive gear assembly can be removed from the engine (see Section 11). If wear this severe is apparent, the entire engine should be disassembled for inspection.

### Installation

**12** Make sure the bearing surfaces on the camshafts and in the holders are clean, then apply molybdenum disulphide oil (a 50/50 mixture of molybdenum disulphide grease and engine oil) to each of them **(see illustration)**. Also apply it to the camshaft lobes.

**13** The camshafts and holders must be installed in their correct location according to their identification marks (see Steps 5 and 6). If separated, install each holder onto its correct side of the camshaft **(see illustration 9.6d)**, with the index line on the end of each shaft on the right-hand side of the engine and facing up and in line with the index line on the holder **(see illustration)**. Do not confuse the index line on the right-hand end of each shaft with the square cutout on the left-hand end of each shaft.

**14** To install the front cylinder camshafts when the rear cylinder shafts are in place, first align the "T1" mark on the timing plate with the static mark on the cover, and check that the index line on the end of each rear cylinder shaft faces away from the head. Now turn the engine 90° (1/4 turn) clockwise until the "T2" mark aligns and the lines on the rear shafts face back at about 10 o'clock. Install the front cylinder camshafts with the index lines facing away from the head.

**15** To install the rear cylinder camshafts when the front cylinder shafts are in place, first align the "T2" mark on the timing plate with the static mark on the cover, and check that the index line on the end of each front cylinder shaft faces away from the head. Now turn the engine 630° (1 3/4 turns) clockwise until the "T1" mark aligns and the lines on the front shafts face forward at about 3 o'clock. Install the rear cylinder camshafts with the

index lines facing away from the head.

**16** If the camshafts have been removed from both heads, install the rear ones first with the index lines facing away from the head and the "T1" mark aligned, then turn the engine 90° (1/4 turn) clockwise until the "T2" mark aligns and the lines on the rear shafts face back at about 10 o'clock, and install the front camshafts with the lines facing away from the head.

**17** Make sure the camshaft holder dowels are installed, and that the cutout in each rocker arm shaft is aligned with the camshaft holder bolt hole in each corner of the cylinder head. Lay the camshafts and holders in place in the cylinder head **(see illustration 9.6c)**, making sure the lines on the camshaft ends and holders remain aligned and the camshaft driven gear meshes correctly with the drive gear **(see illustration)**. Take extra care at this stage as it is easy to be one tooth out on the timing without it appearing as a significant misalignment of the timing marks.

**18** Install the holder bolts, not forgetting to fit the oil pipe assembly and plates, which must be installed with the crescents facing in **(see illustration)**. Note that the bolts are all different lengths – make sure they are installed as shown **(see illustrations overleaf)**. When tightening the camshaft holders, tighten the no. 2 (front left cylinder) holder before the no. 4 (front right cylinder) holder, and the no. 3 (rear right cylinder) holder before the no. 1 (rear left

**2**

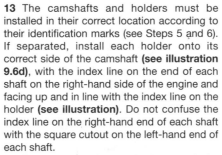

9.17 Make sure the holders locate onto the dowels and the teeth of the gears mesh correctly

9.18a Fit the oil pipe plates with the crescents facing in

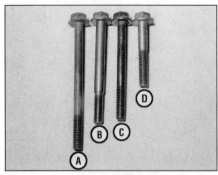

9.18b Install each bolt . . .

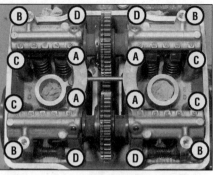

9.18c . . . in its correct location as shown

9.18d Tighten all the bolts as described to the specified torque

9.19a With the T1 mark aligned with the static mark (arrowed) . . .

9.19b . . . and the rear cylinder camshaft lines facing away from the head . . .

cylinder) holder. This is to compress the valves on those cylinders not at TDC on the compression stroke without placing undue strain on the camshafts. Tighten the bolts evenly and a little at a time in a criss-cross pattern, to the torque setting specified at the beginning of the Chapter (see illustration). Whilst tightening the bolts, make sure the holders are being pulled squarely down and are not binding on the dowels. Check that each camshaft is not pinched by turning the engine a few degrees in each direction.
*Caution: The holders are likely to break if they are not tightened down evenly and squarely.*
**19** With all holders tightened down, check that the valve timing marks align as follows. Start with the "T1" mark aligned with the static mark and the index lines on the rear cylinder camshafts facing away from the head (see illustrations). The front cylinder camshaft lines should face forwards at 3 o'clock (see illustration). Now turn the engine 90° clockwise until the "T2" mark aligns with the static mark (see illustration). The front cylinder camshaft lines should now face away from the head and the rear cylinder camshaft lines should face back at about 10 o'clock (see illustrations). Now turn the engine 270° clockwise until the "T1" mark again aligns with the static mark (see illustration 9.19a). The rear cylinder camshaft lines should now face

9.19c . . . the front cylinder camshaft lines should face as shown (arrowed)

9.19d With the T2 mark aligned with the static mark (arrowed) . . .

9.19e . . . the front cylinder camshaft lines should face away from the head (arrowed) . . .

9.19f . . . and the rear cylinder camshaft lines should face as shown (arrowed)

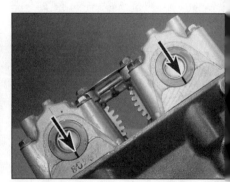

9.19g With the rear cylinder camshaft lines facing the head (arrowed) . . .

**9.19h . . . the front cylinder camshaft lines should face as shown (arrowed)**

**9.19i With the front cylinder camshaft lines facing the head (arrowed) . . .**

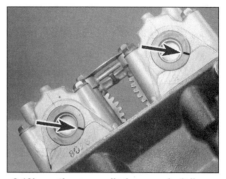

**9.19j . . . the rear cylinder camshaft lines should face as shown (arrows)**

the head and the front cylinder camshaft lines should face back at about 3 o'clock **(see illustrations)**. Now turn the engine 90° clockwise until the "T2" mark again aligns with the static mark **(see illustration 9.19d)**. The front cylinder camshaft lines should now face the head and the rear cylinder camshaft lines should face forward between 3 and 4 o'clock **(see illustrations)**.
*Caution: If the marks are not aligned exactly as described, the valve timing will be incorrect and the valves may strike the pistons, causing extensive damage to the engine.*
**20** Check the valve clearances and adjust them if necessary (see Chapter 1).
**21** Use a new O-ring on the timing inspection cover and smear it and the cover threads with molybdenum disulphide oil (a 50/50 mixture of molybdenum disulphide grease and engine oil) **(see illustration)**. Tighten the cover to the torque setting specified at the beginning of the Chapter **(see illustration)**.
**22** Install the valve covers (see Section 8).

**9.21a Smear the cover threads and new O-ring with molybdenum oil . . .**

**9.21b . . . and tighten it to the specified torque**

*component from dropping into the engine on removal.*

### Removal

**1** Remove the camshafts (see Section 9).
**2** Before proceeding, arrange to label and store the related components of the rocker assemblies in such a way that they can be returned to their original locations without getting mixed up. A good way to do this is to obtain a container which is divided into eight compartments, and to label each compartment with the identity of the rockers which will be stored in it (ie number of cylinder, inlet or exhaust side). Alternatively, labelled plastic bags will do just as well. A similar way of storing the shims is also required, though sixteen compartments are

needed, labelled according to cylinder number, inlet or exhaust side, inner or outer valve.
**3** Lift up each rocker arm and remove each shim from the top of the valve assembly and store it in the container for safekeeping. Remove the shim using a magnet or put a dab of grease onto a small screwdriver – it will stick to the grease **(see illustration)**.
**4** Unscrew the rocker arm shaft plug from the side of the cylinder head **(see illustration)**. Discard the plug as it has special threads and new ones must be used if they are removed. Slide the rocker shaft out, removing the arms and spring as you do **(see illustration)**. Slide the arms and spring back into their original positions on their shaft, and place them in the correct location in the container.

---

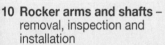

## 10 Rocker arms and shafts –
removal, inspection and installation

*Note: The rocker arms and shafts can be removed with the engine in the frame. Place clean rags over the spark plug holes and the cam gear train holes to prevent any*

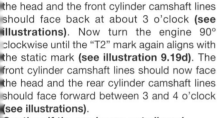

**2**

**10.3 A dab of grease on the end of a screwdriver makes shim removal easy**

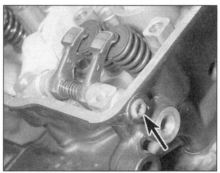

**10.4a Remove the plug (arrowed) . . .**

**10.4b . . . then withdraw the rocker shaft and remove the arms and spring**

10.6  Measure the diameter of the rocker shaft

10.7a  Align the cutout (A) in the shaft with the bolt hole (B) . . .

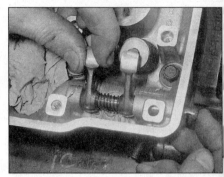

10.7b  . . . and slide the shaft home

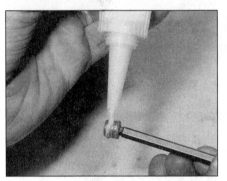

10.7c  Apply a sealant to the plug threads . . .

10.7d  . . . and install it in the head

## Inspection

5 Clean all components with solvent and dry them off. Blow through any oil passages with compressed air, if available. Inspect the rocker arm faces for pits, spalling, score marks and rough spots. Check the rocker arm-to-shaft contact areas. Look for cracks in each rocker arm. If the faces of the rocker arms are damaged, the rocker arms and the camshafts should be replaced as a set.
6 Measure the diameter of the rocker arm shafts, in the area where the rocker arms ride, and compare the results with this Chapter's Specifications **(see illustration)**. Also measure the inside diameter of the rocker arms and compare the results with this Chapter's Specifications. If either the shaft or the rocker arms are worn beyond

the specified limits, replace them as a set.

## Installation

7 Lubricate each shaft with molybdenum disulphide oil (a 50/50 mixture of molybdenum disulphide grease and engine oil). Position the rocker arms onto their correct valves. Slide the rocker shaft into place, noting that the cutout in each shaft must be on the outside, and should be aligned with the camshaft holder corner bolt hole **(see illustration)**. Slide the shaft through each arm and the spring, with the spring between the arms **(see illustration)**. Apply a suitable sealant to the threads of the **new** rocker shaft plug and tighten it to the torque setting specified at the beginning of the Chapter **(see illustrations)**.

8 Lubricate each shim with molybdenum disulphide oil (a 50/50 mixture of molybdenum disulphide grease and engine oil) and install it in the recess in the top of the valve spring retainer, making sure it is returned to its original position **(see illustration)**. Note: *It is most important that the shims are returned to their original valves otherwise the valve clearances will be inaccurate.* Swing the rocker arm down onto the valve **(see illustration)**.
9 Check that each arm moves freely on its shaft, then install the camshafts (see Section 9).

## 11  Camshaft drive gear assemblies – removal, inspection and installation

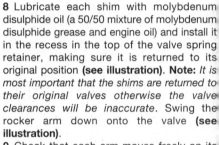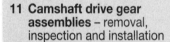

Note: *The camshaft drive gear assemblies can be removed with the engine in the frame. Place clean rags over the spark plug holes and the cam gear train holes to prevent any component from dropping into the engine on removal.*

## Removal

1 Remove the camshafts (see Section 9).
2 Unscrew the bolt securing the camshaft drive gear assembly to the inlet side of the crankcase. The bolt is situated centrally below the two inlet manifolds **(see illustration)**. The rear cylinder bolt does not clear the water pipe, so leave it loosely in place or, i

10.8a  Fit each shim into its recess . . .

10.8b  . . . and position the rocker arm on its valve

11.2  Unscrew the bolt securing the assembly to the crankcase

11.3a Remove the four bolts (arrowed) . . .

11.3b . . . and lift the assembly out of the head

11.3c Remove the dowels (arrowed) if loose

necessary, remove the water pipe (see Chapter 3). Check the condition of the sealing washer and replace it if necessary.

3 Each assembly is marked for identification. The front cylinder assembly is marked with an "F" and the rear with an "R". If the markings are no longer visible, make your own as the assemblies must be installed in their original position. Unscrew and remove the four bolts securing the assembly to the cylinder head **(see illustration)**. Carefully lift the assembly out of the cylinder head, noting how it fits **(see illustration)**. Remove the two dowels if they are loose **(see illustration)**.

### Inspection

4 Wash the assembly in clean solvent and dry it off.

5 Check the teeth on both gears for cracks and other damage and make sure the gears turn smoothly and freely. If the teeth are damaged or worn, the assembly must be replaced. If this is the case, the corresponding teeth on both the camshafts and the crankshaft should be inspected.

### Installation

6 If removed, fit the two dowels into the cylinder head, making sure they are fully pressed home, otherwise the gear assemblies will not sit properly and the gears will not mesh **(see illustration 11.3c)**.

7 Install the gear assembly, making sure it is fitted into its correct head (see Step 3) and with the bolt hole for the crankcase bolt facing

the inlet side of the cylinder. Press the assembly squarely down onto its dowels, making sure the lower gear teeth mesh correctly with those of the drive gear on the crankshaft. This can be done by turning the upper gear back and forth – the whole assembly should be felt to rise off the cylinder head slightly.

8 Install the four mounting bolts and the cylinder block bolt, using a new sealing washer if required, and tighten them all finger-tight **(see illustration and 11.2)**. Tighten the two mounting bolts adjacent to the dowels first, followed by the other two bolts, and finally the crankcase bolt, to the torque settings specified at the beginning of the Chapter **(see illustration)**.

9 Install the camshafts (see Section 9).

### 12 Cylinder heads – removal and installation

**Caution:** *The engine must be completely cool before beginning this procedure or the cylinder head may become warped.*
**Note 1:** *The cylinder head can be removed with the engine in the frame. If the engine has been removed, ignore the steps which don't apply.*
**Note 2:** *If removing the rear cylinder head, a peg spanner is required to slacken and tighten the adjuster bolt locknut on the right-hand engine mounting bolt. If the Honda service*

tool *(Part no. 07HMA-MR70200) is not available, a suitable one will have to fabricated out of a piece of steel tubing.*

### Removal

1 If removing the front cylinder head, remove the radiators and the cooling system thermostat (see Chapter 3).

2 If not already done (Step 1), drain the cooling system (see Chapter 1).

3 Remove the carburettors (see Chapter 4).

4 Remove the exhaust system (see Chapter 4).

5 Remove the camshafts (see Section 9), and if required the rocker arms and shafts (see Section 10). If they are not being removed, it is advisable to cable-tie each rocker arm to its valve to prevent the shim falling out should the cylinder head be moved or turned upside down. Alternatively, lift up each rocker arm and remove each shim from the top of each valve assembly and store it in a marked container (see Section 10, Step 2) for safekeeping. Remove the shim using a magnet or put a dab of grease onto a small screwdriver and remove the shim – it will stick to the grease **(see illustration 10.3)**.

6 Unscrew the bolt securing the camshaft drive gear assembly to the inlet side of the crankcase. The bolt is situated centrally below the two inlet manifolds **(see illustration 11.2)**. The rear cylinder bolt does not clear the water pipe, so leave it loosely in place or, if necessary, remove the water pipe (see Chapter 3). Check the condition of the sealing washer and replace it if necessary.

7 If removing the front cylinder head, on VFR models remove the engine front mounting bolts on each side of the frame, noting the spacer fitted with the right-hand bolt **(see illustrations 5.24b and c)**. On RVF models, remove the engine upper front mounting bolts on each side of the frame, noting the spacer fitted with the left-hand bolt **(see illustration 5.24e)**.

8 If removing the rear cylinder head, remove the upper rear engine mounting bolts on each side of the frame. When removing the right-hand bolt, unscrew the upper rear mounting bolt, then unscrew the adjusting bolt locknut using the peg spanner (see **Note 2** above),

11.8a Install the bolts . . .

11.8b . . . and tighten them as described to the specified torque

**2**

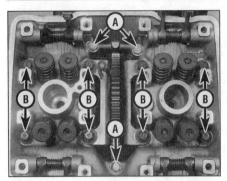

12.9 Cylinder head 6 mm bolts (A) and 8 mm bolts (B)

12.11 Lift the head up off the block

12.12 Remove the dowels (arrowed) if loose

then unscrew the adjuster bolt using an Allen key **(see illustrations 5.23a, b and c).**

**9** Each cylinder head is secured by eight 8 mm bolts and three 6 mm bolts **(see illustration)**. First slacken the 6 mm bolts evenly and a little at a time until they are all slack, then remove the bolts and their washers. Now slacken and remove the 8 mm bolts evenly and a little at a time in a criss-cross pattern until they are all slack, then remove the bolts and their washers.

**10** Each camshaft drive gear assembly is marked for identification. The front cylinder assembly is marked with an "F" and the rear with an "R". If the markings are no longer visible, make your own as the assemblies must be installed in their original position. Lift the assembly out of the head **(see illustration 11.3b)**.

**11** Pull the cylinder head up off the block **(see illustration)**. If it is stuck, tap around the joint faces of the cylinder head with a soft-faced mallet to free the head. Do not attempt to free the head by inserting a screwdriver between the head and cylinder block – you'll damage the sealing surfaces. Remove the old cylinder head gasket and discard it as a new one must be used.

**12** If they are loose, remove the dowels from the cylinder block **(see illustration)**. If they appear to be missing they are probably stuck in the underside of the cylinder head.

**13** Check the cylinder head gasket and the mating surfaces on the cylinder head and

crankcase for signs of leakage, which could indicate warpage. Refer to Section 14 and check the flatness of the cylinder head.

**14** Clean all traces of old gasket material from the cylinder head and crankcase. If a scraper is used, take care not to scratch or gouge the soft aluminium. Be careful not to let any of the gasket material fall into the crankcase, the cylinder bores or the oil passages.

### Installation

**15** If removed, install the dowels onto the cylinder block **(see illustration 12.12)**. Lubricate the cylinder bores with engine oil.

**16** Ensure both cylinder head and crankcase mating surfaces are clean, then lay the new head gasket in place on the cylinder block, making sure all the holes are correctly aligned and the UP mark faces up **(see illustration)**. Never re-use the old gasket.

**17** Carefully fit the cylinder head onto the block, making sure it locates correctly onto the dowels **(see illustration 12.11)**.

**18** Install the camshaft drive gear assembly, making sure it is fitted into its correct head (see Step 11) and with the bolt hole for the crankcase bolt facing the inlet side of the engine. Press the assembly squarely down onto its dowels, making sure the lower gear teeth mesh correctly with those of the drive gear on the crankshaft. This can be done by turning the upper gear back and forth – the whole assembly should be felt to rise off the cylinder head slightly.

**19** Install the eight 8 mm bolts with their washers and the three 6 mm bolts and tighten them all finger-tight **(see illustration 12.9)**. Now tighten the 8 mm bolts evenly and a little at a time in a criss-cross pattern to the torque setting specified at the beginning of the Chapter, then tighten the 6 mm bolts in the same way **(see illustration)**.

**20** If the front cylinder head was removed, install the front engine mounting bolts, making sure the spacer is fitted with the right-hand bolt on VFR models, and the left-hand bolt on RVF models, and tighten them to the specified torque setting.

**21** If the rear cylinder head was removed, install the adjuster bolt into the upper rear right-hand mounting and tighten it finger-tight **(see illustration 5.23c)**. Also fit the left-hand engine bolt finger-tight. On the right-hand side, tighten the adjuster bolt using an Allen key, to the torque setting specified at the beginning of the Chapter **(see illustration 5.26e)**. Make a reference mark between the adjuster bolt and the frame as a check against the adjuster bolt turning while the locknut is being tightened, then fit the locknut and tighten it to the specified torque setting using the peg spanner **(see illustrations 5.26g, 5.23b and 5.26h)**. Check that the reference marks still align – if they don't, repeat the installation and tightening procedure. Now fit the mounting bolt into the adjuster bolt **(see illustration 5.23a)** and tighten it to the specified torque setting. Now tighten the left-hand bolt to the specified torque.

**22** Install the remaining components in a reverse of their removal sequence, referring to the relevant Sections or Chapters (see Steps 1 to 5).

### 13 Valves/valve seats/valve guides – servicing

**1** Because of the complex nature of this job and the special tools and equipment required, most owners leave servicing of the valves, valve seats and valve guides to a professional.

**2** The home mechanic can, however, remove the valves from the cylinder head, clean and

12.16 Make sure the gasket is the correct way round with all holes aligned and the UP mark (arrowed) facing up

12.19 Tighten the cylinder head bolts as described to the specified torque

check the components for wear and assess the extent of the work needed, and, unless a valve service is required, grind in the valves (see Section 14).

**3** The dealer or engineering works will remove the valves and springs, replace the valves and guides, recut the valve seats, check and replace the valve springs, spring retainers and collets (as necessary) and reassemble the valve components.

**4** After the valve service has been performed, the head will be in like-new condition. When the head is returned, be sure to clean it again very thoroughly before installation on the engine to remove any metal particles or abrasive grit that may still be present from the valve service operations. Use compressed air, if available, to blow out all the holes and passages.

## 14 Cylinder head and valves – disassembly, inspection and reassembly

**1** As mentioned in the previous section, valve servicing, valve seat re-cutting and valve guide replacement should be left to a Honda dealer or engineering works. However, disassembly, cleaning and inspection of the valves and related components can be done (if the necessary special tools are available) by the home mechanic. This way no expense is incurred if the inspection reveals that overhaul is not required at this time.

**2** To disassemble the valve components without the risk of damaging them, a valve spring compressor is absolutely necessary.

### Disassembly

**3** Before proceeding, arrange to label and store the valves along with their related components in such a way that they can be returned to their original locations without getting mixed up **(see illustration)**. A good way to do this is to use the same container as the shims are stored in (see Section 10), or to obtain a separate container which is divided into sixteen compartments, and to label each compartment with the identity of the valve which will be stored in it (ie number of cylinder, inlet or exhaust side, inner or outer valve). Alternatively, labelled plastic bags will do just as well.

**4** If not already done, remove the rocker arms and shafts (see Section 10).

**5** If not already done, clean all traces of old gasket material from the cylinder head. If a scraper is used, take care not to scratch or gouge the soft aluminium.

 **HAYNES HINT** *Refer to Tools and Workshop Tips for details of gasket removal methods.*

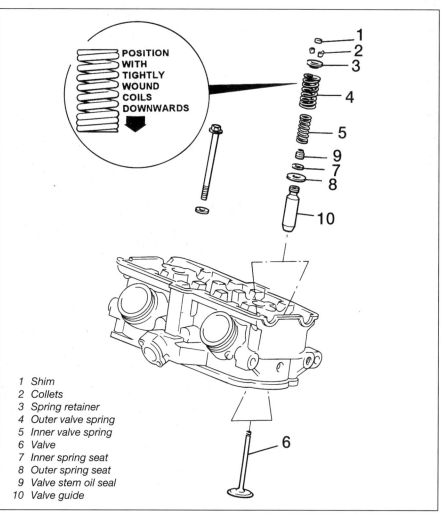

1 Shim
2 Collets
3 Spring retainer
4 Outer valve spring
5 Inner valve spring
6 Valve
7 Inner spring seat
8 Outer spring seat
9 Valve stem oil seal
10 Valve guide

**14.3 Valve components**

**6** Compress the valve spring on the first valve with a spring compressor, making sure it is correctly located onto each end of the valve assembly **(see illustration)**. Do not compress the springs any more than is absolutely necessary. Remove the collets, using either needle-nose pliers, tweezers, a magnet or a screwdriver with a dab of grease on it **(see illustration)**. Carefully release the valve spring compressor and remove the spring retainer, noting which way up it fits, the inner and outer springs, the spring seats (one for each spring, the inner one fits inside the outer one), and the valve from the head **(see illustration 14.3)**. If the valve binds in the guide (won't pull through), push it back into the head and

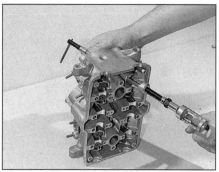
**14.6a Compressing the valve springs using a valve spring compressor**

**14.6b Remove the collets with needle-nose pliers, tweezers, a magnet or a screwdriver with a dab of grease on it**

**2**

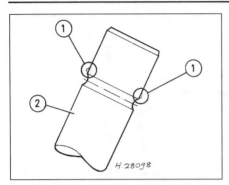
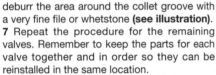

**14.6c If the valve stem (2) won't pull through the guide, deburr the area above the collet groove (1)**

**14.13 Checking the cylinder head gasket face for distortion**

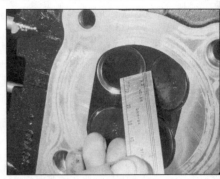

**14.14 Measure the valve seat width with a ruler (or for greater precision use a vernier caliper)**

deburr the area around the collet groove with a very fine file or whetstone **(see illustration)**.
**7** Repeat the procedure for the remaining valves. Remember to keep the parts for each valve together and in order so they can be reinstalled in the same location.
**8** Once the valves have been removed and labelled, pull the valve stem seals off the top of the valve guides with pliers and discard them (the old seals should never be reused).
**9** Next, clean the cylinder head with solvent and dry it thoroughly. Compressed air will speed the drying process and ensure that all holes and recessed areas are clean.
**10** Clean all of the valve springs, collets, retainers and spring seats with solvent and dry them thoroughly. Do the parts from one

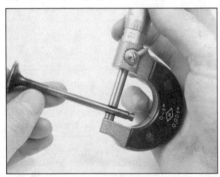

**14.15a Measure the valve stem diameter with a micrometer**

valve at a time so that no mixing of parts between valves occurs.
**11** Scrape off any deposits that may have formed on the valve, then use a motorised wire brush to remove deposits from the valve heads and stems. Again, make sure the valves do not get mixed up.

### Inspection

**12** Inspect the head very carefully for cracks and other damage. If cracks are found, a new head will be required. Check the cam bearing surfaces for wear and evidence of seizure. Check the camshafts for wear as well (see Section 9).
**13** Using a precision straight-edge and a feeler gauge set to the warpage limit listed in the specifications at the beginning of the Chapter, check the head gasket mating surface for warpage. Refer to *Tools and Workshop Tips* in the Reference section for details of how to use the straight-edge.
**14** Examine the valve seats in the combustion chamber. If they are pitted, cracked or burned, the head will require work beyond the scope of the home mechanic. Measure the valve seat width and compare it to this Chapter's Specifications **(see illustration)**. If it exceeds the service limit, or if it varies around its circumference, valve overhaul is required. If available, use Prussian blue to determine the extent of valve seat wear. Uniformly coat the seat with the

Prussian blue, then install the valve and rotate it back and forth using a lapping tool. Remove the valve and check whether the ring of blue on the valve is uniform and continuous around the valve, and of the correct width as specified.
**15** Measure the valve stem diameter **(see illustration)**. Clean the valve guides to remove any carbon build-up, then measure the inside diameters of the guides (at both ends and the centre of the guide) with a small hole gauge and micrometer **(see illustrations)**. The guides are measured at the ends and at the centre to determine if they are worn in a bell-mouth pattern (more wear at the ends). Subtract the stem diameter from the valve guide diameter to obtain the valve stem-to-guide clearance. If the stem-to-guide clearance is greater than listed in this Chapter's Specifications, the guides and valves will have to be replaced with new ones. If the valve stem or guide is worn beyond its limit, or if the guide is worn unevenly, it must be replaced.
**16** Carefully inspect each valve face for cracks, pits and burned spots. Check the valve stem and the collet groove area for cracks **(see illustration)**. Rotate the valve and check for any obvious indication that it is bent. Check the end of the stem for pitting and excessive wear. The presence of any of the above conditions indicates the need for

**14.15b Insert a small hole gauge into the valve guide and expand it so there's a slight drag when it's pulled out**

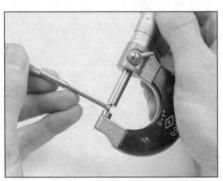

**14.15c Measure the small hole gauge with a micrometer**

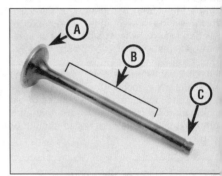

**14.16 Check the valve face (A), stem (B) and collet groove (C) for signs of wear and damage**

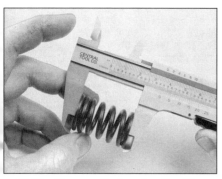

**14.17a Measure the free length of the valve springs**

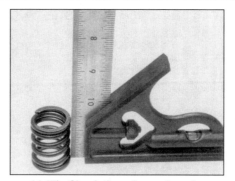

**14.17b Check the valve springs for squareness**

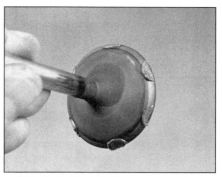

**14.21 Apply the grinding compound very sparingly, in small dabs, to the valve face only**

valve servicing. The stem end can be ground down, provided that the amount of stem above the collet groove after grinding is sufficient.

**17** Check the end of each valve spring for wear and pitting. Measure the spring free length and compare it to that listed in the specifications **(see illustration)**. If any spring is shorter than specified it has sagged and must be replaced. Also place the spring upright on a flat surface and check it for bend by placing a ruler against it **(see illustration)**. If the bend in any spring is excessive, it must be replaced.

**18** Check the spring retainers and collets for obvious wear and cracks. Any questionable parts should not be reused, as extensive damage will occur in the event of failure during engine operation.

**19** If the inspection indicates that no overhaul work is required, the valve components can be reinstalled in the head.

## Reassembly

**20** Unless a valve service has been performed, before installing the valves in the head they should be ground in (lapped) to ensure a positive seal between the valves and seats. This procedure requires coarse and fine valve grinding compound and a valve grinding tool. If a grinding tool is not available, a piece of rubber or plastic hose can be slipped over the valve stem (after the valve has been installed in the guide) and used to turn the valve.

**14.22a Rotate the valve grinding tool back and forth between the palms of your hands**

**21** Apply a small amount of coarse grinding compound to the valve face, then slip the valve into the guide **(see illustration)**. **Note:** *Make sure each valve is installed in its correct guide and be careful not to get any grinding compound on the valve stem.*

**22** Attach the grinding tool (or hose) to the valve and rotate the tool between the palms of your hands. Use a back-and-forth motion (as though rubbing your hands together) rather than a circular motion (ie so that the valve rotates alternately clockwise and anti-clockwise rather than in one direction only) **(see illustration)**. Lift the valve off the seat and turn it at regular intervals to distribute the grinding compound properly. Continue the grinding procedure until the

**14.22b The valve face and seat should show a uniform unbroken ring . . .**

valve face and seat contact area is of uniform width and unbroken around the entire circumference of the valve face and seat **(see illustrations)**.

**23** Carefully remove the valve from the guide and wipe off all traces of grinding compound. Use solvent to clean the valve and wipe the seat area thoroughly with a solvent soaked cloth.

**24** Repeat the procedure with fine valve grinding compound, then repeat the entire procedure for the remaining valves.

**25** Lay the spring seats for all the valves in place in the cylinder head, making sure the inner seat fits flush inside the outer seat, then install new valve stem seals on each of the guides **(see illustrations)**. Use an appropriate

**2**

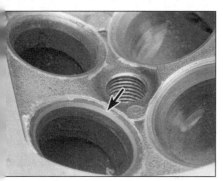

**14.22c . . . and the seat (arrowed) should be the specified width all the way round**

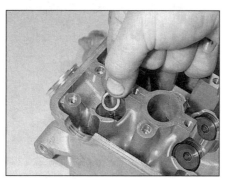

**14.25a Fit the inner spring seat . . .**

**14.25b . . . followed by the outer spring seat . . .**

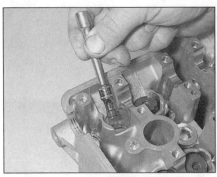

14.25c ... then press the valve stem seal into position using a suitable deep socket

14.26a Lubricate the stem and slide the valve into its correct location

14.26b Fit the inner valve spring ...

size deep socket to push the seals over the end of the valve guide until they are felt to clip into place. Don't twist or cock them, or they will not seal properly against the valve stems. Also, don't remove them again or they will be damaged.

**26** Coat the valve stems with molybdenum disulphide grease, then install one of them into its guide, rotating it slowly to avoid damaging the seal **(see illustration)**. Check that the valve moves up and down freely in the guide. Next, install the inner and outer springs, with their closer-wound coils facing down into the cylinder head, followed by the spring retainer, with its shouldered side facing down so that it fits into the top of the springs **(see illustrations)**.

**27** Apply a small amount of grease to the collets to help hold them in place as the pressure is released from the springs **(see illustration)**. Compress the springs with the valve spring compressor and install the collets **(see illustration)**. When compressing the springs, depress them only as far as is absolutely necessary to slip the collets into place. Make certain that the collets are securely locked in their retaining grooves.

**28** Support the cylinder head on blocks so the valves can't contact the workbench top, then very gently tap each of the valve stems with a soft-faced hammer. This will help seat the collets in their grooves.

14.26c ... and the outer valve spring, with their closer-wound coils facing down ...

 **HAYNES HiNT** *Check for proper sealing of the valves by pouring a small amount of solvent into each of the valve ports. If the solvent leaks past any valve into the combustion chamber area the valve grinding operation on that valve should be repeated.*

## 15 Starter clutch and primary drive gear – removal, inspection and installation

**1** Remove the lower fairing (see Chapter 8).

14.26d ... then fit the spring retainer

**2** Drain the engine oil (see Chapter 1).
**3** Unscrew the twelve bolts securing the right-hand crankcase cover and remove the cover, being prepared to catch any residue oil, and noting the positions of the wiring clips **(see illustration)**. Discard the gasket as a new one must be used. Remove the dowels from either the cover or the crankcase if they are loose.
**4** Remove the pulse generator coil assembly (see Chapter 5).
**5** Withdraw the starter idle/reduction gear shaft from the centre of the gear, then remove the gear, noting how it fits **(see illustration)**.
**6** Turn the starter clutch in a clockwise

14.27a A small dab of grease will help to keep the collets in place on the valve while the spring is released

14.27b Compress the springs and install the collets, making sure they locate in the groove

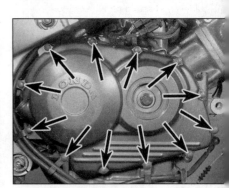

15.3 The cover is secured by twelve bolts (arrowed)

15.5 Withdraw the shaft and remove the idle/reduction gear

15.8a Remove the bolt . . .

15.8b . . . and draw the starter clutch off the shaft

15.9 Remove the thrust washer (A), the spacer (B) and the primary drive gear (C) if required

15.11 Withdraw the needle bearing and drive gear from the starter clutch

direction using a 14 mm spanner or socket on the bolt, until the recessed section in the main clutch housing aligns with the starter clutch **(see illustration 15.18b)**. This provides clearance for the starter clutch to be removed.

**7** To remove the starter clutch bolt, the primary drive gear on the back of the starter clutch and the primary driven gear on the back of the main clutch housing must be locked together. If the engine is in the frame, engage 6th gear and have an assistant hold the rear brake on hard with the rear tyre in firm contact with the ground. Alternatively, Honda provide a special tool (Part no. 00724-001010) which locks the gears, or a stout piece of cloth, such as denim, can be jammed between them, without the risk of any damage should the bolt prove tight.

**8** Slacken and remove the bolt and its washer, then draw the starter clutch off the end of the crankshaft **(see illustrations)**. Note how the wider groove in the starter clutch fits over the wider spline on the shaft.

**9** If required, draw the thrust washer, spacer and primary drive gear off the end of the crankshaft, noting which way round they fit **(see illustration)**.

### Inspection

**10** With the starter clutch face down on a workbench, check that the starter driven gear rotates freely in a clockwise direction and locks against the rotor in an anti-clockwise direction. If it doesn't, the starter clutch should be dismantled for further investigation.

**11** Withdraw the needle roller bearing and starter driven gear from the starter clutch **(see**

illustration). If the gear appears stuck, rotate it clockwise as you withdraw it to free it from the starter clutch.

**12** Check the condition of the rollers inside the clutch body **(see illustration)**. If they are damaged, marked or flattened at any point, they should be replaced. Unscrew the three cover bolts and remove the cover, noting how the small hole locates over the pin **(see illustration)**. Remove the rollers, plungers and

**2**

15.12a Check the rollers (arrowed) for signs of wear

15.12b Unscrew the three bolts and remove the cover, noting the hole (arrowed) for the locating pin

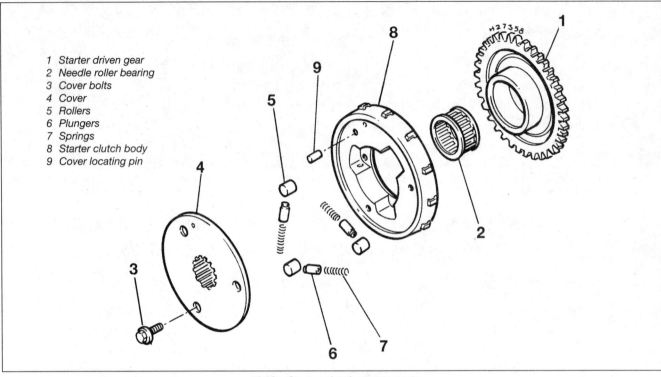

1 Starter driven gear
2 Needle roller bearing
3 Cover bolts
4 Cover
5 Rollers
6 Plungers
7 Springs
8 Starter clutch body
9 Cover locating pin

15.12c Starter clutch components

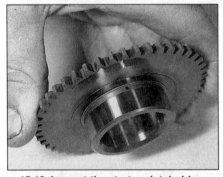

15.13 Inspect the starter clutch driven gear contact surface

springs, noting how they fit **(see illustration)**. Install the new components in a reverse sequence. Make sure the small hole in the cover locates over the pin. Apply a suitable non-permanent thread locking compound to the bolts and tighten them to the torque setting specified at the beginning of the Chapter.

**13** Check the bearing surface of the starter driven gear hub and the needle roller bearing **(see illustration)**. If the bearing surface shows signs of excessive wear or the bearing itself is worn or damaged, they should be replaced.

**14** Check the teeth of the starter idle/reduction gear and the corresponding teeth of the starter driven gear and starter motor drive shaft. Replace the gears and/or starter motor if worn or chipped teeth are discovered on related gears. Also check the idle/reduction gear shaft for damage, and check that the gear is not a

loose fit on the shaft. Replace the shaft if necessary.

**15** Check the teeth of the primary drive gear and the corresponding teeth of the primary driven gear on the back of the main clutch housing. Replace the gear and/or clutch housing if worn or chipped teeth are discovered.

### Installation

**16** If removed, slide the primary drive gear, spacer and thrust washer onto the crankshaft, making sure the teeth of the gear mesh correctly with those of the primary driven gear on the back of the main clutch housing **(see illustrations)**.

**17** Lubricate the hub of the starter driven gear with clean engine oil, then install the starter driven gear into the clutch, rotating

15.16a Slide the primary drive gear . . .

15.16b . . . the spacer . . .

15.16c . . . and the thrust washer onto the shaft

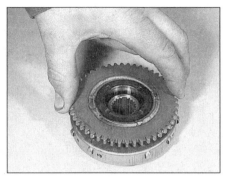

15.17a  Fit the driven gear into the starter clutch body . . .

15.17b  . . . then fit the needle roller bearing

15.18a  The wide spline (arrowed) in the starter clutch must align with that on the crankshaft . . .

clockwise as you do so to spread the rollers and allow the hub of the gear to enter **(see illustration)**. Fit the needle roller bearing into the driven gear **(see illustration)**.

18  Make sure the recessed section in the main clutch housing aligns with the starter clutch, then install the starter clutch assembly onto the end of the crankshaft, aligning the wider groove in the starter clutch with the wider spline on the shaft **(see illustrations)**. Install the starter clutch bolt and its washer **(see illustration 15.8a)**, and using the method employed on removal to stop the clutch from

turning, tighten the bolt to the torque setting specified at the beginning of the Chapter **(see illustration)**.

19  Lubricate the idle/reduction gear shaft with clean engine oil. Install the gear assembly, making sure the smaller pinion faces outwards and meshes correctly with the teeth of the starter driven gear, and the teeth of the larger pinion mesh correctly with the teeth of the starter motor shaft, then slide the shaft into the gear **(see illustration)**.

20  Install the pulse generator coil assembly (see Chapter 5).

21  If removed, insert the dowels in the crankcase, then install the crankcase cover using a new gasket, making sure it locates correctly onto the dowels and the idle/reduction gear shaft **(see illustration)**. Tighten the cover bolts evenly in a criss-cross sequence to the specified torque setting, making sure the wiring clips are correctly installed **(see illustration)**.

22  Refill the engine with oil (see Chapter 1) and check the level (see *Daily (pre-ride) checks*).

23  Install the lower fairing (see Chapter 8).

15.18b  . . and the cutout in the main clutch housing must be positioned to allow clearance for the starter driven gear

15.18c  Tighten the starter clutch bolt to the specified torque

15.19  Install the idle/reduction gear as shown and slide the shaft into its bore

**2**

15.21a  Position a new gasket onto the dowels (arrowed) . . .

15.21b  . . . then fit the cover

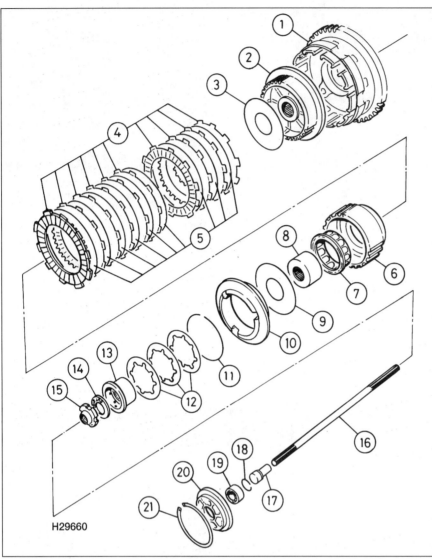

**16.2b Remove the circlip (arrowed) . . .**

**16.2c . . . and withdraw the pressure plate lifter**

**16 Clutch** – removal, inspection and installation

**16.2a Clutch components**

| | | |
|---|---|---|
| 1 Clutch housing | 8 One-way clutch hub | 15 Clutch nut |
| 2 Inner clutch centre | 9 Outer thrust washer | 16 Pushrod |
| 3 Inner thrust washer | 10 Pressure plate | 17 Pushrod end-piece |
| 4 Friction plates | 11 Spring seat | 18 Circlip |
| 5 Plain plates | 12 Diaphragm springs | 19 Bearing |
| 6 Outer clutch centre | 13 Diaphragm spring holder | 20 Pressure plate lifter |
| 7 One-way clutch sprag | 14 Lockwasher | 21 Circlip |

**Note 1:** *The clutch can be removed with the engine in the frame. If the engine has been removed, ignore the steps which don't apply.*
**Note 2:** *A peg spanner is required to slacken and tighten the clutch nut. If the Honda service tool (Part no. 07716-0020203) is not available, a suitable one will have to be fabricated out of a piece of steel tubing with an ID of 27 mm and an OD of 30 mm, or an old socket.*

### Removal

**1** Remove the starter clutch (see Section 15).
**2** Remove the circlip securing the pressure plate lifter inside the pressure plate and remove the lifter **(see illustrations)**.
**3** Remove the pushrod end piece from either the back of the pressure plate lifter or the end of the input shaft **(see illustration)**. Withdraw the clutch pushrod from the input shaft, noting which way round it fits – it may have to be poked through from the other side, requiring removal of the engine sprocket cover, or the engine will have to be tipped on its side **(see illustration)**.
**4** The clutch nut is staked against the input shaft. Unstake the nut using a screwdriver, a

**16.3a Remove the end-piece . . .**

**16.3b . . . and withdraw the pushrod**

16.4  Unstake the clutch nut

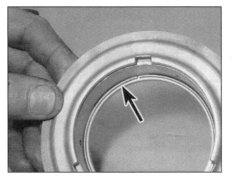

16.6  Do not remove the spring seat (arrowed) unless a new one is being fitted

16.7  Remove the clutch plates as an assembly

punch, or a drill **(see illustration)**. To remove the clutch nut, the input shaft must be locked. If the engine is in the frame, engage 6th gear and have an assistant hold the rear brake on hard with the rear tyre in firm contact with the ground. Alternatively, fit the primary drive gear back onto the end of the crankshaft (if removed) – the primary drive gear and the primary driven gear on the back of the main clutch housing can be locked together using the special tool (Part no. 00724-001010), or a stout piece of cloth, such as denim, can be jammed between them, without the risk of any damage should the bolt prove tight. Unscrew the nut using the peg spanner (see **Note 2**) **(see illustration 16.32c)** and remove the lockwasher from the input shaft, noting which way round it fits **(see illustration 16.32a)**. Discard the nut, and if it is worn or damaged the lockwasher, as new ones must be used.

> **HAYNES HINT**
> *If the engine is being completely disassembled or the oil pump driven sprocket is being removed, also slacken the sprocket bolt while the input shaft is locked.*

**5**  Draw the diaphragm spring holder off the shaft, noting how it fits **(see illustration 16.31)**.
**6**  Remove the three diaphragm springs,

noting how they fit, followed by the pressure plate **(see illustrations 16.30b and a)**. Do not remove the spring seat from the pressure plate unless it is being replaced **(see illustration)**.
**7**  Remove the outer thrust washer **(see illustration 16.29)**, then pull the clutch friction and plain plates off the input shaft as an assembly **(see illustration)**.
**8**  Pull the outer clutch centre and one-way clutch out of the clutch as an assembly, then remove the inner thrust washer, the inner clutch centre and the clutch housing **(see illustrations 16.27, 16.25b and a, and 16.24b)**.
**9**  Note the tabs on the oil pump drive sprocket behind the clutch housing which must locate in the slots in the back of the housing on reassembly. If required, unscrew the oil pump driven sprocket bolt and remove the drive and driven sprocket together with the drive chain **(see illustrations)**. If the sprocket bolt was not previously slackened, lock the sprocket to prevent it from turning (see **Tool Tip**). Also remove the clutch housing guide from the input shaft **(see illustration 16.22)**.

### Inspection

#### Clutch unit

**10**  After an extended period of service the clutch friction plates will wear and promote clutch slip. Measure the thickness of each

friction plate using a vernier caliper **(see illustration)**. If any plate has worn to or beyond the service limits given in the Specifications at the beginning of the Chapter, the friction plates must be replaced as a set. Also, if any of the plates smell burnt or are glazed, they must be replaced as a set.
**11**  The plain plates should not show any signs of excess heating (bluing). Check for warpage using a flat surface and feeler gauges **(see illustration)**. If any plate exceeds the maximum permissible amount of warpage, or shows signs of bluing, all plain plates must be replaced as a set.
**12**  Lay the diaphragm springs on top of each other on a flat surface (such as a piece of plate glass) and measure the height to the surface of the inner edge of the top spring

16.9a  Remove the sprocket bolt . . .

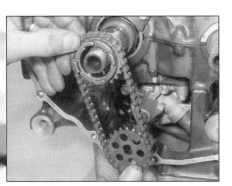

16.9b  . . . and draw the chain and sprockets off the shafts

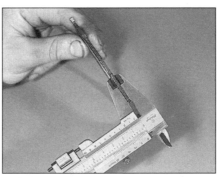

16.10  Measuring clutch friction plate thickness

16.11  Check the plain plates for warpage

**2**

**16.12 Measure the height of all three diaphragm springs as shown**

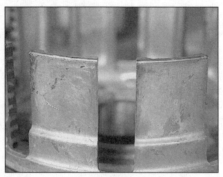

**16.13 Inspect the clutch housing edges for indentations**

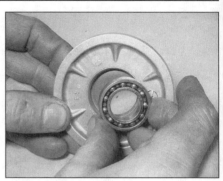

**16.14 Replace the bearing if required**

**(see illustration)**. Replace the springs if the height measured is less than the limit specified at the beginning of the Chapter.

**13** Inspect the clutch assembly for burrs and indentations on the edges of the protruding tangs of the friction plates and/or slots in the edge of the housing with which they engage **(see illustration)**. Similarly check for wear between the inner tongues of the plain plates and the slots in the clutch centre. Wear of this nature will cause clutch drag and slow disengagement during gear changes, since the plates will snag when the pressure plate is lifted. With care, a small amount of wear can be corrected by dressing with a fine file, but if this is excessive the worn components should be replaced.

**14** Check the pressure plate lifter, bearing and pushrod end-piece for signs of roughness,

wear or damage, and replace any parts as necessary. Check that the bearing outer race is a tight fit in the centre of the lifter, and that the inner race rotates freely without any rough spots. Replace the bearing if necessary **(see illustration)**. Check that the pushrod is straight by rolling it on a flat surface.

**15** Using a vernier caliper, measure the internal and external diameter of the clutch housing guide, and the internal diameter of the clutch housing and the oil pump drive sprocket. Compare the measurements to the specifications at the beginning of the Chapter and replace any components that are worn beyond their service limit. Also check all the above components for signs of damage or scoring, and replace if necessary.

**16** Check the teeth of the primary driven gear on the back of the clutch housing and the

corresponding teeth of the primary drive gear on the back of the starter clutch. Replace the clutch housing and/or gear if worn or chipped teeth are discovered.

**17** Check the pressure plate and thrust washer for signs of roughness, wear or damage, and replace any parts as necessary.

**18** Check the diaphragm spring seat for distortion, wear or damage, and replace it if necessary **(see illustration 16.6)**.

**19** With the one-way clutch face up on a workbench, check that the hub rotates freely in an anti-clockwise direction and locks against the sprags in a clockwise direction. If it doesn't, replace the one-way clutch. Check the condition of the sprags inside the clutch body **(see illustration)**. If they are damaged, marked or flattened at any point, they should be replaced. Check the bearing surface of the hub. If the hub surface shows signs of excessive wear or has flat spots, it should be replaced.

### Release mechanism

**20** Unscrew the bolt securing the clutch cable holder to the alternator cover, then detach the bracket and slip the cable end out of the release lever on the engine sprocket cover **(see illustrations)**. Unscrew the two bolts securing the speedometer drive box to the engine sprocket cover and detach the box, noting how the drive tab locates in the slot in the sprocket bolt cap **(see illustration)**. Unscrew the bolts securing the engine sprocket cover to the crankcase and draw the cover away from the engine **(see illustration)**.

**16.19 Check the one-way clutch as described**

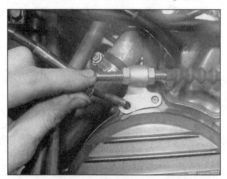

**16.20a Remove the clutch cable bracket bolt . . .**

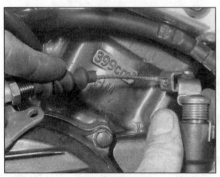

**16.20b . . . and detach the cable end from the lever**

**16.20c Remove the two bolts and detach the speedometer drive box from the cover**

**16.20d The sprocket cover is secured by four bolts (arrowed)**

16.20e Remove and clean the release mechanism components, noting how they fit

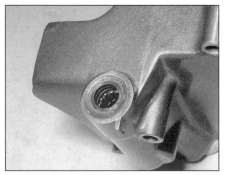

16.20f Check the oil seal and needle bearing in the cover

16.20g Note the locations of the different bolts . . .

Note the positions of the bolts as they are all different lengths. Remove the dowels if they are loose. Check the clutch release actuating mechanism for smooth operation and any signs of wear or damage. Remove the components, noting how the return spring ends locate, and clean and grease them if required (see illustrations). On assembly, align the shaft so that the release rod fits into its recess in the shaft. Check the pushrod oil seal in the crankcase joint for signs of leakage and replace it if necessary (see illustration 21.11); this seal is accessed by separating the crankcase halves, but if care is exercised it may be possible to lever the seal out and press a new one in without separating the crankcases (main pushrod removed). Refit the cover and the speedometer drive gear,

making sure the cover bolts are in their correct location and the drive gear tab locates correctly onto the slot in the engine sprocket bolt cap (see illustrations).

## Installation

21 Remove all traces of old gasket from the crankcase and cover surfaces.
22 Smear the inside and outside of the clutch housing guide with molybdenum disulphide oil (a 50/50 mixture of molybdenum disulphide grease and engine oil), then install the guide onto the input shaft (see illustration).
23 Install the oil pump drive chain onto its drive and driven sprockets, then install the sprockets and chain as an assembly onto the clutch housing guide and oil pump; ensure that the scribed lines on the driven sprocket

face the engine and that the tabs on the drive sprocket face out (see illustration). Apply a suitable non-permanent thread locking compound to the sprocket bolt and tighten it to the torque setting specified at the beginning of the chapter (see Tool Tip), not forgetting its washer (see illustration). Alternatively, tighten the bolt when tightening the clutch nut (see Step 29).

Insert a screwdriver through one of the holes in the sprocket and lock it against the crankcase to prevent the sprocket from turning whilst tightening the bolt.

24 Install the clutch housing over the housing guide on the mainshaft, making sure that the tabs on the oil pump drive sprocket engage with the slots in the rear of the housing (see illustrations).

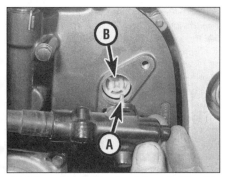

16.20h . . . and align the drive tab (A) with the slot (B)

16.22 Slide the guide onto the input shaft . . .

16.23a . . . then fit the oil pump chain and sprockets . . .

16.23b . . . and tighten the bolt to the specified torque

16.24a Align the tabs (A) with the slots (B) . . .

2

16.24b . . . then slide the housing onto the shaft . . .

16.25a . . . followed by the inner clutch centre . . .

16.25b . . . and the inner thrust washer

16.26 Start to build up the clutch plates as described . . .

16.27 . . . then fit the one-way clutch and outer clutch centre . . .

16.28 . . . build up the remaining clutch plates . . .

16.29 . . . and fit the outer thrust washer

**25** Slide the inner clutch centre and the inner thrust washer onto the shaft **(see illustrations)**.

**26** Start to build up the clutch plates in the housing, starting with a friction plate, then a plain plate and alternating friction and plain plates until four friction and three plain plates are installed **(see illustration)**. Coat the plates with oil before installing them.

**27** Apply clean engine oil to the one-way clutch sprags, then install the one-way clutch assembly and outer clutch centre **(see illustration)**.

**28** Build up the remaining clutch plates, starting with a plain plate and alternating them as before **(see illustration)**. Coat the plates with oil before installing them.

**29** Coat the outer thrust washer with clean engine oil and fit it into the clutch centre **(see illustration)**.

**30** If removed, install the diaphragm spring seat into the pressure plate **(see illustration 16.6)**. Install the pressure plate into the clutch centre, then Install the three diaphragm springs, making sure their higher inner edges face out **(see illustrations)**.

**31** Install the diaphragm spring holder, making sure its stepped inner edge fits into the inner edge of the outer thrust washer **(see illustration)**.

**32** Fit the lockwasher, using a new one if necessary, with its "OUTSIDE" mark facing

16.30a Install the pressure plate . . .

16.30b . . . and the three diaphragm springs

16.31 Install the spring holder . . .

16.32a ... the lockwasher (note OUTSIDE marking) ...

16.32b ... and the clutch nut

16.32c Fit the peg spanner or fabricated tool ...

out, onto the shaft splines (see illustration). Install the *new* clutch nut and, using the method employed on dismantling to lock the input shaft and the peg spanner used to unscrew it, tighten the nut to the torque setting specified at the beginning of the Chapter (see illustrations). Stake the nut shoulder against the detent in the shaft using a punch (see illustration). Take care not to damage the shaft threads.

33 Lubricate the longer unpolished end of the pushrod with molybdenum disulphide grease and install it into the end of the input shaft, making sure the longer end faces the left-hand side of the engine (see illustration). Install the pushrod end-piece (see illustration).

34 Install the pressure plate lifter and secure it with the circlip, making sure it is properly seated in its groove (see illustrations).

35 Install the starter clutch (see Section 15).

16.32d ... and tighten the clutch nut to the specified torque

16.32e Stake the nut against the cutout in the shaft

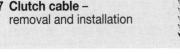

## 17 Clutch cable –
removal and installation

1 Remove the fairing left-hand side panel (see Chapter 8). Working at the lower end of the clutch cable, fully slacken the front adjuster nut and thread the rear nut off the end of the threaded section in the cable bracket on the alternator cover (see illustration). Disconnect

16.33a Slide the pushrod into the shaft ...

16.33b ... then fit the end-piece

16.34a Install the pressure plate lifter ...

16.34b ... and secure it with the circlip

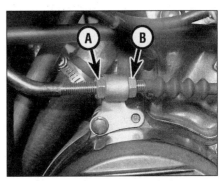

17.1a Fully slacken the front nut (A) and thread the rear nut (B) off the adjuster ...

**2**

17.1b . . . then release the cable end from the lever . . .

17.1c . . . and draw the adjuster out of the bracket

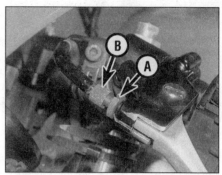

17.2 Fully slacken the lockring (A) and thread the adjuster (B) into the bracket

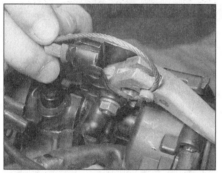

17.3 Align the slots as shown and detach the inner cable

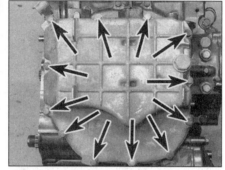

18.4 The sump is secured by twelve bolts (arrowed)

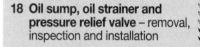

### 18 Oil sump, oil strainer and pressure relief valve – removal, inspection and installation

**Note:** *The oil sump, strainer and pressure relief valve can be removed with the engine in the frame. If the engine has been removed, ignore the steps which don't apply.*

### Removal

1 Remove the lower fairing (see Chapter 8).
2 Drain the engine oil (see Chapter 1).
3 Remove the front cylinder exhaust downpipes (see Chapter 4).
4 Unscrew the twelve sump bolts, slackening them evenly in a criss-cross sequence to prevent distortion, and remove the sump **(see illustration)**. Discard the gasket as a new one must be used.
5 Remove the oil strainer from the oil pump scavenge pipe – it is a push fit **(see illustration)**. Remove the rubber seal and discard it as a new one must be used.
6 The pressure relief valve is a push-fit into its socket in the crankcase. Remove it, and discard the O-ring as a new one must be used.

### Inspection

7 Remove all traces of gasket from the sump

the cable end from the clutch release mechanism lever, noting how it fits and release the adjuster from the bracket **(see illustrations)**.
2 Fully slacken the lockring on the adjuster at the handlebar end of the cable then screw the adjuster fully in **(see illustration)**. This resets it to the beginning of its adjustment span.
3 Align the slots in the adjuster and lockwheel with that in the lever bracket, then pull the outer cable end from the socket in the adjuster and release the inner cable from the lever **(see illustration)**. Remove the cable from the machine, noting its routing through the guide on the top yoke.

 **HAYNES HiNT** *Before removing the cable from the bike, tape the lower end of the new cable to the upper end of the old cable. Slowly pull the lower end of the old cable out, guiding the new cable down into position. Using this method will ensure the cable is routed correctly.*

4 Installation is the reverse of removal. Apply grease to the cable ends. Make sure the cable is correctly routed. Adjust the amount of clutch lever freeplay (see Chapter 1).

18.5 Remove the strainer (arrowed) . . .

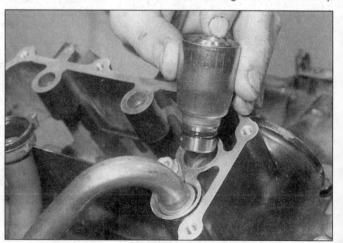

18.6 . . . and the pressure relief valve

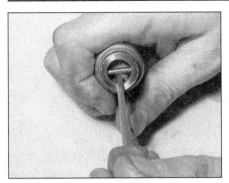

**18.9  Check that the plunger moves freely in the valve body**

**18.10  Smear clean oil onto the new relief valve O-ring**

**18.11  Fit the seal into the pipe . . .**

and crankcase mating surfaces, and clean the inside of the sump with solvent.

**8** Clean the oil strainer in solvent and remove any debris caught in the mesh. If the strainer gauze is damaged, replace the strainer with a new one.

**9** Push the relief valve plunger into the valve body and check that it moves smoothly and freely against spring pressure **(see illustration)**. If not, replace the relief valve – individual components are not available.

### Installation

**10** Fit a new O-ring onto the relief valve and smear it with clean oil, then push the valve into its socket in the crankcase **(see illustration)**.

**11** Fit a new rubber seal into the oil pump scavenge pipe **(see illustration)**. Do not fit it onto the strainer as it will distort when the strainer is fitted onto the pipe.

**12** Install the strainer onto the pipe, locating the cutout in the strainer base over the lug on the pipe **(see illustration)**.

**13** Lay a new gasket onto the sump (if the engine is in the frame) or onto the crankcase (if the engine has been removed and is positioned upside down on the work surface) **(see illustration)**. Make sure the holes in the gasket align correctly with the bolt holes.

**14** Position the sump onto the crankcase and install the bolts finger-tight **(see illustration)**. Tighten the bolts evenly in a criss-cross pattern.

**15** Install the front cylinder exhaust downpipes (see Chapter 4).

**16** Fill the engine with the correct type and quantity of oil as described in Chapter 1. Start the engine and check that there are no leaks around the sump.

**17** Install the lower fairing (see Chapter 8).

### 19  Oil pump – removal, inspection and installation

**Note:** *The oil pump can be removed with the engine in the frame. If the engine has been removed, ignore the steps which don't apply.*

#### Removal

**1** Remove the sump and oil strainer (see Section 18).

**2** Unscrew the twelve bolts securing the right-hand crankcase cover and remove the cover, being prepared to catch any residue oil, and noting the positions of the wiring clips **(see illustration 15.3)**. Discard the gasket as a new one must be used. Remove the dowels from either the cover or the crankcase if they are loose.

**3** Unscrew the bolt securing the oil pump driven sprocket **(see illustration 16.9a)**. To prevent the sprocket from turning, engage 6th gear and have an assistant hold the rear brake on (if the engine is in the frame). Alternatively, Honda provide a special tool (Part no. 00724-001010) which locks the primary drive and

**18.12  . . . then install the strainer, aligning the cutout (A) with the lug (B)**

driven gears on the starter clutch and main clutch respectively, or a stout piece of cloth, such as denim, can be jammed between them, or use a screwdriver through one of the holes in the sprocket (see **Tool Tip**, Section 16). Draw the sprocket off the oil pump and slip it out of the chain.

**4** On UK VFR L and M models, pull the two small-bore oil pipes from their sockets in the oil pump and crankcase – they are a push-fit. On all models, unscrew the bolts securing the large-bore oil pipe to the pump and the crankcase and remove the pipe **(see illustration)**. Remove the O-rings from the oil pipe sockets or the pipes themselves. The O-rings can be reused if they are in good condition, but should be replaced if they are in any way damaged or deteriorated.

**2**

**18.13  Lay the new gasket on the sump or crankcase as appropriate . . .**

**18.14  . . . then install the sump**

**19.4  Unscrew the two bolts (arrowed) and remove the pipe**

19.5 The oil pump is secured by three bolts (arrowed)

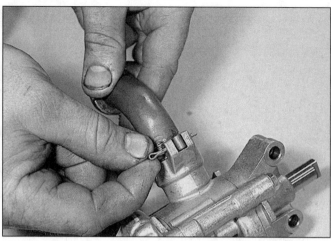

19.6 Remove the split pin and remove the scavenge pipe

5 Unscrew the three bolts securing the pump to the crankcase, then remove the pump, noting how it fits (see illustration). Note that you may need to rotate the oil pump driveshaft to aid its disconnection with the water pump driveshaft. Remove the pump dowels from either the crankcase or the pump if they are loose. Also remove the oil orifice and its O-ring from the crankcase. The O-ring can be reused if it is in good condition, but should be replaced if it is in any way damaged or deteriorated.

### Inspection

6 Withdraw the split pin securing the scavenge pipe to the pump, then pull the pipe out of the pump (see illustration). Discard the O-ring as a new one must be used.
7 On UK VFR L and M models, unscrew the three bolts securing the covers to the pump body, then remove the outer (cooling circuit) cover (see illustration). Remove the cover dowels if they are loose. Remove the outer and inner rotors, noting which way round they fit. Remove the inner (feed circuit) cover and its dowels if they are loose. Remove the inner and outer rotors, noting which way round they fit, then slide the drive pin out of the driveshaft. Push the shaft through the pump body and withdraw it from the cooling circuit side, then remove the drive pin and thrust washer. Note which way round the driveshaft fits in the pump. Remove the split pin securing the cooling circuit regulator in the outer cover, noting that the regulator is under spring pressure, then remove the spring retainer, the spring and the plunger, noting which way round each fits.
8 On all other models, unscrew the three bolts securing the cover to the pump body, then remove cover (see illustration). Remove the cover dowels if they are loose. Remove the outer and inner rotors, noting which way round they fit. Withdraw the driveshaft through the pump body and remove the drive pin and thrust washer. Note which way round the driveshaft fits in the pump.
9 Clean all the components in solvent.
10 Inspect the pump body and rotors for scoring and wear. If any damage, scoring or

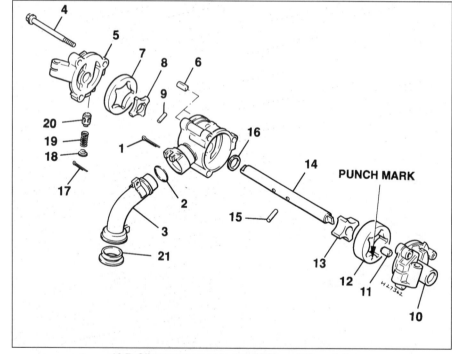

19.7 Oil pump components – UK L and M models

| | | |
|---|---|---|
| 1 Split pin | 8 Cooling circuit inner rotor | 15 Drive pin |
| 2 O-ring | 9 Drive pin | 16 Thrust washer |
| 3 Scavenge pipe | 10 Inner cover | 17 Split pin |
| 4 Cover bolts | 11 Dowels | 18 Spring retainer |
| 5 Outer cover | 12 Feed circuit outer rotor | 19 Spring |
| 6 Dowels | 13 Feed circuit inner rotor | 20 Plunger |
| 7 Cooling circuit outer rotor | 14 Driveshaft | 21 Strainer seal |

19.8 Unscrew the bolts and remove the cover

19.10  Look for scoring and wear, such as on this outer rotor

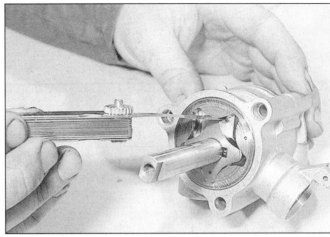

19.11  Measure the inner rotor tip-to-outer rotor clearance as shown

uneven or excessive wear is evident, replace the pump (individual components are not available) **(see illustration)**.

**11**  Fit the inner and outer rotors into the pump body (on UK VFR L and M models with the dual circuit pump, make sure the thinner rotors are fitted in the cooling circuit side, and the thicker rotors in the feed side). Measure the clearance between the inner rotor tip and the outer rotor with a feeler gauge and compare it to the service limit listed in the specifications at the beginning of the Chapter **(see illustration)**. If the clearance measured is greater than the maximum listed, replace the pump.

**12**  Measure the clearance between the outer rotor and the pump body with a feeler gauge and compare it to the maximum clearance listed in the specifications at the beginning of the Chapter **(see illustration)**. If the clearance measured is greater than the maximum listed, replace the pump.

**13**  Lay a straight-edge across the rotors and the pump body and, using a feeler gauge, measure the rotor end-float (the gap between the rotors and the straight-edge **(see illustration)**. If the clearance measured is greater than the maximum listed, replace the pump.

**14**  Check the pump drive chain and driven sprockets for wear or damage, and replace them as a set along with the drive sprocket if necessary. To access the drive sprocket, remove the clutch (see Section 16).

**15**  If the pump is good, make sure all the components are clean, then lubricate them with new engine oil.

**16**  On UK VFR L and M models, slide the thrust washer onto the shaft and fit the cooling circuit drive pin into the central hole in the driveshaft **(see illustration 19.7)**. Slide the driveshaft through the pump body from the outer cooling circuit side, making sure the end with the tab goes through to the inner feed circuit side. Fit the feed circuit drive pin into its hole in the driveshaft, then slide the inner

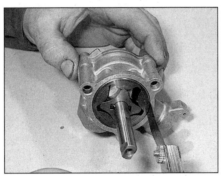

19.12  Measure the outer rotor-to-body clearance as shown

feed circuit rotor onto the shaft so that the cutouts on the inside of the rotor locate over the ends of the drive pin. Slide the outer rotor, with its punch mark facing out, onto the shaft and over the inner rotor. Remember that the feed circuit rotors are thicker than the cooling circuit rotors. Lubricate the rotors with clean engine oil. Fit the inner cover dowels if removed, the fit the cover. Slide the inner cooling circuit rotor onto the driveshaft so that the cutouts on the inside of the rotor locate over the ends of the drive pin. Slide the outer rotor, with its punch mark facing out, onto the driveshaft and over the inner rotor. Lubricate

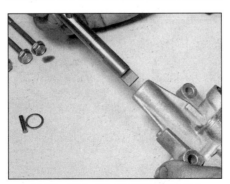

19.17a  Slide the shaft through the pump . . .

19.13  Measure the rotor end-float as shown

the rotors with clean engine oil. Fit the outer cover dowels if removed, the fit the cover and tighten the bolts to the torque setting specified at the beginning of the Chapter. Install the cooling circuit regulator plunger, spring and spring retainer into the cover and secure them using a new split pin.

**17**  On all other models, slide the driveshaft through the pump body from the outside, making sure the end with the bolt hole is on the outside **(see illustration)**. Slide the thrust washer onto the driveshaft and fit the drive pin into the central hole in the driveshaft **(see illustrations)**. Slide the inner rotor onto the

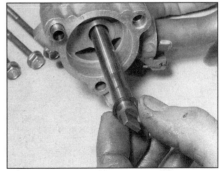

19.17b  . . . then fit the thrust washer . . .

**2**

19.17c . . . and the drive pin

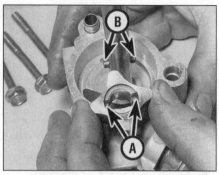

19.17d The cutouts (A) on the inside of the inner rotor locate onto the drive pin ends (B)

19.17e Fit the outer rotor with the punch mark (arrowed) facing out

19.17f Lubricate the rotors . . .

19.17g . . . then install the cover . . .

shaft so that the cutouts on the inside of the rotor locate over the ends of the drive pin (see illustrations). Slide the outer rotor, with its punch mark facing out, onto the driveshaft and over the inner rotor (see illustration). Lubricate the rotors with clean engine oil (see illustration). Fit the outer cover dowels if removed, then fit the cover and tighten the bolts to the torque setting specified at the beginning of the Chapter (see illustrations).

18 Rotate the pump shaft by hand and check that the rotors turn smoothly and freely.

19 Fit a new O-ring onto the pump end of the scavenge pipe and smear it with clean oil. Fit the pipe into the pump, aligning the holes in the tab on the pipe with those in the lugs on the pump (see illustration). Secure them using a new split pin inserted through the holes. Bend over the ends of the split pin.

### Installation

20 Check that the oil orifice is clear. Smear its O-ring with clean engine oil, using a new one if required, then fit the orifice and the O-ring into the crankcase (see illustrations).

21 If removed, fit the pump dowels into the crankcase (see illustration). Position the water pump and oil pump driveshaft slots vertically so that they engage easily when the pump is installed.

22 Manoeuvre the pump into position, making sure it engages correctly with the water pump and locates correctly onto the

19.17h . . . and tighten the bolts to the specified torque

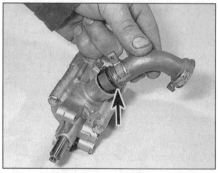

19.19 Fit the scavenge pipe using a new O-ring (arrowed)

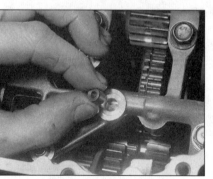

19.20a Fit the oil orifice . . .

19.20b . . . then fit the O-ring around it

19.21 Make sure the dowels (arrowed) are in place . . .

19.22a ... then install the pump ...

19.22b ... and tighten the bolts to the specified torque

19.24a Smear the O-rings with clean oil ...

dowels **(see illustration)**. Fit the pump mounting bolts and tighten them to the torque setting specified at the beginning of the Chapter **(see illustration)**.

**23** Slip the oil pump driven sprocket into the drive chain, then fit the sprocket onto the pump. Clean the threads of the sprocket bolt, then apply a suitable non-permanent thread locking compound and tighten the bolt to the specified torque, using the method employed on removal to prevent the sprocket turning.

**24** The oil pipe O-rings can be re-used if they are in good condition, but should be replaced if they are in any way damaged or deteriorated. Smear them with clean oil before fitting the pipes **(see illustration)**. On all models, fit the large bore oil pipe into the pump and the crankcase and secure it with the bolts **(see illustration)**. On UK VFR L and M models, fit the two small bore oil pipes into their sockets in the oil pump and crankcase – they are a push-fit.

**25** If removed, fit the right-hand crankcase cover dowels into the crankcase, then install the cover using a new gasket, making sure it locates correctly onto the dowels and the idle/reduction gear shaft **(see illustration 15.21a)**. Tighten the cover bolts evenly in a criss-cross sequence to the specified torque setting, making sure the wiring clips are correctly installed **(see illustration 15.21b)**.

**26** Install the oil strainer and sump (see Section 18).

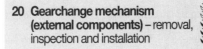

## 20 Gearchange mechanism (external components) – removal, inspection and installation

**Note:** *The gearchange mechanism (external components) can be removed with the engine in the frame. If the engine has been removed, ignore the steps which don't apply.*

### Removal

**1** Remove the lower fairing (see Chapter 8).

**2** Unscrew the gearchange lever linkage arm pinch bolt and remove the arm from the shaft, noting the alignment punch marks **(see illustrations)**. If no marks are visible, make your own before removing the arm so that it can be correctly aligned with the shaft on installation. Unscrew the bolt securing the clutch cable holder to the alternator cover, then detach the bracket and slip the cable end out of the release lever on the engine sprocket cover **(see illustrations 16.20a and b)**. Unscrew the two bolts securing the speedometer drive box to the engine sprocket cover and detach the box, noting how the drive tab locates in the slot in the sprocket bolt cap **(see illustration 16.20c)**. Unscrew the bolts securing the engine sprocket cover to the crankcase and draw the cover away from the engine **(see illustration 16.20d)**. Note the positions of the

19.24b ... then fit the pipe and tighten the bolts

bolts as they are all different lengths. Note the position of the dowels and remove them if they are loose.

**3** Remove the water pump (see Chapter 3).

**4** Wrap some insulating tape around the gearchange shaft splines to protect the oil seal lips as the gearchange mechanism cover is removed. Unscrew the bolts and remove the cover **(see illustration)**. Remove the dowels if they are loose. Discard the gasket as a new one must be used.

**5** Note how the gearchange shaft centralising spring ends fit on each side of the locating pin in the casing, and how the eye of the selector arm locates over the collar on the drum shift assembly **(see**

**2**

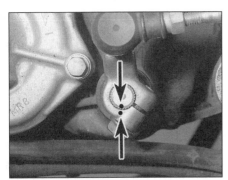

20.2a Note the alignment of the punch marks (arrowed) ...

20.2b ... then remove the bolt and slide the arm off the shaft

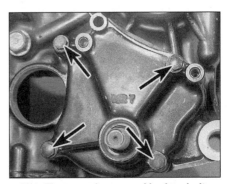

20.4 The cover is secured by four bolts (arrowed)

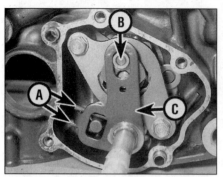

20.5 Note how the spring ends (A) locate, and how the eye of the arm locates over the collar (B), then withdraw the shaft/arm assembly (C)

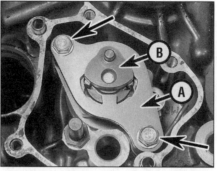

20.6 Unscrew the two bolts (arrowed) and remove the guide plate (A) and drum shift assembly (B)

20.7 Remove the stopper arm assembly

illustration). Withdraw the gearchange shaft and its thrust washer from the casing. Remove the collar from the pin on the drum shift assembly.

6 Unscrew the two bolts securing the drum shift guide plate, then remove the plate along with the drum shift assembly, noting that the pawls of the drum shift are under spring pressure (see illustration). Use your fingers to prevent them from pinging out. Note the correct fitted position of all components. Remove the spacer from the guide plate upper mounting dowel and the thrust washer from the lower one.

7 Lift the stopper arm off the stopper plate on the selector drum and remove the arm with its

return spring and collar, noting how they fit (see illustration).

8 If the selector drum and forks are to be removed from the transmission casing, unscrew the pin bolt securing the drum shift cam to the selector drum, then remove the cam and the rear guide plate (see illustration). Note the locating pin between the shift cam and the selector drum and remove it for safe keeping if required (see illustration). Also remove the dowels if they are loose.

### Inspection

9 Inspect the stopper arm return spring and the shaft centralising spring. If they are

fatigued, worn or damaged they must be replaced. Also check that the centralising spring locating pin in the casing is securely tightened. If it is loose, remove it and apply a suitable non-permanent thread locking compound, then tighten it to the specified torque.

10 Check the gearchange shaft for straightness and damage to the splines. If the shaft is bent you can attempt to straighten it, but if the splines are damaged the shaft must be replaced. Also check the condition of the shaft oil seal in the casing and replace it if damaged or deteriorated. Lever the old seal out using a screwdriver and drive the new seal in squarely (see illustration).

11 Inspect the selector arm eye and the drum shift collar, and the stopper arm roller and the stopper plates. If they are worn or damaged they must be replaced.

12 Check the drum shift, pawls, pins and springs for wear and damage. Replace them if defects are found.

### Installation

13 If removed, install the locating pin in the offset hole in the end of the selector drum, and the guide plate dowels (see illustration). Fit the rear guide plate onto the dowels, then install the drum shift cam, locating the slot in the back over the locating pin in the selector drum (see illustrations). Clean the threads of the pin bolt, then apply a suitable non-

20.8a Unscrew the pin bolt and remove the cam (arrowed) . . .

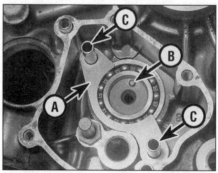

20.8b . . . the rear guide plate (A), the locating pin (B) and the dowels (C) if loose

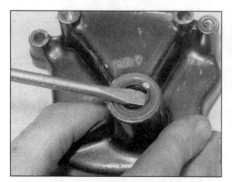

20.10 Replace the gearchange cover oil seal if required

20.13a Fit the locating pin and the dowels (arrowed) . . .

20.13b . . . then fit the rear guide plate over the dowels

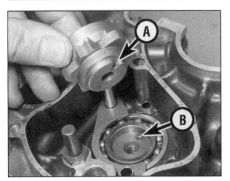

20.13c Fit the cam so the cutout (A) locates over the pin (B)

20.13d Apply a thread locking compound to the bolt . . .

20.13e . . . and tighten it to the specified torque

permanent thread locking compound (see illustration). Install the pin bolt and tighten it to the torque setting specified at the beginning of the Chapter, using a rod inserted between the cam and the crankcase to prevent the drum from turning (see illustration).

14 Fit the spacer onto the guide plate upper mounting dowel (see illustration).

15 Fit the stopper arm assembly onto the lower mounting dowel, positioning the stopper arm roller into the neutral detent in the shift cam (identified by the triangle on the top of the cam) and making sure the spring ends are located correctly over the stopper arm and against the casing (see illustration). Make sure the stopper arm is free to move and is returned by the pressure of the spring. Fit the thrust washer onto the stopper arm (see illustration).

16 If the drum shift assembly was disassembled, install the springs, pins and pawls, making sure the rounded end of each pawl fits into the rounded cut-out in the drum shift, and that the pins locate correctly in the cut-outs in the pawls (see illustrations).

17 Depress the pawls and fit the drum shift assembly into the shift cam, locating the pin bolt through the hole in the drum shift (see illustration). Make sure the pawls locate correctly in the cutouts in the cam. Fit the guide plate around the drum shift and locate it

20.14 Fit the spacer onto the upper dowel

20.15a Install the stopper arm

20.15b Align the cam so that the stopper arm locates against the neutral detent, identified by the triangle (arrowed)

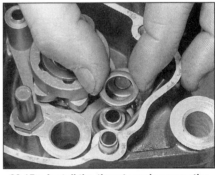

20.15c Install the thrust washer over the stopper arm

2

20.16a Drum shift pawl assembly

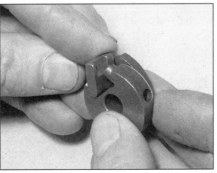

20.16b Note that the pawl cut-out is offset – ensure they are fitted correctly

20.17a Fit the drum shift assembly into the cam . . .

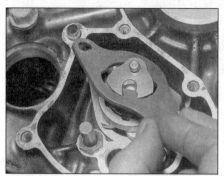

20.17b ... then fit the guide plate ...

20.17c ... and tighten the bolts to the specified torque

20.18 Fit the collar onto the pin

onto the dowels **(see illustration)**. Clean the threads of the guide plate bolts, then apply a suitable non-permanent thread locking compound and tighten them to the specified torque setting **(see illustration)**.

**18** Fit the collar onto the pin on the drum shift assembly, noting that its shouldered side faces the shift assembly **(see illustration)**.

**19** Check that the gearchange shaft centralising spring is correctly positioned, then fit the thrust washer onto the inner end of the shaft **(see illustrations)**. Fit the shaft into its hole in the casing. Make sure the centralising spring ends are correctly located on each side of the tab on the arm and the pin in the casing, and that the eye of the arm locates around the collar **(see illustration 20.5)**.

**20** Fit the cover dowels in the casing if removed, then install the cover using a new gasket and tighten the bolts evenly **(see illustration)**. Remove the tape from around the shaft splines.

**21** Install the water pump (see Chapter 3).

**22** If removed, fit the engine sprocket cover dowels into the casing, then fit the cover and tighten the bolts securely, making sure the bolts are in their correct locations **(see illustration 16.20g)**. Fit the speedometer drive gear onto the cover, making sure the drive gear tab locates correctly into the slot in the engine sprocket bolt cap **(see illustration 16.20h)**. Fit the clutch cable end into the release lever, then mount the cable bracket onto the alternator cover and tighten its bolts securely **(see illustrations 16.20b and a)**.

**23** Install the gearchange linkage arm onto the end of the shaft, aligning the punch marks, and check that the mechanism works correctly **(see illustrations 20.2a and b)**. Tighten the pinch bolt.

**24** Install the lower fairing (see Chapter 8).

## 21 Crankcase halves –
separation and reassembly

**Note:** *To separate the crankcase halves, the engine must be removed from the frame.*

### Separation

**1** To access the pistons, connecting rods, crankshaft, bearings, transmission shafts and the selector drum and forks, the crankcase must be split into two parts.

**2** To enable the crankcases to be separated, the engine must be removed from the frame (see Section 5). Before the crankcases can be separated the following components must be removed:

  a) Oil cooler (UK VFR L and M models) (Section 7).
  b) Valve covers (Section 8).
  c) Camshafts (Section 9).
  d) Camshaft drive gear assemblies (Section 11).
  e) Cylinder heads (Section 12).
  f) Ignition pulse generator assembly (Chapter 5).
  g) Starter clutch and primary drive gear (Section 15).
  h) Clutch (Section 16).
  i) Water pump (Chapter 3).
  j) Gearchange mechanism external components (Section 20) – see note below.
  k) Oil sump (Section 18).
  l) Oil pump (Section 19).
  m) Alternator rotor and stator (Chapter 9).
  n) Starter motor (Chapter 9).

**Note:** *If the crankcases are being separated to inspect the crankshaft without removing it, or to remove the crankshaft without removing the connecting rods and pistons, the front cylinder head can remain in situ. The rear head must be removed, otherwise access for*

20.19a Check that the spring ends are correctly located ...

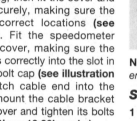

20.19b ... then fit the thrust washer and install the shaft

20.20a Lay the gasket onto the dowels (arrowed) ...

20.20b ... then install the gearchange cover

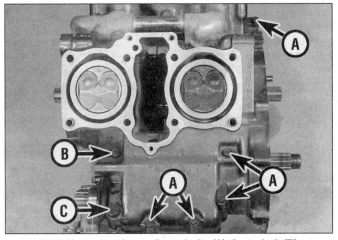

**21.4 Upper crankcase 6 mm bolts (A), 8 mm bolt (B) and 10 mm bolt (C)**

**21.6 Lower crankcase 6 mm bolts (A) and 8 mm bolts (B)**

tightening one of the crankcase bolts with a torque wrench is too restricted. However, if removal of the connecting rod assemblies is intended, full disassembly of the top-end is necessary. The gearchange mechanism external components can also remain in situ unless the selector drum and forks are being removed.

**3** If the transmission shafts are being removed, unscrew the two bolts securing the transmission input shaft bearing retainer plate to the right-hand side of the crankcase and remove the plate **(see illustration 28.2a)**.

**4** Unscrew the five 6 mm, one 8 mm and one 10 mm upper crankcase bolts **(see illustration)**. Unscrew the bolts evenly, a little at a time and in a criss-cross sequence until they are finger-tight, then remove them. **Note:** *As each bolt is removed, store it in its relative position in a cardboard template of the crankcase halves. This will ensure all bolts are installed in the correct location on reassembly.*

**5** Turn the engine upside down.

**6** Unscrew the seven 6 mm lower crankcase bolts, followed by the ten 8 mm bolts **(see**

**illustration)**. Unscrew the bolts evenly, a little at a time and in a criss-cross sequence until they are finger-tight, then remove them. **Note:** *As each bolt is removed, store it in its relative position in a cardboard template of the crankcase halves. This will ensure all bolts are installed in the correct location on reassembly.*

**7** Carefully lift the lower crankcase half off the upper half, using a soft-faced hammer to tap around the joint to initially separate the halves if necessary. **Note:** *If the halves do not separate easily, make sure all fasteners have been removed. Do not try and separate the halves by levering against the crankcase mating surfaces as they are easily scored and will leak oil in the future if damaged.* The lower crankcase half will come away with the gearchange mechanism external components (if not already removed) and the selector drum and forks, leaving the crankshaft and transmission shafts in the upper crankcase half.

**8** Remove the three locating dowels from the crankcase if they are loose (they could be in either crankcase half), noting their locations **(see illustration)**.

**9** Refer to Sections 22 to 30 for the removal and installation of the components housed within the crankcases.

### Reassembly

**10** Remove all traces of sealant from the crankcase mating surfaces.

**11** Ensure that all components and their bearings are in place in the upper and lower crankcase halves. If the transmission shafts have not been removed, check the condition of the output shaft oil seal on the left-hand end of the shaft and the clutch pushrod oil seal on the left-hand end of the input shaft and replace them if they are damaged or deteriorated **(see illustration)**.

**12** Generously lubricate the crankshaft and transmission shafts, particularly around the bearings, with clean engine oil, then use a rag soaked in high flash-point solvent to wipe over the mating surfaces of both crankcase halves to remove all traces of oil.

**13** If removed, install the three locating dowels in the upper crankcase half **(see illustration 21.8)**.

**2**

**21.8 Remove the dowels (arrowed) if they are loose**

**21.11 Check the output shaft seal (A) and the pushrod seal (B)**

**21.14 Apply sealant to one crankcase half**

**21.15 Make sure the selector forks locate in their pinion grooves (arrowed)**

**21.17 Tighten the bolts as described to the specified torque**

**14** Apply a small amount of suitable sealant to the outer mating surface of one crankcase half **(see illustration)**.
*Caution: Do not apply an excessive amount of sealant as it will ooze out when the case halves are assembled and may obstruct oil passages. Do not apply the sealant on or too close to any of the bearing inserts or surfaces.*
**15** Check again that all components are in position, particularly that the bearing shells are still correctly located in the lower crankcase half. Carefully install the lower crankcase half down onto the upper crankcase half, making sure each selector fork locates correctly in the groove in its pinion, and the dowels all locate correctly into the lower crankcase half **(see illustration)**.
**16** Check that the lower crankcase half is correctly seated. **Note:** *The crankcase halves should fit together without being forced. If the casings are not correctly seated, remove the lower crankcase half and investigate the problem. Do not attempt to pull them together using the crankcase bolts as the casing will crack and be ruined.*
**17** Clean the threads of the ten 8 mm lower crankcase bolts and insert them in their original locations **(see illustration 21.6)**. Secure all bolts finger-tight at first, then tighten them evenly a little at a time in a criss-cross sequence to the torque setting specified at the beginning of the Chapter **(see illustration)**.
**18** Clean the threads of the seven 6 mm lower crankcase bolts and insert them in their original locations **(see illustration 21.6)**. Secure all bolts finger-tight at first, then tighten them evenly a little at a time in a criss-cross sequence to the torque setting specified at the beginning of the Chapter.
**19** Turn the engine over. Clean the threads of the five 6 mm, one 8 mm and one 10 mm upper crankcase bolts and insert them in their original locations **(see illustration 21.4)**. Secure all bolts finger-tight at first, then tighten them evenly a little at a time in a criss-cross sequence to the torque setting specified at the beginning of the Chapter.
**20** With all crankcase fasteners tightened,

check that the crankshaft and transmission shafts rotate smoothly and easily. Check that the transmission shafts rotate freely and independently in neutral, then rotate the selector drum by hand and select each gear in turn whilst rotating the input shaft. Check that all gears can be selected and that the shafts rotate freely in every gear. If there are any signs of undue stiffness, tight or rough spots, or of any other problem, the fault must be rectified before proceeding further.
**21** Install the transmission input shaft bearing retainer plate onto the right-hand side of the crankcase. Apply a suitable non-permanent thread locking compound to the threads of the screws and tighten them securely.
**22** Install all other removed assemblies in the reverse of the sequence given in Step 2.

## 22 Crankcase halves and cylinder bores – inspection and servicing

### Crankcase halves

**1** After the crankcases have been separated, remove the crankshaft, connecting rods and pistons, transmission shafts, selector drum and forks, neutral switch oil pressure switch, and, if required, the cooling system unions, referring to the relevant Sections of this Chapter, to Chapter 9 for the oil pressure and neutral switches, and to Chapter 3 for the coolant unions.
**2** The crankcases should be cleaned thoroughly with new solvent and dried with compressed air. All oil passages should be blown out with compressed air.
**3** All traces of old gasket sealant should be removed from the mating surfaces. Minor damage to the surfaces can be cleaned up with a fine sharpening stone or grindstone.
*Caution: Be very careful not to nick or gouge the crankcase mating surfaces or oil leaks will result. Check both crankcase halves very carefully for cracks and other damage.*
**4** Small cracks or holes in aluminium castings may be repaired with an epoxy resin adhesive

as a temporary measure. Permanent repairs can only be effected by argon-arc welding, and only a specialist in this process is in a position to advise on the economy or practical aspect of such a repair. If any damage is found that can't be repaired, replace the crankcase halves as a set.
**5** Damaged threads can be economically reclaimed by using a diamond section wire insert, of the Heli-Coil type, which is easily fitted after drilling and re-tapping the affected thread.
**6** Sheared studs or screws can usually be removed with screw extractors, which consist of a tapered, left-hand thread screw of very hard steel. These are inserted into a pre-drilled hole in the stud, and usually succeed in dislodging the most stubborn stud or screw.

> **HAYNES HiNT** *Refer to Tools and Workshop Tips for details of installing a thread insert and using screw extractors.*

**7** Install all components and assemblies, referring to the relevant Sections of this Chapter and to Chapter 9, before reassembling the crankcase halves.

### Cylinder bores

**8** Do not attempt to separate the cylinder liners from the cylinder block.
**9** Check the cylinder walls carefully for scratches and score marks.
**10** Using a precision straight-edge and a feeler gauge set to the warpage limit listed in the specifications at the beginning of the Chapter, check the block gasket mating surface for warpage. Refer to *Tools and Workshop Tips* in the Reference section for details of how to use the straight-edge. If warpage is excessive the block must be replaced with a new one.
**11** Using telescoping gauges and a micrometer (see *Tools and Workshop Tips*), check the dimensions of each cylinder to assess the amount of wear, taper and ovality. Measure near the top (but below the level of the top piston ring at TDC), centre and bottom (but above the level of the oil ring at BDC) of

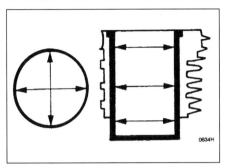

**22.11 Measure each cylinder bore in the directions shown**

the bore, both parallel to and across the crankshaft axis **(see illustration)**. Compare the results to the specifications at the beginning of the Chapter. If the cylinders are worn, oval or tapered beyond the service limit the crankcases will have to be renewed, oversize pistons and rings and not available.

**12** If the precision measuring tools are not available, take the crankcases to a Honda dealer or specialist motorcycle repair shop for assessment and advice.

**13** If the cylinder bores are in good condition and the piston-to-bore clearance is within specifications (see Section 25), the cylinders should be honed (de-glazed). To perform this operation you will need the proper size flexible hone with fine stones, or a bottle-brush type hone, plenty of light oil or honing oil, some clean rags and an electric drill motor.

**14** Hold the block sideways (so that the bores are horizontal rather than vertical) in a vice with soft jaws or cushioned with wooden blocks. Mount the hone in the drill motor, compress the stones and insert the hone into the cylinder. Thoroughly lubricate the cylinder, then turn on the drill and move the hone up and down in the cylinder at a pace which produces a fine cross-hatch pattern on the cylinder wall with the lines intersecting at an angle of approximately 60∞. Be sure to use plenty of lubricant and do not take off any more material than is necessary to produce the desired effect. Do not withdraw the hone from the cylinder while it is still turning. Switch off the drill and continue to move it up and down in the cylinder until it has stopped turning, then compress the stones and withdraw the hone. Wipe the oil from the cylinder and repeat the procedure on the other cylinders. Remember, do not take too much material from the cylinder wall.

**15** Wash the bores thoroughly with warm soapy water to remove all traces of the abrasive grit produced during the honing operation. Be sure to run a brush through the stud holes and flush them with running water. After rinsing, dry the cylinders thoroughly and apply a thin coat of light, rust-preventative oil to all machined surfaces.

**16** If you do not have the equipment or desire to perform the honing operation, take the crankcase to a Honda dealer or specialist motorcycle repair shop.

## 23 Main and connecting rod bearings – general information

**1** Even though main and connecting rod bearings are generally replaced with new ones during the engine overhaul, the old bearings should be retained for close examination as they may reveal valuable information about the condition of the engine.

**2** Bearing failure occurs mainly because of lack of lubrication, the presence of dirt or other foreign particles, overloading the engine and/or corrosion. Regardless of the cause of bearing failure, it must be corrected before the engine is reassembled to prevent it from happening again.

**3** When examining the connecting rod bearings, remove them from the connecting rods and caps and lay them out on a clean surface in the same general position as their location on the crankshaft journals. This will enable you to match any noted bearing problems with the corresponding crankshaft journal.

**4** Dirt and other foreign particles get into the engine in a variety of ways. It may be left in the engine during assembly or it may pass through filters or breathers. It may get into the oil and from there into the bearings. Metal chips from machining operations and normal engine wear are often present. Abrasives are sometimes left in engine components after reconditioning operations, especially when parts are not thoroughly cleaned using the proper cleaning methods. Whatever the source, these foreign objects often end up imbedded in the soft bearing material and are easily recognised. Large particles will not imbed in the bearing and will score or gouge the bearing and journal. The best prevention for this cause of bearing failure is to clean all parts thoroughly and keep everything spotlessly clean during engine reassembly. Frequent and regular oil and filter changes are also recommended.

**5** Lack of lubrication or lubrication breakdown has a number of interrelated causes. Excessive heat (which thins the oil), overloading (which squeezes the oil from the bearing face) and oil leakage or throw off (from excessive bearing clearances, worn oil pump or high engine speeds) all contribute to lubrication breakdown. Blocked oil passages will also starve a bearing and destroy it. When lack of lubrication is the cause of bearing failure, the bearing material is wiped or extruded from the steel backing of the bearing. Temperatures may increase to the point where the steel backing and the journal turn blue from overheating.

 *Refer to Tools and Workshop Tips for bearing fault finding.*

**6** Riding habits can have a definite effect on bearing life. Full throttle low speed operation, or labouring the engine, puts very high loads on bearings, which tend to squeeze out the oil film. These loads cause the bearings to flex, which produces fine cracks in the bearing face (fatigue failure). Eventually the bearing material will loosen in pieces and tear away from the steel backing. Short trip riding leads to corrosion of bearings, as insufficient engine heat is produced to drive off the condensed water and corrosive gases produced. These products collect in the engine oil, forming acid and sludge. As the oil is carried to the engine bearings, the acid attacks and corrodes the bearing material.

**7** Incorrect bearing installation during engine assembly will lead to bearing failure as well. Tight fitting bearings which leave insufficient bearing oil clearances result in oil starvation. Dirt or foreign particles trapped behind a bearing insert result in high spots on the bearing which lead to failure.

**8** To avoid bearing problems, clean all parts thoroughly before reassembly, double check all bearing clearance measurements and lubricate the new bearings with clean engine oil during installation.

## 24 Connecting rods – removal, inspection and installation

**Note:** *To remove the connecting rods the engine must be removed from the frame and the crankcases separated.*

### Removal

**1** Remove the engine from the frame (see Section 5) and separate the crankcase halves (see Section 21).

**2** Before removing the rods from the crankshaft, measure the clearance between each pair of rods with a feeler gauge **(see illustration)**. If the clearance is greater than the service limit listed in this Chapter's Specifications, replace that pair of rods with new ones.

**3** Using paint or a felt marker pen, mark the relevant cylinder identity on each connecting rod and cap. Mark across the cap-to-

**24.2 Measure the connecting rod side clearance using a feeler gauge**

**2**

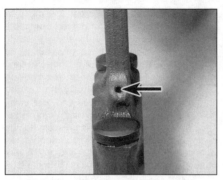

24.3 The oil hole (arrowed) in each connecting rod faces the back of the engine

24.4 Unscrew the nuts and remove the connecting rod cap

24.5 Withdraw the piston and connecting rod assembly from the top of the cylinder

connecting rod join and note which side of the rod faces the front of the engine to ensure that the cap and rod are fitted the correct way around on reassembly. Note that the number already across the rod and cap indicates rod size grade, not cylinder number, and the letter indicates rod weight grade. The oil hole in the big-end of each connecting rod should face the back of the engine **(see illustration)**.
4 Unscrew the big-end cap nuts and separate the cap from the crankpin **(see illustration)**.
5 Push each piston/connecting rod assembly up and remove it from the top of the bore making sure the connecting rod does not mark the cylinder bore walls **(see illustration)**. Do not remove the bolts from the connecting rods. Keep the rod, cap, bolts, nuts and (if

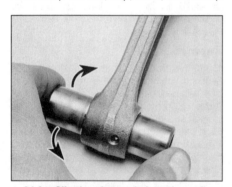

24.9a Slip the piston pin into the rod's small-end and rock it back and forth to check for looseness

they are to be reused) the bearing shells together in their correct positions to ensure correct installation.

>  **To ease removal of the pistons, remove any ridge of carbon built up on the top of each cylinder bore. If there is a pronounced wear ridge, remove it using a ridge reamer.**

*Caution: Do not try to remove the piston/connecting rod from the bottom of the cylinder bore. The piston will not pass the crankcase main bearing webs. If the piston is pulled right to the bottom of the bore the oil control ring will expand and lock the piston in position. If this happens it is likely the ring will be broken.*
6 Immediately install the relevant bearing shells (if removed), bearing cap, and nuts on each piston/connecting rod assembly so that they are all kept together as a matched set.
7 Remove the pistons from the connecting rods (see Section 25).

### Inspection
8 Check the connecting rods for cracks and other obvious damage.
9 Apply clean engine oil to the piston pin, insert it into the connecting rod small-end and check for any freeplay between the two **(see illustration)**. Measure the pin external diameter and the small-end bore diameter, then calculate the difference to obtain the small-

end-to-piston pin clearance **(see illustrations)**. Compare the result to the specifications at the beginning of the Chapter. If the clearance is greater than specified, replace the components that are worn beyond their specified limits.
10 Refer to Section 23 and examine the connecting rod bearing shells. If they are scored, badly scuffed or appear to have seized, new shells must be installed. Always replace the shells in the connecting rods as a set. If they are badly damaged, check the corresponding crankpin. Evidence of extreme heat, such as discoloration, indicates that lubrication failure has occurred. Be sure to thoroughly check the oil pump and pressure regulator as well as all oil holes and passages before reassembling the engine.
11 Have the rods checked for twist and bend by a Honda dealer if you are in doubt about their straightness.

### Oil clearance check
12 Whether new bearing shells are being fitted or the original ones are being re-used, the connecting rod bearing oil clearance should be checked prior to reassembly. If not already done, remove the crankshaft from the crankcase (see Section 27).
13 Clean the backs of the bearing shells and the bearing locations in both the connecting rod and cap.
14 Press the bearing shells into their locations, ensuring that the tab on each shell engages the notch in the connecting rod/cap **(see illustration)**. Make sure the bearings are

24.9b Measure the external diameter of the pin . . .

24.9c . . . and the internal diameter of the connecting rod small-end

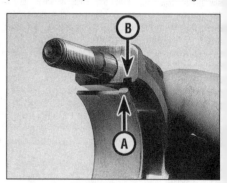

24.14 Make sure the tab (A) locates in the notch (B)

24.21a Crankpin journal size letters (arrowed)

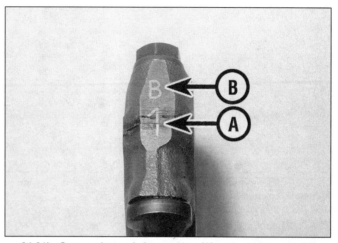

24.21b Connecting rod size number (A) and weight code (B)

fitted in the correct locations and take care not to touch any shell's bearing surface with your fingers.

15 Cut a length of the appropriate size Plastigauge (it should be slightly shorter than the width of the crankpin). Place a strand of Plastigauge on the (cleaned) crankpin journal and fit the (clean) connecting rod, shells and cap. Make sure the cap is fitted the correct way around so the previously made markings align, and that the rod is facing the right way, and tighten the cap nuts evenly, in two or three stages, to the torque setting specified at the beginning of the Chapter, whilst ensuring that the connecting rod does not rotate on the crankshaft. Slacken the cap nuts and remove the connecting rod, again taking great care not to rotate the rod or crankshaft.

16 Compare the width of the crushed Plastigauge on the crankpin to the scale printed on the Plastigauge envelope to obtain the connecting rod bearing oil clearance (see illustration 27.18). Compare the reading to the specifications at the beginning of the Chapter.

17 On completion carefully scrape away all traces of the Plastigauge material from the crankpin and bearing shells using a fingernail or other object which is unlikely to score the shells.

18 If the clearance is within the range listed in this Chapter's Specifications and the bearings are in perfect condition, they can be reused. If the clearance is beyond the service limit, replace the bearing shells with new ones (see Steps 21 and 22). Check the oil clearance once again (the new shells may be thick enough to bring bearing clearance within the specified range). Always replace all of the shells at the same time.

19 If the clearance is still greater than the service limit listed in this Chapter's Specifications, the crankpin is worn and the crankshaft should be replaced

20 Repeat the bearing selection procedure for the remaining connecting rods.

### Bearing shell selection

21 Replacement bearing shells for the big-end bearings are supplied on a selected fit basis. Code letters and numbers stamped on various components are used to identify the correct replacement bearings. The crankpin journal size letters are stamped on the crankshaft webs and will be either an A or a B (see illustration). Each letter is adjacent to the crankpin journal it represents. The connecting rod size code number is marked on the flat face of the connecting rod and cap and will be either a 1 or a 2 (see illustration).

22 A range of bearing shells is available. To select the correct bearing shell colour code for a particular big-end, using the table below cross-refer the crankpin journal size letter (stamped on the web) with the connecting rod size number (stamped on the rod). For example, if the connecting rod size is 2, and the crankpin size is A, then the bearing required is Green. The colour is marked on the side of the shell (see illustration). Note: *Replacement shells for the front cylinder bearings are marked by a single colour mark, while replacement bearings for the rear cylinder bearings are marked by a double colour mark. Be sure to fit the correct shells on the relevant bearing.*

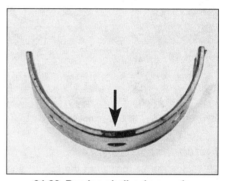

24.22 Bearing shell colour code location

### Connecting rod selection

23 If a connecting rod needs to be replaced, the weight of the replacement rod needs to be matched to the other rod on the same crankpin. If both rods are being replaced, they need to be matched together. The connecting rod weight code is marked on the flat face of the connecting rod and cap and will be either an A, B, or C (see illustration 24.21b).

24 Select the rod in accordance with the table below.

| Weight code of rod being replaced | Weight code of other rod on crankpin | Weight code of new rod |
|---|---|---|
| A | B | A, B or C |
| A | C | A or B |
| B | A | B or C |
| B | B | A, B or C |
| B | C | A or B |
| C | A | B or C |
| C | B | A, B or C |

| Crankpin code | Connecting rod code | |
|---|---|---|
| | 1 – (33.000 to 33.008 mm) | 2 – (33.008 to 33.016 mm) |
| A – (29.992 to 30.008 mm) | C – Yellow | B – Green |
| B – (29.984 to 29.992 mm) | B – Green | A – Brown |

2

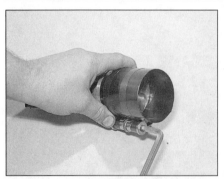

24.27a Clamp the rings in position by tightening the bands on the compressor . . .

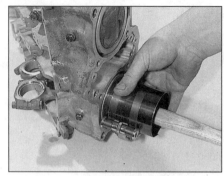

24.27b . . . then push the piston into its bore

24.28a Lubricate the crankpin journal . . .

24.28b . . . and fit the connecting rod to it

## Installation

**25** Install the pistons onto the connecting rods (see Section 25). If removed, install the crankshaft (see Section 27).
**26** Install the bearing shells in the connecting rods and caps, aligning the notch in the bearing with the groove in the rod or cap **(see illustration 24.14)**. Lubricate the shells with molybdenum disulphide oil (a 50/50 mixture of molybdenum disulphide grease and clean engine oil).
**27** Lubricate the pistons, rings and cylinder bore with clean engine oil. Insert the piston/connecting rod assembly into the top of its bore, taking care not to allow the connecting rod to mark the bore. Make sure the "IN" mark on the piston crown is on the inlet side of the bore and the connecting rod is

the right way round (see Step 3), then carefully compress and feed each piston ring into the bore until the piston crown is flush with the top of the bore **(see illustration 24.5)**. If available, a piston ring compressor makes installation a lot easier **(see illustrations)**.
**28** Ensure that the connecting rod bearing insert is still correctly installed. Liberally lubricate the crankpin with molybdenum disulphide oil (a 50/50 mixture of molybdenum disulphide grease and clean engine oil) **(see illustration)**. Taking care not to mark the cylinder bores, pull the piston/connecting rod assembly down its bore and onto the crankpin **(see illustration)**.
**29** Fit the bearing cap with its shell onto the connecting rod **(see illustration)**. Make sure the cap is fitted the correct way around so the connecting rod and bearing cap weight/size markings are correctly aligned.
**30** Fit the nuts to the connecting rod and tighten them evenly, in two or three stages, to the specified torque setting **(see illustration)**.
**31** Check that the crankshaft is free to rotate easily, then install the three remaining assemblies in the same way. Check to make sure that all components have been returned to their original locations using the marks made on disassembly.
**32** Check that the rods rotate smoothly and freely on the crankpin. If there are any signs of roughness or tightness, remove the rods and re-check the bearing clearance. Sometimes tapping the bottom of the connecting rod cap

will relieve tightness, but if in doubt, recheck the clearances.
**33** Reassemble the crankcase halves (see Section 21).

## 25 Pistons – removal, inspection and installation

**Note:** *To remove the pistons the engine must be removed from the frame and the crankcase halves separated.*

### Removal

**1** Remove the engine from the frame (see Section 5) and separate the crankcase halves (see Section 21).
**2** Separate the connecting rods from the crankshaft (see Section 24).
**3** Before removing the piston from the connecting rod, use a sharp scriber or felt marker pen to write the cylinder identity on the crown of each piston (or on the inside of the skirt if the piston is dirty and going to be cleaned). Each piston should also have an "IN" mark on its crown which should face the inlet side of the bore **(see illustration)**. If this is not visible, mark the piston accordingly so that it can be installed the correct way round.
**4** Carefully prise out the circlip on one side of the piston using needle-nose pliers or a small flat-bladed screwdriver inserted into the notch

24.29 Fit the connecting rod cap . . .

24.30 . . . and tighten the nuts to the specified torque

25.3 Note the IN mark which faces the inlet side of the cylinder

**25.4a Prise out the circlip . . .**

**25.4b . . . then push out the pin and remove the piston**

**25.6 Removing the piston rings using a ring removal and installation tool**

(see illustration). Push the piston pin out from the other side to free the piston from the connecting rod (see illustration). Remove the other circlip and discard them as new ones must be used. When the piston has been removed, install its pin back into its bore so that related parts do not get mixed up.

*If a piston pin is a tight fit in the piston bosses, soak a rag in boiling water then wring it out and wrap it around the piston – this will expand the alloy piston sufficiently to release its grip on the pin. If the piston pin is particularly stubborn, extract it using a drawbolt tool, but be careful to protect the piston's working surfaces.*

### Inspection

5 Before the inspection process can be carried out, the pistons must be cleaned and the old piston rings removed.

6 Using your thumbs or a piston ring removal and installation tool, carefully remove the rings from the pistons (see illustration). Do not nick or gouge the pistons in the process. Carefully note which way up each ring fits and in which groove as they must be installed in their original positions if being re-used. The upper surface of each ring is marked with a letter at one end. The top ring is identified by the letter R, and the second (middle) ring by a mark "•" or the letters RN.

7 Scrape all traces of carbon from the tops of the pistons. A hand-held wire brush or a piece of fine emery cloth can be used once most of the deposits have been scraped away. Do not, under any circumstances, use a wire brush mounted in a drill motor to remove deposits from the pistons; the piston material is soft and will be eroded away by the wire brush.

8 Use a piston ring groove cleaning tool to remove any carbon deposits from the ring grooves. If a tool is not available, a piece broken off an old ring will do the job. Be very careful to remove only the carbon deposits. Do not remove any metal and do not nick or gouge the sides of the ring grooves.

9 Once the deposits have been removed, clean the pistons with solvent and dry them thoroughly. If the identification previously marked on the piston is cleaned off, be sure to re-mark it with the correct identity. Make sure the oil return holes below the oil ring groove are clear.

10 Carefully inspect each piston for cracks around the skirt, at the pin bosses and at the ring lands. Normal piston wear appears as even, vertical wear on the thrust surfaces of the piston and slight looseness of the top ring in its groove. If the skirt is scored or scuffed, the engine may have been suffering from overheating and/or abnormal combustion, which caused excessively high operating temperatures. The oil pump should be checked thoroughly. Also check that the circlip grooves are not damaged.

11 A hole in the piston crown, an extreme to be sure, is an indication that abnormal combustion (pre-ignition) was occurring. Burned areas at the edge of the piston crown are usually evidence of spark knock (detonation). If any of the above problems exist, the causes must be corrected or the damage will occur again.

12 Measure the piston ring-to-groove clearance by laying each piston ring in its groove and slipping a feeler gauge in beside it (see illustration). Make sure you have the correct ring for the groove (see Step 6). Check the clearance at three or four locations around the groove. If the clearance is greater than specified, replace both the piston and rings as a set. If new rings are being used, measure the clearance using the new rings. If the clearance is greater than that specified, the piston is worn and must be replaced.

13 Check the piston-to-bore clearance by measuring the bore (see Section 22) and the piston diameter. Make sure each piston is matched to its correct cylinder. Measure the piston 10.0 mm up from the bottom of the skirt and at 90° to the piston pin axis (see illustration). Subtract the piston diameter from the bore diameter to obtain the clearance. If it is greater than the specified figure, the piston must be replaced (assuming the bore itself is within limits).

14 If not already done (see Section 24), apply clean engine oil to the piston pin, insert it into the piston and check for any freeplay between the two (see illustration). Measure the pin

**2**

**25.12 Measure the piston ring-to-groove clearance with a feeler gauge**

**25.13 Measure the piston diameter with a micrometer at the specified distance from the bottom of the skirt**

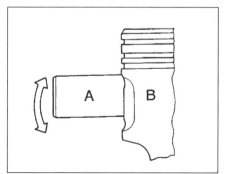

**25.14a Slip the pin (A) into the piston (B) and try to rock it back and forth. If it's loose, replace the piston and pin**

**25.14b Measure the internal diameter of the bore in the piston**

**25.17 Do not over-compress the circlip when fitting it into the piston**

**26.3 Measuring piston ring installed end gap**

external diameter **(see illustration 24.9b)**, and the pin bore in the piston **(see illustration)**. Calculate the difference to obtain the piston pin-to-piston pin bore clearance. Compare the result to the specifications at the beginning of the Chapter. If the clearance is greater than specified, replace the components that are worn beyond their specified limits. Repeat the measurements between the pin and the connecting rod small-end **(see illustration 24.9c)**.

### *Installation*

**15** Inspect and install the piston rings (see Section 26).

**16** Lubricate the piston pin, the piston pin bore and the connecting rod small-end bore with molybdenum disulphide oil (a 50/50 mixture of molybdenum disulphide grease and clean engine oil).

**17** When installing the pistons onto the connecting rods, make sure that the "IN" mark is on the same side as the oil hole in the connecting rod on the front cylinder pistons, but is on the opposite side to the hole on the rear cylinder pistons **(see illustration 24.3)**. Install a *new* circlip in one side of the piston (do not re-use old circlips). Line up the piston on its correct connecting rod, and insert the piston pin from the other side **(see illustration 25.4b)**. Secure the pin with the other *new* circlip. When installing the circlips, compress them only just enough to fit them in the piston,

and make sure they are properly seated in their grooves with the open end away from the removal notch **(see illustration)**.

**18** Install the connecting rods onto the crankshaft (see Section 24) and reassemble the crankcase halves (see Section 21).

### 26 Piston rings –
### inspection and installation

**1** It is good practice to replace the piston rings when an engine is being overhauled. Before installing the new piston rings, the ring end gaps must be checked with the rings installed in the bore.

**2** Lay out the pistons and the new ring sets so the rings will be matched with the same piston and bore during the end gap measurement procedure and engine assembly.

**3** To measure the installed ring end gap, insert the top ring into the top of the bore and square it up with the bore walls by pushing it in with the top of the piston. The ring should be about 20 mm below the top edge of the bore. To measure the end gap, slip a feeler gauge between the ends of the ring and compare the measurement to the specifications at the beginning of the Chapter **(see illustration)**.

**4** If the gap is larger or smaller than specified, double check to make sure that you have the correct rings before proceeding.

**5** If the gap is too small, it must be enlarged or the ring ends may come in contact with each other during engine operation, which can cause serious damage. The end gap can be increased by filing the ring ends very carefully with a fine file. When performing this operation, file only from the outside in **(see illustration)**.

**6** Excess end gap is not critical unless it exceeds the service limit. Again, double-check to make sure you have the correct rings for your engine and check that the bore is not worn.

**7** Repeat the procedure for each ring that will be installed in the bore. Remember to keep the rings, pistons and bores matched up.

**8** Once the ring end gaps have been checked/corrected, the rings can be installed on the pistons.

**9** The oil control ring (lowest on the piston) is installed first. It is composed of three separate components, namely the expander and the upper and lower side rails. Slip the expander into the groove, then install the upper side rail. Do not use a piston ring installation tool on the oil ring side rails as they may be damaged. Instead, place one end of the side rail into the groove between the expander and the ring land. Hold it firmly in place and slide a finger around the piston while pushing the rail into the groove. Next, install the lower side rail in the same manner **(see illustrations)**. Make sure the ends of the expander do not overlap.

**26.5 Ring end gap can be enlarged by clamping a file in a vice and filing the ring ends**

**26.9a Install the oil ring expander in its groove . . .**

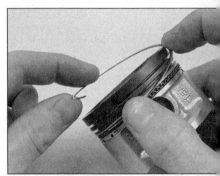

**26.9b . . . and fit the side rails each side of it. The oil ring must be installed by hand**

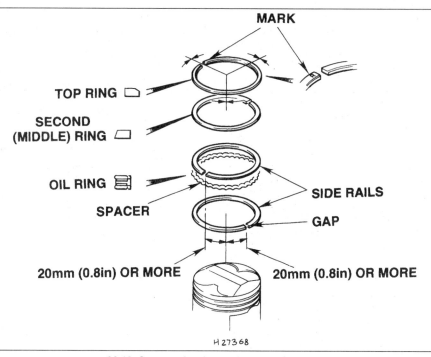

MARK

TOP RING

SECOND
(MIDDLE) RING

OIL RING

SIDE RAILS

SPACER

GAP

20mm (0.8in) OR MORE          20mm (0.8in) OR MORE

H 27368

**26.13 Stagger the ring end gaps as shown**

**0** After the three oil ring components have been installed, check to make sure that both the upper and lower side rails can be turned smoothly in the ring groove.

**1** The upper surface of each compression ring is marked with a mark or letter at one end. The top ring is identified by the letter R, and the second (middle) ring by the mark "●" or letters RN. Install the second (middle) ring next. Make sure that the identification mark or letter near the end gap is facing up. Fit the ring into the middle groove in the piston. Do not expand the ring any more than is necessary to slide it into place. To avoid breaking the ring, use a piston ring installation tool.

**2** Finally, install the top ring in the same manner into the top groove in the piston. Make sure the identification letter near the end gap is facing up.

**3** Once the rings are correctly installed,

check they move freely without snagging and stagger their end gaps as shown (see illustration).

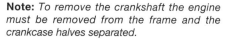

**27 Crankshaft and main bearings** – removal, inspection and installation

**Note:** *To remove the crankshaft the engine must be removed from the frame and the crankcase halves separated.*

### Removal

**1** Remove the engine from the frame (see Section 5) and separate the crankcase halves (see Section 21).

**2** Separate the connecting rods from the crankshaft (see Section 24).

**Note:** *If no work is to be carried out on the piston/connecting rod assemblies there is no*

need to remove them from the bores, although the connecting rod bearing caps must be removed (see Section 24, Steps 3 and 4) and the pistons pushed up to the top of the bores so that the connecting rod ends are positioned clear of the crankshaft.

**3** Lift the crankshaft out of the upper crankcase half, taking care not to dislodge the main bearing shells (see illustration).

**4** The main bearing shells can be removed from the crankcase halves by pushing their centres to the side, then lifting them out (see illustration). Keep the shells in order.

### Inspection

**5** Clean the crankshaft with solvent, using a rifle-cleaning brush to scrub out the oil passages. If available, blow the crank dry with compressed air, and also blow through the oil passages. Check the drive gear for wear or damage (see illustration). If any of the gear teeth are excessively worn, chipped or broken, the crankshaft must be replaced. If wear or damage is found, also inspect the camshaft drive gear assemblies (see Section 11).

**6** Refer to Section 23 and examine the main bearing shells. If they are scored, badly scuffed or appear to have been seized, new bearings must be installed. Always replace the main bearings as a set. If they are badly damaged, check the corresponding crankshaft journals. Evidence of extreme heat, such as discoloration, indicates that lubrication failure has occurred. Be sure to thoroughly check the oil pump and pressure regulator as well as all oil holes and passages before reassembling the engine.

**7** The crankshaft journals should be given a close visual examination, paying particular attention where damaged bearings have been discovered. If the journals are scored or pitted in any way a new crankshaft will be required. Note that undersizes are not available, precluding the option of re-grinding the crankshaft.

**8** Place the crankshaft on V-blocks and check the runout at the main bearing journals using a dial gauge. Compare the reading to the maximum specified at the beginning of the Chapter. If the runout exceeds the limit, the crankshaft must be replaced.

**2**

**27.3 Lift the crankshaft out of the crankcase . . .**

**27.4 . . . and remove the shells if required**

**27.5 Check the teeth of the drive gear as described**

27.9a  Main bearing journal size numbers (arrowed)

27.9b  Main bearing housing size letters (arrowed)

### Main bearing shell selection

9  Replacement bearing shells for the main bearings are supplied on a selected fit basis. Code letters and numbers stamped on various components are used to identify the correct replacement bearings. The crankshaft main bearing journal size numbers are stamped on the crankshaft webs and will be either a 1 or a 2 (see illustration). Each number is adjacent to the journal it represents. The corresponding main bearing housing size letters are stamped into the upper crankcase half and will be either an A or a B. The left-hand letter corresponds to the left-hand journal, the right-hand letter to the right-hand journal, and the inner left- and right-hand letters to the inner left- and right-hand journals respectively (see illustration).

10  A range of bearing shells is available. To select the correct bearing for a particular journal, using the accompanying table cross-refer the main bearing journal size number (stamped on the crank web) with the main bearing housing size letter (stamped on the crankcase) to determine the colour code of the bearing required. For example, if the journal code is 1, and the housing code is B, then the bearing required is Yellow. The colour is marked on the side of the shell (see illustration 24.22).

| Crankcase code | Main journal code | |
| --- | --- | --- |
| | 1 – (29.994 to 30.002 mm) | 2 – (30.002 to 30.010 mm) |
| A – (33.000 to 33.008 mm) | C – Yellow | B – Green |
| B – (33.008 to 33.016 mm) | B – Green | A – Brown |

### Oil clearance check

11  Whether new bearing shells are being fitted or the original ones are being re-used, the main bearing oil clearance should be checked before the engine is reassembled. Main bearing oil clearance is measured with a product known as Plastigauge.

12  Clean the backs of the bearing shells and the bearing housings in both crankcase halves.

13  Press the bearing shells into their cut-outs, ensuring that the tab on each shell engages in the notch in the crankcase (see illustration). Make sure the bearings are fitted in the correct locations and take care not to touch any shell's bearing surface with your fingers.

14  Ensure the shells and crankshaft are clean and dry. Lay the crankshaft in position in the upper crankcase.

15  Cut several lengths of the appropriate size Plastigauge (they should be slightly shorter than the width of the crankshaft journals). Place a strand of Plastigauge on each

(cleaned) journal (see illustration). Make sur the crankshaft is not rotated.

16  Carefully install the lower crankcase half o to the upper half. Check that the lowe crankcase half is correctly seated. Note: Do no tighten the crankcase bolts if the casing is no correctly seated. Install the lower crankcase mm bolts in their original locations and tighte them evenly a little at a time in a criss-cros sequence to the torque setting specified at th beginning of the Chapter (see illustration 21.6 Make sure that the crankshaft is not rotated a the bolts are tightened.

17  Slacken each bolt evenly a little at a tim in a criss-cross sequence until they are a finger-tight, then remove the bolts. Careful lift off the lower crankcase half, making sur the Plastigauge is not disturbed.

18  Compare the width of the crushe Plastigauge on each crankshaft journal to th scale printed on the Plastigauge envelope t obtain the main bearing oil clearanc (see illustration). Compare the reading t

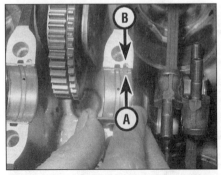

27.13  Fit the shells, locating the tab (A) in the notch (B)

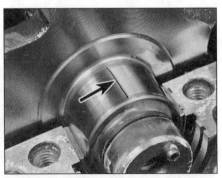

27.15  Lay a strip of Plastigauge (arrowed) on each journal parallel to the crankshaft centreline

27.18  Measure the width of the crushed Plastigauge

**27.23 Generously lubricate all the bearing shells**

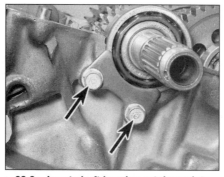

**28.2a Input shaft bearing retainer plate bolts (arrowed)**

**28.2b Lift the input shaft (A) and the output shaft (B) out of the crankcase**

the specifications at the beginning of the Chapter.

**19** On completion carefully scrape away all traces of the Plastigauge material from the crankshaft journal and bearing shells; use a fingernail or other object which is unlikely to score them.

**20** If the oil clearance falls into the specified range, no bearing shell replacement is required (provided they are in good condition). If the clearance is beyond the service limit, refer to the marks on the case and the marks on the crankshaft and select new bearing shells (see Steps 9 and 10). Install the new shells and check the oil clearance once again (the new shells may bring bearing clearance within the specified range). Always replace all of the shells at the same time.

**21** If the clearance is still greater than the service limit listed in this Chapter's Specifications (even with replacement shells), the crankshaft journal is worn and the crankshaft should be replaced. Measure the diameter of each journal and compare the measurements to the table above to confirm that the journals are worn beyond the standard specification.

### Installation

**22** Clean the backs of the bearing shells and the bearing cut-outs in both crankcase halves. If new shells are being fitted, ensure that all traces of the protective grease are cleaned off using paraffin (kerosene). Wipe dry the shells and crankcase halves with a lint-free cloth. Make sure all the oil passages and holes are clear, and blow them through with compressed air if it is available.

**23** Press the bearing shells into their locations. Make sure the tab on each shell engages in the notch in the casing **(see illustration 27.13)**. Make sure the bearings are fitted in the correct locations and take care not to touch any shell's bearing surface with your fingers. Lubricate each shell with molybdenum disulphide oil (a 50/50 mixture of molybdenum disulphide grease and clean engine oil) **(see illustration)**.

**24** Lower the crankshaft into position in the upper crankcase, making sure all bearings remain in place **(see illustration 27.3)**. If the front cylinder head was not removed, make sure the teeth of the drive gear on the crankshaft mesh with those on the camshaft drive gear assembly.

**25** Fit the connecting rods to the crankshaft (see Section 24).

**26** Reassemble the crankcase halves (see Section 21).

### 28 Transmission shafts and bearings – removal and installation

**Note:** *To remove the transmission shafts the engine must be removed from the frame and the crankcases separated. If the engine has already been removed, ignore the steps which do not apply.*

### Removal

**1** Remove the engine from the frame (see Section 5) and separate the crankcase halves (see Section 21). Remove the clutch pushrod oil seal **(see illustration 28.8a)**.

**2** Remove the bearing retainer plate from the input shaft right-hand end **(see illustration)**. Lift the input shaft and output shaft out of the casing, noting their relative positions and how

they fit together **(see illustration)**. If they are stuck, use a soft-faced hammer and gently tap on the ends of the shafts to free them. Remove the bearing half-ring retainer from the left-hand end of the output shaft and the needle bearing dowel from the left-hand end of the input shaft, noting how they fit **(see illustrations 28.4a and b)**. If they are not in their slot or hole in the crankcase, remove them from the bearings themselves on the shafts. If necessary, the input shaft and output shaft can be disassembled and inspected for wear or damage (see Section 29).

**3** Referring to *Tools and Workshop Tips* (Section 5) in the Reference Section, check the bearings on the transmission shafts. Replace the bearings if necessary, noting that the output shaft left-hand bearing is not available separately from the shaft. Also check the condition of the output shaft oil seal and replace it if it is worn or damaged **(see illustration 28.5b)**.

### Installation

**4** Install the bearing half-ring retainer for the left-hand end of the output shaft into its slot in the upper crankcase half, and the needle bearing dowel for the left-hand end of the input shaft into its hole **(see illustrations)**.

**5** Lubricate the left-hand end of the output shaft with clean oil and slide the *new*

**2**

**28.4a Fit the half-ring retainer into its slot . . .**

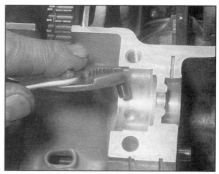

**28.4b . . . and the dowel pin into its hole**

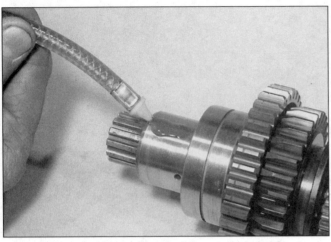

28.5a Lubricate the end of the output shaft . . .

28.5b . . . then fit the oil seal . . .

28.5c . . . and lubricate the seal lips

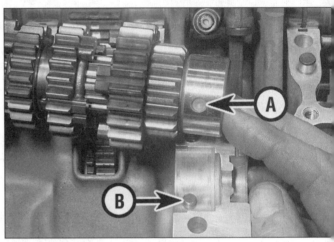

28.6 Locate the bearing hole (A) over the dowel (B)

output shaft oil seal onto the shaft (see illustrations). Smear the seal lips with oil (see illustration).

6 Lower the input shaft into position in the upper crankcase, making sure the hole in the needle bearing engages correctly with the dowel (see illustration).

7 Lower the output shaft into position in the crankcase half, making sure the groove in the bearing engages correctly with the bearing half-ring retainer (see illustration). Also

ensure that the oil seal lip locates in the crankcase groove.

8 Make sure both transmission shafts are correctly seated and their related pinions are correctly engaged (see illustration 28.2). Fit a new clutch pushrod oil seal into its seat (see illustration). Position the input shaft bearing retainer plate on the crankcase, apply a non-permanent thread locking compound to its bolts and tighten them securely (see illustration).

Caution: If the bearing half-ring retainer or dowel are not correctly engaged with their bearings, the crankcase halves will not seat correctly.

9 Position the gears in the neutral position and check the shafts are free to rotate easily and independently (ie the input shaft can turn whilst the output shaft is held stationary before proceeding further.

10 Reassemble the crankcase halves (see Section 21).

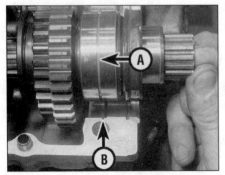

28.7 Locate the bearing groove (A) onto the half-ring retainer (B)

28.8a Fit the new pushrod oil seal

28.8b Apply thread locking compound to the input shaft bearing retainer bolts

## 29 Transmission shafts –
disassembly, inspection and reassembly

**1** Remove the transmission shafts from the casing (see Section 28). Always disassemble the transmission shafts separately to avoid mixing up the components.

### Input shaft disassembly

**HAYNES HiNT** *When disassembling the transmission shafts, place the parts on a long rod or thread a wire through them to keep them in order and facing the proper direction.*

**2** Slide the needle bearing cage and bearing off the left-hand end of the shaft, followed by the thrust washer, the 2nd gear pinion, the splined washer, the 6th gear pinion and its bush, and the splined washer **(see illustration)**.
**3** Remove the circlip securing the combined 3rd/4th gear pinion, then slide the pinion off the shaft.
**4** Remove the circlip securing the 5th gear pinion **(see illustration 29.14f)**, then slide the splined washer, the pinion and its bush, and the thrust washer off the shaft.
**5** The 1st gear pinion is integral with the shaft.

### Input shaft inspection

**6** Wash all of the components in clean solvent and dry them off.
**7** Check the gear teeth for cracking, chipping, pitting and other obvious wear or damage. Any pinion that is damaged as such must be replaced.
**8** Inspect the dogs and the dog holes in the gears for cracks, chips, and excessive wear especially in the form of rounded edges. Make sure mating gears engage properly. Replace the paired gears as a set if necessary.
**9** Check for signs of scoring or bluing on the pinions, bushes and shaft. This could be caused by overheating due to inadequate lubrication. Check that all the oil holes and passages are clear. Replace any damaged pinions or bushes.
**10** Check that each pinion moves freely on the shaft or bush but without undue freeplay. Check that each bush moves freely on the shaft but without undue freeplay. If the necessary equipment is available the individual components can be measured and the results compared with the specifications at the beginning of this Chapter.
**11** The shaft is unlikely to sustain damage unless the engine has seized, placing an unusually high loading on the transmission, or the machine has covered a very high mileage. Check the surface of the shaft, especially where a pinion turns on it, and replace the shaft if it has scored or picked up, or if there are any cracks. Damage of any kind can only be cured by replacement.

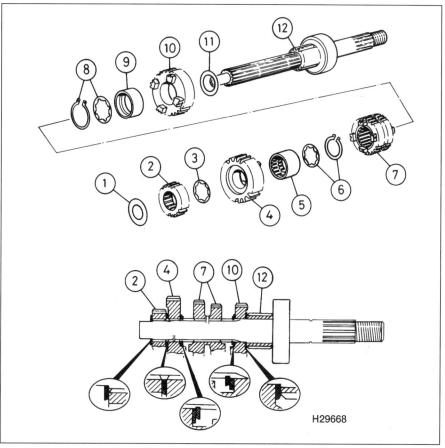
**29.2 Transmission input shaft components**

| | |
|---|---|
| 1 Thrust washer | 6 Splined washer and circlip |
| 2 2nd gear pinion | 7 Combined 3rd/4th gear pinion |
| 3 Splined washer | 8 Circlip and splined washer |
| 4 6th gear pinion | 9 5th gear pinion bush |
| 5 6th gear pinion bush | 10 5th gear pinion |
| | 11 Thrust washer |
| | 12 Input shaft with integral 1st gear pinion |

**12** Check the washers and circlips and replace any that are bent or appear weakened or worn. Use new ones if in any doubt. Note that it is good practice to renew all circlips when overhauling gearshafts.

### Input shaft reassembly

**13** During reassembly, apply engine oil to the mating surfaces of the shaft, pinions and bushes. When installing the circlips, do not expand their ends any further than is necessary. Install the stamped circlips and washers so that their chamfered side faces the pinion it secures **(see illustration 29.2)**.
**14** Slide the thrust washer onto the left-hand end of the shaft, followed by the 5th gear pinion bush, aligning the oil hole in the bush with the hole in the shaft. Fit the 5th gear pinion with its dogs facing away from the integral 1st gear **(see illustrations)**. Slide the

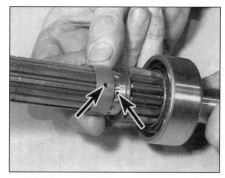
**29.14a Slide the thrust washer ...**    **29.14b ... the 5th gear pinion bush (oil holes arrowed) ...**

**2**

29.14c . . . the 5th gear pinion . . .

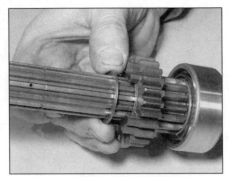

29.14d . . . and the splined washer onto the shaft . . .

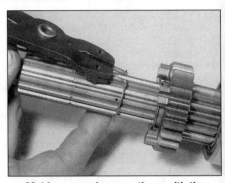

29.14e . . . and secure them with the circlip . . .

29.14f . . . making sure it locates properly in its groove

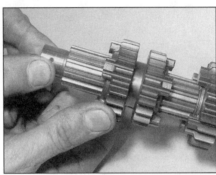

29.15a Slide the combined 3rd/4th gear pinion onto the shaft . . .

splined washer onto the shaft, then fit the circlip, making sure that it locates correctly in the groove in the shaft (see illustrations).

15 Slide the combined 3rd/4th gear pinion onto the shaft with the smaller 3rd gear pinion facing the 5th gear pinion (see illustration). Fit the circlip, making sure it is locates correctly in its groove in the shaft (see illustration).

16 Slide the splined washer onto the shaft, followed by the 6th gear pinion bush, aligning the oil hole in the bush with the hole in the shaft, and the 6th gear pinion, making sure its dogs face the 3rd/4th gear pinion (see illustrations). Slide the splined washer, the 2nd gear pinion and the thrust washer onto

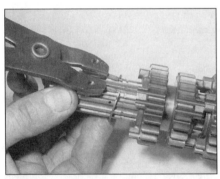

29.15b . . . and secure it with the circlip

29.16a Slide the splined washer . . .

29.16b . . . the 6th gear pinion bush (oil holes arrowed) . . .

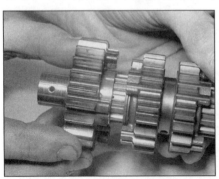

29.16c . . . the 6th gear pinion . . .

29.16d . . . the splined washer . . .

29.16e . . . the 2nd gear pinion . . .

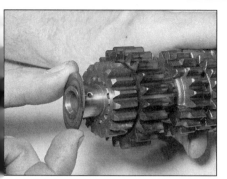

**29.16f ... the thrust washer ...**

**29.16g ... the needle bearing ...**

**29.16h ... and the bearing cage onto the shaft**

the end of the shaft, then fit the needle roller bearing and its cage over the end of the shaft **(see illustrations)**.

**17** Check that all components have been correctly installed **(see illustration)**.

## Output shaft disassembly

**18** Remove the caged ball bearing from the right-hand end of the shaft, referring to *Tools and Workshop Tips (*Section 5) in the Reference Section if required **(see illustration 29.34)**.

**19** Slide the thrust washer off the shaft, followed by the 1st gear pinion and its needle roller bearing, the thrust washer and the 5th gear pinion **(see illustration)**.

**20** Remove the circlip securing the 3rd gear pinion, then slide the splined washer, the pinion and its splined bush off the shaft.

**21** Slide the lockwasher and the splined washer off the shaft, noting how they fit together.

**22** Slide the 4th gear pinion and its splined bush, followed by the splined washer, off the shaft.

**23** Remove the circlip securing the 6th gear pinion, then slide the pinion off the shaft.

**29.17 The complete input shaft assembly should be as shown**

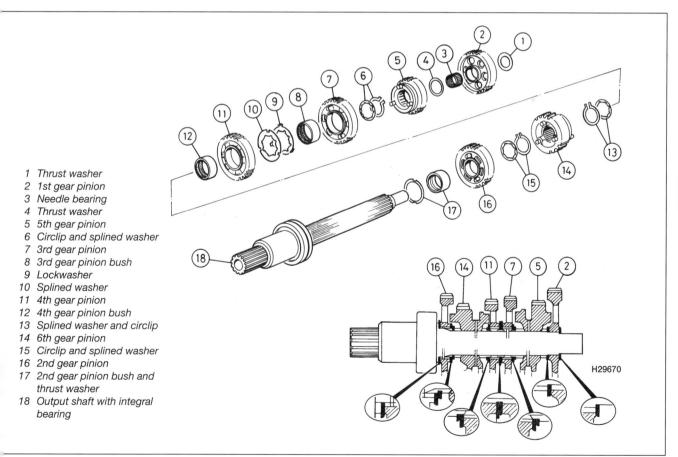

1  *Thrust washer*
2  *1st gear pinion*
3  *Needle bearing*
4  *Thrust washer*
5  *5th gear pinion*
6  *Circlip and splined washer*
7  *3rd gear pinion*
8  *3rd gear pinion bush*
9  *Lockwasher*
10 *Splined washer*
11 *4th gear pinion*
12 *4th gear pinion bush*
13 *Splined washer and circlip*
14 *6th gear pinion*
15 *Circlip and splined washer*
16 *2nd gear pinion*
17 *2nd gear pinion bush and thrust washer*
18 *Output shaft with integral bearing*

H29670

**29.19 Transmission output shaft components**

2

29.27a Slide the thrust washer . . .

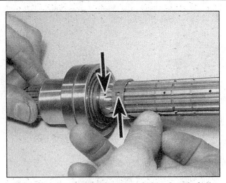

29.27b . . . the 2nd gear pinion bush (oil holes arrowed) . . .

29.27c . . . the 2nd gear pinion . . .

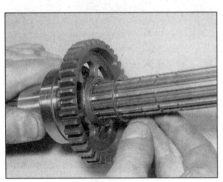

29.27d . . . and the splined washer onto the shaft . . .

29.27e . . . and secure them with the circlip

**24** Remove the circlip securing the 2nd gear pinion, then slide the splined washer, the pinion and its bush, and the thrust washer off the shaft.

### Output shaft inspection

**25** Refer to Steps 6 to 12 above.

### Output shaft reassembly

**26** During reassembly, apply engine oil to the mating surfaces of the shaft, pinions and bushes. When installing the circlips, do not expand the ends any further than is necessary. Install the stamped circlips and washers so that their chamfered side faces the pinion it secures (see illustration 29.19).

**27** Slide the thrust washer onto the right-hand end of the shaft, followed by the 2nd gear pinion bush, aligning the oil hole in the bush with the hole in the shaft, the 2nd gear pinion and the splined washer, then fit the circlip, making sure it is locates correctly in its groove in the shaft.

**28** Slide the 6th gear pinion with its selector fork groove facing away from the 2nd gear pinion, then fit the circlip, making sure it is locates correctly in its groove in the shaft (see illustrations).

**29** Slide the splined washer and the 4th gear pinion bush onto the shaft, making sure the oil hole in the bush aligns with the hole in the shaft, followed by the 4th gear pinion; note that the dished side of the 4th gear pinion faces the sixth gear pinion (see illustrations)

29.28a Slide the 6th gear pinion onto the shaft . . .

29.28b . . . and secure it with the circlip

29.29a Slide the splined washer . . .

29.29b . . . the 4th gear pinion bush . . .

29.29c . . . and the 4th gear pinion onto the shaft

29.30a Slide the slotted splined washer onto the shaft . . .

29.30b . . . and locate it as shown

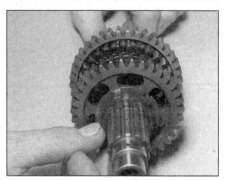

29.30c Slide the lockwasher onto the shaft . . .

**30** Slide the slotted splined washer onto the shaft and locate it in its groove, then turn it in the groove so that the splines on the washer locate between the splines of the shaft and secure the washer in the groove **(see illustrations)**. Slide the lockwasher onto the shaft, so that the tabs on the lockwasher face the left-hand end of the shaft and locate into the slots in the outer rim of the spline washer **(see illustrations)**.

**31** Slide the 3rd gear pinion bush onto the shaft, making sure the oil hole in the bush aligns with the hole in the shaft, followed by the 3rd gear pinion and the splined washer, then fit the circlip, making sure it is locates correctly in its groove in the shaft **(see illustrations)**. Note that the 3rd gear pinion is fitted so that its dished side faces away from the 4th gear pinion.

**32** Slide the 5th gear pinion onto the shaft with its selector fork groove facing the 3rd gear pinion, followed by the thrust washer **(see illustrations)**.

**33** Slide the 1st gear pinion needle roller bearing onto the shaft, followed by the 1st gear pinion and the thrust washer **(see illustrations overleaf)**. Note that the 1st gear pinion is fitted so that its dished side faces the 5th gear pinion.

**34** Fit the caged ball bearing onto the right-hand end of the shaft, referring to *Tools and Workshop Tips* (Section 5) in the

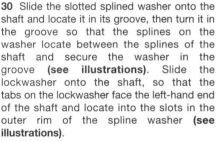

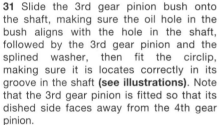

29.30d . . . and locate it as shown

29.31a Slide the 3rd gear pinion bush (oil holes arrowed) . . .

29.31b . . . the 3rd gear pinion . . .

29.31c . . . and the splined washer onto the shaft . . .

**2**

29.31d . . . and secure them with the circlip

29.32a Slide the 5th gear pinion . . .

29.32b . . . and the thrust washer onto the shaft

**29.33a Slide the needle bearing . . .**

**29.33b . . . the 1st gear pinion . . .**

**29.33c . . . and the thrust washer onto the shaft . . .**

**29.34 . . . then fit the bearing onto the end of the shaft**

**29.35 The assembled output shaft should be as shown**

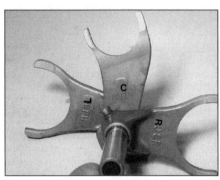

**30.3 The letters R, C and L identify each fork's position on the shaft**

Reference Section if required **(see illustration)**.

**35** Check that all components have been correctly installed **(see illustration)**.

## 30 Selector drum and forks – removal, inspection and installation

**Note:** *To remove the selector drum and forks the engine must be removed from the frame and the crankcases separated.*

### Removal

**1** Remove the engine (see Section 5) and separate the crankcase halves (see Section 21). The selector drum and forks are located in the lower crankcase half.

**2** If not already done, remove the gearchange mechanism external components (see Section 20).

**3** Before removing the selector forks, note that each fork carries an identification letter. The right-hand fork has an "R", the centre fork a "C", and the left-hand fork an "L" **(see illustration)**. These letters face the right-hand side of the engine. If no letters are visible, mark them yourself using a felt pen.

**4** Unscrew the bolt retaining the fork shaft **(see illustration)**. Support the selector forks and withdraw the shaft from the casing, then remove the forks **(see illustration)**. Once removed from the case, slide the forks back onto the shaft in their correct order and way round **(see illustration 30.3)**.

**5** Remove the selector drum **(see illustration)**.

### Inspection

**6** Inspect the selector forks for any signs of wear or damage, especially around the fork ends where they engage with the groove in the pinion. Check that each fork fits correctly in its pinion groove. Check closely to see if the forks are bent. If the forks are in any way damaged they must be replaced.

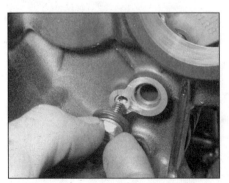

**30.4a Remove the bolt retaining the shaft . . .**

**30.4b . . . then withdraw the shaft and remove the forks . . .**

**30.5 . . . and the selector drum**

**30.7  Measure the fork end thickness as shown**

**30.11  Replace the bearing if necessary**

**30.12a  Locate the drum end into its bore . . .**

**7** Measure the thickness of the fork ends and compare the readings to the specifications **(see illustration)**. Replace the forks if they are worn beyond their specifications.

**8** Check that the forks fit correctly on their shaft. They should move freely with a light fit but no appreciable freeplay. Measure the internal diameter of the fork bores and the corresponding diameter of the fork shaft. Replace the forks and/or shaft if they are worn beyond their specifications. Check that the fork shaft holes in the casing are neither worn nor damaged.

**9** The selector fork shaft can be checked for trueness by rolling it along a flat surface. A bent rod will cause difficulty in selecting gears

and make the gearshift action heavy. Replace the shaft if it is bent.

**10** Inspect the selector drum grooves and selector fork guide pins for signs of wear or damage. If either component shows signs of wear or damage the selector(s) and drum must be replaced.

**11** Check that the selector drum bearing rotates freely and has no sign of freeplay between it and the casing. Replace the bearing if necessary (see *Tools and Workshop Tips* (Section 5) in the Reference Section) **(see illustration)**.

### Installation

**12** Slide the selector drum into position in the crankcase **(see illustration 30.5)**. Make sure

the drum end locates into its bore in the casing, and position it so that the neutral contact is against the neutral switch **(see illustrations)**.

**13** Refer to Step 3 for the correct location of each fork **(see illustration 30.3)**. Lubricate the selector fork shaft with clean engine oil and slide it through the crankcase and each fork in turn, and into its bore, locating the guide pin on the end of each fork into its groove in the drum **(see illustrations)**. Clean the threads of the fork shaft bolt, then apply a suitable non-permanent thread locking compound and tighten the bolt to the torque setting specified at the beginning of the Chapter **(see illustrations)**.

**14** Reassemble the crankcase halves (see Section 21).

**30.12b  . . . and position it in the neutral position (arrowed)**

**30.13a  Slide the shaft through each fork . . .**

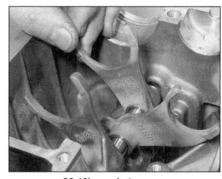

**30.13b  . . . in turn . . .**

**30.13c  . . . locating the guide pins in the drum grooves (A) and the shaft end in its bore (B)**

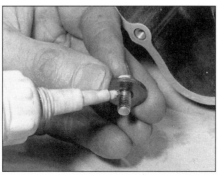

**30.13d  Apply a thread locking compound to the bolt . . .**

**30.13e  . . . and tighten it to the specified torque**

**2**

## 31 Initial start-up after overhaul

| Up to 600 miles (1000 km) | 6000 rpm max | Vary throttle position/speed |
|---|---|---|
| 600 to 1000 miles (1000 to 1600 km) | 8000 rpm max | Vary throttle position/speed. Use full throttle for short bursts |
| Over 1000 miles (1600 km) | 14,500 rpm max | Do not exceed tachometer red line |

**1** Make sure the engine oil level and coolant level are correct (see *Daily (pre-ride) checks*). Turn the fuel tap to the "OFF" position.

**2** Turn the engine kill switch to the OFF position and shift the gearbox into neutral. Turn the ignition ON and crank the engine over with the starter until the oil pressure indicator light goes off (which indicates that oil pressure exists). Turn the ignition OFF and turn the engine kill switch back to the RUN position.

**3** Make sure there is fuel in the tank, then turn the fuel tap to the "ON" or "RES" position as required, and set the choke.

**4** Start the engine and allow it to run at a moderately fast idle until it reaches operating temperature.

 **Warning: If the oil pressure warning light doesn't go off, or it comes on while the engine is running, stop the engine immediately.**

**5** Check carefully for oil and coolant leaks and make sure the transmission and controls, especially the brakes, function properly before road testing the machine. Refer to Section 32 for the recommended running-in procedure.

**6** Upon completion of the road test, and after the engine has cooled down completely, recheck the valve clearances (see Chapter 1) and check the engine oil and coolant levels (see *Daily (pre-ride) checks*).

## 32 Recommended running-in procedure

**1** Treat the machine gently for the first few miles to make sure oil has circulated throughout the engine and any new parts installed have started to seat.

**2** Even greater care is necessary if new pistons/rings or a new crankcase/bores have been fitted, and the bike will have to be run in as when new. This means greater use of the transmission and a restraining hand on the throttle until at least 600 miles (1000 km) have been covered. There's no point in keeping to any set speed limit – the main idea is to keep from labouring the engine and to gradually increase performance up to the 600 mile (1000 km) mark. Experience is the best guide, since it's easy to tell when an engine is running freely. The above maximum engine speed limitations, which Honda provide for new motorcycles, can be used as a guide.

**3** If a lubrication failure is suspected, stop the engine immediately and try to find the cause. If an engine is run without oil, even for a short period of time, severe damage will occur.

# Chapter 3
## Cooling system

## Contents

## Degrees of difficulty

| Easy, suitable for novice with little experience  | Fairly easy, suitable for beginner with some experience  | Fairly difficult, suitable for competent DIY mechanic | Difficult, suitable for experienced DIY mechanic | Very difficult, suitable for expert DIY or professional |
|---|---|---|---|---|

## Specifications

**Coolant**
Mixture type and capacity . . . . . . . . . . . . . . . . . . . . . . . . . . . . . . . . . . . see Chapter 1

**Radiator**
Cap valve opening pressure . . . . . . . . . . . . . . . . . . . . . . . . . . . . . . . . . 16 to 20 psi (1.1 to 1.4 Bar)

**Fan switch**
Cooling fan cut-in temperature . . . . . . . . . . . . . . . . . . . . . . . . . . . . . . 98 to 102°C
Cooling fan cut-out temperature . . . . . . . . . . . . . . . . . . . . . . . . . . . . 93 to 97°C

**Coolant temperature sender**
Resistance
   @ 50°C . . . . . . . . . . . . . . . . . . . . . . . . . . . . . . . . . . . . . . . . . . . . . . 130 to 180 ohms
   @ 80°C . . . . . . . . . . . . . . . . . . . . . . . . . . . . . . . . . . . . . . . . . . . . . . 45 to 60 ohms
   @ 120°C . . . . . . . . . . . . . . . . . . . . . . . . . . . . . . . . . . . . . . . . . . . . . 10 to 20 ohms

**Thermostat**
Opening temperature . . . . . . . . . . . . . . . . . . . . . . . . . . . . . . . . . . . . . 80 to 84°C
Valve lift . . . . . . . . . . . . . . . . . . . . . . . . . . . . . . . . . . . . . . . . . . . . . . . 8 mm (min) @ 95°C

**Torque settings – specific components**
Fan switch . . . . . . . . . . . . . . . . . . . . . . . . . . . . . . . . . . . . . . . . . . . . . . 18 Nm
Coolant temperature sender . . . . . . . . . . . . . . . . . . . . . . . . . . . . . . . . 10 Nm
Water pump cover bolts . . . . . . . . . . . . . . . . . . . . . . . . . . . . . . . . . . . 10 Nm
Water pump mounting bolts . . . . . . . . . . . . . . . . . . . . . . . . . . . . . . . . 10 Nm

**Torque settings – non-specified components**
**Note:** *Where a specific setting is not given for a particular bolt/nut, these general settings apply. The dimension given applies to the diameter of the thread, not the head.*
5 mm bolt/nut . . . . . . . . . . . . . . . . . . . . . . . . . . . . . . . . . . . . . . . . . . . 5 Nm
6 mm bolt/nut . . . . . . . . . . . . . . . . . . . . . . . . . . . . . . . . . . . . . . . . . . . 10 Nm
8 mm bolt/nut . . . . . . . . . . . . . . . . . . . . . . . . . . . . . . . . . . . . . . . . . . . 22 Nm
10 mm bolt/nut . . . . . . . . . . . . . . . . . . . . . . . . . . . . . . . . . . . . . . . . . . 35 Nm
12 mm bolt/nut . . . . . . . . . . . . . . . . . . . . . . . . . . . . . . . . . . . . . . . . . . 55 Nm
6 mm flange bolt with 8 mm head . . . . . . . . . . . . . . . . . . . . . . . . . . . 9 Nm
6 mm flange bolt/nut with 10 mm head . . . . . . . . . . . . . . . . . . . . . . . 12 Nm
8 mm flange bolt/nut . . . . . . . . . . . . . . . . . . . . . . . . . . . . . . . . . . . . . 27 Nm
10 mm flange bolt/nut . . . . . . . . . . . . . . . . . . . . . . . . . . . . . . . . . . . . 40 Nm

**3**

## 1  General information

The cooling system uses a water/antifreeze coolant to carry away excess energy in the form of heat. The cylinders are surrounded by a water jacket from which the heated coolant is circulated by thermo-syphonic action in conjunction with a water pump, driven by the oil pump. The hot coolant passes upwards to the thermostat and through to the radiator. The coolant then flows across the core of the upper radiator, then via two hoses to the lower radiator, to the water pump and back to the engine where the cycle is repeated.

A thermostat is fitted in the system to prevent the coolant flowing through the radiator when the engine is cold, therefore accelerating the speed at which the engine reaches normal operating temperature. A coolant temperature sender mounted in the thermostat housing transmits information to the temperature gauge on the instrument panel. A cooling fan is fitted to the rear of the lower radiator to aid cooling in extreme conditions; a thermostatically-controlled switch fitted to the side of the lower radiator triggers the operation of the fan motor.

The complete cooling system is partially sealed and pressurised, the pressure being controlled by a valve contained in the spring-loaded radiator cap. By pressurising the coolant the boiling point is raised, preventing premature boiling in adverse conditions. The overflow pipe from the system is connected to a reservoir into which excess coolant is expelled under pressure. The discharged coolant automatically returns to the radiator when the engine cools.

⚠ *Warning: Do not remove the pressure cap from the radiator when the engine is hot. Scalding hot coolant and steam may be blown out under pressure, which could cause serious injury. When the engine has cooled, place a thick rag, like a towel over the pressure cap; slowly rotate the cap anti-clockwise to the first stop. This procedure allows any residual pressure to escape. When the steam has stopped escaping, press down on the cap while turning it anti-clockwise and remove it.*
*Do not allow antifreeze to come in contact with your skin or painted surfaces of the motorcycle. Rinse off any spills immediately with plenty of water.*
*Antifreeze is highly toxic if ingested. Never leave antifreeze lying around in an open container or in puddles on the floor; children and pets are attracted by its sweet smell and may drink it. Check with the local authorities about disposing of used antifreeze. Many communities will have collection centres which will see that antifreeze is disposed of safely.*

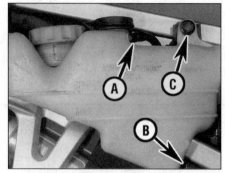

3.2a  Detach the breather/overflow hose (A) and the reservoir hose (B), then unscrew the bolt (C) and remove the reservoir . . .

*Caution: At all times use the specified type of antifreeze, and always mix it with distilled water in the correct proportion. The antifreeze contains corrosion inhibitors which are essential to avoid damage to the cooling system. A lack of these inhibitors could lead to a build-up of corrosion which would block the coolant passages, resulting in overheating and severe engine damage. Distilled water must be used as opposed to tap water to avoid a build-up of scale which would also block the passages.*

## 2  Radiator pressure cap – check

1  If problems such as overheating or loss of coolant occur, check the entire system as described in Chapter 1. The radiator cap opening pressure should be checked by a Honda dealer with the special tester required to do the job. If the cap is defective, replace it with a new one.

## 3  Coolant reservoir – removal and installation

### Removal

1  The coolant reservoir is located behind the seat cowl on the right-hand side. Remove the seat cowl for access (see Chapter 8).
2  Release the clamp securing the breather/overflow hose (coming out of the top of the reservoir) and detach the hose **(see illustrations)**.
3  Place a suitable container underneath the reservoir, then release the clamp securing the radiator overflow hose to the base of the reservoir. Detach the hose and allow the coolant to drain into the container **(see illustration 3.2a)**.
4  Unscrew the reservoir mounting bolt and remove the reservoir, noting how the lugs at the back locate in the bracket **(see illustration 3.2b)**.

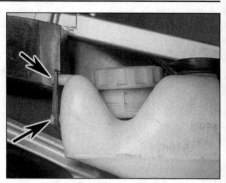

3.2b  . . . noting how the lugs (arrowed) locate in the bracket

### Installation

5  Installation is the reverse of removal. Make sure the hoses are correctly installed and secured with their clamps. On completion refill the reservoir as described in *Daily (pre-ride) checks*.

## 4  Cooling fan and fan switch – check and replacement

### Cooling fan

#### Check

1  If the engine is overheating and the cooling fan isn't coming on, first check the cooling fan circuit fuse (see Chapter 9) and then the fan switch as described in Steps 8 to 12 below.
2  If the fan does not come on, (and the fan switch is good), the fault lies in either the cooling fan motor or the relevant wiring. Test all the wiring and connections as described in Chapter 9.
3  To test the cooling fan motor, remove the lower fairing (see Chapter 8), and disconnect the fan wiring connector on the left-hand side of the lower radiator **(see illustration)**. Using a 12 volt battery and two jumper wires, connect the battery positive (+ve) lead to the black/blue fan wire and the battery negative (–ve) lead to earth. Once connected the fan should operate. If it does not, and the wiring is

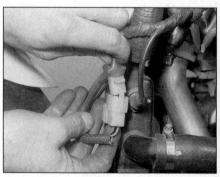

4.3  Disconnect the cooling fan wiring connector

4.5a The fan assembly is secured by three bolts (arrowed). Note the fan switch earth lead secured by the top bolt

4.5b The fan motor is secured to the shroud by three nuts (arrowed)

4.9 Disconnect the fan switch wiring connector

all good, then the fan is faulty. Individual components are available for the fan assembly.

### Replacement

 **Warning: The engine must be completely cool before carrying out this procedure.**

4  Remove the lower radiator (see Section 7).

5  Unscrew the three bolts securing the fan shroud and fan assembly to the radiator, noting that the upper bolt also secures the earth (ground) cable **(see illustration)**. Unscrew the three nuts on the front of the fan securing it to the shroud and remove the shroud **(see illustration)**.

6  Installation is the reverse of removal. Do not forget to attach the earth (ground) cable to the upper mounting bolt securing the shroud to the radiator.

7  Install the lower radiator (see Section 7).

### *Cooling fan switch*

#### Check

8  If the engine is overheating and the cooling fan isn't coming on, first check the cooling fan circuit fuse (see Chapter 9). If the fuse is blown, check the fan circuit for a short to earth (see the wiring diagrams at the end of this book).

9  If the fuse is good, remove the lower fairing (see Chapter 8), and disconnect the wiring connector from the fan switch on the left-hand side of the lower radiator **(see illustration)**. Using a jumper wire if necessary, connect the wire to earth (ground). The fan should come on. If it does, the fan switch is defective and must be replaced. If it does not come on, the fan should be tested (see Step 3).

10  If the fan is on the whole time, disconnect the wiring connector. The fan should stop. If it does, the switch is defective and must be replaced. If it doesn't, check the wiring between the switch and the fan, and the fan itself.

11  If the fan works but is suspected of cutting in at the wrong temperature, a more comprehensive test of the switch can be made as follows.

12  Remove the switch (see Steps 14 to 17). Fill a small heatproof container with coolant

and place it on a stove. Connect the positive (+ve) probe of an ohmmeter to the terminal of the switch and the negative (–ve) probe to the switch body, and using some wire or other support suspend the switch in the coolant so that just the sensing portion and the threads are submerged **(see illustration)**. Also place a thermometer capable of reading temperatures up to 110°C in the coolant so that its bulb is close to the switch. **Note:** *None of the components should be allowed to directly touch the container.*

13  Initially the ohmmeter reading should be very high indicating that the switch is open (OFF). Heat the coolant, stirring it gently.

 **Warning: This must be done very carefully to avoid the risk of personal injury.**

When the temperature reaches around 98 to 102°C the meter reading should drop to around zero ohms, indicating that the switch has closed (ON). Now turn the heat off. As the temperature falls below 93 to 97°C the meter reading should show infinite (very high) resistance, indicating that the switch has opened (OFF). If the meter readings obtained are different, or they are obtained at different temperatures, then the switch is faulty and must be replaced.

#### Replacement

 **Warning: The engine must be completely cool before carrying out this procedure.**

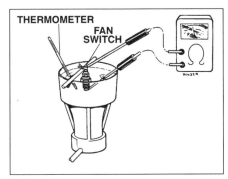

4.12 Fan switch testing set-up

14  Drain the cooling system (see Chapter 1).

15  Remove the lower fairing (see Chapter 8), and disconnect the wiring connector from the fan switch on the left-hand side of the lower radiator **(see illustration 4.9)**. Unscrew the switch and withdraw it from the radiator. Discard the O-ring as a new one must be used.

16  Apply a suitable sealant to the switch threads, then install the switch using a new O-ring and tighten it to the torque setting specified at the beginning of the Chapter. Take care not to overtighten the switch as the radiator could be damaged.

17  Reconnect the switch wiring and refill the cooling system (see Chapter 1).

### 5  Coolant temperature gauge and sender – check and replacement

### *Coolant temperature gauge*

#### Check

1  The circuit consists of the sender mounted in the bottom of the thermostat housing and the gauge assembly mounted in the instrument panel. If the system malfunctions check first that the battery is fully charged and that the fuses are all good.

2  If the gauge is not working, remove the right-hand fairing side panel (see (Chapter 8). Disconnect the wire from the sender and turn the ignition switch ON **(see illustration)**. The

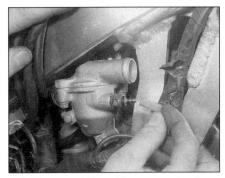

5.2 Disconnect the wiring connector from the sender

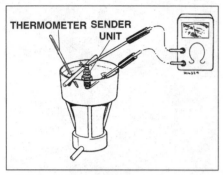

5.7 Temperature gauge sender testing
set-up

temperature gauge needle should be on the 'C' on the gauge. Now earth the sender wire on the engine. The needle should swing immediately over to the 'H' on the gauge. *Caution: Do not earth the wire for any longer than is necessary to take the reading, or the gauge may be damaged.*
If the needle moves as described above, the sender is proven defective and must be replaced.

**3** If the needle movement is still faulty, or if it does not move at all, the fault lies in the wiring or the gauge itself. Check all the relevant wiring and wiring connectors (see Chapter 9). If all appears to be well, the gauge is defective and must be replaced.

## Replacement

**4** See Chapter 9.

6.3a Slacken the clamp and detach the
hose from the cover . . .

6.3c . . . and remove the cover . . .

## Temperature gauge sender

### Check

**5** Remove the lower fairing (see Chapter 8) and drain the cooling system (see Chapter 1). The sender is fitted to the bottom of the thermostat housing.
**6** Disconnect the sender wiring connector **(see illustration 5.2)**. Using a continuity tester, check for continuity between the sender body and earth (ground). There should be continuity. If there is no continuity, check that the thermostat mounting is secure.
**7** Remove the sender (see Steps 9 to 11 below). Fill a small heatproof container with oil and place it on a stove. Using an ohmmeter, connect the positive (+ve) probe of the meter to the terminal on the sender, and the negative (–ve) probe to the body of the sender. Using some wire or other support suspend the sender in the coolant so that just the sensing portion and the threads are submerged. Also place a thermometer capable of reading temperatures up to 120°C in the water so that its bulb is close to the sender **(see illustration)**. Note: *None of the components should be allowed to directly touch the container.*
**8** Heat the oil, stirring it gently.

> ⚠ *Warning: This must be done very carefully to avoid the risk of personal injury.*

When the temperature reaches around 50°C the meter should read between 130 and 180

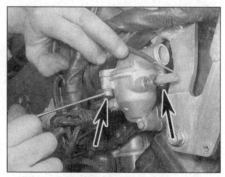

6.3b . . . then unscrew the cover bolts
(arrowed) . . .

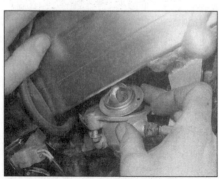

6.3d . . . and the thermostat

ohms. When the temperature reaches around 80°C the meter should read between 45 and 60 ohms. When the temperature reaches around 120°C the meter should read between 10 and 20 ohms. If the meter readings obtained are different, or they are obtained at different temperatures, then the sender is faulty and must be replaced.

### Replacement

> ⚠ *Warning: The engine must be completely cool before carrying out this procedure.*

**9** Remove the lower fairing (see Chapter 8) and drain the cooling system (see Chapter 1). The sender is fitted to the bottom of the thermostat housing.
**10** Disconnect the sender wiring connector **(see illustration 5.2)**. Unscrew the sender and remove it from the thermostat housing.
**12** Apply a smear of sealant to the threads of the new sender, then install it into the thermostat housing and tighten it to the torque setting specified at the beginning of the Chapter. Connect the sender wiring.
**11** Refill the cooling system (see Chapter 1).
**12** Install the lower fairing (see Chapter 8).

## 6 Thermostat and housing – removal, check and installation

### Removal

**Note:** *The complete thermostat housing can be removed without removing the thermostat itself – ignore the points in Step 3 relating to cover and thermostat removal.*

> ⚠ *Warning: The engine must be completely cool before carrying out this procedure.*

**1** The thermostat is automatic in operation and should give many years service without requiring attention. In the event of a failure, the valve will probably jam open, in which case the engine will take much longer than normal to warm up. Conversely, if the valve jams shut, the coolant will be unable to circulate and the engine will overheat. Neither condition is acceptable, and the fault must be investigated promptly.
**2** Remove the lower fairing (see Chapter 8) and drain the cooling system (see Chapter 1).
**3** The thermostat is located in the thermostat housing on the right-hand end of the front cylinder head. Slacken the clamp securing the hose to the housing cover and detach the hose **(see illustration)**. Unscrew the two bolts securing the cover and separate it from the housing, noting that the rear bolt cannot be fully withdrawn as it does not clear the housing bolt **(see illustration)**. Withdraw the thermostat, noting how it fits **(see illustration)**. Discard the cover O-ring as a new one must be used.
**4** The thermostat housing is secured to the engine by two bolts. Slacken the clamp

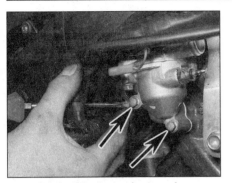

6.4a  Slacken the hose clamp and remove the bolts (arrowed) . . .

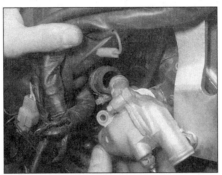

6.4b  . . . then detach the housing from the hose

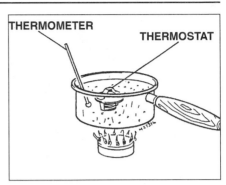

6.6  Thermostat testing set-up

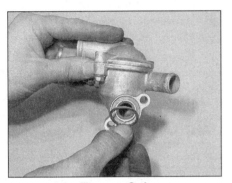

6.8a  Fit a new O-ring . . .

6.8b  . . . then install the thermostat housing (housing cover already fitted)

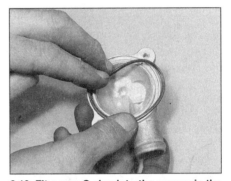

6.10  Fit a new O-ring into the groove in the cover

securing the hose to the housing, then unscrew the bolts and remove the housing **(see illustrations)**. Discard the O-ring as a new one must be used.

### Check

**5** Examine the thermostat visually before carrying out the test. If it remains in the open position at room temperature, it should be replaced.

**6** Suspend the thermostat by a piece of wire in a container of cold water. Place a thermometer in the water so that the bulb is close to the thermostat **(see illustration)**. Heat the water, noting the temperature when the thermostat opens, and compare the result with the specifications given at the beginning of the Chapter. Also check the amount the valve opens after it has been heated at 95°C

for a few minutes and compare the measurement to the specifications. If the readings obtained differ from those given, the thermostat is faulty and must be replaced.

**7** In the event of thermostat failure, as an emergency measure only, it can be removed and the machine used without it. **Note:** *Take care when starting the engine from cold as it will take much longer than usual to warm up.* Ensure that a new unit is installed as soon as possible.

### Installation

**8** Install the thermostat housing using a new O-ring and tighten the bolts and the hose clamp securely **(see illustrations)**.

**9** Fit the thermostat into the housing, making sure that it seats correctly and that the hole is at the front **(see illustration 6.3d)**.

**10** Fit a new O-ring onto the cover, using a dab of grease to keep it in place if required **(see illustration)**. Fit the cover onto the housing, then install the two bolts and tighten them securely and the hose clamp securely **(see illustrations 6.3c, b and a)**.

**11** Refill the cooling system (see Chapter 1).

**12** Install the lower fairing (see Chapter 8).

### 7  Radiators – removal and installation

### Removal

⚠️ *Warning: The engine must be completely cool before carrying out this procedure.*

**1** Remove the lower fairing (see Chapter 8) and drain the cooling system (see Chapter 1).

**2** Disconnect the fan wiring connector on the left-hand end of the radiator **(see illustration 3.3)**. Also disconnect the wiring connector from the fan switch in the radiator **(see illustration 4.9)**.

**3** Slacken the clamps securing the radiator hose to the top right-hand side of the upper radiator, and the reservoir hose to the filler neck, and detach them from the radiator **(see illustration)**.

**4** Slacken the clamp securing the radiator hose to the bottom left-hand side of the lower radiator and detach it from the radiator **(see illustration)**. The connecting hoses between

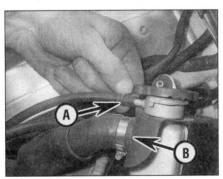

7.3  Release the clamps and detach the overflow hose (A) and the radiator hose (B)

7.4  Slacken the clamp and detach the hose (arrowed) from the lower radiator

**3**

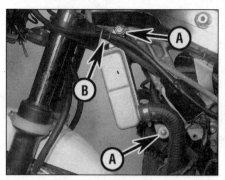

**7.5a Unscrew the upper radiator mounting bolts (A) and free the speedometer cable from its guide (B) . . .**

**7.5b . . . then unscrew the lower radiator upper mounting bolt (arrowed) . . .**

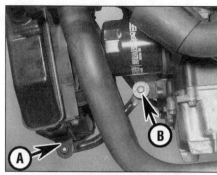

**7.5c . . . and lower mounting bolt, either at the radiator (A) or at the engine (B)**

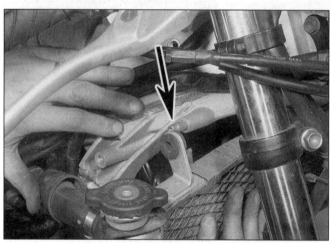

**7.6a Free the upper radiator from its lug (arrowed) . . .**

**7.6b . . . and the lower radiator from its lug (arrowed) and remove the assembly**

the radiators can be left in situ and the radiators removed together.

**5** Unscrew the two bolts securing the upper radiator and the two bolts securing the lower radiator **(see illustrations)**. Note the arrangement of the collars and rubber grommets, and how the upper radiator top bolt secures the fairing trim panel, which also has a collar. Free the speedometer cable from its guide on the left-hand side of the upper radiator.

**7.9 With the exception of the mounting bolt on the bottom of the lower radiator, each bolt has a collar that fits into the rubber grommet**

**6** Carefully manoeuvre the radiators sideways to the right until they are clear of their mounting lugs, then remove the radiator assembly **(see illustrations)**.

**7** If necessary, remove the cooling fan (see Section 4) from the radiator.

**8** Remove the stone guard from the upper radiator. Check the stone guard and the radiator for signs of damage and clear any dirt or debris that might obstruct air flow and inhibit cooling. If the radiator fins are badly damaged or broken the radiator must be replaced. Also check the rubber mounting grommets, and replace them if necessary.

### Installation

**9** Installation is the reverse of removal, noting the following.
  a) *Make sure the locating lugs fit correctly into the rubber grommets (see illustrations 7.6a and b).*
  b) *Make sure the various collars are correctly installed with the mounting bolts (see illustration).*
  c) *Make sure that the fan wiring is correctly connected.*
  d) *Ensure the coolant hoses are in good condition (see Chapter 1), and are*

  *securely retained by their clamps, using new ones if necessary.*
  e) *On completion refill the cooling system as described in Chapter 1.*

## 8 Water pump – check, removal and installation

### Check

**1** The water pump is located on the lower left side of the engine. Visually check the area around the pump for signs of leakage.

**2** To prevent leakage of water from the cooling system to the lubrication system and vice versa, two seals are fitted on the pump shaft. On the underside of the pump body there is also a drainage hole. If either seal fails, this hole should allow the coolant or oil to escape and prevent the oil and coolant mixing.

**3** The seal on the water pump side is of the mechanical type which bears on the rear face of the impeller. The second seal, which is mounted behind the mechanical seal is of the normal feathered lip type. However, neither seal is available as a separate item as the

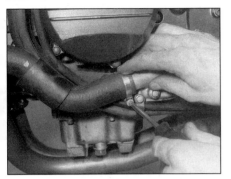

8.5a  Slacken the clamp . . .

8.5b  . . . and detach the hose from the
pump

8.6a  Unscrew the four bolts (arrowed) . . .

pump is sold as an assembly. Therefore, if on inspection the drainage hole shows signs of leakage, the pump must be removed and replaced.

## Removal

**4**  Drain the coolant (see Chapter 1). Place a suitable container below the water pump to catch any residue oil as the water pump is removed.
**5**  Slacken the clamp securing the coolant hose to the pump cover and detach the hose **(see illustrations)**.
**6**  Unscrew the bolts securing the pump cover to the pump and the pump to the crankcase, noting the hose clip fitted with the lower bolt, and remove the cover **(see illustrations)**. Note the position of each bolt as hey are different lengths. Discard the cover O-ring as a new one must be used. Remove the dowel from the pump or the cover if it is loose.
**7**  Slacken the clamp securing the coolant hose to the pump body and detach the hose. Carefully draw the pump from the crankcase, noting how it fits **(see illustration 8.9b)**. Remove the O-ring from the rear of the pump body and discard it as a new one must be used.
**8**  Wiggle the water pump impeller back-and-forth and in-and-out **(see illustration)**. If there is excessive movement the pump must be replaced. Also check for corrosion or a build-up of scale in the pump body and clean or replace the pump as necessary.

8.6b  . . . and remove the cover, noting the
dowel (arrowed)

## Installation

**9**  Apply a smear of engine oil to the new pump body O-ring and install it onto the rear of the pump body **(see illustration)**. Install the pump into the crankcase, aligning the slot in the impeller shaft with the tab on the oil pump shaft **(see illustration)**.
**10**  Attach the coolant hose to the pump body and secure it with its clamp.
**11**  Install the new cover O-ring into its groove in the pump **(see illustration)**. Fit the pump dowel into its hole in the pump.
**12**  Install the cover onto the pump, then install the four bolts and tighten them to the torque setting specified at the beginning of the Chapter **(see illustrations 8.6b and a)**. Make sure the different bolts are in their correct locations – the longest is for bottom

8.8  Check for freeplay between the
impeller and the housing

left, the next longest for the bottom right, and the two shortest are for the top.
**14**  Attach the coolant hose to the pump cover and secure it with its clamp **(see illustrations 8.5b and a)**.
**15**  Refill the cooling system (see Chapter 1).

## 9  Coolant hoses –
### removal and installation

## Removal

**1**  Before removing a hose, drain the coolant (see Chapter 1).
**2**  Use a screwdriver to slacken the larger-bore hose clamps, then slide them back along

**3**

8.9a  Fit a new O-ring . . .

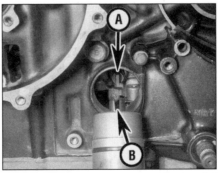

8.9b  . . . then install the pump, aligning the
slot (B) with the drive tab (A)

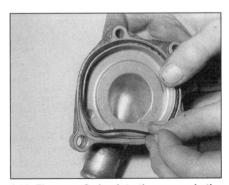

8.10  Fit a new O-ring into the groove in the
cover

the hose and clear of the union spigot **(see illustrations 8.5a and b)**. The smaller-bore hoses are secured by spring clamps which can be expanded by squeezing their ears together with pliers **(see illustration 7.3)**. *Caution: The radiator unions are fragile. Do not use excessive force when attempting to remove the hoses.*

**3** If a hose proves stubborn, release it by rotating it on its union before working it off. If all else fails, cut the hose with a sharp knife then slit it at each union so that it can be peeled off in two pieces. Whilst this means replacing the hose, it is preferable to buying a new radiator.

**4** The water pipe inlet unions to the cylinder block can be removed by unscrewing the retaining bolts **(see illustration)**. If they are removed, the O-rings must be replaced. The

outlet union is also secured by two bolts. If it is removed, the O-ring must be replaced.

### Installation

**5** Slide the clips onto the hose and then work it on to its respective union.

 *If the hose is difficult to push on its union, it can be softened by soaking it in very hot water, or alternatively a little soapy water can be used as a lubricant.*

**6** Rotate the hose on its unions to settle it in position before sliding the clamps into place and tightening them securely.

**7** If either the inlet unions to the cylinder block or the outlet union from the cylinder

9.4 Water pipe union bolts (arrowed)

heads have been removed, fit a new O-ring, then install the union and tighten the mounting bolts securely.

# Chapter 4
# Fuel and exhaust systems

## Contents

## Degrees of difficulty

| **Easy,** suitable for novice with little experience  | **Fairly easy,** suitable for beginner with some experience  | **Fairly difficult,** suitable for competent DIY mechanic | **Difficult,** suitable for experienced DIY mechanic | **Very difficult,** suitable for expert DIY or professional |
|---|---|---|---|---|

## Specifications

### Fuel

| | |
|---|---|
| Grade ................................................. | Unleaded, minimum 91 RON (Research Octane Number) |
| Fuel tank capacity (including reserve) ......................... | 15.0 litres |
| Reserve ............................................... | 2.0 litres |

### Carburettors

| | |
|---|---|
| Type ................................................. | CV |
| Pilot screw setting (turns out) | |
|   VFR models ........................................ | 2 turns out |
|   RVF models ........................................ | 1 5/8 turns out |
| Float height | |
|   VFR models ........................................ | 6.8 mm |
|   RVF models ........................................ | 12.5 mm |
| Idle speed ............................................. | see Chapter 1 |

### Carburettor jet sizes

| | |
|---|---|
| Pilot jet .............................................. | 35 |
| Main jet | |
|   VFR K grey import models | |
|     Front cylinder carburettors ............................ | 110 |
|     Rear cylinder carburettors ............................ | 110 |
|   VFR L and N grey import models | |
|     Front cylinder carburettors ............................ | 115 |
|     Rear cylinder carburettors ............................ | 118 |
|   VFR UK spec models | |
|     Front cylinder carburettors ............................ | 122 |
|     Rear cylinder carburettors ............................ | 120 |
|   RVF models (all carburettors) ............................ | 108 |

4

## Torque settings – specific components

| | |
|---|---|
| Front cylinder exhaust downpipe nuts | 8 Nm |
| Rear cylinder exhaust header pipe nuts | 8 Nm |
| Right-hand footrest bracket bolts | 27 Nm |

## Torque settings – non-specified components

**Note:** *Where a specific setting is not given for a particular bolt/nut, these general settings apply. The dimension given applies to the diameter of the thread, not the head.*

| | |
|---|---|
| 5 mm bolt/nut | 5 Nm |
| 6 mm bolt/nut | 10 Nm |
| 8 mm bolt/nut | 22 Nm |
| 10 mm bolt/nut | 35 Nm |
| 12 mm bolt/nut | 55 Nm |
| 6 mm flange bolt with 8 mm head | 9 Nm |
| 6 mm flange bolt/nut with 10 mm head | 12 Nm |
| 8 mm flange bolt/nut | 27 Nm |
| 10 mm flange bolt/nut | 40 Nm |

---

### 1 General information and precautions

## General information

The fuel system consists of the fuel tank, fuel tap with integral filter, carburettors, fuel hoses and control cables.

The fuel tap is automatic and opens by vacuum when the engine is turned. The fuel filter is fitted inside the fuel tank and is part of the tap.

The carburettors used on all models are CV types. On all models there is a carburettor for each cylinder. For cold starting, a choke lever (VFR models) or knob (RVF models) is mounted between the fairing side panel and the frame on the left-hand side, and is connected to the carburettors by a cable.

Air is drawn into the carburettors via an air filter which is housed under the fuel tank. On RVF models, air ducts mounted between intakes in the fairing and the fuel tank direct air under force to the air filter housing intake.

The exhaust system is a four-into-one design.

Many of the fuel system service procedures are considered routine maintenance items and for that reason are included in Chapter 1.

## Precautions

 *Warning: Petrol (gasoline) is extremely flammable, so take extra precautions when you work on any part of the fuel system. Don't smoke or allow open flames or bare light bulbs near the work area, and don't work in a garage where a natural gas-type appliance is present. If you spill any fuel on your skin, rinse it off immediately with soap and water. When you perform any kind of work on the fuel system, wear safety glasses and have a fire extinguisher suitable for a class B type fire (flammable liquids) on hand.*

Always perform service procedures in a well-ventilated area to prevent a build-up of fumes.

Never work in a building containing a gas appliance with a pilot light, or any other form of naked flame. Ensure that there are no naked light bulbs or any sources of flame or sparks nearby.

Do not smoke (or allow anyone else to smoke) while in the vicinity of petrol (gasoline) or of components containing it. Remember the possible presence of vapour from these sources and move well clear before smoking.

Check all electrical equipment belonging to the house, garage or workshop where work is being undertaken (see the Safety first! section of this manual). Remember that certain electrical appliances such as drills, cutters etc. create sparks in the normal course of operation and must not be used near petrol (gasoline) or any component containing it. Again, remember the possible presence of fumes before using electrical equipment.

Always mop up any spilt fuel and safely dispose of the rag used.

Any stored fuel that is drained off during servicing work must be kept in sealed containers that are suitable for holding petrol (gasoline), and clearly marked as such; the containers themselves should be kept in a safe place. Note that this last point applies equally to the fuel tank if it is removed from the machine; also remember to keep its filler cap closed at all times.

Read the Safety first! section of this manual carefully before starting work.

### 2 Fuel tank and fuel tap – removal and installation

 *Warning: Refer to the precautions given in Section 1 before starting work.*

## Fuel tank

### Removal

**1** Make sure the fuel cap is secure. Remove the seat cowling (see Chapter 8).

**2** On VFR models, pull the tank breather hose off the breather union at the front of the tank **(see illustration)**.

**3** On RVF models, remove the screw securing each air duct to the tank and remove the ducts **(see illustration)**.

**4** Unscrew the bolt securing the rear of the

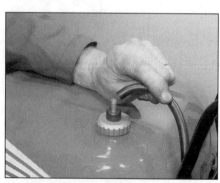

**2.2 Detach the breather hose from its union**

**2.3 Each duct is secured by a single screw**

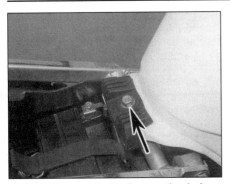

2.4a  Remove the tank mounting bolt (arrowed) . . .

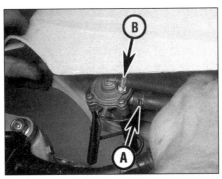

2.4b  . . . then raise the tank at the rear and detach the fuel hose (A) and the vacuum hose (B)

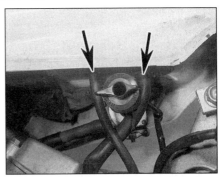

2.4c  On RVF models, also detach the breather and drain hoses (arrowed)

tank to the frame (see illustration). Raise the tank at the rear and release the clamps securing the fuel hose and the vacuum hose to the unions on the tap, noting which fits where, and detach the hoses (see illustration). On RVF models, also detach the breather and water drain hoses from their unions (see illustration).

5 Check that all hoses have been disconnected, then carefully draw the tank back, noting how the tab locates at the front, and lift the tank away.

6 Inspect the tank mounting rubbers for signs of damage or deterioration and replace them if necessary.

## Installation

7 Check that the tank mounting rubbers are fitted, then carefully lower the fuel tank into position. Keeping the tank raised at the rear, connect the fuel and vacuum hoses to their unions on the tap and secure them with the clamps (see illustration 2.4b). On RVF models, also connect the breather and drain hoses (see illustration 2.4c).

8 Locate the tab at the front of the tank under the frame and lower it into position (see illustration). Push the tank forward to align the mounting bolt holes, then install the bolt with its collar and tighten it securely (see illustration).

9 On VFR models, attach the breather hose to the union on the breather (see illustration 2.2).

10 On RVF models, install the air ducts and secure them with the screws (see illustration).

11 Start the engine and check that there is no sign of fuel leakage, then shut if off.

12 Install the seat cowling (see (Chapter 8).

## *Fuel tap*

### Removal

13 The tap should not be removed unnecessarily from the tank to prevent the possibility of damaging the O-ring or the filter.

14 The fuel tap is automatic, operated by a vacuum created when the engine is turned over. If it is faulty, it can be disassembled and

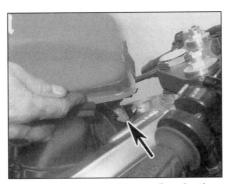

2.8a  Locate the tab (arrowed) under the frame

inspected. The most likely problem is a hole or split in the diaphragm. Before removing and dismantling the tap, check that the vacuum hose is securely attached at both ends, and that there are no splits or cracks in the hose. If in doubt, attach a spare hose to the vacuum union on the tap and apply a vacuum to the hose. If fuel does not flow through the tap (make sure it is turned to ON or RES), remove it and disassemble it to check the diaphragm. The diaphragm cover and components are available as an assembly.

15 Remove the fuel tank as described above. Connect a drain hose to the fuel hose union

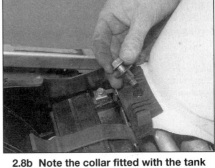

2.8b  Note the collar fitted with the tank bolt

and insert its end in a container suitable and large enough for storing the petrol. Turn the fuel tap to the RES position, then attach a suitable hose to the vacuum union and apply a vacuum to allow the tank to drain.

16 Unscrew the two bolts securing the tap and the bolt securing the tap knob holder and withdraw the tap assembly (see illustration). Check the condition of the O-ring. If it is in good condition it can be re-used, though it is better to use a new one. If it is in any way deteriorated or damaged it must be replaced.

17 If the fuel tap has been leaking, tightening the assembly screws on the back of the tap

2.10  Make sure the duct locates correctly onto both the fairing and the tank

2.16  The tap is secured to the tank by two bolts (A). Also remove the bolt (B) securing the knob holder

4

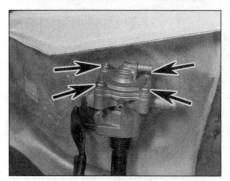

2.17 If the tap is leaking, tighten the screws (arrowed)

4.1 Remove the sub-air cleaner element if required

may help **(see illustration)**. Slacken all the screws a little first, then tighten them evenly a little at a time to ensure the cover seats properly on the tap body. If leakage persists, the tap should be replaced, however nothing is lost by dismantling the tap for further inspection. Unscrew the screws and disassemble the tap, noting how the components fit. Inspect all components for wear or damage, and replace them as necessary, if available. If any of the components are worn or damaged beyond repair and are not available individually, a new tap must be fitted.

18 Clean the gauze filters to remove all traces of dirt and fuel sediment. Check the gauze for holes. If any are found, a new tap should be fitted as the filters are not available individually.

### Installation

19 Install the fuel tap into the tank, using a new O-ring if required, and tighten the bolts securely **(see illustration 2.16)**.

20 Install the fuel tank (see above).

## 3 Fuel tank – cleaning and repair

1 All repairs to the fuel tank should be carried out by a professional who has experience in this critical and potentially dangerous work. Even after cleaning and flushing of the fuel

system, explosive fumes can remain and ignite during repair of the tank.

2 If the fuel tank is removed from the bike, it should not be placed in an area where sparks or open flames could ignite the fumes coming out of the tank. Be especially careful inside garages where a natural gas-type appliance is located, because the pilot light could cause an explosion.

## 4 Air filter housing – removal and installation

### Removal

1 Remove the fuel tank (see Section 2), and the air filter (see Chapter 1). Also remove the sub-air cleaner for safekeeping if required **(see illustration)**.

2 Release the clamp securing the engine breather hose to the breather union on the rear cylinder valve cover and detach the hose **(see illustration)**.

3 Remove the four screws securing the filter housing to the carburettor air duct holder **(see illustration)**. Lift the housing up off the air duct holder and remove it **(see illustration)**.

### Installation

4 Installation is the reverse of removal. Check the condition of the various hoses and their clamps and replace them if necessary.

## 5 Idle fuel/air mixture adjustment – general information

1 Due to the increased emphasis on controlling exhaust emissions, certain governmental regulations have been formulated which directly affect the carburation of this machine. The pilot screws can be adjusted, but the use of an exhaust gas analyser and an auxiliary tachometer capable of accurately displaying changes of 50 rpm is the only certain way to adjust the idle fuel/air mixture and be sure the machine doesn't exceed the emissions regulations.

2 The pilot screws are set to their correct position by the manufacturer and should not be adjusted or removed unless it is necessary to do so during a carburettor overhaul. If the screws are to be removed, record the pilot screw's current setting by turning the screw it in until it seats lightly, counting the number of turns necessary to achieve this, then fully unscrew it. On installation, the screw is simply backed out the number of turns you've recorded.

3 If the engine runs extremely rough at idle or continually stalls, and if a carburettor overhaul does not cure the problem, take the motorcycle to a Honda dealer equipped with an exhaust gas analyser. They will be able to properly adjust the idle fuel/air mixture to achieve a smooth idle and restore low speed performance.

## 6 Carburettor overhaul – general information

1 Poor engine performance, hesitation, hard starting, stalling, flooding and backfiring are all signs that major carburettor maintenance may be required.

2 Keep in mind that many so-called carburettor problems are really not carburettor problems at all, but mechanical problems within the engine or ignition system malfunctions. Try to establish for certain that

4.2 Release the clamp and detach the hose from the breather

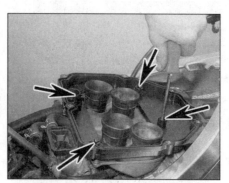

4.3a Remove the four screws (arrowed) . . .

4.3b . . . and lift the housing off the carburettors

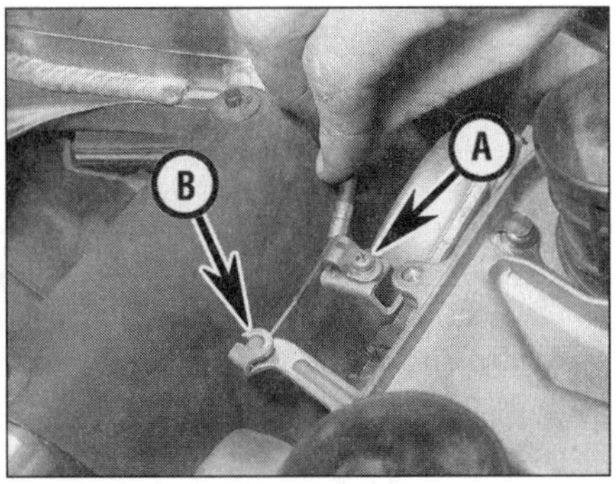


**7.2 Slacken the clamp screw (A) and detach the outer cable, then free the nipple from the lever (B)**

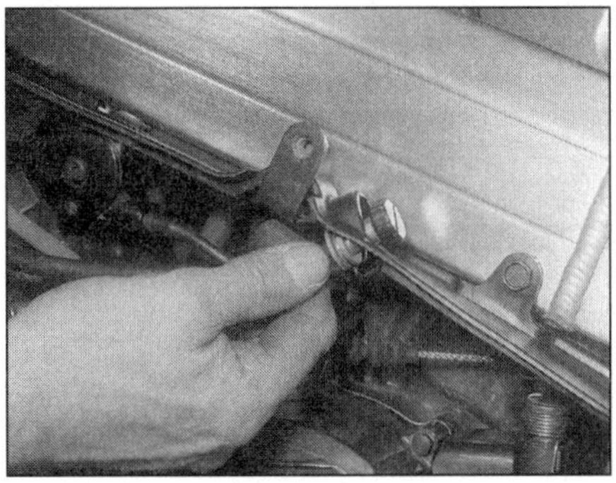

**7.4 Release the idle speed adjuster from its holder**

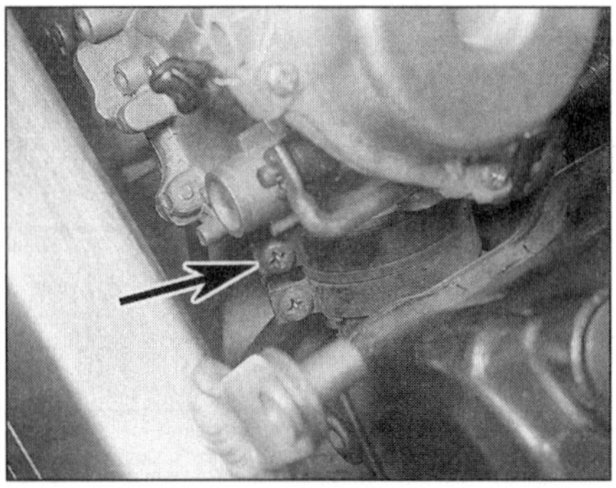

**7.5a Slacken the upper clamp (arrowed) on each intake rubber . . .**

the carburettors are in need of maintenance before beginning a major overhaul.

**3** Check the fuel tap and filter, the fuel and vacuum hoses, the intake manifold joint clamps, the air filter, the ignition system, the spark plugs and carburettor synchronisation before assuming that a carburettor overhaul is required.

**4** Most carburettor problems are caused by dirt particles, varnish and other deposits which build up in and block the fuel and air passages. Also, in time, gaskets and O-rings shrink or deteriorate and cause fuel and air leaks which lead to poor performance.

**5** When overhauling the carburettors, disassemble them completely and clean the parts thoroughly with a carburettor cleaning solvent and dry them with filtered, unlubricated compressed air. Blow through the fuel and air passages with compressed air to force out any dirt that may have been loosened but not removed by the solvent. Once the cleaning process is complete, reassemble the carburettor using new gaskets and O-rings.

**6** Before disassembling the carburettors, make sure you have all necessary O-rings and other parts, some carburettor cleaner, a supply of clean rags, some means of blowing out the carburettor passages and a clean place to work. It is recommended that only one carburettor be overhauled at a time to avoid mixing up parts.

## 7 Carburettors – removal and installation

***Warning: Refer to the precautions given in Section 1 before starting work.***

### *Removal*

**1** Remove the fuel tank and the air filter housing (see Sections 2 and 4).

**2** Slacken the choke outer cable bracket screw and free the cable from the bracket on the front of the carburettors, then detach the inner cable nipple from the choke linkage lever **(see illustration)**.

**3** Detach the throttle cables from the carburettors (see Section 11, Steps 2 and 3 or 4, according to model). If access is too restricted, detach them after the carburettors have been lifted off the cylinder head intakes.

**4** Release the idle speed adjuster from its holder and feed it through to the base of the carburettors **(see illustration)**. Remove the rear bolt securing the left-hand fairing side panel trim to provide more clearance if required.

**5** Fully slacken the upper clamps on the cylinder head intake rubbers, then ease the carburettors off the intakes, noting that they are quite a tight fit, and remove them **(see illustrations)**. **Note:** *Keep the carburettors upright to prevent fuel spillage from the float chambers and the possibility of the piston diaphragms being damaged.*

***Caution: Stuff clean rag into each cylinder head intake after removing the carburettors to prevent anything from falling in.***

**6** Place a suitable container below the float chambers, then slacken the drain screw on each chamber in turn and drain all the fuel from the carburettors **(see illustration)**. Discard the drain screw O-rings as new ones must be used. Once all the fuel has been drained, fit the new O-rings and tighten the drain screws securely.

**7** If necessary, slacken the clamps securing the intake rubbers to the cylinder head and remove the rubbers, noting which way up and round they fit **(see illustration 7.8b)**.

### *Installation*

**8** Installation is the reverse of removal, noting the following.

a) *Check for cracks or splits in the cylinder head intake rubbers, and replace them if necessary.*
b) *If removed, make sure the intake rubbers are installed with the CARB marking facing out (towards the carburettor), and so that the arrow next to the UP mark points upwards. If this is not visible, the smaller cutout in the rubber should be central at the top and the large one central at the bottom **(see illustration)**. If*



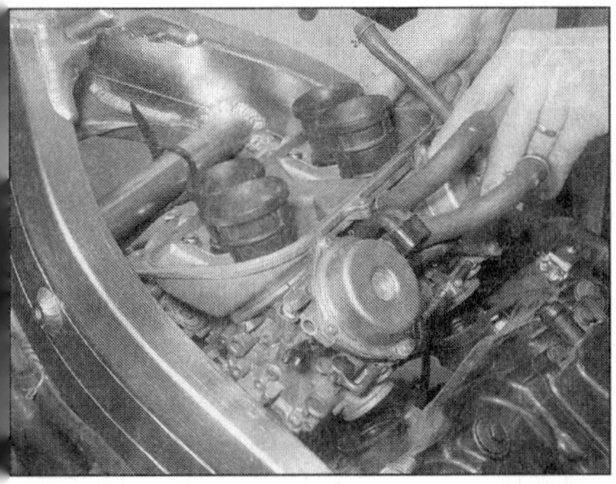

**7.5b . . . and lift the carburettors off the intakes**

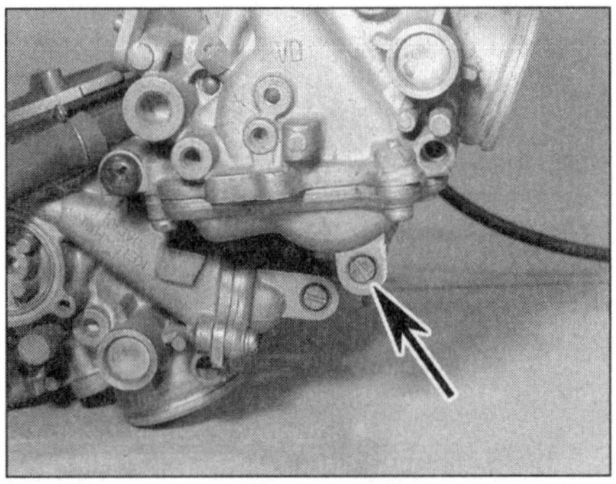

**7.6 Slacken the drain screw (arrowed) on each float chamber in turn and drain the carburettors**

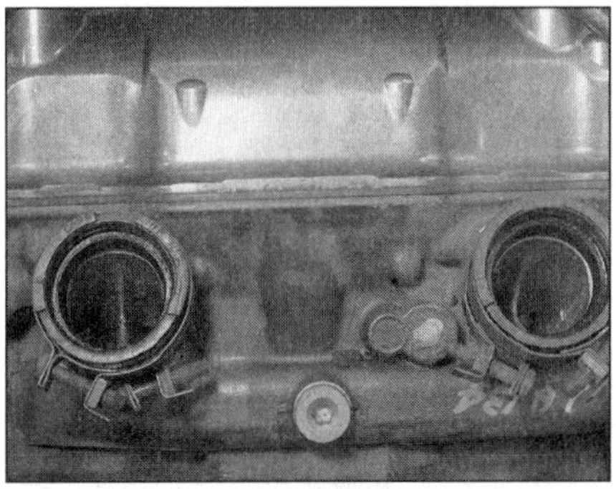

**7.8 Make sure the rubbers are fitted as described**

**8.3a Remove the screws (arrowed) and the cover . . .**

**8.3b . . . then withdraw the spring**

**8.4 Peel the diaphragm off the carburettor and withdraw the diaphragm and piston assembly**

the rubbers are not correctly aligned, the carburettors will not seat properly and there could be an air leak.

c) *Make sure the carburettors are fully engaged with the intake rubbers and the clamps are securely tightened.*

d) *Make sure all hoses are correctly routed and secured and not trapped or kinked.*

e) *Refer to Section 11 for installation of the throttle cables. Check the operation of the cables and adjust them as necessary (see Chapter 1).*

f) *Check idle speed and carburettor synchronisation and adjust as necessary (see Chapter 1).*

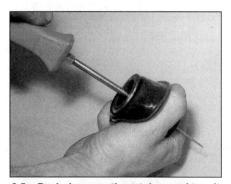

**8.5a Push down on the retainer and turn it to release it . . .**

---

## 8 Carburettors – disassembly, cleaning and inspection

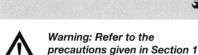

> ⚠ **Warning: Refer to the precautions given in Section 1 before starting work.**

### Disassembly

**1** Remove the carburettors from the machine as described in the previous Section. **Note:** *Do not separate the carburettors unless absolutely necessary; each carburettor can be dismantled sufficiently for all normal cleaning and adjustments while in place on the mounting brackets. Dismantle the carburettors separately to avoid interchanging parts.*

**2** If required, remove the air duct assembly from the carburettors (see Section 9, Step 3), but note that this is not necessary for carburettor disassembly and cleaning, unless they are being separated.

**3** Unscrew and remove the top cover retaining screws, noting the position of any hose clips **(see illustration)**. Lift off the cover and remove the spring from inside the piston **(see illustration)**.

**4** Carefully peel the diaphragm away from its sealing groove in the carburettor and

withdraw the diaphragm and piston assembly **(see illustration)**. Note how the tab on the diaphragm fits in the recess in the carburettor body.

***Caution: Do not use a sharp instrument to displace the diaphragm as it is easily damaged.***

**5** On VFR models, if required, gently push down on the jet needle retainer using a Phillips screwdriver and rotate it until its tab is released from the protrusions inside the piston, then remove the retainer **(see illustrations)**. Push the needle up from the bottom of the piston and withdraw it from the top **(see illustration)**. Take care not to lose the spring and the washer that fits between the head of the needle and the piston.

**6** On RVF models, if required, thread a 4 mm screw into the top of the needle holder (one of the top cover retaining screws is ideal), then grasp the screw head using a pair of pliers and carefully draw the holder out of the piston **(see illustration)**. Push the needle up from the bottom of the piston and withdraw it from the top **(see illustration 8.5c)**. Take care not to lose the spring and note the washer that fits between the head of the needle and the piston. Discard the O-ring on the holder as a new one must be used.

**7** Remove the screws securing the float chamber to the base of the carburettor and

**8.5b . . . then remove the retainer . . .**

**8.5c . . . and push the needle up from the bottom**

**8.6 Draw the holder out of the piston using a 4 mm screw**

8.7  Remove the three screws (arrowed) and lift off the chamber

8.8a  Withdraw the float pin and remove the float assembly

8.8b  Unscrew the float needle valve seat (arrowed)

remove it **(see illustration)**. Remove the rubber gasket and discard it as a new one must be used.

**8** Using a pair of thin-nose pliers, carefully withdraw the float pin **(see illustration)**. If necessary, displace the pin using a small punch or a nail. Remove the float and unhook the float needle valve, noting how it fits onto the tab on the float **(see illustration 10.8a)**. On VFR models, unscrew and remove the float needle valve seat and its sealing washer, taking care not to damage its gauze filter **(see illustration)**.

**9** Unscrew and remove the pilot jet **(see illustration)**.

**10** Unscrew and remove the main jet from the base of the needle jet holder **(see illustration)**.

**11** Unscrew and remove the needle jet holder **(see illustration)**.

**12** The pilot screw can be removed if required, but note that its setting will be disturbed (see **Haynes Hint**). Unscrew and remove the pilot screw along with its spring, washer and O-ring **(see illustration)**. Discard the O-ring as a new one must be used.

**13** On VFR models, slacken the screw on the inner arm securing the choke linkage bar, then lift the bar arm off the outer choke plunger **(see illustrations)**. If working on a carburettor with an inward facing plunger, withdraw the bar to free the inner arms, noting how the spring fits **(see illustrations 9.19a and b)**. Unscrew the choke plunger nut and withdraw the plunger and spring from the carburettor body, noting how they fit **(see**

> **HAYNES HINT**  *To record the pilot screw's current setting, turn the screw it in until it seats lightly, counting the number of turns necessary to achieve this, then fully unscrew it. On installation, the screw is simply backed out the number of turns you've recorded.*

8.9  Remove the pilot jet (arrowed) . . .

8.10  . . . the main jet (arrowed) . . .

8.11  . . . and the needle jet holder (arrowed)

**4**

8.12  If required, remove the pilot screw along with its O-ring, washer and spring

8.13a  Slacken the screw . . .

8.13b  . . . then lift the arm off the plunger

**8.13c Unscrew the nut and remove the plunger and spring**

**8.14a Undo the choke linkage bar screws . . .**

**8.14b . . . and remove the plastic washers . . .**

illustration). Take care not to lose the spring when removing the nut.

**14** On RVF models, remove the screws securing the choke plunger linkage bar to the carburettors, then remove the plastic washers **(see illustrations)**. Lift off the bar, noting how it fits, and remove the collars and the return spring, noting how it fits **(see illustrations)**. Unscrew the choke plunger nut and withdraw the plunger and spring from the carburettor body, noting how they fit **(see illustration 8.13c)**. Take care not to lose the spring when removing the nut.

### Cleaning

*Caution: Use only a petroleum based solvent for carburettor cleaning. Don't use caustic cleaners.*

**8.14c . . . then lift off the bar and remove the collars . . .**

**15** Submerge the metal components in the solvent for approximately thirty minutes (or longer, if the directions recommend it).

**16** After the carburettor has soaked long enough for the cleaner to loosen and dissolve most of the varnish and other deposits, use a nylon-bristled brush to remove the stubborn deposits. Rinse it again, then dry it with compressed air.

**17** Use a jet of compressed air to blow out all of the fuel and air passages in the main and upper body, not forgetting the air jets in the carburettor intake.

*Caution: Never clean the jets or passages with a piece of wire or a drill bit, as they will be enlarged, causing the fuel and air metering rates to be upset.*

**8.14d . . . and the return spring**

### Inspection

**18** Check the operation of the choke plunger. If it doesn't move smoothly, inspect the needle on the end of the choke plunger, the spring and the plunger linkage bar **(see illustration)**. Replace any component that is worn, damaged or bent.

**19** If removed from the carburettor, check the tapered portion of the pilot screw and the spring and O-ring for wear or damage**(see illustration)**. Replace them if necessary.

**20** Check the carburettor body, float chamber and top cover for cracks, distorted sealing surfaces and other damage. If any defects are found, replace the faulty component, although replacement of the entire carburettor will probably be necessary (check with a Honda dealer on the availability of separate components).

**21** Check the piston diaphragm for splits, holes and general deterioration **(see illustration)**. Holding it up to a light will help to reveal problems of this nature.

**22** Insert the piston in the carburettor body and check that the piston moves up-and-down smoothly. Check the surface of the piston for wear. If it's worn excessively or doesn't move smoothly in the guide, replace the components as necessary.

**23** Check the jet needle for straightness by rolling it on a flat surface such as a piece of

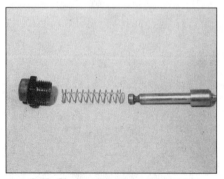

**8.18 Choke plunger components**

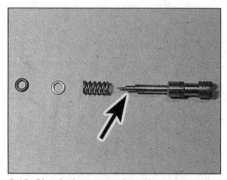

**8.19 Check the tapered portion of the pilot screw (arrowed) for wear**

**8.21 Check the piston diaphragm for splits or other damage**

glass. Replace it if it's bent or if the tip is worn.

**24** Check the tip of the float needle valve and the valve seat (see illustrations). If either has grooves or scratches in it, or is in any way worn, they must be replaced as a set. Gently push down on the rod on the top of the needle valve then release it – if it doesn't spring back, replace the valve. On VFR models, also check the condition of the valve seat filter and of the sealing washer.

**25** Operate the throttle shaft to make sure the throttle butterfly valve opens and closes smoothly. If it doesn't, cleaning the throttle linkage may help. Otherwise, replace the carburettor.

**26** Check the float for damage. This will usually be apparent by the presence of fuel inside the float. If the float is damaged, it must be replaced.

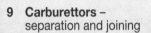

**9  Carburettors –**
separation and joining

*Warning: Refer to the precautions given in Section 1 before proceeding*

### Separation

**1** The carburettors do not need to be separated for normal overhaul. If you need to separate them (to replace a carburettor body, for example), refer to the following procedure.

**2** Remove the carburettors from the machine (see Section 7). Mark the body of each carburettor with its cylinder location to ensure that it is positioned correctly on reassembly.

**3** Bend back the tabs on the lockplates between each pair of screws securing the air duct assembly to the carburettors, then remove the screws and lift off the duct assembly, noting which way round it fits and how it locates onto the dowels (see illustrations). Also note how the rubber flanges locate around the air pipes. Remove the dowels from each carburettor intake if

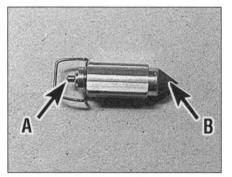

**8.24a  Check the valve's spring loaded rod (A) and tip (B) for wear or damage**

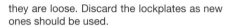

they are loose. Discard the lockplates as new ones should be used.

**4** On VFR models, slacken the screws on the inner arms securing the choke linkage bars, then lift the bar outer arms off the outer plungers and withdraw the bars, recovering the springs and inner arms as you do (see illustrations 8.13a and b).

**5** On RVF models, remove the screws securing the choke plunger linkage bar to the carburettors, then remove the plastic washers (see illustrations 8.14a and b). Lift off the bar, noting how it fits, and remove the collars and the return spring, noting how it fits (see illustrations 8.14c and d).

**8.24b  Check the valve seat for wear and the gauze filter for holes and splits**

**6** On VFR models, remove the screws securing the left-hand pair of carburettors to the right-hand pair (see illustration). Also remove the screws which join the front and rear carburettors together (see illustration).

**7** On RVF models, unscrew the nut on the left-hand end of each bar which joins each front and rear pair of carburettors together, then withdraw the bars, noting the hose clip fitted on the end of the bar on the no. 3 carburettor.

**8** On VFR models, remove the split pin securing each end of the choke linkage joining bar, then remove the bar, noting the

**9.3a  Bend back the tabs . . .**

**9.3b  . . . then remove the screws (arrowed) . . .**

**4**

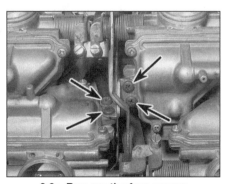

**9.3c  . . . and lift off the duct holder**

**9.6a  Remove the four screws (arrowed) . . .**

**9.6b  . . . and remove the single screw (arrowed) on each side**

**9.8 Remove the split pin (arrowed) on each end of the choke linkage bar**

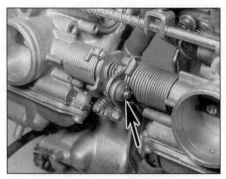

**9.9 Remove the split pin (arrowed) on each end of the throttle linkage bar**

**9.13 Make sure all the hoses are correctly installed – VFR model shown**

arrangement of the washers and collars **(see illustration)**.

**9** Remove the split pin securing each end of the throttle linkage joining bar, then remove the bar, noting the arrangement of the washers **(see illustration)**. The bar can be left in situ and removed as the carburettors are separated if required.

**10** Make a careful note of how the carburettor synchronisation springs and thrust springs are arranged to ensure that they are fitted correctly on reassembly. Also note the arrangement of the various hoses and their unions.

**11** Carefully separate the carburettors. Retrieve the thrust springs between each left- and right-hand pair of carburettors and note the fitting of the two fuel joint pipes, the two

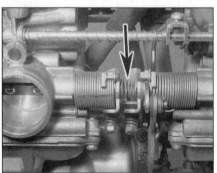

**9.18 Fit the thrust spring (arrowed) between each pair**

air joint pipes, and the two sub air cleaner joint pipes, as they are separated. Where fitted, discard the O-rings as new ones must be used. On RVF models, remove the choke linkage joining bracket and its support rods. The synchronisation springs can be left in situ, but take care that they do not spring out when handling the carburettors.

### Joining

**12** Where removed, fit a new O-ring onto each end of the fuel, air and sub-air cleaner joint pipes. Fit the two fuel joint pipes, the two air joint pipes, and the two sub air cleaner joint pipes into one of the carburettors for each front and rear pair. On RVF models, also fit the choke linkage joining bar support rods between the carburettors, then locate the joining bracket between each rod.

**13** Carefully join the carburettors together, making sure the fuel joint pipes, air vent joint pipes, sub air cleaner joint pipes, and on RVF models the choke linkage support rods and bracket, all locate correctly into their bores **(see illustration)**.

**14** On VFR models, install the choke linkage joining bar with its collars and washers and secure it using new split pins **(see illustration 8.8)**.

**15** Install the throttle linkage joining bar with its washers and secure it using new split pins **(see illustration 8.9)**.

**16** On VFR models, install all the screws which join the carburettors to each other, but

do not yet fully tighten any of them until they are all installed **(see illustrations 9.6a and b)**. Now tighten all the screws securely.

**17** On RVF models, slide the joining bars, from the right-hand side, through each front and rear pair of carburettors, then fit the nuts onto the left-hand ends of the bars and tighten them securely. Make sure the hose clip is on the no. 3 (right-hand rear) carburettor.

**18** Install the two thrust springs between each pair of carburettors, making sure it sits squarely **(see illustration)**.

**19** On VFR models, slide the choke linkage bar through the no. 1 carburettor (rear pair) and the no. 4 carburettor (front pair), then slide the spring onto the bar **(see illustration)**. Fit the arm onto its plunger, then slide the bar through the inner arm and into its bore in the other carburettor **(see illustrations)**. Fit each choke linkage arm onto the outer plungers **(see illustration 8.13b)**. Align each arm on each plunger so that the freeplay between them is equidistant, so that each plunger opens simultaneously with the rest when the choke is activated, then tighten the clamp screws onto the bars **(see illustration 8.13a)**.

**20** On RVF models, fit the choke linkage bar return springs and inner plastic washers, then locate the bars, fit the outer plastic washers and secure the bars with the screws **(see illustrations 8.14d, c, b and a)**.

**21** If removed, fit the dowels into each carburettor intake **(see illustration 9.3c)**. Fit

**9.19a Slide the bar through the correct carburettor and fit the spring onto it . . .**

**9.19b . . . then locate the inner arm onto its plunger . . .**

**9.19c . . . and slide the bar through it and into its bore**

10.1a  Fit the plunger and spring . . .

10.1b  . . . and secure them with the nut

the air duct assembly onto the carburettors, making sure the assembly locates correctly onto the dowels and that each rubber flange locates correctly around the air pipes. This can be a tricky operation, but great care must be taken to ensure that the holes in each flange locate correctly around each pipe, as they can easily become distorted by the pipes as you fit them, resulting in the rubbers being damaged and air leaks occurring. If the assembly does not want to locate easily, tighten it down using the screws after installing the lockplates.

22  Install the air duct assembly lockplates, using new ones if required and install the screws **(see illustration 9.3b)**. Tighten the screws evenly and a little at a time to ensure that the assembly is drawn down evenly and squarely onto the carburettors. Bend the tabs on the lockplates up onto the screws **(see illustration 9.3a)**.

23  Install the carburettors (see Section 7).

## 10  Carburettors – reassembly and float height check

**Warning: Refer to the precautions given in Section 1 before proceeding.**
**Note:** When reassembling the carburettors, be sure to use new O-rings and seals. Do not overtighten the carburettor jets and screws as they are easily damaged.

1  Install the choke plunger and spring into the carburettor body and tighten the nut to secure it **(see illustrations)**.

2  On VFR models, if completely removed, slide the choke linkage bar through the no. 1 carburettor (rear pair) and the no. 4 carburettor (front pair), then slide the spring onto the bar **(see illustration 9.19a)**. Fit the arm onto its plunger, then slide the bar through the inner arm and into its bore in the other carburettor **(see illustrations 9.19b and c)**. Fit each choke linkage arm onto the outer

plungers **(see illustration 8.13b)**. Align each arm on each plunger so that the freeplay between them is equidistant, so that each plunger opens simultaneously with the rest when the choke is activated, then tighten the clamp screws onto the bars **(see illustration 8.13a)**.

3  On RVF models, fit the choke linkage bar return spring and inner plastic washers, then locate the bar, fit the outer plastic washers and secure the bar with the screws **(see illustrations 8.14d, c, b and a)**.

4  Install the pilot screw (if removed) along with its spring, washer and O-ring, turning it in until it seats lightly **(see illustration 8.12)**. Now, turn the screw out the number of turns previously recorded on disassembly.

5  Install the needle jet holder into the carburettor **(see illustration)**. Screw the main jet into the end of the needle jet holder **(see illustration)**.

6  Install the pilot jet into the carburettor **(see illustration)**.

7  On VFR models, install the float needle valve seat and its sealing washer, making sure the filter is attached **(see illustration)**.

10.5a  Install the needle jet holder . . .

10.5b  . . . the main jet . . .

10.6  . . . and the pilot jet

10.7  Install the needle valve seat, using a new sealing washer if required

**4**

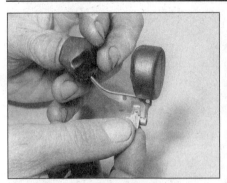

**10.8a Hook the needle valve onto the tab ...**

**10.8b ... then fit the float assembly, making sure the valve enters the seat (arrow) ...**

**10.8c ... and secure it with the pin**

**8** Hook the float needle valve onto the float tab, then position the float assembly in the carburettor and install the pin, making sure it is secure **(see illustrations)**.

**9** To check the float height, hold the carburettor so the float hangs down, then tilt it back until the needle valve is just seated, but not so far that the needle's spring-loaded tip is compressed. Measure the distance between the gasket face (with the gasket removed) and the bottom of the float with an accurate ruler **(see illustration)**. The correct setting should be as given in the Specifications at the beginning of the

Chapter. If it is incorrect, adjust the float height by carefully bending the float tab a little at a time until the correct height is obtained. Repeat the procedure for all carburettors.

**10** With the float height checked, fit a new rubber gasket onto the float chamber, making sure it is seated properly in its groove, and install the chamber onto the carburettor **(see illustrations)**.

**11** On VFR models, if removed, fit the washer onto the needle and insert the needle into the piston **(see illustration)**. Fit the spring into the retainer then fit the retainer into the piston,

then push down on the needle retainer using a Phillips screwdriver and rotate it until its tab locks under the protrusion in the piston **(see illustration)**.

**12** On RVF models, fit the washer onto the needle and insert the needle into the piston **(see illustration 10.11a)**. Fit a new O-ring into the groove in the needle holder. Fit the spring into the holder, then insert the holder into the centre of the piston and push it down until the O-ring is felt to locate in its groove in the piston **(see illustration)**. Remove the bolt used on removal from the holder, if not already done.

**10.9 Measuring float height**

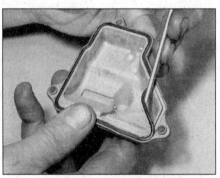

**10.10a Fit a new gasket into the groove ...**

**10.10b ... and install the float chamber**

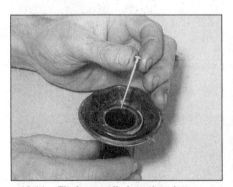

**10.11a Fit the needle into the piston ...**

**10.11b ... and secure it with the retainer as described**

**10.12 Install the needle holder using a new O-ring (arrowed)**

10.13a  Install the piston assembly . . .

10.13b  . . . making sure the diaphragm edge  fits into the groove and the tab is correctly positioned around the air hole (arrow)

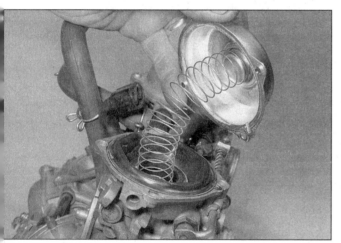

10.14a  Fit the top cover onto the spring . . .

10.14b  . . . and fit it so that the protrusion (arrowed) fits over the diaphragm tab

**13** Insert the piston assembly into the body and lightly push it down, ensuring the needle is correctly aligned with the needle jet **(see illustration)**. Align the tab on the diaphragm with the recess in the carburettor body, then press the diaphragm outer edge into its groove, making sure it is correctly seated and that the tab locates in the recess around the air hole **(see illustration)**. Check the diaphragm is not creased, and that the piston moves smoothly up and down in its guide.
**14** Install the spring into the piston **(see illustration 8.3b)**. Fit the top cover to the carburettor, making sure the top of the spring locates over the raised section on the inside of the cover, and aligning the protrusion on the cover with the tab on the diaphragm and, and tighten its screws securely **(see illustrations)**.
**15** If removed, install the air duct assembly (see Section 9, Steps 21 and 22).
**15** Install the carburettors (see Section 7).

## 11 Throttle cables – removal and installation

⚠️ *Warning: Refer to the precautions given in Section 1 before proceeding.*

### Removal

**1** Remove the fuel tank and the air filter housing (see Sections 2 and 4). Whilst it is possible to detach the throttle cables with the carburettors in situ, there is a limited amount of space to work in and it can be tricky. If required, displace the carburettors to improve access (see Section 7).
**2** Turn the handlebars onto full left lock to provide the maximum freeplay in the cables. Mark each cable according to its location. On VFR models, the base carburettor is no. 2 and the accelerator cable is the upper cable in the bracket, the decelerator cable is the lower. On RVF models the base is no. 1 and the

accelerator cable is the lower cable in the bracket, the decelerator cable is the upper.
**3** On VFR models, slacken the accelerator cable adjuster locknut, then unscrew the adjuster so that it threads out of the captive nut, until it is clear of the small lug on the bracket **(see illustration)**. Slip the adjuster

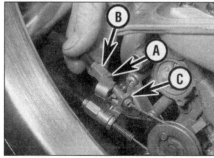

11.3a  Slacken the locknut (A), then unscrew the adjuster (B) until the captive nut (C) is free of its lug, then slip the cable out of the bracket

**4**

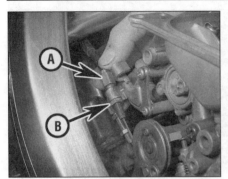

11.3b Unscrew the adjuster (A) until the captive nut (B) is clear of its lug, then slip the cable out of the bracket

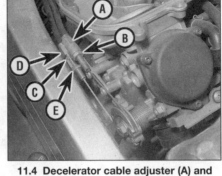

11.4 Decelerator cable adjuster (A) and captive nut (B). Accelerator cable locknut (C), adjuster (D) and captive nut (E)

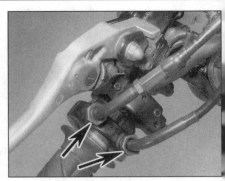

11.5a Slacken the elbow nuts (arrowed) . . .

out of the bracket and detach the cable nipple from the carburettors. Now unscrew the decelerator cable adjuster until the captive nut is free, then slip the adjuster out of the bracket and detach the cable nipple from the carburettors **(see illustration)**. Withdraw the cables from the machine noting the correct routing of each cable.

**4** On RVF models, unscrew the decelerator cable adjuster until the captive nut is free, then slip the adjuster out of the bracket and detach the cable nipple from the carburettors **(see illustration)**. Slacken the accelerator cable adjuster locknut, then unscrew the adjuster so that it threads out of the captive nut, which locates against a small lug on the

bracket. Thread the captive nut off the adjuster, then slip the adjuster out of the bracket and detach the cable nipple from the carburettors. Withdraw the cables from the machine noting the correct routing of each cable.

**5** Slacken the cable elbow nuts at the throttle pulley housing, then remove the housing screws and lift off the top half **(see illustrations)**. Detach the cable nipples from the pulley and detach the lower housing half from the handlebar **(see illustrations)**. Fully unscrew the decelerator cable elbow nut, then remove the cable from the housing **(see illustration)**. Thread the housing off the accelerator cable elbow and withdraw the

cable **(see illustration)**. Mark each cable to ensure it is connected correctly on installation.

### Installation

**6** Fit the accelerator cable elbow into the forward socket of the lower half of the throttle pulley housing and thread the housing onto it **(see illustration 11.5f)**. Fit the decelerator cable into the rear socket and tighten the nut **(see illustration 11.5e)**. Fit the lower half of the housing onto the handlebar, then lubricate the cable nipples with multi-purpose grease and install them into the throttle pulley **(see illustration)**.

**7** Fit the top half of the housing onto the

11.5b . . . and remove the screws (arrowed) . . .

11.5c . . . then lift off the housing and detach the cable ends from the pulley . . .

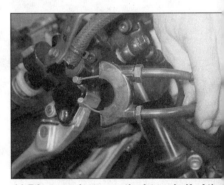

11.5d . . . and remove the lower half of the housing

11.5e Unscrew the decelerator cable elbow nut and withdraw the cable from the housing . . .

11.5f . . . then thread the housing off the accelerator cable elbow

11.6 Fit the nipples into their sockets in the pulley

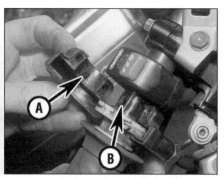

11.7a  Locate the pin (A) into the hole (B) . . .

11.7b  . . . then tighten the housing screws

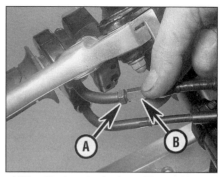

11.7c  Slacken the locknut (A) and thread the adjuster (B) fully in

handlebar, making sure the pin locates in the hole in the top of the handlebar, and install the screws, tightening them securely (see illustrations). Slacken the locknut on the cable adjuster and thread the adjuster fully in, then tighten the locknut against it (see illustration). This resets the adjuster to the start of its range.

8  Feed the cables through to the carburettors, making sure they are correctly routed. The cables must not interfere with any other component and should not be kinked or bent sharply.

9  On VFR models, lubricate the decelerator cable nipple with multi-purpose grease and fit it into the lower socket on the carburettor throttle cam (see illustration). Fit the cable

adjuster into the lower bracket, locating the nut against the lug so that it is captive, then thread the adjuster into the nut until it is tight (see illustration). Lubricate the accelerator cable nipple with multi-purpose grease and fit it into the upper socket on the carburettor throttle cam. Fit the accelerator cable adjuster into the upper bracket, then thread the lower nut up the adjuster (see illustration 11.3a). Locate the nut against the lug so that it is captive, then thread the adjuster into the nut until the specified amount of cable freeplay is obtained (see Chapter 1). Tighten the locknut against the bracket.

10  On RVF models, lubricate the accelerator cable nipple with multi-purpose grease and fit it into the lower socket on the carburettor

throttle cam. Fit the accelerator cable adjuster into the inner bracket, then thread the lower nut onto the end of the adjuster (see illustration 11.4). Locate the nut against the lug so that it is captive, then thread the adjuster into the nut until the specified amount of cable freeplay is obtained (see Chapter 1). Tighten the locknut against the bracket. Lubricate the decelerator cable nipple with multi-purpose grease and fit it into the upper socket on the carburettor throttle cam. Fit the cable adjuster into the upper bracket, locating the nut against the lug so that it is captive, then thread the adjuster into the nut until it is tight.

11  Operate the throttle to check that it opens and closes freely.

12  Check and adjust the throttle cable freeplay if required (see Chapter 1). Turn the handlebars back and forth to make sure the cable doesn't cause the steering to bind.

13  Install the carburettors (if displaced), the air filter housing and the fuel tank (see Sections 7, 4 and 2).

14  Start the engine and check that the idle speed does not rise as the handlebars are turned. If it does, the throttle cable is routed incorrectly. Correct the problem before riding the motorcycle.

11.9a  Fit the decelerator cable nipple into its socket in the cam . . .

11.9b  . . . then locate the cable in the bracket and fully tighten the adjuster

## 12  Choke cable – removal and installation

### Removal

1  Remove the fuel tank and the air filter housing (see Sections 2 and 4).

2  Remove the left-hand fairing side panel, and on VFR models also remove the trim panel (see Chapter 8).

3  Slacken the choke outer cable bracket screw and free the cable from the bracket on the front of the carburettors, then detach the inner cable nipple from the choke linkage lever (see illustrations). Withdraw the cable from the machine noting the correct routing.

4  On VFR models, remove the screw securing the choke lever, then remove the lever and

12.3a  Slacken the bracket screw and release the outer cable . . .

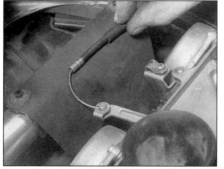

12.3b  . . . then free the inner cable nipple from the lever

**4**

12.4a Remove the screw (arrowed) . . .

12.4b . . . and detach the nipple from the lever . . .

12.4c . . . then draw the outer cable from its socket

detach the cable nipple, noting how it fits **(see illustrations)**. Draw the outer cable out of the housing **(see illustration)**. Note the star washer in the lever housing and remove it for safekeeping if required, noting which way round it fits.

5 On RVF models unscrew the nut securing the choke knob in the fairing trim panel and draw the cable out of the panel, feeding the nut off the end of the cable as you do **(see illustration)**.

### Installation

6 On VFR models, lubricate the lever-end cable nipple with multi-purpose grease and the rubber protector on the end of the outer cable with WD40 and fit the outer cable into the choke lever housing. If removed, fit the star washer into the housing, with its curved ends facing in **(see illustration)**. Attach the nipple to the choke lever and fit the lever onto the housing, making sure the nipple stays in place, and tighten the screw **(see illustration 12.4b an a)**.

7 On RVF models, pass the cable down through the hole in the trim panel and locate the knob in the hole. Feed the nut onto the end of the cable and up to the knob and tighten it to secure the knob **(see illustration 12.5)**.

8 Feed the cable through to the carburettors, making sure it is correctly routed. The cable must not interfere with any other component and should not be kinked or bent sharply.

9 Lubricate the cable nipple with multi-purpose grease and attach it to the choke linkage lever on the carburettor **(see illustration 12.3b)**. Fit the outer cable into its bracket, making sure there is a small amount of freeplay in the inner cable, and tighten the screw **(see illustration 12.3a)**.

10 Check the operation of the choke cable (see Chapter 1).

11 Install the air filter housing and the fuel tank (see Sections 4 and 2).

12 Install the fairing side panel trim (VFR models) and the panel (see Chapter 8).

---

### 13 Exhaust system – removal and installation

> ⚠️ **Warning: If the engine has been running the exhaust system will be very hot. Allow the system to cool before carrying out any work.**

**Note:** The exhaust system can be removed as a complete assembly (with the exception of the rear cylinder header pipes), but it can be tricky to install it as such without the aid of an assistant. It is better to separate the rear section from the front cylinder downpipes as described. To remove the system complete, do not slacken the clamp bolts between the rear section and the front downpipes and unscrew the front downpipe nuts at the same time as the rear ones. The rear section can be removed leaving the front cylinder downpipes in place, though it is not advised as it is difficult to locate the section back into the downpipes without damaging the sealing rings. On RVF models, the silencer can be separated from the rear section leaving the rear section pipes in place, or after the section has been removed as an assembly.

### Removal

1 Remove the seat cowling and the lower fairing (see Chapter 8). Also remove the bolt securing the bottom of the lower radiator to its bracket and swing the radiator forward. Tie it in this position to provide access to the front downpipes.

2 Slacken the clamp bolts securing the front cylinder downpipes in the rear section pipes

12.5 Fully unscrew the nut (arrowed) and draw the cable out

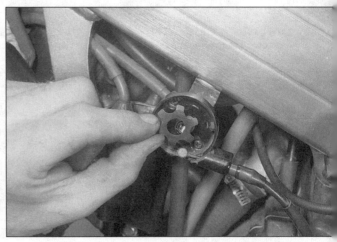

12.6 Fit the star washer with its curved ends facing in

13.2a  Slacken the clamp bolts (arrowed) . . .

13.2b  . . . then unscrew the downpipe nuts . . .

13.2c  . . . and swing the downpipe down and out of the rear section

(see illustration). Unscrew the two nuts securing each downpipe to the front cylinder head, then swing each pipe outwards and free them from the rear section using a twisting motion (see illustrations). Remove the gasket from each port in the cylinder head and discard them as new ones must be used (see illustration).

HAYNES HiNT   Exhaust system clamp bolts tend to become corroded and seized. It is advisable to spray them with WD40 or a similar product before attempting to slacken them.

3 Unscrew the two bolts securing the rider's right-hand footrest bracket and the bolt securing the top of the heat shield to the frame, then swing the whole footrest/rear brake master cylinder/heat shield assembly up and secure it to the rear sub-frame, making sure no strain is placed on the brake and reservoir hoses (see illustration). This provides access to the rear cylinder downpipe joint nuts.
4 On VFR models, unscrew the two nuts securing the passenger's left-hand footrest bracket and the silencer bracket to the frame and leave the assembly loose on the studs (see illustration).
5 On RVF models, unscrew the nut on the

silencer mounting bolt, but the leave the bolt loosely in place.
6 Unscrew the three nuts securing the rear cylinder downpipes to the header pipes (see illustration).
7 On VFR models draw the footrest assembly with the silencer attached off the studs, then lower the rear section to the ground (see illustrations). If required, separate the footrest bracket and silencer bracket from the silencer.
8 On RVF models, withdraw the silencer mounting bolt, then lower the rear section to the ground.
9 Remove the gasket from each rear cylinder header pipe and discard them as new ones

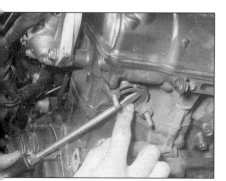

13.2d  Remove the gasket from the cylinder head

13.3  Unscrew the footrest bracket bolts (A) and the heat shield bolt (B) and swing the assembly up

13.4  Remove the two nuts (arrowed)

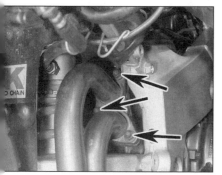

13.6  Remove the nuts (arrowed) securing the rear cylinder downpipes . . .

13.7a  . . . then draw the silencer and bracket off the studs . . .

13.7b  . . . and the downpipes off the header pipes

**13.9 Remove the gaskets from the header pipes**

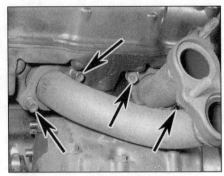

**13.10 The rear cylinder header pipes are secured by four nuts (arrowed)**

**13.11 Always use new gaskets**

must be used **(see illustration)**. Also remove the sealing rings from the rear section pipes where they join the front downpipes and discard them as new ones should be used.

**10** If required, unscrew the two nuts securing each header pipe to the rear cylinder head and remove the header pipe assembly **(see illustration)**. Access to these nuts is difficult and is best achieved using a universal drive adapter and socket extension. Remove the gasket from each port in the cylinder head and discard them as new ones must be used.

## Installation

**11** Installation is the reverse of removal, noting the following:

a) *Leave all fasteners loose until the entire system has been installed, making alignment of the various sections easier. Tighten the silencer mountings last.*

b) *Use new gaskets in each cylinder head port and between the rear cylinder header pipes and downpipes* **(see illustration)**.

c) *Use new sealing rings between the rear section pipes and the front downpipes.*

d) *Apply some copper grease to the rear section clamp bolts to prevent them from seizing up.*

e) *Tighten the front downpipe nuts and the rear header pipe nuts to the torque setting specified at the beginning of the Chapter.*

f) *Tighten the right-hand footrest bracket and on VFR models the left-hand passenger's footrest bracket nuts to the specified torque setting.*

g) *Run the engine and check the system for leaks.*

# Chapter 5
# Ignition system

## Contents

## Degrees of difficulty

| Easy, suitable for novice with little experience |  | Fairly easy, suitable for beginner with some experience |  | Fairly difficult, suitable for competent DIY mechanic | | Difficult, suitable for experienced DIY mechanic | | Very difficult, suitable for expert DIY or professional | |

## Specifications

### General information

Firing order . . . . . . . . . . . . . . . . . . . . . . . . . . . . . . . . . . . . . . . . . . . 1-4-3-2

Cylinder numbering
  Rear left . . . . . . . . . . . . . . . . . . . . . . . . . . . . . . . . . . . . . . . . . . . . . 1
  Front left . . . . . . . . . . . . . . . . . . . . . . . . . . . . . . . . . . . . . . . . . . . . . 2
  Rear right . . . . . . . . . . . . . . . . . . . . . . . . . . . . . . . . . . . . . . . . . . . . 3
  Front right . . . . . . . . . . . . . . . . . . . . . . . . . . . . . . . . . . . . . . . . . . . . 4

Spark plugs . . . . . . . . . . . . . . . . . . . . . . . . . . . . . . . . . . . . . . . . . . . . See Chapter 1

```
        ↑
      FRONT

   ┌────┬────┐
   │ 2  │ 4  │
   └────┴────┘

   ┌────┬────┐
   │ 1  │ 3  │
   └────┴────┘
```

### Ignition timing

At idle
  VFR models . . . . . . . . . . . . . . . . . . . . . . . . . . . . . . . . . . . . . . . . . . 18° BTDC
  RVF models . . . . . . . . . . . . . . . . . . . . . . . . . . . . . . . . . . . . . . . . . . 15° BTDC

Full advance
  VFR models . . . . . . . . . . . . . . . . . . . . . . . . . . . . . . . . . . . . . . . . . . 35 to 37° BTDC @ 12,000 rpm
  RVF models . . . . . . . . . . . . . . . . . . . . . . . . . . . . . . . . . . . . . . . . . . 36° BTDC @ 7400 to 7600 rpm

### Pulse generator coil(s)

Resistance . . . . . . . . . . . . . . . . . . . . . . . . . . . . . . . . . . . . . . . . . . . . 450 to 550 ohms @ 20°C

### Ignition HT coils

Primary winding resistance . . . . . . . . . . . . . . . . . . . . . . . . . . . . . . . . 2.5 to 3.5 ohms @ 20°C
Secondary winding resistance
  With plug cap . . . . . . . . . . . . . . . . . . . . . . . . . . . . . . . . . . . . . . . . . 14.0 to 25.0 K ohms @ 20°C
  Without plug cap . . . . . . . . . . . . . . . . . . . . . . . . . . . . . . . . . . . . . . . 11.0 to 14.0 K ohms @ 20°C

5

## Torque settings – specific components

Timing inspection cover . . . . . . . . . . . . . . . . . . . . . . . . . . . . . . . . . . 18 Nm

## Torque settings – non-specified components

**Note:** *Where a specific setting is not given for a particular bolt/nut, these general settings apply. The dimension given applies to the diameter of the thread, not the head.*

5 mm bolt/nut . . . . . . . . . . . . . . . . . . . . . . . . . . . . . . . . . . . . . . . . . . 5 Nm
6 mm bolt/nut . . . . . . . . . . . . . . . . . . . . . . . . . . . . . . . . . . . . . . . . . . 10 Nm
8 mm bolt/nut . . . . . . . . . . . . . . . . . . . . . . . . . . . . . . . . . . . . . . . . . . 22 Nm
10 mm bolt/nut . . . . . . . . . . . . . . . . . . . . . . . . . . . . . . . . . . . . . . . . . 35 Nm
12 mm bolt/nut . . . . . . . . . . . . . . . . . . . . . . . . . . . . . . . . . . . . . . . . . 55 Nm
6 mm flange bolt with 8 mm head . . . . . . . . . . . . . . . . . . . . . . . . . . 9 Nm
6 mm flange bolt/nut with 10 mm head . . . . . . . . . . . . . . . . . . . . . 12 Nm
8 mm flange bolt/nut . . . . . . . . . . . . . . . . . . . . . . . . . . . . . . . . . . . . 27 Nm
10 mm flange bolt/nut . . . . . . . . . . . . . . . . . . . . . . . . . . . . . . . . . . . 40 Nm

## 1 General information

All models are fitted with a fully transistorised electronic ignition system, which due to its lack of mechanical parts is totally maintenance free. The system comprises a rotor, pulse generator coil(s), ignition control unit and ignition HT coils (refer to the wiring diagrams at the end of Chapter 9 for details). VFR models are fitted with two pulse generator coils, while RVF models have one.

The ignition triggers, which are on the starter clutch housing on the right-hand end of the crankshaft, magnetically operate the pulse generator coil(s) as the crankshaft rotates. The pulse generator coil(s) sends a signal to the ignition control unit which then supplies the ignition HT coils with the power necessary to produce a spark at the plugs.

The system uses two HT coils, the front supplying nos. 2 and 4 cylinder spark plugs and the rear coil supplying nos. 1 and 3 cylinder plugs. On VFR models, the front cylinder coil is mounted on the left-hand side of the engine by the front cylinders, while on RVF models it is mounted on the right-hand side. On both models, the rear coil is mounted on the outside of the left-hand side of the frame, to the rear of the engine.

The system incorporates an electronic advance system controlled by signals generated by the pulse generator coil(s) and the ignition control unit.

On Japanese home market versions (grey imports) a rev limiter set in the speedometer tranmits a signal to the ignition control unit when 180 kmh (112 mph) is reached. At this road speed, the ignition cuts out. Note that most grey imports sold in the UK will have had this system disabled at the time of first registration.

On RVF models the system incorporates a safety interlock circuit which will cut the ignition if the sidestand is extended whilst the engine is running and in gear, or if a gear is selected whilst the engine is running and the sidestand is down. It also prevents the engine from being started if the sidestand is down and the engine is in gear unless the clutch lever is pulled in. VFR models have a simpler system, which does not include a sidestand switch, but prevents the engine from being started if it is in gear unless the clutch lever is pulled in, and it cuts the starter circuit rather than the ignition circuit.

Because of their nature, the individual ignition system components can be checked but not repaired. If ignition system troubles occur, and the faulty component can be isolated, the only cure for the problem is to replace the part with a new one. Keep in mind that most electrical parts, once purchased, cannot be returned. To avoid unnecessary expense, make very sure the faulty component has been positively identified before buying a replacement part.

Note that there is no provision for adjusting the ignition timing on these models.

## 2 Ignition system – check

 *Warning: The energy levels in electronic systems can be very high. On no account should the ignition be switched on whilst the plugs or plug caps are being held. Shocks from the HT circuit can be most unpleasant. Secondly, it is vital that the engine is not turned over or run with any of the plug caps removed, and that the plugs are soundly earthed (grounded) when the system is checked for sparking. The ignition system components can be seriously damaged if the HT circuit becomes isolated.*

**1** As no means of adjustment is available, any failure of the system can be traced to failure of a system component or a simple wiring fault. Of the two possibilities, the latter is by far the most likely. In the event of failure, check the system in a logical fashion, as described below.

**2** Disconnect the HT leads from the spark plugs. Connect each lead to a spare spark plug and lay each plug on the engine with the threads contacting the engine. If necessary, hold each spark plug with an insulated tool.

 *Warning: Do not remove any of the spark plugs from the engine to perform this check – atomised fuel being pumped out of the open spark plug hole could ignite, causing severe injury!*

**3** Having observed the above precautions, check that the kill switch is in the RUN position and the transmission is in neutral, then turn the ignition switch ON and turn the engine over on the starter motor. If the system is in good condition a regular, fat blue spark should be evident at each plug electrode. If the spark appears thin or yellowish, or is non-existent, further investigation will be necessary. Before proceeding further, turn the ignition off and remove the key as a safety measure.

**4** The ignition system must be able to produce a spark which is capable of jumping a particular size gap. Honda do not provide a specification, but a healthy system should produce a spark capable of jumping at least 6 mm. A simple testing tool can be made to test the minimum gap across which the spark will jump (see **Tool Tip**).

*A simple spark gap testing tool can be made from a block of wood, a large alligator clip and two nails, one of which is fashioned so that a spark plug cap or bare HT lead end can be connected to its end. Make sure the gap between the two nail ends is the same as specified.*

3.4a Front cylinder coil – VFR models

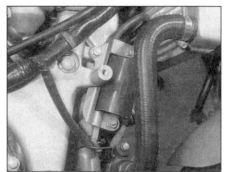

3.4b Front cylinder coil – RVF models

3.4c Rear cylinder coil – all models

**5** Connect one of the spark plug HT leads from one coil to the protruding electrode on the test tool, and clip the tool to a good earth (ground) on the engine or frame. Check that the kill switch is in the RUN position, turn the ignition switch ON and turn the engine over on the starter motor. If the system is in good condition a regular, fat blue spark should be seen to jump the gap between the nail ends. Repeat the test for the other coil. If the test results are good the entire ignition system can be considered good. If the spark appears thin or yellowish, or is non-existent, further investigation will be necessary.

**6** Ignition faults can be divided into two categories, namely those where the ignition system has failed completely, and those which are due to a partial failure. The likely faults are listed below, starting with the most probable source of failure. Work through the list systematically, referring to the subsequent sections for full details of the necessary checks and tests. **Note:** *Before checking the following items ensure that the battery is fully charged and that all fuses are in good condition.*

a) *Loose, corroded or damaged wiring connections, broken or shorted wiring between any of the component parts of the ignition system (see Chapter 9).*

b) *Faulty HT lead or spark plug cap, faulty spark plug, dirty, worn or corroded plug electrodes, or incorrect gap between electrodes.*

c) *Faulty ignition (main) switch or engine kill switch (see Chapter 9).*

d) *Faulty neutral, clutch or sidestand switch (RVF models only) (see Chapter 9).*

e) *Faulty pulse generator coil or damaged rotor.*

f) *Faulty ignition HT coil(s).*

g) *Faulty ignition control unit.*

**7** If the above checks don't reveal the cause of the problem, have the ignition system tested by a Honda dealer. Honda produce a tester which can perform a complete diagnostic analysis of the ignition system.

## 3 Ignition HT coils – check, removal and installation

### Check

**1** In order to determine conclusively that the ignition coils are defective, they should be tested by a Honda dealer equipped with the special diagnostic tester.

**2** However, the coils can be checked visually (for cracks and other damage) and the primary and secondary coil resistance can be measured with a multimeter. If the coils are undamaged, and if the resistance readings are as specified at the beginning of the Chapter, they are probably capable of proper operation.

**3** Remove the left-hand (VFR models) or the right-hand (RVF) fairing side panel and the seat cowling (see Chapter 8). Disconnect the battery negative (–ve) lead.

**4** On VFR models, the front cylinder coil is mounted on the left-hand side of the engine by the front cylinders, while on RVF models it is mounted on the right-hand side **(see illustrations)**. On both models, the rear coil is mounted on the outside of the left-hand side of the frame, to the rear of the engine **(see illustration)**.

**5** Disconnect the primary circuit electrical connectors from the coil being tested and the HT leads from the spark plugs **(see illustration)**. Mark the locations of all wires and leads before disconnecting them.

**6** Set the meter to the ohms x 1 scale and measure the resistance between the primary circuit terminals on the coil **(see illustration)**. This will give a resistance reading of the primary windings of the coil and should be consistent with the value given in the Specifications at the beginning of the Chapter.

**7** To check the condition of the secondary windings, set the meter to the K ohm scale. Connect one meter probe to one spark plug cap and the other probe to the other spark plug cap **(see illustration)**. If the reading obtained is not within the range shown in the Specifications, remove the caps from the ends of the HT leads and repeat the measurement. If the reading is now as specified, replace the spark plug caps with

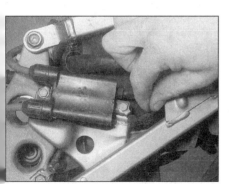

3.5 Disconnect the coils' primary circuit wiring connector

3.6 To test the coil primary resistance, connect the multimeter leads between the primary circuit terminals on the coil

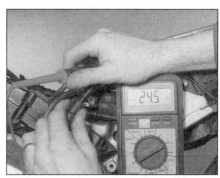

3.7 To test the coil secondary resistance, connect the multimeter leads between the spark plug leads

**4.3a Pulse generator coil wiring connector (arrowed) – VFR models**

**4.3b Pulse generator coil wiring connector (arrowed) – RVF models**

**4.8a Disconnect the neutral switch wiring connector . . .**

new ones. If the reading is still outside the specified range, it is likely that the coil is defective.

**8** Should any of the above checks not produce the expected result, have your findings confirmed on the diagnostic tester (see Step 1). If the coil is confirmed to be faulty, it must be replaced; the coil is a sealed unit and cannot therefore be repaired.

### Removal

**9** On VFR models, the front cylinder coil is mounted on the left-hand side of the engine by the front cylinders, while on RVF models it is mounted on the right-hand side **(see illustration 3.4a and b)**. On both models, the rear coil is mounted on the outside of the left-hand side of the frame, to the rear of the engine **(see illustration 3.4c)**. Access the front coil by removing the relevant fairing side panel, and the rear coil by removing the seat cowling (see Chapter 8).

**10** If not already done, remove the seat cowling (see Chapter 8) and disconnect the battery negative (–ve) lead.

**11** Disconnect the primary circuit electrical connectors from the coil **(see illustration 3.5)** and disconnect the HT leads from the spark plugs. Mark the locations of all wires and leads before disconnecting them.

**12** Unscrew the two bolts securing each coil, noting the spacers, and remove the coils. Note the routing of the HT leads.

### Installation

**13** Installation is the reverse of removal. Make sure the wiring connectors and HT leads are securely connected.

---

**4 Pulse generator coil assembly** – check, removal and installation

---

### Check

**1** Remove the seat cowling (see Chapter 8) and disconnect the battery negative (–ve) lead.

**2** Remove the lower fairing (see Chapter 8).

**3** Trace the pulse generator coil/neutral switch/oil pressure switch wiring back from the top of the right-hand crankcase cover and disconnect it at the black 4-pin connector **(see illustrations)**. Using a multimeter set to the ohms x 100 scale, measure the resistance between the white/yellow and yellow terminals on the pulse generator coil side of the connector. On VFR models with two coils, also measure the resistance between white/blue and blue terminals.

**4** Compare the reading obtained with that given in the Specifications at the beginning of this Chapter. The pulse generator coil must be replaced if the reading obtained differs greatly from that given, particularly if the meter indicates a short circuit (no measurable

resistance) or an open circuit (infinite, or very high resistance).

**5** If the pulse generator coil is thought to be faulty, first check that this is not due to a damaged or broken wire from the coil to the connector; pinched or broken wires can usually be repaired.

### Removal

**6** Remove the seat cowling (see Chapter 8) and disconnect the battery negative (–ve) lead.

**7** Remove the lower fairing (see Chapter 8).

**8** Trace the pulse generator coil/neutral switch/oil pressure switch wiring back from the top of the right-hand crankcase cover and disconnect it at the black 4-pin connector **(see illustrations 4.3a and b)**. Disconnect the neutral switch wiring connector from its terminal on the switch and release it from its clip, then remove the screw securing the oil pressure switch wiring connector and disconnect it **(see illustrations)**.

**9** Unscrew the twelve bolts securing the right-hand crankcase cover and remove the cover, being prepared to catch any residue oil, and noting the positions of the wiring clips **(see illustration)**. Discard the gasket as a new one must be used. Remove the dowels from either the cover or the crankcase if they are loose.

**10** Unscrew the bolt securing the pulse generator coil(s) to the crankcase **(see illustration)**. Remove the rubber wiring

**4.8b . . . and the oil pressure switch wiring connector**

**4.9 The right-hand crankcase cover is secured by twelve bolts (arrowed)**

**4.10 Pulse generator coil assembly bolts (arrowed) – VFR models**

**4.12 Fit the grommet (arrowed) into its recess**

**4.13a Place a new gasket onto the dowels . . .**

**4.13b . . . then install the cover**

grommet from its recess, then remove the coil(s).

**11** Examine the triggers on the starter clutch for signs of damage and replace the clutch housing if necessary (see Chapter 2).

### Installation

**12** Install the pulse generator coil(s) onto the crankcase and tighten the bolt(s) securely **(see illustration 4.12)**. Apply a suitable sealant to the wiring grommet and fit it into its recess **(see illustration)**.

**13** If removed, insert the dowels in the crankcase, then install the crankcase cover using a new gasket, making sure it locates correctly onto the dowels and the idle/reduction gear shaft **(see illustrations)**. Tighten the cover bolts evenly in a criss-cross sequence to the specified torque setting, making sure the wiring clips are correctly installed.

**14** Connect the oil pressure switch wire to its terminal on the switch and tighten the screw securely, then connect the neutral switch wiring connector to the switch terminal and place the wiring in its guide **(see illustrations 4.8b and a)**. Connect the pulse generator coil/neutral switch/oil pressure switch wiring at the black 4-pin connector **(see illustrations 4.3a and b)**.

**15** Install the lower fairing (see Chapter 8).

**16** Reconnect the battery negative (–ve) lead and install the seat cowling (see Chapter 8).

### 5 Ignition control unit – check, removal and installation

#### Check

**1** If the tests shown in the preceding Sections have failed to isolate the cause of an ignition fault, it is possible that the ignition control unit itself is faulty. No test details are available with which the unit can be tested on home workshop equipment. Take the machine to a Honda dealer for testing on the diagnostic tester..

#### Removal

**2** Remove the seat cowling (see Chapter 8) and disconnect the battery negative (–ve) lead.

**3** On VFR models the control unit is mounted on the rear mudguard at the back, and on RVF models it is mounted on the left-hand side of the rear sub-frame **(see illustrations)**.

**4** Disconnect the wiring connector(s) from the ignition control unit **(see illustration)**.

**5** On VFR models, remove the screw securing the ignition control unit clip and remove the unit **(see illustration)**. On RVF models, remove the ignition control unit from its rubber sleeve, or lift the sleeve and unit together off the sleeve's mounting lugs, and remove the unit **(see illustration 5.3b)**.

#### Installation

**6** Installation is the reverse of removal. Make sure the wiring connector(s) are correctly and securely connected.

### 6 Ignition timing – general information and check

#### General information

**1** Since no provision exists for adjusting the ignition timing and since no component is subject to mechanical wear, there is no need for regular checks; only if investigating a fault such as a loss of power or a misfire, should the ignition timing be checked.

**5.3a Ignition control unit – VFR models**

**5.3b Ignition control unit – RVF models**

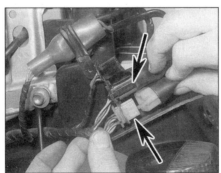

**5.4 Ignition control unit wiring connectors (arrowed) – VFR models**

**5.5 Remove the screw to release the clip**

**5**

**2** The ignition timing is checked dynamically (engine running) using a stroboscopic lamp. The inexpensive neon lamps should be adequate in theory, but in practice may produce a pulse of such low intensity that the timing mark remains indistinct. If possible, one of the more precise xenon tube lamps should be used, powered by an external source of the appropriate voltage. **Note:** *Do not use the machine's own battery as an incorrect reading may result from stray impulses within the machine's electrical system.*

## Check

**3** Warm the engine up to normal operating temperature then stop it.
**4** Unscrew the timing inspection cover from the right-hand crankcase cover **(see illustration)**. Discard the cover O-ring as a new one must be used.
**5** The timing mark on the starter clutch which indicates the firing point at idle speed for the nos. 1 and 3 cylinders is a line with the letter F next to the T1 mark **(see illustration)**. The timing mark which indicates the firing point at idle speed for the nos. 2 and 4 cylinders is a line with the letter F next to the T2 mark. The static timing mark with which these should align is the index mark on the crankcase cover.

**HAYNES HiNT** *The timing marks can be highlighted with white paint to make them more visible under the stroboscope light.*

**6** Connect the timing light to the no. 1 cylinder HT lead as described in the manufacturer's instructions.
**7** Start the engine and aim the light at the static timing mark.
**8** With the machine idling, the timing mark F

6.4 Remove the timing inspection cover

next to the T1 mark should align with the static timing mark.
**9** Slowly increase the engine speed whilst observing the timing mark. The timing mark should move anti-clockwise, increasing in relation to the engine speed until it reaches full advance (no identification mark).
**10** Repeat Steps 6 to 9 for the other cylinders, using the relevant F mark.
**11** As already stated, there is no means of adjustment of the ignition timing on these machines. If the ignition timing is incorrect, or

6.12a Fit a new O-ring and lubricate it . . .

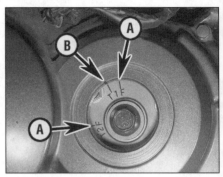
6.5 "F" marks (A), static timing mark (B)

suspected of being incorrect, one of the ignition system components is at fault, and the system must be tested as described in the preceding Sections of this Chapter.
**12** When the check is complete, install the timing inspection cover using a new O-ring and smear it and the cover threads with molybdenum disulphide oil (a 50/50 mixture of molybdenum disulphide grease and engine oil) **(see illustration)**. Tighten the cover to the torque setting specified at the beginning of the Chapter **(see illustration)**.

6.12b . . . then tighten the cover to the specified torque

# Chapter 6
# Frame, suspension and final drive

## Contents

## Degrees of difficulty

| Easy, suitable for novice with little experience  | Fairly easy, suitable for beginner with some experience  | Fairly difficult, suitable for competent DIY mechanic 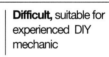 | Difficult, suitable for experienced DIY mechanic | Very difficult, suitable for expert DIY or professional |
| --- | --- | --- | --- | --- |

## Specifications

### Front forks

Fork oil type . . . . . . . . . . . . . . . . . . . . . . . . . . . . . . . . . . . . . . . . . . . 10W fork oil
Fork oil capacity
    VFR K models . . . . . . . . . . . . . . . . . . . . . . . . . . . . . . . . . . . . . . . . 450 cc
    VFR L, M and N models . . . . . . . . . . . . . . . . . . . . . . . . . . . . . . . . 390 cc
    RVF models . . . . . . . . . . . . . . . . . . . . . . . . . . . . . . . . . . . . . . . . . 445 cc
Fork oil level*
    VFR K models . . . . . . . . . . . . . . . . . . . . . . . . . . . . . . . . . . . . . . . . 90 mm
    VFR L, M and N models . . . . . . . . . . . . . . . . . . . . . . . . . . . . . . . . 122 mm
    RVF models . . . . . . . . . . . . . . . . . . . . . . . . . . . . . . . . . . . . . . . . . 74 mm

| | Standard | Service limit |
| --- | --- | --- |
| Fork spring free length (min) | | |
|     VFR K models . . . . . . . . . . . . . . . . . . . . . . . . . . . . . . . | Not available | Not available |
|     VFR L, M and N models . . . . . . . . . . . . . . . . . . . . . . . | 277.3 mm | 271.8 mm |
|     RVF models . . . . . . . . . . . . . . . . . . . . . . . . . . . . . . . | 234.2 mm | 229.5 mm |

Fork tube runout limit . . . . . . . . . . . . . . . . . . . . . . . . . . . . . . . . . . . . 0.2 mm
*Oil level is measured from the top of the tube with the fork spring removed and the leg fully compressed.

### Rear suspension

| | Standard | Service limit |
| --- | --- | --- |
| Shock absorber spring free length | | |
|     VFR K models . . . . . . . . . . . . . . . . . . . . . . . . . . . . . . . | Not available | Not available |
|     VFR L, M and N models . . . . . . . . . . . . . . . . . . . . . . . | 158.7 mm | 155.5 mm |
|     RVF models . . . . . . . . . . . . . . . . . . . . . . . . . . . . . . . | 121 mm | Not available |

### Final drive

Drive chain slack and lubricant . . . . . . . . . . . . . . . . . . . . . . . . . . . . See Chapter 1
Drive chain size . . . . . . . . . . . . . . . . . . . . . . . . . . . . . . . . . . . . . . . . 525, 104 links (VFR), 102 links (RVF)
Sprocket sizes
    Front (engine) sprocket . . . . . . . . . . . . . . . . . . . . . . . . . . . . . . . . . 15T
    Rear (wheel) sprocket . . . . . . . . . . . . . . . . . . . . . . . . . . . . . . . . . . 40T (VFR), 38T (RVF)

6

## Torque settings – specific components

| | |
|---|---|
| Footrest holder bolt | 45 Nm |
| Footrest bracket bolts | 27 Nm |
| Sidestand pivot bolt nut | 38 Nm |
| Sidestand bracket bolt | 35 Nm |
| Handlebar holder clamp bolts | |
|    VFR models | 12 Nm |
|    RVF models | 27 Nm |
| Top yoke fork clamp bolts | |
|    VFR models | 11 Nm |
|    RVF models | 23 Nm |
| Bottom yoke fork clamp bolts | 40 Nm |
| Steering stem nut | |
|    VFR models | 140 Nm |
|    RVF models | 105 Nm |
| Front brake master cylinder clamp bolts | 12 Nm |
| Fork damper rod bolt | 20 Nm |
| Fork top bolt | |
|    VFR K models | Not available |
|    VFR L, M and N models | 20 Nm |
|    RVF models | 35 Nm |
| Steering head bearing adjuster nut (see text) | |
|    VFR models | 50 Nm |
|    RVF models | 25 Nm |
| Shock absorber mounting bolt nuts | 45 Nm |
| Shock absorber linkage pivot bolt nuts | 45 Nm |
| Shock absorber linkage arm bolt nuts | 45 Nm |
| Swingarm pivot adjuster bolt | 15 Nm |
| Swingarm pivot adjuster bolt locknut | |
|    VFR models | 80 Nm |
|    RVF models | 65 Nm |
| Swingarm pivot bolt nut | 95 Nm |
| Front sprocket bolt | 55 Nm |
| Rear sprocket nuts | 35 Nm |
| Rear wheel bearing holder pinch bolt | 55 Nm |

## Torque settings – non-specified components

**Note:** *Where a specific setting is not given for a particular bolt/nut, these general settings apply. The dimension given applies to the diameter of the thread, not the head.*

| | |
|---|---|
| 5 mm bolt/nut | 5 Nm |
| 6 mm bolt/nut | 10 Nm |
| 8 mm bolt/nut | 22 Nm |
| 10 mm bolt/nut | 35 Nm |
| 12 mm bolt/nut | 55 Nm |
| 6 mm flange bolt with 8 mm head | 9 Nm |
| 6 mm flange bolt/nut with 10 mm head | 12 Nm |
| 8 mm flange bolt/nut | 27 Nm |
| 10 mm flange bolt/nut | 40 Nm |

## 1 General information

All models use a twin spar box-section aluminium frame which uses the engine as a stressed member.

Front suspension is by a pair of oil-damped telescopic forks. On VFR K models, the forks have a conventional damper system, while L, M and N models have a cartridge damper. RVF models have upside down forks with a cartridge damper. On all except VFR K models, the forks are adjustable for preload and damping.

At the rear, an alloy swingarm acts on a single shock absorber via a three-way linkage. The shock absorber is adjustable for spring preload and damping. On VFR L, M and N models, the shock absorber has a remote reservoir.

The drive to the rear wheel is by chain.

## 2 Frame – inspection and repair

1 The frame should not require attention unless accident damage has occurred. In most cases, frame replacement is the only satisfactory remedy for such damage. A few frame specialists have the jigs and other equipment necessary for straightening the frame to the required standard of accuracy, but even then there is no simple way of assessing to what extent the frame may have been over stressed.

2 After the machine has accumulated a lot of miles, the frame should be examined closely for signs of cracking or splitting at the welded joints. Loose engine mount bolts can cause ovaling or fracturing of the mounting tabs. Minor damage can often be repaired by welding, depending on the extent and nature of the damage.

3 Remember that a frame which is out of alignment will cause handling problems. If misalignment is suspected as the result of an accident, it will be necessary to strip the machine completely so the frame can be thoroughly checked.

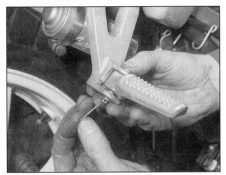

**3.1a  Remove the split pin and washer . . .**

**3.1b  . . . and withdraw the pivot pin**

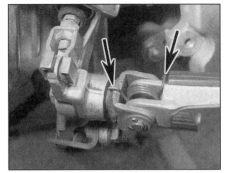

**3.1c  Note how the spring ends (arrowed) locate on the front footrest . . .**

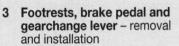

## 3  Footrests, brake pedal and gearchange lever – removal and installation

### Footrests

#### Removal

**1**  Remove the split pin and washer from the bottom of the footrest pivot pin, then withdraw the pivot pin and remove the footrest **(see illustrations)**. On the front footrests, note the fitting of the return spring **(see illustration)**. On the rear footrests, note the fitting of the detent plate, ball and spring, and take care that they do not spring out when removing the footrest **(see illustration)**.

#### Installation

**2**  Installation is the reverse of removal.

### Brake pedal

#### Removal

**3**  Unhook the brake pedal return spring and the brake light switch spring from the bracket on the pedal **(see illustration)**.
**4**  Remove the split pin from the clevis pin securing the brake pedal to the master cylinder pushrod **(see illustration)**. Remove the clevis pin and separate the pedal from the pushrod.
**5**  The pedal pivots on the footrest holder. Remove the bolt on the inside of the footrest bracket and remove the footrest and its holder

**(see illustration 3.3)**. Remove the thrust washer and slide the pedal off the holder. If required, remove the bolt securing the spring bracket and remove the bracket.

#### Installation

**6**  Installation is the reverse of removal, noting the following:
  a) *Apply molybdenum disulphide oil to the brake pedal pivot.*
  b) *Align the flat on the footrest holder with that in the bracket.*
  c) *Tighten the footrest holder bolt to the torque setting specified at the beginning of the Chapter.*
  d) *Use a new split pin on the clevis pin securing the brake pedal to the master cylinder pushrod.*
  e) *Check the operation of the rear brake light switch (see Chapter 1).*

### Gearchange lever

#### Removal

**7**  Slacken the gearchange lever linkage rod locknuts, then unscrew the rod and separate it from the lever and the arm (the rod is reverse-threaded on one end and so will simultaneously unscrew from both lever and arm when turned in the one direction) **(see illustration)**. Note how far the rod is threaded into the lever and arm as this determines the height of the lever relative to the footrest.

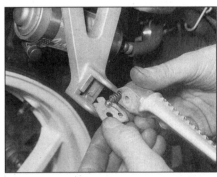

**3.1d  . . . and how the spring, ball and detent plate fit on the rear footrest**

**8**  The lever pivots on the footrest holder. Remove the bolt on the inside of the footrest bracket and remove the footrest and its holder. Slide the lever off the holder.

#### Installation

**9**  Installation is the reverse of removal, noting the following:
  a) *Apply molybdenum disulphide oil to the gear lever pivot.*
  b) *Align the flat on the footrest holder with that in the bracket.*
  c) *Tighten the footrest holder bolt to the torque setting specified at the beginning of the Chapter.*
  d) *Adjust the gear lever height as required by screwing the rod in or out of the lever and arm. Tighten the locknuts securely.*

**6**

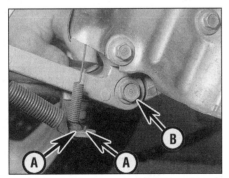

**3.3  Unhook the springs (A) from the bracket. Brake pedal/footrest holder bolt (B)**

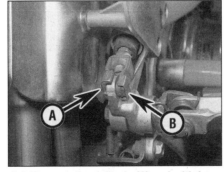

**3.4  Remove the split pin (A) and withdraw the clevis pin (B)**

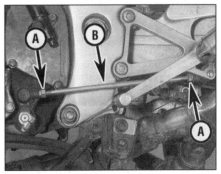

**3.7  Slacken the locknuts (A), then unscrew the linkage rod (B)**

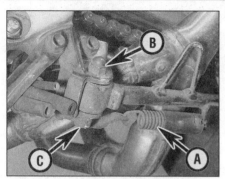

4.3 Unhook the spring (A), then unscrew the nut (B) and remove the bolt (C)

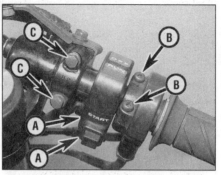

5.1 Handlebar switch screws (A), throttle housing screws (B), master cylinder clamp bolts (C)

5.6 Remove the clutch lever bracket bolts and the switch housing screws

## 4 Sidestand – removal and installation

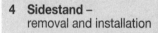

1 The sidestand is attached to a bracket on the frame. A spring anchored to the stand ensures that it is held in the retracted or extended position.

2 Support the bike using an auxiliary stand. On RVF models, remove the sidestand switch (see Chapter 9).

3 Unhook the stand spring and unscrew the nut securing the stand on the pivot bolt (see illustration). Remove the pivot bolt from the inside of the bracket and remove the stand, and on VFR models the thrust washers.

4 If required, unscrew the bolts securing the bracket to the frame and remove the bracket.

5 On installation apply grease to the pivot bolt shank and tighten the nut to the torque setting specified at the beginning of the Chapter. Reconnect the sidestand spring and check that it holds the stand securely up when not in use – an accident is almost certain to occur if the stand extends while the machine is in motion.

6 On RVF models, check the operation of the sidestand switch (see Chapter 1).

## 5 Handlebars and levers – removal and installation

### Right handlebar

#### Removal

**Note:** *On VFR models, the handlebars can be removed from the handlebar holders which clamp around the top of the forks, leaving the holders in place. On RVF models, the bars and holders cannot be separated.*

1 Unscrew the two handlebar switch screws and free the switch from the handlebar (see illustration). Unscrew the two throttle cable housing screws and release the throttle cables from the throttle grip. Position the switch housing and the throttle housing away from the handlebar.

2 Disconnect the brake light switch wires from the master cylinder assembly. Unscrew the two master cylinder assembly clamp bolts and position the assembly clear of the handlebar, making sure no strain is placed on the hydraulic hose (see illustration 5.1). Keep the master cylinder reservoir upright to prevent possible fluid leakage.

3 On VFR models, if removing the handlebar leaving the holder in place, unscrew the handlebar end-weight retaining screw, then remove the weight from the end of the handlebar and slide off the throttle twistgrip (see illustration 5.7a). Unscrew and remove the fork clamp bolt in the top yoke, then unscrew and remove the handlebar clamp bolt in the handlebar holder, noting how it locates in the cutout in the handlebar (see illustrations 5.7b and c). Using a flat-bladed screwdriver, spread the clamp slit to free the bar, then knock it through the holder from the outer end and withdraw it from the holder (see illustration 5.7d).

4 On VFR models, if removing the handlebar and holder together, and on RVF models, remove the steering stem nut cap, then unscrew the steering stem nut. Slacken both fork clamp bolts in the top yoke, then ease the yoke up and off the forks and position it aside (see illustrations in Section 18 of Chapter 1). Slacken the handlebar holder pinch bolts, then ease the handlebar up and off the fork (see illustrations 5.8a and b). If necessary, unscrew the handlebar end-weight retaining

screw, then remove the weight from the end of the handlebar and slide off the throttle twistgrip (see illustration 5.7a).

### Left handlebar
#### Removal

**Note:** *On VFR models, the handlebars can be removed from the handlebar holders which clamp around the top of the forks, leaving the holders in place. On RVF models, the bars and holders cannot be separated.*

5 Unscrew the two handlebar switch screws and free the switch from the handlebar. Position the switch housing away from the handlebar.

6 Disconnect the clutch switch wires from the switch in the clutch lever bracket. Unscrew the two lever assembly clamp bolts and position the assembly clear of the handlebar, making sure the cable is not unduly bent or kinked (see illustration).

7 On VFR models, if removing the handlebar leaving the holder in place, unscrew the handlebar end-weight retaining screw, then remove the weight from the end of the handlebar and remove the grip (see illustration). It may be necessary to slit the grip open using a sharp blade in order to remove it as they are sometimes stuck in place. This will mean using a new grip on assembly. Unscrew and remove the fork clamp bolt in the top yoke, then unscrew and remove the handlebar clamp bolt in the handlebar holder, noting how it locates in the cutout in the handlebar (see illustrations).

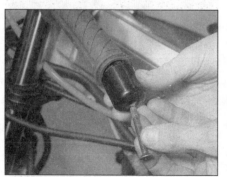

5.7a Remove the screw and the end-weight

5.7b Remove the fork clamp bolt . . .

5.7c ... and the handlebar clamp bolt ...

5.7d ... then spread the clamp and remove the handlebar

5.8a Handlebar holder pinch bolts (arrowed) – VFR models

Using a flat bladed screwdriver, spread the clamp slit to free the bar, then knock it through the holder from the outer end and withdraw it from the holder **(see illustration)**.
**8** On VFR models, if removing the handlebar and holder together, and on RVF models, remove the steering stem nut cap, then unscrew the steering stem nut. Slacken both fork clamp bolts in the top yoke, then ease the yoke up and off the forks and position it aside **(see illustrations in Section 18 of Chapter 1)**. Slacken the handlebar holder clamp bolts, then ease the handlebar up and off the fork **(see illustrations)**. If necessary, unscrew the handlebar end-weight retaining screw, then remove the weight from the end of the handlebar and remove the grip **(see illustration 5.7a)**. It may be necessary to slit the grip open using a sharp blade in order to remove it as they are sometimes stuck in place. This will mean using a new grip on assembly.

### Installation

**9** Installation is the reverse of removal, noting the following.
a) On VFR models, when installing the handlebar into the holder, align the cutout in the bar with the bolt hole in the holder, so that the bolt locates the bar in the correct position **(see illustration)**.
b) When fitting the top yoke onto the forks, align the lug on the top of each handlebar holder with the slot in the yoke, so that

the handlebars are set in the correct position **(see illustration)**.
c) Refer to the Specifications at the beginning of the Chapter and tighten the handlebar holder clamp bolts, the fork clamp bolts and the steering stem nut to the specified torque settings.
d) Make sure the front brake and clutch lever assembly clamps are installed with the UP mark facing up. Tighten the brake master cylinder clamp bolts to the torque setting specified at the beginning of the Chapter.
e) Make sure the pin in the lower half of each switch housing locates in the hole in the underside of the handlebar **(see illustration)**.

5.8b Handlebar holder pinch bolt (arrowed) – RVF models

f) If removed, apply a suitable non-permanent locking compound to the handlebar end-weight retaining screws. If new grips are being fitted, secure them using a suitable adhesive.
g) Do not forget to reconnect the front brake light switch and clutch switch wiring connectors.

### Clutch lever
#### Removal

**10** Slacken the clutch cable adjuster lockring and thread the adjuster fully into the bracket to provide maximum freeplay in the cable **(see illustration)**. Unscrew the lever pivot bolt locknut, then withdraw the pivot bolt and

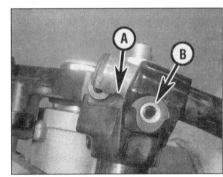

5.9a Align the cutout (A) with the bolt hole (B)

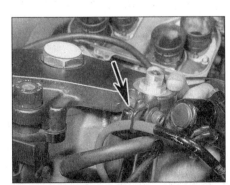

5.9b Make sure the lug (arrowed) on the holder locates correctly into the top yoke – VFR model shown

5.9c Locate the pin (arrowed) into the hole in the handlebar

5.10a Slacken the lockring (arrowed) and thread the adjuster into the bracket

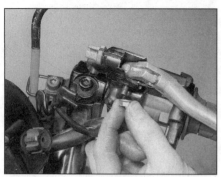

5.10b Remove the locknut, then withdraw the pivot bolt and remove the lever

5.11a Unscrew the nut . . .

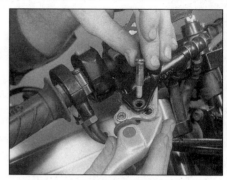

5.11b . . . withdraw the bolt and remove the lever

5.11c Note how the span adjuster assembly fits

remove the lever, detaching the cable nipple as you do (see illustration).

### Front brake lever

#### Removal

**11** Unscrew the lever pivot bolt locknut, then withdraw the pivot bolt and remove the lever **(see illustrations)**. If required, separate the lever from the span adjuster assembly, noting how it fits **(see illustration)**.

#### Installation

**12** Installation is the reverse of removal. Apply grease to the pivot bolt shafts and the contact areas between the lever and its bracket, and to the clutch cable nipple **(see illustration)**. Adjust the clutch cable freeplay (see Chapter 1).

5.12 Apply grease to the pivot bolt shaft

## 6  Forks –
removal and installation

### Removal

*Caution: Although not strictly necessary, before removing the forks it is recommended that the fairing and fairing panels are removed (see Chapter 8). This will prevent accidental damage to the paintwork.*

**1** Remove the front wheel (see Chapter 7).
**2** Remove the front mudguard (see Chapter 8).
**3** Slacken the handlebar holder clamp bolts **(see illustration 5.8a and b)** and the fork

clamp bolts in the top yoke **(see illustration)**. If the forks are to be disassembled, or if the fork oil is being changed, it is advisable to slacken the fork top bolts at this stage **(see illustration)**.

> **HAYNES HINT** *Slackening the fork clamp bolts in the top yoke before slackening the fork top bolts releases pressure on the top bolt. This makes it much easier to remove and helps to preserve the threads.*

**4** Slacken but do not remove the fork clamp bolts in the bottom yoke, and remove the forks by twisting them and pulling them downwards **(see illustration)**. As the forks drop clear of the top yoke, draw the handlebar assemblies and the wiring ties or hose guide (VFR models) off the top, and remove the circlip, which supports the handlebar holders, from its groove in the fork **(see illustration)**. Support the right handlebar so that no strain is placed on the brake master cylinder hose and the reservoir is upright.

> **HAYNES HINT** *If the fork legs are seized in the yokes, spray the area with penetrating oil and allow time for it to soak in before trying again.*

6.3a Fork clamp bolts (arrowed)

6.3b Fork top bolt (arrowed)

6.4a Slacken the bottom yoke fork clamp bolt (arrowed) . . .

**6.4b . . . and withdraw the fork, removing the handlebar, cable ties or hose guide, and the circlip (arrowed) as you do**

**6.5a Fit the circlip . . .**

**6.5b . . . making sure it fits into its groove . . .**

## Installation

**5** Remove all traces of corrosion from the fork tubes and the yokes. Slide the forks up through the bottom yoke, then install the circlip, wiring ties and the handlebars onto the forks **(see illustration)**. Make sure the circlip locates properly into the groove in the fork, and press the handlebar holders down onto the ring so that it locates up inside the base of the holder **(see illustration)**. Slide the forks up into the top yoke, aligning the handlebar holders so that the lug on the top locates into its slot in the top yoke **(see illustration 5.9b)**. Make sure the forks are pushed fully home, so that the handlebar holders are held securely between the top yoke and the circlip. Check that the amount of protrusion of the fork tube above the top yoke is equal on both sides.

**6** Tighten the fork clamp bolts in the bottom yoke to the torque setting specified at the beginning of the Chapter **(see illustration)**. If the fork legs have been dismantled or if the fork oil has been changed, the fork top bolts should now be tightened to the specified torque setting. Now tighten the fork clamp bolts in the top yoke and the handlebar holder clamp bolts to the specified torque setting.

**7** Install the front wheel (see Chapter 7), and the front brace and mudguard (see Chapter 8).

**8** Check the operation of the front forks and brakes before taking the machine out on the road.

**6.5c . . . and that it locates into the base of the handlebar holder**

**6.6 Tighten the various clamp bolts to their specified torque settings**

## 7 Forks – disassembly, inspection and reassembly

## VFR K models

### Disassembly

**1** Always dismantle the fork legs separately to avoid interchanging parts and thus causing an accelerated rate of wear. Store all components in separate, clearly marked containers **(see illustration)**.

**2** Before dismantling the fork, it is advised that the damper rod bolt be slackened at this stage. Compress the fork tube in the slider so

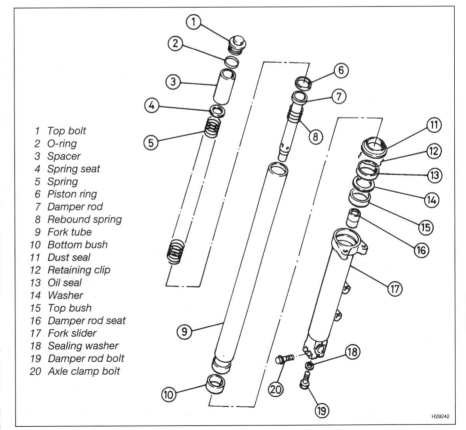

1  Top bolt
2  O-ring
3  Spacer
4  Spring seat
5  Spring
6  Piston ring
7  Damper rod
8  Rebound spring
9  Fork tube
10  Bottom bush
11  Dust seal
12  Retaining clip
13  Oil seal
14  Washer
15  Top bush
16  Damper rod seat
17  Fork slider
18  Sealing washer
19  Damper rod bolt
20  Axle clamp bolt

**7.1 Front fork components – VFR K models**

H29242

**6**

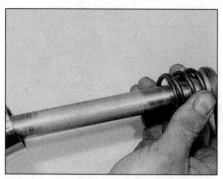

7.8 Withdraw the damper rod and rebound spring from the tube

7.9 Prise out the dust seal using a flat-bladed screwdriver

7.10 Prise out the retaining clip using a flat-bladed screwdriver

that the spring exerts maximum pressure on the damper rod head, then have an assistant slacken the damper rod bolt in the base of the fork slider **(see illustration 7.31)**. If an assistant is not available, clamp the brake caliper mounting lugs in a soft-jawed vice to support the fork. If required, remove the circlip securing the mudguard holder to the top of the fork slider and remove the holder.

3 If the fork top bolt was not slackened with the fork in situ, carefully clamp the fork tube in a vice equipped with soft jaws, taking care not to overtighten or score its surface, and slacken the top bolt.

4 Unscrew the fork top bolt from the top of the fork tube.

 *Warning: The fork spring is pressing on the fork top bolt with considerable pressure. Unscrew the bolt very carefully, keeping a downward pressure on it and release it slowly as it is likely to spring clear. It is advisable to wear some form of eye and face protection when carrying out this operation.*

5 Slide the fork tube down into the slider and withdraw the spacer, spring seat and the spring from the tube **(see illustrations 7.26c, b and a)**. Note which way up the spring is fitted, ie whether the closer-spaced spring coils are at the top or bottom of the spring.

6 Invert the fork leg over a suitable container and pump the fork vigorously to expel as much fork oil as possible.

7 Remove the previously slackened damper rod bolt and its copper sealing washer from the bottom of the slider. Discard the sealing washer as a new one must be used on reassembly. If the damper rod bolt was not slackened before dismantling the fork, it may be necessary to re-install the spring, spring seat, spacer and top bolt to prevent the damper rod from turning. Alternatively, a long metal bar or length of wood doweling (such as a broom handle) passed down through the fork tube and pressed hard into the damper rod head quite often suffices.

8 Invert the fork and withdraw the damper rod from inside the fork tube. Remove the rebound spring from the damper rod **(see illustration)**.

9 Carefully prise out the dust seal from the top of the slider to gain access to the oil seal retaining clip **(see illustration)**. Discard the dust seal as a new one must be used.

10 Carefully remove the retaining clip, taking care not to scratch the surface of the tube **(see illustration)**.

11 To separate the tube from the slider it is necessary to displace the top bush and oil seal. The bottom bush should not pass through the top bush, and this can be used to good effect. Push the tube gently inwards until it stops against the damper rod seat. Take care not to do this forcibly or the seat may be damaged. Then pull the tube sharply outwards until the bottom bush strikes the top

bush. Repeat this operation until the top bush and seal are tapped out of the slider **(see illustration)**.

12 With the tube removed, slide off the oil seal and its washer, noting which way up they fit **(see illustration)**. Discard the oil seal as a new one must be used. The top bush can then also be slid off its upper end.

*Caution: Do not remove the bottom bush from the tube unless it is to be replaced.*

13 Tip the damper rod seat out of the slider, noting which way up it fits.

### Inspection

14 Clean all parts in solvent and blow them dry with compressed air, if available. Check the fork tube for score marks, scratches, flaking of the chrome finish and excessive or abnormal wear. Look for dents in the tube and replace the tube in both forks if any are found. Check the fork seal seat for nicks, gouges and scratches. If damage is evident, leaks will occur. Also check the oil seal washer for damage or distortion and replace it if necessary.

15 Check the fork tube for runout using V-blocks and a dial gauge, or have it done at a dealer service department or other repair shop **(see illustration)**. If the amount of runout exceeds the service limit specified, the tube should be replaced.

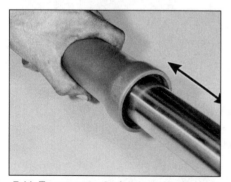

7.11 To separate the inner and outer fork tubes, pull them apart firmly several times – the slide hammer effect will pull the tubes apart

7.12 The oil seal (1), washer (2), top bush (3) and bottom bush (4) will come out with the fork tube

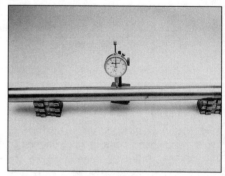

7.15 Check the fork tube for runout using V-blocks and a dial indicator

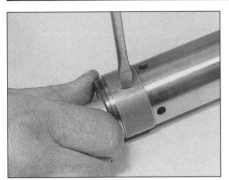

**7.17  Prise off the bottom bush using a flat-bladed screwdriver**

**7.18  Replace the damper rod piston ring if it is worn or damaged**

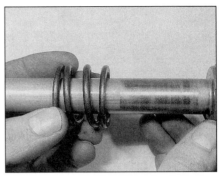

**7.19a  Slide the rebound spring onto the damper rod**

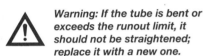

*Warning: If the tube is bent or exceeds the runout limit, it should not be straightened; replace it with a new one.*

**16**  Check the spring for cracks and other damage. Measure the spring free length and compare the measurement to the specifications at the beginning of the Chapter. If it is defective or sagged below the service limit, replace the springs in both forks with new ones. Never replace only one spring. Also check the rebound spring.

**17**  Examine the working surfaces of the two bushes; if worn or scuffed they must be replaced. To remove the bottom bush from the fork tube, prise it apart at the slit using a flat-bladed screwdriver and slide it off **(see illustration)**. Make sure the new one seats properly.

**18**  Check the damper rod and its piston ring for damage and wear, and replace them if necessary **(see illustration)**. Do not remove the rings from the piston unless they are being replaced

### Reassembly

**19**  If removed, install the piston ring into the groove in the damper rod head, then slide the rebound spring onto the rod **(see illustration)**. Insert the damper rod into the fork tube and slide it into place so that it projects fully from the bottom of the tube, then install the seat on the bottom of the damper rod **(see illustration)**.

**20**  Oil the fork tube and bottom bush with the specified fork oil and insert the assembly into the slider **(see illustration)**. Fit a new copper sealing washer to the damper rod bolt and apply a few drops of a suitable non-permanent thread locking compound, then install the bolt into the bottom of the slider **(see illustration)**. Tighten the bolt to the specified torque setting. If the damper rod rotates inside the tube, temporarily install the fork spring and top bolt (see Steps 26 and 27) and compress the fork to hold the damper rod. Alternatively, a long metal bar or length of wood doweling (such as a broom handle) pressed hard into the damper rod head quite often suffices. Otherwise, wait until the fork is fully reassembled before tightening the bolt.

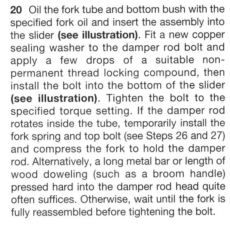

**7.19b  Fit the seat to the bottom of the rod**

**7.20b  Apply a thread locking compound to the damper rod bolt and use a new sealing washer**

**21**  Push the fork tube fully into the slider, then oil the top bush and slide it down over the tube **(see illustration)**. Press the bush squarely into its recess in the slider as far as possible, then install the oil seal washer **(see illustration)**. Either use the Honda service tool or a suitable piece of tubing to tap the bush fully into place; the tubing must be slightly larger in diameter than the fork tube and slightly smaller in diameter than the bush recess in the slider. Take care not to scratch the fork tube during this operation; it is best to make sure that the fork tube is pushed fully into the slider so that any accidental scratching is confined to the area above the oil seal.

**22**  When the bush is seated fully and

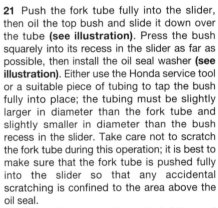

**7.20a  Slide the tube into the slider**

**7.21a  Install the top bush . . .**

**7.21b  . . . followed by the washer**

**6**

7.22 Make sure the oil seal is the correct way up

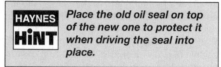

7.23 Install the retaining clip . . .

7.24 . . . followed by the dust seal . . .

squarely in its recess in the slider, (remove the washer to check, wipe the recess clean, then reinstall the washer), install the new oil seal.

 **HAYNES HiNT** *Wrap some insulating tape around the circlip groove in the top of the fork tube – this will prevent the possibility of damage to the oil seal lips as it is slid down the tube.*

Smear the seal's lips with fork oil and slide it over the tube so that its markings face upwards and drive the seal into place as described in Step 21 until the retaining clip groove is visible above the seal.**(see illustration)**.

**HAYNES HiNT** *Place the old oil seal on top of the new one to protect it when driving the seal into place.*

23 Once the seal is correctly seated, fit the retaining clip, making sure it is correctly located in its groove **(see illustration)**.
24 Lubricate the lips of the new dust seal then slide it down the fork tube and press it into position **(see illustration)**.
25 Slowly pour in the specified quantity of the specified grade of fork oil and pump the fork at least ten times to distribute it evenly **(see illustration)**; the oil level should also be measured and adjustment made by adding or subtracting oil. Fully compress the fork tube

into the slider and measure the fork oil level from the top of the tube **(see illustration)**. Add or subtract fork oil until it is at the level specified at the beginning of the Chapter.
26 Clamp the slider in a soft-jawed vice using the brake caliper mounting lugs, taking care not to overtighten and damage them. Pull the fork tube out of the slider as far as possible then install the spring with its closer-spaced coils at the top, followed by the spring seat and the spacer **(see illustrations)**.
27 Fit a new O-ring to the fork top bolt and thread the bolt into the top of the fork tube.

⚠️ *Warning: It will be necessary to compress the spring by pressing it down using the top bolt to engage the threads of the top bolt with the fork tube. This is a potentially dangerous operation and should be performed with care, using an assistant if necessary. Wipe off any excess oil before starting to prevent the possibility of slipping.*

Keep the fork tube fully extended whilst pressing on the spring. Screw the top bolt carefully into the fork tube making sure it is not cross-threaded. **Note:** *The top bolt can be tightened to the specified torque setting at this stage if the tube is held between the padded jaws of a vice, but do not risk distorting the tube by doing so. A better method is to tighten the top bolt when the fork has been installed in the bike and is securely held in the bottom yoke.*

7.25a Pour the oil into the top of the tube

7.25b Measure the oil level with the fork held vertical

7.26a Install the spring . . .

7.26b . . . followed by the spring seat . . .

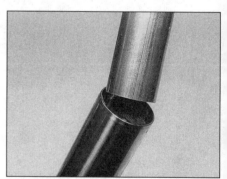

7.26c . . . and the spacer . . .

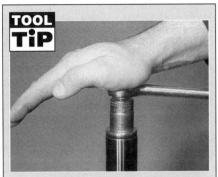

*Use a ratchet-type tool when installing the fork top bolt. This makes it unnecessary to remove the tool from the bolt whilst threading it in, making it easier to maintain a downward pressure on the spring.*

**28**  Remove the insulating tape from around the circlip groove in the fork tube. If removed, fit the mudguard holder onto the top of the slider, noting that each is marked L or R according to its side, and secure it with its circlip.

**29**  Install the forks (see Section 6). Set the spring preload adjuster as required (see Section 11).

## VFR L, M and N models

### Disassembly

**30**  Always dismantle the fork legs separately to avoid interchanging parts and thus causing an accelerated rate of wear. Store all components in separate, clearly marked containers **(see illustration)**.

**31**  Before dismantling the fork, it is advised that the damper rod bolt be slackened at this stage. Compress the fork tube in the slider so that the spring exerts maximum pressure on the damper rod head, then have an assistant slacken the damper rod bolt in the base of the fork slider **(see illustration)**. If required, remove the circlip securing the mudguard holder to the top of the fork slider and remove the holder.

**32**  Set the spring preload adjuster to its minimum setting (see Section 11). If the fork top bolt was not slackened with the fork in situ, carefully clamp the fork tube in a vice equipped with soft jaws, taking care not to overtighten or score its surface, and slacken the top bolt.

**33**  Unscrew the fork top bolt from the top of the fork tube **(see illustration 7.59)**. The bolt will remain threaded on the damper rod.

**34**  Carefully clamp the fork slider in a vice and slide the fork tube down into the slider a little way (wrap a rag around the top of the tube to minimise oil spillage) while, with the aid of an assistant if necessary, keeping the damper rod fully extended. Counter-hold the preload adjuster and unscrew the fork top bolt from the damper rod **(see illustration 7.30)**.

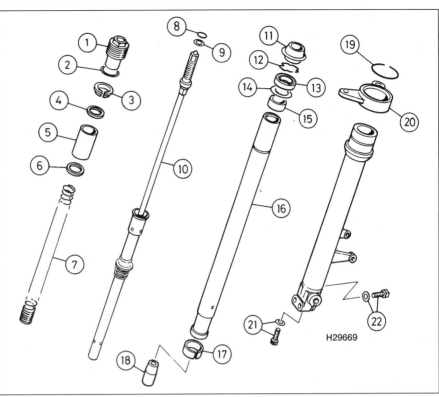

**7.30  Front fork components – VFR L, M and N models**

| 1 | Top bolt | 9 | Circlip | 16 | Fork tube |
|---|----------|---|---------|----|-----------|
| 2 | O-ring | 10 | Damper rod | 17 | Bottom bush |
| 3 | Slotted spring collar | 11 | Dust seal | 18 | Damper rod seat |
| 4 | Washer | 12 | Retaining clip | 19 | Circlip |
| 5 | Spacer | 13 | Oil seal | 20 | Mudguard holder |
| 6 | Spring seat | 14 | Washer | 21 | Damper rod bolt and |
| 7 | Spring | 15 | Top bush | | sealing washer |
| 8 | O-ring | | | | |

**35**  Remove the slotted spring collar by slipping it out to the side **(see illustration 7.57)**, then remove the washer, the spacer and the spring seat **(see illustration 7.56d, c and b)**. Note which way up the spring is fitted, ie whether the closer-spaced spring coils are at the top or bottom of the spring **(see illustration 7.56a)**.

**36**  Invert the fork leg over a suitable container and pump the fork vigorously to expel as much fork oil as possible.

**37**  Remove the previously slackened damper rod bolt and its copper sealing washer from the bottom of the slider **(see illustration)**. Discard the sealing washer as a new one must be used on reassembly.

**38**  Invert the fork and withdraw the damper rod from inside the fork tube **(see illustration 7.49a)**.

**7.31  Slacken the damper rod bolt**

**7.37  Unscrew and remove the damper rod bolt**

**6**

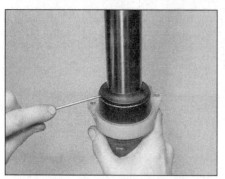
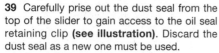

**7.39 Prise out the dust seal using a flat-bladed screwdriver**

**7.40 Prise out the retaining clip using a flat-bladed screwdriver**

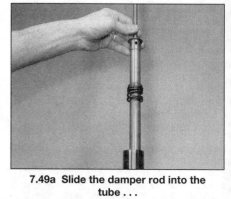

**7.49a Slide the damper rod into the tube . . .**

39 Carefully prise out the dust seal from the top of the slider to gain access to the oil seal retaining clip **(see illustration)**. Discard the dust seal as a new one must be used.

40 Carefully remove the retaining clip, taking care not to scratch the surface of the tube **(see illustration)**.

41 To separate the tube from the slider it is necessary to displace the top bush and oil seal. The bottom bush should not pass through the top bush, and this can be used to good effect. Push the tube gently inwards until it stops against the damper rod seat. Take care not to do this forcibly or the seat may be damaged. Then pull the tube sharply outwards until the bottom bush strikes the top bush. Repeat this operation until the top bush and seal are tapped out of the slider **(see illustration 7.11)**.

42 With the tube removed, slide off the oil seal, washer and top bush, noting which way up they fit **(see illustration 7.12)**. Discard the oil seal as a new one must be used.

*Caution: Do not remove the bottom bush from the tube unless it is to be replaced.*

43 Tip the damper rod seat out of the slider, noting which way up it fits.

## Inspection

44 Clean all parts in solvent and blow them dry with compressed air, if available. Check the fork tube for score marks, scratches, flaking of the chrome finish and excessive or abnormal wear. Look for dents in the tube and replace the tube

in both forks if any are found. Check the fork seal seat for nicks, gouges and scratches. If damage is evident, leaks will occur. Also check the oil seal washer for damage or distortion and replace it if necessary.

45 Check the fork tube for runout using V-blocks and a dial gauge **(see illustration 7.15)**. If the amount of runout exceeds the service limit specified, the tube should be replaced.

⚠ *Warning: If the tube is bent or exceeds the runout limit, it should not be straightened; replace it with a new one.*

46 Check the spring for cracks and other damage. Measure the spring free length and compare the measurement to the specifications at the beginning of the Chapter. If it is defective or sagged below the service limit, replace the springs in both forks with new ones. Never replace only one spring.

47 Examine the working surfaces of the two bushes; if worn or scuffed they must be replaced. To remove the bottom bush from the fork tube, prise it apart at the slit using a flat-bladed screwdriver and slide it off **(see illustration 7.17)**. Make sure the new one seats properly.

48 Check the damper rod assembly for damage and wear, and replace it if necessary. Holding the outside of the damper, pump the rod in and out of the damper. If the rod does not move smoothly in the damper it must be replaced.

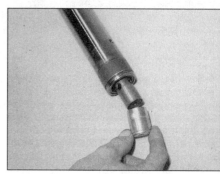

**7.49b . . . and fit the seat to the bottom of the rod**

## Reassembly

49 Insert the damper rod into the fork tube and slide it into place so that it projects fully from the bottom of the tube, then install the seat on the bottom of the damper rod **(see illustrations)**.

50 Oil the fork tube and bottom bush with the specified fork oil and insert the assembly into the slider **(see illustration)**. Fit a new copper sealing washer to the damper rod bolt and apply a few drops of a suitable non-permanent thread locking compound, then install the bolt into the bottom of the slider **(see illustration)**. Tighten the bolt to the specified torque setting **(see illustration)**. If the damper rod rotates inside the tube, wait until the fork is fully reassembled before tightening the bolt.

**7.50a Slide the tube into the slider**

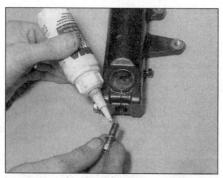

**7.50b Apply a thread locking compound to the damper rod bolt and use a new sealing washer . . .**

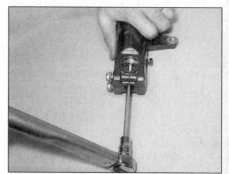

**7.50c . . . and tighten the bolt to the specified torque**

**51** Push the fork tube fully into the slider, then oil the top bush and slide it down over the tube **(see illustration)**. Press the bush squarely into its recess in the slider as far as possible, then install the oil seal washer with its flat side facing up **(see illustration)**. Either use the service tool (Pt. Nos. 07947-KA50100 and 07947-KF00100) or a suitable piece of tubing to tap the bush fully into place; the tubing must be slightly larger in diameter than the fork tube and slightly smaller in diameter than the bush recess in the slider. Take care not to scratch the fork tube during this operation; it is best to make sure that the fork tube is pushed fully into the slider so that any accidental scratching is confined to the area above the oil seal.

**52** When the bush is seated fully and squarely in its recess in the slider, (remove the washer to check, wipe the recess clean, then reinstall the washer), install the new oil seal.

**HAYNES HINT**

*Wrap some insulating tape around the circlip groove in the top of the fork tube – this will prevent the possibility of damage to the oil seal lips as it is slid down the tube.*

Smear the seal's lips with fork oil and slide it over the tube so that its markings face upwards and drive the seal into place as described in Step 51 until the retaining clip groove is visible above the seal **(see illustration)**.

**HAYNES HINT**

*Place the old oil seal on top of the new one to protect it when driving the seal into place.*

7.51a  Install the top bush . . .

7.52  Make sure the oil seal is the correct way up

**53** Once the seal is correctly seated, fit the retaining clip, making sure it is correctly located in its groove **(see illustration)**.

**54** Lubricate the lips of the new dust seal then slide it down the fork tube and press it into position **(see illustration)**.

**55** Slowly pour in the specified quantity of the specified grade of fork oil and pump the fork and damper rod at least ten times each to distribute it evenly **(see illustration)**; the oil level should also be measured and adjustment made by adding or subtracting oil. Fully compress the fork tube and damper rod into the slider and measure the fork oil level from the top of the tube **(see illustration)**. Add or subtract fork oil until it is at the level specified at the beginning of the Chapter.

**56** Clamp the slider in a vice via the brake caliper mounting lugs, taking care not to

7.51b  . . . followed by the washer

7.53  Install the retaining clip . . .

7.54  . . . followed by the dust seal

overtighten and damage them. Pull the fork tube and damper rod out of the slider as far as possible then install the spring with its closer-wound coils at the bottom **(see illustration)**.

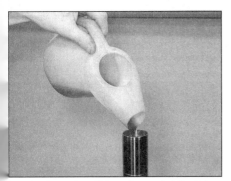

7.55a  Pour the oil into the top of the tube

7.55b  Measure the oil level with the fork held vertical

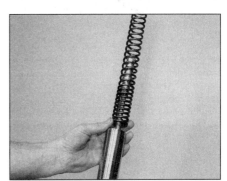

7.56a  Install the spring . . .

7.56b ... followed by the spring seat ...

7.56c ... the spacer ...

7.56d ... and the washer

7.57 Fit the slotted collar between the nut and the upper spring seat

7.58a Fit a new O-ring ...

7.58b ... then thread the top bolt onto the damper rod

7.59 Thread the top bolt into the tube

Install the spring seat, the spacer and the washer **(see illustrations)**.
**57** Slide the slotted spring collar into position between the upper spring seat and the nut on the damper rod **(see illustration)**.
**58** Fit a new O-ring onto the fork top bolt, then thread the top bolt fully, but not tightly, onto the damper rod, using a spanner on either the nut or the preload adjuster to prevent the rod from turning **(see illustrations)**.
**59** Withdraw the tube fully from the slider and carefully screw the top bolt into the fork tube making sure it is not cross-threaded **(see illustration)**. **Note:** *The top bolt can be tightened to the specified torque setting at this stage if the tube is held between the padded jaws of a vice, but do not risk distorting the tube by doing so. A better*

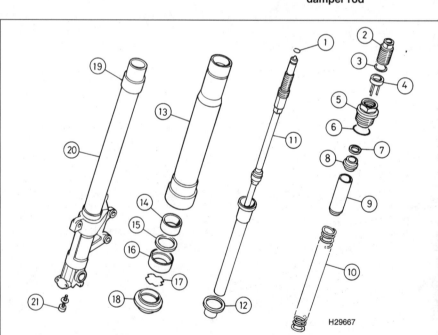

7.62 Front fork components – RVF models

| | | |
|---|---|---|
| 1  Circlip | 9  Spacer and lower spring seat | 16  Oil seal |
| 2  Pre-load adjuster | | 17  Retaining clip |
| 3  O-ring | 10  Spring | 18  Dust seal |
| 4  Adjuster tripod | 11  Damper rod | 19  Top bush |
| 5  Top bolt | 12  Damper rod seat | 20  Fork slider |
| 6  O-ring | 13  Fork tube | 21  Damper rod bolt and sealing washer |
| 7  Washer | 14  Bottom bush | |
| 8  Upper spring seat | 15  Washer | |

H29667

7.64a  Remove the circlip . . .

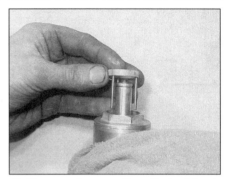

7.64b  . . . then unscrew the pre-load
adjuster . . .

7.46c  . . . and remove the adjuster tripod

*method is to tighten the top bolt when the fork leg has been installed and is securely held in the triple clamps.*

**TOOL TiP** *Use a ratchet-type tool when installing the fork top bolt. This makes it unnecessary to remove the tool from the bolt whilst threading it in making it easier to maintain a downward pressure on the spring.*

If the damper rod Allen bolt requires tightening (see Step 50), clamp the fork slider between the padded jaws of a vice and have an assistant compress the tube into the slider so that maximum spring pressure is placed on the damper rod head – tighten the damper Allen bolt to the specified torque setting **(see illustration 7.50c)**.

60  Remove the insulating tape from around the circlip groove in the fork tube. If removed, fit the mudguard holder onto the top of the slider, noting that each is marked L or R according to its side, and secure it with its circlip.

61  Install the forks (see Section 6). Set the spring preload adjuster as required (see Section 11).

## RVF models

### Disassembly

62  Always dismantle the fork legs separately to avoid interchanging parts and thus causing

an accelerated rate of wear. Store all components in separate, clearly marked containers **(see illustration on opposite page)**.

63  Before dismantling the fork, it is advised that the damper rod bolt be slackened at this stage. Compress the fork tube in the slider so that the spring exerts maximum pressure on the damper rod head, then have an assistant slacken the damper rod bolt in the base of the fork slider **(see illustration 7.31)**.

64  Remove the circlip from the top of the damper rod protruding from the fork top bolt **(see illustration)**. Unscrew and remove the preload adjuster, then withdraw the adjuster tripod using either a magnet, or a piece of wire or welding rod, flattened at the end and hooked over slightly, to remove it **(see illustrations)**. If the fork top bolt was not slackened with the fork in situ, carefully clamp the fork tube in a vice equipped with soft jaws, taking care not to overtighten or score its surface, and slacken the top bolt.

65  Unscrew the fork top bolt from the top of the fork tube **(see illustration 7.91)**. The bolt will remain threaded on the damper rod.

66  Carefully clamp the fork slider in a vice and slide the fork tube fully down onto the slider (wrap a rag around the top of the tube to minimise oil spillage) while, with the aid of an assistant if necessary, keeping the damper rod fully extended. Push down on the spacer and insert a spanner between the washer and the bottom of the top bolt and fit it onto the flats on the damper rod, Use it to counter-

hold the damper rod, then unscrew the fork top bolt from the rod **(see illustration)**.

67  Remove the washer, then remove the seat, the spacer and the spring seat (which fits into the bottom of the spacer and will probably come away with it). Note which way up the spring is fitted, ie whether the taped end is positioned downwards or upwards.

68  Invert the fork leg over a suitable container and pump the fork vigorously to expel as much fork oil as possible.

69  Remove the previously slackened damper rod bolt and its copper sealing washer from the bottom of the slider **(see illustration 7.37)**. Discard the sealing washer as a new one must be used on reassembly.

70  Invert the fork and withdraw the damper rod from inside the fork tube. The damper rod seat may come away with the rod, otherwise remove it later (see Step 75).

71  Carefully prise out the dust seal from the bottom of the tube to gain access to the oil seal retaining clip **(see illustration)**. Discard the dust seal as a new one must be used.

72  Carefully remove the retaining clip, taking care not to scratch the surface of the tube **(see illustration)**.

73  To separate the slider from the tube it is necessary to displace the bottom bush and oil seal. The top bush should not pass through the bottom bush, and this can be used to good effect. Push the slider gently inwards until it stops. Take care not to do this forcibly. Then pull the slider sharply outwards until the

7.66  Locate the spanner as described and unscrew the top bolt (arrowed)

7.71  Prise off the dust seal . . .

7.72  . . . then lever out the retaining clip using a flat-bladed screwdriver

**6**

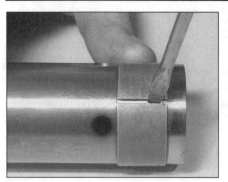

7.74a Carefully lever apart the ends of the top bush and remove it from the slider

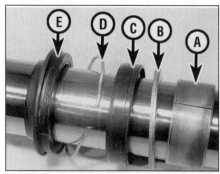

7.74b Bottom bush (A), oil seal washer (B), oil seal (C), retaining clip (D), dust seal (E)

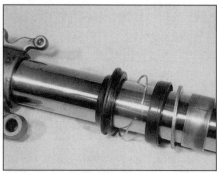

7.81a Slide the dust seal, the retaining clip, the oil seal, the oil seal washer and the bottom bush onto the slider as shown

top bush strikes the bottom bush. Repeat this operation until the bottom bush and seal are tapped out of the slider (see illustration 7.11).

74 With the tube and slider separated, remove the top bush from the slider by carefully levering its ends apart using a screwdriver (see illustration). Slide the bottom bush, the oil seal washer, the oil seal, the retaining clip and the dust seal off the slider, noting which way up they fit (see illustration). Discard the oil seal and the dust seal as new ones must be used.

75 If the damper rod seat did not come out with the rod, tip it out of the slider, noting which way up it fits.

### Inspection

76 Clean all parts in solvent and blow them dry with compressed air, if available. Check the fork tube for score marks, scratches, flaking of the chrome finish and excessive or abnormal wear. Look for dents in the tube and replace the tube in both forks if any are found. Check the fork seal seat for nicks, gouges and scratches. If damage is evident, leaks will occur. Also check the oil seal washer for damage or distortion and replace it if necessary.

77 Check the fork slider for runout using V-blocks and a dial gauge, or have it done at a dealer service department or other repair shop (see illustration 7.15). If the amount of

runout exceeds the service limit specified, the slider should be replaced.

> ⚠️ **Warning: If the slider is bent or exceeds the runout limit, it should not be straightened; replace it with a new one.**

78 Check the spring for cracks and other damage. Measure the spring free length and compare the measurement to the specifications at the beginning of the Chapter. If it is defective or sagged below the service limit, replace the springs in both forks with new ones. Never replace only one spring.

79 Examine the working surfaces of the two bushes; if worn or scuffed they must be replaced.

80 Check the damper rod assembly for damage and wear, and replace it if necessary. Holding the outside of the damper, pump the rod in and out of the damper. If the rod does not move smoothly in the damper it must be replaced.

### Reassembly

81 Wrap some insulating tip over the ridges on the end of the fork slider to protect the lips of the new oil seal as it is installed. Apply a smear of the specified clean fork oil to the lips of the oil seal and the inner surface of each bush, then slide the new dust seal, the retaining clip, the oil seal, the oil seal washer and the bottom bush onto the fork slider, making sure that the marked side of the oil

seal faces the dust seal (see illustration). Remove the insulating tape and fit the top bush into its recess in the slider (see illustration).

82 Apply a smear of the specified clean fork oil to the outer surface of each bush, then carefully insert the slider fully into the fork tube (see illustration).

83 Support the fork upside down, then press the bottom bush squarely into its recess in the fork tube as far as possible (see illustration). Slide the oil seal washer on top of the bush, and keep the oil seal, the retaining clip and the dust seal out of the way by sliding them up the slider. If necessary, tape them to the slider to prevent them from falling down and interfering as the bush is drifted into place.

84 Using either the special service tool (part nos. 07KMD-KZ30100 and 07RMD-MW40100) or a suitable drift, carefully drive the bottom bush fully into its recess using the oil seal washer to prevent damaging the edges of the bush. Make sure the bush enters the recess squarely, and take care not to scratch or gouge the slider (it is best to make sure that the fork slider is pushed fully into the tube so that any accidental scratching is confined to the area that does not affect the oil seal).

85 When the bush is seated fully and squarely in its recess in the tube, (remove the washer to check, wipe the recess clean, then reinstall the washer), drive the oil seal into

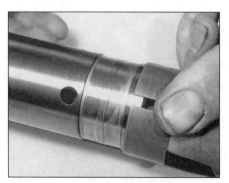

7.81b Make sure the top bush seats properly in its recess

7.82 Fit the slider into the bottom of the fork tube

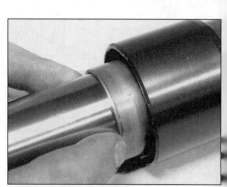

7.83 Make sure the bottom bush enters the fork tube squarely

7.85  Drive the oil seal into the bottom of the tube . . .

7.86a  . . . and fit its retaining clip, making sure it is properly seated . . .

7.86b  . . . then press the dust seal into place

place as described in Step 84 until the retaining clip groove is visible above the seal **(see illustration)**.

**86**  Once the oil seal is correctly seated, fit the retaining clip, making sure it is correctly located in its groove, then press the dust seal into position **(see illustrations)**.

**87**  Lay the fork flat and slide the tube fully onto the slider. Install the damper rod seat onto the bottom of the damper rod **(see illustration)**, then insert the damper rod into the top of the fork tube and through the slider until it seats on the bottom of the slider. Fit a new copper sealing washer to the damper rod bolt and apply a few drops of a suitable non-permanent thread locking compound, then install the bolt into the bottom of the slider and tighten it to the

torque setting specified at the beginning of the Chapter **(see illustrations 7.50b and c)**.

**88**  Stand the fork upright and slowly pour in the specified quantity of the specified grade of fork oil, then pump the damper and tube at least ten times each to distribute the oil evenly **(see illustration 7.55a)**.

*Caution: When pumping the fork, do not withdraw the slider from the tube by more than 230 mm.*

The oil level should also be measured and adjustment made by adding or subtracting oil. Fully compress the fork tube and the damper and measure the fork oil level from the top of the tube **(see illustration 7.55b)**. Add or subtract fork oil until it is at the level specified at the beginning of the Chapter.

**89**  If removed, fit the spring seat into the bottom of the spacer. Withdraw the damper rod as far as possible out of the fork tube, and keep it extended using the aid of an assistant **(see illustration)**. Install the spring with its tapered end upwards into the fork tube, then install the spacer, making sure the lip on the bottom of the spring seat fits into the top of the spring **(see illustration)**. Fit the seat into the top of the spacer, then fit the washer **(see illustrations)**.

**90**  Fit a new O-ring to the fork top bolt and thread the bolt onto the damper rod **(see illustration)**. Push down on the spacer and insert a spanner between the washer and the bottom of the top bolt and fit it onto the flats on the damper rod. Use it to counter-hold the

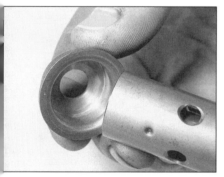

7.87  Fit the damper rod seat onto the end of the end of the damper rod

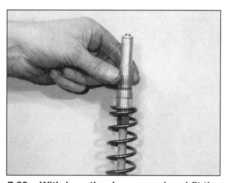

7.89a  Withdraw the damper rod and fit the spring . . .

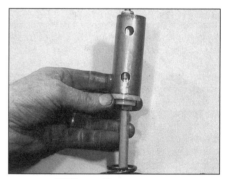

7.89b  . . . the spacer . . .

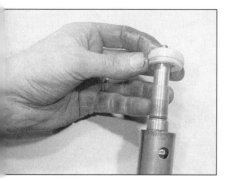

7.89c  . . . the seat . . .

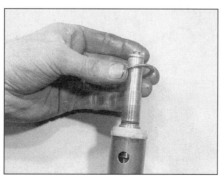

7.89d  . . . and the washer

7.90a  Thread the top bolt onto the damper rod . . .

6

damper rod, then tighten the top bolt to the specified torque setting **(see illustration)**.
**91** Apply a smear of the specified clean oil to the top bolt O-ring. Fully extend the fork tube and screw the bolt securely into the tube **(see illustration)**.

**TOOL TiP** *Use a ratchet-type tool when installing the fork top bolt. This makes it unnecessary to remove the tool from the bolt whilst threading it in making it easier to maintain a downward pressure on the spring.*

**92** Fit the preload adjuster tripod into the top bolt, making sure the leg ends locate into the holes **(see illustration 7.64c)**. Check the condition of the adjuster O-rings and replace them if necessary. Thread the adjuster into the top bolt, then fit the circlip into its groove in the top of the damper rod **(see illustrations)**.
**93** Install the forks as described in Section 6. Set the spring preload adjuster as required (see Section 11).

**8  Steering stem –**
removal and installation

### Removal

**1** Remove the front forks (see Section 6) and the horn (see Chapter 9). On VFR models, unscrew the bolt securing the front brake hose guide **(see illustration)**. On RVF models, unscrew the bolt securing each front brake hose union. Take care not to strain or knock the hoses when removing the steering stem.
**2** Remove the steering stem nut cap and unscrew the nut **(see illustration)**. Lift the top yoke off the steering stem and place it aside, making sure no strain is placed on the ignition switch wiring. If required, trace the wiring and disconnect it at the connector. On VFR models, this will mean removing the right-hand fairing side panel (see Chapter 8), and on RVF models, the air filter housing (see Chapter 4).
**3** Bend down the tabs on the steering stem

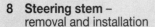

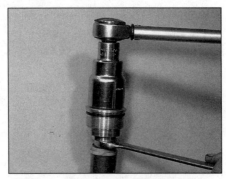

**7.90b** . . . then counter-hold the damper rod as described and tighten the top bolt to the specified torque

**7.91** Thread the top bolt into the tube

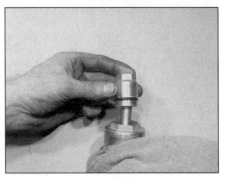

**7.92a** Thread the adjuster into the top bolt . . .

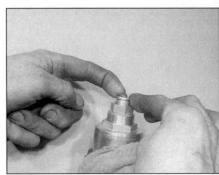

**7.92b** . . . and fit the circlip

**8.1** Remove the bolt (arrowed) and detach the brake hose clamp

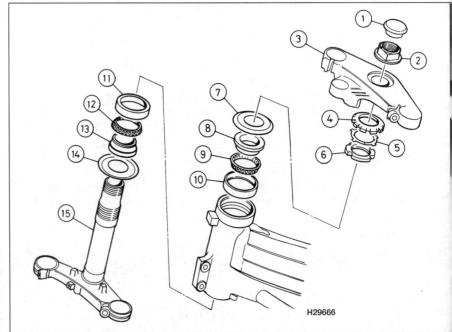

**8.2 Steering stem components**

1 Steering stem nut cap
2 Steering stem nut
3 Top yoke
4 Locknut
5 Lockwasher
6 Adjuster nut
7 Bearing cover
8 Upper bearing inner race
9 Upper bearing
10 Upper bearing outer race
11 Lower bearing outer race
12 Lower bearing
13 Lower bearing inner race
14 Dust seal
15 Bottom yoke and steering stem

lockwasher to release it from the locknut, then unscrew and remove the locknut using either a suitable C-spanner or a drift located in one of the notches. Remove the lockwasher, bending up the remaining tabs to release it from the adjuster nut if necessary. Inspect the tabs for cracks or signs of fatigue. If there are any, discard the lockwasher and use a new one; otherwise the old one can be reused.

4 Supporting the bottom yoke, unscrew the adjuster nut using either a C-spanner, a peg-spanner or a drift located in one of the notches, then remove the adjuster nut and the bearing cover from the steering stem.

5 Gently lower the bottom yoke and steering stem out of the frame.

6 Remove the upper bearing and its inner race from the top of the steering head. Remove all traces of old grease from the bearings and races and check them for wear or damage as described in Section 9. **Note:** *Do not attempt to remove the races from the frame or the lower bearing from the steering stem unless they are to be replaced.*

## Installation

7 Smear a liberal quantity of grease on the bearing races in the frame. Work the grease well into both the upper and lower bearings.

8 Carefully lift the steering stem/bottom yoke up through the frame. Install the upper bearing and its inner race in the top of the steering head, then install the bearing cover. Apply some clean engine oil to the adjuster nut and thread the nut on the steering stem.

9 If the Honda service tool (Part no. 07HMD-MR70100) is available, use this with a torque wrench to tighten the adjuster nut to preload the bearings. Tighten the adjuster nut to the torque setting specified at the beginning of the Chapter, then turn the steering stem through its full lock four or five times and re-tighten the adjuster nut to the specified setting. Ensure that the steering stem is able to move freely from lock to lock following adjustment – if necessary reset the bearing adjustment as described in Chapter 1.

10 If the service tool is not available, tighten the nut using a C-spanner so that bearing play is eliminated, but the steering stem is able to move freely from lock to lock – refer to the procedure in Chapter 1 for details.

*Caution: Take great care not to apply excessive pressure because this will cause premature failure of the bearings.*

11 When the bearings are correctly adjusted, install the lockwasher, using a new one if the tabs are weakened or cracked, onto the adjuster nut and fit two tabs into the slots in the adjuster nut. Install the locknut and tighten it finger-tight, then tighten it further (to a maximum of 90°) until the remaining tabs on the lockwasher align with the slots in the locknut. Hold the adjuster nut to prevent it from moving if necessary. Bend up the lockwasher tabs to secure the locknut.

12 Install the top yoke onto the steering stem. Install the steering stem nut and its washer and tighten it finger-tight at this stage. Temporarily install one of the forks to align the top and bottom yokes, and secure it by tightening the bottom yoke clamp bolt only.

13 Tighten the steering stem nut to the specified torque setting.

14 On VFR models attach the front brake hose guide, and on RVF models the hose unions, to the bottom yoke. Reconnect the ignition switch wiring connector if it was disconnected.

15 Install the horn (see Chapter 9) and the front forks (see Section 6).

16 Carry out a check of the steering head bearing freeplay as described in Chapter 1, and if necessary re-adjust.

---

## 9  Steering head bearings – inspection and replacement

### Inspection

1 Remove the steering stem (see Section 8).

2 Remove all traces of old grease from the bearings and races and check them for wear or damage.

3 The outer races should be polished and free from indentations. Inspect the bearing

rollers for signs of wear, damage or discoloration, and examine the bearing roller retainer cage for signs of cracks or splits. Spin the bearings by hand. They should spin freely and smoothly. If there are any signs of wear on any of the above components both upper and lower bearing assemblies must be replaced as a set. Only remove the races if they need to be replaced – do not re-use them once they have been removed.

### Replacement

4 The outer races are an interference fit in the steering head and can be tapped from position with a suitable drift **(see illustration)**. Tap firmly and evenly around each race to ensure that it is driven out squarely. It may prove advantageous to curve the end of the drift slightly to improve access.

5 Alternatively, the races can be removed using a slide-hammer type bearing extractor; these can often be hired from tool shops.

6 The new outer races can be pressed into the head using a drawbolt arrangement **(see illustration)**, or by using a large diameter tubular drift which bears only on the outer edge of the race. Ensure that the drawbolt washer or drift (as applicable) bears only on the outer edge of the race and does not contact the working surface. Alternatively, have the races installed by a Honda dealer equipped with the bearing race installing tools.

> **HAYNES HINT** *Installation of new bearing outer races is made much easier if the races are left overnight in the freezer. This causes them to contract slightly making them a looser fit.*

7 To remove the lower bearing from the steering stem, use two screwdrivers placed on opposite sides of the race to work it free. If the bearing is firmly in place it will be necessary to use a bearing puller, or in extreme circumstances to split the bearing's inner section using an angle grinder **(see illustration)**. Take the steering stem to a

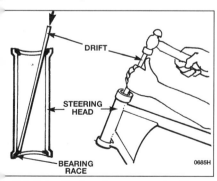

**9.4  Drive the bearing races out with a brass drift as shown**

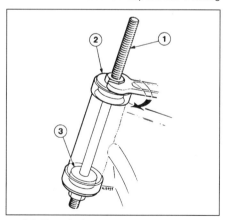

**9.6  Drawbolt arrangement for fitting steering stem bearing races**

1  Long bolt or threaded bar
2  Thick washer
3  Guide for lower race

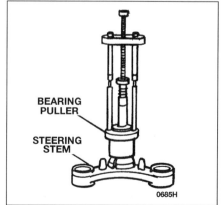

**9.7  It is best to remove the lower bearing using a puller**

6

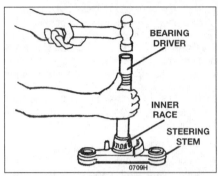

9.8 Drive the new bearing on using a suitable bearing driver or a length of pipe that bears only against the inner race and not against the balls or cage

10.3a Remove the footrest bracket bolts . . .

10.3b . . . and the heat shield bolt, and swing the assembly clear

Honda dealer if required. Check the condition of the dust seal that fits under the lower bearing and replace it if it is worn, damaged or deteriorated.

**8** Fit the new lower bearing onto the steering stem. A length of tubing with an internal diameter slightly larger than the steering stem will be needed to tap the new bearing into position **(see illustration)**. Ensure that the drift bears only on the inner edge of the bearing and does not contact the rollers.

**9** Install the steering stem (see Section 8).

## 10 Rear shock absorber and linkage – removal, inspection and installation

**Note:** *Although the shock absorber and linkage can be removed with the exhaust system in situ, the procedure is quite complicated and access to certain bolts is very difficult, especially for a torque wrench, which is essential for the installation procedure. It is therefore recommended that the exhaust system is removed (see Chapter 4). A procedure for each situation is given.*

### Removal with exhaust system in place

**1** Place the machine on an auxiliary stand. Position a support under the rear wheel so

that it does not drop when the shock absorber is removed, but also making sure that the weight of the machine is off the rear suspension so that the shock is not compressed.

**2** Note the shock absorber spring preload current setting, then adjust it to its softest setting (see Section 11).

**3** Remove the seat cowling (see Chapter 8). Unscrew the two bolts securing the rider's right-hand footrest bracket and the bolt securing the top of the heat shield to the frame, then swing the whole footrest/rear brake master cylinder/heat shield assembly up and secure it to the rear sub-frame, making sure no strain is placed on

the brake and reservoir hoses **(see illustrations)**.

**4** On VFR models, using socket extensions inserted through the holes in the frame, counter-hold the shock absorber upper mounting bolt and unscrew the nut, then withdraw the bolt **(see illustrations)**. On RVF models, unscrew the nut securing the upper mounting bracket to the top of the frame cross-member **(see illustration)**. On VFR L, M and N models, remove the screw caps and slacken the clamps securing the shock absorber reservoir, located behind the passenger's right-hand footrest bracket. Free the reservoir from the clamps **(see illustration)**.

10.4a On VFR models, unscrew the shock absorber upper mounting bolt nut using a socket extension as shown . . .

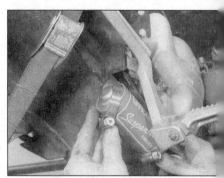

10.4b . . . and withdraw the bolt

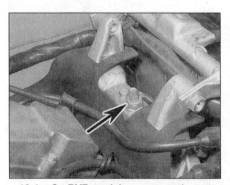

10.4c On RVF models, unscrew the nut (arrowed)

10.4d Remove the caps and slacken the clamps . . .

10.4e . . . then free the reservoir

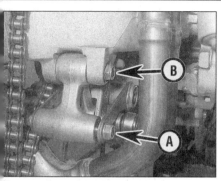

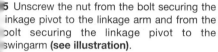

10.5 Remove the linkage pivot-to-linkage arm nut (A) and the linkage pivot-to-swingarm nut (B)

10.6 Unscrew the nut and withdraw the bolt, then swing the linkage arm down

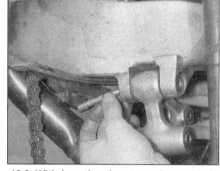

10.8 Withdraw the pivot-to-swingarm bolt

5 Unscrew the nut from the bolt securing the linkage pivot to the linkage arm and from the bolt securing the linkage pivot to the swingarm (see illustration).

6 Unscrew the nut and withdraw the bolt securing the linkage arm to the frame, then swing the linkage arm down (see illustration).

7 Raise the swingarm and withdraw the bolt securing the linkage arm to the linkage pivot and remove the arm.

8 Withdraw the bolt securing the linkage pivot to the swingarm (see illustration).

9 Raise the swingarm, then remove the shock absorber with the linkage pivot still attached. On VFR L, M and N models, free the reservoir hose from its guide and feed the reservoir through as you remove the shock, noting the routing of the hose (see illustration). On all VFR models, also note the routing of the drain hose.

10 On VFR models, a metelastic bush rather than a needle bearing is fitted between the linkage pivot and the shock absorber, meaning there is very little free movement between them when the bolt is tight. As the bolt has to be tightened before installation due to the lack of access with the exhaust in place, it is essential to mark the relative positions of the shock and the pivot before separation to ensure they can be fitted together in the same position. If they are installed out of position it will either be impossible to align the linkage pivot with the swingarm and linkage arm, or if it is possible it will probably mean that the bush is under some preload which will affect the overall performance of the suspension and accelerate wear of the bush. Mark their relative positions using a permanent marker or scribe, then unscrew the nut and withdraw the bolt and separate the shock from the pivot.

11 On RVF models, unscrew the nut and withdraw the bolt securing the linkage pivot to the shock absorber and separate them.

### Removal with exhaust system removed

12 Place the machine on an auxiliary stand. Position a support under the rear wheel so that it does not drop when the shock absorber

is removed, but also making sure that the weight of the machine is off the rear suspension so that the shock is not compressed.

13 Note the shock absorber spring preload current setting, then adjust it to its softest setting (see Section 11).

14 Remove the seat cowling (see Chapter 8).

15 Remove the exhaust system (see Chapter 4).

16 Unscrew the nut and withdraw the bolt securing the linkage arm to the linkage pivot, then swing the linkage arm down. If required, unscrew the nut and withdraw the bolt securing the linkage arm to the frame and remove the arm, noting which way up it fits. The linkage arm can be left in place if only the shock needs to be removed.

17 Unscrew the nut and withdraw the bolt securing the shock absorber to the linkage pivot, then swing the pivot down. If required, unscrew the nut and withdraw the bolt securing the linkage pivot to the swingarm and remove the pivot, noting which way it fits. The linkage pivot can be left in place if only the shock needs to be removed.

18 On VFR L, M and N models, slacken the clamps securing the shock absorber reservoir, located behind the passenger's right-hand footrest bracket (see illustrations 10.4d and e). On VFR models, using socket extensions inserted through the holes in the frame, counter-hold the bolt and unscrew the nut, then withdraw the bolt (see illus-

trations 10.4a and b). On RVF models, unscrew the nut securing the upper mounting bracket to the top of the frame cross-member (see illustration 10.4c).

19 Raise the swingarm, then remove the shock absorber. On VFR L, M and N models, free the reservoir hose from its guide and feed the reservoir through as you remove the shock, noting the routing of the hose (see illustration 10.9). On all VFR models, also note the routing of the drain hose.

### Inspection

20 Inspect the shock absorber for obvious physical damage and the coil spring for looseness, cracks or signs of fatigue.

21 Inspect the damper rod for signs of bending, pitting and oil leakage (see illustration).

22 Inspect the pivot hardware at the top and bottom of the shock for wear or damage.

23 To measure the shock absorber spring free length, compress the spring using a coil spring compressor by just enough to access the spring stopper ring. Remove the ring and the spring seat, then carefully release the compressor until the spring is relaxed. Remove the spring, noting which way it fits. Measure the free length of the spring and compare it to the specifications. If the spring has relaxed below its service limit, it must be replaced. Individual components for the rear shock absorber are available for VFR models. Check with your Honda dealer for availability.

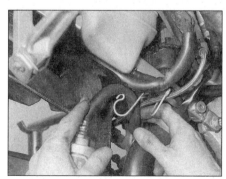

10.9 Free the reservoir hose from its guide

10.21 Look for pitting and oil leakage on the rod (arrow)

6

**10.24 Withdraw the spacers and remove the seals**

On RVF models, the entire unit must be replaced if it is worn or damaged.

**24** Withdraw the spacers and lever out the dust seals from the linkage pivot and arm, noting their different sizes **(see illustration)**. Thoroughly clean all components, removing all traces of dirt, corrosion and grease.

**25** Inspect all components closely, looking for obvious signs of wear such as heavy scoring, or for damage such as cracks or distortion.

**26** Check the condition of the needle roller bearings in the linkage pivot and arm. On VFR models, also check the condition of the metelastic bush.

**27** Worn bearings or bushes can be drifted out of their bores, but note that removal will destroy them; new components should be obtained before work commences. The new ones should be pressed or drawn into their bores rather than driven into position. In the absence of a press, a suitable drawbolt arrangement can be made up as described below.

**28** It will be necessary to obtain a long bolt or a length of threaded rod from a local engineering works or some other supplier. The bolt or rod should be about one inch longer than the combined width of the linkage piece and one bearing. Also required are suitable nuts and two large and robust washers having a larger outside diameter than the bearing housing. In the case of the threaded rod, fit one nut to one end of the rod and stake it in place for convenience.

**29** Fit one of the washers over the bolt or rod so that it rests against the head or staked nut, then pass the assembly through the relevant bore. Over the projecting end place the bearing, which should be greased to ease installation, followed by the remaining washer and nut.

**30** Holding the bearing or bush to ensure that it is kept square, slowly tighten the nut so that the bearing or bush is drawn into its bore.

**31** Once it is fully home, remove the drawbolt arrangement and, if necessary, repeat the procedure to fit the other bearings.

**32** Lubricate the needle roller bearings and the spacers with molybdenum disulphide grease and install the spacers **(see illustration 10.24)**.

**33** Check the condition of the dust seals and replace them if they are damaged or deteriorated. Press the seals squarely into place.

### Installation

**34** Installation is the reverse of removal, noting the following.

a) *Apply molybdenum disulphide grease to the pivot points.*

b) *Make sure the linkage arm is installed with the ends curving downwards.*

c) *On VFR L, M and N models, make sure the reservoir hose is correctly routed and secured in its guide (see illustration 10.9). On all VFR models, make sure the drain hose is routed between the front of the linkage arm and the frame and out through the breather hose guide on the left-hand side of the bike.*

d) *If the exhaust system was not removed, tighten the shock absorber to linkage pivot nut to the specified torque setting before installing the shock, making sure on VFR models that their relative positions are as noted or marked on removal (see Step 10).*

e) *With the exception of the above, install the bolts and nuts finger-tight only until all components are in position, then tighten the nuts to the torque settings specified at the beginning of the Chapter.*

f) *Adjust the suspension as required (see Section 11).*

## 11 Suspension – adjustments

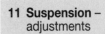

### Front forks

**1** On VFR K models, the front forks are not adjustable.

**2** On all other VFR models and RVF models, the front forks are adjustable for spring preload and damping. Spring preload is adjusted using a suitable spanner on the adjuster flats **(see illustrations)**. Turn it clockwise to increase preload and anti-clockwise to decrease it. The amount of preload is indicated by lines on the adjuster. Always make sure both adjusters are set equally. Damping is adjusted using a screwdriver in the slot in the top of the damper rod protruding from the preload adjuster. Turn it clockwise to increase damping and anti-clockwise to decrease it.

### Rear shock absorber

**3** On all models the rear shock absorber is adjustable for spring preload and damping.

**4** On VFR K models, preload adjustment is made using a suitable C-spanner (one is provided in the toolkit) to turn the spring seat on the top of the shock absorber. There are six positions. Position 1 is the softest setting, position 6 is the hardest. Align the setting required with the adjustment stopper. To increase the preload, turn the spring seat clockwise. To decrease the preload, turn the spring seat anti-clockwise.

**5** On all other VFR models and RVF models, preload adjustment is made by turning the adjuster nut on the threads of the shock absorber body **(see illustration)**. Slacken the locknut, then turn the adjuster nut clockwise to increase preload and anti-clockwise to decrease it. Tighten the locknut securely after adjustment.

**6** Damping adjustment is made by turning the adjuster on the bottom of the shock absorber using a flat-bladed screwdriver **(see**

**11.2a Pre-load adjuster (A), damping adjuster (B) – VFR models**

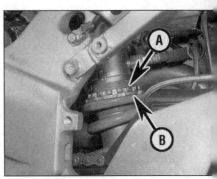

**11.5 Pre-load adjuster locknut (A) and adjuster nut (B)**

11.6 Damping adjuster (arrowed)

12.2 Free the brake hose from its clamps (arrowed)

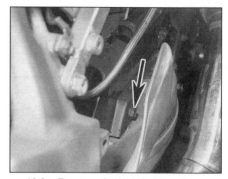

12.3a Remove the bolt (arrowed) . . .

**illustration)**. To set the standard position, turn the adjuster clockwise until it stops, then turn it anti clockwise 1 turn until the punch mark on the adjuster aligns with the index mark on the shock absorber. To increase the damping, turn the adjuster clockwise. To decrease the damping, turn the adjuster anti-clockwise.

## 12 Swingarm –
removal and installation

### Removal

**Note:** *If the rear wheel hub assembly is to be removed from the swingarm, it is advisable to do it at this stage (see Chapter 7) so that the rear brake can be used to prevent the assembly from rotating while slackening the hub nut, which is very tight.*

**1** Remove the rear wheel (see Chapter 7). Slacken the bearing holder pinch bolt in the rear wheel **(see illustration 15.9c)**. Using the pin spanner tool provided in the toolkit or a suitable drift located in one of the notches, turn the bearing holder until the drive chain is fully slack, then disengage the chain from the sprocket **(see illustration 15.14)**.

**2** Remove the rear brake caliper, noting that there is no need to disconnect the brake hose

12.3b . . . and the nut (arrowed), then remove the chain guard

12.5 Unscrew the nut (arrowed)

(see Chapter 7). Release the rear brake hose from its clamps on the chain guard and support the caliper so that no strain is placed on the hose **(see illustration)**.

**3** Unscrew the bolt and nut securing the chain guard to the swingarm and remove the guard, noting how it locates over the lugs on the swingarm **(see illustrations)**.

**4** Remove the rear shock absorber and linkage (see Section 10).

**5** Unscrew the nut on the left-hand end of the swingarm pivot bolt **(see illustration)**.

**6** Unscrew the locknut on the adjuster bolt on the right-hand end of the pivot bolt **(see illustration)**. This requires the use of a Honda service tool, Pt. No. 07908-4690001, which is

a special wrench that fits the locknut **(see illustration)**. There is no alternative to the use of this tool, particularly for the tightening procedure (see Step 16); if you do not have access to it, the swingarm pivot locknut can be unscrewed using a suitable peg spanner, but must be later tightened by a Honda dealer service department.

**7** The swingarm pivot bolt fits into the head of the adjuster bolt (actually a threaded sleeve). Using an Allen key, unscrew the pivot bolt which will also unscrew the adjuster bolt **(see illustration)**.

**8** When the adjuster bolt is fully unscrewed, support the swingarm then withdraw the pivot bolt and the adjuster bolt and remove the

12.6a Unscrew the locknut . . .

12.6b . . . using the special tool. This tool MUST be used for the swingarm tightening procedure

12.7 Unscrew the pivot bolt and the adjuster bolt together (arrow)

**6**

12.8a Withdraw the pivot bolt . . .

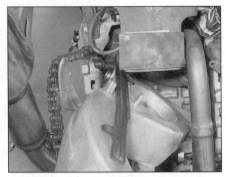

12.8b . . . and remove the swingarm as described

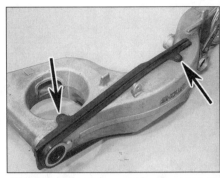

12.9 The slider is secured by four screws, two on the top (arrowed) and two on the bottom

swingarm **(see illustration)**. If the exhaust system is still in place, draw the swingarm back a little, then twist the left-hand side up and the back round to the right to manoeuvre it around the exhaust **(see illustration)**.

9 Remove the chain slider from the swingarm if necessary **(see illustration)**. If it is badly worn or damaged, it should be replaced.

10 Remove the collar from the left-hand side of the swingarm **(see illustration)**. Inspect all components for wear or damage as described in Section 13.

### *Installation*

11 If removed, apply a suitable non-permanent thread locking compound to the chain slider mounting screws and install the slider **(see illustration 12.9)**.

12 Lubricate the dust seals, bearings, collar, and the pivot bolt with grease.

13 Fit the collar into the left-hand side of the swingarm **(see illustration 12.10)**.

14 Offer up the swingarm, manoeuvring it as described in Step 8 if the exhaust is in place, and have an assistant hold it in place. Make sure the drive chain is looped over the front of the swingarm. Slide the pivot adjuster bolt onto the pivot bolt and engage its flats with those of the pivot bolt **(see illustrations)**. Install the pivot bolt through the swingarm,

and tighten it as much as possible by hand **(see illustration)**. Tighten the adjuster bolt further by turning the pivot bolt using a suitable Allen key. Tighten the adjuster bolt in this way to the torque setting specified at the beginning of the Chapter **(see illustration)**.

15 Thread the pivot bolt nut finger-tight onto the left-hand end of the bolt **(see illustration)**.

16 Install the adjuster bolt locknut and tighten it as much as possible by hand **(see illustration)**. Tighten the locknut further using the service tool as described in Step 6, and using an Allen key applied through its middle to counter-hold the pivot bolt and adjuster

12.10 Remove the collar

12.14a Slide the adjuster bolt onto the pivot bolt . . .

12.14b . . . and engage them together

12.14c Slide the bolt through the swingarm . . .

12.14d . . . and tighten it to the specified torque

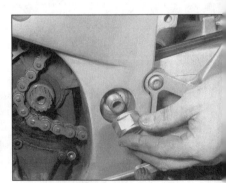

12.15 Thread the nut onto the left-hand end of the bolt

12.16a Fit the locknut . . .

12.16b . . . and tighten it as described to the specified torque

12.17 Tighten the nut to the specified torque

bolt and prevent them from turning. Then, using a torque wrench applied to the hole in the arm of the service tool, tighten the locknut to the specified torque setting **(see illustration)**. **Note:** *The specified torque setting takes into account the extra leverage provided by the service tool and cannot be duplicated without it.*

**17** Tighten the pivot bolt nut to the specified torque setting, again using an Allen key to counter-hold the pivot bolt and adjuster bolt and prevent them from turning **(see illustration)**.

**18** Install the rear shock absorber and linkage (see Section 10).

**19** If removed, install the hub assembly (see Chapter 7).

**20** Install the chain guard, making sure it locates correctly over the lugs on the swingarm **(see illustrations)**. Apply a suitable non-permanent thread locking compound to the nut and the bolt and tighten them securely **(see illustrations 12.3a and b)**.

**21** If not already done (See Step 19), install the rear brake caliper (see Chapter 7). Secure the brake hose in its clamps on the chain guard **(see illustration 12.2)**.

**22** Install the rear wheel (see Chapter 7).

**23** Check and adjust the drive chain slack (see Chapter 1). Make sure the bearing holder pinch bolt is tightened to the specified torque setting. Check the operation of the rear suspension before taking the machine on the road.

12.20a Install the chain guard . . .

12.20b . . . making sure it locates correctly (arrow)

## 13 Swingarm – inspection and bearing replacement

### Inspection

**1** If required, remove the wheel hub assembly (see Chapter 7).

**2** Thoroughly clean all components, removing all traces of dirt, corrosion and grease.

**3** Inspect all components closely, looking for obvious signs of wear such as heavy scoring, and cracks or distortion due to accident damage. Any damaged or worn component must be replaced.

**4** Check the swingarm pivot bolt for straightness by rolling it on a flat surface such

as a piece of plate glass (first wipe off all old grease and remove any corrosion using fine emery cloth). If the equipment is available, place the axle in V-blocks and measure the runout using a dial indicator. If the axle is bent or the runout exceeds the limit specified, replace it.

### Bearing replacement

**5** Withdraw the bearing spacer **(see illustration)**. Lever out the dust seal on each side of the swingarm, and remove the circlip from the right-hand side **(see illustrations)**. Refer to *Tools and Workshop Tips (Section 5)* in the Reference section and remove the bearings, then clean them and inspect them for wear or damage. A needle bearing is fitted in the left-hand side, and a ball bearing in the

13.5a Withdraw the spacer . . .

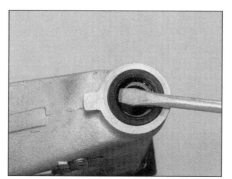

13.5b . . . then lever out the seals . . .

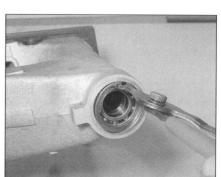

13.5c . . . and remove the circlip

**6**

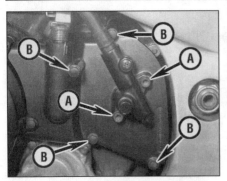

14.2a Speedometer drivebox bolts (A),
sprocket cover bolts (B)

14.2b Note how the tab (A) locates in the
slot (B)

14.3 Unscrew the bolt (arrowed) and
detach the bracket

right-hand side. If the bearings do not run smoothly and freely or if there is excessive freeplay, they must be replaced. The needle bearing in the left-hand side of the swingarm should be replaced as a matter of course if it is removed.

**6** Do not forget to install the bearing spacer between the bearings in the swingarm **(see illustration 13.5a)**. When installing the new needle bearing, lubricate it with molybdenum disulphide grease and set it in the swingarm to a depth of exactly 4 mm. Check the condition of the dust seals and replace them if they are damaged or deteriorated.

### 14 Drive chain – removal, cleaning and installation

#### Removal

**Note:** *The original equipment drive chain fitted to all models is an endless chain, which means it doesn't have a split link and therefore cannot be split. Removal requires the removal of the swingarm.*

**Warning: NEVER install a drive chain which uses a clip-type master (split) link.**

**1** Remove the swingarm (see Section 12).
**2** Unscrew the two bolts securing the speedometer drive box to the engine sprocket cover and detach the box, noting how the drive tab locates in the slot in the sprocket bolt cap **(see illustrations)**.
**3** Unscrew the bolt securing the clutch cable bracket to the alternator cover **(see illustration)**. There is no need to separate the cable from the bracket.
**4** Unscrew the bolts securing the engine sprocket cover, noting their different lengths, and position the cover aside, letting it dangle by the clutch cable **(see illustration 14.2)**. If required, detach the cable end from the release lever on the cover. Remove the dowels if they are loose.
**5** Slip the chain off the front sprocket and remove it from the bike.

#### Cleaning

**6** Soak the chain in paraffin (kerosene) for approximately five or six minutes.

*Caution: Don't use gasoline (petrol), solvent or other cleaning fluids. Don't use high-pressure water. Remove the chain, wipe it off, then blow dry it with compressed air immediately. The entire process shouldn't take longer than ten minutes – if it does, the O-rings in the chain rollers could be damaged.*

#### Installation

**7** Installation is the reverse of removal. On completion adjust and lubricate the chain following the procedures described in Chapter 1.

*Caution: Use only the recommended lubricant.*

### 15 Sprockets – check and replacement

#### Check

**1** Unscrew the two bolts securing the speedometer drive box to the engine sprocket cover and detach the box, noting how the drive tab locates in the slot in the sprocket bolt cap **(see illustrations 14.2a and b)**.
**2** Unscrew the bolt securing the clutch cable bracket to the alternator cover **(see illustration 14.3)**. There is no need to separate the cable from the bracket.
**3** Unscrew the bolts securing the engine sprocket cover, noting their different lengths, and position the cover aside, letting it dangle

by the clutch cable **(see illustration 14.2)**. If required, detach the cable end from the release lever on the cover. Remove the dowels if they are loose.

**4** Check the wear pattern on both sprockets (see Chapter 1, Section 1). If the sprocket teeth are worn excessively, replace the chain and both sprockets as a set. Whenever the sprockets are inspected, the drive chain should be inspected also (see Chapter 1). If you are replacing the chain, also replace the sprockets.
**5** Adjust and lubricate the chain following the procedures described in Chapter 1.

*Caution: Use only the recommended lubricant.*

#### Replacement

##### Front sprocket

**6** Unscrew the two bolts securing the speedometer drive box to the engine sprocket cover and detach the box, noting how the drive tab locates in the slot in the sprocket bolt cap **(see illustrations 14.2a and b)**.
**7** Unscrew the bolt securing the clutch cable bracket to the alternator cover **(see illustration 14.3)**. There is no need to separate the cable from the bracket.
**8** Unscrew the bolts securing the engine sprocket cover and position the cover aside, letting it dangle by the clutch cable **(see illustration 14.2)**. If required, detach the cable end from the release lever on the cover. Remove the dowels if they are loose.
**9** Remove the cap from the engine sprocket bolt **(see illustration)**. Have an assistant

15.9a Remove the cap . . .

15.9b . . . then unscrew the bolt and
remove the washer

**15.9c Slacken the bearing holder pinch bolt and turn the holder to provide chain slack**

**15.10 Draw the sprocket off the shaft and disengage the chain**

**15.12 Tighten the sprocket bolt to the specified torque**

apply the rear brake, then unscrew the sprocket bolt and remove the washer **(see illustration)**. Slacken the bearing holder pinch bolt in the rear wheel **(see illustration)**. Using the pin spanner tool provided in the toolkit or a suitable drift located in one of the notches, turn the bearing holder until the drive chain is fully slack.

**10** Slide the sprocket and chain off the shaft and slip the sprocket out of the chain **(see illustration)**. If there is not enough slack on the chain to remove the sprocket, disengage the chain from the rear wheel.

**11** Engage the new sprocket with the chain and slide it on the shaft. Take up the slack in the chain by turning the bearing holder using the tool, then temporarily tighten the pinch bolt.

**12** Install the sprocket bolt with its washer and tighten it to the torque setting specified at the beginning of the Chapter, using the method employed on removal to prevent the sprocket from turning **(see illustration)**. Fit the bolt cap **(see illustration 15.9a)**.

**13** Install the sprocket cover and the speedometer drive box, aligning the drive tab with the slot in the sprocket bolt cap **(see illustrations 14.2b and 14.2a)**. Adjust and lubricate the chain following the procedures described in Chapter 1.

**Rear sprocket**

**14** Slacken the bearing holder pinch bolt in the rear wheel **(see illustration 15.9c)**. Using the pin spanner tool provided in the toolkit or a suitable drift located in one of the notches, turn the bearing holder until the drive chain is

fully slack. Disengage the chain from the rear wheel **(see illustration)**.

**15** Have an assistant apply the rear brake, the unscrew the nuts securing the sprocket to the hub assembly **(see illustration)**. Remove the sprocket, noting which way round it fits.

**16** Check that the sprocket bolts are correctly located with their flat sides located in the cutouts in the rear of the sprocket holder **(see illustration)**. Install the sprocket onto the hub with the stamped mark facing out, then fit the washers and nuts **(see illustrations)**. Apply the rear brake and tighten the nuts to the torque setting specified at the beginning of the Chapter.

**17** Fit the chain around the sprocket, then adjust and lubricate the chain following the procedures described in Chapter 1.

**15.14 Slip the chain off the sprocket**

**15.15 The sprocket is secured by six nuts (arrowed)**

**15.16a Check the sprocket bolts as described . . .**

**15.16b . . . then install the sprocket . . .**

**15.16c . . . fit the washers and nuts . . .**

**15.16d . . . and tighten them to the specified torque**

**6**

**Notes**

# Chapter 7
# Brakes, wheels and tyres

## Contents

## Degrees of difficulty

| **Easy,** suitable for novice with little experience  | **Fairly easy,** suitable for beginner with some experience  | **Fairly difficult,** suitable for competent DIY mechanic  | **Difficult,** suitable for experienced DIY mechanic  | **Very difficult,** suitable for expert DIY or professional |
|---|---|---|---|---|

## Specifications

### Brakes

| | Standard | Service limit |
|---|---|---|
| Brake fluid type . . . . . . . . . . . . . . . . . . . . . . . . . . . . . . . . . . . . . . | DOT 4 | |
| Front caliper bore ID | | |
|   VFR models | | |
|     Upper bore . . . . . . . . . . . . . . . . . . . . . . . . . . . . . . . . . . . . | 32.030 to 32.080 mm | 32.09 mm |
|     Lower bore . . . . . . . . . . . . . . . . . . . . . . . . . . . . . . . . . . . . | 30.230 to 30.280 mm | 30.29 mm |
|   RVF models | | |
|     Upper bore . . . . . . . . . . . . . . . . . . . . . . . . . . . . . . . . . . . . | 30.230 to 30.280 mm | 30.29 mm |
|     Lower bore . . . . . . . . . . . . . . . . . . . . . . . . . . . . . . . . . . . . | 27.000 to 27.050 mm | 27.06 mm |
| Front caliper piston OD | | |
|   VFR models | | |
|     Upper piston . . . . . . . . . . . . . . . . . . . . . . . . . . . . . . . . . . | 31.984 to 31.998 mm | 31.94 mm |
|     Lower piston . . . . . . . . . . . . . . . . . . . . . . . . . . . . . . . . . . | 30.148 to 30.198 mm | 30.14 mm |
|   RVF models | | |
|     Upper piston . . . . . . . . . . . . . . . . . . . . . . . . . . . . . . . . . . | 30.148 to 30.198 mm | 30.14 mm |
|     Lower piston . . . . . . . . . . . . . . . . . . . . . . . . . . . . . . . . . . | 26.916 to 26.968 mm | 26.91 mm |
| Front disc minimum thickness . . . . . . . . . . . . . . . . . . . . . . . . . . | 3.8 to 4.2 mm | 3.5 mm |
| Disc maximum runout (front and rear) . . . . . . . . . . . . . . . . . . . . . | – | 0.3 mm |
| Front master cylinder bore ID . . . . . . . . . . . . . . . . . . . . . . . . . . . | 14.000 to 14.043 mm | 14.06 mm |
| Front master cylinder piston OD . . . . . . . . . . . . . . . . . . . . . . . . . | 13.957 to 13.984 mm | 13.95 mm |
| Rear caliper bore ID . . . . . . . . . . . . . . . . . . . . . . . . . . . . . . . . . . | 25.400 to 25.450 mm | 25.46 mm |
| Rear caliper piston OD . . . . . . . . . . . . . . . . . . . . . . . . . . . . . . . . | 25.318 to 25.368 mm | 25.31 mm |
| Rear disc minimum thickness . . . . . . . . . . . . . . . . . . . . . . . . . . . | 5.8 to 6.2 mm | 5.0 mm |
| Rear master cylinder bore ID . . . . . . . . . . . . . . . . . . . . . . . . . . . | 14.000 to 14.043 mm | 14.06 mm |
| Rear master cylinder piston OD . . . . . . . . . . . . . . . . . . . . . . . . . | 13.957 to 13.984 mm | 13.95 mm |

**7**

## Wheels

Maximum wheel runout (front and rear)
    Axial (side-to-side) ........................................ 2.0 mm
    Radial (out-of-round) ...................................... 2.0 mm
Maximum axle runout (front and rear) .......................... 0.20 mm

## Tyres

Tyre pressures ............................................. see *Daily (pre-ride)* checks
Tyre sizes*
  VFR models
    Front .................................................. 120/60-VR17
    Rear ................................................... 150/60-VR18
  RVF models
    Front .................................................. 120/60-R17 55H
    Rear .................................................. 150/60-R17 66H
*Refer to the owners handbook or the tyre information label on the swingarm for approved tyre brands.*

## Torque settings – specific components

Front brake pad retaining pin
  VFR models ............................................. 17 Nm
  RVF models ............................................. 18 Nm
Front brake pad retaining pin plug .......................... 2.5 Nm
Front brake caliper mounting bolts
  VFR models ............................................. 27 Nm
  RVF models ............................................. 31 Nm
Front brake caliper Torx bolts
  VFR models ............................................. 27 Nm
  RVF models ............................................. 33 Nm
Front brake disc bolts ..................................... 20 Nm
Front brake master cylinder clamp bolts ..................... 12 Nm
Rear brake pad retaining pin
  VFR models ............................................. 17 Nm
  RVF models ............................................. 18 Nm
Rear brake pad retaining pin plug ........................... 2.5 Nm
Rear brake caliper mounting bolts .......................... 27 Nm
Rear brake caliper bracket slider pins
  Front .................................................. 23 Nm
  Rear ................................................... 13 Nm
Rear brake disc nuts ...................................... 35 Nm
Rear brake master cylinder bolts ........................... 12 Nm
Brake hose banjo bolts .................................... 35 Nm
Rear brake hose caliper joint nut .......................... 14 Nm
Rear brake hose caliper joint bolt ......................... 35 Nm
Brake caliper bleed valves ................................ 6 Nm
Front axle bolt ........................................... 60 Nm
Front axle clamp bolts .................................... 22 Nm
Rear wheel nut ........................................... 120 Nm
Rear wheel drive pins ..................................... 15 Nm
Rear brake torque arm nuts (VFR models) ................... 35 Nm
Rear hub assembly nut
  VFR models ............................................. 165 Nm
  RVF models ............................................. 205 Nm
Rear wheel bearing holder pinch bolt ........................ 55 Nm

## Torque settings – non-specified components

**Note:** *Where a specific setting is not given for a particular bolt/nut, these general settings apply. The dimension given applies to the diameter of the thread, not the head.*
5 mm bolt/nut ............................................. 5 Nm
6 mm bolt/nut ............................................. 10 Nm
8 mm bolt/nut ............................................. 22 Nm
10 mm bolt/nut ............................................ 35 Nm
12 mm bolt/nut ............................................ 55 Nm
6 mm flange bolt with 8 mm head ........................... 9 Nm
6 mm flange bolt/nut with 10 mm head ...................... 12 Nm
8 mm flange bolt/nut ...................................... 27 Nm
10 mm flange bolt/nut ..................................... 40 Nm

2.1a Pad cover removal – VFR models

2.1b Pad cover removal – RVF models

2.1c Unscrew the pad pin plug and the pad pin . . .

## 1 General information

All models covered in this manual are fitted with cast alloy wheels designed for tubeless tyres only. Both front and rear brakes are hydraulically operated disc brakes.

On all models, the front brakes are twin opposed-piston calipers, and the rear brake is a twin piston sliding caliper.

*Caution: Disc brake components rarely require disassembly. Do not disassemble components unless absolutely necessary. If a hydraulic brake line is loosened, the entire system must be disassembled, drained, cleaned and then properly filled and bled upon reassembly. Do not use solvents on internal brake components. Solvents will cause the seals to swell and distort. Use only clean brake fluid or denatured alcohol for cleaning. Use care when working with brake fluid as it can injure your eyes and it will damage painted surfaces and plastic parts.*

## 2 Front brake pads – replacement

 *Warning: The dust created by the brake system may contain asbestos, which is harmful to your health. Never blow it out with compressed air and don't inhale any of it. An approved filtering mask should be worn when working on the brakes.*

1 Remove the pad cover on the top of the caliper **(see illustrations)**. Unscrew the pad retaining pin plug followed by the pad retaining pin and withdraw the pin, noting how it keeps the pad spring pressed onto the pads **(see illustrations)**. Remove the spring, then lift out the pads **(see illustrations)**.

2 Inspect the surface of each pad for contamination and check that the friction material has not worn level with or beyond the wear grooves in the pad face **(see illustration)**. If either pad is worn down to, or

2.1d . . . then withdraw the pin and remove the spring . . .

beyond, the service limit, fouled with oil or grease, or heavily scored or damaged by dirt and debris, both pads must be replaced as a set. Note that it is not possible to degrease the friction material; if the pads are contaminated in any way they must be replaced.

3 If the pads are in good condition clean them carefully, using a fine wire brush which is completely free of oil and grease to remove all traces of road dirt and corrosion. Using a pointed instrument, clean out the grooves in the friction material and dig out any embedded particles of foreign matter. Any areas of glazing may be removed using emery cloth.

4 Check the condition of the brake disc (see Section 4).

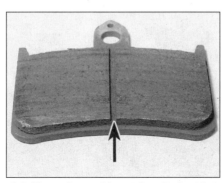

2.2 The pads must be replaced when the wear groove (arrowed) is no longer visible

2.1e . . . and lift out the pads

5 Remove all traces of corrosion from the pad pin. Inspect the pin for signs of damage and replace it if necessary.

6 Push the pistons as far back into the caliper as possible using hand pressure or a piece of wood as leverage. Due to the increased friction material thickness of new pads, it may be necessary to remove the master cylinder reservoir cover and diaphragm and siphon out some fluid.

7 Smear the backs of the pads and the shank of the pad pin with copper-based grease, making sure that none gets on the front or sides of the pads **(see illustrations)**.

8 Installation of the pads is the reverse of removal. Insert the pads into the caliper so that the friction material faces the disc, then slide the pad retaining pin through the hole in

2.7a Apply copper grease to the back of each pad . . .

**7**

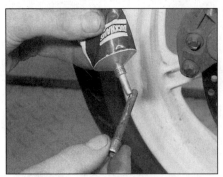

2.7b . . . and to the pad pin

2.8a Install the pads . . .

2.8b . . . then slide the pad pin into the outer pad

2.8c Fit the spring and slide the pad pin onto it and through the inner pad . . .

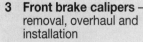

2.8d . . . and tighten it to the specified torque

the outer pad **(see illustrations)**. Fit the pad spring with its narrower end at the top, making sure it locates correctly onto the pads. Press down on the spring and slide the pin across so that it locates in the groove in the middle of the spring and passes through the hole in the inner pad **(see illustration)**. Tighten the pad retaining pin to the torque setting specified at the beginning of the Chapter **(see illustration)**. Install the pad pin plug and tighten it to the specified torque **(see illustration 2.1c)**. Fit the caliper cover **(see illustrations 2.1a or b)**.

**9** Top up the master cylinder reservoir if necessary (see *Daily (pre-ride) checks*), and replace the reservoir cover and diaphragm.

**10** Operate the brake lever several times to bring the pads into contact with the disc.

Check the operation of the brake before riding the motorcycle.

### 3 Front brake calipers – removal, overhaul and installation

⚠️ *Warning: If a caliper indicates the need for an overhaul (usually due to leaking fluid or sticky operation), all old brake fluid should be flushed from the system. Also, the dust created by the brake system may contain asbestos, which is harmful to your health. Never blow it out with compressed air and don't inhale any of it. An approved filtering mask should be worn when*

*working on the brakes. Do not, under any circumstances, use petroleum-based solvents to clean brake parts. Use clean brake fluid, brake cleaner or denatured alcohol only.*

#### Removal

**1** If the calipers are being overhauled, remove the brake pads (see Section 2), then slacken and lightly retighten the four Torx bolts which join the caliper halves **(see illustration)**. If the calipers are just being to work on the front forks or wheel, the pads can be left in place and the Torx bolts should not be disturbed.

**2** If the calipers are just being displaced and not completely removed or overhauled, do not disconnect the brake hose. If the calipers are being overhauled, remove the brake hose banjo bolt. Note the alignment of the hose on the caliper and separate the hose from the caliper **(see illustration)**. Plug the hose end or wrap a plastic bag tightly around it to minimise fluid loss and prevent dirt entering the system. Discard the sealing washers as new ones must be used on installation. **Note:** *If you are planning to overhaul the caliper and don't have a source of compressed air to blow out the pistons, just loosen the banjo bolt at this stage and retighten it lightly. The bike's hydraulic system can then be used to force the pistons out of the body once the pads have been removed. Disconnect the hose once the pistons have been sufficiently displaced.*

**3** Unscrew the caliper mounting bolts, and

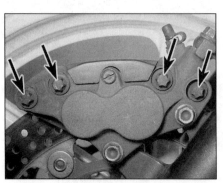

3.1 The caliper halves are joined by four Torx bolts (arrowed)

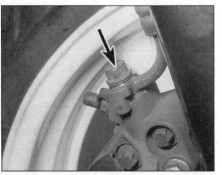

3.2 Note the alignment of the hose before removing the banjo bolt (arrowed)

3.3a Unscrew the caliper mounting bolts (arrowed) . . .

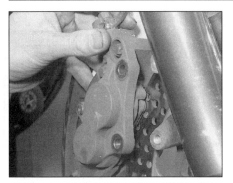

3.3b . . . and slide the caliper off the disc

slide the caliper off the disc **(see illustrations)**.

## Overhaul

**4** Clean the exterior of the caliper with denatured alcohol or brake system cleaner **(see illustration)**.

**5** Displace the pistons as far as possible from the caliper body, either by pumping them out by operating the front brake lever, or by forcing them out using compressed air. If the compressed air method is used, place a wad of rag between the pistons and the caliper to act as a cushion, then use compressed air directed into the fluid inlet to force the pistons out of the body. Use only low pressure to ease the pistons out and make sure both pistons are displaced at the same time. If the air pressure is too high and the pistons are forced out, the caliper and/or pistons may be damaged. Unscrew the Torx bolts and separate the caliper halves. Mark each piston head and caliper body with a felt marker to ensure that the pistons can be matched to their original bores on reassembly. Remove the seals from either half of the caliper body and discard them as new ones must be used.

 **Warning: Never place your fingers in front of the pistons in an attempt to catch or protect them when applying compressed air, as serious injury could result.**

3.6 **Remove the dust seal with a plastic or wooden tool (a pencil works well) to avoid damage to the bore and seal groove**

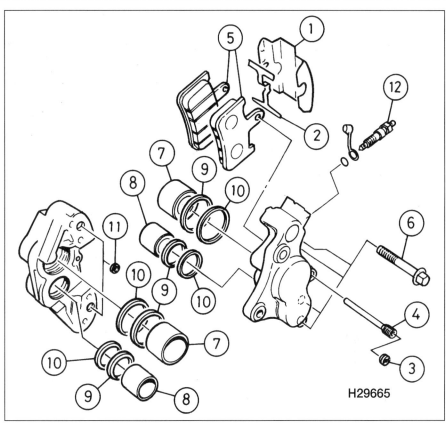

3.4 **Front brake caliper components**

| | | |
|---|---|---|
| 1  Pad cover | 5  Brake pads | 9  Dust seals |
| 2  Pad spring | 6  Caliper Torx bolts | 10  Piston seals |
| 3  Pad retaining pin plug | 7  Pistons – large diameter | 11  Caliper seals |
| 4  Pad retaining pin | 8  Pistons – small diameter | 12  Bleed valve |

**6** Using a wooden or plastic tool, remove the dust seals from the caliper bores **(see illustration)**. Discard them as new ones must be used on installation. If a metal tool is being used, take great care not to damage the caliper bores.

**7** Remove and discard the piston seals in the same way.

**8** Clean the pistons and bores with denatured alcohol, clean brake fluid or brake system cleaner. If compressed air is available, use it to dry the parts thoroughly (make sure it's filtered and unlubricated).

**Caution: Do not, under any circumstances, use a petroleum-based solvent to clean brake parts.**

**9** Inspect the caliper bores and pistons for signs of corrosion, nicks and burrs and loss of plating. If surface defects are present, the caliper assembly must be replaced. If the necessary measuring equipment is available, compare the dimensions of the pistons and bores to those given in the Specifications Section of this Chapter, replacing any component that is worn beyond the service limit. If the caliper is in bad shape the master cylinder should also be checked.

**10** Lubricate the new piston seals with clean

brake fluid and install them in their grooves in the caliper bores. Note that different sizes of bore and piston are used (see Specifications), and care must therefore be taken to ensure that the correct size seals are fitted to the correct bores. The same applies when fitting the new dust seals and pistons.

**11** Lubricate the new dust seals with clean brake fluid and install them in their grooves in the caliper bores.

**12** Lubricate the pistons with clean brake fluid and install them closed-end first into the caliper bores. Using your thumbs, push the pistons all the way in, making sure they enter the bore squarely.

**13** Fit new seals into one half of the caliper body, then join the halves together and tighten the four Torx bolts lightly. They can be fully tightened after the calipers have been installed.

## Installation

**14** Install the caliper on the brake disc making sure the pads sit squarely either side of the disc (if they weren't removed) **(see illustration 3.3b)**.

**15** Install the caliper mounting bolts, and tighten them to the torque setting specified at

**7**

3.15a Install the bolts . . .

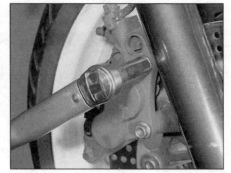

3.15b . . . and tighten them to the specified torque

4.2 Set up a dial indicator with the probe contacting the brake disc, then rotate the wheel to check for runout

the beginning of the Chapter (see illustrations).

**16** If the calipers were overhauled, tighten the four Torx bolts to the specified torque setting.

**17** If removed, connect the brake hose to the caliper, using new sealing washers on each side of the fitting. Align the hose as noted on removal. Tighten the banjo bolt to the torque setting specified at the beginning of the Chapter. Top up the master cylinder reservoir with DOT 4 brake fluid (see *Daily (pre-ride) checks*) and bleed the hydraulic system as described in Section 11.

**18** If removed, install the brake pads (see Section 2).

**19** Check for leaks and thoroughly test the operation of the brake before riding the motorcycle.

```
4   Front brake discs –
    inspection, removal and
    installation
```

### Inspection

**1** Visually inspect the surface of the disc for score marks and other damage. Light scratches are normal after use and won't affect brake operation, but deep grooves and heavy score marks will reduce braking efficiency and accelerate pad wear. If a disc is badly grooved it must be machined or replaced.

**2** To check disc runout, position the bike on an auxiliary stand and support it so that the wheel is raised off the ground. Mount a dial gauge on a fork leg, with the plunger on the gauge touching the surface of the disc about 10 mm (1/2 in) from the outer edge (see illustration). Rotate the wheel and watch the indicator needle, comparing the reading with the limit listed in the Specifications at the beginning of the Chapter. If the runout is greater than the service limit, check the wheel bearings for play (see Chapter 1). If the bearings are worn, replace them (see Section 16) and repeat this check. If the disc runout is still excessive, it will have to be replaced, although machining by an engineer may be possible.

**3** The disc must not be machined or allowed to wear down to a thickness less than the service limit as listed in this Chapter's Specifications and as marked on the disc itself (see illustration). The thickness of the disc can be checked with a micrometer (see illustration). If the thickness of the disc is less than the service limit, it must be replaced.

### Removal

**4** Remove the front wheel (see Section 14). *Caution: Do not lay the wheel down and allow it to rest on the disc – the disc could become warped. Set the wheel on wood blocks so the disc doesn't support the weight of the wheel.*

**5** Mark the relationship of the disc to the wheel, so it can be installed in the same

position. Unscrew the disc retaining bolts, loosening them a little at a time in a criss-cross pattern to avoid distorting the disc, then remove the disc from the wheel (see illustration).

### Installation

**6** Install the disc on the wheel, making sure the marked side is on the outside. Align the previously applied matchmarks (if you're reinstalling the original disc).

**7** Install the bolts and tighten them in a criss-cross pattern evenly and progressively to the torque setting specified at the beginning of the Chapter. Clean off all grease from the brake disc(s) using acetone or brake system cleaner. If a new brake disc has been installed, remove any protective coating from its working surfaces.

**8** Install the wheel (see Section 14).

**9** Operate the brake lever several times to bring the pads into contact with the disc. Check the operation of the brakes carefully before riding the bike.

```
5   Front brake master cylinder
    – removal, overhaul and
    installation
```

**1** If the master cylinder is leaking fluid, or if the lever does not produce a firm feel when the brake is applied, and bleeding the brakes does not help (see Section 11), and the

4.3a The minimum disc thickness is marked on each disc

4.3b Using a micrometer to measure disc thickness

4.5 Each disc is secured by six bolts (arrowed)

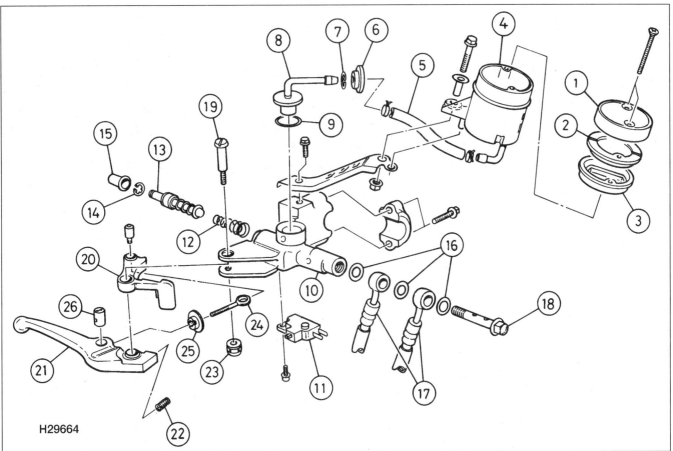

**5.1 Front brake master cylinder components**

| | | | |
|---|---|---|---|
| 1 Reservoir cap | 8 Reservoir hose union | 15 Rubber boot | 21 Brake lever |
| 2 Diaphragm plate | 9 O-ring | 16 Sealing washers | 22 Spring |
| 3 Diaphragm | 10 Master cylinder | 17 Brake hoses | 23 Nut |
| 4 Reservoir | 11 Brake light switch | 18 Brake hose banjo bolt | 24 Span adjuster |
| 5 Reservoir hose | 12 Spring | 19 Brake lever pivot bolt | 25 Span adjuster wheel |
| 6 Rubber cap | 13 Piston assembly | 20 Span adjuster bracket | 26 Trunnion |
| 7 Circlip | 14 Circlip | | |

hydraulic hoses are all in good condition, then master cylinder overhaul is recommended **(see illustration)**.

**2** Before disassembling the master cylinder, read through the entire procedure and make sure that you have the correct rebuild kit. Also, you will need some new DOT 4 brake fluid, some clean rags and internal circlip pliers. **Note:** *To prevent damage to the paint from spilled brake fluid, always cover the fuel tank when working on the master cylinder.* ***Caution: Disassembly, overhaul and reassembly of the brake master cylinder must be done in a spotlessly clean work area to avoid contamination and possible failure of the brake hydraulic system components.***

## Removal

**3** Loosen, but do not remove, the screws holding the reservoir cover in place **(see**

**illustration)**. Access to the front reservoir cap screws is restricted by the windshield. If a short or angled screwdriver is not available, remove the fairing to access the screws (see Chapter 8).

**5.3 Slacken the two reservoir cover screws**

**4** Disconnect the electrical connectors from the brake light switch **(see illustration)**.
**5** Remove the front brake lever (see Chapter 6).
**6** Unscrew the brake hose banjo bolt and

**5.4 Disconnect the brake light switch wiring connectors (arrowed)**

**7**

5.6 Note the alignment of the hose before removing the banjo bolt (arrowed)

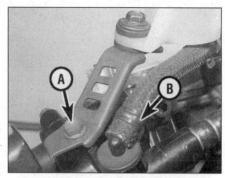

5.7 Unscrew the bracket bolt (A) and release the hose clamp (B)

5.8 Unscrew the clamp bolts (arrowed) and remove the master cylinder assembly

separate the hose from the master cylinder, noting its alignment (see illustration). Discard the sealing washers as they must be replaced with new ones. Wrap the end of the hose in a clean rag and suspend it in an upright position or bend it down carefully and place the open end in a clean container. The objective is to prevent excessive loss of brake fluid, fluid spills and system contamination.

7  Unscrew the bolt securing the reservoir bracket to the master cylinder, then release the clamp securing the reservoir hose to the union on the master cylinder (see illustration). Remove the reservoir cover retaining screws and lift off the cover, the diaphragm plate and the rubber diaphragm. Drain the brake fluid from the reservoir into a suitable container, then detach the reservoir hose from its union on the master cylinder. Wipe any remaining fluid out of the reservoir with a clean rag.

8  Unscrew the master cylinder clamp bolts, then lift the master cylinder away from the handlebar (see illustration).

9  Remove the screw securing the brake light switch to the bottom of the master cylinder and remove the switch.

Caution: Do not tip the master cylinder upside down or brake fluid will run out.

## Overhaul

10  Carefully remove the dust boot from the end of the piston (see illustration).

11  Using circlip pliers, remove the circlip and slide out the piston assembly and the spring, noting how they fit (see illustration). Lay the parts out in the proper order to prevent confusion during reassembly (see illustration).

12  Remove the fluid reservoir hose union rubber cap, then remove the circlip and detach the union from the master cylinder. Discard the O-ring as a new one must be used. Inspect the reservoir hose for cracks or splits and replace if necessary.

13  Clean all parts with clean brake fluid or denatured alcohol. If compressed air is available, use it to dry the parts thoroughly (make sure it's filtered and unlubricated).

Caution: Do not, under any circumstances, use a petroleum-based solvent to clean brake parts.

14  Check the master cylinder bore for corrosion, scratches, nicks and score marks. If the necessary measuring equipment is available, compare the dimensions of the piston and bore to those given in the Specifications Section of this Chapter. If damage or wear is evident, the master cylinder must be replaced with a new one. If the master cylinder is in poor condition, then the caliper(s) should be checked as well. Check that the fluid inlet and outlet ports in the master cylinder are clear.

15  The dust boot, circlip, piston, seal, primary cup and spring are included in the rebuild kit. Use all of the new parts, regardless of the apparent condition of the old ones. If the seal and cup are not already on the piston, fit them according to the layout of the old piston assembly.

16  Install the spring in the master cylinder so that its tapered end faces the piston.

17  Lubricate the piston, seal and cup with clean brake fluid. Install the assembly into the master cylinder, making sure it is the correct way round (see illustration 5.11b). Make sure the lips on the cup do not turn inside out when they are slipped into the bore. Depress the piston and install the new circlip, making sure that it locates in the master cylinder groove (see illustration 5.11a).

18  Install the rubber dust boot, making sure the lip is seated correctly in the piston groove (see illustration 5.10).

19  Fit a new O-ring onto the reservoir hose union, then press the union into the master cylinder and secure it with the circlip. Fit the rubber cap over the circlip.

20  Inspect the reservoir cover rubber diaphragm and replace it if it is damaged or deteriorated.

## Installation

21  Install the brake light switch.

22  Attach the master cylinder to the handlebar and fit the clamp with its UP mark facing up, then tighten the bolts to the torque

5.10 Remove the rubber boot from the end of the master cylinder piston . . .

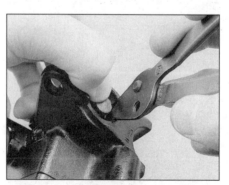

5.11a . . . then depress the piston and remove the circlip using a pair of internal circlip pliers

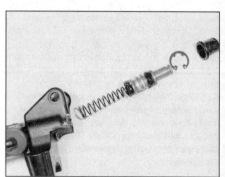

5.11b Lay out the internal parts as shown, even if new parts are being used, to avoid confusion on reassembly

**5.22a Install the clamp with the UP mark facing up . . .**

**5.22b . . . and tighten the bolts to the specified torque**

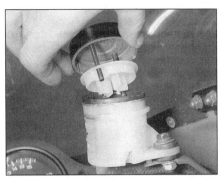

**5.28 Make sure the diaphragm is correctly seated, then fit the plate and cover**

setting specified at the beginning of the Chapter **(see illustrations)**.

**23** Connect the brake hose to the master cylinder, using new sealing washers on each side of the union, and aligning the hose as noted on removal **(see illustration 5.6)**. Tighten the banjo bolt to the torque setting specified at the beginning of this Chapter.

**24** Install the brake lever (see Chapter 6).

**25** Mount the reservoir onto the master cylinder and tighten its bolt securely **(see illustration 5.7)**. Connect the reservoir hose to the union and secure it with the clamp.

**26** Connect the brake light switch wiring **(see illustration 5.4)**.

**27** Fill the fluid reservoir with new DOT 4 brake fluid as described in *Daily (pre-ride) checks*. Refer to Section 11 of this Chapter and bleed the air from the system.

**28** Fit the rubber diaphragm, making sure it is correctly seated, the diaphragm plate and the cover onto the master cylinder reservoir **(see illustration)**.

**29** Check the operation of the front brake before riding the motorcycle.

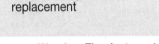

**6 Rear brake pads – replacement**

*Warning: The dust created by the brake system may contain asbestos, which is harmful to*

*your health. Never blow it out with compressed air and don't inhale any of it. An approved filtering mask should be worn when working on the brakes.*

**1** Unscrew the pad retaining pin plug and slacken the pad retaining pin, then remove the caliper upper mounting bolt and slacken the lower one and swing the caliper down at the front **(see illustrations)**. Access the upper caliper bolt using a socket extension inserted through one of the holes in the rear sprocket **(see illustration)**.

**2** Remove the pad retaining pin, then draw out the pads **(see illustration)**.

**3** Inspect the surface of each pad for contamination and check that the friction material has not worn level with or beyond the wear grooves in the pad face or the cutouts in

the pad edge. If either pad is worn down to, or beyond, the service limit, fouled with oil or grease, or heavily scored or damaged by dirt and debris, both pads must be replaced as a set. Note that it is not possible to degrease the friction material; if the pads are contaminated in any way they must be replaced.

**4** If the pads are in good condition clean them carefully, using a fine wire brush which is completely free of oil and grease to remove all traces of road dirt and corrosion. Using a pointed instrument, clean out the grooves in the friction material and dig out any embedded particles of foreign matter. Any areas of glazing may be removed using emery cloth.

**5** Check the condition of the brake disc (see Section 8).

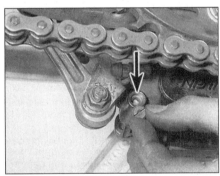

**6.1a Remove the plug and slacken the pad pin (arrowed)**

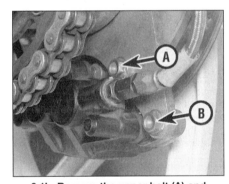

**6.1b Remove the upper bolt (A) and slacken the lower one (B) . . .**

**6.1c . . . accessing the upper bolt as shown . . .**

**6.1d . . . and swing the caliper down**

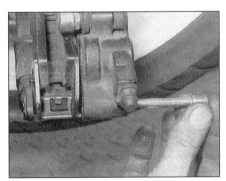

**6.2 Withdraw the pin and remove the pads**

**7**

6.7 Push the pistons back into the caliper

6.8 Apply copper grease to the back of each pad and to the pad pin

6.9a Check that the rear spring (arrowed) . . .

6.9b . . . and the front spring are correctly positioned (arrowed)

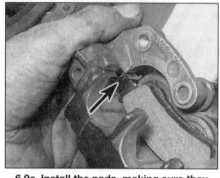

6.9c Install the pads, making sure they locate correctly against the rear spring (arrow) . . .

6.9d . . . then install the pad pin

6 Remove all traces of corrosion from the pad pin. Inspect the pin for signs of damage and replace if necessary.

7 Push the pistons as far back into the caliper as possible using hand pressure, a brake pad or a piece of wood as leverage (see illustration). Due to the increased friction material thickness of new pads, it may be necessary to remove the master cylinder reservoir cover and diaphragm and siphon out some fluid.

8 Smear the backs of the pads and the shank of the pad pin with copper-based grease, making sure that none gets on the front or sides of the pads (see illustration).

9 Installation of the pads is the reverse of removal. Make sure the pad springs are correctly positioned in the caliper (see illustrations). Insert the pads into the caliper so that the friction material faces the disc, making sure they locate correctly against the springs, then slide the pad retaining pin through (see illustrations). Make sure the pin passes through the hole in each pad. Tighten the pad retaining pin finger tight.

10 Swing the caliper up onto the disc and tighten the mounting bolts to the torque setting specified at the beginning of the Chapter (see illustration). Tighten the pad retaining pin to the specified torque, then install the pad pin plug (see illustration).

11 Top up the master cylinder reservoir if necessary (see Daily (pre-ride) checks), and replace the reservoir cover and diaphragm.

12 Operate the brake pedal several times to bring the pads into contact with the disc. Check the operation of the brake before riding the motorcycle.

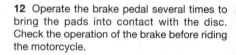

7 Rear brake caliper – removal, overhaul and installation

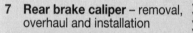

Warning: If a caliper indicates the need for an overhaul (usually due to leaking fluid or sticky operation), all old brake fluid should be flushed from the system. Also, the dust created by the brake system may contain asbestos, which is harmful to your health. Never blow it out with compressed air and don't inhale any of it. An approved filtering mask should be worn when working on the brakes. Do not, under any circumstances, use petroleum-based solvents to clean brake parts. Use clean brake fluid, brake cleaner or denatured alcohol only.

### Removal

1 If the caliper is being overhauled, remove the brake pads (see Section 6). If the caliper is just being removed, the pads can be left in place.

2 If the caliper is just being displaced and not completely removed or overhauled, do not disconnect the brake hose. If the caliper is

6.10a Tighten the caliper mounting bolts . . .

6.10b . . . and the pad pin to the specified torque

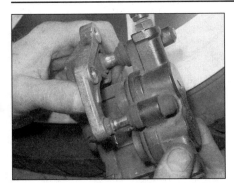

**7.4 Slide the caliper bracket out of the caliper**

being overhauled, counter-hold the hose nut and slacken the joint nut, then unscrew the hose bolt in the caliper and separate the hose from the caliper. Plug the hose end or wrap a plastic bag tightly around it to minimise fluid loss and prevent dirt entering the system. Discard the sealing washers as new ones must be used on installation. **Note:** *If you are planning to overhaul the caliper and don't have a source of compressed air to blow out the pistons, just loosen the banjo bolt at this stage and retighten it lightly. The bike's hydraulic system can then be used to force the pistons out of the body once the pads have been removed. Disconnect the hose once the pistons have been sufficiently displaced.*

**3** Unscrew the caliper mounting bolts, and slide the caliper off the disc **(see illustrations 6.1b and c)**. If the caliper is being overhauled, remove the pad springs, noting carefully how they fit.

## Overhaul

**4** Slide the caliper off the caliper bracket **(see illustration)**. If required, remove the pad spring from the bracket, noting how it fits.
**5** Clean the exterior of the caliper with denatured alcohol or brake system cleaner **(see illustrations)**.
**6** Remove the pistons from the caliper body, either by pumping them out by operating the rear brake pedal until the pistons are displaced, or by forcing them out using compressed air. Mark each piston head and the caliper body with a felt marker to ensure that the pistons can be matched to their original bores on reassembly. If the compressed air method is used, place a wad of rag over the pistons to act as a cushion, then use compressed air directed into the fluid inlet to force the pistons out of the body. Use only low pressure to ease the pistons out and make sure both pistons are displaced at the same time. If the air pressure is too high and the pistons are forced out, the caliper and/or pistons may be damaged.

 **Warning: Never place your fingers in front of the pistons in an attempt to catch or protect them when applying**

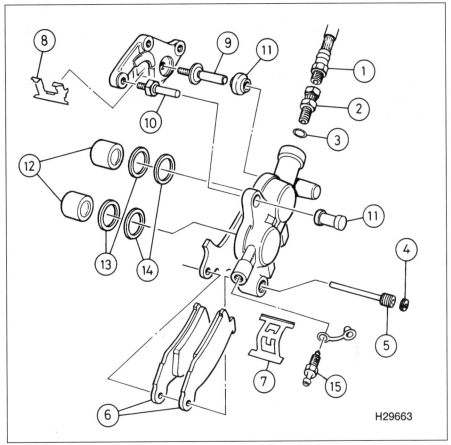

H29663

**7.5 Rear brake caliper components**

| | |
|---|---|
| 1 Hose nut | 6 Brake pads | 11 Rubber boots |
| 2 Joint nut and hose bolt | 7 Front pad spring | 12 Pistons |
| 3 Sealing washer | 8 Rear pad spring | 13 Dust seals |
| 4 Pad retaining pin plug | 9 Rear slider pin | 14 Piston seals |
| 5 Pad retaining pin | 10 Front slider pin | 15 Bleed valve |

*compressed air, as serious injury could result.*

**7** Using a wooden or plastic tool, remove the dust seals from the caliper bores **(see illustration 3.6)**. Discard them as new ones must be used on installation. If a metal tool is being used, take great care not to damage the caliper bores.
**8** Remove and discard the piston seals in the same way.
**9** Clean the pistons and bores with denatured alcohol, clean brake fluid or brake system cleaner. If compressed air is available, use it to dry the parts thoroughly (make sure it's filtered and unlubricated).
*Caution: Do not, under any circumstances, use a petroleum-based solvent to clean brake parts.*
**10** Inspect the caliper bores and pistons for signs of corrosion, nicks and burrs and loss of plating. If surface defects are present, the caliper assembly must be replaced. If the necessary measuring equipment is available, compare the dimensions of the pistons and bores to those given in the Specifications Section of this Chapter, replacing any

component that is worn beyond the service limit. If the caliper is in bad shape the master cylinder should also be checked.
**11** Check that the caliper body is able to slide freely on the slider pins. If not, clean off all traces of corrosion and hardened grease. Apply a smear of copper or silicone based grease to the slider pins and reassemble the two components and check again. Replace the rubber boots if they are damaged or deteriorated. If a pin is loose, remove them both and clean the threads. Apply a suitable non-permanent thread locking compound and tighten them to the specified torque.
**12** Lubricate the new piston seals with clean brake fluid and install them in their grooves in the caliper bores.
**13** Lubricate the new dust seals with clean brake fluid and install them in their grooves in the caliper bores.
**14** Lubricate the pistons with clean brake fluid and install them closed-end first into the caliper bores. Using your thumbs, push the pistons all the way in, making sure they enter the bore squarely.
**15** Make sure the rear pad spring is correctly

**7**

7.15 Make sure the spring is correctly fitted in the bracket

8.3 The minimum disc thickness is marked on each disc

8.5 The disc is secured by four bolts (arrowed)

positioned, then slide the caliper bracket into the caliper **(see illustration)**.

### Installation

**16** If removed, make sure that the pad springs are correctly fitted, then install the brake pads (see Section 6).

**17** Install the caliper on the brake disc making sure the pads sit squarely either side of the disc, then tighten the caliper mounting bolts to the torque setting specified at the beginning of the Chapter. If the pads were removed, tighten the pad retaining pin to the specified torque.

**18** Connect the brake hose to the caliper, using a new sealing washer. Tighten the hose bolt to the torque setting specified at the beginning of the Chapter. Now counter-hold the hose nut and tighten the joint nut to the specified torque.

**19** Remove the seat cowling (see Chapter 8). Top up the master cylinder reservoir with DOT 4 brake fluid (see *Daily (pre-ride) checks*) and bleed the hydraulic system as described in Section 11.

**20** Check for leaks and thoroughly test the operation of the brake before riding the motorcycle.

---

### 8 Rear brake disc – inspection, removal and installation

### Inspection

**1** Visually inspect the surface of the disc for score marks and other damage. Light scratches are normal after use and won't affect brake operation, but deep grooves and heavy score marks will reduce braking efficiency and accelerate pad wear. If a disc is badly grooved it must be machined or replaced.

**2** To check disc runout, position the bike on an auxiliary stand and support it so that the wheel is raised off the ground. Mount a dial gauge on the swingarm, with the plunger on the gauge touching the surface of the disc about 10 mm (1/2 in) from the outer edge **(see illustration 4.3a)**. Rotate the wheel and watch

the indicator needle, comparing the reading with the limit listed in the Specifications at the beginning of the Chapter. If the runout is greater than the service limit, check the bearings for play (see Chapter 1). If the bearings are worn, replace them (see Section 16) and repeat this check. If the disc runout is still excessive, it will have to be replaced, although machining by an engineer may be possible.

**3** The disc must not be machined or allowed to wear down to a thickness less than the service limit as listed in this Chapter's Specifications and as marked on the disc itself **(see illustration)**. The thickness of the disc can be checked with a micrometer **(see illustration 4.3b)**. If the thickness of the disc is less than the service limit, it must be replaced.

### Removal

**4** Remove the rear wheel and hub assembly (see Section 16).

**5** Mark the relationship of the disc to the hub, so it can be installed in the same position. Counter-hold the disc bolts and unscrew the nuts, loosening them a little at a time in a criss-cross pattern to avoid distorting the disc, then withdraw the bolts and remove the disc from the wheel **(see illustration)**.

### Installation

**6** Install the disc on the hub, making sure the marked side is on the outside, facing the wheel. Align the previously applied matchmarks (if you're reinstalling the original disc).

**7** Install the bolts and tighten the nuts in a criss-cross pattern evenly and progressively to the torque setting specified at the beginning of the Chapter. Clean off all grease from the brake disc(s) using acetone or brake system cleaner. If a new brake disc has been installed, remove any protective coating from its working surfaces.

**8** Install the hub assembly and the wheel (see Section 16).

**9** Operate the brake lever several times to bring the pads into contact with the disc. Check the operation of the brakes carefully before riding the bike.

---

### 9 Rear brake master cylinder – removal, overhaul and installation

**1** If the master cylinder is leaking fluid, or if the lever does not produce a firm feel when the brake is applied, and bleeding the brakes does not help (see Section 11), and the hydraulic hoses are all in good condition, then master cylinder overhaul is recommended.

**2** Before disassembling the master cylinder, read through the entire procedure and make sure that you have the correct rebuild kit. Also, you will need some new DOT 4 brake fluid, some clean rags and internal circlip pliers. **Note:** *To prevent damage to the paint from spilled brake fluid, always cover the surrounding components when working on the master cylinder.*

*Caution: Disassembly, overhaul and reassembly of the brake master cylinder must be done in a spotlessly clean work area to avoid contamination and possible failure of the brake hydraulic system components.*

### Removal

**3** Remove the seat cowling (see Chapter 8).

**4** Unscrew the bolt securing the master cylinder fluid reservoir to the frame, then remove the reservoir cover and pour the fluid into a container. Release the clamp securing the reservoir hose to the union on the master cylinder and detach the hose **(see illustration)**.

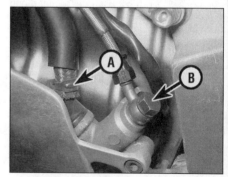

9.4 Reservoir hose clamp (A). Note the alignment of the hose before removing the banjo bolt (B)

**5** Unscrew the brake hose banjo bolt and separate the brake hose from the master cylinder, noting its alignment **(see illustration 9.4)**. Discard the two sealing washers as they must be replaced with new ones. Wrap the end of the hose in a clean rag and suspend the hose in an upright position or bend it down carefully and place the open end in a clean container. The objective is to prevent excessive loss of brake fluid, fluid spills and system contamination.

**6** Remove the split pin from the clevis pin securing the brake pedal to the master cylinder pushrod **(see illustration)**. Withdraw the clevis pin and separate the pedal from the pushrod. Discard the split pin as a new one must be used.

**7** Unscrew the two bolts securing the master cylinder to the bracket and remove the master cylinder **(see illustration)**.

### Overhaul

**8** If required, mark the position of the clevis locknut on the pushrod, then slacken the locknut and thread the clevis and its base nut off the pushrod **(see illustration)**.

**9** Dislodge the rubber dust boot from the base of the master cylinder to reveal the pushrod retaining circlip.

**10** Depress the pushrod and, using circlip pliers, remove the circlip. Slide out the piston assembly and spring. If they are difficult to remove, apply low pressure compressed air to the fluid outlet. Lay the parts out in the proper order to prevent confusion during reassembly.

**11** Clean all of the parts with clean brake fluid or denatured alcohol.

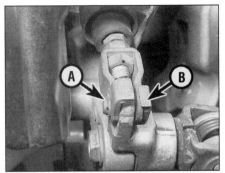

**9.6 Remove the split pin (A) and withdraw the clevis pin (B)**

*Caution:* **Do not, under any circumstances, use a petroleum-based solvent to clean brake parts.** *If compressed air is available, use it to dry the parts thoroughly (make sure it's filtered and unlubricated).*

**12** Check the master cylinder bore for corrosion, scratches, nicks and score marks. If the necessary measuring equipment is available, compare the dimensions of the piston and bore to those given in the Specifications Section of this Chapter. If damage is evident, the master cylinder must be replaced with a new one. If the master cylinder is in poor condition, then the caliper should be checked as well.

**13** If required, unscrew the fluid reservoir hose union screw and detach the elbow from the master cylinder. Discard the O-ring as a new one must be used. Inspect the reservoir hose for cracks or splits and replace if necessary.

**14** The dust boot, circlip, piston, seal,

**9.7 The master cylinder is secured to the bracket by two bolts (arrowed)**

primary cup and spring are included in the rebuild kit. Use all of the new parts, regardless of the apparent condition of the old ones. If the seal and cup are not already on the piston, fit them according to the layout of the old piston assembly.

**15** Install the spring in the master cylinder so that its tapered end faces the piston.

**16** Lubricate the piston, seal and cup with clean brake fluid. Install the assembly into the master cylinder, making sure it is the correct way round. Make sure the lips on the cup do not turn inside out when they are slipped into the bore.

**17** Install and depress the pushrod, then fit a new circlip, making sure it is properly seated in the groove.

**18** Install the rubber dust boot, making sure the lip is seated properly in the groove.

**19** If removed, fit a new O-ring to the fluid reservoir hose union, then install the union onto the master cylinder and secure it with its screw.

### Installation

**20** If removed, install the clevis locknut, the clevis and the base nut onto the master cylinder pushrod end. Position the clevis as noted on removal, then tighten the clevis locknut securely. If in doubt, Honda recommend that the distance between the lower mounting bolt hole on the master cylinder and the pin hole on the clevis is 67.5 mm **(see illustration 9.8)**. However the pedal height can be altered to suit individual tastes. This is best done after the assembly is installed, and is done by slackening the clevis locknut, then turning the pushrod itself using a spanner on the flats on the top of the rod, until the desired pedal height is obtained. Tighten the clevis locknut securely on completion.

**21** Install the master cylinder onto the footrest bracket and tighten its mounting bolts to the torque setting specified at the beginning of the Chapter **(see illustration 9.7)**.

**22** Align the brake pedal with the master cylinder pushrod clevis, then slide in the clevis pin and secure it using a new split pin **(see illustration 9.6)**.

**23** Connect the brake hose banjo bolt to the master cylinder, using a new sealing washer

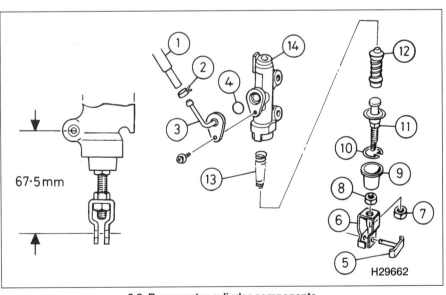

**9.8 Rear master cylinder components**

| | | |
|---|---|---|
| 1 *Reservoir hose* | 6 *Clevis* | 11 *Pushrod* |
| 2 *Reservoir hose clamp* | 7 *Clevis base nut* | 12 *Piston and cup assembly* |
| 3 *Reservoir hose union* | 8 *Locknut* | 13 *Spring* |
| 4 *O-ring* | 9 *Rubber boot* | 14 *Master cylinder* |
| 5 *Clevis pin* | 10 *Circlip* | |

**7**

on each side of the banjo union. Ensure that the hose is positioned so that it butts against the lug and tighten the banjo bolt to the specified torque setting (see illustration 9.5).

24 Secure the fluid reservoir to the frame with its retaining bolt. Ensure that the hose is correctly routed behind the coolant reservoir, then connect it to the union on the master cylinder and secure it with the clamp. Check that the hose is secure and clamped at the reservoir end as well. If the clamps have weakened, use new ones.

25 Fill the fluid reservoir with new DOT 4 brake fluid (see *Daily (pre-ride) checks*) and bleed the system following the procedure in Section 11.

26 Install the seat cowling (see Chapter 8). Check the operation of the brake carefully before riding the motorcycle.

## 10 Brake hoses, pipes and unions – inspection and replacement

### Inspection

1 Brake hose and pipe condition should be checked regularly and the hoses replaced at the specified interval (see Chapter 1).

2 Twist and flex the rubber hoses while looking for cracks, bulges and seeping fluid (see illustration). Check extra carefully around the areas where the hoses connect with the banjo fittings, as these are common areas for hose failure.

3 Inspect the metal brake pipe (RVF models) and the banjo union fittings connected to the brake hoses. If the fittings are rusted, scratched or cracked, replace them.

### Replacement

4 The brake hoses have banjo union fittings on each end, with the exception of the rear caliper hose which has a joint bolt and nut, and the brake pipe (RVF model) has joint nuts. Cover the surrounding area with plenty of rags and unscrew the banjo bolt or joint nut at each end of the hose or pipe, noting its alignment. Free the hose or pipe from any clips or guides and remove it. Discard the sealing washers on the hose banjo unions (see illustration).

5 Position the new hose or pipe, making sure it isn't twisted or otherwise strained, and abut the tab on the hose union with the lug on the component casting, where present. Otherwise align the hose or pipe as noted on removal. Install the hose banjo bolts using new sealing washers on both sides of the unions, and the joint bolt on the rear caliper using one new sealing washer. Tighten the banjo bolts and the rear joint bolt and nut to the torque settings specified at the beginning of this Chapter. Make sure the hoses and pipes are correctly aligned and routed clear of all moving components.

6 Flush the old brake fluid from the system, refill with new DOT 4 brake fluid (see *Daily*

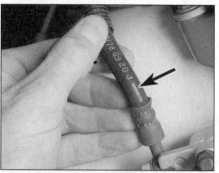

**10.2 Flex the brake hoses and check for cracks, bulges and leaking fluid**

*(pre-ride) checks*) and bleed the air from the system (see Section 10). Check the operation of the brakes carefully before riding the motorcycle.

## 11 Brake system bleeding

1 Bleeding the brakes is simply the process of removing all the air bubbles from the brake fluid reservoirs, the hoses and the brake calipers. Bleeding is necessary whenever a brake system hydraulic connection is loosened, when a component or hose is replaced, or when the master cylinder or caliper is overhauled. Leaks in the system may also allow air to enter, but leaking brake fluid will reveal their presence and warn you of the need for repair.

2 To bleed the brakes, you will need some new DOT 4 brake fluid, a length of clear vinyl or plastic tubing, a small container partially filled with clean brake fluid, some rags and a spanner to fit the brake caliper bleed valves.

3 Cover the fuel tank and other painted components to prevent damage in the event that brake fluid is spilled.

4 If bleeding the rear brake, remove the seat cowling (see Chapter 8) for access to the fluid reservoir.

5 Remove the reservoir cover, diaphragm plate (where fitted) and diaphragm and slowly

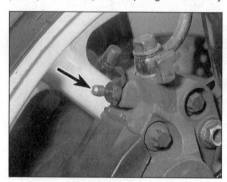

**11.6a Brake caliper bleed valve (arrowed)**

**10.4 Remove the banjo bolt and separate the hose from the caliper; there is a sealing washer on each side of the fitting**

pump the brake lever or pedal a few times, until no air bubbles can be seen floating up from the holes in the bottom of the reservoir. Doing this bleeds the air from the master cylinder end of the line. Loosely refit the reservoir cover.

6 Pull the dust cap off the bleed valve (see illustration). Attach one end of the clear vinyl or plastic tubing to the bleed valve and submerge the other end in the brake fluid in the container (see illustration).

7 Remove the reservoir cover and check the fluid level. Do not allow the fluid level to drop below the lower mark during the bleeding process.

8 Carefully pump the brake lever or pedal three or four times and hold it in (front) or down (rear) while opening the caliper bleed valve. When the valve is opened, brake fluid will flow out of the caliper into the clear tubing and the lever will move toward the handlebar or the pedal will move down.

9 Retighten the bleed valve, then release the brake lever or pedal gradually. Repeat the process until no air bubbles are visible in the brake fluid leaving the caliper and the lever or pedal is firm when applied. On completion, disconnect the bleeding equipment, then tighten the bleed valve to the torque setting specified at the beginning of the chapter and install the dust cap.

10 Install the diaphragm and cover assembly, wipe up any spilled brake fluid and check the entire system for leaks.

**11.6b To bleed the brakes, you need a spanner, a short section of clear tubing, and a clear container half-filled with brake fluid**

**HAYNES HiNT** *If it's not possible to produce a firm feel to the lever or pedal the fluid my be aerated. Let the brake fluid in the system stabilise for a few hours and then repeat the procedure when the tiny bubbles in the system have settled out. To speed this process up, tie the front brake lever to the handlebar or tie a weight to the rear brake pedal so that the system is pressurised.*

## 12 Wheels – inspection and repair

**1** In order to carry out a proper inspection of the wheels, it is necessary to support the bike upright so that the wheel being inspected is raised off the ground. Position the motorcycle on an auxiliary stand. Clean the wheels thoroughly to remove mud and dirt that may interfere with the inspection procedure or mask defects. Make a general check of the wheels (see Chapter 1) and tyres (see *Daily (pre-ride) checks*).
**2** Attach a dial gauge to the fork slider or the swingarm and position its stem against the side of the rim **(see illustration)**. Spin the wheel slowly and check the axial (side-to-side) runout of the rim. In order to accurately check radial (out of round) runout with the dial gauge, the wheel would have to be removed from the machine, and the tyre from the wheel. With the axle clamped in a vice and the dial gauge positioned on the top of the rim, the wheel can be rotated to check the runout.
**3** An easier, though slightly less accurate, method is to attach a stiff wire pointer to the fork slider or the swingarm and position the end a fraction of an inch from the wheel (where the wheel and tyre join). If the wheel is true, the distance from the pointer to the rim will be constant as the wheel is rotated. **Note:** *If wheel runout is excessive, check the wheel or hub bearings very carefully before replacing the wheel.*
**4** The wheels should also be visually

inspected for cracks, flat spots on the rim and other damage. Look very closely for dents in the area where the tyre bead contacts the rim. Dents in this area may prevent complete sealing of the tyre against the rim, which leads to deflation of the tyre over a period of time. If damage is evident, or if runout in either direction is excessive, the wheel will have to be replaced with a new one. Never attempt to repair a damaged cast alloy wheel.

## 13 Wheels – alignment check

**1** Misalignment of the wheels, which may be due to a cocked rear wheel or a bent frame or fork yokes, can cause strange and possibly serious handling problems. If the frame or yokes are at fault, repair by a frame specialist or replacement with new parts are the only alternatives.
**2** To check the alignment you will need an assistant, a length of string or a perfectly straight piece of wood and a ruler. A plumb bob or other suitable weight will also be required.
**3** In order to make a proper check of the wheels it is necessary to support the bike in an upright position, using an auxiliary stand. Measure the width of both tyres at their widest points. Subtract the smaller measurement from the larger measurement, then divide the difference by two. The result is the amount of offset that should exist between the front and rear tyres on both sides.
**4** If a string is used, have your assistant hold one end of it about halfway between the floor and the rear axle, touching the rear sidewall of the tyre.
**5** Run the other end of the string forward and pull it tight so that it is roughly parallel to the floor. Slowly bring the string into contact with the front sidewall of the rear tyre, then turn the front wheel until it is parallel with the string. Measure the distance from the front tyre sidewall to the string.
**6** Repeat the procedure on the other side of the motorcycle. The distance from the front

tyre sidewall to the string should be equal on both sides.
**7** As was previously pointed out, a perfectly straight length of wood may be substituted for the string. The procedure is the same.
**8** If the front-to-back alignment is correct, the wheels still may be out of alignment vertically.
**9** Using the plumb bob, or other suitable weight, and a length of string, check the rear wheel to make sure it is vertical. To do this, hold the string against the tyre upper sidewall and allow the weight to settle just off the floor. When the string touches both the upper and lower tyre sidewalls and is perfectly straight, the wheel is vertical. If it is not, place thin spacers under one leg of the stand.
**10** Once the rear wheel is vertical, check the front wheel in the same manner. If both wheels are not perfectly vertical, the frame and/or major suspension components are bent.

## 14 Front wheel – removal and installation

### *Removal*

**1** Position the motorcycle on an auxiliary stand and support it under the crankcase so that the front wheel is off the ground. Always make sure the motorcycle is properly supported.
**2** Remove the brake caliper mounting bolts and slide the caliper off the disc **(see illustration 3.3a and b)**. Support the caliper with a piece of wire or a bungee cord so that no strain is placed on its hydraulic hose. There is no need to disconnect the hose from the caliper. **Note:** *Do not operate the front brake lever with the calipers removed.*
**3** Slacken the axle clamp bolts on the bottom of the right-hand fork, then unscrew the axle bolt from the right-hand end of the axle **(see illustration)**.
**4** Slacken the axle clamp bolts on the bottom of the left-hand fork **(see illustration)**. Support the wheel, then withdraw the axle from the left-hand side and carefully lower the wheel. Use a screwdriver inserted through the

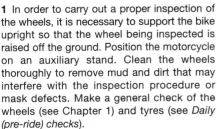

**12.2 Check the wheel for radial (out-of-round) runout (A) and axial (side-to-side) runout (B)**

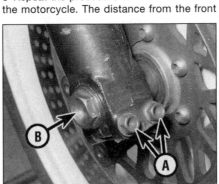

**14.3 Slacken the axle clamp bolts (A), then remove the axle bolt (B)**

**14.4a Slacken the axle clamp bolts (arrowed), then withdraw the axle**

**7**

14.4b Use a screwdriver to aid axle removal

14.5 Remove the spacers from the wheel

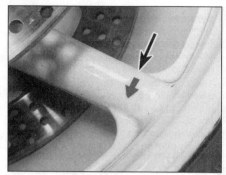

14.8 Note the directional arrow on the wheel (arrowed)

14.10 Slide the axle in from the left . . .

14.11a . . . then install the axle bolt . . .

holes in the end of the axle as a lever to aid removal (see illustration).

5 Remove the long wheel spacer from the right-hand side of the wheel and the short spacer from the left-hand side (see illustration).

Caution: Don't lay the wheel down and allow it to rest on a disc – the disc could become warped. Set the wheel on wood blocks so the disc doesn't support the weight of the wheel.

6 Check the axle for straightness by rolling it on a flat surface such as a piece of plate glass (first wipe off all old grease and remove any corrosion using fine emery cloth). If the

equipment is available, place the axle in V-blocks and measure the runout using a dial gauge. If the axle is bent or the runout exceeds the limit specified, replace it.

7 Check the condition of the wheel bearings (see Section 16).

### Installation

8 Apply a smear of grease to the inside of the wheel spacers, and also to the outside where they fit into the wheel. Fit the long spacer into the right-hand side of the wheel and the short spacer into the left-hand side (see illustration 14.5). Each side of the wheel can be identified using the directional arrow cast into one of the

spokes near the rim (see illustration). The arrow denotes the normal direction of rotation of the wheel.

9 Manoeuvre the wheel into position, making sure the directional arrow is pointing in the normal direction of rotation. Apply a thin coat of grease to the axle.

10 Lift the wheel into place between the fork sliders, making sure the spacers remain in position. Slide the axle in from the left-hand side (see illustration).

11 Install the axle bolt and tighten it to the torque setting specified at the beginning of the Chapter (see illustrations). Use a screwdriver inserted through the holes in the end of the axle to counter-hold it (see illustration 14.4b).

12 Tighten the axle clamp bolts on the bottom of each fork to the specified torque setting (see illustration).

13 Install the brake calipers, making sure the pads sit squarely on either side of the disc (see illustration 3.15a). Tighten the caliper mounting bolts to the specified torque setting (see illustration 3.15b).

14 Apply the front brake a few times to bring the pads back into contact with the discs. Move the motorcycle off its stand, apply the front brake and pump the front forks a few times to settle all components in position.

15 Check for correct operation of the front brake before riding the motorcycle.

14.11b . . . and tighten it to the specified torque

14.12 Tighten all the clamp bolts to the specified torque

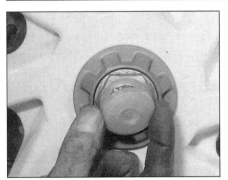

15.2a Remove the cap . . .

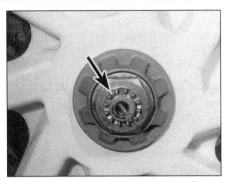

15.2b . . . and the split pin (arrowed) . . .

15.3a . . . then unscrew the nut . . .

15.3b . . . remove the shim . . .

15.3c . . . and the spacer . . .

15.3d . . . and draw the wheel off the hub

## 15 Rear wheel and hub assembly – removal, inspection and installation

### Rear wheel

#### Removal

**1** Position the motorcycle on an auxiliary stand and support it so that the rear wheel is off the ground. Always make sure the motorcycle is properly supported.
**2** Remove the wheel nut cap **(see illustration)**. Remove the split pin from the wheel nut and discard it as a new one must be used **(see illustration)**.

**3** Unscrew the wheel nut, using the rear brake to prevent the wheel from turning **(see illustration)**. Remove the shim and spacer and draw the wheel off its drive pins on the hub flange **(see illustrations)**.

#### Inspection

**4** Check the wheel drive pins on the hub flange for wear, damage and looseness, and replace them if necessary **(see illustration 15.6)**. If any are loose, remove them all – they are secured by bolts on the inside of the flange. Also check the corresponding drive pin holes in the wheel for damage or ovalling. If any is evident, replace the wheel. When installing the drive pins, apply a suitable non-permanent thread locking compound to the

bolts and tighten them to the torque setting specified at the beginning of the Chapter.
**5** Refer to Chapter 1 for further wheel checks.

#### Installation

**6** Lift the wheel into position on the hub, making sure the drive pins on the hub flange locate into the holes in the inside of the wheel **(see illustration)**.
**7** Fit the spacer, the shim and the wheel nut **(see illustrations 15.3c, b and a)**, then tighten the wheel nut to the torque setting specified at the beginning of the Chapter, using the rear brake to prevent the wheel from turning **(see illustration)**.
**8** Secure the nut using a new split pin, then fit the nut cap **(see illustration)**.

15.6 Locate the drive pins (A) in the holes (B)

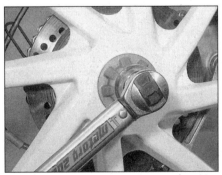

15.7 Tighten the wheel nut to the specified torque . . .

15.8 . . . then fit a new split pin

7

15.10a Unstake the hub nut . . .

15.10b . . . then remove the nut along with the spring washer and thrust washer

15.12a Slacken the pinch bolt (A) and turn the bearing holder (B) to provide chain slack, then disengage the chain and remove the sprocket assembly

15.12b Draw the hub assembly out of the bearing holder

15.13 Draw the axle bolt out of the hub, noting how it fits

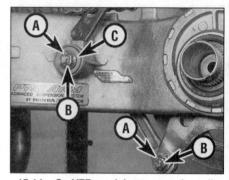

15.14a On VFR models, remove the split pins (A), nuts (B) and the collar (C) . . .

## Hub assembly

### Removal

**9** Remove the rear wheel (see above).
**10** Unstake the hub nut on the left-hand side of the hub using a suitable drift **(see illustration)**. Have an assistant apply the rear brake hard, then unscrew the hub nut, noting that it is very tight **(see illustration)**. Remove the spring washer and the thrust washer from behind the nut **(see illustration)**. Discard the nut as a new one must be used.
**11** Remove the brake caliper mounting bolts and slide the caliper off the disc **(see illustrations 6.1b and c)**. Support the caliper with a piece of wire or a bungee cord so that no strain is placed on its hydraulic hose. There is no need to disconnect the hose from the

caliper. **Note**: *Do not operate the rear brake pedal with the caliper removed.*
**12** Slacken the bearing holder pinch bolt and turn the holder using the pin spanner tool provided in the toolkit, until the drive chain is fully slack **(see illustration)**. Disengage the drive chain from the rear sprocket and draw the sprocket off the hub assembly. Now grasp the brake disc and draw the hub assembly out of the bearing holder from the right-hand side **(see illustration)**.
**13** Tap the right-hand end of the axle bolt using a soft-faced hammer and withdraw it from the left-hand side of the hub assembly **(see illustration)**. Note how the splines on the head of the bolt locate in the splines on the inside of the hub.
**14** On VFR models, if the bearing holder is

being removed, remove the split pins from the brake torque arm nuts on the left-hand side of the swingarm, then unscrew the nuts and remove the torque arm, noting the arrangement of the various collars **(see illustrations)**. Discard the split pins as new ones must be used. On RVF models, the caliper bracket doubles as a torque arm, with the slot in the bracket locating over the long lug on the swingarm, and the bracket can be simply drawn off the bearing holder after removing the circlip.
**15** Remove the circlip securing the brake caliper bracket to the holder and remove the bracket **(see illustration)**. If not already done, slacken the bearing holder pinch bolt and draw the holder out from the left-hand side of the swingarm **(see illustration)**.

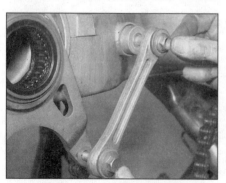

15.14b . . . and withdraw the bolts and torque arm from the other side

15.15a Remove the circlip and the caliper bracket . . .

15.15b . . . then draw the bearing holder out

15.22a  Install the bearing holder . . .

15.22b  . . . and fit the caliper bracket

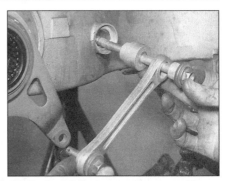

15.22c  Install the torque arm assembly . . .

15.22d  . . . and fit the collar . . .

15.22e  . . . and nut onto the swingarm mount . . .

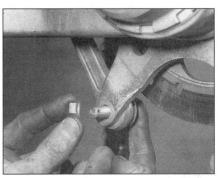

15.22f  . . . and the nut onto the bracket mount

**16**  If required, separate the brake disc from the hub assembly (see Section 8).

### Inspection

**17**  Check the axle bolt for straightness by rolling it on a flat surface such as a piece of plate glass (if the axle is corroded, first remove the corrosion with fine emery cloth). If the equipment is available, place the axle in V-blocks and measure the runout using a dial gauge. If the axle is bent or the runout exceeds the limit specified at the beginning of the Chapter, replace it.

**18**  Check the condition of the bearings in the bearing holder (see Section 16).
**19**  Inspect the splines on the hub for damage and wear and replace it if necessary. Also check the corresponding splines in the rear sprocket holder.
**20**  If not already done, check the wheel drive pins on the hub flange (see Step 4).

### Installation

**21**  If removed, fit the brake disc onto the hub assembly (see Section 8).
**22**  If removed, fit the bearing holder into the

swingarm, then locate the caliper bracket onto the right-hand end of the holder **(see illustrations)**. On RVF models make sure the slot locates over the long lug on the swingarm. Secure the bracket with the circlip, making sure it fits properly into its groove **(see illustration 15.15a)**. On VFR models, install the brake torque arm onto the caliper bracket and the swingarm, making sure the various collars are correctly installed **(see illustration)**. Tighten the nuts to the torque setting specified at the beginning of the Chapter and secure them using new split pins **(see illustration)**.

15.22g  Tighten the nuts to the specified torque . . .

15.22h  . . . and fit new split pins

**7**

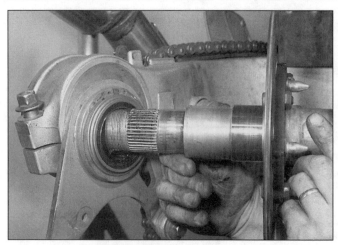

15.23a  Install the hub assembly . . .

15.23b  . . . and fit the sprocket

23  Apply grease to the needle bearing in the right-hand side of the bearing holder. Slide the hub assembly through the bearing holder from the right-hand side **(see illustration)**. Make sure the hub assembly is pushed fully into the bearing holder. Slide the rear sprocket onto the hub, aligning the splines on the sprocket holder with those on the hub, and push the sprocket fully onto the splines **(see illustration)**.
24  Fit the thrust washer and the spring washer, with its raised inner edge facing out, onto the left-hand side of the hub, then thread the new hub nut on and tighten it hand tight

**(see illustrations)**. On RVF models, oil the threads of the nut before fitting it.
25  Install the caliper on the brake disc making sure the pads sit squarely either side of the disc. Tighten the caliper mounting bolts to the specified torque setting **(see illustration 6.10a)**.
26  Operate the brake pedal several times to bring the pads into contact with the disc. Have an assistant apply the rear brake hard, then tighten the hub nut to the specified torque setting **(see illustration)**. Stake the rim of the nut against the indentation in the hub using a suitable drift **(see illustration)**.

27  Fit the axle bolt into the left-hand side of the hub assembly, making sure the splines on the head of the bolt locate with those on the inside of the hub **(see illustration 15.13)**. Tap the bolt home using a soft-faced hammer to ensure it is properly seated **(see illustration)**.
28  Fit the drive chain around the sprocket and install the rear wheel (see above).
29  Check and adjust the drive chain slack (see Chapter 1). Make sure the bearing holder pinch bolt is tightened to the specified torque setting. Check the operation of the rear brake carefully before riding the bike.

15.24a  Fit the thrust washer . . .

15.24b  . . . the spring washer . . .

15.24c  . . . and the hub nut

15.26a  Tighten the nut to the specified torque . . .

15.26b  . . . and stake its rim against the indentation

15.27  Tap the axle bolt fully home using a suitable drift, making sure the splines engage

16.3 Lever out the grease seals and discard them

16.4a Use a drift to knock out the bearings

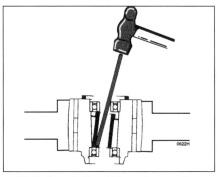

16.4b Locate the drift as shown when driving out the bearing

## 16 Wheel bearings – removal, inspection and installation

### Front wheel bearings

**Note:** *Always replace the wheel bearings in pairs. Never replace the bearings individually. Avoid using a high pressure cleaner on the wheel bearing area.*

**1** Remove the wheel (see Section 14).

**2** Set the wheel on blocks so as not to allow the weight of the wheel to rest on the brake disc. Have the left-hand side of the wheel facing up.

**3** Prise out the seal on each side of the wheel using a flat-bladed screwdriver, taking care not to damage the rim of the hub **(see illustration)**. Discard the seals as new ones should be used.

**4** Using a metal rod (preferably a brass drift punch) inserted through the centre of the left-hand bearing, tap evenly around the inner race of the right-hand bearing to drive it from the hub **(see illustrations)**. The bearing spacer will also come out.

**5** Lay the wheel on its other side so that the left-hand bearing faces down. Drive the bearing out of the wheel using the same technique as above.

**6** If the bearings are of the unsealed type or are only sealed on one side, clean them with a high flash-point solvent (one which won't leave any residue) and blow them dry with compressed air (don't let the bearings spin as you dry them). Apply a few drops of oil to the bearing. **Note:** *If the bearing is sealed on both sides don't attempt to clean it.*

 **Refer to Tools and Workshop Tips (Section 5) for more information about bearings.**

**7** Hold the outer race of the bearing and rotate the inner race – if the bearing doesn't turn smoothly, has rough spots or is noisy, replace it with a new one.

**8** If the bearing is good and can be re-used, wash it in solvent once again and dry it, then pack the bearing with grease.

16.9 The bearing can be driven in using a suitable socket

**9** Thoroughly clean the hub area of the wheel. First install the left-hand side bearing into its recess in the hub, with the marked or sealed side facing outwards. Using the old bearing (if new ones are being fitted), a bearing driver or a socket large enough to contact the outer race of the bearing, drive it in until it's completely seated **(see illustration)**.

**10** Turn the wheel over and install the bearing spacer. Drive the right-hand side bearing into place as described above.

**11** Apply a smear of grease to the lips of the seals, then press them into the wheel. Gently

16.11 The seal can be driven in using a flat piece of wood

drive them into place using a seal or bearing driver, a suitable socket or a flat piece of wood **(see illustration)**.

**12** Clean off all grease from the brake discs using acetone or brake system cleaner then install the wheel (see Section 14).

### Rear wheel bearings

**13** Remove the rear wheel, the hub assembly and the bearing holder (see Section 15).

**14** Remove the collar from the left-hand side of the holder, noting how it fits between the seal and the bearing **(see illustrations)**. Using

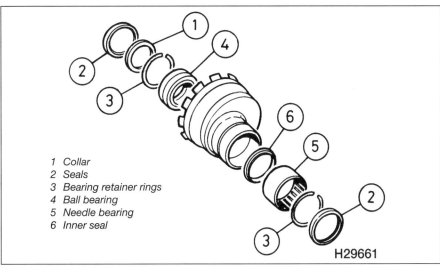

1 Collar
2 Seals
3 Bearing retainer rings
4 Ball bearing
5 Needle bearing
6 Inner seal

H29661

16.14a Bearing holder components

7

a flat-bladed screwdriver, prise out the seal from each side of the holder (see illustration). Also lever out the retaining rings securing each bearing. Discard the seals as new ones should be used.

**15** Set the bearing holder on blocks to allow the bearings to be driven out. Refer to *Tools and Workshop Tips (Section 5)* in the Reference Section and remove the bearings from the holder. Also remove the inner seal.

**16** Check the bearings as described in Steps 6 to 8 above.

**17** Thoroughly clean the holder, then install the inner dust seal, followed by the bearings. Apply grease to the outside of the needle bearing and press, rather than drive, it home until it is fully seated. Install the caged ball bearing with the marked or sealed side facing outwards. Using the old bearing (if a new one is being fitted), a bearing driver or a socket large enough to contact the outer race of the bearing, drive it in squarely until it's completely seated.

**18** Fit the bearing retaining rings, making sure they fit properly in their grooves.

**19** Apply a smear of grease to the lips of the seals, and press them into the holder. Gently drive them into place using a seal or bearing driver, a suitable socket or a flat piece of wood. Fit the collar into the left-hand side of the holder (see illustration 16.14b).

**20** Install the bearing holder, the hub assembly and the wheel (see Section 15).

16.14b Remove the collar, noting how it fits . . .

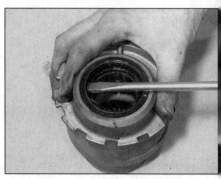

16.14c . . . and lever out the seals

## 17 Tyres –
### general information and fitting

### *General information*

**1** The wheels fitted to all models are designed to take tubeless tyres only. Tyre sizes are given in the Specifications at the beginning of this chapter.

**2** Refer to the Daily (pre-ride) checks listed at the beginning of this manual for tyre maintenance.

### *Fitting new tyres*

**3** When selecting new tyres, refer to the tyre information label on the swingarm and the tyre options listed in the owners handbook. Ensure that front and rear tyre types are compatible, the correct size and correct speed rating; if necessary seek advice from a Honda dealer or tyre fitting specialist (see illustration).

**4** It is recommended that tyres are fitted by a motorcycle tyre specialist rather than attempted in the home workshop. This is particularly relevant in the case of tubeless tyres because the force required to break the seal between the wheel rim and tyre bead is substantial, and is usually beyond the capabilities of an individual working with normal tyre levers. Additionally, the specialist will be able to balance the wheels after tyre fitting.

**5** Note that punctured tubeless tyres can in some cases be repaired. Honda recommend that such repairs are carried out only by an authorised dealer.

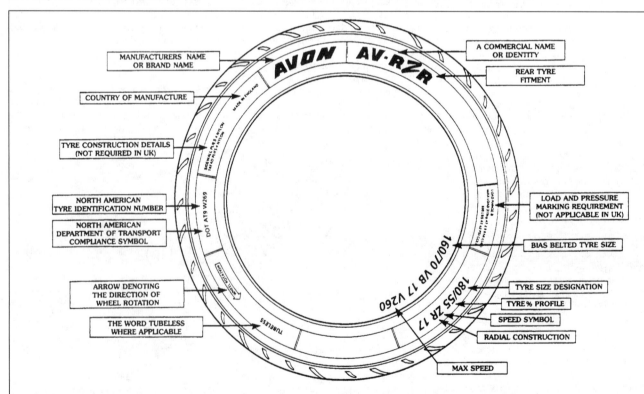

17.3 Common tyre sidewall markings

# Chapter 8
# Bodywork

## Contents

## Degrees of difficulty

| Easy, suitable for novice with little experience |  | Fairly easy, suitable for beginner with some experience |  | Fairly difficult, suitable for competent DIY mechanic | | Difficult, suitable for experienced DIY mechanic |  | Very difficult, suitable for expert DIY or professional | |
|---|---|---|---|---|---|---|---|---|---|

## 1 General information

This Chapter covers the procedures necessary to remove and install the body parts. Since many service and repair operations on these motorcycles require the removal of the body parts, the procedures are grouped here and referred to from other Chapters.

In the case of damage to the body parts, it is usually necessary to remove the broken component and replace it with a new (or used) one. The material that the body panels are composed of doesn't lend itself to conventional repair techniques. There are however some shops that specialise in 'plastic welding', so it may be worthwhile seeking the advice of one of these specialists before consigning an expensive component to the bin.

When attempting to remove any body panel, first study it closely, noting any fasteners and associated fittings, to be sure of returning everything to its correct place on installation. In some cases the aid of an assistant will be required when removing panels, to help avoid the risk of damage to paintwork. Once the evident fasteners have been removed, try to withdraw the panel as described but DO NOT FORCE IT – if it will not release, check that all fasteners have been removed and try again. Where a panel engages another by means of tabs, be careful not to break the tab or its mating slot or to damage the paintwork. Remember that a few moments of patience at this stage will save you a lot of money in replacing broken fairing panels!

When installing a body panel, first study it closely, noting any fasteners and associated fittings removed with it, to be sure of returning everything to its correct place. Check that all fasteners are in good condition, including all trim nuts or clips and damping/rubber mounts; any of these must be replaced if faulty before the panel is reassembled. Check also that all mounting brackets are straight and repair or replace them if necessary before attempting to install the panel. Where assistance was required to remove a panel, make sure your assistant is on hand to install it.

Tighten the fasteners securely, but be careful not to overtighten any of them or the panel may break (not always immediately) due to the uneven stress. Where quick-release fasteners are fitted, turn them 90° anti-clockwise to release them, and 90° clockwise to secure them.

**HAYNES HINT** *Note that a small amount of lubricant (liquid soap or similar) applied to the mounting rubber grommets of the seat cowling will assist the lugs to engage without the need for undue pressure.*

8

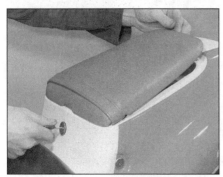

2.1 Remove the passenger seat

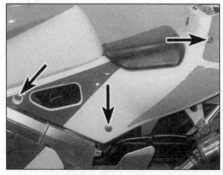

2.2a Remove the three screws (arrowed) on each side . . .

2.2b . . . then lift the cowling out of its grommets (arrow) . . .

## 2 Seat cowling – removal and installation

### Removal

**1** Insert the ignition key into the seat lock located behind the rider's seat, and turn it clockwise to unlock the passenger's seat. Remove the passenger's seat **(see illustration)**.

**2** On VFR models, remove the three screws securing each side of the seat cowling **(see illustration)**. Carefully lift the rear of the cowling to free the two lugs from their rubber grommets **(see illustration)**. Lift the rear of the cowling further to access the taillight assembly wiring connector and disconnect the connector **(see illustration)**. Carefully draw the cowling rearwards and off the bike, taking care not to bend the front sides **(see illustration)**.

**3** On RVF models, lift each side of the rear of the rider's seat and remove the two screws,

then remove the seat **(see illustrations)**. Also remove the screw securing each side of the seat cowling **(see illustration)**. Carefully pull the front top corner on each side of the cowling away from the fuel tank to free each lug from its grommet. Carefully lift the rear of the cowling to free the two lugs from their rubber grommets. Lift the rear of the cowling further to access the taillight assembly wiring connector and disconnect the connector. Carefully draw the cowling rearwards and off the bike, taking care not to bend the front sides.

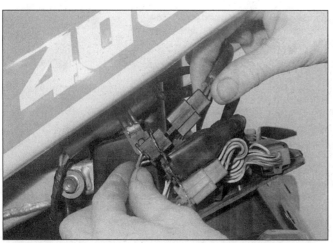

2.2c . . . and raise it to disconnect the taillight wiring connector

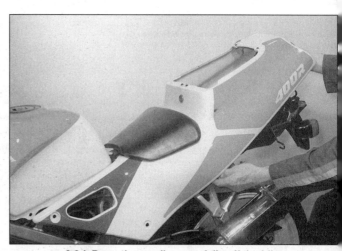

2.2d Draw the cowling carefully off the bike

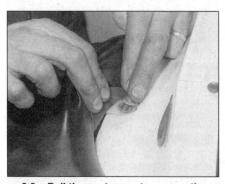

2.3a Pull the seat away to access the screws . . .

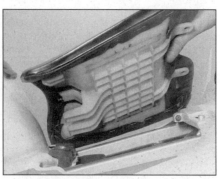

2.3b . . . and remove the seat

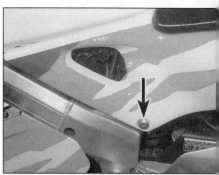

2.3c Remove the single screw (arrowed) on each side

## Installation

**4** Installation is the reverse of removal. Make sure the lugs locate correctly in their rubber grommets **(see illustration 2.2b)**. Make sure the tab at the front of the rider's seat on RVF models, and the tabs at the front of the passenger's seat on all models locate correctly **(see illustration)**. Push down on the rear of the passenger's seat to engage the latch **(see illustration)**.

## 3  Rear view mirrors – removal and installation

### Removal

**1** Unscrew the two nuts securing each mirror and remove the mirror along with its rubber insulator pads **(see illustrations)**.

### Installation

**2** Installation is the reverse of removal.

## 4  Fairing panels – removal and installation

### Fairing

**Note:** The windshield is secured to the fairing with rivets and should not be removed unless it is being replaced. Windshields are available separately from the fairing. The type of rivet supplied by Honda, requires the rivet to be inserted from the outside of the windshield and a keeper pressed onto its inner end.

### VFR models removal

**1** Remove the fairing side panels and the radiator cover (see below).
**2** Remove the rear view mirrors (see Section 3).
**3** Disconnect the turn signal wiring connectors **(see illustration)**.
**4** Unscrew the bolt securing the front of the fairing to the fairing bracket **(see illustration)**. Carefully draw the fairing forward and off the bike **(see illustration)**.

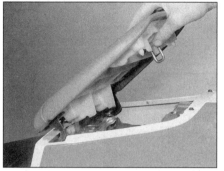
2.4a  Locate the tabs at the front . . .

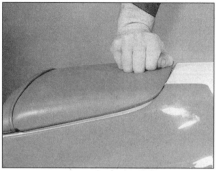
2.4b  . . . and push down to engage the latch

3.1a  Unscrew the two nuts . . .

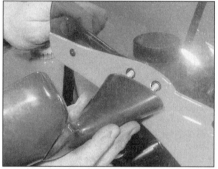
3.1b  . . . and remove the mirror . . .

3.1c  . . . noting how the rubber pad fits between the bracket and the fairing

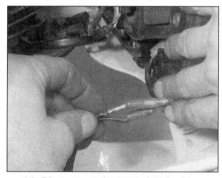
4.3  Disconnect the turn signal wiring connectors . . .

4.4a  . . . then unscrew the bolt . . .

4.4b  . . . and draw the fairing off the bike

8

**4.5a Remove the screw . . .**

**4.5b . . . and lift off the duct**

### RVF models removal

**5** Remove the screw securing each air duct to the tank and remove the ducts **(see illustrations)**.
**6** Disconnect the headlight and turn signal wiring connectors, and carefully pull the sidelight out of its socket in the base of the headlight.
**7** Remove the trim clip securing each inner side of the fairing to the radiator cover.
**8** Unscrew the bolt securing the front of the fairing to the fairing bracket. Carefully draw the fairing forward and off the bike.
**9** If required, remove the headlight from the fairing (see Chapter 9).

### Installation

**11** Installation is the reverse of removal. On VFR models, make sure the rubber headlight surrounds do not turn inside out when installing the fairing. Make sure the wiring connectors are correctly and securely connected.

### *Fairing side panels*
### Removal

**12** Each side panel is secured by two quick-release screws and a normal screw, and has tabs which fit into slots in the fairing **(see illustration)**. On VFR models, there is also a screw securing the inner trim panel to each

side panel **(see illustration)**. Remove the screws, then carefully draw the panel away, releasing its tabs at the front from the fairing, noting how it fits **(see illustration)**. On RVF models, if required, remove the trim clip securing the heat insulator pad and remove the pad, noting how it fits **(see illustration)**.
**13** If required, remove the trim panels. On VFR models, each is secured by two bolts. On RVF models, each is secured by two trim clips, inserted from the underside. When removing the left-hand trim panel, release the idle speed adjuster from its bracket, and on RVF models, remove the choke cable (see Chapter 4).

### Installation

**14** Installation is the reverse of removal. Make sure the tabs locate correctly into the slots in the fairing.

### *Radiator cover*
### Removal

**15** Remove the seven (VFR models) or five (RVF models) fasteners securing the radiator cover to the fairing and the lower fairing **(see illustrations)**. Carefully draw the cover away from the bike, noting how it fits **(see illustration)**.

### Installation

**16** Installation is the reverse of removal.

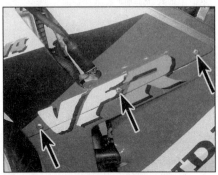

**4.12a Remove the three screws (arrowed) . . .**

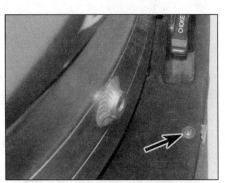

**4.12b . . . and on VFR models the trim panel screw (arrowed)**

**4.12c . . . then remove the panel, releasing the tabs at the front**

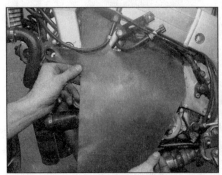

**4.12d Remove the insulator pad on RVF models**

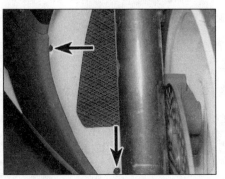

**4.15a Remove the screws . . .**

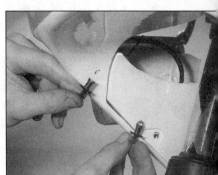

**4.15b . . . and the trim clips (two on VFR models, one on RVF models) . . .**

4.15c ... and remove the radiator cover

4.18a  Remove the two screws (arrowed) on each side ...

4.18b  ... noting the spacers on VFR models ...

## Lower fairing

### Removal

**17**  Remove the fairing side panels and the radiator cover (see above).

**18**  The lower fairing is secured by two screws on each side, one in the middle at the top, the other at the rear on the bottom **(see illustration)**. On VFR models, a spacer fits between the inside of each top mounting and the frame **(see illustration)**. Remove the screws, then carefully lower the fairing and manoeuvre it from under the bike **(see illustration)**.

### Installation

**19**  Installation is the reverse of removal. Do not forget the spacers on the top mountings on VFR models **(see illustration 4.18b)**.

---

**5  Front mudguard** – removal and installation

### Removal

#### VFR models

**1**  Unscrew the four bolts securing the mudguard to the holder on each fork slider and remove the mudguard, noting how it fits **(see illustration)**.

#### RVF models

**2**  Unscrew the nut securing each brake hose clamp to the mudguard, then remove the clamps, noting how they fit, and position the hoses aside **(see illustration)**.

**3**  Unscrew the two bolts securing each side of the mudguard to the fork slider and remove

4.18c  ... and remove the lower fairing

the mudguard, noting how it fits **(see illustration)**.

### Installation

**4**  Installation is the reverse of removal.

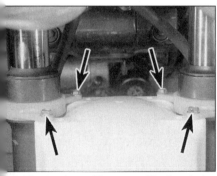

5.1  The mudguard is secured by four bolts (arrowed)

5.2  Unscrew the brake hose clamp nuts ...

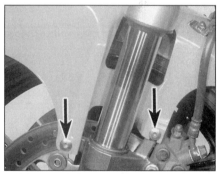

5.3  ... and the two bolts (arrowed) on each side

**8**

Notes

# Chapter 9
# Electrical system

## Contents

## Degrees of difficulty

| Easy, suitable for novice with little experience |  | Fairly easy, suitable for beginner with some experience |  | Fairly difficult, suitable for competent DIY mechanic | | Difficult, suitable for experienced DIY mechanic | | Very difficult, suitable for expert DIY or professional | 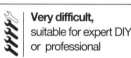 |

## Specifications

### Battery

| | |
|---|---|
| Capacity . . . . . . . . . . . . . . . . . . . . . . . . . . . . . . . . . . . . . . . . . . . . | 12 V, 6 Ah |
| Voltage | |
|   Fully charged . . . . . . . . . . . . . . . . . . . . . . . . . . . . . . . . . . . . . | 13.0 to 13.2 V |
|   Uncharged . . . . . . . . . . . . . . . . . . . . . . . . . . . . . . . . . . . . . . | below 12.3 V |
| Charging rate | |
|   Normal . . . . . . . . . . . . . . . . . . . . . . . . . . . . . . . . . . . . . . . . | 0.7 A for 5 to 10 hrs |
|   Quick . . . . . . . . . . . . . . . . . . . . . . . . . . . . . . . . . . . . . . . . . | 3.0 A for 1hr |
| Current leakage . . . . . . . . . . . . . . . . . . . . . . . . . . . . . . . . . . . . . . | 1 mA (max) |

### Alternator

| | |
|---|---|
| Stator coil resistance . . . . . . . . . . . . . . . . . . . . . . . . . . . . . . . . . . | 0.1 to 1.0 ohms |

### Regulator/rectifier

| | |
|---|---|
| Regulated voltage output . . . . . . . . . . . . . . . . . . . . . . . . . . . . . . . | 13.5 to 15.5 V @ 5000 rpm |
| Regulated current output . . . . . . . . . . . . . . . . . . . . . . . . . . . . . . . | 0 to 6 A @ 5000 rpm |

### Starter motor

| | |
|---|---|
| Brush length | |
|   Standard . . . . . . . . . . . . . . . . . . . . . . . . . . . . . . . . . . . . . . . | 12.0 to 13.0 mm |
|   Service limit (min) . . . . . . . . . . . . . . . . . . . . . . . . . . . . . . . . | 6.5 mm |

## Fuses

VFR models

| | |
|---|---|
| Main | 30 A |
| Others | 10 A x 3, 20 A x 1 |

RVF models

| | |
|---|---|
| Main | 30 A |
| Others | 10 A x 3, 15 A x 1 |

## Bulbs

**Note:** *The following bulb ratings for Japan spec models (greys) are as suited to that market. Certain bulbs may have been uprated to conform to UK requirements (eg the brake/tail light bulb will be uprated to 21/5 W)*

| | |
|---|---|
| Headlight | |
| UK spec | 60/55 W halogen x 2 |
| Japan spec | 60/35 W halogen x 2 |
| Sidelight | |
| UK spec | 5.0 W x 2 |
| Japan spec | 1.7 W x 2 |
| Brake/tail light | |
| UK spec | 21/5 W x 2 |
| Japan spec | 18/5 W x 2 |
| Turn signal lights | |
| UK spec | 21 W x 4 |
| Japan spec | |
| VFR | 15 W x 4 |
| RVF – front (incorporating running lights) | 18/5 W x 2 |
| RVF – rear | 15 W x 2 |
| Instrument lights | 1.7 W |
| Turn signal indicator light | 1.7 W |
| Neutral indicator light | 1.7 W |
| Oil pressure indicator light | 1.7 W |
| High beam indicator light | 1.7 W |
| Sidestand indicator light (RVF models) | 1.7 W |
| Speed limiter light (VFR models – where fitted) | 3.4 W |

## Torque settings – specific components

| | |
|---|---|
| Footrest bracket bolts | 27 Nm |
| Oil pressure switch | 12 Nm |
| Ignition switch Torx bolts | 25 Nm |
| Neutral switch | 12 Nm |
| Alternator rotor bolt | 85 Nm |

## Torque settings – non-specified components

**Note:** *Where a specific setting is not given for a particular bolt/nut, these general settings apply. The dimension given applies to the diameter of the thread, not the head.*

| | |
|---|---|
| 5 mm bolt/nut | 5 Nm |
| 6 mm bolt/nut | 10 Nm |
| 8 mm bolt/nut | 22 Nm |
| 10 mm bolt/nut | 35 Nm |
| 12 mm bolt/nut | 55 Nm |
| 6 mm flange bolt with 8 mm head | 9 Nm |
| 6 mm flange bolt/nut with 10 mm head | 12 Nm |
| 8 mm flange bolt/nut | 27 Nm |
| 10 mm flange bolt/nut | 40 Nm |

## 1 General information

All models have a 12-volt electrical system charged by a three-phase alternator with a separate regulator/rectifier.

The regulator maintains the charging system output within the specified range to prevent overcharging, and the rectifier converts the ac (alternating current) output of the alternator to dc (direct current) to power the lights and other components and to charge the battery. The alternator rotor is mounted on the left-hand end of the crankshaft.

The starter motor is mounted on the front of the engine. The starting system includes the motor, the battery, the relay and the various wires and switches. If the engine kill switch is in the RUN position and the ignition (main) switch is ON, the starter relay allows the starter motor to operate only if the transmission is in neutral (neutral switch on) or, if the transmission is in gear, if the clutch lever is pulled into the handlebar and, on RVF models, the sidestand is up.

**Note:** *Keep in mind that electrical parts, once purchased, cannot be returned. To avoid unnecessary expense, make very sure the faulty component has been positively identified before buying a replacement part.*

## 2  Electrical system – fault finding

**Warning: To prevent the risk of short circuits, the ignition (main) switch must always be OFF and the battery negative (–ve) terminal should be disconnected before any of the bike's other electrical components are disturbed. Don't forget to reconnect the terminal securely once work is finished or if battery power is needed for circuit testing.**

1 A typical electrical circuit consists of an electrical component, the switches, relays, etc. related to that component and the wiring and connectors that hook the component to both the battery and the frame. To aid in locating a problem in any electrical circuit, refer to the wiring diagrams at the end of this Chapter.

2 Before tackling any troublesome electrical circuit, first study the wiring diagram (see end of Chapter) thoroughly to get a complete picture of what makes up that individual circuit. Trouble spots, for instance, can often be narrowed down by noting if other components related to that circuit are operating properly or not. If several components or circuits fail at one time, chances are the fault lies in the fuse or earth (ground) connection, as several circuits often are routed through the same fuse and earth (ground) connections.

3 Electrical problems often stem from simple causes, such as loose or corroded connections or a blown fuse. Prior to any electrical fault finding, always visually check the condition of the fuse, wires and connections in the problem circuit. Intermittent failures can be especially frustrating, since you can't always duplicate the failure when it's convenient to test. In such situations, a good practice is to clean all connections in the affected circuit, whether or not they appear to be good. All of the connections and wires should also be wiggled to check for looseness which can cause intermittent failure.

4 If testing instruments are going to be utilised, use the wiring diagram to plan where you will make the necessary connections in order to accurately pinpoint the trouble spot.

5 The basic tools needed for electrical fault finding include a battery and bulb test circuit, a continuity tester, a test light, and a jumper wire. A multimeter capable of reading volts, ohms and amps is also very useful as an alternative to the above, and is necessary for performing more extensive tests and checks.

**HAYNES HiNT** *Refer to Fault Finding Equipment in the Reference section for details of how to use electrical test equipment.*

## 3  Battery – removal, installation, inspection and maintenance

**Caution: Be extremely careful when handling or working around the battery. The electrolyte is very caustic and an explosive gas (hydrogen) is given off when the battery is charging.**

### Removal and installation

1 On VFR models, remove the seat cowling (see Chapter 8). On RVF models, lift each side of the rear of the rider's seat and remove the two screws, then remove the seat.

2 Unscrew the negative (–ve) terminal bolt first and disconnect the lead from the battery **(see illustration)**. Lift up the red insulating cover to access the positive (+ve) terminal, then unscrew the bolt and disconnect the lead **(see illustration)**. Release the battery strap from its hook and lift the battery from the bike **(see illustrations)**.

3 On installation, clean the battery terminals and lead ends with a wire brush or knife and emery paper. Reconnect the leads, connecting the positive (+ve) terminal first.

**HAYNES HiNT** *Battery corrosion can be kept to a minimum by applying a layer of petroleum jelly to the terminals after the cables have been connected.*

**3.2a  Disconnect the negative lead . . .**

**3.2c  . . . then unhook the strap . . .**

4 Install the seat or seat cowling (see Chapter 8).

### Inspection and maintenance

5 The battery fitted to the models covered in this manual is of the maintenance free (sealed) type, therefore requiring no regular maintenance. However, the following checks should still be regularly performed.

6 Check the battery terminals and leads for tightness and corrosion. If corrosion is evident, unscrew the terminal screws and disconnect the leads from the battery, disconnecting the negative (–ve) terminal first, and clean the terminals and lead ends with a wire brush or knife and emery paper. Reconnect the leads, connecting the negative (–ve) terminal last, and apply a thin coat of petroleum jelly to the connections to slow further corrosion.

7 The battery case should be kept clean to prevent current leakage, which can discharge the battery over a period of time (especially when it sits unused). Wash the outside of the case with a solution of baking soda and water. Rinse the battery thoroughly, then dry it.

8 Look for cracks in the case and replace the battery if any are found. If acid has been spilled on the frame or battery box, neutralise it with a baking soda and water solution, dry it thoroughly, then touch up any damaged paint.

9 If the motorcycle sits unused for long periods of time, disconnect the cables from the battery terminals, negative (–ve) terminal first. Refer to Section 4 and charge the battery once every month to six weeks.

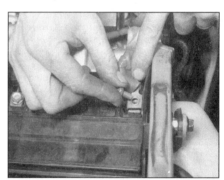

**3.2b  . . . and the positive lead . . .**

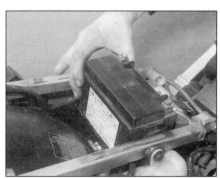

**3.2d  . . . and remove the battery**

**9**

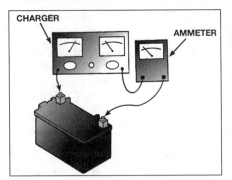

4.2 If the charger doesn't have ammeter built in, connect one in series as shown. DO NOT connect the ammeter between the battery terminals or it will be ruined

5.1a Fusebox location

5.1b The main fuse is located in the starter relay

**10** The condition of the battery can be assessed by measuring the voltage present at the battery terminals. Connect the voltmeter positive (+ve) probe to the battery positive (+ve) terminal, and the negative (–ve) probe to the battery negative (–ve) terminal. When fully charged there should be more than 13.0 volts present. If the voltage falls below 12.3 volts the battery must be removed, disconnecting the negative (–ve) terminal first, and recharged as described below in Section 4.

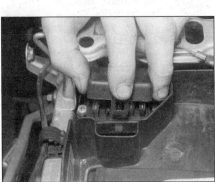

5.2a Unclip the lid to access the fuses

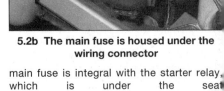

5.2b The main fuse is housed under the wiring connector

### 4  Battery – charging

*Caution: Be extremely careful when handling or working around the battery. The electrolyte is very caustic and an explosive gas (hydrogen) is given off when the battery is charging.*
**1** Remove the battery (see Section 3). Connect the charger to the battery, making sure that the positive (+ve) lead on the charger is connected to the positive (+ve) terminal on the battery, and the negative (–ve) lead is connected to the negative (–ve) terminal.
**2** Honda recommend that the battery is charged at a maximum rate of 0.7 amps for 5 to 10 hours. Exceeding this figure can cause the battery to overheat, buckling the plates and rendering it useless. Few owners will have access to an expensive current controlled charger, so if a normal domestic charger is used check that after a possible initial peak, the charge rate falls to a safe level **(see illustration)**. If the battery becomes hot during charging **stop**. Further charging will cause damage. **Note:** *In emergencies the battery can be charged at a higher rate of around 3.0 amps for a period of 1 hour. However, this is not recommended and the low amp charge is by far the safer method of charging the battery.*
**3** If the recharged battery discharges rapidly if left disconnected it is likely that an internal short caused by physical damage or

sulphation has occurred. A new battery will be required. A sound item will tend to lose its charge at about 1% per day.
**4** Install the battery (see Section 3).
**5** If the motorcycle sits unused for long periods of time, charge the battery once every month to six weeks and leave it disconnected.

### 5  Fuses – check and replacement

**1** The electrical system is protected by fuses of different ratings. All except the main fuse are housed in the fusebox, which is located under the seat cowling **(see illustration)**. The

5.3a Use a pair of pliers to remove a fuse

main fuse is integral with the starter relay, which is under the seat cowling on the right-hand side of the bike, just ahead of the coolant reservoir **(see illustration)**.
**2** To access the fuses, remove the seat cowling (see Chapter 8) and unclip the fusebox lid **(see illustration)**. To access the main fuse, disconnect the starter relay wiring connector **(see illustration)**.
**3** The fuses can be removed and checked visually. If you can't pull the fuse out with your fingertips, use a pair of suitable pliers **(see illustration)**. A blown fuse is easily identified by a break in the element **(see illustration)**. Each fuse is clearly marked with its rating and must only be replaced by a fuse of the correct rating. A spare fuse of each rating is housed in the fusebox, and a spare main fuse is housed

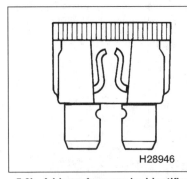

H28946

5.3b A blown fuse can be identified by a break in its element

**5.3c Spare main fuse (arrowed)**

in the bottom of the starter relay **(see illustration)**. If a spare fuse is used, always replace it so that a spare of each rating is carried on the bike at all times.

*Warning: Never put in a fuse of a higher rating or bridge the terminals with any other substitute, however temporary it may be. Serious damage may be done to the circuit, or a fire may start.*

**4** If a fuse blows, be sure to check the wiring circuit very carefully for evidence of a short-circuit. Look for bare wires and chafed, melted or burned insulation. If the fuse is replaced before the cause is located, the new fuse will blow immediately.

**5** Occasionally a fuse will blow or cause an open-circuit for no obvious reason. Corrosion of the fuse ends and fusebox terminals may occur and cause poor fuse contact. If this happens, remove the corrosion with a wire brush or emery paper, then spray the fuse end and terminals with electrical contact cleaner.

## 6 Lighting system – check

**1** The battery provides power for operation of the headlight, tail light, brake light and instrument cluster lights. If none of the lights operate, always check battery voltage before proceeding. Low battery voltage indicates either a faulty battery or a defective charging system. Refer to Section 3 for battery checks and Sections 30 and 31 for charging system tests. Also, check the condition of the fuses.

### Headlight

**2** If the headlight fails to work, first check the fuse with the key ON (see Section 5), and then the bulb (see Section 7). If they are both good, use jumper wires to connect the bulb directly to the battery terminals. If the light comes on, the problem lies in the wiring, the relay(s), or one of the switches in the circuit. Refer to Section 20 for the switch testing procedures, and also the wiring diagrams at the end of this Chapter.

**3** If either the high beam or low beam relay is suspected of being faulty, substitute it with the other relay. Remove the lower fairing to access the high beam relay – it is mounted on the right-hand side of the engine behind the wiring connectors **(see illustration)**. Remove the fairing to access the low beam relay – it is mounted on the right-hand side of the headlight assembly **(see illustration)**. If the beam in question then works, the faulty relay must be replaced. If not, check for voltage at the white/blue terminal of the low beam relay and the blue/white terminal of the high beam relay. If no voltage is present, check the wiring between the relays and the switches (see *wiring diagrams* at the end of the Chapter). If the wiring is good, check for voltage at the black/red terminal on the relay. If voltage is present, and the wiring between the relay and the headlight is good, replace the relay. If no voltage is present, check the wiring between the relay and the fusebox (see *wiring diagrams* at the end of the Chapter).

**Note:** *Japanese market models (greys) using a 35 W low beam are only fitted with a high beam relay, mounted on the right-hand side of the headlight assembly. If this is the case, and a conversion to UK spec has not been done, then the substitution test will not be possible. To check the relay, switch the ignition ON and the light switch ON, then flick the HI/LO beam switch to HI and listen for a click in the relay. If the relay clicks, check for voltage at the black/red terminal of the relay. If voltage is present, and the wiring between the relay and the headlight is good, replace the relay. If no voltage is present, check the wiring between the relay and the fusebox (see wiring diagrams at the end of the Chapter). If the relay does not click, check for voltage at the blue/white terminal of the high beam relay. If voltage is present, replace the relay. If no voltage is present, check the wiring between the relays and the switches (see wiring diagrams at the end of the Chapter).*

### Tail light

**4** If the tail light fails to work, check the bulb and the bulb terminals first, then the fuse, then check for battery voltage at the brown/white terminal on the supply side of the tail light wiring connector. If voltage is present, check the earth (ground) circuit for an open or poor connection.

**5** If no voltage is indicated, check the wiring between the tail light and the ignition switch, then check the switch. Also check the lighting switch.

### Brake light

**6** If the brake light fails to work, check the bulb and the bulb terminals first, then the fuse, then check for battery voltage at the green/yellow terminal on the supply side of the tail light wiring connector, with the brake lever pulled in or the pedal depressed. If voltage is present, check the earth (ground) circuit for an open or poor connection.

**7** If no voltage is indicated, check the brake light switches, then the wiring between the tail light and the switches.

**8** See Section 14 for brake switch check and Section 9 for tail light bulb replacement.

**6.3a Hi-beam relay (arrowed) – UK models**

**6.3b Hi-beam relay (arrowed) – imported models, lo-beam relay – UK models**

## Instrument and warning lights

**9** See Section 17 for instrument and warning light bulb replacement.

## Turn signal lights

**10** See Section 11 for turn signal circuit check.

### 7  Headlight bulb and sidelight bulb – replacement

**Note:** *The headlight bulb is of the quartz-halogen type. Do not touch the bulb glass as skin acids will shorten the bulb's service life. If the bulb is accidentally touched, it should be wiped carefully when cold with a rag soaked in methylated spirit and dried before fitting.*

⚠ **Warning: Allow the bulb time to cool before removing it if the headlight has just been on.**

### Headlight

**1** Disconnect the relevant wiring connector from the back of the headlight assembly and remove the rubber dust cover, noting how it fits **(see illustrations).**
**2** Release the bulb retaining clip, noting how it fits, then remove the bulb **(see illustrations).**
**3** Fit the new bulb, bearing in mind the information in the **Note** above. Make sure the

**7.2a  Release the clip . . .**

**7.6a  Remove the bulbholder . . .**

**7.1a  Disconnect the wiring connector . . .**

tabs on the bulb fit correctly in the slots in the bulb housing, and secure it in position with the retaining clip.
**4** Install the dust cover, making sure it is correctly seated and with the "TOP" mark at the top, and connect the wiring connector.
**5** Check the operation of the headlight.

**HAYNES HiNT** *Always use a paper towel or dry cloth when handling new bulbs to prevent injury if the bulb should break and to increase bulb life.*

### Sidelight

**6** Pull the bulbholder out of its socket in the

**7.2b  . . . and remove the bulb**

**7.6b  . . . and pull out the bulb**

**7.1b  . . . and remove the dust cover**

base of the headlight, then carefully pull the bulb out of the holder **(see illustrations).**
**7** Install the new bulb in the bulbholder, then install the bulbholder by pressing it in. Make sure the rubber cover is correctly seated.
**8** Check the operation of the sidelight.

### 8  Headlight assembly – removal and installation

### VFR models

#### Removal

**1** Remove the fairing (see Chapter 8).
**2** Remove the instrument cluster (see Section 15).
**3** To remove an individual light from the assembly, disconnect the relevant wiring connector from the back of the headlight **(see illustration 7.1a).** Remove the three screws securing each light to the assembly bracket and remove the light **(see illustration).**
**4** To remove the headlight assembly complete, disconnect the wiring connector from the back of each headlight **(see illustration 7.1a).** Release the wiring loom and the headlight wiring from the clamp on

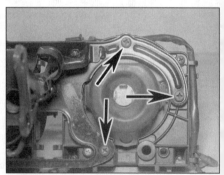
**8.3  Each unit is secured by three screws (arrowed)**

8.4a Release the wiring from its clamp . . .

8.4b . . . then unscrew the nuts and withdraw the bolts . . .

8.4c . . . and remove the assembly

the bracket **(see illustration)**. On UK VFR L and M models, remove the oil cooler mounting bolt. Unscrew the nuts on the bolts securing the assembly bracket to the steering head, then support the assembly and withdraw the bolts **(see illustrations)**. If required, remove the three screws securing each light to the assembly bracket and remove the lights **(see illustration 8.3)**.

5 To separate the beam unit from its holder, first mark each unit according to its side and note the positions of the beam adjusting screws **(see illustration)**. Check the current aim setting by measuring the amount of thread projecting from the holder on each beam adjusting screw. Remove the beam unit pivot screw and open the pivot cover **(see illustration)**. Also remove the two headlight

beam adjusting screws. Lift the beam unit off the holder, noting how the pivot locates, and remove the adjuster springs **(see illustrations)**. Remove the captive nuts from the beam unit.

### Installation

6 Installation is the reverse of removal. Make sure all the wiring is correctly connected and secured. Check the operation of the headlight and sidelight. Check the headlight aim (see Chapter 1).

## RVF models

### Removal

7 Remove the fairing (see Chapter 8).

8 Unscrew the four screws securing the headlight unit to the fairing and remove the headlight, noting how it fits **(see illustration)**.

### Installation

9 Installation is the reverse of removal. Make sure all the wiring is correctly connected and secured. Check the operation of the headlight and sidelight. Check the headlight aim (see Chapter 1).

### 9 Brake/tail light bulb – replacement

1 Insert the ignition key into the seat lock located behind the rider's seat, and turn it clockwise to unlock the passenger's seat. Remove the passenger's seat.

8.5a Beam adjusting screws (arrowed)

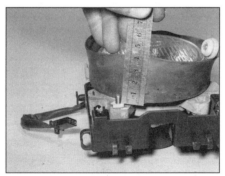

8.5b Measure the projecting thread as an aid to installation

8.5c Remove the pivot cover screw (arrowed) . . .

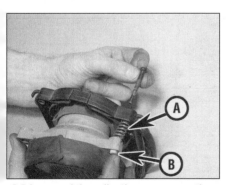

8.5d . . . and the adjusting screws, noting how the spring (A) and captive nut (B) fit . . .

8.5e . . . and how the pivot locates

8.8 The headlight unit is secured by four screws (arrowed)

**9**

9.2  Remove the bulbholder from the taillight . . .

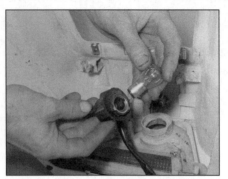

9.3  . . . and the bulb from the holder

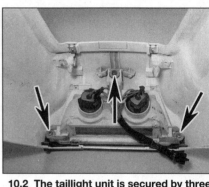

10.2  The taillight unit is secured by three screws

**2** Turn the bulbholder anti-clockwise and withdraw it from the tail light **(see illustration)**.

**3** Push the bulb into the holder and twist it anti-clockwise to remove it **(see illustration)**. Check the socket terminals for corrosion and clean them if necessary. Line up the pins of the new bulb with the slots in the socket, then push the bulb in and turn it clockwise until it locks into place. **Note:** *The pins on the bulb are offset so it can only be installed one way. It is a good idea to use a paper towel or dry cloth when handling the new bulb to prevent injury if the bulb should break and to increase bulb life.*

**4** Install the bulbholder into the tail light and turn it clockwise to secure it.

**5** Locate the tabs at the front of the passenger's seat and push down on the seat to engage the latch.

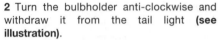

### 10  Tail light assembly – removal and installation

#### Removal

**1** Remove the seat cowling (see Chapter 8).

**2** Remove the three screws securing the tail light assembly and carefully withdraw it from the cowling **(see illustration)**. If required, turn the bulbholders anti-clockwise and withdraw them from the tail light.

11.3  Turn signal relay (arrowed)

#### Installation

**3** Installation is the reverse of removal. Check the operation of the tail light and the brake light.

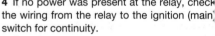

### 11  Turn signal circuit – check

**Note:** *On RVF models the front turn signals also function as running lights and have dual filament bulbs. When checking for faults, refer to the wiring diagram at the end of this Chapter.*

**1** The battery provides power for operation of the turn signal lights, so if they do not operate, always check the battery voltage first. Low battery voltage indicates either a faulty battery or a defective charging system. Refer to Section 3 for battery checks and Sections 34 and 35 for charging system tests. Also, check the fuse (see Section 5) and the switch (see Section 20).

**2** Most turn signal problems are the result of a burned out bulb or corroded socket. This is especially true when the turn signals function properly in one direction, but fail to flash in the other direction. Check the bulbs and the sockets (see Section 12).

**3** If the bulbs and sockets are good, check for power at the turn signal relay black/brown wire (VFR) or brown/white wire (RVF) with the

12.1  Remove the screw and detach the lens . . .

ignition ON. The relay is mounted under the seat cowling on the left-hand side of the bike **(see illustration)**. Remove the seat cowling for access (see Chapter 8). Turn the ignition OFF when the check is complete.

**4** If no power was present at the relay, check the wiring from the relay to the ignition (main) switch for continuity.

**5** If power was present at the relay, using the appropriate wiring diagram at the end of this Chapter, check the wiring between the relay turn signal switch and turn signal lights for continuity. If the wiring and switch are sound replace the relay with a new one.

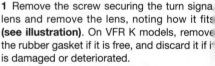

### 12  Turn signal bulbs – replacement

**1** Remove the screw securing the turn signal lens and remove the lens, noting how it fits **(see illustration)**. On VFR K models, remove the rubber gasket if it is free, and discard it if it is damaged or deteriorated.

**2** On all except VFR K models, turn the bulbholder anti-clockwise and withdraw it from the lens **(see illustration)**.

**3** Either a bayont type bulb or a capless type bulb will be fitted. The bayont type has pins which locate in cutouts in the bulbholder and is removed by pushing the bulb into the holder and twisting it anti-clockwise **(see**

12.2  . . . then remove the bulbholder from the lens . . .

illustration). The capless type bulb is simply pulled out of the bulbholder.

**4** Check the socket terminals for corrosion and clean them if necessary. On bayont type bulbs, line up the pins of the new bulb with the slots in the socket, then push the bulb in and turn it clockwise until it locks into place. When fitting the capless bulb, carefully align its fine connecting pins with the holes in the bulbholder and press it into place.

**5** On all except VFR K models, install the bulbholder back into the lens, making sure it is securely held.

**6** Fit the lens onto the holder. On VFR K models, use a new rubber gasket if required, and make sure it is properly seated and not pinched by the lens. On all other models, locate the tab on the back of the lens in the slot in the housing.

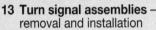

## 13 Turn signal assemblies – removal and installation

### Removal

**1** Disconnect the turn signal wiring connectors. On the front turn signals, they are

**13.1a  Front turn signal wiring connectors (arrowed)**

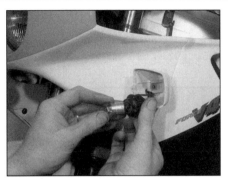

**12.3 . . . and the bulb from the holder**

on the inside of the fairing (see illustration). On the rear turn signals, remove the seat cowling (see Chapter 8) – the connectors are inside a rubber boot which is secured by a clip (see illustration).

**2** On UK VFR L and M models, remove the nut securing the assembly to either the inside of the fairing or rear mudguard. Remove the assembly, noting how the lug locates in the hole in the bracket. Note the mounting rubbers fitted with the front assemblies.

**13.1b  Rear turn signal wiring connectors**

**3** On all other models, remove the screw securing the assembly to either the inside of the fairing or rear mudguard (see illustrations). Remove the assembly, noting the arrangement of the mounting base and collar.

### Installation

**4** Installation is the reverse of removal. Check the operation of the turn signals.

## 14 Brake light switches – check and replacement

### Circuit check

**1** Before checking any electrical circuit, check the bulb (see Section 9) and fuse (see Section 5).

**2** Using a multimeter or test light connected to a good earth (ground), check for voltage at the black/brown terminal on the brake light switch wiring connector (see illustration 14.5 or 14.8). If there's no voltage present, check the wire between the switch and the ignition switch (see the *wiring diagrams* at the end of this Chapter).

**3** If voltage is available, touch the probe of the test light to the other terminal of the switch, then pull the brake lever in or depress the brake pedal. If no reading is obtained or the test light doesn't light up, replace the switch.

**4** If a reading is obtained or the test light does light up, check the wiring between the switch and the brake light bulb (see the *wiring diagrams* at the end of this Chapter).

### Switch replacement

#### Front brake lever switch

**5** The switch is mounted on the underside of the brake master cylinder. Disconnect the

**13.3a  Front turn signal mounting screw (arrowed)**

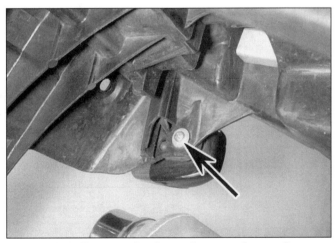

**13.3b  Rear turn signal mounting screw (arrowed)**

14.5  Front brake switch wiring connectors (A), and mounting screw (B)

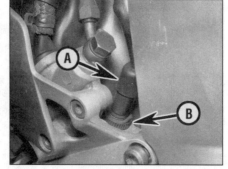

14.8a  Rear brake light switch (A) and its adjuster ring (B)

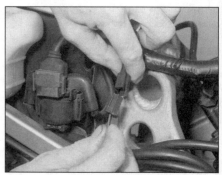

14.8b  Disconnect the wiring connector

wiring connectors from the switch **(see illustration)**.

**6** Remove the single screw securing the switch to the bottom of the master cylinder and remove the switch **(see illustration 14.5)**.

**7** Installation is the reverse of removal. The switch isn't adjustable.

### Rear brake pedal switch

**8** The switch is mounted on the inside of the right-hand footrest bracket **(see illustration)**. Remove the seat cowling for access to the connector (see Chapter 8). Trace the wiring from the switch and disconnect it at the connector **(see illustration)**.

**9** Detach the lower end of the switch spring from the brake pedal, then unscrew and

remove the switch. If access to the switch is too restricted, unscrew the two bolts securing the rider's right-hand footrest bracket and the bolt securing the top of the heat shield to the frame, then swing the whole footrest/rear brake master cylinder/heat shield assembly out, making sure no strain is placed on the brake and reservoir hoses.

**10** Installation is the reverse of removal. If removed, tighten the footrest bracket bolts to the torque setting specified at the beginning of the Chapter. Make sure the brake light is activated just before the rear brake pedal takes effect. If adjustment is necessary, hold the switch and turn the adjusting ring on the switch body until the brake light is activated when required.

## 15 Instruments and speedometer cable – removal and installation

### *Instrument cluster*

#### Removal

**1** Remove the fairing (see Chapter 8).

**2** Unscrew the knurled ring securing the speedometer cable to the back of the speedometer and detach the cable **(see illustration 15.7)**.

**3** Release the clip securing the wiring connector rubber boot and draw the boot back. Disconnect all the wiring connectors **(see illustration)**. Feed the loom and the boot between the speedometer and the tachometer and position it clear **(see illustration)**.

**4** Unscrew the two bolts securing the instrument cluster and remove them with their collars, where fitted **(see illustration)**.

**5** Carefully remove the instrument cluster. On RVF models, note how the two pegs locate in the rubber grommets in the bracket **(see illustration)**.

#### Installation

**6** Installation is the reverse of removal. Make sure that the speedometer cable and wiring connectors are correctly routed and secured.

### *Speedometer cable*

#### Removal

**7** Unscrew the knurled ring securing the

15.3a  Disconnect all the wiring connectors . . .

15.3b  . . . and feed the loom between the instruments

15.4  The instrument cluster is secured by two bolts (arrowed)

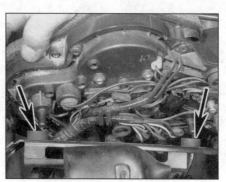

15.5  Locate the pegs in the grommets (arrows)

15.7  Unscrew the ring and detach the cable

15.8a Remove the screw (arrowed) . . .

15.8b . . . and detach the cable

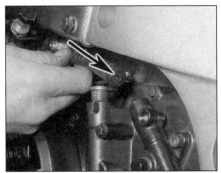

15.12 Align the slot (arrowed) with the drive tab

speedometer cable to the back of the speedometer and detach the cable **(see illustration)**.

**8** Remove the screw securing the lower end of the cable to the drive housing on the engine sprocket cover and detach the cable **(see illustrations)**.

**9** Withdraw the cable, releasing it from its guides, and remove it from the bike, noting its correct routing.

### Installation

**10** Route the cable up through its guides to the back of the instrument cluster.

**11** Connect the cable upper end to the speedometer and tighten the retaining ring securely.

**12** Connect the cable lower end to the drive

housing, aligning the slot in the cable end with the drive tab, and tighten the retaining screw securely **(see illustration)**.

**13** Check that the cable doesn't restrict steering movement or interfere with any other components.

## 16 Instruments –
check and replacement

### *Speedometer*

#### Check

**1** Special instruments are required to properly check the operation of this meter. If it is

believed to be faulty, take the motorcycle to a Honda dealer for assessment.

### Replacement – VFR models

**2** Remove the instrument cluster (see Section 15).

**3** Remove the two nuts securing the speedometer/warning light assembly to the bracket and remove the assembly, feeding the wiring connector under the instrument bracket as you do **(see illustrations)**.

**4** Using a very small Phillips screwdriver, remove the screw in the centre of the odometer trip knob and remove the knob **(see illustrations)**.

**5** Remove the five screws securing the speedometer/warning light assembly front cover and remove the cover **(see illustrations)**.

16.3a Unscrew the two nuts (arrowed) . . .

16.3b . . . and separate the speedometer from the assembly

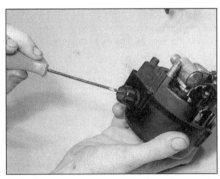

16.4a Remove the screw . . .

16.4b . . . and pull off the knob

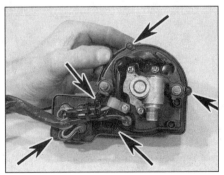

16.5a Remove the screws (arrowed) . . .

16.5b . . . and lift off the front cover

**9**

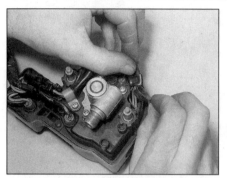

16.6a Remove the blanking cap . . .

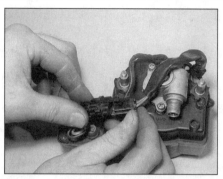

16.6b . . . and disconnect the wiring loom

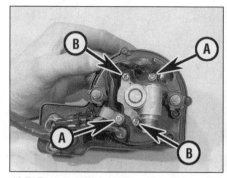

16.7 Remove the two mounting screws (A) and the gearbox screws (B) . . .

16.8a . . . then remove the gearbox . . .

16.8b . . . and the speedometer

**6** Remove the blanking cap from the entry hole for the speedometer wiring **(see illustration)**. Disconnect the wiring connector **(see illustration)**.

**7** Remove the two screws securing the speedometer to the casing, noting that the lower retains a wiring clip **(see illustration)**.

**8** Remove the two screws securing the speedometer gearbox and lift off the box **(see illustration)**. Carefully withdraw the speedometer from the front, feeding the

wiring and its connector through the hole as you do **(see illustration)**.

**9** Installation is the reverse of removal.

### Replacement – RVF models

**10** Remove the instrument cluster (see Section 15).

**11** Using a very small Phillips screwdriver, remove the screw in the centre of the odometer trip knob and remove the knob **(see illustrations 16.4a and b)**.

**12** Remove the two screws securing the

speedometer gearbox, noting the earth wire secured by the upper screw, and lift off the box **(see illustration)**.

**13** Remove the screws securing the instrument cluster front cover, noting the positions of the wiring clips, and remove the cover.

**14** Remove the blanking cap from the entry hole for the speedometer wiring. Disconnect the wiring connector.

**15** Remove the two screws securing the speedometer to the casing. Carefully withdraw the speedometer from the front, feeding the wiring and its connector through the hole as you do.

**16** Installation is the reverse of removal.

### *Tachometer*

#### Check

**17** Special instruments are required to properly check the operation of this meter. If it is believed to be faulty, take the motorcycle to a Honda dealer for assessment.

#### Replacement – VFR models

**18** Remove the instrument cluster (see Section 15).

**19** Disconnect the tachometer wiring connector, and remove the screw securing the earth wire **(see illustration)**.

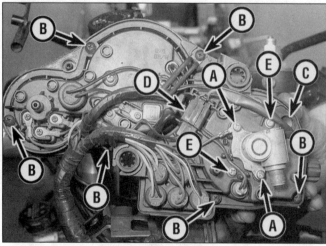

16.12 Speedometer gearbox screws (A), front cover screws (B), blanking cap (C), wiring connector (D), speedometer mounting screws (E)

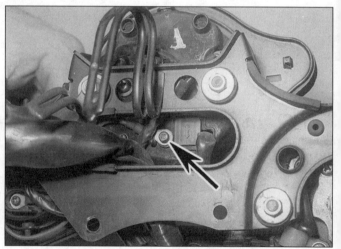

16.19 Remove the screw (arrowed) securing the earth lead . . .

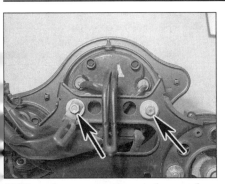

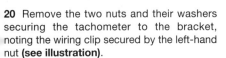

16.20 ... then remove the nuts (arrowed) ...

16.21a ... pull out the bulbholders ...

16.21b ... and remove the tachometer

**20** Remove the two nuts and their washers securing the tachometer to the bracket, noting the wiring clip secured by the left-hand nut **(see illustration)**.
**21** Carefully pull the two tachometer light bulbholders out of the back of the tachometer, and withdraw the tachometer from the front **(see illustrations)**.
**22** Installation is the reverse of removal. Make sure the wires are correctly and securely connected.

### Replacement – RVF models

**23** Remove the instrument cluster (see Section 15).
**24** Using a very small Phillips screwdriver, remove the screw in the centre of the odometer trip knob and remove the knob **(see illustration 16.4a and b)**.
**25** Remove the screws securing the instrument cluster front cover, noting the positions of the wiring clips, and remove the cover **(see illustration)**.
**26** Remove the blanking cap from the entry hole for the tachometer wiring. Disconnect the wiring connector. Also remove the screw securing the earth wire.
**27** Remove the two screws securing the tachometer to the casing. Carefully withdraw the tachometer from the front, feeding the wiring and its connector through the hole as you do.
**28** Installation is the reverse of removal.

## Coolant temperature gauge
### Check
**29** See Chapter 3.
### Replacement – VFR models
**30** Remove the instrument cluster (see Section 15).
**31** Carefully pull the light bulbholder out of the back of the temperature gauge **(see illustration)**.
**32** Remove the screw securing each wiring connector, making a note of which fits where **(see illustration)**.
**33** Remove the two nuts and their washers securing the temperature gauge to the bracket and carefully withdraw the gauge from the front **(see illustrations)**.

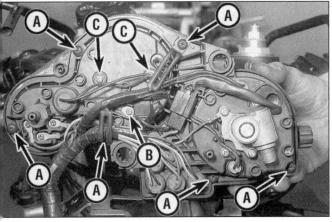

16.25 Front cover screws (A), earth wire screw (B), tachometer mounting screws (C)

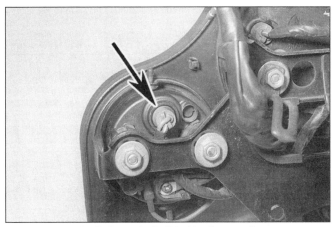

16.31 Pull out the bulbholder (arrowed) ...

16.32 ... and remove the wiring connector screws

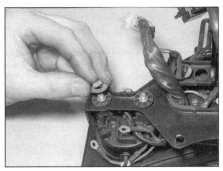

16.33a ... then remove the two nuts ...

16.33b ... and remove the temperature gauge

**9**

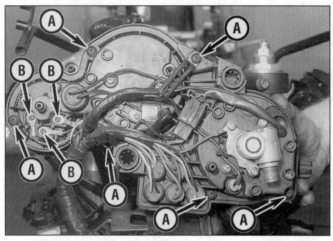

16.37 Front cover screws (A), wiring connector screws (B)

17.2a Pull the bulbholder out of the instrument . . .

**34** Installation is the reverse of removal. Make sure the wires are correctly and securely connected.

### Replacement – RVF models

**35** Remove the instrument cluster (see Section 15).

**36** Using a very small Phillips screwdriver, remove the screw in the centre of the odometer trip knob and remove the knob **(see illustrations 16.4a and b)**.

**37** Remove the screws securing the instrument cluster front cover, noting the positions of the wiring clips, and remove the cover **(see illustration)**.

**38** Remove the screw securing each wiring connector, making a note of which fits where, then carefully withdraw the temperature gauge from the front.

**39** Installation is the reverse of removal. Make sure the wires are correctly and securely connected.

---

**17 Instrument and warning light bulbs** – replacement

---

## Instrument light bulbs

**1** Remove the fairing (see Chapter 8).

**2** Gently pull the bulbholder out of the instrument casing, then pull the bulb out of the bulbholder **(see illustrations)**. If the socket contacts are dirty or corroded, scrape them clean and spray with electrical contact cleaner before a new bulb is installed. Carefully push the new bulb into the holder and install the windshield, trim and inner screen (see Chapter 8).

## Indicator/warning light bulbs

**3** Remove the fairing (see Chapter 8). The bulbs are accessible with the instrument cluster in place, but access is quite restricted. If it is too restricted, unscrew the two bolts

17.2b . . . and the bulb out of the holder

securing the instrument cluster and displace it as required to improve access.

**4** Gently pull the bulbholder out of the panel, then pull the bulb out of the bulbholder **(see illustration)**. If the socket contacts are dirty or corroded, scrape them clean and spray with electrical contact cleaner before a new bulb is installed. Carefully push the new bulb into the holder and install the windshield, trim and inner screen (see Chapter 8).

---

**18 Oil pressure switch** – check, removal and installation

---

## Check

**1** The oil pressure warning light should come on when the ignition (main) switch is turned ON and extinguish a few seconds after the engine is started. If the oil pressure warning light comes on whilst the engine is running, stop the engine immediately and carry out an oil level check, and if the level is correct, an oil pressure check (see Chapter 1).

**2** If the oil pressure warning light does not come on when the ignition is turned on, check the bulb (see Section 17) and fuse (see Section 5).

17.4 Pull the bulbholder out of the panel and remove the bulb

**3** The oil pressure switch is screwed into the crankcase between the cylinders and is accessed by removing the lower fairing (see Chapter 8). Pull the rubber cover off the switch and remove the screw securing the wiring connector **(see illustrations)**. With the ignition switched ON, earth (ground) the wire on the crankcase and check that the warning light comes on. If the light comes on, the switch is defective and must be replaced.

**4** If the light still does not come on, check for voltage at the wire terminal. If there is no voltage present, check the wire between the

18.3a Pull back the rubber cover (arrowed) . . .

**18.3b  . . . then remove the terminal screw and detach the wiring**

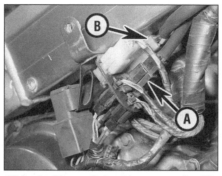

**19.1a  Ignition switch wiring connector (A), right-hand switchgear connector (B) – VFR models**

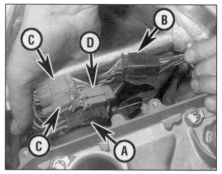

**19.1b  Ignition switch wiring connector (A), right-hand switch gear connector (B), left-hand switchgear connectors (C), sidestand switch connector (D) – RVF models**

switch, the instrument cluster and fusebox for continuity (see the *wiring diagrams* at the end of this Chapter).

5 If the warning light comes on whilst the engine is running, yet the oil pressure is satisfactory, remove the wire from the oil pressure switch. With the wire detached and the ignition switched ON the light should be out. If it is illuminated, the wire between the switch and instrument cluster must be earthed (grounded) at some point. If the wiring is good, the switch must be assumed faulty and replaced.

### Removal

6 Remove the lower fairing (see Chapter 8).
7 Pull the rubber cover off the switch and remove the screw securing the wiring connector **(see illustrations 18.3a and b)**.
8 Unscrew the oil pressure switch and withdraw it from the crankcase.

### Installation

9 Apply a suitable sealant to the upper portion of the switch threads near the switch body, leaving the bottom 3 to 4 mm of thread clean. Install the switch in the crankcase and tighten it to the torque setting specified at the beginning of the Chapter. Attach the wiring connector and secure it with the screw, then fit the rubber cover **(see illustrations 18.3b and a)**.
10 Run the engine and check that the switch operates correctly.
11 Install the middle fairing panel (see Chapter 8).

### 19 Ignition (main) switch – check, removal and installation

 **Warning: To prevent the risk of short circuits, disconnect the battery negative (–ve) lead before making any ignition (main) switch checks.**

### Check

1 On VFR models, remove the lower fairing. On RVF models, remove the air filter housing

(see Chapter 4). Trace the ignition (main) switch wiring back from the base of the switch and disconnect it at the black connector **(see illustrations)**.
2 Using an ohmmeter or a continuity tester, check the continuity of the connector terminal pairs (see the *wiring diagrams* at the end of this Chapter). Continuity should exist between the terminals connected by a solid line on the diagram when the switch is in the indicated position.
3 If the switch fails any of the tests, replace it.

### Removal

**Note:** *Support the bike on an auxiliary stand and tie the back end down so that all weight is off the front end of the bike.*
4 On VFR models, remove the lower fairing. On RVF models, remove the air filter housing (see Chapter 4). Trace the ignition (main) switch wiring back from the base of the switch and disconnect it at the black connector **(see illustrations 19.1a or b)**. Draw the wiring through to the switch, noting its routing.
5 Two Torx bolts mount the ignition switch to the underside of the top yoke **(see illustration)**. Remove the bolts and withdraw the switch from the top yoke.

### Installation

6 Installation is the reverse of removal. Tighten the Torx bolts to the torque setting

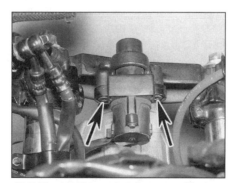

**19.5  The ignition switch is secured by two Torx bolts (arrowed)**

specified at the beginning of the Chapter. Make sure wiring is securely connected and correctly routed.

### 20 Handlebar switches – check

1 Generally speaking, the switches are reliable and trouble-free. Most troubles, when they do occur, are caused by dirty or corroded contacts, but wear and breakage of internal parts is a possibility that should not be overlooked. If breakage does occur, the entire switch and related wiring harness will have to be replaced with a new one, as individual parts are not available.
2 The switches can be checked for continuity using an ohmmeter or a continuity test light. Always disconnect the battery negative (–ve) cable, which will prevent the possibility of a short circuit, before making the checks.
3 Trace the wiring harness of the switch in question back to its connector and disconnect it. On VFR models, the connector for the right-hand switch is below the main frame on the right-hand side – remove the lower fairing for access **(see illustration 19.1a)**. The connectors for the left-hand switch are in a rubber boot behind the left-hand side of the upper radiator – remove the left-hand fairing side panel for access **(see illustration)**. On

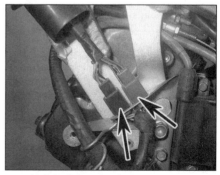

**20.3  Left-hand switchgear wiring connectors (arrowed) – VFR models**

21.3a Remove the screws . . .

21.3b . . . and separate the halves

21.4 Locate the pin (arrowed) in the hole in the handlebar

RVF models, the connectors for both switches are behind the steering stem – remove the air filter housing for access (see Chapter 4) **(see illustration 19.1b)**.

**4** Check for continuity between the terminals of the switch harness with the switch in the various positions (i.e. switch off – no continuity, switch on – continuity) – see the *wiring diagrams* at the end of this Chapter.

**5** If the continuity check indicates a problem exists, refer to Section 21, remove the switch and spray the switch contacts with electrical contact cleaner. If they are accessible, the contacts can be scraped clean with a knife or polished with crocus cloth. If switch components are damaged or broken, it will be obvious when the switch is disassembled.

## 21 Handlebar switches – removal and installation

### Removal

**1** If the switch is to be removed from the bike, rather than just displaced from the handlebar, trace the wiring harness of the switch in question back to its connector and disconnect it. On VFR models, the connector for the right-hand switch is below the main frame on the right-hand side – remove the lower fairing for access **(see illustration 19.1a)**. The connectors for the left-hand switch are in a rubber boot behind the left-hand side of the upper radiator – remove the left-hand fairing side panel for access **(see illustration 20.3)**. On RVF models, the connectors for both switches are behind the steering stem – remove the air filter housing for access (see Chapter 4) **(see illustration 19.1b)**.Work back along the harness, freeing it from all the relevant clips and ties, whilst noting its correct routing.

**2** Disconnect the two wires from the brake light switch (if removing the right-hand switch) or the clutch switch (if removing the left-hand switch) **(see illustration 14.5 or 24.1)**.

**3** Unscrew the two handlebar switch screws and free the switch from the handlebar by separating the halves **(see illustrations)**.

### Installation

**4** Installation is the reverse of removal. Make sure the locating pin in the lower half of the switch locates in the hole in the underside of the handlebar **(see illustration)**.

## 22 Neutral switch – check, removal and installation

### Check

**1** Before checking the electrical circuit, check the bulb (see Section 17) and fuse (see Section 5).

**2** The switch is located in the right-hand side of the transmission casing on the back of the engine **(see illustration)**. Remove the lower fairing for access (see Chapter 8). Detach the wiring connector from the switch **(see illustration)**. Make sure the transmission is in neutral.

**3** With the connector disconnected and the ignition switched ON, the neutral light should be out. If not, the wire between the connector and instrument cluster must be earthed (grounded) at some point.

**4** Check for continuity between the switch terminal and the crankcase. With the transmission in neutral, there should be continuity. With the transmission in gear, there should be no continuity. If the tests prove otherwise, then the switch is faulty.

**5** If the continuity tests prove the switch is good, check for voltage at the wire terminal

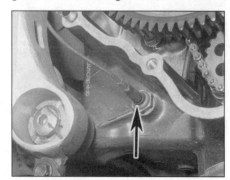

22.2a Neutral switch (arrowed)

using a test light. If there's no voltage present, check the wire between the switch, the instrument cluster and fusebox (see the *wiring diagrams* at the end of this Chapter).

### Removal

**6** Remove the lower fairing (see Chapter 8).

**7** Detach the wiring connector from the switch **(see illustration 22.2b)**.

**8** Unscrew the switch and withdraw it from the transmission casing.

### Installation

**9** Apply a smear of sealant to the threads of the switch, taking care not to cover the contact point.

**10** Install the switch and tighten it to the torque setting specified at the beginning of the Chapter.

**11** Check the operation of the neutral light.

**12** Install the lower fairing (see Chapter 8).

## 23 Sidestand switch (RVF models) – check and replacement

### Check

**1** The sidestand switch is mounted on the back of the sidestand. The switch is part of the safety circuit which prevents or stops the engine running if the transmission is in gear whilst the sidestand is down, and prevents the engine from starting if the transmission is in gear unless the sidestand is up, and unless the clutch is pulled in. Before checking the

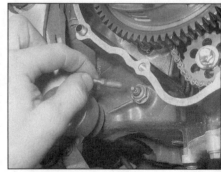

22.2b Disconnect the wiring connector

**23.6 Sidestand switch (arrowed)**

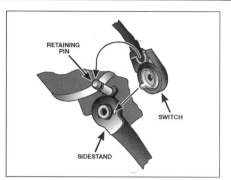

**23.8 Make sure the lug on the switch locates in the hole in the stand, and the cutout in the switch locates around the retaining pin**

**24.2 Disconnect the clutch switch wiring connectors (arrowed)**

electrical circuit, check the indicator bulb (see Section 17) and fuse (see Section 5).

**2** Remove the lower fairing (see Chapter 8) and the air filter housing (see Chapter 4). Trace the wiring back from the switch to its connector and disconnect it **(see illustration 19.1b)**.

**3** Check the operation of the switch using an ohmmeter or continuity test light. Connect the meter to the green/white and green wires on the switch side of the connector. With the sidestand up there should be continuity (zero resistance) between the terminals, and with the stand down there should be no continuity (infinite resistance). Now connect the meter to the yellow/black and green wires on the switch side of the connector. With the sidestand down there should be continuity (zero resistance) between the terminals, and with the stand up there should be no continuity (infinite resistance).

**4** If the switch does not perform as expected, it is defective and must be replaced.

**5** If the switch is good, check the wiring between the various components in the starter safety circuit (see the *wiring diagrams* at the end of this book).

### Replacement

**6** The sidestand switch is mounted on the back of the sidestand **(see illustration)**. Remove the lower fairing (see Chapter 8) and the air filter housing (see Chapter 4). Trace the wiring back from the switch to its connector and disconnect it **(see illustration 19.1b)**. Work back along the switch wiring, freeing it

from any relevant retaining clips and ties, noting its correct routing.

**7** Unscrew the switch bolt and remove the switch from the stand, noting how it fits.

**8** Fit the new switch onto the sidestand, making sure the pin locates in the hole in the sidestand, and the lug for the spring on the stand bracket locates into the cutout in the switch body **(see illustration)**. Secure the switch with its bolt.

**9** Make sure the wiring is correctly routed up to the connector and retained by all the necessary clips and ties.

**10** Reconnect the wiring connector and check the operation of the sidestand switch.

**11** Install the lower fairing (see Chapter 8).

### 24 Clutch switch – check and replacement

#### Check

**1** The clutch switch is housed in the clutch lever bracket. The switch is part of the safety circuit which prevents or stops the engine running if the transmission is in gear whilst the sidestand is down, and prevents the engine from starting if the transmission is in gear unless the sidestand is up and the clutch lever is pulled in. The switch isn't adjustable.

**2** To check the switch, disconnect the wiring connectors from the switch **(see illustration)**.

Connect the probes of an ohmmeter or a continuity test light to the two switch terminals. With the clutch lever pulled in, continuity should be indicated. With the clutch lever out, no continuity (infinite resistance) should be indicated.

**3** If the switch is good, check the other components in the starter circuit as described in the relevant sections of this Chapter. If all components are good, check the wiring between the various components (see the *wiring diagrams* at the end of this book).

### Replacement

**4** Remove the clutch lever (see Chapter 6).

**5** Disconnect the wiring connectors from the clutch switch **(see illustration 24.2)**. Using a small screwdriver, push the switch from the connector end and withdraw it from inside the bracket **(see illustration)**.

**6** Installation is the reverse of removal. Make sure the ridge on the top of the switch locates in the cutout in the lever bracket, and push the switch fully home **(see illustration)**.

### 25 Diode – check and replacement

#### Check

**1** The diode is a small block that plugs into a connector in the main wiring harness, and is located on the left-hand side of the rear sub-frame **(see illustration)**. The diode is part of

**24.5 Push the switch out using a screwdriver**

**24.6 Make sure the ridge locates in the cutout (arrowed)**

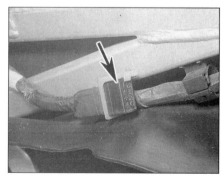

**25.1 Diode (arrowed)**

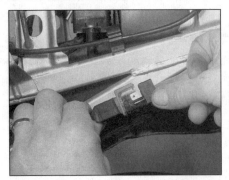

25.2 Pull the diode out of its connector

26.5a Unplug the wiring connectors . . .

26.5b . . . then unscrew the bolt and remove the horn

the safety circuit which prevents or stops the engine running if the transmission is in gear whilst the sidestand is down, and prevents the engine from starting if the transmission is in gear unless the sidestand is up and the clutch lever is pulled in.

2 Remove the seat cowling (see Chapter 8) and disconnect the diode from the harness **(see illustration)**.

3 On models with a two-pin diode connector, using an ohmmeter or continuity tester, connect the positive (+ve) probe to the green/red terminal of the diode and the negative (−ve) probe to the light green/red terminal. The diode should show continuity. Now reverse the probes. The diode should show no continuity. If it doesn't behave as stated, replace the diode.

4 On models with a three-pin diode connector, using an ohmmeter or continuity tester, connect the positive (+ve) probe to one of the outer terminals of the diode and the negative (−ve) probe to the middle terminal of the diode. The diode should show continuity. Now reverse the probes. The diode should show no continuity. Repeat the tests between the other outer terminal and the middle terminal. The same results should be achieved. If it doesn't behave as stated, replace the diode.

5 If the diode is good, check the other components in the starter circuit as described in the relevant sections of this Chapter. If all components are good, check the wiring

between the various components (see the *wiring diagrams* at the end of this book).

### Replacement

6 The diode is a small block that plugs into a connector in the main wiring harness, and is located on the left-hand side of the rear sub-frame **(see illustration 25.1)**. Remove the seat cowling for access (see Chapter 8). Disconnect the diode from the harness and connect the new one **(see illustration 25.2)**.

## 26 Horn – 
check and replacement

### Check

1 The horn is mounted on the underside of the bottom yoke.

2 Unplug the wiring connectors from the horn **(see illustration 26.5a)**. Using two jumper wires, apply battery voltage directly to the terminals on the horn. If the horn sounds, check the switch (see Section 21) and the wiring between the switch and the horn (see the *wiring diagrams* at the end of this Chapter).

3 If the horn doesn't sound, replace it.

### Replacement

4 The horn is mounted on the underside of the bottom yoke.

5 Unplug the wiring connectors from the horn, then unscrew the bolt securing the horn and remove it from the bike **(see illustrations)**.

6 Install the horn and securely tighten the bolt. Connect the wiring connectors to the horn.

## 27 Starter relay – 
check and replacement
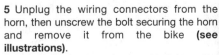

### Check

1 If the starter circuit is faulty, first check the fuse (see Section 5).

2 The starter relay is located under the seat cowling on the right-hand side of the bike, just ahead of the coolant reservoir. Remove the seat cowling for access (see Chapter 8). Disconnect the relay wiring connector to provide access to the rear terminals, then lift the rubber terminal cover and unscrew the bolt securing the starter motor lead **(see illustrations)**; position the lead away from the relay terminal. Reconnect the wiring connector. With the ignition switch ON, the engine kill switch in the RUN position, the transmission in neutral and the clutch pulled in, press the starter switch. The relay should be heard to click.

3 If the relay doesn't click, switch off the ignition and remove the relay as described below; test it as follows.

4 Set a multimeter to the ohms x 1 scale and connect it across the relay's starter motor and battery lead terminals **(see illustration 27.2b)**. Using a fully-charged 12 volt battery and two insulated jumper wires, connect the positive (+ve) terminal of the battery to the yellow/red wire terminal of the relay, and the negative (−ve) terminal to the green/red wire terminal of the relay. At this point the relay should be heard to click and the multimeter read 0 ohms (continuity). If this is the case the relay is proved good. If the relay does not click when battery voltage is applied and indicates no continuity (infinite resistance) across its terminals, it is faulty and must be replaced.

5 If the relay is good, check for battery

27.2a Disconnect the wiring connector (arrowed) . . .

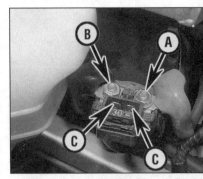

27.2b . . . to access the battery lead (A), the starter motor lead (B) and the wiring terminals (C)

**28.3a Pull back the terminal cover . . .**

**28.3b . . . then unscrew the nut and detach the lead**

**28.4 Unscrew the two bolts (arrowed) and remove the starter motor**

voltage between the yellow/red wire and the green/red wire when the starter button is pressed. Check the other components in the starter circuit as described in the relevant sections of this Chapter. If all components are good, check the wiring between the various components (see the *wiring diagrams* at the end of this book).

### Replacement

**6** Remove the seat cowling (see Chapter 8).
**7** Disconnect the battery terminals, remembering to disconnect the negative (–ve) terminal first.
**8** Disconnect the relay wiring connector, then unscrew the two nuts securing the starter motor and battery leads to the relay and detach the leads (**see illustrations 27.2a and b**). Remove the relay with its rubber sleeve from its mounting lug on the frame.
**9** Installation is the reverse of removal. Make sure the terminal nuts are securely tightened. Connect the negative (–ve) lead last when reconnecting the battery.

### 28 Starter motor – removal and installation

### Removal

**1** Remove the seat cowling and the lower

fairing (see Chapter 8). Disconnect the battery negative (–ve) lead. The starter motor is mounted at the front of the engine.
**2** Remove the bolt securing the bottom of the lower radiator to the bracket, then swing the radiator forward.
**3** Peel back the rubber terminal cover and remove the nut securing the starter lead to the motor (**see illustrations**). Detach the lead and withdraw it from its guide, if required.
**4** Unscrew the two bolts securing the starter motor to the crankcase (**see illustration**). Slide the starter motor out from the crankcase and remove it from the machine.
**5** Remove the O-ring on the end of the starter motor and discard it as a new one must be used (**see illustration**).

### Installation

**6** Install a new O-ring on the end of the starter motor and ensure it is seated in its groove (**see illustration**). Apply a smear of engine oil to the O-ring to aid installation.
**7** Manoeuvre the motor into position and slide it into the crankcase (**see illustration**). Ensure that the starter motor teeth mesh correctly with those of the starter idle/reduction gear. Install the mounting bolts and tighten them securely.
**8** Connect the starter lead to the motor, making sure it is fitted in its guide, and secure it with the nut (**see illustration 28.3b**). Make

sure the rubber cover is correctly seated over the terminal.
**9** Connect the battery negative (–ve) lead and install the lower fairing and the seat cowling (see Chapter 8).

### 29 Starter motor – disassembly, inspection and reassembly

### Disassembly

**1** Remove the starter motor (see Section 28).
**2** Note the alignment marks between the main housing and the front and rear covers, or

**28.5 Remove the O-ring and discard it**

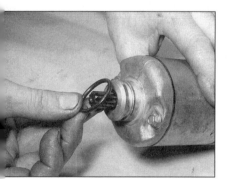

**28.6 Fit a new O-ring . . .**

**28.7a . . . and lubricate it, then install the starter motor . . .**

**28.7b . . . and fit the bolts**

29.2 Note the alignment marks between the housing and the covers (arrows)

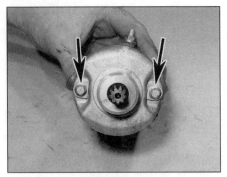

29.3 Unscrew and remove the two bolts (arrowed) . . .

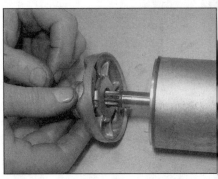

29.4a . . . then remove the front cover . . .

29.4b . . . the shims . . .

29.4c . . . and the tabbed washer

29.5 Remove the rear cover

make your own if they aren't clear **(see illustration)**.

**3** Unscrew the two long bolts, noting how the washers locate, and withdraw them from the starter motor **(see illustration)**. Discard their O-rings as new ones must be used.

**4** Wrap some insulating tape around the teeth on the end of the starter motor shaft – this will protect the oil seal from damage as the front cover is removed. Remove the front cover from the motor **(see illustration)**. Remove the cover O-ring from the main housing and

discard it as a new one must be used. Remove the shims from the front end of the armature shaft or the inside of the front cover, noting their correct fitted locations **(see illustration)**. Also remove the tabbed thrust washer from the front cover **(see illustration)**.

**5** Remove the rear cover and brushplate assembly from the motor **(see illustration)**. Remove the cover O-ring from the main housing and discard it as a new one must be used. Remove the shims from the rear end of the armature shaft or from inside the rear

cover after the brushplate assembly has been removed.

**6** Withdraw the armature from the main housing.

**7** Noting the correct fitted location of each component, unscrew the terminal nut and remove it along with its washer, the insulating washers and O-ring **(see illustration)**. Withdraw the terminal bolt and brushplate assembly from the main housing.

**8** Lift the brush springs and slide the brushes out from their holders **(see illustration)**.

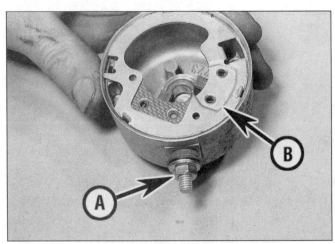

29.7 Unscrew the nut (A) and remove the washers, then remove the brushplate assembly (B)

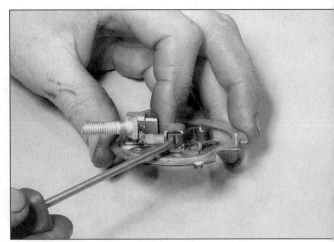

29.8 Lift the brush springs and withdraw the brushes

## Inspection

**9** The parts of the starter motor that are most likely to require attention are the brushes **(see illustration)**. Measure the length of the brushes and compare the results to the brush length listed in this Chapter's Specifications **(see illustration)**. If any of the brushes are worn beyond the service limit, replace the brush assembly with a new one. If the brushes are not worn excessively, nor cracked, chipped, or otherwise damaged, they may be re-used.

**10** Inspect the commutator bars on the armature for scoring, scratches and discoloration. The commutator can be cleaned and polished with crocus cloth, but do not use sandpaper or emery paper. After cleaning, wipe away any residue with a cloth soaked in electrical system cleaner or denatured alcohol.

**11** Using an ohmmeter or a continuity test light, check for continuity between the commutator bars **(see illustration)**. Continuity should exist between each bar and all of the others. Also, check for continuity between the commutator bars and the armature shaft **(see illustration)**. There should be no continuity (infinite resistance) between the commutator and the shaft. If the checks indicate otherwise, the armature is defective.

**12** Check for continuity between each brush and the terminal bolt. There should be continuity (zero resistance). Check for continuity between the terminal bolt and the

housing (when assembled). There should be no continuity (infinite resistance).

**13** Check the front end of the armature shaft for worn, cracked, chipped and broken teeth. If the shaft is damaged or worn, replace the armature.

**14** Inspect the end covers for signs of cracks or wear. Inspect the magnets in the main housing and the housing itself for cracks.

**15** Inspect the insulating washers and front cover oil seal for signs of damage and replace them if necessary.

## Reassembly

**16** Slide the brushes back into position in their holders and place the brush spring ends onto the brushes **(see illustration)**.

**17** Ensure that the inner rubber insulator is in place on the terminal bolt, then insert the bolt through the rear cover and fit the brushplate assembly in the rear cover, making sure its tab is correctly located in the slot in the cover **(see illustrations)**. Fit the O-ring and the insulating washers over the terminal, then fit

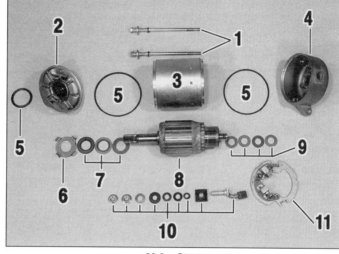

29.9a  Starter motor components

| | |
|---|---|
| 1 | Long bolts |
| 2 | Front cover |
| 3 | Main housing |
| 4 | Rear cover |
| 5 | O-rings |
| 6 | Tabbed washer |
| 7 | Front shims |
| 8 | Armature |
| 9 | Rear shims |
| 10 | Terminal bolt assembly |
| 11 | Brushplate assembly |

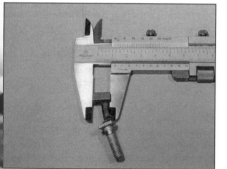

29.9b  Measure the brush length

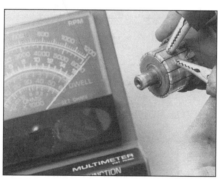

29.11a  Continuity should exist between the commutator bars

29.11b  There should be no continuity between the commutator bars and the armature shaft

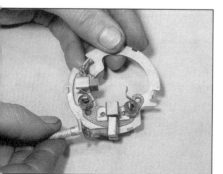

29.16  Fit the brushes into the brushplate and locate the springs . . .

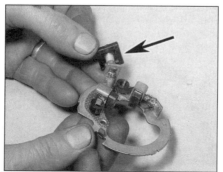

29.17a  . . . then fit the inner insulator (arrowed) onto the terminal bolt

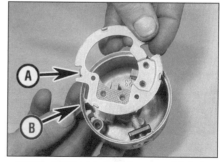

29.17b  Fit the brushplate assembly into the rear cover, aligning the tab (A) with the slot (B) . . .

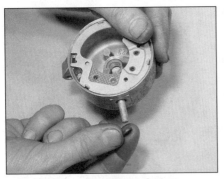

29.17c ... then fit the O-ring ...

29.17d ... the insulating washers ...

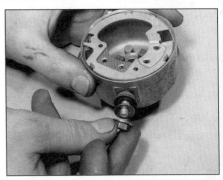

29.17e ... the plain washer and the nut

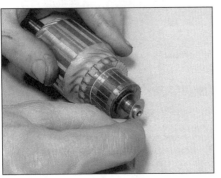

29.18a Fit the shims ...

29.18b ... then insert the armature into the rear cover, making sure the brush ends (arrowed) locate correctly

the standard washer and the nut (see illustrations).

18 Slide the shims onto the rear end of the armature shaft, then lubricate the shaft with a drop of oil (see illustrations). Insert the armature into the rear cover, locating the brushes on the commutator bars as you do, taking care not to damage them (see illustration). Check that each brush is securely pressed against the commutator by its spring and is free to move easily in its holder.

19 Fit a new O-ring onto the main housing, then fit the housing over the armature and onto the rear cover, aligning the marks made on removal (see illustrations).

20 Apply a smear of grease to the lips of the front cover oil seal and fit a new O-ring onto the front of the main housing (see illustration). Fit the tabbed washer onto the cover, making sure the tabs locate correctly (see illustration). Slide the shims onto the front of the armature shaft, then install the cover, aligning the marks made on removal (see illustrations). Remove the protective tape from the shaft end.

21 Slide a new O-ring onto each of the long bolts. Check the marks made on removal are correctly aligned, then install the long bolts and tighten them securely, making sure the flat edge on each washer is against the raised section on the front cover (see illustrations).

22 Install the starter motor (see Section 29).

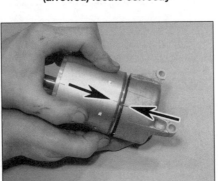

29.19a Fit a new O-ring ...

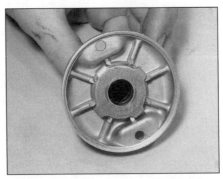

29.19b ... then install the main housing, aligning the marks (arrowed)

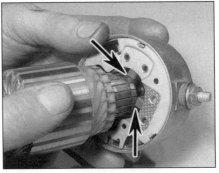

29.20a Fit a new O-ring onto the main housing ...

29.20b ... and locate the tabbed washer in the front cover

29.20c Fit the shims onto the shaft ...

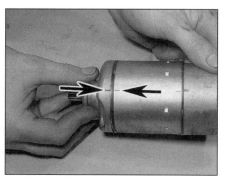

**29.20d ... then install the cover, aligning the marks (arrowed)**

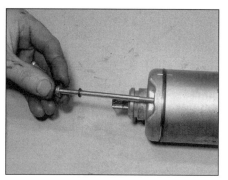

**29.21a Install the long bolts ...**

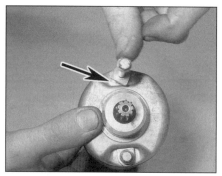

**29.21b ... locating the flat of each washer against the raised edge (arrow)**

## 30 Charging system testing – general information and precautions

**1** If the performance of the charging system is suspect, the system as a whole should be checked first, followed by testing of the individual components. **Note:** *Before beginning the checks, make sure the battery is fully charged and that all system connections are clean and tight.*

**2** Checking the output of the charging system and the performance of the various components within the charging system requires the use of a multimeter (with voltage, current and resistance checking facilities).

**3** When making the checks, follow the procedures carefully to prevent incorrect connections or short circuits, as irreparable damage to electrical system components may result if short circuits occur.

**4** If a multimeter is not available, the job of checking the charging system should be left to a Honda dealer.

## 31 Charging system – leakage and output test

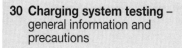

**1** If the charging system of the machine is thought to be faulty, remove the seat cowling (see Chapter 8) and perform the following checks.

### Leakage test

**Caution:** *Always connect an ammeter in series, never in parallel with the battery, otherwise it will be damaged. Do not turn the ignition ON or operate the starter motor when the ammeter is connected – a sudden surge in current will blow the meter's fuse.*

**2** Turn the ignition switch OFF and disconnect the lead from the battery negative (–ve) terminal.

**3** Set the multimeter to the Amps function and connect its negative (–ve) probe to the battery negative (–ve) terminal, and positive (+ve) probe to the disconnected negative (–ve) lead **(see illustration)**. Always set the meter

to a high amps range initially and then bring it down to the mA (milli Amps) range; if there is a high current flow in the circuit it may blow the meter's fuse.

**4** If the current leakage indicated exceeds the amount specified at the beginning of the Chapter, there is probably a short circuit in the wiring. Disconnect the meter and connect the negative (–ve) lead to the battery, tightening it securely.

**5** If leakage is indicated, use the wiring diagrams at the end of this book to systematically disconnect individual electrical components and repeat the test until the source is identified.

### Output test

**6** Start the engine and warm it up to normal operating temperature. Remove the seat cowling (see Chapter 8).

**7** To check the voltage output, allow the engine to idle and connect a multimeter set to the 0-20 volts DC scale (voltmeter) across the terminals of the battery (positive (+ve) lead to battery positive (+ve) terminal, negative (–ve) lead to battery negative (–ve) terminal). Slowly increase the engine speed to 5000 rpm and note the reading obtained. The regulated voltage should be as specified at the beginning of the Chapter. If the voltage is outside these limits, check the alternator and the regulator (see Sections 32 and 33).

**8** To check the current output, disconnect the starter relay wiring connector and remove the main fuse, then reconnect the connector.

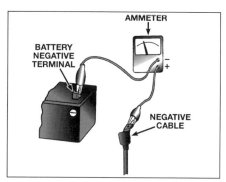

**31.3 Checking the charging system leakage rate – connect the meter as shown**

Connect a multimeter set to the 0-20 amps DC scale (ammeter) between the terminals of the main fuse (positive (+ve) lead to the left-hand (rear) terminal, negative (–ve) lead to right-hand (front) terminal), inserting the probes into the base of the fuse sockets. Allow the engine to idle, then slowly increase the engine speed to 5000 rpm and note the reading obtained. The regulated current should be as specified at the beginning of the Chapter. If the current is outside these limits, check the alternator and the regulator (see Sections 32 and 33).

 **HAYNES HiNT** *Clues to a faulty regulator are constantly blowing bulbs, with brightness varying considerably with engine speed, and battery overheating.*

## 32 Alternator – check, removal and installation

### Check

**1** Remove the lower fairing (see Chapter 8).

**2** Trace the wiring back from the top of the alternator cover on the left-hand side of the engine and disconnect it at the white connector containing the yellow wires below the right-hand side of the frame **(see illustration)**.

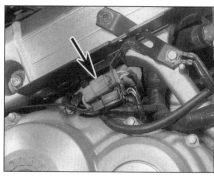

**32.2 Alternator wiring connector (arrowed) – RVF model shown**

32.3 Test the alternator as described

32.6 Remove the alternator cover and discard the gasket

32.7 Hold the rotor using a suitable tool and unscrew the bolt (arrowed)

**3** Using a multimeter set to the ohms x 1 (ohmmeter) scale measure the resistance between each of the yellow wires on the alternator side of the connector, taking a total of three readings, then check for continuity between each terminal and ground (earth) **(see illustration)**. If the stator coil windings are in good condition the three readings should be within the range shown in the Specifications at the start of this Chapter and there should be no continuity (infinite resistance) between any of the terminals and ground (earth). If not, the alternator stator coil assembly is at fault and should be replaced. **Note:** *Before condemning the stator coils, check the fault is not due to damaged wiring between the connector and coils.*

## Removal

**4** Remove the lower fairing (see Chapter 8).
**5** Trace the wiring back from the top of the alternator cover on the left-hand side of the engine and disconnect it at the connector below the right-hand side of the frame **(see illustration 32.2)**. Free the wiring from any clips or guides and feed it through to the alternator cover.
**6** Working in a criss-cross pattern, evenly slacken the alternator cover retaining bolts **(see illustration)**. Lift the cover away from the engine, being prepared to catch any residual oil which may be released as the cover is removed. Remove the gasket and discard it.

**7** To remove the rotor bolt it is necessary to stop the rotor from turning. If a rotor holding strap or tool is not available, place the transmission in gear and have an assistant apply the rear brake, then unscrew the bolt **(see illustration)**.

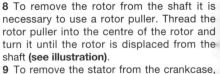

*A rotor holding tool can easily be made using two strips of steel bolted together in the middle, and with a bolt through each end which locate into the recessed bores in the rotor.*

**8** To remove the rotor from the shaft it is necessary to use a rotor puller. Thread the rotor puller into the centre of the rotor and turn it until the rotor is displaced from the shaft **(see illustration)**.
**9** To remove the stator from the crankcase, unscrew the four bolts securing the stator, and the bolt securing the wiring clamp, then remove the assembly, noting how the rubber wiring grommet fits **(see illustration)**.

## Installation

**10** Install the stator onto the crankcase, aligning the rubber wiring grommet with the groove in the case **(see illustration)**. Apply a suitable non-permanent thread locking compound to the stator bolt threads, then install the bolts and tighten them securely **(see illustration)**. Apply a suitable sealant to

32.8 Draw the rotor off the end of the crankshaft using a rotor puller

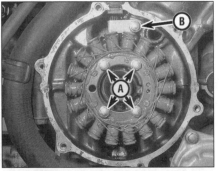

32.9 Unscrew the stator bolts (A) and the wiring clamp bolt (B)

32.10a Fit the stator . . .

32.10b . . . then apply threadlock and install the bolts

32.10c Apply sealant to the wiring grommet . . .

32.10d . . . and press it into its recess . . .

32.10e . . . then secure the wiring with the clamp

32.11 Fit the rotor onto the shaft . . .

32.12a . . . then install the bolt . . .

32.12b . . . and tighten it to the specified torque

the wiring grommet, then install it into the cut-out in the crankcase **(see illustrations)**. Secure the wiring with its clamp **(see illustration)**.

**11** Clean the tapered end of the crankshaft and the corresponding mating surface on the inside of the rotor with a suitable solvent. Make sure that no metal objects have attached themselves to the magnet on the inside of the rotor, then install the rotor onto the shaft **(see illustration)**.

33.1 Disconnect the regulator/rectifier wiring connector

**12** Install the rotor bolt and tighten it to the torque setting specified at the beginning of the Chapter, using the method employed on removal to prevent the rotor from turning **(see illustrations)**.

**13** Install the alternator cover using a new gasket **(see illustration 32.6)**. Tighten the cover bolts evenly in a criss-cross sequence.

**14** Reconnect the wiring at the connector and secure it with any clips or ties.

**15** Install the lower fairing (see Chapter 8).

## 33 Regulator/rectifier –
check and replacement

### Check

**1** Remove the seat cowling (see Chapter 8). The regulator/rectifier is mounted on the left-hand side of the rear sub-frame. Disconnect the wiring connector **(see illustration)**.

**2** Connect the negative (–ve) probe of the multimeter to a suitable ground (earth) point, then switch the ignition switch 'ON' and carry

out the following checks.

**3** Set the multimeter to the 0-20 dc volts setting. Connect the meter positive (+ve) probe to the Red/white terminal and the negative (–ve) probe to the green terminal on the wiring connector and check for voltage. Full battery voltage should be present. Switch the ignition switch 'OFF'.

**4** Switch the multimeter to the resistance (ohms) scale. Check for continuity between the Green terminal of the wiring connector and ground (earth). There should be continuity.

**5** Check the resistance between any two Yellow terminals of the wiring connector. A resistance reading of 0.1 to 1.0 ohms should be obtained between any two Yellow terminals of the wiring connector.

**6** If the above checks do not provide the expected results check the wiring between the battery, regulator/rectifier and alternator (see the *wiring diagrams* at the end of this book).

**7** If the wiring checks out, the regulator/rectifier unit is probably faulty. To check the unit, use a multimeter set to the appropriate resistance scale and check the

**9**

resistance between the various terminals on the regulator/rectifier **(see illustration)**. If the readings do not compare closely with those shown in the accompanying table the regulator/rectifier unit can be considered faulty. **Note:** *The use of certain multimeters could lead to false readings being obtained, as could a low battery in the meter and contact between the meter probes and your fingers. If the above check shows the regulator/rectifier unit to be faulty, take the unit to a Honda dealer for confirmation of its condition before replacing it.*

### Replacement

**8** Remove the seat cowling (see Chapter 8).
**9** The regulator/rectifier is mounted on the left-hand side of the rear sub-frame. Disconnect the wiring connector **(see illustration 33.1)**.

**10** Unscrew the two nuts securing the regulator/rectifier and remove it. Note the wiring clip secured by the rear nut on VFR models.

**11** Install the new unit and tighten its nuts securely, not forgetting the wiring clip on VFR models. Connect the wiring connector.
**12** Install the seat cowling (see Chapter 8).

|  ⊕ probe / ⊖ probe | Red/white | Yellow | Yellow | Yellow | Green |
|---|---|---|---|---|---|
| Red/white |  | ∞ | ∞ | ∞ | ∞ |
| Yellow | 0.5 – 10 |  | 30 – 500 | 30 – 500 | 10 – 200 |
| Yellow | 0.5 – 10 | 30 – 500 |  | 30 – 500 | 10 – 200 |
| Yellow | 0.5 – 10 | 30 – 500 | 30 – 500 |  | 10 – 200 |
| Green | 1 – 20 | 0.5 – 10 | 0.5 – 10 | 0.5 – 10 |  |

K ohms

**33.7 Regulator/rectifier test connections and data**

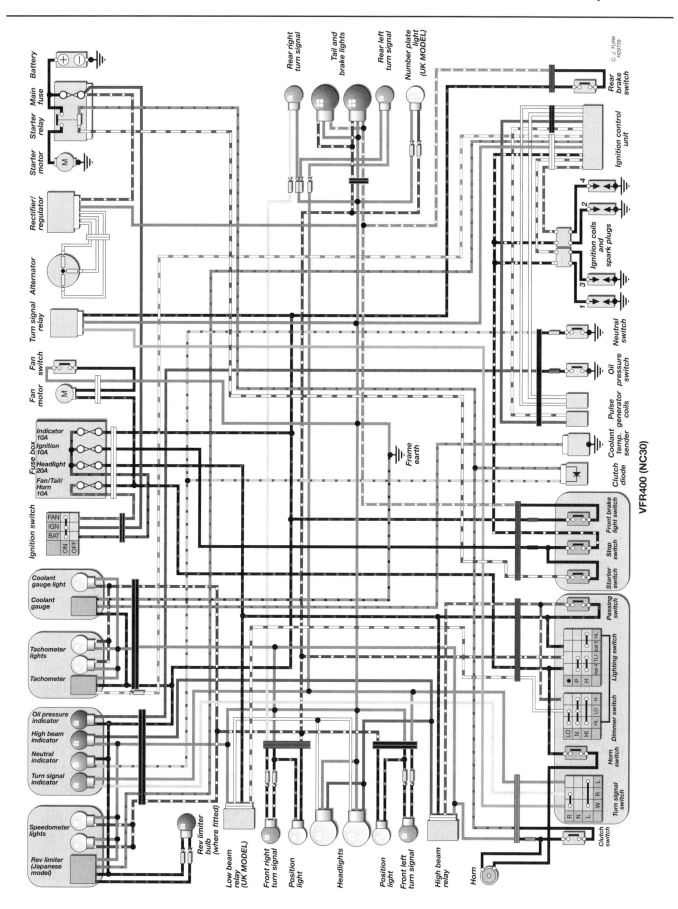

C. J. TURK
H29739

VFR400 (NC30)

9

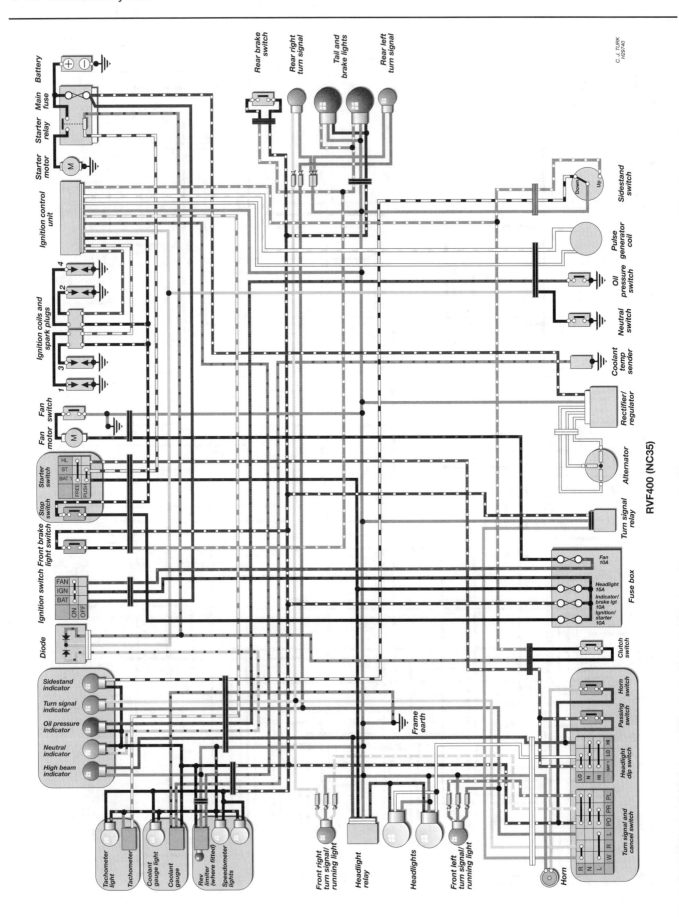

RVF400 (NC35)

# Dimensions and Weights

## VFR400
| | |
|---|---|
| Wheelbase | 1345 mm |
| Overall length | 1985 mm |
| Overall width | 705 mm |
| Overall height | 1075 mm |
| Ground clearance | 125 mm |
| Weight (dry) | 175 kg |

## RVF400
| | |
|---|---|
| Wheelbase | 1335 mm |
| Overall length | 1985 mm |
| Overall width | 685 mm |
| Overall height | 1065 mm |
| Ground clearance | 125 mm |
| Weight (dry) | Not available |

## Buying tools

A toolkit is a fundamental requirement for servicing and repairing a motorcycle. Although there will be an initial expense in building up enough tools for servicing, this will soon be offset by the savings made by doing the job yourself. As experience and confidence grow, additional tools can be added to enable the repair and overhaul of the motorcycle. Many of the specialist tools are expensive and not often used so it may be preferable to hire them, or for a group of friends or motorcycle club to join in the purchase.

As a rule, it is better to buy more expensive, good quality tools. Cheaper tools are likely to wear out faster and need to be renewed more often, nullifying the original saving.

> **Warning: To avoid the risk of a poor quality tool breaking in use, causing injury or damage to the component being worked on, always aim to purchase tools which meet the relevant national safety standards.**

The following lists of tools do not represent the manufacturer's service tools, but serve as a guide to help the owner decide which tools are needed for this level of work. In addition, items such as an electric drill, hacksaw, files, soldering iron and a workbench equipped with a vice, may be needed. Although not classed as tools, a selection of bolts, screws, nuts, washers and pieces of tubing always come in useful.

For more information about tools, refer to the Haynes *Motorcycle Workshop Practice TechBook* (Bk. No. 3470).

## Manufacturer's service tools

Inevitably certain tasks require the use of a service tool. Where possible an alternative tool or method of approach is recommended, but sometimes there is no option if personal injury or damage to the component is to be avoided. Where required, service tools are referred to in the relevant procedure.

Service tools can usually only be purchased from a motorcycle dealer and are identified by a part number. Some of the commonly-used tools, such as rotor pullers, are available in aftermarket form from mail-order motorcycle tool and accessory suppliers.

# Maintenance and minor repair tools

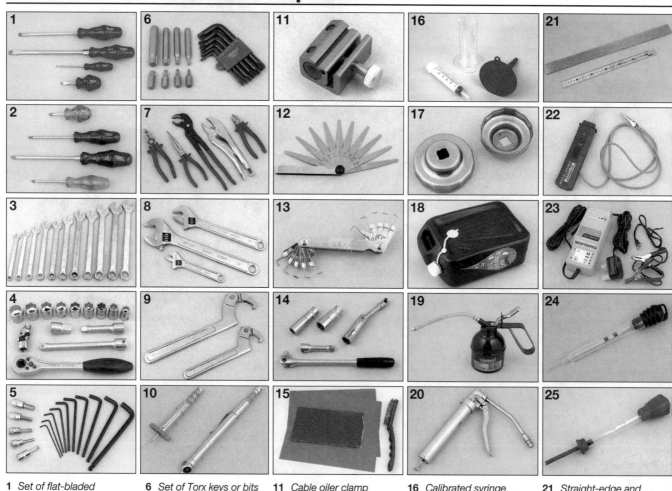

1 Set of flat-bladed screwdrivers
2 Set of Phillips head screwdrivers
3 Combination open-end and ring spanners
4 Socket set (3/8 inch or 1/2 inch drive)
5 Set of Allen keys or bits

6 Set of Torx keys or bits
7 Pliers, cutters and self-locking grips (Mole grips)
8 Adjustable spanners
9 C-spanners
10 Tread depth gauge and tyre pressure gauge

11 Cable oiler clamp
12 Feeler gauges
13 Spark plug gap measuring tool
14 Spark plug spanner or deep plug sockets
15 Wire brush and emery paper

16 Calibrated syringe, measuring vessel and funnel
17 Oil filter adapters
18 Oil drainer can or tray
19 Pump type oil can
20 Grease gun

21 Straight-edge and steel rule
22 Continuity tester
23 Battery charger
24 Hydrometer (for battery specific gravity check)
25 Anti-freeze tester (for liquid-cooled engines)

# Repair and overhaul tools

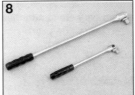

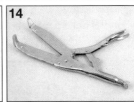

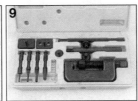

1  Torque wrench
   (small and mid-ranges)
2  Conventional, plastic or
   soft-faced hammers
3  Impact driver set
4  Vernier gauge
5  Circlip pliers (internal and
   external, or combination)
6  Set of cold chisels
   and punches
7  Selection of pullers
8  Breaker bars
9  Chain breaking/
   riveting tool set
10  Wire stripper and
    crimper tool
11  Multimeter (measures
    amps, volts and ohms)
12  Stroboscope (for
    dynamic timing checks)
13  Hose clamp
    (wingnut type shown)
14  Clutch holding tool
15  One-man brake/clutch
    bleeder kit

# Specialist tools

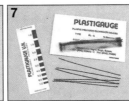

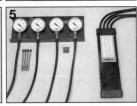
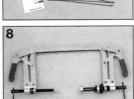
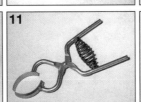

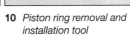
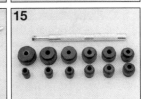

1  Micrometers
   (external type)
2  Telescoping gauges
3  Dial gauge
4  Cylinder
   compression gauge
5  Vacuum gauges (left) or
   manometer (right)
6  Oil pressure gauge
7  Plastigauge kit
8  Valve spring compressor
   (4-stroke engines)
9  Piston pin drawbolt tool
10  Piston ring removal and
    installation tool
11  Piston ring clamp
12  Cylinder bore hone
    (stone type shown)
13  Stud extractor
14  Screw extractor set
15  Bearing driver set

## 1 Workshop equipment and facilities

### The workbench

● Work is made much easier by raising the bike up on a ramp - components are much more accessible if raised to waist level. The hydraulic or pneumatic types seen in the dealer's workshop are a sound investment if you undertake a lot of repairs or overhauls (see illustration 1.1).

1.1 Hydraulic motorcycle ramp

● If raised off ground level, the bike must be supported on the ramp to avoid it falling. Most ramps incorporate a front wheel locating clamp which can be adjusted to suit different diameter wheels. When tightening the clamp, take care not to mark the wheel rim or damage the tyre - use wood blocks on each side to prevent this.
● Secure the bike to the ramp using tie-downs (see illustration 1.2). If the bike has only a sidestand, and hence leans at a dangerous angle when raised, support the bike on an auxiliary stand.

1.2 Tie-downs are used around the passenger footrests to secure the bike

● Auxiliary (paddock) stands are widely available from mail order companies or motorcycle dealers and attach either to the wheel axle or swingarm pivot (see illustration 1.3). If the motorcycle has a centrestand, you can support it under the crankcase to prevent it toppling whilst either wheel is removed (see illustration 1.4).

1.3 This auxiliary stand attaches to the swingarm pivot

1.4 Always use a block of wood between the engine and jack head when supporting the engine in this way

### Fumes and fire

● Refer to the Safety first! page at the beginning of the manual for full details. Make sure your workshop is equipped with a fire extinguisher suitable for fuel-related fires (Class B fire - flammable liquids) - it is not sufficient to have a water-filled extinguisher.
● Always ensure adequate ventilation is available. Unless an exhaust gas extraction system is available for use, ensure that the engine is run outside of the workshop.
● If working on the fuel system, make sure the workshop is ventilated to avoid a build-up of fumes. This applies equally to fume build-up when charging a battery. Do not smoke or allow anyone else to smoke in the workshop.

### Fluids

● If you need to drain fuel from the tank, store it in an approved container marked as suitable for the storage of petrol (gasoline) (see illustration 1.5). Do not store fuel in glass jars or bottles.

1.5 Use an approved can only for storing petrol (gasoline)

● Use proprietary engine degreasers or solvents which have a high flash-point, such as paraffin (kerosene), for cleaning off oil, grease and dirt - never use petrol (gasoline) for cleaning. Wear rubber gloves when handling solvent and engine degreaser. The fumes from certain solvents can be dangerous - always work in a well-ventilated area.

### Dust, eye and hand protection

● Protect your lungs from inhalation of dust particles by wearing a filtering mask over the nose and mouth. Many frictional materials still contain asbestos which is dangerous to your health. Protect your eyes from spouts of liquid and sprung components by wearing a pair of protective goggles (see illustration 1.6).

1.6 A fire extinguisher, goggles, mask and protective gloves should be at hand in the workshop

● Protect your hands from contact with solvents, fuel and oils by wearing rubber gloves. Alternatively apply a barrier cream to your hands before starting work. If handling hot components or fluids, wear suitable gloves to protect your hands from scalding and burns.

### What to do with old fluids

● Old cleaning solvent, fuel, coolant and oils should not be poured down domestic drains or onto the ground. Package the fluid up in old oil containers, label it accordingly, and take it to a garage or disposal facility. Contact your local authority for location of such sites or ring the oil care hotline.

OIL CARE

FOLLOW THE CODE

OIL BANK LINE
**0800 66 33 66**

Note: It is antisocial and illegal to dump oil down the drain. To find the location of your local oil recycling bank, call this number free.

In the USA, note that any oil supplier must accept used oil for recycling.

## 2 Fasteners -
### screws, bolts and nuts

### *Fastener types and applications*

#### Bolts and screws

● Fastener head types are either of hexagonal, Torx or splined design, with internal and external versions of each type **(see illustrations 2.1 and 2.2)**; splined head fasteners are not in common use on motorcycles. The conventional slotted or Phillips head design is used for certain screws. Bolt or screw length is always measured from the underside of the head to the end of the item **(see illustration 2.11)**.

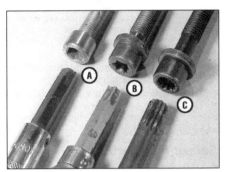

**2.1 Internal hexagon/Allen (A), Torx (B) and splined (C) fasteners, with corresponding bits**

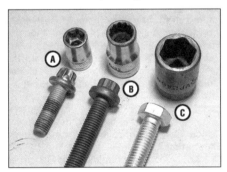

**2.2 External Torx (A), splined (B) and hexagon (C) fasteners, with corresponding sockets**

● Certain fasteners on the motorcycle have a tensile marking on their heads, the higher the marking the stronger the fastener. High tensile fasteners generally carry a 10 or higher marking. Never replace a high tensile fastener with one of a lower tensile strength.

#### Washers (see illustration 2.3)

● Plain washers are used between a fastener head and a component to prevent damage to the component or to spread the load when torque is applied. Plain washers can also be used as spacers or shims in certain assemblies. Copper or aluminium plain washers are often used as sealing washers on drain plugs.

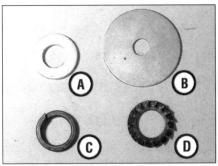

**2.3 Plain washer (A), penny washer (B), spring washer (C) and serrated washer (D)**

● The split-ring spring washer works by applying axial tension between the fastener head and component. If flattened, it is fatigued and must be renewed. If a plain (flat) washer is used on the fastener, position the spring washer between the fastener and the plain washer.
● Serrated star type washers dig into the fastener and component faces, preventing loosening. They are often used on electrical earth (ground) connections to the frame.
● Cone type washers (sometimes called Belleville) are conical and when tightened apply axial tension between the fastener head and component. They must be installed with the dished side against the component and often carry an OUTSIDE marking on their outer face. If flattened, they are fatigued and must be renewed.
● Tab washers are used to lock plain nuts or bolts on a shaft. A portion of the tab washer is bent up hard against one flat of the nut or bolt to prevent it loosening. Due to the tab washer being deformed in use, a new tab washer should be used every time it is disturbed.
● Wave washers are used to take up endfloat on a shaft. They provide light springing and prevent excessive side-to-side play of a component. Can be found on rocker arm shafts.

#### Nuts and split pins

● Conventional plain nuts are usually six-sided **(see illustration 2.4)**. They are sized by thread diameter and pitch. High tensile nuts carry a number on one end to denote their tensile strength.

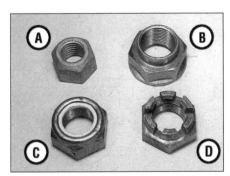

**2.4 Plain nut (A), shouldered locknut (B), nylon insert nut (C) and castellated nut (D)**

● Self-locking nuts either have a nylon insert, or two spring metal tabs, or a shoulder which is staked into a groove in the shaft - their advantage over conventional plain nuts is a resistance to loosening due to vibration. The nylon insert type can be used a number of times, but must be renewed when the friction of the nylon insert is reduced, ie when the nut spins freely on the shaft. The spring tab type can be reused unless the tabs are damaged. The shouldered type must be renewed every time it is disturbed.
● Split pins (cotter pins) are used to lock a castellated nut to a shaft or to prevent slackening of a plain nut. Common applications are wheel axles and brake torque arms. Because the split pin arms are deformed to lock around the nut a new split pin must always be used on installation - always fit the correct size split pin which will fit snugly in the shaft hole. Make sure the split pin arms are correctly located around the nut **(see illustrations 2.5 and 2.6)**.

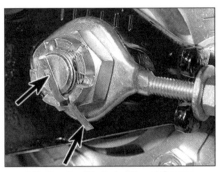

**2.5 Bend split pin (cotter pin) arms as shown (arrows) to secure a castellated nut**

**2.6 Bend split pin (cotter pin) arms as shown to secure a plain nut**

**Caution: If the castellated nut slots do not align with the shaft hole after tightening to the torque setting, tighten the nut until the next slot aligns with the hole - never slacken the nut to align its slot.**

● R-pins (shaped like the letter R), or slip pins as they are sometimes called, are sprung and can be reused if they are otherwise in good condition. Always install R-pins with their closed end facing forwards **(see illustration 2.7)**.

**2.7 Correct fitting of R-pin. Arrow indicates forward direction**

## Circlips (see illustration 2.8)

● Circlips (sometimes called snap-rings) are used to retain components on a shaft or in a housing and have corresponding external or internal ears to permit removal. Parallel-sided (machined) circlips can be installed either way round in their groove, whereas stamped circlips (which have a chamfered edge on one face) must be installed with the chamfer facing away from the direction of thrust load **(see illustration 2.9)**.

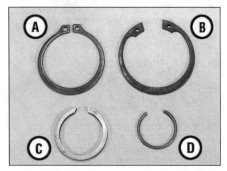

**2.8 External stamped circlip (A), internal stamped circlip (B), machined circlip (C) and wire circlip (D)**

● Always use circlip pliers to remove and install circlips; expand or compress them just enough to remove them. After installation, rotate the circlip in its groove to ensure it is securely seated. If installing a circlip on a splined shaft, always align its opening with a shaft channel to ensure the circlip ends are well supported and unlikely to catch **(see illustration 2.10)**.

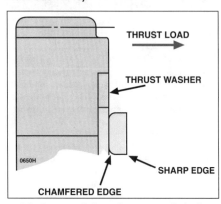

**2.9 Correct fitting of a stamped circlip**

THRUST LOAD
THRUST WASHER
SHARP EDGE
CHAMFERED EDGE
0650H

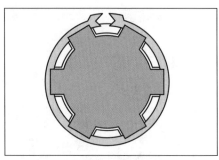

**2.10 Align circlip opening with shaft channel**

● Circlips can wear due to the thrust of components and become loose in their grooves, with the subsequent danger of becoming dislodged in operation. For this reason, renewal is advised every time a circlip is disturbed.

● Wire circlips are commonly used as piston pin retaining clips. If a removal tang is provided, long-nosed pliers can be used to dislodge them, otherwise careful use of a small flat-bladed screwdriver is necessary. Wire circlips should be renewed every time they are disturbed.

## Thread diameter and pitch

● Diameter of a male thread (screw, bolt or stud) is the outside diameter of the threaded portion **(see illustration 2.11)**. Most motorcycle manufacturers use the ISO (International Standards Organisation) metric system expressed in millimetres, eg M6 refers to a 6 mm diameter thread. Sizing is the same for nuts, except that the thread diameter is measured across the valleys of the nut.

● Pitch is the distance between the peaks of the thread **(see illustration 2.11)**. It is expressed in millimetres, thus a common bolt size may be expressed as 6.0 x 1.0 mm (6 mm thread diameter and 1 mm pitch). Generally pitch increases in proportion to thread diameter, although there are always exceptions.

● Thread diameter and pitch are related for conventional fastener applications and the accompanying table can be used as a guide. Additionally, the AF (Across Flats), spanner or socket size dimension of the bolt or nut **(see illustration 2.11)** is linked to thread and pitch specification. Thread pitch can be measured with a thread gauge **(see illustration 2.12)**.

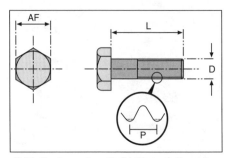

AF
L
D
P

**2.11 Fastener length (L), thread diameter (D), thread pitch (P) and head size (AF)**

**2.12 Using a thread gauge to measure pitch**

| AF size | Thread diameter x pitch (mm) |
|---------|------------------------------|
| 8 mm | M5 x 0.8 |
| 8 mm | M6 x 1.0 |
| 10 mm | M6 x 1.0 |
| 12 mm | M8 x 1.25 |
| 14 mm | M10 x 1.25 |
| 17 mm | M12 x 1.25 |

● The threads of most fasteners are of the right-hand type, ie they are turned clockwise to tighten and anti-clockwise to loosen. The reverse situation applies to left-hand thread fasteners, which are turned anti-clockwise to tighten and clockwise to loosen. Left-hand threads are used where rotation of a component might loosen a conventional right-hand thread fastener.

## Seized fasteners

● Corrosion of external fasteners due to water or reaction between two dissimilar metals can occur over a period of time. It will build up sooner in wet conditions or in countries where salt is used on the roads during the winter. If a fastener is severely corroded it is likely that normal methods of removal will fail and result in its head being ruined. When you attempt removal, the fastener thread should be heard to crack free and unscrew easily - if it doesn't, stop there before damaging something.

● A smart tap on the head of the fastener will often succeed in breaking free corrosion which has occurred in the threads **(see illustration 2.13)**.

● An aerosol penetrating fluid (such as WD-40) applied the night beforehand may work its way down into the thread and ease removal. Depending on the location, you may be able to make up a Plasticine well around the fastener head and fill it with penetrating fluid.

**2.13 A sharp tap on the head of a fastener will often break free a corroded thread**

● If you are working on an engine internal component, corrosion will most likely not be a problem due to the well lubricated environment. However, components can be very tight and an impact driver is a useful tool in freeing them **(see illustration 2.14)**.

**2.14 Using an impact driver to free a fastener**

● Where corrosion has occurred between dissimilar metals (eg steel and aluminium alloy), the application of heat to the fastener head will create a disproportionate expansion rate between the two metals and break the seizure caused by the corrosion. Whether heat can be applied depends on the location of the fastener - any surrounding components likely to be damaged must first be removed **(see illustration 2.15)**. Heat can be applied using a paint stripper heat gun or clothes iron, or by immersing the component in boiling water - wear protective gloves to prevent scalding or burns to the hands.

**2.15 Using heat to free a seized fastener**

● As a last resort, it is possible to use a hammer and cold chisel to work the fastener head unscrewed **(see illustration 2.16)**. This will damage the fastener, but more importantly extreme care must be taken not to damage the surrounding component.

*Caution: Remember that the component being secured is generally of more value than the bolt, nut or screw - when the fastener is freed, do not unscrew it with force, instead work the fastener back and forth when resistance is felt to prevent thread damage.*

**2.16 Using a hammer and chisel to free a seized fastener**

## Broken fasteners and damaged heads

● If the shank of a broken bolt or screw is accessible you can grip it with self-locking grips. The knurled wheel type stud extractor tool or self-gripping stud puller tool is particularly useful for removing the long studs which screw into the cylinder mouth surface of the crankcase or bolts and screws from which the head has broken off **(see illustration 2.17)**. Studs can also be removed by locking two nuts together on the threaded end of the stud and using a spanner on the lower nut **(see illustration 2.18)**.

**2.17 Using a stud extractor tool to remove a broken crankcase stud**

**2.18 Two nuts can be locked together to unscrew a stud from a component**

● A bolt or screw which has broken off below or level with the casing must be extracted using a screw extractor set. Centre punch the fastener to centralise the drill bit, then drill a hole in the fastener **(see illustration 2.19)**. Select a drill bit which is approximately half to three-quarters the

**2.19 When using a screw extractor, first drill a hole in the fastener . . .**

diameter of the fastener and drill to a depth which will accommodate the extractor. Use the largest size extractor possible, but avoid leaving too small a wall thickness otherwise the extractor will merely force the fastener walls outwards wedging it in the casing thread.

● If a spiral type extractor is used, thread it anti-clockwise into the fastener. As it is screwed in, it will grip the fastener and unscrew it from the casing **(see illustration 2.20)**.

**2.20 . . . then thread the extractor anti-clockwise into the fastener**

● If a taper type extractor is used, tap it into the fastener so that it is firmly wedged in place. Unscrew the extractor (anti-clockwise) to draw the fastener out.

⚠ *Warning: Stud extractors are very hard and may break off in the fastener if care is not taken - ask an engineer about spark erosion if this happens.*

● Alternatively, the broken bolt/screw can be drilled out and the hole retapped for an oversize bolt/screw or a diamond-section thread insert. It is essential that the drilling is carried out squarely and to the correct depth, otherwise the casing may be ruined - if in doubt, entrust the work to an engineer.
● Bolts and nuts with rounded corners cause the correct size spanner or socket to slip when force is applied. Of the types of spanner/socket available always use a six-point type rather than an eight or twelve-point type - better grip

**2.21 Comparison of surface drive ring spanner (left) with 12-point type (right)**

is obtained. Surface drive spanners grip the middle of the hex flats, rather than the corners, and are thus good in cases of damaged heads **(see illustration 2.21).**

● Slotted-head or Phillips-head screws are often damaged by the use of the wrong size screwdriver. Allen-head and Torx-head screws are much less likely to sustain damage. If enough of the screw head is exposed you can use a hacksaw to cut a slot in its head and then use a conventional flat-bladed screwdriver to remove it. Alternatively use a hammer and cold chisel to tap the head of the fastener around to slacken it. Always replace damaged fasteners with new ones, preferably Torx or Allen-head type.

HAYNES
**HiNT**

*A dab of valve grinding compound between the screw head and screwdriver tip will often give a good grip.*

### Thread repair

● Threads (particularly those in aluminium alloy components) can be damaged by overtightening, being assembled with dirt in the threads, or from a component working loose and vibrating. Eventually the thread will fail completely, and it will be impossible to tighten the fastener.

● If a thread is damaged or clogged with old locking compound it can be renovated with a thread repair tool (thread chaser) **(see illustrations 2.22 and 2.23);** special thread

**2.22 A thread repair tool being used to correct an internal thread**

**2.23 A thread repair tool being used to correct an external thread**

chasers are available for spark plug hole threads. The tool will not cut a new thread, but clean and true the original thread. Make sure that you use the correct diameter and pitch tool. Similarly, external threads can be cleaned up with a die or a thread restorer file **(see illustration 2.24).**

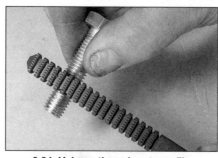

**2.24 Using a thread restorer file**

● It is possible to drill out the old thread and retap the component to the next thread size. This will work where there is enough surrounding material and a new bolt or screw can be obtained. Sometimes, however, this is not possible - such as where the bolt/screw passes through another component which must also be suitably modified, also in cases where a spark plug or oil drain plug cannot be obtained in a larger diameter thread size.

● The diamond-section thread insert (often known by its popular trade name of Heli-Coil) is a simple and effective method of renewing the thread and retaining the original size. A kit can be purchased which contains the tap, insert and installing tool **(see illustration 2.25).** Drill out the damaged thread with the size drill specified **(see illustration 2.26).** Carefully retap the thread **(see illustration 2.27).** Install the

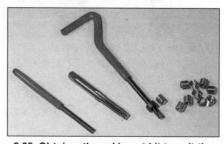

**2.25 Obtain a thread insert kit to suit the thread diameter and pitch required**

**2.26 To install a thread insert, first drill out the original thread . . .**

**2.27 . . . tap a new thread . . .**

**2.28 . . . fit insert on the installing tool . . .**

**2.29 . . . and thread into the component . . .**

**2.30 . . . break off the tang when complete**

insert on the installing tool and thread it slowly into place using a light downward pressure **(see illustrations 2.28 and 2.29).** When positioned between a 1/4 and 1/2 turn below the surface withdraw the installing tool and use the break-off tool to press down on the tang, breaking it off **(see illustration 2.30).**

● There are epoxy thread repair kits on the market which can rebuild stripped internal threads, although this repair should not be used on high load-bearing components.

## Thread locking and sealing compounds

● Locking compounds are used in locations where the fastener is prone to loosening due to vibration or on important safety-related items which might cause loss of control of the motorcycle if they fail. It is also used where important fasteners cannot be secured by other means such as lockwashers or split pins.

● Before applying locking compound, make sure that the threads (internal and external) are clean and dry with all old compound removed. Select a compound to suit the component being secured - a non-permanent general locking and sealing type is suitable for most applications, but a high strength type is needed for permanent fixing of studs in castings. Apply a drop or two of the compound to the first few threads of the fastener, then thread it into place and tighten to the specified torque. Do not apply excessive thread locking compound otherwise the thread may be damaged on subsequent removal.

● Certain fasteners are impregnated with a dry film type coating of locking compound on their threads. Always renew this type of fastener if disturbed.

● Anti-seize compounds, such as copper-based greases, can be applied to protect threads from seizure due to extreme heat and corrosion. A common instance is spark plug threads and exhaust system fasteners.

## 3  Measuring tools and gauges

## Feeler gauges

● Feeler gauges (or blades) are used for measuring small gaps and clearances (see illustration 3.1). They can also be used to measure endfloat (sideplay) of a component on a shaft where access is not possible with a dial gauge.

● Feeler gauge sets should be treated with care and not bent or damaged. They are etched with their size on one face. Keep them clean and very lightly oiled to prevent corrosion build-up.

**3.1 Feeler gauges are used for measuring small gaps and clearances - thickness is marked on one face of gauge**

● When measuring a clearance, select a gauge which is a light sliding fit between the two components. You may need to use two gauges together to measure the clearance accurately.

## Micrometers

● A micrometer is a precision tool capable of measuring to 0.01 or 0.001 of a millimetre. It should always be stored in its case and not in the general toolbox. It must be kept clean and never dropped, otherwise its frame or measuring anvils could be distorted resulting in inaccurate readings.

● External micrometers are used for measuring outside diameters of components and have many more applications than internal micrometers. Micrometers are available in different size ranges, eg 0 to 25 mm, 25 to 50 mm, and upwards in 25 mm steps; some large micrometers have interchangeable anvils to allow a range of measurements to be taken. Generally the largest precision measurement you are likely to take on a motorcycle is the piston diameter.

● Internal micrometers (or bore micrometers) are used for measuring inside diameters, such as valve guides and cylinder bores. Telescoping gauges and small hole gauges are used in conjunction with an external micrometer, whereas the more expensive internal micrometers have their own measuring device.

### External micrometer

**Note:** *The conventional analogue type instrument is described. Although much easier to read, digital micrometers are considerably more expensive.*

● Always check the calibration of the micrometer before use. With the anvils closed (0 to 25 mm type) or set over a test gauge (for

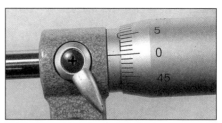

**3.2 Check micrometer calibration before use**

the larger types) the scale should read zero (see illustration 3.2); make sure that the anvils (and test piece) are clean first. Any discrepancy can be adjusted by referring to the instructions supplied with the tool. Remember that the micrometer is a precision measuring tool - don't force the anvils closed, use the ratchet (4) on the end of the micrometer to close it. In this way, a measured force is always applied.

● To use, first make sure that the item being measured is clean. Place the anvil of the micrometer (1) against the item and use the thimble (2) to bring the spindle (3) lightly into contact with the other side of the item (see illustration 3.3). Don't tighten the thimble down because this will damage the micrometer - instead use the ratchet (4) on the end of the micrometer. The ratchet mechanism applies a measured force preventing damage to the instrument.

● The micrometer is read by referring to the linear scale on the sleeve and the annular scale on the thimble. Read off the sleeve first to obtain the base measurement, then add the fine measurement from the thimble to obtain the overall reading. The linear scale on the sleeve represents the measuring range of the micrometer (eg 0 to 25 mm). The annular scale

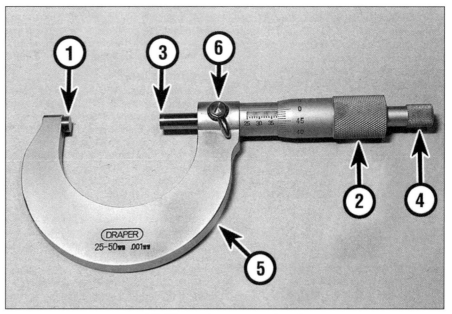

**3.3 Micrometer component parts**

| | | |
|---|---|---|
| 1 *Anvil* | 3 *Spindle* | 5 *Frame* |
| 2 *Thimble* | 4 *Ratchet* | 6 *Locking lever* |

on the thimble will be in graduations of 0.01 mm (or as marked on the frame) - one full revolution of the thimble will move 0.5 mm on the linear scale. Take the reading where the datum line on the sleeve intersects the thimble's scale. Always position the eye directly above the scale otherwise an inaccurate reading will result.

In the example shown the item measures 2.95 mm **(see illustration 3.4)**:

| | |
|---|---|
| Linear scale | 2.00 mm |
| Linear scale | 0.50 mm |
| Annular scale | 0.45 mm |
| **Total figure** | **2.95 mm** |

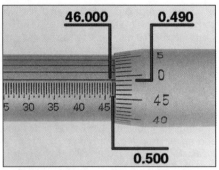

**3.5 Micrometer reading of 46.99 mm on linear and annular scales . . .**

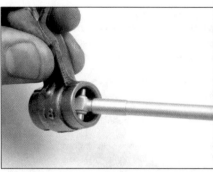

**3.7 Expand the telescoping gauge in the bore, lock its position . . .**

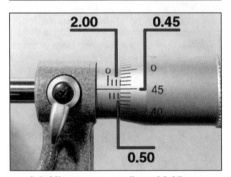

**3.4 Micrometer reading of 2.95 mm**

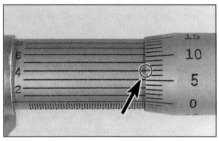

**3.6 . . . and 0.004 mm on vernier scale**

**3.8 . . . then measure the gauge with a micrometer**

Most micrometers have a locking lever (6) on the frame to hold the setting in place, allowing the item to be removed from the micrometer.
● Some micrometers have a vernier scale on their sleeve, providing an even finer measurement to be taken, in 0.001 increments of a millimetre. Take the sleeve and thimble measurement as described above, then check which graduation on the vernier scale aligns with that of the annular scale on the thimble **Note:** *The eye must be perpendicular to the scale when taking the vernier reading - if necessary rotate the body of the micrometer to ensure this.* Multiply the vernier scale figure by 0.001 and add it to the base and fine measurement figures.

In the example shown the item measures 46.994 mm **(see illustrations 3.5 and 3.6)**:

| | |
|---|---|
| Linear scale (base) | 46.000 mm |
| Linear scale (base) | 00.500 mm |
| Annular scale (fine) | 00.490 mm |
| Vernier scale | 00.004 mm |
| **Total figure** | **46.994 mm** |

### Internal micrometer

● Internal micrometers are available for measuring bore diameters, but are expensive and unlikely to be available for home use. It is suggested that a set of telescoping gauges and small hole gauges, both of which must be used with an external micrometer, will suffice for taking internal measurements on a motorcycle.
● Telescoping gauges can be used to

measure internal diameters of components. Select a gauge with the correct size range, make sure its ends are clean and insert it into the bore. Expand the gauge, then lock its position and withdraw it from the bore **(see illustration 3.7)**. Measure across the gauge ends with a micrometer **(see illustration 3.8)**.
● Very small diameter bores (such as valve guides) are measured with a small hole gauge. Once adjusted to a slip-fit inside the component, its position is locked and the gauge withdrawn for measurement with a micrometer **(see illustrations 3.9 and 3.10)**.

### Vernier caliper

**Note:** *The conventional linear and dial gauge type instruments are described. Digital types are easier to read, but are far more expensive.*
● The vernier caliper does not provide the precision of a micrometer, but is versatile in being able to measure internal and external diameters. Some types also incorporate a depth gauge. It is ideal for measuring clutch plate friction material and spring free lengths.
● To use the conventional linear scale vernier, slacken off the vernier clamp screws (1) and set its jaws over (2), or inside (3), the item to be measured **(see illustration 3.11)**. Slide the jaw into contact, using the thumb-wheel (4) for fine movement of the sliding scale (5) then tighten the clamp screws (1). Read off the main scale (6) where the zero on the sliding scale (5) intersects it, taking the whole number to the left of the zero; this provides the base measurement. View along the sliding scale and select the division which

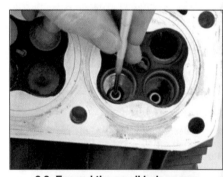

**3.9 Expand the small hole gauge in the bore, lock its position . . .**

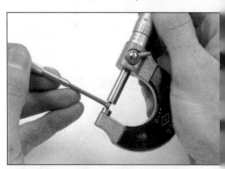

**3.10 . . . then measure the gauge with a micrometer**

lines up exactly with any of the divisions on the main scale, noting that the divisions usually represents 0.02 of a millimetre. Add this fine measurement to the base measurement to obtain the total reading.

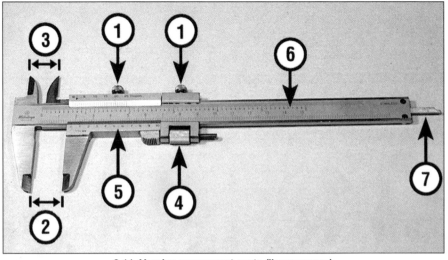

**3.11 Vernier component parts (linear gauge)**

| | | | |
|---|---|---|---|
| 1 | Clamp screws | 3 | Internal jaws | 5 | Sliding scale | 7 | Depth gauge |
| 2 | External jaws | 4 | Thumbwheel | 6 | Main scale | | |

In the example shown the item measures 55.92 mm (see illustration 3.12):

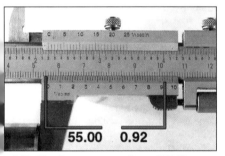

**3.12 Vernier gauge reading of 55.92 mm**

| Base measurement | 55.00 mm |
|---|---|
| Fine measurement | 00.92 mm |
| Total figure | **55.92 mm** |

● Some vernier calipers are equipped with a dial gauge for fine measurement. Before use, check that the jaws are clean, then close them fully and check that the dial gauge reads zero. If necessary adjust the gauge ring accordingly. Slacken the vernier clamp screw (1) and set its jaws over (2), or inside (3), the item to be measured (see illustration 3.13). Slide the jaws into contact, using the thumbwheel (4) for fine movement. Read off the main scale (5) where the edge of the sliding scale (6) intersects it, taking the whole number to the left of the zero; this provides the base measurement. Read off the needle position on the dial gauge (7) scale to provide the fine measurement; each division represents 0.05 of a millimetre. Add this fine measurement to the base measurement to obtain the total reading.

In the example shown the item measures 55.95 mm (see illustration 3.14):

| Base measurement | 55.00 mm |
|---|---|
| Fine measurement | 00.95 mm |
| Total figure | **55.95 mm** |

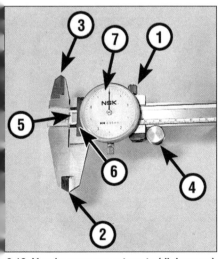

**3.13 Vernier component parts (dial gauge)**

| | |
|---|---|
| 1 | Clamp screw |
| 2 | External jaws |
| 3 | Internal jaws |
| 4 | Thumbwheel |
| 5 | Main scale |
| 6 | Sliding scale |
| 7 | Dial gauge |

**3.14 Vernier gauge reading of 55.95 mm**

## Plastigauge

● Plastigauge is a plastic material which can be compressed between two surfaces to measure the oil clearance between them. The width of the compressed Plastigauge is measured against a calibrated scale to determine the clearance.

● Common uses of Plastigauge are for measuring the clearance between crankshaft journal and main bearing inserts, between crankshaft journal and big-end bearing inserts, and between camshaft and bearing surfaces. The following example describes big-end oil clearance measurement.

● Handle the Plastigauge material carefully to prevent distortion. Using a sharp knife, cut a length which corresponds with the width of the bearing being measured and place it carefully across the journal so that it is parallel with the shaft (see illustration 3.15). Carefully install both bearing shells and the connecting rod. Without rotating the rod on the journal tighten its bolts or nuts (as applicable) to the specified torque. The connecting rod and bearings are then disassembled and the crushed Plastigauge examined.

**3.15 Plastigauge placed across shaft journal**

● Using the scale provided in the Plastigauge kit, measure the width of the material to determine the oil clearance (see illustration 3.16). Always remove all traces of Plastigauge after use using your fingernails.

*Caution: Arriving at the correct clearance demands that the assembly is torqued correctly, according to the settings and sequence (where applicable) provided by the motorcycle manufacturer.*

**3.16 Measuring the width of the crushed Plastigauge**

## Dial gauge or DTI (Dial Test Indicator)

● A dial gauge can be used to accurately measure small amounts of movement. Typical uses are measuring shaft runout or shaft endfloat (sideplay) and setting piston position for ignition timing on two-strokes. A dial gauge set usually comes with a range of different probes and adapters and mounting equipment.
● The gauge needle must point to zero when at rest. Rotate the ring around its periphery to zero the gauge.
● Check that the gauge is capable of reading the extent of movement in the work. Most gauges have a small dial set in the face which records whole millimetres of movement as well as the fine scale around the face periphery which is calibrated in 0.01 mm divisions. Read off the small dial first to obtain the base measurement, then add the measurement from the fine scale to obtain the total reading.

In the example shown the gauge reads 1.48 mm (see illustration 3.17):

| Base measurement | 1.00 mm |
|---|---|
| Fine measurement | 0.48 mm |
| Total figure | **1.48 mm** |

3.17 Dial gauge reading of 1.48 mm

● If measuring shaft runout, the shaft must be supported in vee-blocks and the gauge mounted on a stand perpendicular to the shaft. Rest the tip of the gauge against the centre of the shaft and rotate the shaft slowly whilst watching the gauge reading (see illustration 3.18). Take several measurements along the length of the shaft and record the

3.18 Using a dial gauge to measure shaft runout

maximum gauge reading as the amount of runout in the shaft. **Note:** *The reading obtained will be total runout at that point - some manufacturers specify that the runout figure is halved to compare with their specified runout limit.*
● Endfloat (sideplay) measurement requires that the gauge is mounted securely to the surrounding component with its probe touching the end of the shaft. Using hand pressure, push and pull on the shaft noting the maximum endfloat recorded on the gauge (see illustration 3.19).

3.19 Using a dial gauge to measure shaft endfloat

● A dial gauge with suitable adapters can be used to determine piston position BTDC on two-stroke engines for the purposes of ignition timing. The gauge, adapter and suitable length probe are installed in the place of the spark plug and the gauge zeroed at TDC. If the piston position is specified as 1.14 mm BTDC, rotate the engine back to 2.00 mm BTDC, then slowly forwards to 1.14 mm BTDC.

## Cylinder compression gauges

● A compression gauge is used for measuring cylinder compression. Either the rubber-cone type or the threaded adapter type can be used. The latter is preferred to ensure a perfect seal against the cylinder head. A 0 to 300 psi (0 to 20 Bar) type gauge (for petrol/gasoline engines) will be suitable for motorcycles.
● The spark plug is removed and the gauge either held hard against the cylinder head (cone type) or the gauge adapter screwed into cylinder head (threaded type) (see illustration 3.20). Cylinder compression is measured with the engine turning over, but not running - carry out the compression test as described in

3.20 Using a rubber-cone type cylinder compression gauge

*Fault Finding Equipment.* The gauge will hold the reading until manually released.

## Oil pressure gauge

● An oil pressure gauge is used for measuring engine oil pressure. Most gauges come with a set of adapters to fit the thread of the take-off point (see illustration 3.21). If the take-off point specified by the motorcycle manufacturer is an external oil pipe union, make sure that the specified replacement union is used to prevent oil starvation.

3.21 Oil pressure gauge and take-off point adapter (arrow)

● Oil pressure is measured with the engine running (at a specific rpm) and often the manufacturer will specify pressure limits for a cold and hot engine.

## Straight-edge and surface plate

● If checking the gasket face of a component for warpage, place a steel rule or precision straight-edge across the gasket face and measure any gap between the straight-edge and component with feeler gauges (see illustration 3.22). Check diagonally across the component and between mounting holes (see illustration 3.23).

3.22 Use a straight-edge and feeler gauges to check for warpage

3.23 Check for warpage in these directions

● Checking individual components for warpage, such as clutch plain (metal) plates, requires a perfectly flat plate or piece or plate glass and feeler gauges.

## 4  Torque and leverage

### What is torque?

● Torque describes the twisting force about a shaft. The amount of torque applied is determined by the distance from the centre of the shaft to the end of the lever and the amount of force being applied to the end of the lever; distance multiplied by force equals torque.
● The manufacturer applies a measured torque to a bolt or nut to ensure that it will not slacken in use and to hold two components securely together without movement in the joint. The actual torque setting depends on the thread size, bolt or nut material and the composition of the components being held.
● Too little torque may cause the fastener to loosen due to vibration, whereas too much torque will distort the joint faces of the component or cause the fastener to shear off. Always stick to the specified torque setting.

### Using a torque wrench

● Check the calibration of the torque wrench and make sure it has a suitable range for the job. Torque wrenches are available in Nm (Newton-metres), kgf m (kilograms-force metre), lbf ft (pounds-feet), lbf in (inch-pounds). Do not confuse lbf ft with lbf in.
● Adjust the tool to the desired torque on the scale (see illustration 4.1). If your torque wrench is not calibrated in the units specified, carefully convert the figure (see *Conversion Factors*). A manufacturer sometimes gives a torque setting as a range (8 to 10 Nm) rather than a single figure - in this case set the tool midway between the two settings. The same torque may be expressed as 9 Nm ± 1 Nm. Some torque wrenches have a method of locking the setting so that it isn't inadvertently altered during use.

**4.1  Set the torque wrench index mark to the setting required, in this case 12 Nm**

● Install the bolts/nuts in their correct location and secure them lightly. Their threads must be clean and free of any old locking compound. Unless specified the threads and flange should be dry - oiled threads are necessary in certain circumstances and the manufacturer will take this into account in the specified torque figure. Similarly, the manufacturer may also specify the application of thread-locking compound.
● Tighten the fasteners in the specified sequence until the torque wrench clicks, indicating that the torque setting has been reached. Apply the torque again to double-check the setting. Where different thread diameter fasteners secure the component, as a rule tighten the larger diameter ones first.
● When the torque wrench has been finished with, release the lock (where applicable) and fully back off its setting to zero - do not leave the torque wrench tensioned. Also, do not use a torque wrench for slackening a fastener.

### Angle-tightening

● Manufacturers often specify a figure in degrees for final tightening of a fastener. This usually follows tightening to a specific torque setting.
● A degree disc can be set and attached to the socket (see illustration 4.2) or a protractor can be used to mark the angle of movement on the bolt/nut head and the surrounding casting (see illustration 4.3).

**4.2  Angle tightening can be accomplished with a torque-angle gauge . . .**

**4.3  . . . or by marking the angle on the surrounding component**

### Loosening sequences

● Where more than one bolt/nut secures a component, loosen each fastener evenly a little at a time. In this way, not all the stress of the joint is held by one fastener and the components are not likely to distort.
● If a tightening sequence is provided, work in the REVERSE of this, but if not, work from the outside in, in a criss-cross sequence (see illustration 4.4).

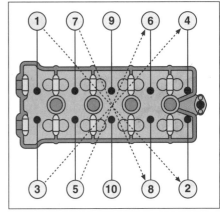

**4.4  When slackening, work from the outside inwards**

### Tightening sequences

● If a component is held by more than one fastener it is important that the retaining bolts/nuts are tightened evenly to prevent uneven stress build-up and distortion of sealing faces. This is especially important on high-compression joints such as the cylinder head.
● A sequence is usually provided by the manufacturer, either in a diagram or actually marked in the casting. If not, always start in the centre and work outwards in a criss-cross pattern (see illustration 4.5). Start off by securing all bolts/nuts finger-tight, then set the torque wrench and tighten each fastener by a small amount in sequence until the final torque is reached. By following this practice,

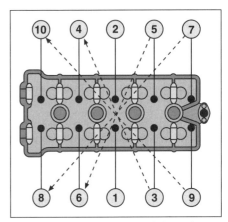

**4.5  When tightening, work from the inside outwards**

the joint will be held evenly and will not be distorted. Important joints, such as the cylinder head and big-end fasteners often have two- or three-stage torque settings.

### Applying leverage

● Use tools at the correct angle. Position a socket wrench or spanner on the bolt/nut so that you pull it towards you when loosening. If this can't be done, push the spanner without curling your fingers around it **(see illustration 4.6)** - the spanner may slip or the fastener loosen suddenly, resulting in your fingers being crushed against a component.

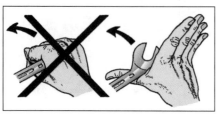

**4.6 If you can't pull on the spanner to loosen a fastener, push with your hand open**

● Additional leverage is gained by extending the length of the lever. The best way to do this is to use a breaker bar instead of the regular length tool, or to slip a length of tubing over the end of the spanner or socket wrench.
● If additional leverage will not work, the fastener head is either damaged or firmly corroded in place (see *Fasteners*).

### 5   Bearings

### Bearing removal and installation

#### Drivers and sockets

● Before removing a bearing, always inspect the casing to see which way it must be driven out - some casings will have retaining plates or a cast step. Also check for any identifying markings on the bearing and if installed to a certain depth, measure this at this stage. Some roller bearings are sealed on one side - take note of the original fitted position.
● Bearings can be driven out of a casing using a bearing driver tool (with the correct size head) or a socket of the correct diameter. Select the driver head or socket so that it contacts the outer race of the bearing, not the balls/rollers or inner race. Always support the casing around the bearing housing with wood blocks, otherwise there is a risk of fracture. The bearing is driven out with a few blows on the driver or socket from a heavy mallet. Unless access is severely restricted (as with wheel bearings), a pin-punch is not recommended unless it is moved around the bearing to keep it square in its housing.

● The same equipment can be used to install bearings. Make sure the bearing housing is supported on wood blocks and line up the bearing in its housing. Fit the bearing as noted on removal - generally they are installed with their marked side facing outwards. Tap the bearing squarely into its housing using a driver or socket which bears only on the bearing's outer race - contact with the bearing balls/rollers or inner race will destroy it **(see illustrations 5.1 and 5.2)**.
● Check that the bearing inner race and balls/rollers rotate freely.

**5.1  Using a bearing driver against the bearing's outer race**

**5.2  Using a large socket against the bearing's outer race**

#### Pullers and slide-hammers

● Where a bearing is pressed on a shaft a puller will be required to extract it **(see illustration 5.3)**. Make sure that the puller clamp or legs fit securely behind the bearing and are unlikely to slip out. If pulling a bearing

**5.3  This bearing puller clamps behind the bearing and pressure is applied to the shaft end to draw the bearing off**

off a gear shaft for example, you may have to locate the puller behind a gear pinion if there is no access to the race and draw the gear pinion off the shaft as well **(see illustration 5.4)**.

> **Caution: Ensure that the puller's centre bolt locates securely against the end of the shaft and will not slip when pressure is applied. Also ensure that puller does not damage the shaft end.**

**5.4  Where no access is available to the rear of the bearing, it is sometimes possible to draw off the adjacent component**

● Operate the puller so that its centre bolt exerts pressure on the shaft end and draws the bearing off the shaft.
● When installing the bearing on the shaft, tap only on the bearing's inner race - contact with the balls/rollers or outer race with destroy the bearing. Use a socket or length of tubing as a drift which fits over the shaft end **(see illustration 5.5)**.

**5.5  When installing a bearing on a shaft use a piece of tubing which bears only on the bearing's inner race**

● Where a bearing locates in a blind hole in a casing, it cannot be driven or pulled out as described above. A slide-hammer with knife-edged bearing puller attachment will be required. The puller attachment passes through the bearing and when tightened expands to fit firmly behind the bearing **(see illustration 5.6)**. By operating the slide-hammer part of the tool the bearing is jarred out of its housing **(see illustration 5.7)**.
● It is possible, if the bearing is of reasonable weight, for it to drop out of its housing if the casing is heated as described opposite. If this

**5.6 Expand the bearing puller so that it locks behind the bearing . . .**

**5.7 . . . attach the slide hammer to the bearing puller**

method is attempted, first prepare a work surface which will enable the casing to be tapped face down to help dislodge the bearing - a wood surface is ideal since it will not damage the casing's gasket surface. Wearing protective gloves, tap the heated casing several times against the work surface to dislodge the bearing under its own weight **(see illustration 5.8)**.

**5.8 Tapping a casing face down on wood blocks can often dislodge a bearing**

● Bearings can be installed in blind holes using the driver or socket method described above.

## Drawbolts

● Where a bearing or bush is set in the eye of a component, such as a suspension linkage arm or connecting rod small-end, removal by drift may damage the component. Furthermore, a rubber bushing in a shock absorber eye cannot successfully be driven out of position. If access is available to a engineering press, the task is straightforward. If not, a drawbolt can be fabricated to extract the bearing or bush.

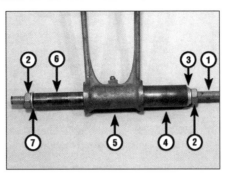

**5.9 Drawbolt component parts assembled on a suspension arm**

1 Bolt or length of threaded bar
2 Nuts
3 Washer (external diameter greater than tubing internal diameter)
4 Tubing (internal diameter sufficient to accommodate bearing)
5 Suspension arm with bearing
6 Tubing (external diameter slightly smaller than bearing)
7 Washer (external diameter slightly smaller than bearing)

**5.10 Drawing the bearing out of the suspension arm**

● To extract the bearing/bush you will need a long bolt with nut (or piece of threaded bar with two nuts), a piece of tubing which has an internal diameter larger than the bearing/bush, another piece of tubing which has an external diameter slightly smaller than the bearing/bush, and a selection of washers **(see illustrations 5.9 and 5.10)**. Note that the pieces of tubing must be of the same length, or longer, than the bearing/bush.
● The same kit (without the pieces of tubing) can be used to draw the new bearing/bush back into place **(see illustration 5.11)**.

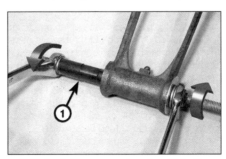

**5.11 Installing a new bearing (1) in the suspension arm**

## Temperature change

● If the bearing's outer race is a tight fit in the casing, the aluminium casing can be heated to release its grip on the bearing. Aluminium will expand at a greater rate than the steel bearing outer race. There are several ways to do this, but avoid any localised extreme heat (such as a blow torch) - aluminium alloy has a low melting point.
● Approved methods of heating a casing are using a domestic oven (heated to 100°C) or immersing the casing in boiling water **(see illustration 5.12)**. Low temperature range localised heat sources such as a paint stripper heat gun or clothes iron can also be used **(see illustration 5.13)**. Alternatively, soak a rag in boiling water, wring it out and wrap it around the bearing housing.

> ⚠ **Warning: All of these methods require care in use to prevent scalding and burns to the hands. Wear protective gloves when handling hot components.**

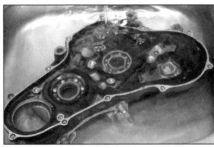

**5.12 A casing can be immersed in a sink of boiling water to aid bearing removal**

**5.13 Using a localised heat source to aid bearing removal**

● If heating the whole casing note that plastic components, such as the neutral switch, may suffer - remove them beforehand.
● After heating, remove the bearing as described above. You may find that the expansion is sufficient for the bearing to fall out of the casing under its own weight or with a light tap on the driver or socket.
● If necessary, the casing can be heated to aid bearing installation, and this is sometimes the recommended procedure if the motorcycle manufacturer has designed the housing and bearing fit with this intention.

Installation of bearings can be eased by placing them in a freezer the night before installation. The steel bearing will contract slightly, allowing easy insertion in its housing. This is often useful when installing steering head outer races in the frame.

### Bearing types and markings

Plain shell bearings, ball bearings, needle roller bearings and tapered roller bearings will all be found on motorcycles (see illustrations 5.14 and 5.15). The ball and roller types are usually caged between an inner and outer race, but uncaged variations may be found.

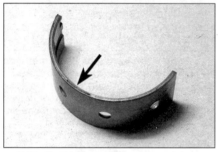

5.14 Shell bearings are either plain or grooved. They are usually identified by colour code (arrow)

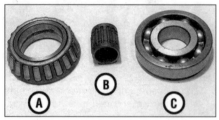

5.15 Tapered roller bearing (A), needle roller bearing (B) and ball journal bearing (C)

Shell bearings (often called inserts) are usually found at the crankshaft main and connecting rod big-end where they are good at coping with high loads. They are made of a phosphor-bronze material and are impregnated with self-lubricating properties.

Ball bearings and needle roller bearings consist of a steel inner and outer race with the balls or rollers between the races. They require constant lubrication by oil or grease and are good at coping with axial loads. Taper roller bearings consist of rollers set in a tapered cage set on the inner race; the outer race is separate. They are good at coping with axial loads and prevent movement along the shaft - a typical application is in the steering head.

Bearing manufacturers produce bearings to ISO size standards and stamp one face of the bearing to indicate its internal and external diameter, load capacity and type (see illustration 5.16).

Metal bushes are usually of phosphor-bronze material. Rubber bushes are used in suspension mounting eyes. Fibre bushes have also been used in suspension pivots.

5.16 Typical bearing marking

### Bearing fault finding

If a bearing outer race has spun in its housing, the housing material will be damaged. You can use a bearing locking compound to bond the outer race in place if damage is not too severe.

Shell bearings will fail due to damage of their working surface, as a result of lack of lubrication, corrosion or abrasive particles in the oil (see illustration 5.17). Small particles of dirt in the oil may embed in the bearing material whereas larger particles will score the bearing and shaft journal. If a number of short journeys are made, insufficient heat will be generated to drive off condensation which has built up on the bearings.

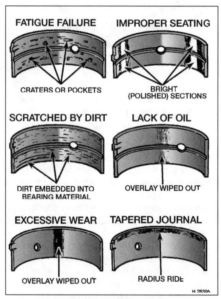

5.17 Typical bearing failures

Ball and roller bearings will fail due to lack of lubrication or damage to the balls or rollers. Tapered-roller bearings can be damaged by overloading them. Unless the bearing is sealed on both sides, wash it in paraffin (kerosene) to remove all old grease then allow it to dry. Make a visual inspection looking to dented balls or rollers, damaged cages and worn or pitted races (see illustration 5.18).

A ball bearing can be checked for wear by listening to it when spun. Apply a film of light oil to the bearing and hold it close to the ear - hold the outer race with one hand and spin the inner

5.18 Example of ball journal bearing with damaged balls and cages

5.19 Hold outer race and listen to inner race when spun

race with the other hand (see illustration 5.19). The bearing should be almost silent when spun; if it grates or rattles it is worn.

## 6 Oil seals

### Oil seal removal and installation

Oil seals should be renewed every time a component is dismantled. This is because the seal lips will become set to the sealing surface and will not necessarily reseal.

Oil seals can be prised out of position using a large flat-bladed screwdriver (see illustration 6.1). In the case of crankcase seals, check first that the seal is not lipped on the inside, preventing its removal with the crankcases joined.

6.1 Prise out oil seals with a large flat-bladed screwdriver

New seals are usually installed with their marked face (containing the seal reference code) outwards and the spring side towards the fluid being retained. In certain cases, such as a two-stroke engine crankshaft seal, a double lipped seal may be used due to there being fluid or gas on each side of the joint.

● Use a bearing driver or socket which bears only on the outer hard edge of the seal to install it in the casing - tapping on the inner edge will damage the sealing lip.

## Oil seal types and markings

● Oil seals are usually of the single-lipped type. Double-lipped seals are found where a liquid or gas is on both sides of the joint.
● Oil seals can harden and lose their sealing ability if the motorcycle has been in storage for a long period - renewal is the only solution.
● Oil seal manufacturers also conform to the ISO markings for seal size - these are moulded into the outer face of the seal (see illustration 6.2).

**6.2 These oil seal markings indicate inside diameter, outside diameter and seal thickness**

## 7 Gaskets and sealants

### Types of gasket and sealant

● Gaskets are used to seal the mating surfaces between components and keep lubricants, fluids, vacuum or pressure contained within the assembly. Aluminium gaskets are sometimes found at the cylinder joints, but most gaskets are paper-based. If the mating surfaces of the components being joined are undamaged the gasket can be installed dry, although a dab of sealant or grease will be useful to hold it in place during assembly.
● RTV (Room Temperature Vulcanising) silicone rubber sealants cure when exposed to moisture in the atmosphere. These sealants are good at filling pits or irregular gasket faces, but will tend to be forced out of the joint under very high torque. They can be used to replace a paper gasket, but first make sure that the width of the paper gasket is not essential to the shimming of internal components. RTV sealants should not be used on components containing petrol (gasoline).
● Non-hardening, semi-hardening and hard setting liquid gasket compounds can be used with a gasket or between a metal-to-metal joint. Select the sealant to suit the application: universal non-hardening sealant can be used on virtually all joints; semi-hardening on joint faces which are rough or damaged; hard setting sealant on joints which require a permanent bond and are subjected to high temperature and pressure. **Note:** *Check first if the paper gasket has a bead of sealant*

*impregnated in its surface before applying additional sealant.*
● When choosing a sealant, make sure it is suitable for the application, particularly if being applied in a high-temperature area or in the vicinity of fuel. Certain manufacturers produce sealants in either clear, silver or black colours to match the finish of the engine. This has a particular application on motorcycles where much of the engine is exposed.
● Do not over-apply sealant. That which is squeezed out on the outside of the joint can be wiped off, whereas an excess of sealant on the inside can break off and clog oilways.

### Breaking a sealed joint

● Age, heat, pressure and the use of hard setting sealant can cause two components to stick together so tightly that they are difficult to separate using finger pressure alone. Do not resort to using levers unless there is a pry point provided for this purpose (see illustration 7.1) or else the gasket surfaces will be damaged.
● Use a soft-faced hammer (see illustration 7.2) or a wood block and conventional hammer to strike the component near the mating surface. Avoid hammering against cast extremities since they may break off. If this method fails, try using a wood wedge between the two components.

*Caution: If the joint will not separate, double-check that you have removed all the fasteners.*

**7.1 If a pry point is provided, apply gently pressure with a flat-bladed screwdriver**

**7.2 Tap around the joint with a soft-faced mallet if necessary - don't strike cooling fins**

### Removal of old gasket and sealant

● Paper gaskets will most likely come away complete, leaving only a few traces stuck on

*Most components have one or two hollow locating dowels between the two gasket faces. If a dowel cannot be removed, do not resort to gripping it with pliers - it will almost certainly be distorted. Install a close-fitting socket or Phillips screwdriver into the dowel and then grip the outer edge of the dowel to free it.*

the sealing faces of the components. It is imperative that all traces are removed to ensure correct sealing of the new gasket.
● Very carefully scrape all traces of gasket away making sure that the sealing surfaces are not gouged or scored by the scraper (see illustrations 7.3, 7.4 and 7.5). Stubborn deposits can be removed by spraying with an aerosol gasket remover. Final preparation of

**7.3 Paper gaskets can be scraped off with a gasket scraper tool . . .**

**7.4 . . . a knife blade . . .**

**7.5 . . . or a household scraper**

**7.6 Fine abrasive paper is wrapped around a flat file to clean up the gasket face**

**7.7 A kitchen scourer can be used on stubborn deposits**

the gasket surface can be made with very fine abrasive paper or a plastic kitchen scourer **(see illustrations 7.6 and 7.7)**.

● Old sealant can be scraped or peeled off components, depending on the type originally used. Note that gasket removal compounds are available to avoid scraping the components clean; make sure the gasket remover suits the type of sealant used.

## 8  Chains

### Breaking and joining final drive chains

● Drive chains for all but small bikes are continuous and do not have a clip-type connecting link. The chain must be broken using a chain breaker tool and the new chain securely riveted together using a new soft rivet-type link. Never use a clip-type connecting link instead of a rivet-type link, except in an emergency. Various chain breaking and riveting tools are available, either as separate tools or combined as illustrated in the accompanying photographs - read the instructions supplied with the tool carefully.

> ⚠ **Warning: The need to rivet the new link pins correctly cannot be overstressed - loss of control of the motorcycle is very likely to result if the chain breaks in use.**

● Rotate the chain and look for the soft link. The soft link pins look like they have been

**8.1 Tighten the chain breaker to push the pin out of the link . . .**

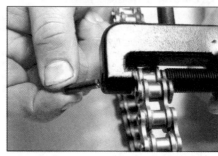

**8.2 . . . withdraw the pin, remove the tool . . .**

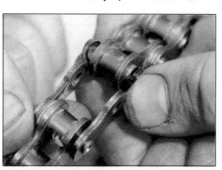

**8.3 . . . and separate the chain link**

deeply centre-punched instead of peened over like all the other pins **(see illustration 8.9)** and its sideplate may be a different colour. Position the soft link midway between the sprockets and assemble the chain breaker tool over one of the soft link pins **(see illustration 8.1)**. Operate the tool to push the pin out through the chain **(see illustration 8.2)**. On an O-ring chain, remove the O-rings **(see illustration 8.3)**. Carry out the same procedure on the other soft link pin.

> **Caution: Certain soft link pins (particularly on the larger chains) may require their ends to be filed or ground off before they can be pressed out using the tool.**

● Check that you have the correct size and strength (standard or heavy duty) new soft link - do not reuse the old link. Look for the size marking on the chain sideplates **(see illustration 8.10)**.

● Position the chain ends so that they are engaged over the rear sprocket. On an O-ring

**8.4 Insert the new soft link, with O-rings, through the chain ends . . .**

**8.5 . . . install the O-rings over the pin ends . . .**

**8.6 . . . followed by the sideplate**

chain, install a new O-ring over each pin of the link and insert the link through the two chain ends **(see illustration 8.4)**. Install a new O-ring over the end of each pin, followed by the sideplate (with the chain manufacturer's marking facing outwards) **(see illustrations 8.5 and 8.6)**. On an unsealed chain, insert the link through the two chain ends, then install the sideplate with the chain manufacturer's marking facing outwards.

● Note that it may not be possible to install the sideplate using finger pressure alone. If using a joining tool, assemble it so that the plates of the tool clamp the link and press the sideplate over the pins **(see illustration 8.7)**. Otherwise, use two small sockets placed over

**8.7 Push the sideplate into position using a clamp**

**8.8 Assemble the chain riveting tool over one pin at a time and tighten it fully**

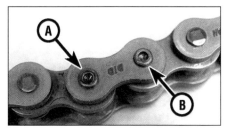

**8.9 Pin end correctly riveted (A), pin end unriveted (B)**

the rivet ends and two pieces of the wood between a G-clamp. Operate the clamp to press the sideplate over the pins.

● Assemble the joining tool over one pin (following the maker's instructions) and tighten the tool down to spread the pin end securely **(see illustrations 8.8 and 8.9)**. Do the same on the other pin.

 **Warning: Check that the pin ends are secure and that there is no danger of the sideplate coming loose. If the pin ends are cracked the soft link must be renewed.**

## Final drive chain sizing

● Chains are sized using a three digit number, followed by a suffix to denote the chain type **(see illustration 8.10)**. Chain type is either standard or heavy duty (thicker sideplates), and also unsealed or O-ring/X-ring type.

● The first digit of the number relates to the pitch of the chain, ie the distance from the centre of one pin to the centre of the next pin **(see illustration 8.11)**. Pitch is expressed in eighths of an inch, as follows:

**8.10 Typical chain size and type marking**

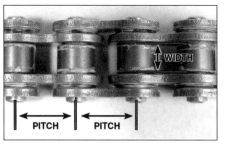

**8.11 Chain dimensions**

Sizes commencing with a 4 (eg 428) have a pitch of 1/2 inch (12.7 mm)

Sizes commencing with a 5 (eg 520) have a pitch of 5/8 inch (15.9 mm)

Sizes commencing with a 6 (eg 630) have a pitch of 3/4 inch (19.1 mm)

● The second and third digits of the chain size relate to the width of the rollers, again in imperial units, eg the 525 shown has 5/16 inch (7.94 mm) rollers **(see illustration 8.11)**.

## 9 Hoses

### Clamping to prevent flow

● Small-bore flexible hoses can be clamped to prevent fluid flow whilst a component is worked on. Whichever method is used, ensure that the hose material is not permanently distorted or damaged by the clamp.
 a) A brake hose clamp available from auto accessory shops **(see illustration 9.1)**.
 b) A wingnut type hose clamp **(see illustration 9.2)**.

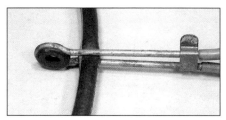

**9.1 Hoses can be clamped with an automotive brake hose clamp . . .**

**9.2 . . . a wingnut type hose clamp . . .**

 c) Two sockets placed each side of the hose and held with straight-jawed self-locking grips **(see illustration 9.3)**.
 d) Thick card each side of the hose held between straight-jawed self-locking grips **(see illustration 9.4)**.

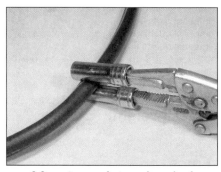

**9.3 . . . two sockets and a pair of self-locking grips . . .**

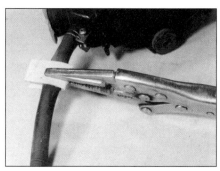

**9.4 . . . or thick card and self-locking grips**

### Freeing and fitting hoses

● Always make sure the hose clamp is moved well clear of the hose end. Grip the hose with your hand and rotate it whilst pulling it off the union. If the hose has hardened due to age and will not move, slit it with a sharp knife and peel its ends off the union **(see illustration 9.5)**.

● Resist the temptation to use grease or soap on the unions to aid installation; although it helps the hose slip over the union it will equally aid the escape of fluid from the joint. It is preferable to soften the hose ends in hot water and wet the inside surface of the hose with water or a fluid which will evaporate.

**9.5 Cutting a coolant hose free with a sharp knife**

# Conversion Factors

## Length (distance)

| | | | | | |
|---|---|---|---|---|---|
| Inches (in) | x 25.4 | = Millimetres (mm) | x 0.0394 | = Inches (in) | |
| Feet (ft) | x 0.305 | = Metres (m) | x 3.281 | = Feet (ft) | |
| Miles | x 1.609 | = Kilometres (km) | x 0.621 | = Miles | |

## Volume (capacity)

| | | | | | |
|---|---|---|---|---|---|
| Cubic inches (cu in; in$^3$) | x 16.387 | = Cubic centimetres (cc; cm$^3$) | x 0.061 | = Cubic inches (cu in; in$^3$) | |
| Imperial pints (Imp pt) | x 0.568 | = Litres (l) | x 1.76 | = Imperial pints (Imp pt) | |
| Imperial quarts (Imp qt) | x 1.137 | = Litres (l) | x 0.88 | = Imperial quarts (Imp qt) | |
| Imperial quarts (Imp qt) | x 1.201 | = US quarts (US qt) | x 0.833 | = Imperial quarts (Imp qt) | |
| US quarts (US qt) | x 0.946 | = Litres (l) | x 1.057 | = US quarts (US qt) | |
| Imperial gallons (Imp gal) | x 4.546 | = Litres (l) | x 0.22 | = Imperial gallons (Imp gal) | |
| Imperial gallons (Imp gal) | x 1.201 | = US gallons (US gal) | x 0.833 | = Imperial gallons (Imp gal) | |
| US gallons (US gal) | x 3.785 | = Litres (l) | x 0.264 | = US gallons (US gal) | |

## Mass (weight)

| | | | | | |
|---|---|---|---|---|---|
| Ounces (oz) | x 28.35 | = Grams (g) | x 0.035 | = Ounces (oz) | |
| Pounds (lb) | x 0.454 | = Kilograms (kg) | x 2.205 | = Pounds (lb) | |

## Force

| | | | | | |
|---|---|---|---|---|---|
| Ounces-force (ozf; oz) | x 0.278 | = Newtons (N) | x 3.6 | = Ounces-force (ozf; oz) | |
| Pounds-force (lbf; lb) | x 4.448 | = Newtons (N) | x 0.225 | = Pounds-force (lbf; lb) | |
| Newtons (N) | x 0.1 | = Kilograms-force (kgf; kg) | x 9.81 | = Newtons (N) | |

## Pressure

| | | | | | |
|---|---|---|---|---|---|
| Pounds-force per square inch (psi; lbf/in$^2$; lb/in$^2$) | x 0.070 | = Kilograms-force per square centimetre (kgf/cm$^2$; kg/cm$^2$) | x 14.223 | = Pounds-force per square inch (psi; lbf/in$^2$; lb/in$^2$) | |
| Pounds-force per square inch (psi; lbf/in$^2$; lb/in$^2$) | x 0.068 | = Atmospheres (atm) | x 14.696 | = Pounds-force per square inch (psi; lbf/in$^2$; lb/in$^2$) | |
| Pounds-force per square inch (psi; lbf/in$^2$; lb/in$^2$) | x 0.069 | = Bars | x 14.5 | = Pounds-force per square inch (psi; lbf/in$^2$; lb/in$^2$) | |
| Pounds-force per square inch (psi; lbf/in$^2$; lb/in$^2$) | x 6.895 | = Kilopascals (kPa) | x 0.145 | = Pounds-force per square inch (psi; lbf/in$^2$; lb/in$^2$) | |
| Kilopascals (kPa) | x 0.01 | = Kilograms-force per square centimetre (kgf/cm$^2$; kg/cm$^2$) | x 98.1 | = Kilopascals (kPa) | |
| Millibar (mbar) | x 100 | = Pascals (Pa) | x 0.01 | = Millibar (mbar) | |
| Millibar (mbar) | x 0.0145 | = Pounds-force per square inch (psi; lbf/in$^2$; lb/in$^2$) | x 68.947 | = Millibar (mbar) | |
| Millibar (mbar) | x 0.75 | = Millimetres of mercury (mmHg) | x 1.333 | = Millibar (mbar) | |
| Millibar (mbar) | x 0.401 | = Inches of water (inH$_2$O) | x 2.491 | = Millibar (mbar) | |
| Millimetres of mercury (mmHg) | x 0.535 | = Inches of water (inH$_2$O) | x 1.868 | = Millimetres of mercury (mmHg) | |
| Inches of water (inH$_2$O) | x 0.036 | = Pounds-force per square inch (psi; lbf/in$^2$; lb/in$^2$) | x 27.68 | = Inches of water (inH$_2$O) | |

## Torque (moment of force)

| | | | | | |
|---|---|---|---|---|---|
| Pounds-force inches (lbf in; lb in) | x 1.152 | = Kilograms-force centimetre (kgf cm; kg cm) | x 0.868 | = Pounds-force inches (lbf in; lb in) | |
| Pounds-force inches (lbf in; lb in) | x 0.113 | = Newton metres (Nm) | x 8.85 | = Pounds-force inches (lbf in; lb in) | |
| Pounds-force inches (lbf in; lb in) | x 0.083 | = Pounds-force feet (lbf ft; lb ft) | x 12 | = Pounds-force inches (lbf in; lb in) | |
| Pounds-force feet (lbf ft; lb ft) | x 0.138 | = Kilograms-force metres (kgf m; kg m) | x 7.233 | = Pounds-force feet (lbf ft; lb ft) | |
| Pounds-force feet (lbf ft; lb ft) | x 1.356 | = Newton metres (Nm) | x 0.738 | = Pounds-force feet (lbf ft; lb ft) | |
| Newton metres (Nm) | x 0.102 | = Kilograms-force metres (kgf m; kg m) | x 9.804 | = Newton metres (Nm) | |

## Power

| | | | | | |
|---|---|---|---|---|---|
| Horsepower (hp) | x 745.7 | = Watts (W) | x 0.0013 | = Horsepower (hp) | |

## Velocity (speed)

| | | | | | |
|---|---|---|---|---|---|
| Miles per hour (miles/hr; mph) | x 1.609 | = Kilometres per hour (km/hr; kph) | x 0.621 | = Miles per hour (miles/hr; mph) | |

## Fuel consumption*

| | | | | | |
|---|---|---|---|---|---|
| Miles per gallon (mpg) | x 0.354 | = Kilometres per litre (km/l) | x 2.825 | = Miles per gallon (mpg) | |

## Temperature

Degrees Fahrenheit = (°C x 1.8) + 32         Degrees Celsius (Degrees Centigrade; °C) = (°F - 32) x 0.56

*It is common practice to convert from miles per gallon (mpg) to litres/100 kilometres (l/100km), where mpg x l/100 km = 282*

## About the MOT Test

In the UK, all vehicles more than three years old are subject to an annual test to ensure that they meet minimum safety requirements. A current test certificate must be issued before a machine can be used on public roads, and is required before a road fund licence can be issued. Riding without a current test certificate will also invalidate your insurance.

For most owners, the MOT test is an annual cause for anxiety, and this is largely due to owners not being sure what needs to be checked prior to submitting the motorcycle for testing. The simple answer is that a fully roadworthy motorcycle will have no difficulty in passing the test.

This is a guide to getting your motorcycle through the MOT test. Obviously it will not be possible to examine the motorcycle to the same standard as the professional MOT tester, particularly in view of the equipment required for some of the checks. However, working through the following procedures will enable you to identify any problem areas before submitting the motorcycle for the test.

It has only been possible to summarise the test requirements here, based on the regulations in force at the time of printing. Test standards are becoming increasingly stringent, although there are some exemptions for older vehicles. More information about the MOT test can be obtained from the HMSO publications, *How Safe is your Motorcycle* and *The MOT Inspection Manual for Motorcycle Testing*.

Many of the checks require that one of the wheels is raised off the ground. If the motorcycle doesn't have a centre stand, note that an auxiliary stand will be required. Additionally, the help of an assistant may prove useful.

Certain exceptions apply to machines under 50 cc, machines without a lighting system, and Classic bikes - if in doubt about any of the requirements listed below seek confirmation from an MOT tester prior to submitting the motorcycle for the test.

Check that the frame number is clearly visible.

> **HAYNES HiNT** *If a component is in borderline condition, the tester has discretion in deciding whether to pass or fail it. If the motorcycle presented is clean and evidently well cared for, the tester may be more inclined to pass a borderline component than if the motorcycle is scruffy and apparently neglected.*

# Electrical System

## Lights, turn signals, horn and reflector

✔ With the ignition on, check the operation of the following electrical components. **Note:** *The electrical components on certain small-capacity machines are powered by the generator, requiring that the engine is run for this check.*

a) *Headlight and tail light. Check that both illuminate in the low and high beam switch positions.*

b) *Position lights. Check that the front position (or sidelight) and tail light illuminate in this switch position.*

c) *Turn signals. Check that all flash at the correct rate, and that the warning light(s) function correctly. Check that the turn signal switch works correctly.*

d) *Hazard warning system (where fitted). Check that all four turn signals flash in this switch position.*

d) *Brake stop light. Check that the light comes on when the front and rear brakes are independently applied. Models first used on or after 1st April 1986 must have a brake light switch on each brake.*

e) *Horn. Check that the sound is continuous and of reasonable volume.*

✔ Check that there is a red reflector on the rear of the machine, either mounted separately or as part of the tail light lens.

✔ Check the condition of the headlight, tail light and turn signal lenses.

## Headlight beam height

✔ The MOT tester will perform a headlight beam height check using specialised beam setting equipment **(see illustration 1)**. This equipment will not be available to the home mechanic, but if you suspect that the headlight is incorrectly set or may have been maladjusted in the past, you can perform a rough test as follows.

✔ Position the bike in a straight line facing a brick wall. The bike must be off its stand, upright and with a rider seated. Measure the height from the ground to the centre of the headlight and mark a horizontal line on the wall at this height. Position the motorcycle 3.8 metres from the wall and draw a vertical

**Headlight beam height checking equipment**

line up the wall central to the centreline of the motorcycle. Switch to dipped beam and check that the beam pattern falls slightly lower than the horizontal line and to the left of the vertical line **(see illustration 2)**.

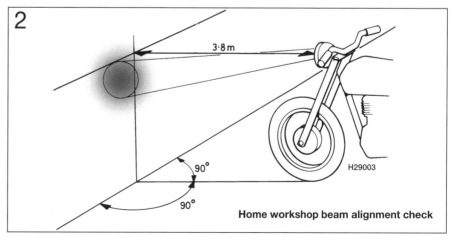

**Home workshop beam alignment check**

# Exhaust System and Final Drive

### Exhaust

✔ Check that the exhaust mountings are secure and that the system does not foul any of the rear suspension components.

✔ Start the motorcycle. When the revs are increased, check that the exhaust is neither holed nor leaking from any of its joints. On a linked system, check that the collector box is not leaking due to corrosion.

✔ Note that the exhaust decibel level ("loudness" of the exhaust) is assessed at the discretion of the tester. If the motorcycle was first used on or after 1st January 1985 the silencer must carry the BSAU 193 stamp, or a marking relating to its make and model, or be of OE (original equipment) manufacture. If the silencer is marked NOT FOR ROAD USE, RACING USE ONLY or similar, it will fail the MOT.

### Final drive

✔ On chain or belt drive machines, check that the chain/belt is in good condition and does not have excessive slack. Also check that the sprocket is securely mounted on the rear wheel hub. Check that the chain/belt guard is in place.

✔ On shaft drive bikes, check for oil leaking from the drive unit and fouling the rear tyre.

# Steering and Suspension

### Steering

✔ With the front wheel raised off the ground, rotate the steering from lock to lock. The handlebar or switches must not contact the fuel tank or be close enough to trap the rider's hand. Problems can be caused by damaged lock stops on the lower yoke and frame, or by the fitting of non-standard handlebars.

✔ When performing the lock to lock check, also ensure that the steering moves freely without drag or notchiness. Steering movement can be impaired by poorly routed cables, or by overtight head bearings or worn bearings. The tester will perform a check of the steering head bearing lower race by mounting the front wheel on a surface plate, then performing a lock to lock check with the weight of the machine on the lower bearing (see illustration 3).

✔ Grasp the fork sliders (lower legs) and attempt to push and pull on the forks (see illustration 4). Any play in the steering head bearings will be felt. Note that in extreme cases, wear of the front fork bushes can be misinterpreted for head bearing play.

✔ Check that the handlebars are securely mounted.

✔ Check that the handlebar grip rubbers are secure. They should by bonded to the bar left end and to the throttle cable pulley on the right end.

### Front suspension

✔ With the motorcycle off the stand, hold the front brake on and pump the front forks up and down (see illustration 5). Check that they are adequately damped.

✔ Inspect the area above and around the front fork oil seals (see illustration 6). There should be no sign of oil on the fork tube (stanchion) nor leaking down the slider (lower leg). On models so equipped, check that there is no oil leaking from the anti-dive units.

✔ On models with swingarm front suspension, check that there is no freeplay in the linkage when moved from side to side.

### Rear suspension

✔ With the motorcycle off the stand and an assistant supporting the motorcycle by its handlebars, bounce the rear suspension (see illustration 7). Check that the suspension components do not foul on any of the cycle parts and check that the shock absorber(s) provide adequate damping.

Front wheel mounted on a surface plate for steering head bearing lower race check

Checking the steering head bearings for freeplay

Hold the front brake on and pump the front forks up and down to check operation

Inspect the area around the fork dust seal for oil leakage (arrow)

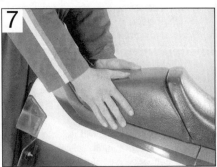

Bounce the rear of the motorcycle to check rear suspension operation

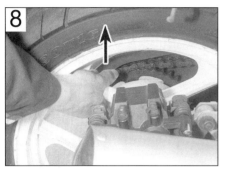

**Checking for rear suspension linkage play**

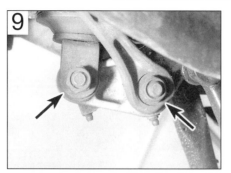

**Worn suspension linkage pivots (arrows) are usually the cause of play in the rear suspension**

**Grasp the swingarm at the ends to check for play in its pivot bearings**

✔ Visually inspect the shock absorber(s) and check that there is no sign of oil leakage from its damper. This is somewhat restricted on certain single shock models due to the location of the shock absorber.

✔ With the rear wheel raised off the ground, grasp the wheel at the highest point and attempt to pull it up **(see illustration 8)**. Any play in the swingarm pivot or suspension linkage bearings will be felt as movement. **Note:** *Do not confuse play with actual suspension movement.* Failure to lubricate suspension linkage bearings can lead to bearing failure **(see illustration 9)**.

✔ With the rear wheel raised off the ground, grasp the swingarm ends and attempt to move the swingarm from side to side and forwards and backwards - any play indicates wear of the swingarm pivot bearings **(see illustration 10)**.

# Brakes, Wheels and Tyres

### Brakes

✔ With the wheel raised off the ground, apply the brake then free it off, and check that the wheel is about to revolve freely without brake drag.

✔ On disc brakes, examine the disc itself. Check that it is securely mounted and not cracked.

✔ On disc brakes, view the pad material through the caliper mouth and check that the pads are not worn down beyond the limit **(see illustration 11)**.

✔ On drum brakes, check that when the brake is applied the angle between the operating lever and cable or rod is not too great **(see illustration 12)**. Check also that the operating lever doesn't foul any other components.

✔ On disc brakes, examine the flexible hoses from top to bottom. Have an assistant hold the brake on so that the fluid in the hose is under pressure, and check that there is no sign of fluid leakage, bulges or cracking. If there are any metal brake pipes or unions, check that these are free from corrosion and damage. Where a brake-linked anti-dive system is fitted, check the hoses to the anti-dive in a similar manner.

✔ Check that the rear brake torque arm is secure and that its fasteners are secured by self-locking nuts or castellated nuts with split-pins or R-pins **(see illustration 13)**.

✔ On models with ABS, check that the self-check warning light in the instrument panel works.

✔ The MOT tester will perform a test of the motorcycle's braking efficiency based on a calculation of rider and motorcycle weight. Although this cannot be carried out at home, you can at least ensure that the braking systems are properly maintained. For hydraulic disc brakes, check the fluid level, lever/pedal feel (bleed of air if its spongy) and pad material. For drum brakes, check adjustment, cable or rod operation and shoe lining thickness.

### Wheels and tyres

✔ Check the wheel condition. Cast wheels should be free from cracks and if of the built-up design, all fasteners should be secure. Spoked wheels should be checked for broken, corroded, loose or bent spokes.

✔ With the wheel raised off the ground, spin the wheel and visually check that the tyre and wheel run true. Check that the tyre does not foul the suspension or mudguards.

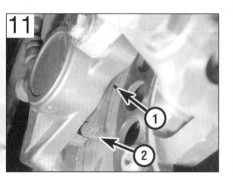

**Brake pad wear can usually be viewed without removing the caliper. Most pads have wear indicator grooves (1) and some also have indicator tangs (2)**

**On drum brakes, check the angle of the operating lever with the brake fully applied. Most drum brakes have a wear indicator pointer and scale.**

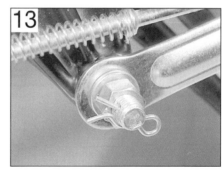

**Brake torque arm must be properly secured at both ends**

Check for wheel bearing play by trying to move the wheel about the axle (spindle)

Checking the tyre tread depth

Tyre direction of rotation arrow can be found on tyre sidewall

Castellated type wheel axle (spindle) nut must be secured by a split pin or R-pin

18

Two straightedges are used to check wheel alignment

✔ With the wheel raised off the ground, grasp the wheel and attempt to move it about the axle (spindle) **(see illustration 14)**. Any play felt here indicates wheel bearing failure.
✔ Check the tyre tread depth, tread condition and sidewall condition **(see illustration 15)**.
✔ Check the tyre type. Front and rear tyre types must be compatible and be suitable for road use. Tyres marked NOT FOR ROAD USE, COMPETITION USE ONLY or similar, will fail the MOT.
✔ If the tyre sidewall carries a direction of rotation arrow, this must be pointing in the direction of normal wheel rotation **(see illustration 16)**.
✔ Check that the wheel axle (spindle) nuts (where applicable) are properly secured. A self-locking nut or castellated nut with a split-pin or R-pin can be used **(see illustration 17)**.
✔ Wheel alignment is checked with the motorcycle off the stand and a rider seated. With the front wheel pointing straight ahead, two perfectly straight lengths of metal or wood and placed against the sidewalls of both tyres **(see illustration 18)**. The gap each side of the front tyre must be equidistant on both sides. Incorrect wheel alignment may be due to a cocked rear wheel (often as the result of poor chain adjustment) or in extreme cases, a bent frame.

# General checks and condition

✔ Check the security of all major fasteners, bodypanels, seat, fairings (where fitted) and mudguards.

✔ Check that the rider and pillion footrests, handlebar levers and brake pedal are securely mounted.

✔ Check for corrosion on the frame or any load-bearing components. If severe, this may affect the structure, particularly under stress.

# Sidecars

A motorcycle fitted with a sidecar requires additional checks relating to the stability of the machine and security of attachment and swivel joints, plus specific wheel alignment (toe-in) requirements. Additionally, tyre and lighting requirements differ from conventional motorcycle use. Owners are advised to check MOT test requirements with an official test centre.

# Preparing for storage

## Before you start

If repairs or an overhaul is needed, see that this is carried out now rather than left until you want to ride the bike again.

Give the bike a good wash and scrub all dirt from its underside. Make sure the bike dries completely before preparing for storage.

## Engine

● Remove the spark plug(s) and lubricate the cylinder bores with approximately a teaspoon of motor oil using a spout-type oil can (see illustration 1). Reinstall the spark plug(s). Crank the engine over a couple of times to coat the piston rings and bores with oil. If the bike has a kickstart, use this to turn the engine over. If not, flick the kill switch to the OFF position and crank the engine over on the starter (see illustration 2). If the nature on the ignition system prevents the starter operating with the kill switch in the OFF position,

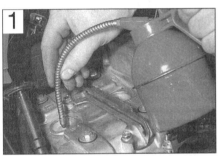

Squirt a drop of motor oil into each cylinder

Flick the kill switch to OFF . . .

. . . and ensure that the metal bodies of the plugs (arrows) are earthed against the cylinder head

remove the spark plugs and fit them back in their caps; ensure that the plugs are earthed (grounded) against the cylinder head when the starter is operated (see illustration 3).

⚠️ **Warning: It is important that the plugs are earthed (grounded) away from the spark plug holes otherwise there is a risk of atomised fuel from the cylinders igniting.**

**HAYNES HiNT** *On a single cylinder four-stroke engine, you can seal the combustion chamber completely by positioning the piston at TDC on the compression stroke.*

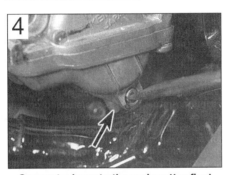

Connect a hose to the carburettor float chamber drain stub (arrow) and unscrew the drain screw

● Drain the carburettor(s) otherwise there is a risk of jets becoming blocked by gum deposits from the fuel (see illustration 4).

● If the bike is going into long-term storage, consider adding a fuel stabiliser to the fuel in the tank. If the tank is drained completely, corrosion of its internal surfaces may occur if left unprotected for a long period. The tank can be treated with a rust preventative especially for this purpose. Alternatively, remove the tank and pour half a litre of motor oil into it, install the filler cap and shake the tank to coat its internals with oil before draining off the excess. The same effect can also be achieved by spraying WD40 or a similar water-dispersant around the inside of the tank via its flexible nozzle.

● Make sure the cooling system contains the correct mix of antifreeze. Antifreeze also contains important corrosion inhibitors.

● The air intakes and exhaust can be sealed off by covering or plugging the openings. Ensure that you do not seal in any condensation; run the engine until it is hot, then switch off and allow to cool. Tape a piece of thick plastic over the silencer end(s) (see illustration 5). Note that some advocate pouring a tablespoon of motor oil into the silencer(s) before sealing them off.

Exhausts can be sealed off with a plastic bag

## Battery

● Remove it from the bike - in extreme cases of cold the battery may freeze and crack its case (see illustration 6).

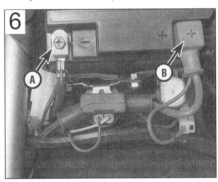

Disconnect the negative lead (A) first, followed by the positive lead (B)

● Check the electrolyte level and top up if necessary (conventional refillable batteries). Clean the terminals.

● Store the battery off the motorcycle and away from any sources of fire. Position a wooden block under the battery if it is to sit on the ground.

● Give the battery a trickle charge for a few hours every month (see illustration 7).

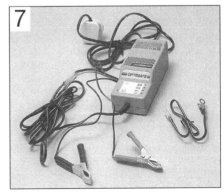

Use a suitable battery charger - this kit also assess battery condition

## Tyres

● Place the bike on its centrestand or an auxiliary stand which will support the motorcycle in an upright position. Position wood blocks under the tyres to keep them off the ground and to provide insulation from damp. If the bike is being put into long-term storage, ideally both tyres should be off the ground; not only will this protect the tyres, but will also ensure that no load is placed on the steering head or wheel bearings.
● Deflate each tyre by 5 to 10 psi, no more or the beads may unseat from the rim, making subsequent inflation difficult on tubeless tyres.

## Pivots and controls

● Lubricate all lever, pedal, stand and footrest pivot points. If grease nipples are fitted to the rear suspension components, apply lubricant to the pivots.
● Lubricate all control cables.

## Cycle components

● Apply a wax protectant to all painted and plastic components. Wipe off any excess, but don't polish to a shine. Where fitted, clean the screen with soap and water.
● Coat metal parts with Vaseline (petroleum jelly). When applying this to the fork tubes, do not compress the forks otherwise the seals will rot from contact with the Vaseline.
● Apply a vinyl cleaner to the seat.

## Storage conditions

● Aim to store the bike in a shed or garage which does not leak and is free from damp.
● Drape an old blanket or bedspread over the bike to protect it from dust and direct contact with sunlight (which will fade paint). This also hides the bike from prying eyes. Beware of tight-fitting plastic covers which may allow condensation to form and settle on the bike.

# Getting back on the road

## Engine and transmission

● Change the oil and replace the oil filter. If this was done prior to storage, check that the oil hasn't emulsified - a thick whitish substance which occurs through condensation.
● Remove the spark plugs. Using a spout-type oil can, squirt a few drops of oil into the cylinder(s). This will provide initial lubrication as the piston rings and bores comes back into contact. Service the spark plugs, or fit new ones, and install them in the engine.
● Check that the clutch isn't stuck on. The plates can stick together if left standing for some time, preventing clutch operation. Engage a gear and try rocking the bike back and forth with the clutch lever held against the handlebar. If this doesn't work on cable-operated clutches, hold the clutch lever back against the handlebar with a strong elastic band or cable tie for a couple of hours **(see illustration 8).**

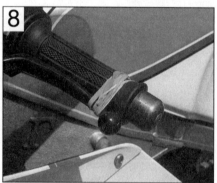

Hold clutch lever back against the handlebar with elastic bands or a cable tie

● If the air intakes or silencer end(s) were blocked off, remove the bung or cover used.
● If the fuel tank was coated with a rust preventative, oil or a stabiliser added to the fuel, drain and flush the tank and dispose of the fuel sensibly. If no action was taken with the fuel tank prior to storage, it is advised that the old fuel is disposed of since it will go off over a period of time. Refill the fuel tank with fresh fuel.

## Frame and running gear

● Oil all pivot points and cables.
● Check the tyre pressures. They will definitely need inflating if pressures were reduced for storage.
● Lubricate the final drive chain (where applicable).
● Remove any protective coating applied to the fork tubes (stanchions) since this may well destroy the fork seals. If the fork tubes weren't protected and have picked up rust spots, remove them with very fine abrasive paper and refinish with metal polish.
● Check that both brakes operate correctly. Apply each brake hard and check that it's not possible to move the motorcycle forwards, then check that the brake frees off again once released. Brake caliper pistons can stick due to corrosion around the piston head, or on the sliding caliper types, due to corrosion of the slider pins. If the brake doesn't free after repeated operation, take the caliper off for examination. Similarly drum brakes can stick due to a seized operating cam, cable or rod linkage.
● If the motorcycle has been in long-term storage, renew the brake fluid and clutch fluid (where applicable).
● Depending on where the bike has been stored, the wiring, cables and hoses may have been nibbled by rodents. Make a visual check and investigate disturbed wiring loom tape.

## Battery

● If the battery has been previously removal and given top up charges it can simply be reconnected. Remember to connect the positive cable first and the negative cable last.
● On conventional refillable batteries, if the battery has not received any attention, remove it from the motorcycle and check its electrolyte level. Top up if necessary then charge the battery. If the battery fails to hold a charge and a visual checks show heavy white sulphation of the plates, the battery is probably defective and must be renewed. This is particularly likely if the battery is old. Confirm battery condition with a specific gravity check.
● On sealed (MF) batteries, if the battery has not received any attention, remove it from the motorcycle and charge it according to the information on the battery case - if the battery fails to hold a charge it must be renewed.

## Starting procedure

● If a kickstart is fitted, turn the engine over a couple of times with the ignition OFF to distribute oil around the engine. If no kickstart is fitted, flick the engine kill switch OFF and the ignition ON and crank the engine over a couple of times to work oil around the upper cylinder components. If the nature of the ignition system is such that the starter won't work with the kill switch OFF, remove the spark plugs, fit them back into their caps and earth (ground) their bodies on the cylinder head. Reinstall the spark plugs afterwards.
● Switch the kill switch to RUN, operate the choke and start the engine. If the engine won't start don't continue cranking the engine - not only will this flatten the battery, but the starter motor will overheat. Switch the ignition off and try again later. If the engine refuses to start, go through the fault finding procedures in this manual. **Note:** *If the bike has been in storage for a long time, old fuel or a carburettor blockage may be the problem. Gum deposits in carburettors can block jets - if a carburettor cleaner doesn't prove successful the carburettors must be dismantled for cleaning.*
● Once the engine has started, check that the lights, turn signals and horn work properly.
● Treat the bike gently for the first ride and check all fluid levels on completion. Settle the bike back into the maintenance schedule.

This Section provides an easy reference-guide to the more common faults that are likely to afflict your machine. Obviously, the opportunities are almost limitless for faults to occur as a result of obscure failures, and to try and cover all eventualities would require a book. Indeed, a number have been written on the subject.

Successful troubleshooting is not a mysterious 'black art' but the application of a bit of knowledge combined with a systematic and logical approach to the problem. Approach any troubleshooting by first accurately identifying the symptom and then checking through the list of possible causes, starting with the simplest or most obvious and progressing in stages to the most complex.

Take nothing for granted, but above all apply liberal quantities of common sense.

The main symptom of a fault is given in the text as a major heading below which are listed the various systems or areas which may contain the fault. Details of each possible cause for a fault and the remedial action to be taken are given, in brief, in the paragraphs below each heading. Further information should be sought in the relevant Chapter.

## 1 Engine doesn't start or is difficult to start

- [ ] Starter motor doesn't rotate
- [ ] Starter motor rotates but engine does not turn over
- [ ] Starter works but engine won't turn over (seized)
- [ ] No fuel flow
- [ ] Engine flooded
- [ ] No spark or weak spark
- [ ] Compression low
- [ ] Stalls after starting
- [ ] Rough idle

## 2 Poor running at low speed

- [ ] Spark weak
- [ ] Fuel/air mixture incorrect
- [ ] Compression low
- [ ] Poor acceleration

## 3 Poor running or no power at high speed

- [ ] Firing incorrect
- [ ] Fuel/air mixture incorrect
- [ ] Compression low
- [ ] Knocking or pinging
- [ ] Miscellaneous causes

## 4 Overheating

- [ ] Engine overheats
- [ ] Firing incorrect
- [ ] Fuel/air mixture incorrect
- [ ] Compression too high
- [ ] Engine load excessive
- [ ] Lubrication inadequate
- [ ] Miscellaneous causes

## 5 Clutch problems

- [ ] Clutch slipping
- [ ] Clutch not disengaging completely

## 6 Gearchange problems

- [ ] Doesn't go into gear, or lever doesn't return
- [ ] Jumps out of gear
- [ ] Overselects

## 7 Abnormal engine noise

- [ ] Knocking or pinking
- [ ] Piston slap or rattling
- [ ] Valve noise
- [ ] Other noise

## 8 Abnormal driveline noise

- [ ] Clutch noise
- [ ] Transmission noise
- [ ] Final drive noise

## 9 Abnormal frame and suspension noise

- [ ] Front end noise
- [ ] Shock absorber noise
- [ ] Brake noise

## 10 Oil pressure warning light comes on

- [ ] Engine lubrication system
- [ ] Electrical system

## 11 Excessive exhaust smoke

- [ ] White smoke
- [ ] Black smoke
- [ ] Brown smoke

## 12 Poor handling or stability

- [ ] Handlebar hard to turn
- [ ] Handlebar shakes or vibrates excessively
- [ ] Handlebar pulls to one side
- [ ] Poor shock absorbing qualities

## 13 Braking problems

- [ ] Brakes are spongy, don't hold
- [ ] Brake lever or pedal pulsates
- [ ] Brakes drag

## 14 Electrical problems

- [ ] Battery dead or weak
- [ ] Battery overcharged

# 1 Engine doesn't start or is difficult to start

### Starter motor doesn't rotate

- ☐ Engine kill switch OFF.
- ☐ Fuse blown. Check main fuse and ignition fuse (Chapter 9).
- ☐ Battery voltage low. Check and recharge battery (Chapter 9).
- ☐ Starter motor defective. Make sure the wiring to the starter is secure. Make sure the starter relay clicks when the start button is pushed. If the relay clicks, then the fault is in the wiring or motor.
- ☐ Starter relay faulty. Check it according to the procedure in Chapter 9.
- ☐ Starter switch not contacting. The contacts could be wet, corroded or dirty. Disassemble and clean the switch (Chapter 9).
- ☐ Wiring open or shorted. Check all wiring connections and harnesses to make sure that they are dry, tight and not corroded. Also check for broken or frayed wires that can cause a short to ground (earth) (see wiring diagram, Chapter 9).
- ☐ Ignition (main) switch defective. Check the switch according to the procedure in Chapter 9. Replace the switch with a new one if it is defective.
- ☐ Faulty neutral, sidestand (RVF only) or clutch switch. Check the wiring to each switch and the switch itself according to the procedures in Chapter 9.

### Starter motor rotates but engine does not turn over

- ☐ Starter motor clutch defective. Inspect and repair or replace (Chapter 2).
- ☐ Damaged idler or starter gears. Inspect and replace the damaged parts (Chapter 2).

### Starter works but engine won't turn over (seized)

- ☐ Seized engine caused by one or more internally damaged components. Failure due to wear, abuse or lack of lubrication. Damage can include seized valves, camshafts, pistons, crankshaft, connecting rod bearings, or transmission gears or bearings. Refer to Chapter 2 for engine disassembly.

### No fuel flow

- ☐ No fuel in tank.
- ☐ Fuel tank breather hose obstructed.
- ☐ Fuel tap filter clogged. Remove the tap and clean it and the filter (Chapter 4).
- ☐ Fuel tap vacuum hose split or detached. Check the hose.
- ☐ Fuel tap diaphragm split. Remove the tap and check the diaphragm (Chapter 4).
- ☐ Fuel line clogged. Pull the fuel line loose and carefully blow through it.
- ☐ Float needle valve clogged. For all of the valves to be clogged, either a very bad batch of fuel with an unusual additive has been used, or some other foreign material has entered the tank. Many times after a machine has been stored for many months without running, the fuel turns to a varnish-like liquid and forms deposits on the inlet needle valves and jets. The carburettors should be removed and overhauled if draining the float chambers doesn't solve the problem.

### Engine flooded

- ☐ Float height too high. Check as described in Chapter 4.
- ☐ Float needle valve worn or stuck open. A piece of dirt, rust or other debris can cause the valve to seat improperly, causing excess fuel to be admitted to the float chamber. In this case, the float chamber should be cleaned and the needle valve and seat inspected. If the needle and seat are worn, then the leaking will persist and the parts should be replaced with new ones (Chapter 4).
- ☐ Starting technique incorrect. Under normal circumstances (ie, if all the carburettor functions are sound) the machine should start with little or no throttle. When the engine is cold, the choke should be operated and the engine started without opening the throttle. When the engine is at operating temperature, only a very slight amount of throttle should be necessary. If the engine is flooded, turn the fuel tap OFF and hold the throttle open while cranking the engine. This will allow additional air to reach the cylinders. Remember to turn the fuel tap back ON after the engine starts.

### No spark or weak spark

- ☐ Ignition switch OFF.
- ☐ Engine kill switch turned to the OFF position.
- ☐ Battery voltage low. Check and recharge the battery as necessary (Chapter 9).
- ☐ Spark plugs dirty, defective or worn out. Locate reason for fouled plugs using spark plug condition chart and follow the plug maintenance procedures (Chapter 1).
- ☐ Spark plug caps or secondary (HT) wiring faulty. Check condition. Replace either or both components if cracks or deterioration are evident (Chapter 5).
- ☐ Spark plug caps not making good contact. Make sure that the plug caps fit snugly over the plug ends.
- ☐ Ignition control unit defective. Check the unit, referring to Chapter 5 for details.
- ☐ Pulse generator defective. Check the unit, referring to Chapter 5 for details.
- ☐ Ignition HT coils defective. Check the coils, referring to Chapter 5.
- ☐ Ignition or kill switch shorted. This is usually caused by water, corrosion, damage or excessive wear. The switches can be disassembled and cleaned with electrical contact cleaner. If cleaning does not help, replace the switches (Chapter 9).
- ☐ Wiring shorted or broken between:
  - a) Ignition (main) switch and engine kill switch (or blown fuse)
  - b) Ignition control unit and engine kill switch
  - c) Ignition control unit and ignition HT coils
  - d) Ignition HT coils and spark plugs
  - e) Ignition control unit and pulse generator
- ☐ Make sure that all wiring connections are clean, dry and tight. Look for chafed and broken wires (Chapters 5 and 9).

### Compression low

- ☐ Spark plugs loose. Remove the plugs and inspect their threads. Reinstall and tighten to the specified torque (Chapter 1).
- ☐ Cylinder heads not sufficiently tightened down. If a cylinder head is suspected of being loose, then there's a chance that the gasket or head is damaged if the problem has persisted for any length of time. The head bolts should be tightened to the proper torque in the correct sequence (Chapter 2).
- ☐ Improper valve clearance. This means that the valve is not closing completely and compression pressure is leaking past the valve. Check and adjust the valve clearances (Chapter 1).
- ☐ Cylinder and/or piston worn. Excessive wear will cause compression pressure to leak past the rings. This is usually accompanied by worn rings as well. A top-end overhaul is necessary (Chapter 2).
- ☐ Piston rings worn, weak, broken, or sticking. Broken or sticking piston rings usually indicate a lubrication or carburation problem that causes excess carbon deposits or seizures to form on the pistons and rings. Top-end overhaul is necessary (Chapter 2).
- ☐ Piston ring-to-groove clearance excessive. This is caused by excessive wear of the piston ring lands. Piston replacement is necessary (Chapter 2).
- ☐ Cylinder head gasket damaged. If a head is allowed to become loose, or if excessive carbon build-up on the piston crown and combustion chamber causes extremely high compression, the head gasket may leak. Retorquing the head is not always sufficient to restore the seal, so gasket replacement is necessary (Chapter 2).

# 1 Engine doesn't start or is difficult to start (continued)

- ☐ Cylinder head warped. This is caused by overheating or improperly tightened head bolts. Machine shop resurfacing or head replacement is necessary (Chapter 2).
- ☐ Valve spring broken or weak. Caused by component failure or wear; the springs must be replaced (Chapter 2).
- ☐ Valve not seating properly. This is caused by a bent valve (from over-revving or improper valve adjustment), burned valve or seat (improper carburation) or an accumulation of carbon deposits on the seat (from carburation or lubrication problems). The valves must be cleaned and/or replaced and the seats serviced if possible (Chapter 2).

## Stalls after starting

- ☐ Improper choke action. Make sure the choke linkage shaft is getting a full stroke and staying in the out position (Chapter 4).
- ☐ Ignition malfunction. See Chapter 5.
- ☐ Carburettor malfunction. See Chapter 4.
- ☐ Fuel contaminated. The fuel can be contaminated with either dirt or water, or can change chemically if the machine is allowed to sit for several months or more. Drain the tank and float chambers (Chapter 4).

- ☐ Intake air leak. Check for loose carburettor-to-intake manifold connections, loose or missing vacuum gauge adapter screws or hoses, or loose carburettor tops (Chapter 4).
- ☐ Engine idle speed incorrect. Turn idle adjusting screw until the engine idles at the specified rpm (Chapter 1).

## Rough idle

- ☐ Ignition malfunction. See Chapter 5.
- ☐ Idle speed incorrect. See Chapter 1.
- ☐ Carburettors not synchronised. Adjust carburettors with vacuum gauge or manometer set as described in Chapter 1.
- ☐ Carburettor malfunction. See Chapter 4.
- ☐ Fuel contaminated. The fuel can be contaminated with either dirt or water, or can change chemically if the machine is allowed to sit for several months or more. Drain the tank and float chambers (Chapter 4).
- ☐ Intake air leak. Check for loose carburettor-to-intake manifold connections, loose or missing vacuum gauge adapter screws or hoses, or loose carburettor tops (Chapter 4).
- ☐ Air filter clogged. Replace the air filter element (Chapter 1).

# 2 Poor running at low speeds

## Spark weak

- ☐ Battery voltage low. Check and recharge battery (Chapter 9).
- ☐ Spark plugs fouled, defective or worn out. Refer to Chapter 1 for spark plug maintenance.
- ☐ Spark plug cap or HT wiring defective. Refer to Chapters 1 and 5 for details on the ignition system.
- ☐ Spark plug caps not making contact.
- ☐ Incorrect spark plugs. Wrong type, heat range or cap configuration. Check and install correct plugs listed in Chapter 1.
- ☐ Ignition control unit defective. See Chapter 5.
- ☐ Pulse generator defective. See Chapter 5.
- ☐ Ignition HT coils defective. See Chapter 5.

## Fuel/air mixture incorrect

- ☐ Pilot screws out of adjustment (Chapter 4).
- ☐ Pilot jet or air passage clogged. Remove and overhaul the carburettors (Chapter 4).
- ☐ Air bleed holes clogged. Remove carburettor and blow out all passages (Chapter 4).
- ☐ Air filter clogged, poorly sealed or missing (Chapter 1).
- ☐ Air filter housing poorly sealed. Look for cracks, holes or loose clamps and replace or repair defective parts.
- ☐ Fuel level too high or too low. Check the float height (Chapter 4).
- ☐ Fuel tank breather hose obstructed.
- ☐ Carburettor inlet manifolds loose. Check for cracks, breaks, tears or loose clamps. Replace the rubber inlet manifold joints if split or perished.

## Compression low

- ☐ Spark plugs loose. Remove the plugs and inspect their threads. Reinstall and tighten to the specified torque (Chapter 1).
- ☐ Cylinder heads not sufficiently tightened down. If a cylinder head is suspected of being loose, then there's a chance that the gasket and head are damaged if the problem has persisted for any length of time. The head bolts should be tightened to the proper torque in the correct sequence (Chapter 2).
- ☐ Improper valve clearance. This means that the valve is not closing completely and compression pressure is leaking past the valve. Check and adjust the valve clearances (Chapter 1).
- ☐ Cylinder and/or piston worn. Excessive wear will cause

compression pressure to leak past the rings. This is usually accompanied by worn rings as well. A top-end overhaul is necessary (Chapter 2).
- ☐ Piston rings worn, weak, broken, or sticking. Broken or sticking piston rings usually indicate a lubrication or carburation problem that causes excess carbon deposits or seizures to form on the pistons and rings. Top-end overhaul is necessary (Chapter 2).
- ☐ Piston ring-to-groove clearance excessive. This is caused by excessive wear of the piston ring lands. Piston replacement is necessary (Chapter 2).
- ☐ Cylinder head gasket damaged. If a head is allowed to become loose, or if excessive carbon build-up on the piston crown and combustion chamber causes extremely high compression, the head gasket may leak. Retorquing the head is not always sufficient to restore the seal, so gasket replacement is necessary (Chapter 2).
- ☐ Cylinder head warped. This is caused by overheating or improperly tightened head bolts. Machine shop resurfacing or head replacement is necessary (Chapter 2).
- ☐ Valve spring broken or weak. Caused by component failure or wear; the springs must be replaced (Chapter 2).
- ☐ Valve not seating properly. This is caused by a bent valve (from over-revving or improper valve adjustment), burned valve or seat (improper carburation) or an accumulation of carbon deposits on the seat (from carburation, lubrication problems). The valves must be cleaned and/or replaced and the seats serviced if possible (Chapter 2).

## Poor acceleration

- ☐ Carburettors leaking or dirty. Overhaul the carburettors (Chapter 4).
- ☐ Timing not advancing. The pulse generator or the ignition control module may be defective. If so, they must be replaced with new ones, as they can't be repaired.
- ☐ Carburettors not synchronised. Adjust them with a vacuum gauge set or manometer (Chapter 1).
- ☐ Engine oil viscosity too high. Using a heavier oil than that recommended in Chapter 1 can damage the oil pump or lubrication system and cause drag on the engine.
- ☐ Brakes dragging. Usually caused by debris which has entered the brake piston seals, or from a warped disc or bent axle. Repair as necessary (Chapter 7).

# 3 Poor running or no power at high speed

## Firing incorrect

☐ Air filter restricted. Clean or replace filter (Chapter 1).
☐ Spark plugs fouled, defective or worn out. See Chapter 1 for spark plug maintenance.
☐ Spark plug caps or HT wiring defective. See Chapters 1 and 5 for details of the ignition system.
☐ Spark plug caps not in good contact. See Chapter 5.
☐ Incorrect spark plugs. Wrong type, heat range or cap configuration. Check and install correct plugs listed in Chapter 1.
☐ Ignition control unit defective. See Chapter 5.
☐ Ignition coils defective. See Chapter 5.

## Fuel/air mixture incorrect

☐ Main jet clogged. Dirt, water or other contaminants can clog the main jets. Clean the fuel tap filter, the float chamber area, and the jets and carburettor orifices (Chapter 4).
☐ Main jet wrong size. The standard jetting is for sea level atmospheric pressure and oxygen content.
☐ Throttle shaft-to-carburettor body clearance excessive. Refer to Chapter 4 for inspection and part replacement procedures.
☐ Air bleed holes clogged. Remove and overhaul carburettors (Chapter 4).
☐ Air filter clogged, poorly sealed, or missing (Chapter 1).
☐ Air filter housing poorly sealed. Look for cracks, holes or loose clamps, and replace or repair defective parts.
☐ Fuel level too high or too low. Check the float height (Chapter 4).
☐ Fuel tank breather hose obstructed.
☐ Carburettor inlet manifolds loose. Check for cracks, breaks, tears or loose clamps. Replace the rubber inlet manifolds if they are split or perished (Chapter 4).

## Compression low

☐ Spark plugs loose. Remove the plugs and inspect their threads. Reinstall and tighten to the specified torque (Chapter 1).
☐ Cylinder heads not sufficiently tightened down. If a cylinder head is suspected of being loose, then there's a chance that the gasket and head are damaged if the problem has persisted for any length of time. The head bolts should be tightened to the proper torque in the correct sequence (Chapter 2).
☐ Improper valve clearance. This means that the valve is not closing completely and compression pressure is leaking past the valve. Check and adjust the valve clearances (Chapter 1).
☐ Cylinder and/or piston worn. Excessive wear will cause compression pressure to leak past the rings. This is usually accompanied by worn rings as well. A top-end overhaul is necessary (Chapter 2).
☐ Piston rings worn, weak, broken, or sticking. Broken or sticking piston rings usually indicate a lubrication or carburation problem that causes excess carbon deposits or seizures to form on the pistons and rings. Top-end overhaul is necessary (Chapter 2).

☐ Piston ring-to-groove clearance excessive. This is caused by excessive wear of the piston ring lands. Piston replacement is necessary (Chapter 2).
☐ Cylinder head gasket damaged. If a head is allowed to become loose, or if excessive carbon build-up on the piston crown and combustion chamber causes extremely high compression, the head gasket may leak. Retorquing the head is not always sufficient to restore the seal, so gasket replacement is necessary (Chapter 2).
☐ Cylinder head warped. This is caused by overheating or improperly tightened head bolts. Machine shop resurfacing or head replacement is necessary (Chapter 2).
☐ Valve spring broken or weak. Caused by component failure or wear; the springs must be replaced (Chapter 2).
☐ Valve not seating properly. This is caused by a bent valve (from over-revving or improper valve adjustment), burned valve or seat (improper carburation) or an accumulation of carbon deposits on the seat (from carburation or lubrication problems). The valves must be cleaned and/or replaced and the seats serviced if possible (Chapter 2).

## Knocking or pinking

☐ Carbon build-up in combustion chamber. Use of a fuel additive that will dissolve the adhesive bonding the carbon particles to the crown and chamber is the easiest way to remove the build-up. Otherwise, the cylinder heads will have to be removed and decarbonised (Chapter 2).
☐ Incorrect or poor quality fuel. Old or improper grades of fuel can cause detonation. This causes the piston to rattle, thus the knocking or pinking sound. Drain old fuel and always use the recommended fuel grade.
☐ Spark plug heat range incorrect. Uncontrolled detonation indicates the plug heat range is too hot. The plug in effect becomes a glow plug, raising cylinder temperatures. Install the proper heat range plug (Chapter 1).
☐ Improper air/fuel mixture. This will cause the cylinders to run hot, which leads to detonation. Clogged jets or an air leak can cause this imbalance. See Chapter 4.

## Miscellaneous causes

☐ Throttle valve doesn't open fully. Adjust the throttle grip freeplay (Chapter 1).
☐ Clutch slipping. May be caused by loose or worn clutch components. Refer to Chapter 2 for clutch overhaul procedures.
☐ Timing not advancing.
☐ Engine oil viscosity too high. Using a heavier oil than the one recommended in Chapter 1 can damage the oil pump or lubrication system and cause drag on the engine.
☐ Brakes dragging. Usually caused by debris which has entered the brake piston seals, or from a warped disc or bent axle. Repair as necessary.

# 4 Overheating

### Engine overheats

- ☐ Coolant level low. Check and add coolant (Chapter 1).
- ☐ Leak in cooling system. Check cooling system hoses and radiator for leaks and other damage. Repair or replace parts as necessary (Chapter 3).
- ☐ Thermostat sticking open or closed. Check and replace as described in Chapter 3.
- ☐ Faulty radiator cap. Remove the cap and have it pressure tested.
- ☐ Coolant passages clogged. Drain and flush the cooling system, then refill with fresh coolant (Chapter 1).
- ☐ Water pump defective. Remove the pump and check the components (Chapter 3).
- ☐ Clogged radiator fins. Clean them by blowing compressed air through the fins from the rear of the radiator.
- ☐ Cooling fan or fan switch fault (Chapter 3).

### Firing incorrect

- ☐ Spark plugs fouled, defective or worn out. See Chapter 1 for spark plug maintenance.
- ☐ Incorrect spark plugs.
- ☐ Ignition control unit defective. See Chapter 5.
- ☐ Faulty ignition HT coils (Chapter 5).

### Fuel/air mixture incorrect

- ☐ Main jet clogged. Dirt, water and other contaminants can clog the main jets. Clean the fuel tap filter, the float chamber area and the jets and carburettor orifices (Chapter 4).
- ☐ Main jet wrong size. The standard jetting is for sea level atmospheric pressure and oxygen content.
- ☐ Air filter clogged, poorly sealed or missing (Chapter 1).
- ☐ Air filter housing poorly sealed. Look for cracks, holes or loose clamps and replace or repair.
- ☐ Fuel level too low. Check float height (Chapter 4).
- ☐ Fuel tank breather hose obstructed.
- ☐ Carburettor inlet manifolds loose. Check for cracks, breaks, tears or loose clamps. Replace the rubber inlet manifold joints if split or perished.

### Compression too high

- ☐ Carbon build-up in combustion chamber. Use of a fuel additive that will dissolve the adhesive bonding the carbon particles to the piston crown and chamber is the easiest way to remove the build-up. Otherwise, the cylinder heads will have to be removed and decarbonised (Chapter 2).
- ☐ Improperly machined head surface or installation of incorrect gasket during engine assembly.

### Engine load excessive

- ☐ Clutch slipping. Can be caused by damaged, loose or worn clutch components. Refer to Chapter 2 for overhaul procedures.
- ☐ Engine oil level too high. The addition of too much oil will cause pressurisation of the crankcase and inefficient engine operation. Check Specifications and drain to proper level (Chapter 1).
- ☐ Engine oil viscosity too high. Using a heavier oil than the one recommended in Chapter 1 can damage the oil pump or lubrication system as well as cause drag on the engine.
- ☐ Brakes dragging. Usually caused by debris which has entered the brake piston seals, or from a warped disc or bent axle. Repair as necessary.

### Lubrication inadequate

- ☐ Engine oil level too low. Friction caused by intermittent lack of lubrication or from oil that is overworked can cause overheating. The oil provides a definite cooling function in the engine. Check the oil level (Chapter 1).
- ☐ Poor quality engine oil or incorrect viscosity or type. Oil is rated not only according to viscosity but also according to type. Some oils are not rated high enough for use in this engine. Check the Specifications section and change to the correct oil (Chapter 1).

### Miscellaneous causes

- ☐ Modification to exhaust system. Most aftermarket exhaust systems cause the engine to run leaner, which make them run hotter. When installing an accessory exhaust system, always rejet the carburettors.

# 5 Clutch problems

### Clutch slipping

- ☐ Insufficient clutch cable freeplay. Check and adjust (Chapter 1).
- ☐ Friction plates worn or warped. Overhaul the clutch assembly (Chapter 2).
- ☐ Plain plates warped (Chapter 2).
- ☐ Clutch springs broken or weak. Old or heat-damaged (from slipping clutch) springs should be replaced with new ones (Chapter 2).
- ☐ Clutch release mechanism defective. Replace any defective parts (Chapter 2).
- ☐ Clutch centre or housing unevenly worn. This causes improper engagement of the plates. Replace the damaged or worn parts (Chapter 2).

### Clutch not disengaging completely

- ☐ Excessive clutch cable freeplay. Check and adjust (Chapter 1).
- ☐ Clutch plates warped or damaged. This will cause clutch drag, which in turn will cause the machine to creep. Overhaul the clutch assembly (Chapter 2).

- ☐ Engine oil deteriorated. Old, thin, worn out oil will not provide proper lubrication for the plates, causing the clutch to drag. Replace the oil and filter (Chapter 1).
- ☐ Engine oil viscosity too high. Using a heavier oil than recommended in Chapter 1 can cause the plates to stick together, putting a drag on the engine. Change to the correct weight oil (Chapter 1).
- ☐ Clutch housing guide seized on mainshaft. Lack of lubrication, severe wear or damage can cause the guide to seize on the shaft. Overhaul of the clutch, and perhaps transmission, may be necessary to repair the damage (Chapter 2).
- ☐ Clutch release mechanism defective. Overhaul the clutch cover components (Chapter 2).
- ☐ Loose clutch centre nut. Causes housing and centre misalignment putting a drag on the engine. Engagement adjustment continually varies. Overhaul the clutch assembly (Chapter 2).

# 6 Gearchange problems

### Doesn't go into gear or lever doesn't return

☐ Clutch not disengaging. See above.
☐ Selector fork(s) bent or seized. Often caused by dropping the machine or from lack of lubrication. Overhaul the transmission (Chapter 2).
☐ Gear(s) stuck on shaft. Most often caused by a lack of lubrication or excessive wear in transmission bearings and bushes. Overhaul the transmission (Chapter 2).
☐ Selector drum binding. Caused by lubrication failure or excessive wear. Replace the drum and bearing (Chapter 2).
☐ Gearchange shaft return spring weak or broken (Chapter 2).
☐ Gearchange lever broken. Splines stripped out of lever or shaft, caused by allowing the lever to get loose or from dropping the machine. Replace necessary parts (Chapter 2).

☐ Gearchange mechanism stopper arm broken or worn. Full engagement and rotary movement of selector drum results. Replace the arm (Chapter 2).
☐ Stopper arm spring broken. Allows arm to float, causing sporadic selector operation. Replace spring (Chapter 2).

### Jumps out of gear

☐ Selector fork(s) worn. Overhaul the transmission (Chapter 2).
☐ Gear groove(s) worn. Overhaul the transmission (Chapter 2).
☐ Gear dogs or dog slots worn or damaged. The gears should be inspected and replaced. No attempt should be made to service the worn parts.

### Overselects

☐ Stopper arm spring weak or broken (Chapter 2).
☐ Gearchange shaft return spring post broken or distorted (Chapter 2).

# 7 Abnormal engine noise

### Knocking or pinking

☐ Carbon build-up in combustion chamber. Use of a fuel additive that will dissolve the adhesive bonding the carbon particles to the piston crown and chamber is the easiest way to remove the build-up. Otherwise, the cylinder head will have to be removed and decarbonised (Chapter 2).
☐ Incorrect or poor quality fuel. Old or improper fuel can cause detonation. This causes the pistons to rattle, thus the knocking or pinking sound. Drain the old fuel and always use the recommended grade fuel (Chapter 4).
☐ Spark plug heat range incorrect. Uncontrolled detonation indicates that the plug heat range is too hot. The plug in effect becomes a glow plug, raising cylinder temperatures. Install the proper heat range plug (Chapter 1).
☐ Improper air/fuel mixture. This will cause the cylinders to run hot and lead to detonation. Clogged jets or an air leak can cause this imbalance. See Chapter 4.

### Piston slap or rattling

☐ Cylinder-to-piston clearance excessive. Caused by improper assembly. Inspect and overhaul top-end (Chapter 2).
☐ Connecting rod bent. Caused by over-revving, trying to start a badly flooded engine or from ingesting a foreign object into the combustion chamber. Replace the damaged parts (Chapter 2).
☐ Piston pin or piston pin bore worn or seized from wear or lack of lubrication. Replace damaged parts (Chapter 2).
☐ Piston ring(s) worn, broken or sticking. Overhaul the top-end (Chapter 2).
☐ Piston seizure damage. Usually from lack of lubrication or overheating. Replace the pistons and renew the crankcase/bores, as necessary (Chapter 2).

☐ Connecting rod upper or lower end clearance excessive. Caused by excessive wear or lack of lubrication. Replace worn parts.

### Valve noise

☐ Incorrect valve clearances. Adjust the clearances by referring to Chapter 1.
☐ Valve spring broken or weak. Check and replace weak valve springs (Chapter 2).
☐ Camshaft or cylinder head worn or damaged. Lack of lubrication at high rpm is usually the cause of damage. Insufficient oil or failure to change the oil at the recommended intervals are the chief causes. Since there are no replaceable bearings in the head, the head itself will have to be replaced if there is excessive wear or damage (Chapter 2).

### Other noise

☐ Cylinder head gasket leaking.
☐ Exhaust pipe leaking at cylinder head connection. Caused by improper fit of pipe(s) or loose exhaust flange. All exhaust fasteners should be tightened evenly and carefully. Failure to do this will lead to a leak.
☐ Crankshaft runout excessive. Caused by a bent crankshaft (from over-revving) or damage from an upper cylinder component failure. Can also be attributed to dropping the machine on either of the crankshaft ends.
☐ Engine mounting bolts loose. Tighten all engine mount bolts (Chapter 2).
☐ Crankshaft bearings worn (Chapter 2).
☐ Camshaft drive gear assembly defective. Replace according to the procedure in Chapter 2.

# 8 Abnormal driveline noise

### Clutch noise

☐ Clutch outer drum/friction plate clearance excessive (Chapter 2).
☐ Loose or damaged clutch pressure plate (Chapter 2).

### Transmission noise

☐ Bearings worn. Also includes the possibility that the shafts are worn. Overhaul the transmission (Chapter 2).
☐ Gears worn or chipped (Chapter 2).
☐ Metal chips jammed in gear teeth. Probably pieces from a broken clutch, gear or selector mechanism that were picked up by the gears. This will cause early bearing failure (Chapter 2).

☐ Engine oil level too low. Causes a howl from transmission. Also affects engine power and clutch operation (Chapter 1).

### Final drive noise

☐ Chain not adjusted properly (Chapter 1).
☐ Front or rear sprocket loose. Tighten fasteners (Chapter 6).
☐ Sprockets worn. Replace sprockets (Chapter 6).
☐ Rear sprocket warped. Replace sprockets (Chapter 6).
☐ Wheel drive pins worn or loose or drive pin holes worn. Check and tighten or replace (Chapter 7).

# 9 Abnormal frame and suspension noise

### Front end noise

☐ Low fluid level or improper viscosity oil in forks. This can sound like spurting and is usually accompanied by irregular fork action (Chapter 6).

☐ Spring weak or broken. Makes a clicking or scraping sound. Fork oil, when drained, will have a lot of metal particles in it (Chapter 6).

☐ Steering head bearings loose or damaged. Clicks when braking. Check and adjust or replace as necessary (Chapters 1 and 6).

☐ Fork yokes loose. Make sure all clamp pinch bolts are tightened to the specified torque (Chapter 6).

☐ Fork tube bent. Good possibility if machine has been dropped. Replace tube with a new one (Chapter 6).

☐ Front axle bolt or axle clamp bolts loose. Tighten them to the specified torque (Chapter 7).

☐ Loose or worn wheel bearings. Check and replace as needed (Chapter 7).

### Shock absorber noise

☐ Fluid level incorrect. Indicates a leak caused by defective seal. Shock will be covered with oil. Replace shock or seek advice on repair from a Honda dealer (Chapter 6).

☐ Defective shock absorber with internal damage. This is in the body of the shock and can't be remedied. The shock must be replaced with a new one (Chapter 6).

☐ Bent or damaged shock body. Replace the shock with a new one (Chapter 6).

☐ Loose or worn suspension linkage components. Check and replace as necessary (Chapter 6).

### Brake noise

☐ Squeal caused by dust on brake pads. Usually found in combination with glazed pads. Clean using brake cleaning solvent (Chapter 7).

☐ Contamination of brake pads. Oil, brake fluid or dirt causing brake to chatter or squeal. Clean or replace pads (Chapter 7).

☐ Pads glazed. Caused by excessive heat from prolonged use or from contamination. Do not use sandpaper, emery cloth, carborundum cloth or any other abrasive to roughen the pad surfaces as abrasives will stay in the pad material and damage the disc. A very fine flat file can be used, but pad replacement is suggested as a cure (Chapter 7).

☐ Disc warped. Can cause a chattering, clicking or intermittent squeal. Usually accompanied by a pulsating lever and uneven braking. Replace the disc (Chapter 7).

☐ Loose or worn wheel bearings. Check and replace as needed (Chapter 7).

# 10 Oil pressure warning light comes on

### Engine lubrication system

☐ Engine oil pump defective, blocked oil strainer gauze or failed relief valve. Carry out oil pressure check (Chapter 2).

☐ Engine oil level low. Inspect for leak or other problem causing low oil level and add recommended oil (Chapter 1).

☐ Engine oil viscosity too low. Very old, thin oil or an improper weight of oil used in the engine. Change to correct oil (Chapter 1).

☐ Camshaft or journals worn. Excessive wear causing drop in oil pressure. Replace cam and/or cylinder head. Abnormal wear could be caused by oil starvation at high rpm from low oil level or improper weight or type of oil (Chapter 1).

☐ Crankshaft and/or bearings worn. Same problems as above. Check and replace crankshaft and/or bearings (Chapter 2).

### Electrical system

☐ Oil pressure switch defective. Check the switch according to the procedure in Chapter 9. Replace it if it is defective.

☐ Oil pressure warning light circuit defective. Check for pinched, shorted, disconnected or damaged wiring (Chapter 9).

# 11 Excessive exhaust smoke

### White smoke

☐ Piston oil ring worn. The ring may be broken or damaged, causing oil from the crankcase to be pulled past the piston into the combustion chamber. Replace the rings with new ones (Chapter 2).

☐ Cylinders worn, cracked, or scored. Caused by overheating or oil starvation. The crankcase/bores will have to be renewed, no oversizes are available.

☐ Valve oil seal damaged or worn. Replace oil seals with new ones (Chapter 2).

☐ Valve guide worn. Perform a complete valve job (Chapter 2).

☐ Engine oil level too high, which causes the oil to be forced past the rings. Drain oil to the proper level (Chapter 1).

☐ Head gasket broken between oil return and cylinder. Causes oil to be pulled into the combustion chamber. Replace the head gasket and check the head for warpage (Chapter 2).

☐ Abnormal crankcase pressurisation, which forces oil past the rings. Clogged breather is usually the cause.

### Black smoke

☐ Air filter clogged. Clean or replace the element (Chapter 1).

☐ Main jet too large or loose. Compare the jet size to the Specifications (Chapter 4).

☐ Choke cable or linkage shaft stuck, causing fuel to be pulled through choke circuit (Chapter 4).

☐ Fuel level too high. Check and adjust the float height(s) as necessary (Chapter 4).

☐ Float needle valve held off needle seat. Clean the float chambers and fuel line and replace the needles and seats if necessary (Chapter 4).

### Brown smoke

☐ Main jet too small or clogged. Lean condition caused by wrong size main jet or by a restricted orifice. Clean float chambers and jets and compare jet size to Specifications (Chapter 4).

☐ Fuel flow insufficient. Float needle valve stuck closed due to chemical reaction with old fuel. Float height incorrect. Restricted fuel line. Clean line and float chamber and adjust floats if necessary.

☐ Carburettor inlet manifold clamps loose (Chapter 4).

☐ Air filter poorly sealed or not installed (Chapter 1).

# 12 Poor handling or stability

## Handlebars hard to turn

- ☐ Steering head bearing adjuster nut too tight. Check adjustment as described in Chapter 1.
- ☐ Bearings damaged. Roughness can be felt as the bars are turned from side-to-side. Replace bearings and races (Chapter 6).
- ☐ Races dented or worn. Denting results from wear in only one position (eg, straight ahead), from a collision or hitting a pothole or from dropping the machine. Replace races and bearings (Chapter 6).
- ☐ Steering stem lubrication inadequate. Causes are grease getting hard from age or being washed out by high pressure car washes. Disassemble steering head and repack bearings (Chapter 6).
- ☐ Steering stem bent. Caused by a collision, hitting a pothole or by dropping the machine. Replace damaged part. Don't try to straighten the steering stem (Chapter 6).
- ☐ Front tyre air pressure too low (Chapter 1).

## Handlebar shakes or vibrates excessively

- ☐ Tyres worn or out of balance (Chapter 7).
- ☐ Swingarm bearings worn. Replace worn bearings (Chapter 6).
- ☐ Wheel rim(s) warped or damaged. Inspect wheels for runout (Chapter 7).
- ☐ Wheel bearings worn. Worn front wheel bearings or rear wheel holder bearings can cause poor tracking. Worn front bearings will cause wobble (Chapter 7).
- ☐ Handlebar clamp bolts loose (Chapter 6).
- ☐ Fork yoke bolts loose. Tighten them to the specified torque (Chapter 6).
- ☐ Engine mounting bolts loose. Will cause excessive vibration with increased engine rpm (Chapter 2).

## Handlebar pulls to one side

- ☐ Frame bent. Definitely suspect this if the machine has been dropped. May or may not be accompanied by cracking near the bend. Replace the frame (Chapter 6).
- ☐ Wheels out of alignment. Caused by improper location of axle spacers or from bent steering stem or frame (Chapter 6).
- ☐ Swingarm bent or twisted. Caused by age (metal fatigue) or impact damage. Replace the arm (Chapter 6).
- ☐ Steering stem bent. Caused by impact damage or by dropping the motorcycle. Replace the steering stem (Chapter 6).
- ☐ Fork tube bent. Disassemble the forks and replace the damaged parts (Chapter 6).
- ☐ Fork oil level uneven. Check and add or drain as necessary (Chapter 6).

## Poor shock absorbing qualities

**Too hard:**
- a) Fork oil level excessive (Chapter 6).
- b) Fork oil viscosity too high. Use a lighter oil (see the Specifications in Chapter 6).
- c) Fork tube bent. Causes a harsh, sticking feeling (Chapter 6).
- d) Shock shaft or body bent or damaged (Chapter 6).
- e) Fork internal damage (Chapter 6).
- f) Shock internal damage.
- g) Tyre pressure too high (Chapter 1).

**Too soft:**
- a) Fork or shock oil insufficient and/or leaking (Chapter 6).
- b) Fork oil level too low (Chapter 6).
- c) Fork oil viscosity too light (Chapter 6).
- d) Fork springs weak or broken (Chapter 6).
- e) Shock internal damage or leakage (Chapter 6).

# 13 Braking problems

## Brakes are spongy, don't hold

- ☐ Air in brake line. Caused by inattention to master cylinder fluid level or by leakage. Locate problem and bleed brakes (Chapter 7).
- ☐ Pad or disc worn (Chapters 1 and 7).
- ☐ Brake fluid leak. See paragraph 1.
- ☐ Contaminated pads. Caused by contamination with oil, grease, brake fluid, etc. Clean or replace pads. Clean disc thoroughly with brake cleaner (Chapter 7).
- ☐ Brake fluid deteriorated. Fluid is old or contaminated. Drain system, replenish with new fluid and bleed the system (Chapter 7).
- ☐ Master cylinder internal parts worn or damaged causing fluid to bypass (Chapter 7).
- ☐ Master cylinder bore scratched by foreign material or broken spring. Repair or replace master cylinder (Chapter 7).
- ☐ Disc warped. Replace disc (Chapter 7).

## Brake lever or pedal pulsates

- ☐ Disc warped. Replace disc (Chapter 7).
- ☐ Axle bent. Replace axle (Chapter 7).

- ☐ Brake caliper bolts loose (Chapter 7).
- ☐ Brake caliper sliders damaged or sticking (rear caliper), causing caliper to bind. Lubricate the sliders or replace them if they are corroded or bent (Chapter 7).
- ☐ Wheel warped or otherwise damaged (Chapter 7).
- ☐ Wheel bearings damaged or worn (Chapter 7).

## Brakes drag

- ☐ Master cylinder piston seized. Caused by wear or damage to piston or cylinder bore (Chapter 7).
- ☐ Lever balky or stuck. Check pivot and lubricate (Chapter 7).
- ☐ Brake caliper binds. Caused by inadequate lubrication or damage to caliper sliders (Chapter 7).
- ☐ Brake caliper piston seized in bore. Caused by wear or ingestion of dirt past deteriorated seal (Chapter 7).
- ☐ Brake pad damaged. Pad material separated from backing plate. Usually caused by faulty manufacturing process or from contact with chemicals. Replace pads (Chapter 7).
- ☐ Pads improperly installed (Chapter 7).

# 14 Electrical problems

## Battery dead or weak

☐ Battery faulty. Caused by sulphated plates which are shorted through sedimentation. Also, broken battery terminal making only occasional contact (Chapter 9).
☐ Battery cables making poor contact (Chapter 9).
☐ Load excessive. Caused by addition of high wattage lights or other electrical accessories.
☐ Ignition (main) switch defective. Switch either grounds (earths) internally or fails to shut off system. Replace the switch (Chapter 9).
☐ Regulator/rectifier defective (Chapter 9).

☐ Alternator stator coil open or shorted (Chapter 9).
☐ Wiring faulty. Wiring grounded (earthed) or connections loose in ignition, charging or lighting circuits (Chapter 9).

## Battery overcharged

☐ Regulator/rectifier defective. Overcharging is noticed when battery gets excessively warm (Chapter 9).
☐ Battery defective. Replace battery with a new one (Chapter 9).
☐ Battery amperage too low, wrong type or size. Install manufacturer's specified amp-hour battery to handle charging load (Chapter 9).

# Fault Finding Equipment

## Checking engine compression

● Low compression will result in exhaust smoke, heavy oil consumption, poor starting and poor performance. A compression test will provide useful information about an engine's condition and if performed regularly, can give warning of trouble before any other symptoms become apparent.
● A compression gauge will be required, along with an adapter to suit the spark plug hole thread size. Note that the screw-in type gauge/adapter set up is preferable to the rubber cone type.

● Before carrying out the test, first check the valve clearances as described in Chapter 1.
1 Run the engine until it reaches normal operating temperature, then stop it and remove the spark plug(s), taking care not to scald your hands on the hot components.
2 Install the gauge adapter and compression gauge in No. 1 cylinder spark plug hole (see illustration 1).
3 On kickstart-equipped motorcycles, make sure the ignition switch is OFF, then open the throttle fully and kick the engine over a couple of times until the gauge reading stabilises.
4 On motorcycles with electric start only, the procedure will differ depending on the nature of the ignition system. Flick the engine kill switch (engine stop switch) to OFF and turn

**Screw the compression gauge adapter into the spark plug hole, then screw the gauge into the adapter**

the ignition switch ON; open the throttle fully and crank the engine over on the starter motor for a couple of revolutions until the gauge reading stabilises. If the starter will not operate with the kill switch OFF, turn the ignition switch OFF and refer to the next paragraph.

5 Install the spark plugs back into their suppressor caps and arrange the plug electrodes so that their metal bodies are earthed (grounded) against the cylinder head; this is essential to prevent damage to the ignition system as the engine is spun over **(see illustration 2)**. Position the plugs well away from the plug holes otherwise there is a risk of atomised fuel escaping from the combustion chambers and igniting. As a safety precaution, cover the top of the valve cover with rag. Now turn the ignition switch ON and kill switch ON, open the throttle fully and crank the engine over on the starter motor for a couple of revolutions until the gauge reading stabilises.

All spark plugs must be earthed (grounded) against the cylinder head

6 After one or two revolutions the pressure should build up to a maximum figure and then stabilise. Take a note of this reading and on multi-cylinder engines repeat the test on the remaining cylinders.

7 The correct pressures are given in Chapter 2 Specifications. If the results fall within the specified range and on multi-cylinder engines all are relatively equal, the engine is in good condition. If there is a marked difference between the readings, or if the readings are lower than specified, inspection of the top-end components will be required.

8 Low compression pressure may be due to worn cylinder bores, pistons or rings, failure of the cylinder head gasket, worn valve seals, or poor valve seating.

9 To distinguish between cylinder/piston wear and valve leakage, pour a small quantity of oil into the bore to temporarily seal the piston rings, then repeat the compression tests **(see illustration 3)**. If the readings show a noticeable increase in pressure this confirms that the cylinder bore, piston, or rings are worn. If, however, no change is indicated, the cylinder head gasket or valves should be examined.

Bores can be temporarily sealed with a squirt of motor oil

10 High compression pressure indicates excessive carbon build-up in the combustion chamber and on the piston crown. If this is the case the cylinder head should be removed and the deposits removed. Note that excessive carbon build-up is less likely with the used on modern fuels.

## Checking battery open-circuit voltage

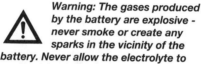

**⚠ Warning: The gases produced by the battery are explosive - never smoke or create any sparks in the vicinity of the battery. Never allow the electrolyte to contact your skin or clothing - if it does, wash it off and seek immediate medical attention.**

● Before any electrical fault is investigated the battery should be checked.

● You'll need a dc voltmeter or multimeter to check battery voltage. Check that the leads are inserted in the correct terminals on the meter, red lead to positive (+ve), black lead to negative (-ve). Incorrect connections can damage the meter.

● A sound fully-charged 12 volt battery should produce between 12.3 and 12.6 volts across its terminals (12.8 volts for a maintenance-free battery). On machines with a 6 volt battery, voltage should be between 6.1 and 6.3 volts.

1 Set a multimeter to the 0 to 20 volts dc range and connect its probes across the

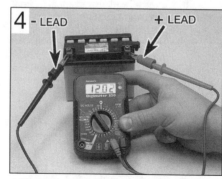

Measuring open-circuit battery voltage

battery terminals. Connect the meter's positive (+ve) probe, usually red, to the battery positive (+ve) terminal, followed by the meter's negative (-ve) probe, usually black, to the battery negative terminal (-ve) **(see illustration 4)**.

2 If battery voltage is low (below 10 volts on a 12 volt battery or below 4 volts on a six volt battery), charge the battery and test the voltage again. If the battery repeatedly goes flat, investigate the motorcycle's charging system.

## Checking battery specific gravity (SG)

**⚠ Warning: The gases produced by the battery are explosive - never smoke or create any sparks in the vicinity of the battery. Never allow the electrolyte to contact your skin or clothing - if it does, wash it off and seek immediate medical attention.**

● The specific gravity check gives an indication of a battery's state of charge.

● A hydrometer is used for measuring specific gravity. Make sure you purchase one which has a small enough hose to insert in the aperture of a motorcycle battery.

● Specific gravity is simply a measure of the electrolyte's density compared with that of water. Water has an SG of 1.000 and fully-charged battery electrolyte is about 26% heavier, at 1.260.

● Specific gravity checks are not possible on maintenance-free batteries. Testing the open-circuit voltage is the only means of determining their state of charge.

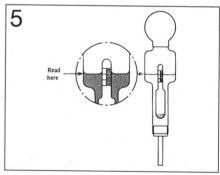

Read here

Float-type hydrometer for measuring battery specific gravity

1 To measure SG, remove the battery from the motorcycle and remove the first cell cap. Draw some electrolyte into the hydrometer and note the reading **(see illustration 5)**. Return the electrolyte to the cell and install the cap.

2 The reading should be in the region of 1.260 to 1.280. If SG is below 1.200 the battery needs charging. Note that SG will vary with temperature; it should be measured at 20°C (68°F). Add 0.007 to the reading for

every 10°C above 20°C, and subtract 0.007 from the reading for every 10°C below 20°C. Add 0.004 to the reading for every 10°F above 68°F, and subtract 0.004 from the reading for every 10°F below 68°F.

**3** When the check is complete, rinse the hydrometer thoroughly with clean water.

## Checking for continuity

● The term continuity describes the uninterrupted flow of electricity through an electrical circuit. A continuity check will determine whether an **open-circuit** situation exists.

● Continuity can be checked with an ohmmeter, multimeter, continuity tester or battery and bulb test circuit **(see illustrations 6, 7 and 8)**.

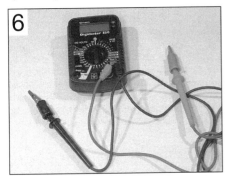

Digital multimeter can be used for all electrical tests

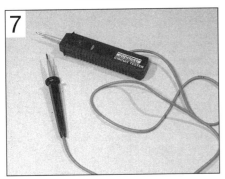

Battery-powered continuity tester

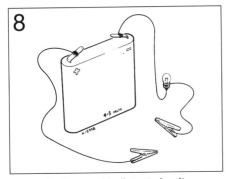

Battery and bulb test circuit

● All of these instruments are self-powered by a battery, therefore the checks are made with the ignition OFF.

● As a safety precaution, always disconnect the battery negative (-ve) lead before making checks, particularly if ignition switch checks are being made.

● If using a meter, select the appropriate ohms scale and check that the meter reads infinity (∞). Touch the meter probes together and check that meter reads zero; where necessary adjust the meter so that it reads zero.

● After using a meter, always switch it OFF to conserve its battery.

### Switch checks

**1** If a switch is at fault, trace its wiring up to the wiring connectors. Separate the wire connectors and inspect them for security and condition. A build-up of dirt or corrosion here will most likely be the cause of the problem - clean up and apply a water dispersant such as WD40.

Continuity check of front brake light switch using a meter - note split pins used to access connector terminals

**2** If using a test meter, set the meter to the ohms x 10 scale and connect its probes across the wires from the switch **(see illustration 9)**. Simple ON/OFF type switches, such as brake light switches, only have two wires whereas combination switches, like the ignition switch, have many internal links. Study the wiring diagram to ensure that you are connecting across the correct pair of wires. Continuity (low or no measurable resistance - 0 ohms) should be indicated with the switch ON and no continuity (high resistance) with it OFF.

**3** Note that the polarity of the test probes doesn't matter for continuity checks, although care should be taken to follow specific test procedures if a diode or solid-state component is being checked.

**4** A continuity tester or battery and bulb circuit can be used in the same way. Connect its probes as described above **(see illustration 10)**. The light should come on to indicate continuity in the ON switch position, but should extinguish in the OFF position.

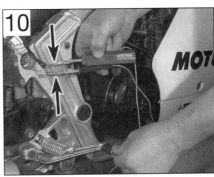

Continuity check of rear brake light switch using a continuity tester

### Wiring checks

● Many electrical faults are caused by damaged wiring, often due to incorrect routing or chaffing on frame components.

● Loose, wet or corroded wire connectors can also be the cause of electrical problems, especially in exposed locations.

**1** A continuity check can be made on a single length of wire by disconnecting it at each end and connecting a meter or continuity tester across both ends of the wire **(see illustration 11)**.

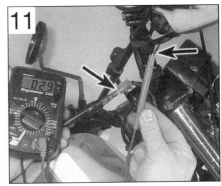

Continuity check of front brake light switch sub-harness

**2** Continuity (low or no resistance - 0 ohms) should be indicated if the wire is good. If no continuity (high resistance) is shown, suspect a broken wire.

## Checking for voltage

● A voltage check can determine whether current is reaching a component.

● Voltage can be checked with a dc voltmeter, multimeter set on the dc volts scale, test light or buzzer **(see illustrations 12 and 13)**. A meter has the advantage of being able to measure actual voltage.

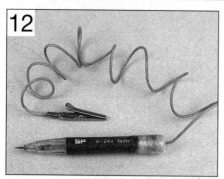

A simple test light can be used for voltage checks

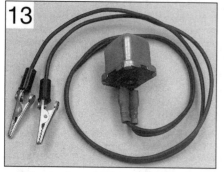

A buzzer is useful for voltage checks

● When using a meter, check that its leads are inserted in the correct terminals on the meter, red to positive (+ve), black to negative (-ve). Incorrect connections can damage the meter.

● A voltmeter (or multimeter set to the dc volts scale) should always be connected in parallel (across the load). Connecting it in series will destroy the meter.

● Voltage checks are made with the ignition ON.

1 First identify the relevant wiring circuit by referring to the wiring diagram at the end of this manual. If other electrical components share the same power supply (ie are fed from the same fuse), take note whether they are working correctly - this is useful information in deciding where to start checking the circuit.

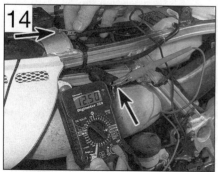

Checking for voltage at the rear brake light power supply wire using a meter . . .

2 If using a meter, check first that the meter leads are plugged into the correct terminals on the meter (see above). Set the meter to the dc volts function, at a range suitable for the battery voltage. Connect the meter red probe (+ve) to the power supply wire and the black probe to a good metal earth (ground) on the motorcycle's frame or directly to the battery negative (-ve) terminal (see illustration 14). Battery voltage should be shown on the meter with the ignition switched ON.

3 If using a test light or buzzer, connect its positive (+ve) probe to the power supply terminal and its negative (-ve) probe to a good earth (ground) on the motorcycle's frame or directly to the battery negative (-ve) terminal (see illustration 15). With the ignition ON, the test light should illuminate or the buzzer sound.

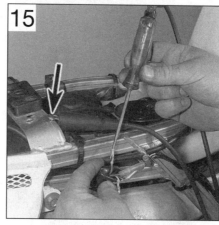

. . . or a test light - note the earth connection to the frame (arrow)

4 If no voltage is indicated, work back towards the fuse continuing to check for voltage. When you reach a point where there is voltage, you know the problem lies between that point and your last check point.

## Checking the earth (ground)

● Earth connections are made either directly to the engine or frame (such as sensors, neutral switch etc. which only have a positive feed) or by a separate wire into the earth circuit of the wiring harness. Alternatively a short earth wire is sometimes run directly from the component to the motorcycle's frame.

● Corrosion is often the cause of a poor earth connection.

● If total failure is experienced, check the security of the main earth lead from the negative (-ve) terminal of the battery and also the main earth (ground) point on the wiring harness. If corroded, dismantle the connection and clean all surfaces back to bare metal.

1 To check the earth on a component, use an insulated jumper wire to temporarily bypass its earth connection (see illustration 16). Connect one end of the jumper wire between the earth terminal or metal body of the component and the other end to the motorcycle's frame.

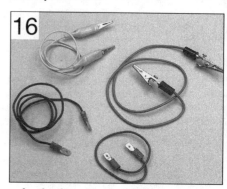

A selection of jumper wires for making earth (ground) checks

2 If the circuit works with the jumper wire installed, the original earth circuit is faulty. Check the wiring for open-circuits or poor connections. Clean up direct earth connections, removing all traces of corrosion and remake the joint. Apply petroleum jelly to the joint to prevent future corrosion.

## Tracing a short-circuit

● A short-circuit occurs where current shorts to earth (ground) bypassing the circuit components. This usually results in a blown fuse.

● A short-circuit is most likely to occur where the insulation has worn through due to wiring chafing on a component, allowing a direct path to earth (ground) on the frame.

1 Remove any bodypanels necessary to access the circuit wiring.

2 Check that all electrical switches in the circuit are OFF, then remove the circuit fuse and connect a test light, buzzer or voltmeter (set to the dc scale) across the fuse terminals. No voltage should be shown.

3 Move the wiring from side to side whilst observing the test light or meter. When the test light comes on, buzzer sounds or meter shows voltage, you have found the cause of the short. It will usually shown up as damaged or burned insulation.

4 Note that the same test can be performed on each component in the circuit, even the switch.

# A

**ABS (Anti-lock braking system)** A system, usually electronically controlled, that senses incipient wheel lockup during braking and relieves hydraulic pressure at wheel which is about to skid.

**Aftermarket** Components suitable for the motorcycle, but not produced by the motorcycle manufacturer.

**Allen key** A hexagonal wrench which fits into a recessed hexagonal hole.

**Alternating current (ac)** Current produced by an alternator. Requires converting to direct current by a rectifier for charging purposes.

**Alternator** Converts mechanical energy from the engine into electrical energy to charge the battery and power the electrical system.

**Ampere (amp)** A unit of measurement for the flow of electrical current. Current = Volts ˆ Ohms.

**Ampere-hour (Ah)** Measure of battery capacity.

**Angle-tightening** A torque expressed in degrees. Often follows a conventional tightening torque for cylinder head or main bearing fasteners **(see illustration)**.

**Angle-tightening cylinder head bolts**

**Antifreeze** A substance (usually ethylene glycol) mixed with water, and added to the cooling system, to prevent freezing of the coolant in winter. Antifreeze also contains chemicals to inhibit corrosion and the formation of rust and other deposits that would tend to clog the radiator and coolant passages and reduce cooling efficiency.

**Anti-dive** System attached to the fork lower leg (slider) to prevent fork dive when braking hard.

**Anti-seize compound** A coating that reduces the risk of seizing on fasteners that are subjected to high temperatures, such as exhaust clamp bolts and nuts.

**API** American Petroleum Institute. A quality standard for 4-stroke motor oils.

**Asbestos** A natural fibrous mineral with great heat resistance, commonly used in the composition of brake friction materials. Asbestos is a health hazard and the dust created by brake systems should never be inhaled or ingested.

**ATF** Automatic Transmission Fluid. Often used in front forks.

**ATU** Automatic Timing Unit. Mechanical device for advancing the ignition timing on early engines.

**ATV** All Terrain Vehicle. Often called a Quad.

**Axial play** Side-to-side movement.

**Axle** A shaft on which a wheel revolves. Also known as a spindle.

# B

**Backlash** The amount of movement between meshed components when one component is held still. Usually applies to gear teeth.

**Ball bearing** A bearing consisting of a hardened inner and outer race with hardened steel balls between the two races.

**Bearings** Used between two working surfaces to prevent wear of the components and a build-up of heat. Four types of bearing are commonly used on motorcycles: plain shell bearings, ball bearings, tapered roller bearings and needle roller bearings.

**Bevel gears** Used to turn the drive through 90°. Typical applications are shaft final drive and camshaft drive **(see illustration)**.

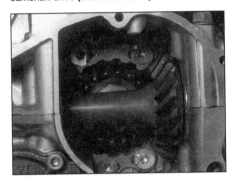

**Bevel gears are used to turn the drive through 90°**

**BHP** Brake Horsepower. The British measurement for engine power output. Power output is now usually expressed in kilowatts (kW).

**Bias-belted tyre** Similar construction to radial tyre, but with outer belt running at an angle to the wheel rim.

**Big-end bearing** The bearing in the end of the connecting rod that's attached to the crankshaft.

**Bleeding** The process of removing air from an hydraulic system via a bleed nipple or bleed screw.

**Bottom-end** A description of an engine's crankcase components and all components contained there-in.

**BTDC** Before Top Dead Centre in terms of piston position. Ignition timing is often expressed in terms of degrees or millimetres BTDC.

**Bush** A cylindrical metal or rubber component used between two moving parts.

**Burr** Rough edge left on a component after machining or as a result of excessive wear.

# C

**Cam chain** The chain which takes drive from the crankshaft to the camshaft(s).

**Canister** The main component in an evaporative emission control system (California market only); contains activated charcoal granules to trap vapours from the fuel system rather than allowing them to vent to the atmosphere.

**Castellated** Resembling the parapets along the top of a castle wall. For example, a castellated wheel axle or spindle nut.

**Catalytic converter** A device in the exhaust system of some machines which converts certain pollutants in the exhaust gases into less harmful substances.

**Charging system** Description of the components which charge the battery, ie the alternator, rectifier and regulator.

**Circlip** A ring-shaped clip used to prevent endwise movement of cylindrical parts and shafts. An internal circlip is installed in a groove in a housing; an external circlip fits into a groove on the outside of a cylindrical piece such as a shaft. Also known as a snap-ring.

**Clearance** The amount of space between two parts. For example, between a piston and a cylinder, between a bearing and a journal, etc.

**Coil spring** A spiral of elastic steel found in various sizes throughout a vehicle, for example as a springing medium in the suspension and in the valve train.

**Compression** Reduction in volume, and increase in pressure and temperature, of a gas, caused by squeezing it into a smaller space.

**Compression damping** Controls the speed the suspension compresses when hitting a bump.

**Compression ratio** The relationship between cylinder volume when the piston is at top dead centre and cylinder volume when the piston is at bottom dead centre.

**Continuity** The uninterrupted path in the flow of electricity. Little or no measurable resistance.

**Continuity tester** Self-powered bleeper or test light which indicates continuity.

**Cp** Candlepower. Bulb rating common found on US motorcycles.

**Crossply tyre** Tyre plies arranged in a criss-cross pattern. Usually four or six plies used, hence 4PR or 6PR in tyre size codes.

**Cush drive** Rubber damper segments fitted between the rear wheel and final drive sprocket to absorb transmission shocks **(see illustration)**.

**Cush drive rubbers dampen out transmission shocks**

# D

**Degree disc** Calibrated disc for measuring piston position. Expressed in degrees.

**Dial gauge** Clock-type gauge with adapters for measuring runout and piston position. Expressed in mm or inches.

**Diaphragm** The rubber membrane in a master cylinder or carburettor which seals the upper chamber.

**Diaphragm spring** A single sprung plate often used in clutches.

**Direct current (dc)** Current produced by a dc generator.

**Decarbonisation** The process of removing carbon deposits - typically from the combustion chamber, valves and exhaust port/system.

**Detonation** Destructive and damaging explosion of fuel/air mixture in combustion chamber instead of controlled burning.

**Diode** An electrical valve which only allows current to flow in one direction. Commonly used in rectifiers and starter interlock systems.

**Disc valve (or rotary valve)** A induction system used on some two-stroke engines.

**Double-overhead camshaft (DOHC)** An engine that uses two overhead camshafts, one for the intake valves and one for the exhaust valves.

**Drivebelt** A toothed belt used to transmit drive to the rear wheel on some motorcycles. A drivebelt has also been used to drive the camshafts. Drivebelts are usually made of Kevlar.

**Driveshaft** Any shaft used to transmit motion. Commonly used when referring to the final driveshaft on shaft drive motorcycles.

# E

**Earth return** The return path of an electrical circuit, utilising the motorcycle's frame.

**ECU (Electronic Control Unit)** A computer which controls (for instance) an ignition system, or an anti-lock braking system.

**EGO** Exhaust Gas Oxygen sensor. Sometimes called a Lambda sensor.

**Electrolyte** The fluid in a lead-acid battery.

**EMS (Engine Management System)** A computer controlled system which manages the fuel injection and the ignition systems in an integrated fashion.

**Endfloat** The amount of lengthways movement between two parts. As applied to a crankshaft, the distance that the crankshaft can move side-to-side in the crankcase.

**Endless chain** A chain having no joining link. Common use for cam chains and final drive chains.

**EP (Extreme Pressure)** Oil type used in locations where high loads are applied, such as between gear teeth.

**Evaporative emission control system** Describes a charcoal filled canister which stores fuel vapours from the tank rather than allowing them to vent to the atmosphere. Usually only fitted to California models and referred to as an EVAP system.

**Expansion chamber** Section of two-stroke engine exhaust system so designed to improve engine efficiency and boost power.

# F

**Feeler blade or gauge** A thin strip or blade of hardened steel, ground to an exact thickness, used to check or measure clearances between parts.

**Final drive** Description of the drive from the transmission to the rear wheel. Usually by chain or shaft, but sometimes by belt.

**Firing order** The order in which the engine cylinders fire, or deliver their power strokes, beginning with the number one cylinder.

**Flooding** Term used to describe a high fuel level in the carburettor float chambers, leading to fuel overflow. Also refers to excess fuel in the combustion chamber due to incorrect starting technique.

**Free length** The no-load state of a component when measured. Clutch, valve and fork spring lengths are measured at rest, without any preload.

**Freeplay** The amount of travel before any action takes place. The looseness in a linkage, or an assembly of parts, between the initial application of force and actual movement. For example, the distance the rear brake pedal moves before the rear brake is actuated.

**Fuel injection** The fuel/air mixture is metered electronically and directed into the engine intake ports (indirect injection) or into the cylinders (direct injection). Sensors supply information on engine speed and conditions.

**Fuel/air mixture** The charge of fuel and air going into the engine. See **Stoichiometric ratio**.

**Fuse** An electrical device which protects a circuit against accidental overload. The typical fuse contains a soft piece of metal which is calibrated to melt at a predetermined current flow (expressed as amps) and break the circuit.

# G

**Gap** The distance the spark must travel in jumping from the centre electrode to the side electrode in a spark plug. Also refers to the distance between the ignition rotor and the pickup coil in an electronic ignition system.

**Gasket** Any thin, soft material - usually cork, cardboard, asbestos or soft metal - installed between two metal surfaces to ensure a good seal. For instance, the cylinder head gasket seals the joint between the block and the cylinder head.

**Gauge** An instrument panel display used to monitor engine conditions. A gauge with a movable pointer on a dial or a fixed scale is an analogue gauge. A gauge with a numerical readout is called a digital gauge.

**Gear ratios** The drive ratio of a pair of gears in a gearbox, calculated on their number of teeth.

**Glaze-busting** see **Honing**

**Grinding** Process for renovating the valve face and valve seat contact area in the cylinder head.

**Gudgeon pin** The shaft which connects the connecting rod small-end with the piston. Often called a piston pin or wrist pin.

# H

**Helical gears** Gear teeth are slightly curved and produce less gear noise that straight-cut gears. Often used for primary drives.

**Installing a Helicoil thread insert in a cylinder head**

**Helicoil** A thread insert repair system. Commonly used as a repair for stripped spark plug threads **(see illustration)**.

**Honing** A process used to break down the glaze on a cylinder bore (also called glaze-busting). Can also be carried out to roughen a rebored cylinder to aid ring bedding-in.

**HT High Tension** Description of the electrical circuit from the secondary winding of the ignition coil to the spark plug.

**Hydraulic** A liquid filled system used to transmit pressure from one component to another. Common uses on motorcycles are brakes and clutches.

**Hydrometer** An instrument for measuring the specific gravity of a lead-acid battery.

**Hygroscopic** Water absorbing. In motorcycle applications, braking efficiency will be reduced if DOT 3 or 4 hydraulic fluid absorbs water from the air - care must be taken to keep new brake fluid in tightly sealed containers.

# I

**lbf ft** Pounds-force feet. An imperial unit of torque. Sometimes written as ft-lbs.

**lbf in** Pound-force inch. An imperial unit of torque, applied to components where a very low torque is required. Sometimes written as in-lbs.

**IC** Abbreviation for Integrated Circuit.

**Ignition advance** Means of increasing the timing of the spark at higher engine speeds. Done by mechanical means (ATU) on early engines or electronically by the ignition control unit on later engines.

**Ignition timing** The moment at which the spark plug fires, expressed in the number of crankshaft degrees before the piston reaches the top of its stroke, or in the number of millimetres before the piston reaches the top of its stroke.

**Infinity ($\infty$)** Description of an open-circuit electrical state, where no continuity exists.

**Inverted forks (upside down forks)** The sliders or lower legs are held in the yokes and the fork tubes or stanchions are connected to the wheel axle (spindle). Less unsprung weight and stiffer construction than conventional forks.

# J

**JASO** Quality standard for 2-stroke oils.

**Joule** The unit of electrical energy.

**Journal** The bearing surface of a shaft.

# K

**Kickstart** Mechanical means of turning the engine over for starting purposes. Only usually fitted to mopeds, small capacity motorcycles and off-road motorcycles.

**Kill switch** Handebar-mounted switch for emergency ignition cut-out. Cuts the ignition circuit on all models, and additionally prevent starter motor operation on others.

**km** Symbol for kilometre.

**kph** Abbreviation for kilometres per hour.

# L

**Lambda ($\lambda$) sensor** A sensor fitted in the exhaust system to measure the exhaust gas oxygen content (excess air factor).

**Lapping** see **Grinding**.
**LCD** Abbreviation for Liquid Crystal Display.
**LED** Abbreviation for Light Emitting Diode.
**Liner** A steel cylinder liner inserted in a aluminium alloy cylinder block.
**Locknut** A nut used to lock an adjustment nut, or other threaded component, in place.
**Lockstops** The lugs on the lower triple clamp (yoke) which abut those on the frame, preventing handlebar-to-fuel tank contact.
**Lockwasher** A form of washer designed to prevent an attaching nut from working loose.
**LT Low Tension** Description of the electrical circuit from the power supply to the primary winding of the ignition coil.

# M

**Main bearings** The bearings between the crankshaft and crankcase.
**Maintenance-free (MF) battery** A sealed battery which cannot be topped up.
**Manometer** Mercury-filled calibrated tubes used to measure intake tract vacuum. Used to synchronise carburettors on multi-cylinder engines.
**Micrometer** A precision measuring instrument that measures component outside diameters **(see illustration)**.

**Tappet shims are measured with a micrometer**

**MON (Motor Octane Number)** A measure of a fuel's resistance to knock.
**Monograde oil** An oil with a single viscosity, eg SAE80W.
**Monoshock** A single suspension unit linking the swingarm or suspension linkage to the frame.
**mph** Abbreviation for miles per hour.
**Multigrade oil** Having a wide viscosity range (eg 10W40). The W stands for Winter, thus the viscosity ranges from SAE10 when cold to SAE40 when hot.
**Multimeter** An electrical test instrument with the capability to measure voltage, current and resistance. Some meters also incorporate a continuity tester and buzzer.

# N

**Needle roller bearing** Inner race of caged needle rollers and hardened outer race. Examples of uncaged needle rollers can be found on some engines. Commonly used in rear suspension applications and in two-stroke engines.
**Nm** Newton metres.
**NOx** Oxides of Nitrogen. A common toxic pollutant emitted by petrol engines at higher temperatures.

# O

**Octane** The measure of a fuel's resistance to knock.
**OE (Original Equipment)** Relates to components fitted to a motorcycle as standard or replacement parts supplied by the motorcycle manufacturer.
**Ohm** The unit of electrical resistance. Ohms = Volts ÷ Current.
**Ohmmeter** An instrument for measuring electrical resistance.
**Oil cooler** System for diverting engine oil outside of the engine to a radiator for cooling purposes.
**Oil injection** A system of two-stroke engine lubrication where oil is pump-fed to the engine in accordance with throttle position.
**Open-circuit** An electrical condition where there is a break in the flow of electricity - no continuity (high resistance).
**O-ring** A type of sealing ring made of a special rubber-like material; in use, the O-ring is compressed into a groove to provide the
**Oversize (OS)** Term used for piston and ring size options fitted to a rebored cylinder.
**Overhead cam (sohc) engine** An engine with single camshaft located on top of the cylinder head.
**Overhead valve (ohv) engine** An engine with the valves located in the cylinder head, but with the camshaft located in the engine block or crankcase.
**Oxygen sensor** A device installed in the exhaust system which senses the oxygen content in the exhaust and converts this information into an electric current. Also called a Lambda sensor.

# P

**Plastigauge** A thin strip of plastic thread, available in different sizes, used for measuring clearances. For example, a strip of Plastigauge is laid across a bearing journal. The parts are assembled and dismantled; the width of the crushed strip indicates the clearance between journal and bearing.
**Polarity** Either negative or positive earth (ground), determined by which battery lead is connected to the frame (earth return). Modern motorcycles are usually negative earth.
**Pre-ignition** A situation where the fuel/air mixture ignites before the spark plug fires. Often due to a hot spot in the combustion chamber caused by carbon build-up. Engine has a tendency to 'run-on'.
**Pre-load (suspension)** The amount a spring is compressed when in the unloaded state. Preload can be applied by gas, spacer or mechanical adjuster.
**Premix** The method of engine lubrication on older two-stroke engines. Engine oil is mixed with the petrol in the fuel tank in a specific ratio. The fuel/oil mix is sometimes referred to as "petroil".
**Primary drive** Description of the drive from the crankshaft to the clutch. Usually by gear or chain.
**PS** Pfedestärke - a German interpretation of BHP.
**PSI** Pounds-force per square inch. Imperial measurement of tyre pressure and cylinder pressure measurement.
**PTFE** Polytetrafluroethylene. A low friction substance.

**Pulse secondary air injection system** A process of promoting the burning of excess fuel present in the exhaust gases by routing fresh air into the exhaust ports.

# Q

**Quartz halogen bulb** Tungsten filament surrounded by a halogen gas. Typically used for the headlight **(see illustration)**.

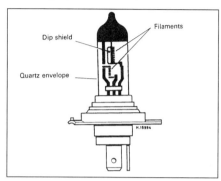

**Quartz halogen headlight bulb construction**

# R

**Rack-and-pinion** A pinion gear on the end of a shaft that mates with a rack (think of a geared wheel opened up and laid flat). Sometimes used in clutch operating systems.
**Radial play** Up and down movement about a shaft.
**Radial ply tyres** Tyre plies run across the tyre (from bead to bead) and around the circumference of the tyre. Less resistant to tread distortion than other tyre types.
**Radiator** A liquid-to-air heat transfer device designed to reduce the temperature of the coolant in a liquid cooled engine.
**Rake** A feature of steering geometry - the angle of the steering head in relation to the vertical **(see illustration)**.

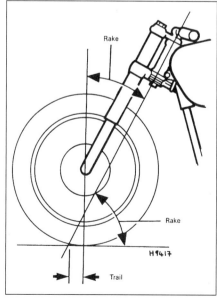

**Steering geometry**

**Rebore** Providing a new working surface to the cylinder bore by boring out the old surface. Necessitates the use of oversize piston and rings.

**Rebound damping** A means of controlling the oscillation of a suspension unit spring after it has been compressed. Resists the spring's natural tendency to bounce back after being compressed.

**Rectifier** Device for converting the ac output of an alternator into dc for battery charging.

**Reed valve** An induction system commonly used on two-stroke engines.

**Regulator** Device for maintaining the charging voltage from the generator or alternator within a specified range.

**Relay** A electrical device used to switch heavy current on and off by using a low current auxiliary circuit.

**Resistance** Measured in ohms. An electrical component's ability to pass electrical current.

**RON (Research Octane Number)** A measure of a fuel's resistance to knock.

**rpm** revolutions per minute.

**Runout** The amount of wobble (in-and-out movement) of a wheel or shaft as it's rotated. The amount a shaft rotates 'out-of-true'. The out-of-round condition of a rotating part.

# S

**SAE (Society of Automotive Engineers)** A standard for the viscosity of a fluid.

**Sealant** A liquid or paste used to prevent leakage at a joint. Sometimes used in conjunction with a gasket.

**Service limit** Term for the point where a component is no longer useable and must be renewed.

**Shaft drive** A method of transmitting drive from the transmission to the rear wheel.

**Shell bearings** Plain bearings consisting of two shell halves. Most often used as big-end and main bearings in a four-stroke engine. Often called bearing inserts.

**Shim** Thin spacer, commonly used to adjust the clearance or relative positions between two parts. For example, shims inserted into or under tappets or followers to control valve clearances. Clearance is adjusted by changing the thickness of the shim.

**Short-circuit** An electrical condition where current shorts to earth (ground) bypassing the circuit components.

**Skimming** Process to correct warpage or repair a damaged surface, eg on brake discs or drums.

**Slide-hammer** A special puller that screws into or hooks onto a component such as a shaft or bearing; a heavy sliding handle on the shaft bottoms against the end of the shaft to knock the component free.

**Small-end bearing** The bearing in the upper end of the connecting rod at its joint with the gudgeon pin.

**Spalling** Damage to camshaft lobes or bearing journals shown as pitting of the working surface.

**Specific gravity (SG)** The state of charge of the electrolyte in a lead-acid battery. A measure of the electrolyte's density compared with water.

**Straight-cut gears** Common type gear used on gearbox shafts and for oil pump and water pump drives.

**Stanchion** The inner sliding part of the front forks, held by the yokes. Often called a fork tube.

**Stoichiometric ratio** The optimum chemical air/fuel ratio for a petrol engine, said to be 14.7 parts of air to 1 part of fuel.

**Sulphuric acid** The liquid (electrolyte) used in a lead-acid battery. Poisonous and extremely corrosive.

**Surface grinding (lapping)** Process to correct a warped gasket face, commonly used on cylinder heads.

# T

**Tapered-roller bearing** Tapered inner race of caged needle rollers and separate tapered outer race. Examples of taper roller bearings can be found on steering heads.

**Tappet** A cylindrical component which transmits motion from the cam to the valve stem, either directly or via a pushrod and rocker arm. Also called a cam follower.

**TCS** Traction Control System. An electronically-controlled system which senses wheel spin and reduces engine speed accordingly.

**TDC** Top Dead Centre denotes that the piston is at its highest point in the cylinder.

**Thread-locking compound** Solution applied to fastener threads to prevent slackening. Select type to suit application.

**Thrust washer** A washer positioned between two moving components on a shaft. For example, between gear pinions on gearshaft.

**Timing chain** See **Cam Chain.**

**Timing light** Stroboscopic lamp for carrying out ignition timing checks with the engine running.

**Top-end** A description of an engine's cylinder block, head and valve gear components.

**Torque** Turning or twisting force about a shaft.

**Torque setting** A prescribed tightness specified by the motorcycle manufacturer to ensure that the bolt or nut is secured correctly. Undertightening can result in the bolt or nut coming loose or a surface not being sealed. Overtightening can result in stripped threads, distortion or damage to the component being retained.

**Torx key** A six-point wrench.

**Tracer** A stripe of a second colour applied to a wire insulator to distinguish that wire from another one with the same colour insulator. For example, Br/W is often used to denote a brown insulator with a white tracer.

**Trail** A feature of steering geometry. Distance from the steering head axis to the tyre's central contact point.

**Triple clamps** The cast components which extend from the steering head and support the fork stanchions or tubes. Often called fork yokes.

**Turbocharger** A centrifugal device, driven by exhaust gases, that pressurises the intake air. Normally used to increase the power output from a given engine displacement.

**TWI** Abbreviation for Tyre Wear Indicator. Indicates the location of the tread depth indicator bars on tyres.

# U

**Universal joint or U-joint (UJ)** A double-pivoted connection for transmitting power from a driving to a driven shaft through an angle. Typically found in shaft drive assemblies.

**Unsprung weight** Anything not supported by the bike's suspension (ie the wheel, tyres, brakes, final drive and bottom (moving) part of the suspension).

# V

**Vacuum gauges** Clock-type gauges for measuring intake tract vacuum. Used for carburettor synchronisation on multi-cylinder engines.

**Valve** A device through which the flow of liquid, gas or vacuum may be stopped, started or regulated by a moveable part that opens, shuts or partially obstructs one or more ports or passageways. The intake and exhaust valves in the cylinder head are of the poppet type.

**Valve clearance** The clearance between the valve tip (the end of the valve stem) and the rocker arm or tappet/follower. The valve clearance is measured when the valve is closed. The correct clearance is important - if too small the valve won't close fully and will burn out, whereas if too large noisy operation will result.

**Valve lift** The amount a valve is lifted off its seat by the camshaft lobe.

**Valve timing** The exact setting for the opening and closing of the valves in relation to piston position.

**Vernier caliper** A precision measuring instrument that measures inside and outside dimensions. Not quite as accurate as a micrometer, but more convenient.

**VIN** Vehicle Identification Number. Term for the bike's engine and frame numbers.

**Viscosity** The thickness of a liquid or its resistance to flow.

**Volt** A unit for expressing electrical "pressure" in a circuit. Volts = current x ohms.

# W

**Water pump** A mechanically-driven device for moving coolant around the engine.

**Watt** A unit for expressing electrical power. Watts = volts x current.

**Wear limit** see **Service limit**

**Wet liner** A liquid-cooled engine design where the pistons run in liners which are directly surrounded by coolant **(see illustration)**.

**Wet liner arrangement**

**Wheelbase** Distance from the centre of the front wheel to the centre of the rear wheel.

**Wiring harness or loom** Describes the electrical wires running the length of the motorcycle and enclosed in tape or plastic sheathing. Wiring coming off the main harness is usually referred to as a sub harness.

**Woodruff key** A key of semi-circular or square section used to locate a gear to a shaft. Often used to locate the alternator rotor on the crankshaft.

**Wrist pin** Another name for gudgeon or piston pin.

# Specifications

The following specifications apply to the NC21 and NC24 models only. Identification details are as follows:

| Model | Year | Code | Engine no. | Frame no. | Carb ID |
|---|---|---|---|---|---|
| VFR400Z (NC21) | 1986 | ZG | NC13E-1030098 to 1045640 | NC21-1000077 to 1015556 | VDA0A A |
| VFR400Z (NC21) | 1987 | ZH | NC13E-1050034 to 1076150 | NC21-1020013 to 1021407 | VDE2A A |
| VFR400R (NC21) | 1986 | RG | NC13E-1030017 to 1045836 | NC21-1000011 to 1015756 | VDA0A A |
| VFR400R (NC21) | 1986 | RG-YA | NC13E-1030065 to 1042932 | NC21-1000074 to 1012861 | VDA0A A |
| VFR400R (NC24) | 1987 | RH | NC13E-1050019 to 1075630 | NC24-1000010 to 1017050 | VDE2C A |
| VFR400R (NC24) | 1987 | RH-II | NC13E-1059737 to 1069166 | NC24-1009051 to 1016630 | VDE2C A |
| VFR400R (NC24) | 1988 | RJ-III | NC13E-1070023 to 1082667 | NC24-1020011 to 1032667 | VDE2C E |

**Note:** *Procedures for these models are not included in this manual – all preceding pages of this manual apply only to the NC30 and NC35 models.*

# Engine, clutch and transmission

## General

| | |
|---|---|
| Type | Four-stroke 90° V-four |
| Capacity | 399 cc |
| Bore | 55.0 mm |
| Stroke | 42.0 mm |
| Compression ratio | |
| VFR400 RG and ZG | 11.0 to 1 |
| VFR400 RH, RJ and ZH | 11.3 to 1 |
| Cylinder compression | 142 to 200 psi (9.8 to 13.8 Bar) |
| Firing order | 1-3-2-4 |
| Cylinder numbering | |
| Rear left | 1 |
| Front left | 2 |
| Rear right | 3 |
| Front right | 4 |
| Clutch | Wet multi-plate |
| Transmission | Six-speed constant mesh |
| Final drive | Chain |

## Camshafts

| | |
|---|---|
| Inlet lobe height | |
| Standard | 31.05 to 31.21 mm |
| Service limit (min) | 31.01 mm |
| Exhaust lobe height | |
| Standard | 31.11 to 31.27 mm |
| Service limit (min) | 31.07 mm |
| Journal diameter | |
| Standard | 27.929 to 27.950 mm |
| Service limit (min) | 27.925 mm |
| Journal holder diameter | |
| Standard | 28.000 to 28.021 mm |
| Service limit (max) | 28.025 mm |
| Journal oil clearance | |
| Standard | 0.050 to 0.092 mm |
| Service limit (max) | 0.096 mm |
| Runout (max) | 0.03 mm |

## Cylinder head

| | |
|---|---|
| Warpage (max) | 0.10 mm |

## Valves, guides and springs

Valve clearances (COLD engine)
Inlet valves . . . . . . . . . . . . . . . . . . . . . . . . . . . . . . . . . . . . . . . . . 0.11 to 0.15 mm
Exhaust valves . . . . . . . . . . . . . . . . . . . . . . . . . . . . . . . . . . . . . . . 0.18 to 0.22 mm
Inlet valve
Stem diameter
VFR400 RG and ZG
Standard . . . . . . . . . . . . . . . . . . . . . . . . . . . . . . . . . . . . . . . . 4.975 to 4.990 mm
Service limit (min) . . . . . . . . . . . . . . . . . . . . . . . . . . . . . . . . . . 4.97 mm
VFR400 RH, RJ and ZH
Standard . . . . . . . . . . . . . . . . . . . . . . . . . . . . . . . . . . . . . . . . 4.475 to 4.490 mm
Service limit (min) . . . . . . . . . . . . . . . . . . . . . . . . . . . . . . . . . . 4.46 mm
Guide bore diameter
VFR400 RG and ZG
Standard . . . . . . . . . . . . . . . . . . . . . . . . . . . . . . . . . . . . . . . . 5.000 to 5.012 mm
Service limit (max) . . . . . . . . . . . . . . . . . . . . . . . . . . . . . . . . . 5.04 mm
VFR400 RH, RJ and ZH
Standard . . . . . . . . . . . . . . . . . . . . . . . . . . . . . . . . . . . . . . . . 4.500 to 4.512 mm
Service limit (max) . . . . . . . . . . . . . . . . . . . . . . . . . . . . . . . . . 4.54 mm
Stem-to-guide clearance
Standard . . . . . . . . . . . . . . . . . . . . . . . . . . . . . . . . . . . . . . . . . . . 0.010 to 0.037 mm
Service limit (max) . . . . . . . . . . . . . . . . . . . . . . . . . . . . . . . . . . . . 0.07 mm
Seat width . . . . . . . . . . . . . . . . . . . . . . . . . . . . . . . . . . . . . . . . . . . . . 1.70 to 2.30 mm
Valve guide height above cylinder head . . . . . . . . . . . . . . . . . . . . . . 10.0 mm
Exhaust valve
Stem diameter
VFR400 RG and ZG
Standard . . . . . . . . . . . . . . . . . . . . . . . . . . . . . . . . . . . . . . . . 4.955 to 4.970 mm
Service limit (min) . . . . . . . . . . . . . . . . . . . . . . . . . . . . . . . . . . 4.94 mm
VFR400 RH, RJ and ZH
Standard . . . . . . . . . . . . . . . . . . . . . . . . . . . . . . . . . . . . . . . . 4.455 to 4.470 mm
Service limit (min) . . . . . . . . . . . . . . . . . . . . . . . . . . . . . . . . . . 4.44 mm
Guide bore diameter
VFR400 RG and ZG
Standard . . . . . . . . . . . . . . . . . . . . . . . . . . . . . . . . . . . . . . . . 5.000 to 5.012 mm
Service limit (max) . . . . . . . . . . . . . . . . . . . . . . . . . . . . . . . . . 5.04 mm
VFR400 RH, RJ and ZH
Standard . . . . . . . . . . . . . . . . . . . . . . . . . . . . . . . . . . . . . . . . 4.500 to 4.512 mm
Service limit (max) . . . . . . . . . . . . . . . . . . . . . . . . . . . . . . . . . 4.54 mm
Stem-to-guide clearance
Standard . . . . . . . . . . . . . . . . . . . . . . . . . . . . . . . . . . . . . . . . . . . 0.030 to 0.057 mm
Service limit (max) . . . . . . . . . . . . . . . . . . . . . . . . . . . . . . . . . . . . 0.10 mm
Valve springs free length (inlet and exhaust)
VFR400 RG and ZG
Inner spring
Standard . . . . . . . . . . . . . . . . . . . . . . . . . . . . . . . . . . . . . . . . 29.84 mm
Service limit (min) . . . . . . . . . . . . . . . . . . . . . . . . . . . . . . . . . . 28.50 mm
Outer spring
Standard . . . . . . . . . . . . . . . . . . . . . . . . . . . . . . . . . . . . . . . . 32.89 mm
Service limit (min) . . . . . . . . . . . . . . . . . . . . . . . . . . . . . . . . . . 31.60 mm
VFR400 RH, RJ and ZH
Inner spring
Standard . . . . . . . . . . . . . . . . . . . . . . . . . . . . . . . . . . . . . . . . 29.28 or 28.89 mm
Service limit (min) . . . . . . . . . . . . . . . . . . . . . . . . . . . . . . . . . . 28.80 or 28.60 mm
Outer spring
Standard . . . . . . . . . . . . . . . . . . . . . . . . . . . . . . . . . . . . . . . . 31.90 or 32.08 mm
Service limit (min) . . . . . . . . . . . . . . . . . . . . . . . . . . . . . . . . . . 30.60 or 30.80 mm

## Clutch

Friction plate thickness
Standard . . . . . . . . . . . . . . . . . . . . . . . . . . . . . . . . . . . . . . . . . . . . . . 2.90 to 3.0 mm
Service limit (min) . . . . . . . . . . . . . . . . . . . . . . . . . . . . . . . . . . . . . . . 2.7 mm
Plain plate warpage (max) . . . . . . . . . . . . . . . . . . . . . . . . . . . . . . . . . 0.3 mm
Spring free height
VFR400 RG and ZG
Standard . . . . . . . . . . . . . . . . . . . . . . . . . . . . . . . . . . . . . . . . 41.2 mm
Service limit (min) . . . . . . . . . . . . . . . . . . . . . . . . . . . . . . . . . . 40 mm
VFR400 RH, RJ and ZH
Standard . . . . . . . . . . . . . . . . . . . . . . . . . . . . . . . . . . . . . . . . 37.6 mm
Service limit (min) . . . . . . . . . . . . . . . . . . . . . . . . . . . . . . . . . . 36.5 mm

Clutch housing ID at guide bore
    Standard . . . . . . . . . . . . . . . . . . . . . . . . . . . . . . . . . . . . . . . . . . . . . . 29.000 to 29.021 mm
    Service limit (max) . . . . . . . . . . . . . . . . . . . . . . . . . . . . . . . . . . . . . . 29.06 mm
Clutch housing guide OD
    Standard . . . . . . . . . . . . . . . . . . . . . . . . . . . . . . . . . . . . . . . . . . . . . . 28.967 to 28.980 mm
    Service limit (min) . . . . . . . . . . . . . . . . . . . . . . . . . . . . . . . . . . . . . . . 28.93 mm
Clutch housing guide ID
    Standard . . . . . . . . . . . . . . . . . . . . . . . . . . . . . . . . . . . . . . . . . . . . . . 21.995 to 22.015 mm
    Service limit (max) . . . . . . . . . . . . . . . . . . . . . . . . . . . . . . . . . . . . . . 22.05 mm
Master cylinder bore diameter
    Standard . . . . . . . . . . . . . . . . . . . . . . . . . . . . . . . . . . . . . . . . . . . . . . 14.000 to 14.043 mm
    Service limit (max) . . . . . . . . . . . . . . . . . . . . . . . . . . . . . . . . . . . . . . 14.055 mm
Master cylinder piston diameter
    Standard . . . . . . . . . . . . . . . . . . . . . . . . . . . . . . . . . . . . . . . . . . . . . . 13.957 to 13.984 mm
    Service limit (min) . . . . . . . . . . . . . . . . . . . . . . . . . . . . . . . . . . . . . . . 13.945 mm
Release (slave) cylinder bore diameter
    Standard . . . . . . . . . . . . . . . . . . . . . . . . . . . . . . . . . . . . . . . . . . . . . . 35.700 to 35.762 mm
    Service limit (max) . . . . . . . . . . . . . . . . . . . . . . . . . . . . . . . . . . . . . . 35.78 mm
Master cylinder piston diameter
    Standard . . . . . . . . . . . . . . . . . . . . . . . . . . . . . . . . . . . . . . . . . . . . . . 35.650 to 35.675 mm
    Service limit (min) . . . . . . . . . . . . . . . . . . . . . . . . . . . . . . . . . . . . . . . 35.62 mm

## Lubrication system

Oil type . . . . . . . . . . . . . . . . . . . . . . . . . . . . . . . . . . . . . . . . . . . . . . . . . . . API grade SE, SF or SG motor oil
Oil viscosity . . . . . . . . . . . . . . . . . . . . . . . . . . . . . . . . . . . . . . . . . . . . . . . . SAE 10W40
Oil capacity
    At oil change . . . . . . . . . . . . . . . . . . . . . . . . . . . . . . . . . . . . . . . . . . . 2.4 litres
    At oil and filter change . . . . . . . . . . . . . . . . . . . . . . . . . . . . . . . . . . . 2.6 litres
    Following engine overhaul – dry engine, new filter
        VFR400 R . . . . . . . . . . . . . . . . . . . . . . . . . . . . . . . . . . . . . . . . . . . 3.1 litres
        VFR400 Z . . . . . . . . . . . . . . . . . . . . . . . . . . . . . . . . . . . . . . . . . . . 3.0 litres
Oil pressure (with engine warm)
    VFR400 RG and ZG . . . . . . . . . . . . . . . . . . . . . . . . . . . . . . . . . . . . . 76 psi (5.3 Bar) at 5000 rpm, oil at 80°C
    VFR400 RH, RJ and ZH . . . . . . . . . . . . . . . . . . . . . . . . . . . . . . . . . . 62 psi (4.3 Bar) at 5000 rpm, oil at 80°C
Oil pump
    Inner rotor tip-to-outer rotor clearance
        Standard . . . . . . . . . . . . . . . . . . . . . . . . . . . . . . . . . . . . . . . . . . 0.15 mm
        Service limit (max) . . . . . . . . . . . . . . . . . . . . . . . . . . . . . . . . . . . 0.20 mm
    Outer rotor-to-body clearance
        Standard . . . . . . . . . . . . . . . . . . . . . . . . . . . . . . . . . . . . . . . . . . 0.15 to 0.21 mm
        Service limit (max) . . . . . . . . . . . . . . . . . . . . . . . . . . . . . . . . . . . 0.35 mm
    Rotor endfloat
        Standard . . . . . . . . . . . . . . . . . . . . . . . . . . . . . . . . . . . . . . . . . . 0.04 to 0.09 mm
        Service limit (max) . . . . . . . . . . . . . . . . . . . . . . . . . . . . . . . . . . . 0.12 mm
Oil pump drive sprocket ID
    Standard . . . . . . . . . . . . . . . . . . . . . . . . . . . . . . . . . . . . . . . . . . . . . . 29.025 to 29.075 mm
    Service limit (max) . . . . . . . . . . . . . . . . . . . . . . . . . . . . . . . . . . . . . . 29.11 mm

## Cylinder block

Bore
    Standard . . . . . . . . . . . . . . . . . . . . . . . . . . . . . . . . . . . . . . . . . . . . . . 55.000 to 55.015 mm
    Service limit (max) . . . . . . . . . . . . . . . . . . . . . . . . . . . . . . . . . . . . . . 55.10 mm
Warpage (max) . . . . . . . . . . . . . . . . . . . . . . . . . . . . . . . . . . . . . . . . . . . . 0.10 mm
Ovality (out-of-round) (max) . . . . . . . . . . . . . . . . . . . . . . . . . . . . . . . . . . 0.10 mm
Taper (max) . . . . . . . . . . . . . . . . . . . . . . . . . . . . . . . . . . . . . . . . . . . . . . 0.10 mm

## Connecting rods

Small-end internal diameter
    Standard . . . . . . . . . . . . . . . . . . . . . . . . . . . . . . . . . . . . . . . . . . . . . . 14.016 to 14.034 mm
    Service limit (max) . . . . . . . . . . . . . . . . . . . . . . . . . . . . . . . . . . . . . . 14.05 mm
Small-end-to-piston pin clearance
    Standard . . . . . . . . . . . . . . . . . . . . . . . . . . . . . . . . . . . . . . . . . . . . . . 0.016 to 0.040 mm
    Service limit (max) . . . . . . . . . . . . . . . . . . . . . . . . . . . . . . . . . . . . . . 0.06 mm
Big-end side clearance
    Standard . . . . . . . . . . . . . . . . . . . . . . . . . . . . . . . . . . . . . . . . . . . . . . 0.1 to 0.3 mm
    Service limit (max) . . . . . . . . . . . . . . . . . . . . . . . . . . . . . . . . . . . . . . 0.4 mm
Big-end oil clearance
    Standard . . . . . . . . . . . . . . . . . . . . . . . . . . . . . . . . . . . . . . . . . . . . . . 0.028 to 0.052 mm
    Service limit (max) . . . . . . . . . . . . . . . . . . . . . . . . . . . . . . . . . . . . . . 0.07 mm

## Pistons

Piston diameter (measured 10.0 mm up from skirt, at 90° to piston pin axis)
Standard . . . . . . . . . . . . . . . . . . . . . . . . . . . . . . . . . . . . . . . . . . . . 54.960 to 54.990 mm
Service limit (min) . . . . . . . . . . . . . . . . . . . . . . . . . . . . . . . . . . . . . 54.85 mm
Piston-to-bore clearance
Standard . . . . . . . . . . . . . . . . . . . . . . . . . . . . . . . . . . . . . . . . . . . . 0.010 to 0.055 mm
Service limit (max) . . . . . . . . . . . . . . . . . . . . . . . . . . . . . . . . . . . . . 0.10 mm
Piston pin diameter
Standard . . . . . . . . . . . . . . . . . . . . . . . . . . . . . . . . . . . . . . . . . . . . 13.994 to 14.000 mm
Service limit (min) . . . . . . . . . . . . . . . . . . . . . . . . . . . . . . . . . . . . . 13.98 mm
Piston pin bore diameter in piston
Standard . . . . . . . . . . . . . . . . . . . . . . . . . . . . . . . . . . . . . . . . . . . . 14.002 to 14.008 mm
Service limit (max) . . . . . . . . . . . . . . . . . . . . . . . . . . . . . . . . . . . . . 14.06 mm
Piston pin-to-piston pin bore clearance
Standard . . . . . . . . . . . . . . . . . . . . . . . . . . . . . . . . . . . . . . . . . . . . 0.002 to 0.014 mm
Service limit (max) . . . . . . . . . . . . . . . . . . . . . . . . . . . . . . . . . . . . . 0.04 mm

## Piston rings

Ring end gap (installed)
Top ring
Standard . . . . . . . . . . . . . . . . . . . . . . . . . . . . . . . . . . . . . . . . . 0.18 to 0.33 mm
Service limit (max) . . . . . . . . . . . . . . . . . . . . . . . . . . . . . . . . . . 0.5 mm
2nd ring
Standard . . . . . . . . . . . . . . . . . . . . . . . . . . . . . . . . . . . . . . . . . 0.18 to 0.33 mm
Service limit (max) . . . . . . . . . . . . . . . . . . . . . . . . . . . . . . . . . . 0.5 mm
Oil ring side-rail
Standard . . . . . . . . . . . . . . . . . . . . . . . . . . . . . . . . . . . . . . . . . 0.20 to 0.70 mm
Service limit (max) . . . . . . . . . . . . . . . . . . . . . . . . . . . . . . . . . . 0.90 mm
Ring-to-groove clearance
Top ring
Standard . . . . . . . . . . . . . . . . . . . . . . . . . . . . . . . . . . . . . . . . . 0.015 to 0.050 mm
Service limit (max) . . . . . . . . . . . . . . . . . . . . . . . . . . . . . . . . . . 0.10 mm
2nd ring
Standard . . . . . . . . . . . . . . . . . . . . . . . . . . . . . . . . . . . . . . . . . 0.015 to 0.050 mm
Service limit (max) . . . . . . . . . . . . . . . . . . . . . . . . . . . . . . . . . . 0.10 mm
Ring identification
Top ring . . . . . . . . . . . . . . . . . . . . . . . . . . . . . . . . . . . . . . . . . . . . "R" (facing up)
2nd ring . . . . . . . . . . . . . . . . . . . . . . . . . . . . . . . . . . . . . . . . . . . . "•" mark or "RN" (facing up)

## Crankshaft and bearings

Main bearing oil clearance
Standard . . . . . . . . . . . . . . . . . . . . . . . . . . . . . . . . . . . . . . . . . . . . 0.025 to 0.049 mm
Service limit (max) . . . . . . . . . . . . . . . . . . . . . . . . . . . . . . . . . . . . . 0.07 mm
Runout (max) . . . . . . . . . . . . . . . . . . . . . . . . . . . . . . . . . . . . . . . . . . 0.03 mm

## Transmission

Gear ratios (no. of teeth)
Primary reduction . . . . . . . . . . . . . . . . . . . . . . . . . . . . . . . . . . . . . . 2.117 to 1
Final reduction . . . . . . . . . . . . . . . . . . . . . . . . . . . . . . . . . . . . . . . . 3.000 to 1
1st gear . . . . . . . . . . . . . . . . . . . . . . . . . . . . . . . . . . . . . . . . . . . . . . 3.307 to 1
2nd gear . . . . . . . . . . . . . . . . . . . . . . . . . . . . . . . . . . . . . . . . . . . . . 2.352 to 1
3rd gear . . . . . . . . . . . . . . . . . . . . . . . . . . . . . . . . . . . . . . . . . . . . . 1.850 to 1
4th gear . . . . . . . . . . . . . . . . . . . . . . . . . . . . . . . . . . . . . . . . . . . . . 1.545 to 1
5th gear . . . . . . . . . . . . . . . . . . . . . . . . . . . . . . . . . . . . . . . . . . . . . 1.333 to 1
6th gear
VFR400 RG and ZG . . . . . . . . . . . . . . . . . . . . . . . . . . . . . . . . . . 1.192 to 1
VFR400 RH, RJ and ZH . . . . . . . . . . . . . . . . . . . . . . . . . . . . . . . 1.227 to 1
Input shaft 5th and 6th gears ID
Standard . . . . . . . . . . . . . . . . . . . . . . . . . . . . . . . . . . . . . . . . . . . . 25.000 to 25.021 mm
Service limit (max) . . . . . . . . . . . . . . . . . . . . . . . . . . . . . . . . . . . . . 25.05 mm
Input shaft 5th and 6th gears bush OD
Standard . . . . . . . . . . . . . . . . . . . . . . . . . . . . . . . . . . . . . . . . . . . . 24.959 to 24.980 mm
Service limit (min) . . . . . . . . . . . . . . . . . . . . . . . . . . . . . . . . . . . . . 24.92 mm
Input shaft 5th and 6th gears gear-to-bush clearance
Standard . . . . . . . . . . . . . . . . . . . . . . . . . . . . . . . . . . . . . . . . . . . . 0.020 to 0.062 mm
Service limit (max) . . . . . . . . . . . . . . . . . . . . . . . . . . . . . . . . . . . . . 0.10 mm
Input shaft 5th gear bush ID
Standard . . . . . . . . . . . . . . . . . . . . . . . . . . . . . . . . . . . . . . . . . . . . 21.985 to 22.006 mm
Service limit (max) . . . . . . . . . . . . . . . . . . . . . . . . . . . . . . . . . . . . . 22.02 mm

| | |
|---|---|
| Input shaft OD at 5th gear bush point | |
| Standard | 21.959 to 21.980 mm |
| Service limit (min) | 21.92 mm |
| Input shaft-to-bush clearance at 5th gear bush point | |
| Standard | 0.005 to 0.047 mm |
| Service limit (max) | 0.10 mm |
| Output shaft 2nd, 3rd and 4th gears ID | |
| Standard | 28.000 to 28.021 mm |
| Service limit (max) | 28.05 mm |
| Output shaft 2nd, 3rd and 4th gears bush OD | |
| Standard | 27.959 to 27.980 mm |
| Service limit (min) | 27.92 mm |
| Output shaft 2nd, 3rd and 4th gears gear-to-bush clearance | |
| Standard | 0.020 to 0.062 mm |
| Service limit (max) | 0.10 mm |
| Output shaft 2nd gear bush ID | |
| Standard | 25.030 to 25.051 mm |
| Service limit (max) | 25.051 mm |
| Output shaft OD at 2nd gear bush point | |
| Standard | 25.002 to 25.015 mm |
| Service limit (min) | 24.97 mm |
| Output shaft-to-bush clearance at 2nd gear bush point | |
| Standard | 0.015 to 0.049 mm |
| Service limit (max) | 0.081 mm |

## Selector drum and forks

| | |
|---|---|
| Selector fork end thickness | |
| Standard | 5.93 to 6.00 mm |
| Service limit (min) | 5.60 mm |
| Selector fork bore ID | |
| Standard | 12.000 to 12.021 mm |
| Service limit (max) | 12.04 mm |
| Selector fork shaft OD | |
| Standard | 11.969 to 11.980 mm |
| Service limit (min) | 11.90 mm |

# Cooling system

## Coolant

| | |
|---|---|
| Coolant type | 50% distilled water, 50% corrosion inhibited ethylene glycol anti-freeze |
| Coolant capacity | |
| Radiator and engine | 1.7 litres |
| Reservoir | 0.25 litre |

## Radiator

| | |
|---|---|
| Cap valve opening pressure | |
| VFR400 RG and ZG | 10 to 15 psi (0.7 to 1.0 Bar) |
| VFR400 RH, RJ and ZH | 13.5 to 17.8 psi (0.9 to 1.2 Bar) |

## Fan switch

| | |
|---|---|
| Cooling fan cut-in temperature | 95 to 105°C |

## Coolant temperature sensor

| | |
|---|---|
| Resistance | |
| @ 60°C | 94 to 117 ohms |
| @ 118°C | 16 to 19 ohms |
| @ 122°C | 14.4 to 17.3 ohms |

## Thermostat

| | |
|---|---|
| Opening temperature | 80 to 84°C |
| Valve lift | 8 mm (min) @ 95°C |

# Fuel and exhaust systems

## Fuel
Grade ............................................................. Unleaded, minimum 91 RON (Research Octane Number)
Fuel tank capacity (including reserve) .......................... 16.0 litres

## Carburettors
Type ............................................................. CV
Pilot screw setting (turns out) ................................. 2 turns out
Float height .................................................... 6.8 mm
Engine idle speed ............................................... 1300 ± 100 rpm
Throttle cable freeplay ......................................... 2 to 6 mm

## Carburettor jet sizes
Pilot jet ....................................................... 35
Main jet
   Front cylinder carburettors ................................. 112
   Rear cylinder carburettors .................................. 110

# Ignition system

## General
Firing order .................................................... 1-3-2-4

## Spark plugs
Type
   Standard .................................................... NGK C8EH-9 or Nippondenso U24FE9
   For extended high speed riding ............................... NGK C9EH-9 or Nippondenso U27FE9
   For cold climate (below 5°C) ................................ NGK C7EH-9 or Nippondenso U22FE9
Electrode gap ................................................... 0.8 to 0.9 mm

## Ignition timing
At idle
   VFR400 RG and ZG ............................................ 15° BTDC
   VFR400 RH, RJ and ZH ........................................ 18° BTDC
Full advance .................................................... 37° BTDC

## Pulse generator coils
Resistance
   VFR400 RG and ZG ............................................ 350 to 430 ohms
   VFR400 RH, RJ and ZH ........................................ 400 to 500 ohms

## Ignition HT coils
Primary winding resistance
   VFR400 RG and ZG ............................................ 2.6 to 3.2 ohms
   VFR400 RH, RJ and ZH ........................................ 2.0 to 4.0 ohms
Secondary winding resistance
   VFR400 RG and ZG
      with plug cap ........................................... 15.0 to 20.6 K ohms
      without plug cap ........................................ 11.7 to 14.3 K ohms
   VFR400 RH, RJ and ZH
      with plug cap ........................................... 15.0 to 21.0 K ohms
      without plug cap ........................................ 11.0 to 15.0 K ohms

## Suspension and final drive

### Front forks

| | |
|---|---|
| Fork oil type | 10W fork oil |
| Fork oil capacity | |
|   VFR400 RG and ZG | |
|     Right fork | 340 cc |
|     Left fork | 345 cc |
|   VFR400 RH, RJ and ZH | |
|     Right fork | 389 cc |
|     Left fork | 392 cc |
| Fork oil level* | |
|   VFR400 RG and ZG | 151 mm |
|   VFR400 RH, RJ and ZH | 90 mm |
| Fork spring free length (min) | |
|   VFR400 RG and ZG | |
|     Standard | 379.0 mm |
|     Service limit | 371.4 mm |
|   VFR400 RH, RJ and ZH | |
|     Standard | 396.8 mm |
|     Service limit | 388.9 mm |
| Fork tube runout limit | 0.2 mm |

*Oil level is measured from the top of the tube with the fork spring removed and the leg fully compressed.

### Rear suspension

| | |
|---|---|
| Shock absorber spring free length | |
|   Standard | 153.1 mm |
|   Service limit | 150.0 mm |

### Final drive

| | |
|---|---|
| Drive chain slack | 15 to 25 mm |
| Drive chain lubricant | SAE 80 or 90 gear oil, or aerosol chain lubricant suitable for O-ring chains |
| Drive chain size | 525, 106 links |
| Sprocket sizes | |
|   Front (engine) sprocket | 15T |
|   Rear (wheel) sprocket | 45T |

## Brakes, wheels and tyres

### Brakes

| | |
|---|---|
| Brake fluid | DOT 4 |
| Front caliper bore ID | |
|   Standard | 27.000 to 27.050 mm |
|   Service limit | 27.060 mm |
| Front caliper piston OD | |
|   Standard | 26.918 to 26.968 mm |
|   Service limit | 26.910 mm |
| Front disc minimum thickness | |
|   VFR400 RG and ZG | |
|     Standard | 3.8 to 4.2 mm |
|     Service limit | 3.5 mm |
|   VFR400 RH, RJ and ZH | |
|     Standard | 4.3 to 4.7 mm |
|     Service limit | 4.0 mm |
| Disc maximum runout (front and rear, all models) | 0.3 mm |
| Front master cylinder bore ID | |
|   Standard | 14.000 to 14.043 mm |
|   Service limit (max) | 14.055 mm |
| Front master cylinder piston OD | |
|   Standard | 13.957 to 13.984 mm |
|   Service limit (min) | 13.945 mm |
| Rear caliper bore ID | |
|   VFR400 RG and ZG | |
|     Standard | 27.000 to 27.050 mm |
|     Service limit (max) | 27.060 mm |
|   VFR400 RH, RJ and ZH | |
|     Standard | 38.180 to 38.230 mm |
|     Service limit (max) | 38.240 mm |

## Brakes (continued)

Rear caliper piston OD
  VFR400 RG and ZG
    Standard .................................................. 26.918 to 26.968 mm
    Service limit (min) ..................................... 26.910 mm
  VFR400 RH, RJ and ZH
    Standard .................................................. 38.115 to 38.148 mm
    Service limit (min) ..................................... 38.105 mm
Rear disc minimum thickness
  Standard .................................................. 4.8 to 5.2 mm
  Service limit (min) ..................................... 4.0 mm
Disc maximum runout (front and rear, all models) ................. 0.3 mm
Rear master cylinder bore ID
  VFR400 RG and ZG
    Standard .................................................. 12.700 to 12.743 mm
    Service limit (max) ..................................... 12.755 mm
  VFR400 RH, RJ and ZH
    Standard .................................................. 14.000 to 14.043 mm
    Service limit (max) ..................................... 14.055 mm
Rear master cylinder piston OD
  VFR400RG and ZG
    Standard .................................................. 12.657 to 12.684 mm
    Service limit (min) ..................................... 12.645 mm
  VFR400RH, RJ and ZH
    Standard .................................................. 13.957 to 13.984 mm
    Service limit (min) ..................................... 13.945 mm

## Wheels

Maximum wheel runout (front and rear)
  Axial (side-to-side) ..................................... 2.0 mm
  Radial (out-of-round) ................................... 2.0 mm
Maximum axle runout (front and rear) ........................ 0.20 mm

## Tyres

| Tyre pressures (cold) | Front | Rear |
| --- | --- | --- |
| Rider only | 32 psi (2.20 Bar) | 36 psi (2.50 Bar) |
| Rider and passenger | 32 psi (2.20 Bar) | 40 psi (2.75 Bar) |

Tyre sizes*
  Front .................................................. 100/90-16 54H
  Rear ................................................... 130/70-18 63H
*Refer to the owners handbook or the tyre information label on the swingarm for approved tyre brands.

# Electrical system

## Battery

Capacity ................................................... 12 V, 9 Ah
Voltage
  Fully charged ........................................... 13.0 V
  Uncharged ............................................... Below 12.0 V
Charging rate
  Normal .................................................. 0.9 A for 5 to 10 hrs
  Quick ................................................... 3.0 A for 1hr
Current leakage ........................................... 1 mA (max)

## Alternator

Power output
  VFR400 RG and ZG ........................................ 270 W @ 5000 rpm
  VFR400 RH, RJ and ZH .................................... 350 W @ 5000 rpm
Stator coil resistance
  VFR400 RG and ZG ........................................ 0.28 to 0.65 ohms
  VFR400 RH, RJ and ZH .................................... 0.30 to 0.45 ohms

## Regulator/rectifier

Regulated voltage output .................................. 14.1 to 15.1 V

## Starter motor

Brush length
  Standard .................................................. 12.0 to 13.0 mm
  Service limit (min) ..................................... 6.5 mm

## Fuses

Main ...................................................... 30 A
Others .................................................... 10 A x 6, 15 A x 1

# Torque settings

## Specific components

| | |
|---|---|
| Oil drain plug | 35 Nm |
| Oil filter | 15 Nm |
| Timing inspection cover | 17.5 Nm |
| Engine mountings | |
|    Adjuster bolt | 11 Nm |
|    Adjuster bolt locknut | 55 Nm |
|    Adjuster bolt nut | 55 Nm |
| Valve cover bolts | 10 Nm |
| Camshaft holder bolts | 12 Nm |
| Camshaft drive gear assemblies | |
|    Mounting bolts | 32 Nm |
|    Crankcase bolt | 12 Nm |
| Cylinder head 6 mm bolts | 12 Nm |
| Cylinder head 8 mm bolts | 32 Nm |
| Starter clutch bolt | 85 Nm |
| Starter clutch cover bolts | 28 Nm |
| Clutch nut | 65 Nm |
| Oil pump cover bolts | 12 Nm |
| Oil pump mounting bolts | 12 Nm |
| Crankcase 6 mm bolts | 12 Nm |
| Crankcase 8 mm bolts | 23 Nm |
| Crankcase 10 mm bolt | 40 Nm |
| Connecting rod cap nuts | 24 Nm |
| Handlebar holder clamp bolts | 27.5 Nm |
| Top yoke fork clamp bolts | 11 Nm |
| Bottom yoke fork clamp bolts | 35 Nm |
| Steering stem nut | 105 Nm |
| Fork damper rod bolt | 30 Nm |
| Fork top bolt | 22 Nm |
| Shock absorber mounting bolt nuts | 45 Nm |
| Shock absorber linkage pivot bolt nuts | 45 Nm |
| Shock absorber linkage arm bolt nuts | 45 Nm |
| Swingarm pivot left-hand bolt | 95 Nm |
| Swingarm pivot right-hand bolt | 60 Nm |
| Front sprocket bolts | 12 Nm |
| Rear sprocket nuts | |
|    VFR400 RG and ZG | 65 Nm |
|    VFR400 RH, RJ and ZH | 42.5 Nm |
| Oil pressure switch | 12 Nm |
| Neutral switch | 12 Nm |
| Alternator rotor bolt | 85 Nm |
| Front brake disc bolts | 40 Nm |
| Rear brake disc bolts – VFR400 RG and ZG | 40 Nm |
| Rear brake disc nuts – VFR400 RH, RJ and ZH | 35 Nm |
| Brake hose banjo bolts | 30 Nm |
| Brake caliper bleed valves | 6 Nm |
| Front axle bolt | 60 Nm |
| Front axle clamp bolts | 22 Nm |
| Rear axle nut – VFR400 RG and ZG | 90 Nm |
| Rear hub assembly nut – VFR400 RH, RJ and ZH | 165 Nm |
| Rear wheel nuts – VFR400 RH, RJ and ZH | 110 Nm |
| Rear wheel bearing holder pinch bolt – VFR400 RH, RJ and ZH | 27 Nm |

## Non-specified components

**Note:** *Where a specific setting is not given for a particular bolt/nut, these general settings apply. The dimension given applies to the diameter of the thread, not the head.*

| | |
|---|---|
| 5 mm bolt/nut | 5 Nm |
| 6 mm bolt/nut | 10 Nm |
| 8 mm bolt/nut | 22 Nm |
| 10 mm bolt/nut | 35 Nm |
| 12 mm bolt/nut | 55 Nm |
| 6 mm flange bolt with 8 mm head | 9 Nm |
| 6 mm flange bolt/nut with 10 mm head | 12 Nm |
| 8 mm flange bolt/nut | 27 Nm |
| 10 mm flange bolt/nut | 40 Nm |

**Note:** *References throughout this index relate to Chapter•page number*

# O

Oil, engine/transmission - 0•11, 1•2, 1•10, REF•45
Oil cooler and pipes - 2•11
Oil filter - 1•10
Oil pressure
   check - 1•22
   relief valve - 2•34
   switch - 9•14
   warning light comes on - REF•33
Oil pump - 2•35
Oil seals - REF•16
Oil strainer - 2•34
Oil sump - 2•34
Overheating - REF•31

# P

Pads - 1•7, 7•3, 7•9
Pistons - 2•48
   rings - 2•50
Poor engine running - REF•29, REF•30
Poor handling or stability - REF•34
Pressure
   cylinder compression - 1•22
   oil - 1•22
   tyre - 0•14
Pulse generator coil assembly - 5•4

# R

Radiator - 3•5
   pressure cap - 3•2
Rear view mirrors - 8•3
Rear wheel and hub assembly - 7•17
Reference - REF•1 et seq
Refilling the cooling system - 1•21
Regulator/rectifier - 9•25
Rings, piston - 2•50
Rocker arms and shafts - 2•17
Routine maintenance and servicing - 1•1 et seq
Running-in procedure - 2•62

# S

Safety checks - 0•11
Safety first - 0•10
Sealants - REF•17
Seals - 1•23
Seat cowling - 8•2
Selector drum and forks - 2•60
Servicing see Routine maintenance
Shock absorber and linkage - 6•20
Short-circuit - REF•38
Sidelight bulb - 9•6
Sidestand - 1•15, 6•4
   switch - 9•16
Spare parts - 0•9
Spark plugs - 1•13
   gaps - 1•8
Speedometer cable - 9•10
Sprockets - 6•26

Stand lubrication - 1•10
Starter clutch and primary drive gear -2•24
Starter motor - 9•19
Starter relay - 9•18
Starting problems - REF•28
Steering - 0•13
   head bearings - 1•16, 1•23, 6•19
   stem - 6•18
Storage - REF•25
Suspension - 6•1 et seq
   adjustment - 6•22
   check - 0•13, 1•15
   noise - REF•33
Suspension linkage, rear - 1•23, 6•20
Swingarm - 1•23, 6•23, 6•25
Switches - 9•9, 9•14, 9•15, 9•16, 9•17

# T

Tail light
   assembly - 9•8
   bulb - 9•7
Technical terms explained - REF•39
Thermostat and housing - 3•4
Throttle cable - 1•12, 4•13
Tools - REF•2
Torque - REF•13
Transmission - 2•1 et seq
   bearings - 2•53
   oil - 0•11, 1•2, 1•10, REF•45
   shafts - 2•53, 2•55
Turn signal
   assemblies - 9•9
   bulbs - 9•8
   circuit - 9•8
Tyres - 7•1 et seq
   check - 1•18
   fitting - 7•22
   pressure - 0•14

# V

Valves
   clearances - 1•19
   covers - 2•12
   seats and guides - 2•20, 2•21
Voltage regulator - 9•25

# W

Warning light bulbs - 9•14
Water pump - 3•6
Weights - REF•1
Wheels - 7•1 et seq
   alignment check - 7•15
   bearings - 1•22, 7•21
   check - 1•18
   inspection and repair - 7•15
   removal - 7•15, 7•17
Wiring diagrams - 9•27, 9•28
Workshop tips - REF•4

# Haynes Motorcycle Manuals – The Complete List

| Title | Book No |
|---|---|
| **BMW** | |
| **BMW 2-valve Twins (70 - 96)** | 0249 |
| **BMW K100 & 75 2-valve Models (83 - 96)** | 1373 |
| **BMW R850 & R1100 4-valve Twins (93 - 97)** | 3466 |
| **BSA** | |
| BSA Bantam (48 - 71) | 0117 |
| BSA Unit Singles (58 - 72) | 0127 |
| BSA Pre-unit Singles (54 - 61) | 0326 |
| BSA A7 & A10 Twins (47 - 62) | 0121 |
| BSA A50 & A65 Twins (62 - 73) | 0155 |
| **DUCATI** | |
| **Ducati 600, 750 & 900 2-valve V-Twins (91 - 96)** | 3290 |
| **Ducati 748, 916 & 996 4-valve V-Twins (94 - 01)** | 3756 |
| **HARLEY-DAVIDSON** | |
| Harley-Davidson Sportsters (70 - 00) | 0702 |
| Harley-Davidson Big Twins (70 - 99) | 0703 |
| **HONDA** | |
| Honda NB, ND, NP & NS50 Melody (81 - 85) ◊ | 0622 |
| Honda NE/NB50 Vision & SA50 Vision Met-in (85 - 95) ◊ | 1278 |
| Honda MB, MBX, MT & MTX50 (80 - 93) | 0731 |
| Honda C50, C70 & C90 (67 - 99) | 0324 |
| Honda XR80R & XR100R (85 - 96) | 2218 |
| Honda XL/XR 80, 100, 125, 185 & 200 2-valve Models (78 - 87) | 0566 |
| Honda H100 & H100S Singles (80 - 92) ◊ | 0734 |
| Honda CB/CD125T & CM125C Twins (77 - 88) ◊ | 0571 |
| Honda CG125 (76 - 00) ◊ | 0433 |
| Honda NS125 (86 - 93) ◊ | 3056 |
| Honda MBX/MTX125 & MTX200 (83 - 93) ◊ | 1132 |
| Honda CD/CM185 200T & CM250C 2-valve Twins (77 - 85) | 0572 |
| Honda XL/XR 250 & 500 (78 - 84) | 0567 |
| Honda XR250L, XR250R & XR400R (86 - 01) | 2219 |
| Honda CB250 & CB400N Super Dreams (78 - 84) ◊ | 0540 |
| Honda CR Motocross Bikes (86 - 01) | 2222 |
| Honda Elsinore 250 (73 - 75) | 0217 |
| **Honda CBR400RR Fours (88 - 99)** | 3552 |
| **Honda VFR400 (NC30) & RVF400 (NC35) V-Fours (89 - 98)** | 3496 |
| **Honda CB500 (93 - 01)** | 3753 |
| Honda CB400 & CB550 Fours (73 - 77) | 0262 |
| Honda CX/GL500 & 650 V-Twins (78 - 86) | 0442 |
| Honda CBX550 Four (82 - 86) ◊ | 0940 |
| Honda XL600R & XR600R (83 - 00) | 2183 |
| **Honda CBR600F1 & 1000F Fours (87 - 96)** | 1730 |
| **Honda CBR600F2 & F3 Fours (91 - 98)** | 2070 |
| **Honda CBR600F4 (99 - 02)** | 3911 |
| **Honda CB600F Hornet** | 3915 |
| Honda CB650 sohc Fours (78 - 84) | 0665 |
| Honda NTV600/650/Deauville V-Twins (88 - 01) | 3243 |
| Honda Shadow VT600 & 750 (USA) (88 - 99) | 2312 |
| Honda CB750 sohc Four (69 - 79) | 0131 |
| Honda V45/65 Sabre & Magna (82 - 88) | 0820 |
| **Honda VFR750 & 700 V-Fours (86 - 97)** | 2101 |
| **Honda VFR800 V-Fours (97 - 99)** | 3703 |
| Honda CB750 & CB900 dohc Fours (78 - 84) | 0535 |
| **Honda VTR1000 (FireStorm, Super Hawk) & XL1000V (Varadero) (97 - 00)** | 3744 |
| **Honda CBR900RR FireBlade (92 - 99)** | 2161 |
| **Honda CBR1100 XX Super Blackbird (96 - 01)** | 3901 |
| **Honda ST1100 Pan European V-Fours (90 - 01)** | 3384 |
| Honda Shadow VT1100 (USA) (85 - 98) | 2313 |

| Title | Book No |
|---|---|
| Honda GL1000 Gold Wing (75 - 79) | 0309 |
| Honda GL1100 Gold Wing (79 - 81) | 0669 |
| Honda Gold Wing 1200 (USA) (84 - 87) | 2199 |
| Honda Gold Wing 1500 (USA) (88 - 00) | 2225 |
| **KAWASAKI** | |
| Kawasaki AE/AR 50 & 80 (81 - 95) | 1007 |
| Kawasaki KC, KE & KH100 (75 - 99) | 1371 |
| Kawasaki KMX125 & 200 (86 - 96) ◊ | 3046 |
| Kawasaki 250, 350 & 400 Triples (72 - 79) | 0134 |
| Kawasaki 400 & 440 Twins (74 - 81) | 0281 |
| Kawasaki 400, 500 & 550 Fours (79 - 91) | 0910 |
| Kawasaki EN450 & 500 Twins (Ltd/Vulcan) (85 - 93) | 2053 |
| **Kawasaki EX & ER500 (GPZ500S & ER-5) Twins (87 - 99)** | 2052 |
| **Kawasaki ZX600 (Ninja ZX-6, ZZ-R600) Fours (90 - 00)** | 2146 |
| **Kawasaki ZX-6R Ninja Fours (95 - 98)** | 3541 |
| **Kawasaki ZX600 (GPZ600R, GPX600R, Ninja 600R & RX & ZX750 (GPX750R, Ninja 750R) Fours (85 - 97)** | 1780 |
| Kawasaki 650 Four (76 - 78) | 0373 |
| Kawasaki 750 Air-cooled Fours (80 - 91) | 0574 |
| **Kawasaki ZR550 & 750 Zephyr Fours (90 - 97)** | 3382 |
| **Kawasaki ZX750 (Ninja ZX-7 & ZXR750) Fours (89 - 96)** | 2054 |
| **Kawasaki Ninja ZX-7R & ZX-9R (ZX750P, ZX900B/C/D/E) (94 - 00)** | 3721 |
| Kawasaki 900 & 1000 Fours (73 - 77) | 0222 |
| **Kawasaki ZX900, 1000 & 1100 Liquid-cooled Fours (83 - 97)** | 1681 |
| **Moto Guzzi** | |
| Moto Guzzi 750, 850 & 1000 V-Twins (74 - 78) | 0339 |
| **MZ ETZ** | |
| MZ ETZ Models (81 - 95) ◊ | 1680 |
| **NORTON** | |
| Norton 500, 600, 650 & 750 Twins (57 - 70) | 0187 |
| Norton Commando (68 - 77) | 0125 |
| **PIAGGIO** | |
| Piaggio (Vespa) Scooters (91 - 98) | 3492 |
| **SUZUKI** | |
| Suzuki GT, ZR & TS50 (77 - 90) ◊ | 0799 |
| Suzuki TS50X (84 - 00) ◊ | 1599 |
| Suzuki 100, 125, 185 & 250 Air-cooled Trail bikes (79 - 89) | 0797 |
| Suzuki GP100 & 125 Singles (78 - 93) ◊ | 0576 |
| Suzuki GS, GN, GZ & DR125 Singles (82 - 99) ◊ | 0888 |
| Suzuki GT250X7, GT200X5 & SB200 Twins (78 - 83) ◊ | 0469 |
| Suzuki GS/GSX250, 400 & 450 Twins (79 - 85) | 0736 |
| **Suzuki GS500E Twin (89 - 97)** | 3238 |
| Suzuki GS550 (77 - 82) & GS750 Fours (76 - 79) | 0363 |
| Suzuki GS/GSX550 4-valve Fours (83 - 88) | 1133 |
| **Suzuki GSX-R600 & 750 (96 - 99)** | 3553 |
| **Suzuki GSF600 & 1200 Bandit Fours (95 - 01)** | 3367 |
| Suzuki GS850 Fours (78 - 88) | 0536 |
| Suzuki GS1000 Four (77 - 79) | 0484 |
| **Suzuki GSX-R750, GSX-R1100 (85 - 92), GSX600F, GSX750F, GSX1100F (Katana) Fours (88 - 96)** | 2055 |
| Suzuki GS/GSX1000, 1100 & 1150 4-valve Fours (79 - 88) | 0737 |
| **TRIUMPH** | |
| Triumph 350 & 500 Unit Twins (58 - 73) | 0137 |
| Triumph Pre-Unit Twins (47 - 62) | 0251 |
| Triumph 650 & 750 2-valve Unit Twins (63 - 83) | 0122 |
| Triumph Trident & BSA Rocket 3 (69 - 75) | 0136 |
| **Triumph Fuel Injected Triples (97 - 00)** | 3755 |
| **Triumph Triples & Fours (carburettor engines) (91 - 99)** | 2162 |
| **VESPA** | |
| Vespa P/PX125, 150 & 200 Scooters (78 - 95) | 0707 |
| Vespa Scooters (59 - 78) | 0126 |

| Title | Book No |
|---|---|
| **YAMAHA** | |
| Yamaha DT50 & 80 Trail Bikes (78 - 95) ◊ | 0800 |
| Yamaha T50 & 80 Townmate (83 - 95) ◊ | 1247 |
| Yamaha YB100 Singles (73 - 91) ◊ | 0474 |
| Yamaha RS/RXS100 & 125 Singles (74 - 95) | 0331 |
| Yamaha RD & DT125LC (82 - 87) ◊ | 0887 |
| Yamaha TZR125 (87 - 93) & DT125R (88 - 95) ◊ | 1655 |
| Yamaha TY50, 80, 125 & 175 (74 - 84) ◊ | 0464 |
| Yamaha XT & SR125 (82 - 96) | 1021 |
| Yamaha Trail Bikes (81 - 00) | 2350 |
| Yamaha 250 & 350 Twins (70 - 79) | 0040 |
| Yamaha XS250, 360 & 400 sohc Twins (75 - 84) | 0378 |
| Yamaha RD250 & 350LC Twins (80 - 82) | 0803 |
| Yamaha RD350 YPVS Twins (83 - 95) | 1158 |
| Yamaha RD400 Twin (75 - 79) | 0333 |
| Yamaha XT, TT & SR500 Singles (75 - 83) | 0342 |
| Yamaha XZ550 Vision V-Twins (82 - 85) | 0821 |
| Yamaha FJ, FZ, XJ & YX600 Radian (84 - 92) | 2100 |
| **Yamaha XJ600S (Diversion, Seca II) & XJ600N Fours (92 - 99)** | 2145 |
| **Yamaha YZF600R Thundercat & FZS600 Fazer (96 - 00)** | 3702 |
| **Yamaha YZF-R6 (98 - 01)** | 3900 |
| Yamaha 650 Twins (70 - 83) | 0341 |
| Yamaha XJ650 & 750 Fours (80 - 84) | 0738 |
| Yamaha XS750 & 850 Triples (76 - 85) | 0340 |
| **Yamaha TDM850, TRX850 & XTZ750 (89 - 99)** | 3540 |
| **Yamaha YZF750R & YZF1000R Thunderace (93 - 00)** | 3720 |
| **Yamaha FZR600, 750 & 1000 Fours (87 - 96)** | 2056 |
| **Yamaha XV V-Twins (81 - 96)** | 0802 |
| **Yamaha XJ900F Fours (83 - 94)** | 3239 |
| **Yamaha XJ900S Diversion (94 - 01)** | 3739 |
| **Yamaha YZF-R1 (98 - 01)** | 3754 |
| **Yamaha FJ1100 & 1200 Fours (84 - 96)** | 2057 |
| **ATVs** | |
| Honda ATC70, 90, 110, 185 & 200 (71 - 85) | 0565 |
| Honda TRX300 Shaft Drive ATVs (88 - 95) | 2125 |
| Honda TRX300EX & TRX400EX ATVs (93 - 99) | 2318 |
| Kawasaki Bayou 220/300 & Prairie 300 ATVs (86 - 01) | 2351 |
| Polaris ATVs (85 to 97) | 2302 |
| Yamaha YT, YFM, YTM & YTZ ATVs (80 - 85) | 1154 |
| Yamaha YFS200 Blaster ATV (88 - 98) | 2317 |
| Yamaha YFB250 Timberwolf ATV (92 - 96) | 2217 |
| Yamaha YFM350 (ER and Big Bear) ATVs (87 - 99) | 2126 |
| Yamaha Warrior and Banshee ATVs (87 - 99) | 2314 |
| ATV Basics | 10450 |
| **MOTORCYCLE TECHBOOKS** | |
| Motorcycle Basics TechBook (2nd Edition) | 3515 |
| Motorcycle Electrical TechBook (3rd Edition) | 3471 |
| Motorcycle Fuel Systems TechBook | 3514 |
| Motorcycle Workshop Practice TechBook (2nd Edition) | 3470 |

◊ = not available in the USA    **Bold type** = Superbike

The manuals on this page are available through good motorcycle dealers and accessory shops. In case of difficulty, contact: **Haynes Publishing** (UK) +44 1963 442030    (USA) +1 805 4986703 (FR) +33 1 47 78 50 50    (SV) +46 18 124016 (Australia/New Zealand) +61 3 9763 8100

# Preserving Our Motoring Heritage

<
*The Model J Duesenberg Derham Tourster. Only eight of these magnificent cars were ever built – this is the only example to be found outside the United States of America*

Almost every car you've ever loved, loathed or desired is gathered under one roof at the Haynes Motor Museum. Over 300 immaculately presented cars and motorbikes represent every aspect of our motoring heritage, from elegant reminders of bygone days, such as the superb Model J Duesenberg to curiosities like the bug-eyed BMW Isetta. There are also many old friends and flames. Perhaps you remember the 1959 Ford Popular that you did your courting in? The magnificent 'Red Collection' is a spectacle of classic sports cars including AC, Alfa Romeo, Austin Healey, Ferrari, Lamborghini, Maserati, MG, Riley, Porsche and Triumph.

## A Perfect Day Out

Each and every vehicle at the Haynes Motor Museum has played its part in the history and culture of Motoring. Today, they make a wonderful spectacle and a great day out for all the family. Bring the kids, bring Mum and Dad, but above all bring your camera to capture those golden memories for ever. You will also find an impressive array of motoring memorabilia, a comfortable 70 seat video cinema and one of the most extensive transport book shops in Britain. The Pit Stop Cafe serves everything from a cup of tea to wholesome, home-made meals or, if you prefer, you can enjoy the large picnic area nestled in the beautiful rural surroundings of Somerset.

>
*John Haynes O.B.E., Founder and Chairman of the museum at the wheel of a Haynes Light 12.*

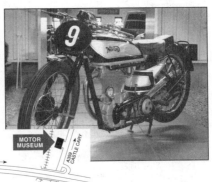

<
*The 1936 490cc sohc-engined International Norton – well known for its racing success*

The Museum is situated on the A359 Yeovil to Frome road at Sparkford, just off the A303 in Somerset. It is about 40 miles south of Bristol, and 25 minutes drive from the M5 intersection at Taunton.

Open 9.30am - 5.30pm (10.00am - 4.00pm Winter) 7 days a week, *except Christmas Day, Boxing Day and New Years Day*
Special rates available for schools, coach parties and outings Charitable Trust No. 292048